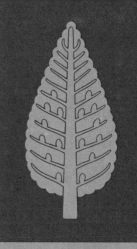

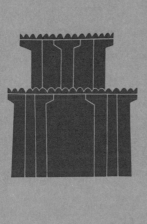

RAND McNALLY

BIBLE
ATLAS

RAND McNALLY

BIBLE ATLAS

Emil G. Kraeling, Ph.D.

Rand McNally & Company   NEW YORK   CHICAGO   SAN FRANCISCO

Acknowledgment

The quotations from *The Holy Bible, Revised Standard Version,* copyrighted 1946, 1952 and published by Thomas Nelson & Sons, are used by permission of the copyright owners, The National Council of the Churches of Christ in the U.S.A.

Preface

A good companion is a real treasure. That holds true not only of persons but of books like this *Bible Atlas,* the proper companion to Sacred Writ for Bible readers and Bible students everywhere. It enhances the value of the written word by clarifying the dimensions of time and place and is particularly helpful because it adds pictures and commentary to the maps illustrating the several periods of Biblical history.

Bible readers in America owe a special debt of gratitude to Rand McNally & Company for the part it has played in supplying the present and the past with a Bible atlas. As long ago as 1884, Rand McNally & Company commissioned and published the first American *Bible Atlas,* a handsome volume of 180 pages with numerous photographs and color maps. This pioneer effort has since then been widely imitated.

Now, as one of the publications of its Centennial Year, Rand McNally & Company is issuing its new *Bible Atlas,* up to date in all technical and scholarly details, more helpful than ever in its interpretative text, beautiful in its make-up and lay-out, yet in a size appropriate to the standard bookshelf, table or desk and to the format of the Bible itself.

Several years ago Rand McNally & Company inquired whether I would assume editorial responsibility for and contribute to the text of the book. The circumstances in which I was involved made it impossible for me to accept the invitation, and I am happy that eventually my brother, Dr. Emil G. Kraeling, was found willing to undertake the work. In him the *Bible Atlas* has found an author whose standing in the scholarly and religious community, established by his many publications, is of the highest order. What he has written should commend itself to the new generation of Bible students, who, as intelligent men and women, still find the Scripture a foundation stone of the understanding of history and the well-spring of their religious life and inspiration.

If by means of this Preface I appear at all in the book, it is only to express my genuine interest in the subject, my hearty commendation of the product and my pleasure at being even remotely associated in the enterprise with my brother and with Rand McNally & Company.

Carl H. Kraeling, Director
THE ORIENTAL INSTITUTE

The Sacred Scriptures of Jews and Christians are read mainly for their religious and moral content. But they can also be read with an eye to what they tell us of the days in which they were written and of the events and conditions which they relate or reflect. To render that which they report geographically understandable is the task to which the author has addressed himself. Text, color maps, photos and black-and-white maps combined are to give a picture of the world of which the Bible tells and take the reader back to those ancient times and places of which he may have read. Attention has been given to archaeological matters, where these were pertinent, and use has been made of the most recent discoveries, including those connected with the Dead Sea Scrolls, the historical information provided by the new Nebuchadnezzar Chronicle and the decision of the Gibeonite question.

The author wishes to thank Rand McNally & Company for producing a work of this nature, which greatly exceeds in size what was originally foreseen. Their counsel and judgment have been most helpful, and they most considerately extended the time necessary for the completion of this work. Thanks are due also to all those who placed photographs at our disposal; their names will be found in the credit lines. I can here only mention two gentlemen whose names do not appear in credit lines, M. E. L. Mallowan and H. Seyrig, both of whom gave me access to photos that have greatly enriched the book.

A few hints as to the use of the book may be added here. Rand McNally & Company are map makers and the book exists for the maps. Every effort has been made to make the maps attractive to the eye and easy to use. Indeed, utility is their aim and for this reason they have not been burdened with names of places that do not play any role in the Biblical history but occur only in name lists and obscure connections. Where the localization of a site is not definite, a question mark follows the place name. Special color maps for particular periods and black-and-white maps for situations where the local factors are important have been provided. The text in the main follows the order of the Old Testament historical books, Genesis through Nehemiah. Since for the period of the monarchy the Books of the Kings are primary, they are followed, but side glances at the Books of Chronicles and the prophetic books are built into the narrative. In the New Testament history the Gospel of Mark and the Book of Acts are basic, but supplementary information from the other sources is similarly drawn in at pertinent points. The sub-heads and the analytical Table of Contents should permit speedy locating of what the reader wishes to look up. There is an index of geographical names for text and maps and a subject index.

In the field of Biblical history the fruits of a century of Biblical "criticism" cannot be left aside entirely, though in a work such as this the reader should not be burdened with matters that are too technical. However, one may assume that a great many people are asking why and wherefore when they read the Biblical narratives, and the text is written in a manner to answer such questions and raise others. If there are a great many "possibly's" in the text, that is in the nature of the case.

I had originally desired to include more material about the history of the Oriental peoples, but that proved impracticable. The Chronological tables provided give the reader a suggestion of that background which is so rich and colorful. Chronology of the period before 1300 B.C. has recently been in a somewhat chaotic state. The so-called "low chronology," reducing the dates considerably, has been followed, even though some of the foremost authorities are not convinced of it. However, for the present purpose it makes little difference whether Hammurabi lived 50 to 100 years earlier than the date given. The time is drawing near when all these problems will be solved with the aid of new cuneiform texts as yet unstudied or undiscovered. For Hebrew chronology we have less prospects of obtaining certainty, since the discovery of Hebrew records comparable to those of Assyria or Babylonia is out of the question owing to the perishable writing material used. A number of chronologies are "on the market," so to speak. We have followed that of Mowinckel. It is a real joy when some new discovery delivers us from combinations and speculations, as occurred this year when a cuneiform text gave us the date of the first capture of Jerusalem (see page 314).

In dealing with the Pentateuchal narratives in which parallel strands have been combined by an editor, according to a hypothesis almost universally accepted, we have refrained from using the language of the schools and instead speak of the older or earlier author, the younger author, the youngest author and of the editor or compiler. The first of these writers may have written in the tenth to ninth century B.C., the second in the eighth to seventh century B.C., and the third *c.* 500 B.C. We give these dates merely as a rough guide to current scholarly opinion.

To the extent that Palestinian topographical research is involved, I must acknowledge my indebtedness to those men who have ridden on horseback or walked on foot over the tells of that land and have carried the research in this field to its present high state of excellence. Dalman, Albright, Alt, Glueck, Noth, Abel and Avi Jonah are among those from whose labors I have profited.

Emil G. Kraeling

THE LAND OF THE BIBLE

I. *JOURNEY INTO THE PAST* 15
   Caves and Scholars   The World of the Patriarchs   Key Ancient Sources
   Enter the Archaeologist   Far Horizons

II. *PASS THROUGH THE LAND* 24
   What's in a Name?   The Central Rift   Hermon, Monarch of All It Surveys
   "Roll, Jordan, Roll"   The Earth's Deepest Valley   In and Around the
   Dead Sea
   The Other Side of the Jordan 28
   "Is There No Balm in Gilead?"   The Lands of Ammon and Moab
   Western Palestine 29
   Galilee and the Plain of Esdraelon   Hills and Valleys of Samaria   Judaea
   and Its Wilderness   The Southern Border and Beyond   Up the Coast from
   Gaza   The Background in Nature   From Forest to Desert   Desert and
   Steppe   Weather and Climate   Beulah Land

THE ANCIENT HEBREW TRADITION

III. *IN THE BEGINNING* 41
   "As It Was in the Beginning"   "O Paradise, O Paradise!"   The Land of
   Nod   The Land of the Flood   Ararat   A Small Horizon   The First Empire
   Builder   A Changing International Scene   The Tower of Babel   Hebrew
   Origins   The Migration of Terah

IV. *WANDERINGS OF ABRAHAM* 62
   To God's Country   A Round Trip to Egypt   Lot's Choice   Abraham as
   Military Leader   The Promised Land   Hagar   The Oaks of Mamre   The
   Cities of the Plain   Ammonites and Moabites   Abraham in the Negeb   Call
   His Name Ishmael   How Beersheba Got Its Name   The Sacrifice of Isaac
   The Tomb of the Patriarchs

V. *THE TENTS OF ISAAC AND THE STAR OF JACOB* . . 79
   At the City of Nahor   The High Places of Isaac
   The Wanderings of Jacob 81
   Jacob's Flight to Gilead   The Last Lap of Jacob's Journey   Jacob's Arrival
   at Shechem   Simeon and Levi Bring Jacob into Disrepute   The Journey from
   Shechem to Bethel   The Oak of Weeping   The Tomb of Rachel   Migdal
   Eder   The Passing of Isaac
   The Edomites 89
   Joseph and His Brethren 90
   Jacob's Sons Go to Egypt   The Young Joseph's Errand and Fate   Joseph in
   Egypt   Jacob's Journey   Requiem

VI. *FROM EGYPT TO THE HOLY MOUNT* 95
   The World Historical Background
   The Oppression and the Mission of Moses 98
   Birth and Youth of Moses   Escape of Moses   Moses in Midian   Moses at
   the Holy Mount   Preliminary Considerations   Geography of the Crucial Area
   The Crossing of the Sea 102
   The Red Sea   The Old Testament Tradition   The Theory of a Southern
   Crossing   The Theory of a Central Crossing   The Theory of a Northern
   Crossing
   From the Sea Crossing to Sinai 107
   Northern Sinais   An Arabian Sinai   To the Traditional Sinai   The Moun-

tain of Moses   Final Observations on the Exodus

VII. *THE WILDERNESS SOJOURN* 114
Paran   To Kadesh   Journey to Mount Hor   Israel and Edom   Stations
after Kadesh in the List of Numbers 33   The Israelite Expansion in Transjordan   Last Encampments of the Israelites   The Scenes of the Balaam Narrative   Events in the Plains of Moab   The Death of Moses

THE PROMISED LAND

VIII. *THE CONQUEST AND DIVISION* 131
Nature of the Conquest Narratives
The Conquest of Jericho 132
Gilgal   The Fall of Jericho
The Conquest of Ai 135
First Attack on Ai   The Vale of Achor   The Capture of Ai   Canaanite
Cities in Israel
Defeat of the League of Kings 137
The Battle of Gibeon   The Kings in the Cave of Makkedah   The Capture
of Cities of the Shephelah   The Conquest of Galilee   Retrospects
The Apportionment of Palestine Among the Tribes 141
The Distribution   The Altar on the Other Side of the Jordan   Joshua's Fare-
well Address

IX. *THE PERIOD OF THE JUDGES* 144
Deliverers and Judges
Review of the Conquest 146
Judah's Role   Joseph's Expansion   The Negative Account   From Gilgal to
Bochim   Ehud's Daring Deed   Shamgar and the Philistines   The Battle of
Taanach   The Midianite Oppression   The Ophrah of the Abiezrites   Gid-
eon's Band   Abimelech's Rise and Fall   Two Minor Judges   A Hero of
Transjordan
The Story of Samson 162
The Scene of Manoah's Sacrifice   The Scenes of Samson's Adventures   Sam-
son and Gaza   The Migration of the Danites
The Story of Ruth 167

THE GREAT KINGS

X. *SAUL FORMS A HEBREW NATION* 171
World Historical Background
The Ephraimite Supremacy 172
From Ramah to Shiloh   The Philistine War   Fortunes of the Ark   Another
Philistine War
Saul's Kingship 176
How Saul Gained the Crown   Saul Delivers Jabesh   The Uprising against
the Philistines   The Amalekite Campaign   David and Goliath   David's Life
at Court and His Flight   David in Exile   Further Incidents of David's Fugi-
tive Life   The Philistine War Begins   David Pursues the Amalekites   Saul's
Defeat   Burial of Saul and Jonathan

XI. *THE STORY OF DAVID* 191
Hebron and Mahanaim   War between the Kingdoms   Abner's Death   On
Beeroth and Gittaim   David Becomes King of Israel and Acquires a Capital
Two Victories over the Philistines   David Brings the Ark to Zion   Further
Wars of David   The Ammonite War   Absalom's Vengeance   Absalom's

Rebellion   The Situation at Jerusalem   Mahanaim   David's Return   David
Exterminates the House of Saul   The Mighty Men of David   A Census and
Its Sequel

XII. *SOLOMON IN ALL HIS GLORY* 210
Adonijah's First Mistake   Passing of David   Solomon Holds a Reckoning
Consolidation of Affairs   Solomon's Reorganization of the Kingdom   The
Empire of Solomon   Solomon and Hiram of Tyre   The Acropolis of Jeru-
salem   Metal Work and Foundry   Debtor of the King of Tyre   Fortifica-
tions   Navigating the Red Sea   The State Visit of an Arabian Queen   The
Ophir Journeys   The Armaments Trade   Seeds of Future Trouble

COLOR MAP SECTION 225

THE DIVIDED KINGDOM

XIII. *THE SECESSION AND THE SUPREMACY OF ISRAEL* . 267
Israel Goes Its Own Way   Jeroboam's Cities   Jeroboam and Ahijah of Shiloh
On Rehoboam's Reign   Shishak's Invasion   Jeroboam and Abijam   Asa and
Baasha   How the House of Omri Was Established   Ahab of Israel   Elijah's
Ministry   The Journey to Horeb   The Calling of Elisha   First Siege of Sa-
maria   The Battle of Aphek   Naboth's Vineyard   Ahab's Last Battle   Aha-
ziah of Israel and Jehoshaphat of Judah

XIV. *THE DOWNFALL OF ISRAEL* 282
Last Story of Elijah   Elisha's Beginnings   Israel and Moab   Elisha's Min-
istry   Two Kings of Judah: Jehoram and Ahaziah   Founding of the Jehu
Dynasty   Judah Ruled by an Israelite Princess   Jehoash of Judah   Events in
Israel   Amaziah of Judah   Israel's Brief Revival   Amos and Hosea   Mena-
hem of Israel   Renewed Rise of Judah   The Aramaean Peril   Exit Israel
Colonization of Israel's Cities

XV. *JUDAH'S VAIN STRUGGLE FOR SURVIVAL* 299
Hezekiah of Judah   The Assyrian Comes to Micah's Home   The Assyrian
Account of the War   Judaean Versions of the Events   The Lesson of the
Fate of the Kingdoms   An Official of Hezekiah   The Era of Assyrian Vassal-
dom   King Josiah   And Great Was the Fall Thereof   King Jehoahaz
Carchemish: One of History's Decisive Battles   King Jehoiachin   Prophet of
the Exile   Disaster Descends   The Lachish Ostraca   Tragedy   Destruction
of the City   Governor Gedaliah   Prophet of the Fugitives   The Fate of the
Mizpah Remnant

BABYLON TO JERUSALEM

XVI. *IN THE LAND OF EXILE* 321
Ezekiel's Prophecy   Daniel   The Image in the Plain of Dura   Is Not This
Great Babylon?   Nebuchadnezzar's Dwelling with the Beasts of the Field
Events under Nebuchadnezzar and His Successors   Nabonidus and Belshazzar
The Last Years of Babylon   Shadow of Things to Come   A Servant of the
Lord and His Home   Hammer Strokes of History   Belshazzar's Feast   The
Fall of Babylon

XVII. *THE RECONSTRUCTION* 329
The Historical Background   Zerubbabel   The "Golah" List   The Satrap
Steps In   An Incident from the Reign of Xerxes   The Glory That Was Susa
By the River Ulai   Persepolis   Decisive Developments   The Coming of Ezra
Nehemiah Goes to Jerusalem   Tour of the Walls   Rebuilding the Walls
The Supporting Jewish Community   Jealous Neighbors   Nehemiah Sees It
Through   Later Trip of Nehemiah   Light on Judah under Darius II   The
Journey of Ezra   The Publication of the Law   Jews in Egypt   Artaxerxes III

Geographical Elements in Some Late Prophetic Writings   Geography in the
Wisdom Literature

THE TIME OF JESUS

XVIII. *THE WORLD INTO WHICH JESUS WAS BORN* . . . 351
The Caesars Appear on the Scene   The Provinces of the Roman Empire   The
Political Situation in Palestine   The Jews under the Procurators

XIX. *THE GOSPEL STORY* 356
The Home of John the Baptist
The Early Life of Jesus 358
Nazareth   "O Little Town of Bethlehem"   The Magi   Herod and the
Herodium   "Out of Egypt Have I Called My Son"   Going to Jerusalem
"A City That Is Compact Together"
The Baptism and Ministry 367
In the Wilderness   Was John at Qumran?   The Scene of Christ's Baptism
Scene of the Temptation   From the Jordan to Galilee (According to John)
The Transfer to Capernaum   Galilean Wanderings   A Special Journey in
Luke's Narrative   Lakeside Scenes   Journey to Nazareth   Tiberias and
Machaerus   Scene of the Miracle of the Loaves   The Journey to Phoenician
Territory   In the Tetrarchy of Philip   Caesarea Philippi   The Scene of the
Transfiguration   Special Journeyings of Luke's Central Section   Journeys
of Jesus in the Gospel of John   At the Well of Jacob   Bethesda   Further
Journeyings   Bethany   Ephraim   The Last Journey to Jerusalem   The
Mount of Olives   Entering Jerusalem   Jesus Visits the Temple   Scene of the
Last Supper   Gethsemane   The Scenes of the Proceedings   Golgotha   The
Holy Sepulchre   Scenes of the Easter Visions   In Galilee and on the Way to
Olivet

THE GROWTH OF CHRISTIANITY

XX. *THE EARLY CHURCH OF PALESTINE* 413
Olivet Once More   The Upper Room   In and Around the Temple   The
Stoning of Stephen   The Travels of Philip   A Chapter in the Travels of
Peter   The Dispersal of the Apostles

XXI. *FROM ANTIOCH TO ROME* 423
The Road to Damascus   In and Out of Damascus   Jerusalem and Tarsus
Antioch the Beautiful   The Church at Antioch
Paul's First Missionary Journey 430
Cyprus   Asia Minor Ahead   Penetrating Pamphylia and Galatia   Back at
Antioch
The Second Missionary Journey 436
From Antioch to the Aegean Sea   On to Macedonia   Athens   Corinth
The Third Missionary Journey 446
Ephesus   A Visit to Macedonia and Greece   From Troas to Assos   Around
the Coast of Asia Minor   To Syria and Palestine   Jerusalem and Caesarea
The Journey to Rome 454
Sidon to Myra   Myra to Crete   Danger at Sea   Malta   To Sicily and Italy
Along the Appian Way   Rome
A Possible Journey to Spain 461
Crete and Nicopolis 463

XXII. *THE GEOGRAPHY OF REVELATION* 465
Patmos   Smyrna   Pergamum   Thyatira   Sardis   Philadelphia   Laodicea
Armageddon
Jerusalem the Golden 474

Color Maps

I.   GEOGRAPHIC REGIONS OF PALESTINE 225

II.   PHYSIOGRAPHIC MAP OF ANCIENT PALESTINE 226

III.   ANCIENT WORLD IN THE DAYS OF THE PATRIARCHS
(1300 B.C.) 228

IV.   THE TABLE OF NATIONS ACCORDING TO GENESIS 10 . . 230

V.   EGYPT AND LANDS OF THE EXODUS (13th Century B.C.) . . . 232

VI.   PALESTINE UNDER JOSHUA AND THE JUDGES
(12th and 11th Centuries B.C.) 234

VII.   PALESTINE IN THE TIME OF SAUL (1000 B.C.) 236

VIII.   THE KINGDOM OF DAVID AND SOLOMON (10th Century B.C.) 238

IX.   ISRAEL AND JUDAH — THE DIVIDED MONARCHY (c. 850 B.C.) 240

X.   PALESTINE AFTER THE FALL OF THE NORTHERN
KINGDOM 242

XI.   THE ASSYRIAN EMPIRE UNDER ASHURBANIPAL
(7th Century B.C.) 244

XII.   THE PERSIAN EMPIRE UNDER CYRUS, DARIUS I AND
XERXES (c. 500 B.C.) 246

XIII.   THE HELLENISTIC WORLD (185 B.C.) 248

XIV.   PALESTINE IN THE MACCABEAN PERIOD 250

XV.   PALESTINE UNDER HEROD THE GREAT (37–4 B.C.) 252

XVI.   PALESTINE IN THE TIME OF JESUS (28 A.D.) 254

XVII.   JERUSALEM UNDER NEHEMIAH (445 B.C.) 256

XVIII.   JERUSALEM FROM 20 B.C. to 70 A.D. 257

XIX.   THE ROMAN EMPIRE IN THE FIRST CENTURY (A.D.) . . . 258

XX.   PAUL'S JOURNEYS 260

XXI.   IMPORTANT ARCHAEOLOGICAL EXCAVATIONS IN
WESTERN ASIA 262

XXII.   PALESTINE TODAY 264

THE DEAD SEA SCROLLS AREA 16
PEUTINGER'S TABLE 22
THE BASIC GEOLOGICAL DEVELOPMENT OF PALESTINE 34
PRIMEVAL ZONES 35
BAROMETRIC PRESSURE PATTERNS 37
PRECIPITATION PATTERNS 38
BABYLONIAN WORLD VIEW 42
EARLY HEBREW WORLD 42
BABYLONIAN WORLD MAP 43
TABLE OF NATIONS 48
TABLE OF EARLY CIVILIZATION 58
WANDERINGS OF ABRAHAM 63
FROM BEERSHEBA TO EL-PARAN 64
AN EARLY INVASION OF PALESTINE 67
DOWN SODOM WAY 70
TABLE OF PEOPLES RELATED TO ISRAEL 73
HEBRON AND VICINITY 78
WANDERINGS OF JACOB 83
SHECHEM AND ITS ENVIRONS 85
WESTERN ASIA AT THE TIME OF HAMMURABI 97
KADESH-BARNEA AND ITS ENVIRONS 118
WHERE THE WALLS CAME TUMBLING DOWN 133
GIBEON AND THE NORTHERN APPROACHES TO JERUSALEM . . . 193
SOLOMON'S PROVINCIAL SYSTEM 213
SOLOMON'S TEMPLE AND PALACE 218
DISTRICTS OF JUDAH UNDER JOSIAH 310
NINEVEH 311
BABYLON 322
FROM PASARGADAE TO PERSEPOLIS 326
PALACE OF NEBUCHADNEZZAR 327
TABLE OF BIBLE HISTORY 344
THE HERODIUM 363
FROM NAZARETH TO CAPERNAUM 372
WHERE THE BIG FISHERMAN WAS AT HOME 376
JOURNEYS OF JESUS ACCORDING TO MARK 387
FROM BETHSAIDA TO CAESAREA PHILIPPI 389
JOURNEYS OF JESUS ACCORDING TO JOHN 391
BETHESDA, THE REDISCOVERED POOLS 393
THE MOUNT OF OLIVES 396
PLAN OF TEMPLE COURT 400
THE ANTONIA 402
THE TEMPLE OF HEROD 402
THE LITHOSTROTOS 403
CAESAREA 419
ANTIOCH 428
ATHENS 441
CRETE 455
THE WIND EUROCLYDON 456
PAUL'S FOURTH SHIPWRECK 457
ROME 460
FINAL SCENE OF PAUL'S MINISTRY 462

THE LAND OF THE BIBLE

TOP, *it was in jars like these that the Dead Sea Scrolls were stored.* (E. L. Sukenik). BOTTOM, *the cave in which the first Dead Sea Scrolls were found.* (E. L. Sukenik)

The DESIGN on the preceding page shows an Achaemenid doorway from Persepolis, an Assyrian winged bull from Khorsabad and a fragment of Dead Sea Scroll writing.

CHAPTER I

JOURNEY INTO THE PAST

IN THE EARLY SPRING of 1947, an exciting event took place in the "little town of Bethlehem" in the Holy Land. Yet the town was as unconscious of its significance as it was of the importance of a much greater event nearly two thousand years ago. One day, three Ta'āmireh Bedouin from the Dead Sea region to the east came into the marts of the town bearing some wrapped parcels. Bethlehem is used to seeing these people in its streets, and had no particular curiosity about their errand. The three men went into the house of a Syrian-Christian merchant and unpacked their parcels to show him the contents—the first of the now famous Dead Sea Scrolls!

These leather rolls had been found in a cave high up in a cliff about a mile from the Dead Sea. A shepherd boy when following a stray goat had noticed a gaping hole in the rock. Out of curiosity, he had thrown a stone into the opening. There was a resounding crash which frightened him so that he ran away. The tribesmen then had crawled into the cave and had found some jars of large size without handles and some of smaller size with little looped handles. The jars were empty, save one large one, in which the men had found three leather scrolls. These they had brought to the merchant at Bethlehem.

The Bedouin offered to sell all the scrolls for twenty pounds (at the time about $80.00). The merchant was reluctant to risk his money on this fragile, decaying material, but promised to see what he could do about finding a buyer. And so the three Arabs left,

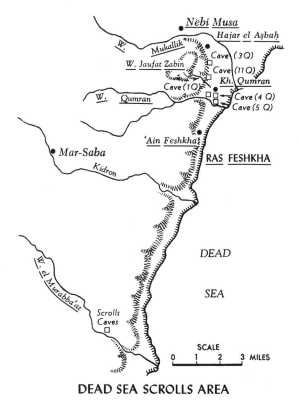

DEAD SEA SCROLLS AREA

the impression that the manuscript was one that had long lain in the Convent library. Some held it to be a forgery, for there had been some notorious forging of inscriptions and of a roll of Deuteronomy back in the eighties of the last century. He did learn, however, from a Dutch scholar and subsequently had it confirmed by a young American scholar at the American School of Oriental Research, Dr. John C. Trever, that it was an almost complete copy of the Book of Isaiah, written in a script different from that of the oldest Hebrew Bible-manuscripts.

Announcement of the great find came from the American School after a few photographs taken by Trever had been submitted to Professor William F. Albright of Johns Hopkins University, a leading expert in the history of Semitic writing. He proclaimed it "the greatest manuscript discovery of modern times," and dated the Isaiah scroll around 100 B.C. When it is realized that the oldest known Hebrew Biblical manuscripts only go back to about 1000 A.D., it can be understood why this discovery was, indeed, an "archaeological bombshell."

All these events took place around the time when the British Mandate over Palestine came to an end and when the state of Israel was establishing itself. The Holy City now became divided between it and the Hashemite Kingdom of Jordan. Fighting

1.1 *Trever and the Archbishop examine the scrolls. (John C. Trever)*

perhaps by the very road once taken by the three departing Wise Men of old, but unlike them taking their treasures back with them.

Contacts in Jerusalem were made by the dealer and soon the matter was brought to the attention of the head of the Syrian Orthodox community, the Metropolitan Archbishop Mar Athanasius Jeshue Samuel. A meeting with the Arabs was arranged and the Archbishop was shown the three scrolls. He was very definitely interested. He thought the documents were written in Hebrew, although the letters looked different and he suspected that they were probably *very* old. He decided that he would like to buy these scrolls, and in time the transaction was completed. Subsequently he obtained a number of other scrolls in a manner not fully clarified.

One of the original three scrolls was very large, but as yet Mar Athanasius was totally ignorant of what he had. Persons in various places were guardedly approached, and given

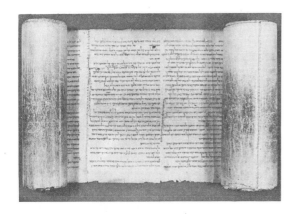

1.2 *The Isaiah Scroll opened to Is. 39–40. Jesus held such a scroll in his hands, unrolling it to the right and rolling it upon the left as he read. (Courtesy American Schools of Oriental Research)*

was going on and there was danger that the city might be destroyed and the precious scrolls lost. The Archbishop went off to America with four scrolls, while six got into the hands of Professor E. L. Sukenik of the Hebrew University, apparently through one of the Archbishop's representatives. Sukenik was first in the field, publishing excerpts from his manuscripts in 1948—a piece of still another scroll of Isaiah and the others non-Biblical texts of great interest. The Isaiah scroll and two other manuscripts of the Archbishop were published in America in 1950–1951, edited by Professor Millar Burrows of Yale University with the aid of Trever and Dr. William H. Brownlee. The fourth scroll of the Archbishop, which was submitted to museum experts for unrolling, was withdrawn by him and finally sold to the State of Israel with the ones already opened. It proved to be an Aramaic *Genesis Apocryphon,* when edited in 1956.

Caves and Scholars

When the dust of battle cleared in the Holy Land, the scrolls cave was in Jordan territory. It was rediscovered in January, 1949, by a Belgian United Nations observer, and a guard of the Arab Legion was set over it. The cave was explored and some six hun-

dred fragments of manuscript recovered out of the rubble.

Where the *Wadi Qumrān,* the valley in which the cave lies, approaches a drop-off some distance below the cave, there are some old ruins, long known but never investigated, and a cemetery with at least one thousand ancient burials. The ruins were called *Khirbet Qumrān.* It was apparent that the scrolls must have belonged to the people that had lived there, perhaps in caves and tents. Scholars at once called to mind the reports about an Essene community supposed to have been in this region. The Essenes were a sect of Jewish ascetics, about whom we hear in ancient sources. According to Pliny the Elder (*c.* 77 A.D.) they had a settlement "above En-gedi," which excellently suits Qumran, and with this tallies the fact that a gate on the south side of Jerusalem was called "Gate of the Essenes." From here they could enter or leave the Holy City in going to and fro between it and Qumran.

The excitement engendered by the scrolls had sent the Bedouin scurrying around investigating all the old caves they had ever noticed. Their search, which was later joined by an organized expedition of several institutions, including the American School of Oriental Research, produced staggering results. Each new cave that yielded manuscript materials was numbered, the original cave being labeled 1Q. The prize discovery of the Bedouin was the cave numbered 4Q. When the authorities stopped all unauthorized

1.3 *Ruins of the Qumran settlement. (Palestine Archaeological Museum)*

1.4 *Copper Scroll, recording where national treasures of the Jews were concealed. (Palestine Archaeological Museum)*

searching there in September, 1952, they still found in it a vast number of book-fragments, many of them belonging to non-Biblical works. In clearing this cave the archaeologists found another cave nearby (5Q), also containing some manuscript remains. They were soon able to chalk up still another find to their credit; about a mile and a half north of the original cave, two copper scrolls were extracted from a cave, the roof of which had collapsed (3Q). These scrolls, one could discern, were inscribed within with Hebrew characters, but they were so oxidized as to create quite a problem for the unrolling. Subsequently fresh cave finds were made by Bedouin in the *Wadi Murabba'āt,* twelve miles farther south; the documents obtained there could be dated as coming from the second century A.D.

The Bedouin of course had been selling fragments found by them to the highest bidder, and it took strenuous efforts on the part of the Jordan authorities to prevent these materials from being scattered. A scrolls assembly project was organized with funds provided by John D. Rockefeller Jr. An international team of scholars was set to work, assorting and fitting together fragments in one of the most gigantic jigsaw puzzles in history.

But the scrolls story was not yet ended. In the years that followed, the ransacking of caves and searching for concealed entrances by the Bedouin brought about more finds constantly. Thus in the spring of 1956 another highly important discovery was made by them—that of Cave 11Q, half a mile north of the original cave (1Q). The hoard obtained from this cave promises to rival the initial one.

The Copper Scrolls, which proved to be a single text, were given preliminary publication in French by Milik in 1959 (English by John Allegro, 1960). This text is written in late Hebrew, like that of the Mishnah. It records where a vast amount of treasure, whether that of the Herodian temple or of the Solomonic temple, is buried. If written *c.* 100 A.D. it may be a product of the imagination.

At the time of the first publication of the scrolls there was much debate about the time of their origin. Some held that they were second or third century A.D. or even from the Middle Ages, while others argued that they were from the time of Christ or even earlier. The only comparable writing was that of a column of Hebrew on the so-called Nash papyrus, found in Egypt and probably dating from the second century B.C.

Two developments led to a certainty of their early date. One was the rise of a whole science of Hebrew palaeography on the part of those who had all the unpublished material before them. They were able to perceive the development the script underwent from shortly before 200 B.C. to 135 A.D. and to date all materials by this means. The second was the archaeological exploration of the Qumran ruins, which was carried out in five seasons of digging (1951–56). Sherds proved that there had been a Judean settlement here in the eighth to seventh centuries B.C. Part of the walls were reused for the structures built by the Qumran community. The first phase (Ia) was one of modest beginnings. A coin of John Hyrcanus (135–104 B.C.) was found and probably dates it. The second phase (Ib) followed closely and is marked by numerous coins of Alexander Jannaeus (103–76 B.C.). At this time the community expanded greatly and most of its installations were constructed (see page 368 f.). The earthquake of the year 31 B.C. did grave damage, and the settlement was abandoned for the rest of the reign of Herod. This may have been the time of the hegira to Damascus, which is mentioned in the so-called "Damascus Document" or "the Zadokite fragments," found in 1910 in the Genizah of the Ezra synagogue in Old Cairo by Solomon Schechter, but originally derived from the Qumran sect, as fragments of the work found there have proved. Period II exhibits coins of Archelaus (4 B.C.–6 A.D.) and is marked by a general revival of life at this center. It ended with the destruction of the buildings by the Romans in 68 A.D. Period III shows a brief occupation by Roman soldiery. The results gained at Qumran were confirmed by the excavations in 1958 at nearby 'Ain Feshkha. The buildings there evidently belonged to the same group, and had the same history. It seems to have been a center for their agriculture, notably growing of date palms. There can be no doubt but that the scrolls of the Qumran library were hidden away when the Roman invasion of Palestine began in 68 A.D.

Fresh scroll discoveries were made in Israeli territory in 1961. News of Bedouin finds led to the sending out of an expedition to search the region between En-gedi and Masada. A group under Y. Yadin succeeded in locating the cave of the Bedouin in the *Nahal Hever* area. Part of a Psalms scroll of the late first century A.D. was discovered, and a bundle of papyrus letters—some of them by Simeon bar Kosebah, "prince over Israel" (known to history as Barcochba), indicating that some of the revolutionists of 135 A.D. took refuge in this cave.

The Land and the Book

The Dead Sea Scrolls turned the eyes of many toward the Holy Land. That land has played a great role in the life of western humanity, and to journey there is among the secret desires of many hearts. Millions of Americans can say with the Philadelphia-born Biblical scholar, Caspar René Gregory, who toured the land of his dreams alone and on foot, "From earliest childhood I looked up to Abraham and Moses, Joshua and David as my ancestors, not in the flesh but in the spirit and imagination. The scenes of the Bible inducted me, a child of the city, into the wonders of rural life. The struggles of its heroes, tribes and kings were the first wars that interested me. The Hebrew names of mountains, plains, rivers and brooks conjured ever new and beautiful scenes before my eyes." That this was true to an even greater degree of our forefathers is obvious from the Biblical place names they sprinkled all over the map of our own land. We are surrounded by reminders of Palestine and beset with invitations to visit it.

There is, however, a special reason for our interest in this land. Our concern is not so much with the Palestine of today, as it is with that country as it once was in a remote past—in Biblical times. And the question is how can we find our way back to that bygone situation?

Key Ancient Sources

In going back through history to Bible times we need various helps. Above all we need to know what the Bible tells us about the countries, cities, villages and roads of the Near East. And it is surprising how much the Bible does have to say on these points, if all the information is put together. But for the interpretation of what the Bible tells us, we need also the help of the scholars who can read it in the original languages, who know the general history of the ancient world of which Biblical history is a part, and who can give the Biblical documents their proper places in that history.

Of course the physical geography of Palestine has not changed and some vestiges of its ancient buildings and sites are still visible. But no country stays the same even for a generation, and most of the ancient roads and towns are gone or buried. So a second thing we need for a journey to Biblical Palestine is the information lent by the historians, geographers and map makers. We cannot list all these sources here, but will single out some to which we will refer frequently in the following pages.

JOSEPHUS. He was a leader in the Jewish revolution of 68 A.D., but was captured by the Romans in an early stage of the war. Among other things he wrote a history of his people (*The Antiquities*) as well as a history of the struggle in which he had participated (*The Jewish War*). His books were preserved by Christians, who found the information he gave valuable. He mentions many cities and towns of Palestine of his time and thus becomes an important witness of the Palestine of the time of Christ.

EUSEBIUS. Fourth century A.D. bishop, who lived in Palestine, and to whom we are immensely indebted for various works of importance in history and geography. His *Onomasticon,* a dictionary of the geographical names of the Bible, locates many Biblical places that still had the old names in his day by stating their distance from some road center. While it is not known whether he had a map to accompany his work, such maps must have been made. We have a valuable old map—though only partially preserved—which seems to be based on his identifications of places.

THE MOSAIC OF MADEBA. This is the map connected with Eusebius. It decorated the floor of an old Christian Basilica of the sixth century at Madeba in the land of Moab, east of the Dead Sea. It was accidentally discovered by refugees from Mohammedan persecution in 1896, when they dug here in order to build a new church for themselves on the site. Figure 7.18 on page 370 shows a section of the mosaic. The map as a whole portrayed Palestine as it presented itself to a pilgrim coming from western lands.

PALESTINE PILGRIMS. These are of consequence chiefly for what they tell us about the holy places shown them in their time. The most important are those who traveled before the Mohammedan conquest in the seventh century. The oldest is the anonymous Pilgrim of Bordeaux (333 A.D.). Two pious women, Paula (386 A.D.) and Silvia (400 A.D.), and Antoninus Martyr (570 A.D.) and the Anglo-Saxon Arculf (670 A.D.) are particularly valuable witnesses.

For the broader geographical picture the following sources require especial mention.

HERODOTUS. The father of History who traveled in the Orient c. 450 B.C.

STRABO. The father of Geography, who wrote a great Greek work describing the known world of his day (*c.* 20 B.C.) and giving rich information of historical nature for the places and regions he mentions.

CLAUDIUS PTOLEMAEUS (PTOLEMY). Great Greek astronomer and mathematician of about 150 A.D. He listed some eight thousand places of the world of his day with their latitude and longitude, and remained the great authority on geography until the Middle Ages. His map is not preserved, but a medieval cartographer drew one on the basis of his facts.

PEUTINGER'S TABLE. This is a thirteenth century map, drawn by an Alsatian monk and named after a gentleman who once owned the manuscript (which is now in the National Library at Vienna). Some believed it to be a "descendant" of the Roman map that was completed in 7 B.C., a few years before Christ was born; others hold it to go back to a second century map. It is a sort of strip-map, twenty-one feet long, and shows the roads of the Roman empire, with distances in Roman miles from town to town. Small places are indicated by two or three houses, but large ones by walls with towers. In arid regions a watering place is marked by a tank surrounded by a bathhouse. It would be difficult to exaggerate the importance of this map. Until recently all attempts to enter roads on modern maps of the ancient world followed Peutinger's Table (see page 22).

Enter the Archaeologist

The study of all these sources is most useful, as we try to move back in time toward Biblical Palestine, but it gets us only part way back. The men to whom we owe these helps were Greeks and Romans, or wrote in Greek and Latin, and so what they tell us does not get us much beyond the early days of the present era. Consequently as we embark upon our trip back through time, we need still a third help—a knowledge of the ancient remains of Palestine as they are understood by the archaeologist.

This archaeological study is something relatively new and new discoveries are constantly being made. It all began back in the eighteenth century, when the first scientifically interested European travelers began to visit the East and to publish reports of what they had seen there. Astonishing progress in the location of Palestinian places was made when the American theologian Edward Robinson traveled in the land in 1838. He found that many ancient place names have survived in Arabic dress to this very day. He assumed that the Biblical towns had lain where those names lingered. He was quite helpless, however, in dating ancient ruins. Proper interpretation of these only began with the use of an archaeological method, which came up long after his time. Since the last decade of the nineteenth century much information has been provided by scientific excavations, which tell us of ancient cities such as Jericho, Gezer, Samaria and Megiddo. More will be produced in the years ahead, but what we can learn about the most important of the ancient cities such as Jerusalem is limited, because they have been destroyed and built over so many times and are still inhabited.

The happy hunting grounds of the archaeologist are the tell and *khirbeh*. Khirbet Qumran, the settlement at which the Dead Sea Scrolls community lived, is a *khirbeh*. The term pertains to a low ruin mound. The tell is usually a high mound and often looks like a natural elevation. Edward Robinson stood on *Tell el Mutesellim* at the edge of the Plain of Esdraelon in 1852 thinking it would present a splendid site for a city, but finding no trace of any kind to show that a city had ever stood there. Actually he was standing on top of the city of Megiddo whose location he was seeking. It was only after the British Archaeologist Sir Flinders Petrie had dug at *Tell el Ḥesī,* a small mound in the low country of southwestern Judaea, in 1890 that the nature of a Palestinian tell became understood. Such a mound represents an old walled city, with successive layers of occupation. When one city was destroyed, a new one would be built on top of the debris and new city walls constructed. As this process repeated itself again and again in thousands of years, the mound grew higher and higher. The old city walls are like so many collars holding in the soil and preventing the forces of erosion from leveling the hill. The high tells all have a history going back to an age long before Israel entered the land. Cities newly founded by the Israelites did not exist long enough to create prominent tells unless an overlay of Greek, Roman, Byzantine and Arabic structures brought about such a result.

Modern archaeology has developed a way of talking about the history of these tells and *khirbeh*s which needs a word of explanation. The humble potsherd or piece of broken earthenware has provided scholars with a master key for the history of the human occupation of any site. This is because there were styles in pottery-shape and ornamentation, just as there were changing styles in clothes. Careful excavations, which went down through layer after layer in the history of a city, have made it possible to corre-

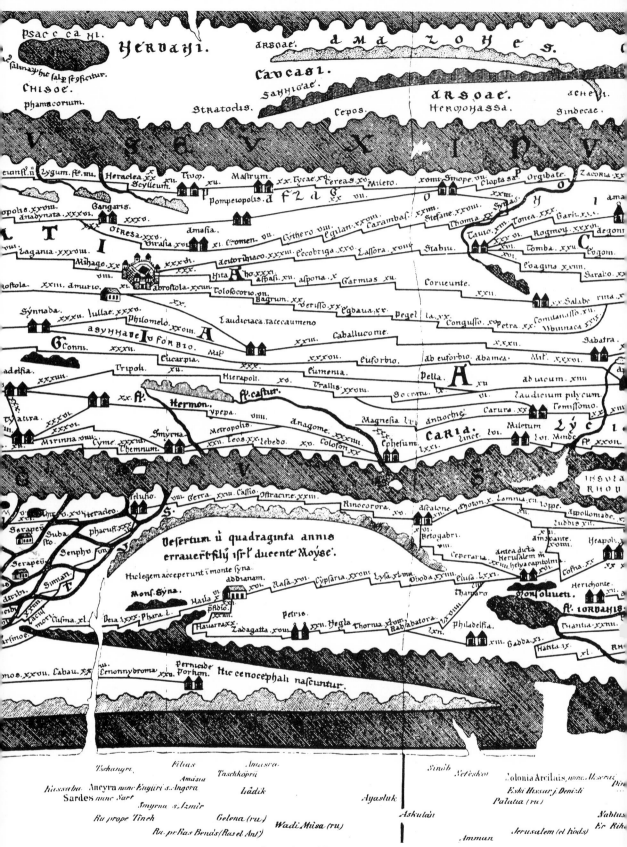

1.5 *A portion of Peutinger's Table, a medieval map believed to be a copy of a Roman map of the second century* A.D. *or earlier (after Miller).*

late the pottery styles with their time. Dateable objects, such as Egyptian scarabs or imported wares, often provided important clues. It is possible today for an expert to walk around a mound and after picking up sample sherds of all kinds to say in what periods the city flourished, or in what periods it probably lay desolate. One can thus know in advance of excavation whether or not a city existed in old Canaanite, Israelite or Jewish times or in the time of Christ. Indeed, "ceramic chronology" is now so exact that one can pin things down almost to the quarter-century.

Since the full history of a city cannot be told without historical records and since in most cases Palestine has not produced these, scholars have found it very convenient to use broad archaeological terminology for a time chart. In so doing they followed the example set by experts in European archaeology. The system rests on the observation that men first used stone implements, then copper or bronze, and finally iron. We give here for convenient reference a list of the main periods with their approximate dates in terms of historical chronology.

Neolithic Age	6000–4500 B.C.
(men still use stone implements)	
Chalcolithic Age	4500–3200 B.C.
(some use of copper along with stone)	
Early Bronze Age	3200–2200 B.C.
Middle Bronze Age	2200–1550 B.C.
Late Bronze Age	1550–1200 B.C.
Iron Age	1200–330 B.C.
Iron I	1200–900 B.C.
Iron II	900–650 B.C.
Iron III	650–330 B.C.

Far Horizons

Finally for our journey back through Biblical history we need to give heed to what archaeology has taught us about the ancient world outside of Palestine. The activity here has been tremendous and the revelations far more spectacular. Though there are still large gaps in our knowledge concerning some of the peoples of the ancient world, notably the close neighbors of Israel (such as Aramaeans, Ammonites, Moabites, Edomites and early Arabians), much has been done to inform us about Egyptians, Phoenicians, Babylonians, Hurrians, Hittites, Assyrians, Elamites and Persians during the many centuries of Oriental history. The archaeological investigations carried on in the lands of all these peoples have produced a vast amount of written records. Mysterious scripts have been made to give up their secrets. Tongues that were unknown have been brought back into existence through the skill of the philologists. For the history and geography of Palestine no other outside sources can equal the Egyptian and Assyrian texts in informativeness. All this material, however, needs interpretation, and had best be mentioned only where it serves our insight. Vast knowledge, too, has accrued in modern times concerning the Hellenistic-Roman East, through Greek papyri and inscriptions, and through excavations carried on in so many ancient cities by classical archaeologists. And all this is not without relevance for our purpose.

So a journey back into the past to Biblical times is something that we can undertake only if we are well equipped. In the preparation of this Bible Atlas all these means have been used to make the trip informative and the information as reliable as possible.

CHAPTER II

PASS THROUGH THE LAND

AMONG the Dead Sea Scrolls from the first Qumran cave there is one that is written in the Aramaic dialect of the time of Christ. It belonged to the Syrian Archbishop, but passed into the ownership of the state of Israel with the rest of his scrolls. When it was opened at the Hebrew University early in 1956 it was found to contain an elaboration of some points in the story of Genesis. Among the things on which it dwells is how Abraham availed himself of the LORD's invitation and walked through the land to its length and its breadth (GEN. 13:17).

What's in a Name?

We too must briefly explore this land in which we are to visit so many individual places. But we must first be clear as to its extent. Names are rather variable in what they cover, depending on political history or other factors. In the patriarchal story we hear about the "land of Canaan" (GEN. 11:31). The term applies only to the region between the Jordan and the Mediterranean Sea. That, in the view of the Genesis writers, is the Promised Land or Holy Land. The familiar term Palestine means "the Philistine country"; this seems strange since only a small corner of the land belonged to that people. The name first was conferred on the coastal region by the Greek navigators, for whom the interior, that seems to us to be the heart of Palestine, was just a hinterland. The term was later stretched to cover the coastal and interior regions quite to the north of Philistaea proper, just as in earlier days "Phoenicia" was sometimes used broadly for the whole coast down to the border of Egypt. The Romans in the second century A.D. designated the entire country *Syria Palaestina,* meaning "the Palestinian part of Syria," for they held Palestine to be a portion of Syria.

Nevertheless, Palestine has a sufficiently distinct northern boundary and enough inner complexity to mark it off as an independent segment of the greater territory. In times when strong political or military pressure could be exercised by Egypt, it was likely to be under Egyptian domination, rather than Syrian or of nations controlling Syria. In Roman times, when Egypt was a Roman province and hence impotent, the natural balance reasserted itself and Palestine became part of Syria.

Modern geographers use the term Palestine differently than the ancients. For them the lands east of the Jordan and Dead Sea also are part of the country. The northern limits of Palestine start in the west at the Leontes River (the *Nahr el Qasimīyeh*) and the southern limits at the valley of Gaza (*Wadi Ghazzeh*). In each case the boundary line may be drawn, roughly speaking, along the same parallel to the desert in the east.

The Central Rift

Palestine is cut into two parts by a deep, wide trough passing through it longitudinally. Through it runs the river Jordan and here too lie the three lakes supplied with water by that stream. Because of the width and depth of the trough, the division made by the Jordan is a far more fundamental one than those marked by the Mississippi, the Rhine, or the Danube. For at its greatest depth, *el Ghōr* or "the valley," as the trough is called, is 1286 feet below sea level and the high country drops off to it very steeply from an elevation of 3000 feet.

Eastern and western Palestine both represent elevated table lands. This is particularly clear in the east, while western Palestine has been serried more deeply in the geological

ages, owing largely to the greater amount of rainfall and consequent erosion in this area.

Hermon, Monarch of All It Surveys

At the head of the great Jordan country stands majestic Mount Hermon (9232 feet). It is really outside of Palestine and yet dominates it, and that seems symbolic of the fact that the region is really a part of Syria. Its fifteen mile comb ascends gradually on the western side, but drops off steeply on the eastern side. The summit area is near the center. There are really three tops, of which the two easterly ones are slightly higher than the one to the west. The upper parts of the mountain are bare and the white stone shines afar. In the winter the mountain is covered with snow from the 2800 foot line upwards, but by September only patches of snow remain. The steep eastern slopes have little vegetation, but the western slopes have some forest growth, partly of evergreens and partly of wild fruit trees.

According to Deuteronomy 3:9, the Amorites called the mountain Shenir (R.S.V. *Senir*), but that name probably applied only to the part of it lying north of Damascus.

With its huge bulk and towering height Mount Hermon is an immense landmark. The visitor to the Lake of Galilee is awed by its majesty. *Jebel esh Sheikh,* or Sheikh Mountain, the Arabs call it and rightly, for it is the sheikh or chief of mountains hereabouts. It can be seen at times by the sharp eyes of a Bedouin from as far south as the "Frank Mountain" near Bethlehem.

"Roll, Jordan, Roll"

Palestine's main river is formed by four separate tributaries coming down from the Hermon region. The most westerly issues from a plain that extends up into the range east of the Leontes River. The central and longest one taps the territory to the west and north of Hermon. Next comes a stream originating in foothills southwest of Mount Hermon near the site of the old Israelite city of

Dan. The easternmost tributary drains the south side of Mount Hermon in several branches. It also receives the waters of the famous grotto of Paneas which was named after the Greek god "Pan" in Hellenistic times and so gets the name of the "River of Paneas" (*Nahr Baniyās*). These streams descend sharply, and this soon becomes true also of the combined current called the Jordan—a name of doubtful origin and meaning. In this area must have sojourned the Psalmist, who amid the noise of the rapids remembers the LORD and his temple "from the land of Jordan, and of the Hermonites, from the hill Mizar" (Ps. 42:6).

The Jordan very soon reaches a marshy area. The papyrus plant formerly grew in profusion in these marshes (which are now being drained by Israeli enterprise), and was used by the local Arabs for mat making. In antiquity, no doubt, the inhabitants of the area also manufactured "paper" for writing material by gluing together strips of papyrus to make sheets and the sheets to make rolls. Many a chapter of the Old Testament must originally have been written on papyrus that came from here. Josephus calls the region Ulatha (*Khŭlethā*). This name has survived in the Arabic designation *Arḍ el Ḥūleh.* At the southern end of the marshy area lies a shallow, heart-shaped body of water three miles long and two miles wide and with a maximum depth of sixteen feet. Contrary to some maps the lake is not called *Ḥūleh* by the natives, but rather *el Khēṭ.* Many modern writers have mistakenly connected it with the waters of Merom (JOSH. 11:5) and called it Lake Merom on their maps. Its ancient name is given by Josephus as Semechonitis; the Talmud preserves it as *Sibkē* or *Subkē, "*thicket-place."

After leaving this lake the Jordan starts southward with new vigor. In noisy rapids and cascades it passes through a gorge. Emerging, it then takes a slower pace as it approaches the entrance to a larger sheet of water—the Lake of Galilee. But it has de-scended nearly 689 feet in the ten mile course from lake to lake.

The Lake of Galilee is thirteen miles long by eight miles wide at the widest point and its surface lies 682 feet below sea level. Where the river enters the lake the land is marshy. On the northwestern shore is a strip of land called nowadays "the little valley" (*el Ghuweir*), but known as the plain of Ginnesar in the time of Jesus. We will speak later of the various names used for the lake in the New Testament age (see page 375). In the Old Testament it is referred to as the Lake of Chinneroth or Chinnereth (JOSH. 12:3; 13:27), after a city which lay enthroned above its northwestern shore (*Tell el ʻOreimeh* or "mound of the little sand hill").

The Earth's Deepest Valley

After leaving this lake the Jordan again drops off swiftly to a third level. The Ghor, which is only four miles wide at first, now broadens out to a width of thirteen to fourteen miles. As the crow flies it is sixty-five miles from the Lake of Galilee to the Dead Sea, but as the river loops (see page 24) it is two hundred miles. The Dead Sea is 1286 feet below sea level, so the Jordan must descend about six hundred feet more before reaching it.

Within the widened trough of the Ghor there is a narrower depression one hundred feet or more in depth which forms the actual river bottom. The transition to this lower level is marked by weird, gray hills called *qaṭṭāra*s ("humps") in Arabic. The depression itself is called the *Zōr,* or "thicket" and is well named, for in a considerable part of its course it is still covered by a jungle. In ancient times this formed a great haven for wild animals (JER. 49:19). A late prophetic writer once refers to it as "the pride of the Jordan" (ZECH. 11:3).

As one goes farther south the river bottom narrows, and there is less vegetation in it. The nature of the bottom lands makes them unsuitable for town sites, generally speaking, and renders the river itself useless for irrigation purposes. What settlements there were grew up in the Ghor above the narrow Zor, at points where streams or brooks came down to join the river.

On its western side, the Ghor was not very favorable for settlements until one neared the vicinity of Jericho, for rainfall is rare and little water seeps down from the parched ravines of western Palestine. A notable exception is provided by the valley coming down from the spring of 'Ain Fār'ah, northeast of Shechem. Another oasis exists farther to the south at the foot of the *Wadi el Qelt.* Here one of the best springs in the whole country, 'Ain es Sultān, gushes forth, making this a most attractive place for a town. Recent excavations have shown that *Tell es Sultān* contained the remains of one of the oldest cities on the face of the earth (see page 134). Established before advances in the art of warfare dictated the choice of hill-top locations, this city, Biblical Jericho, lay hard by the great spring, baking under the fierce sun and, as its name shows, dedicated to the beneficent god of the moon.

On the eastern side of the Jordan Valley, however, there are the rivers *Yarmuk* (not mentioned in the Bible) and Jabbok (*ez Zerqā*) and some smaller streams and brooks. These create pockets of fertile ground, where irrigation is possible and where a goodly number of towns could flourish. The low country just north of the Dead Sea, between the Jordan and the high country to the east, is called "the plains of Moab" in the Old Testament. This designation, no doubt, is of political origin and reflects a time when the Moabites held control of the area. Such, for example, was the case in the days of King Eglon (JUDGES 3:14).

In and Around the Dead Sea

The Dead Sea halts the progress of the Jordan. This is because the Jordan once was part of a much larger lake that filled the whole rift in earlier geological periods. Had the Jordan River been able to carve its own way down to the Gulf of Aqabah and to the Red Sea the whole history of Palestine would have been different. But the Jordan waves lose their punch as they hit the Dead Sea. So great is the absorption of moisture by the hot sun and dry air of this area that the incoming waters are entirely lost by evaporation. The lake water is so salty that a body will not sink in it. Quite appropriately, therefore, "Sea of Salt" is its Hebrew name. To the Greeks the asphalt that occasionally comes to the surface and washes ashore here seemed more remarkable, and led them to call it the "Asphalt Lake."

The Dead Sea is fifty-three miles long, nine to ten miles wide, and lies 1286 feet below sea level. It fills the great rift to such an extent that travel along its western shore is interrupted by the promontory of *Rās Feshkha,* near the northern end of the lake, but still south of the Qumran area and scrolls caves. The water level is currently in a rising phase, and has drowned the trees at various points along the shore. In antiquity the level was lower; one could even wade across the southern part of the lake to "the tongue" (*Lisān*), a flat peninsula-platform that juts out from the eastern shore. The main, upper part of the lake, however, is very deep with a maximum depth of thirteen hundred feet.

Both to the northeast and on the southeast of the Dead Sea there are small districts where fresh-water brooks come down, creating habitable lands, in which there were towns in ancient times. Directly south of the southern end of the Dead Sea is a barren and swampy area called "the ground on which a salt crust has formed" (*es-Sebkha*). From here on the great rift continues riverless for a hundred miles all the way to the Gulf of Aqabah. From the point where the ground begins to ascend, a few miles from the southern end of the Dead Sea, it is no longer called the Ghor, but rather the *Wadi el 'Arabah,* or "valley of the desert."

The Other Side of the Jordan

Let us now look at the northeastern quarter of Palestine. Where would Abraham or Jacob, after skirting Damascus on the east, as they probably would have had to do, have reached the border? There is no clear line of demarcation between Palestine and Syria in this sector as is the case in the central and western ones. But it is logical to continue the northern boundary line from the southern base of Mount Hermon eastward to the headwaters of the *Ruqqād* River, a tributary of the Yarmuk, or to the little crater lake that Josephus calls Phiala (*Birḳet Rān*), and that he believed to be connected in subterranean manner with the Jordan. The territory north of that and east of Mount Hermon, is the *Jedūr,* and thus belongs geographically to Syria. South of it one enters the *Jaulān,* which gets its name from an ancient city, Golan (DEUT. 4:43).

The Jaulan extends from the latitude of the foot of Mount Hermon to the Yarmuk River. The northern part of this region is a high, rolling, rocky country, suited only for nomadic existence. There are numerous volcanic hills with craters; a regular row of these summits extends southeast across the plateau to the Ruqqad River. These hills look much like city mounds and are also named tells by the Arabs. The southern Jaulan, with its volcanic craters and hollows, presents better opportunities for agriculture than the northern portion. A part of this area, *en Nuqrā* ("the depression") is particularly fertile, because of the good brown earth that results from the disintegration of lava. The district as a whole was called Bashan in Old Testament days—a word whose etymology suggests a stoneless, fruitful plain. The term was sometimes used in a broader manner (cf. DEUT. 3:8 f.), and the name became Batanaea in the Graeco-Roman period. The region was famed in Hebrew History for its cattle and its great oak trees (cf. AMOS 4:1; Is. 2:13). But the Israelites who lived there faced dire peril from the expanding power of the Aramaeans of Damascus and the inroads of Arabs from the desert.

After crossing the Yarmuk, Abraham or Jacob would have come next to an upland country extending south to the River Jabbok. This region, today called the *'Ajlūn,* was decidedly more attractive than much of the Jaulan. On crossing the upper reaches of the Jabbok such a nomad would then have come to what is now called the *Belqā,* a name some think is derived from that of King Balak of Numbers 22; it extends all the way to the southern border of eastern Palestine and thus embraces the land of Moab.

"Is There No Balm in Gilead?"

In Old Testament times the southern part of the 'Ajlun and the northern part of the Belqa were called *Gilead,* though that name originally applied only to the country south of Jabbok (see page 84).

Gilead is a fine country, and there are still remnants there of the oak forests that once covered much of it. "Hosea's Mountain" (*Jebel 'Ōsha,* 3597 feet) is the name conferred by the Arabs on the highest summit of the land south of there. In the district north of the Jabbok the crowning height is 4137 feet.

Since this region east of the Ghor receives good rainfall, perennial streams exist here. These have cut steep valleys through the high tableland and on its western side. The Yarmuk carries almost as much water into the Jordan as the latter brings with it up to that point. The Jabbok is likewise a good stream and its valley constitutes the best avenue of entry into western Palestine from Gilead. Important cities were bound to develop, both on the eastern side of the Jordan

Valley where the streams come down, and farther up these watercourses, wherever fertile pockets made agriculture inviting and where good defensive situations existed.

The Lands of Ammon and Moab

As one proceeds southward in the Belqa one perceives a ridge extending from the Jabbok to beyond Madeba (page 123). This ridge constitutes a divide and creates an important geographical division. East of this divide is the Ammonite country, and here lay its capital, Rabbath Ammon, on the very site of 'Ammān, the present capital of the Hashemite Kingdom of Jordan. Much of this Ammonite land is level or rolling. The region west of the divide as far south as the river Arnon (*Wadi el Mōjib*), which cuts a deep valley down to the Dead Sea, was inhabited by Israelites in the time of the early monarchy. But they had only a precarious hold here, since Ammonites and Moabites

were already established in Transjordan before the Hebrews expanded across the river to the east. The best the Hebrew tribes could hope for was to maintain what had been won in the early days. As people of the border, they were under constant peril of being subjugated whenever the west Palestinian brethren were too weak to lend them aid.

South of the Arnon began the land of Moab proper. It extended as far as another deep valley, which is usually identified with the Valley of Zered of Numbers 21:12 (*Wadi el Ḥesā*). It is a fairly fruitful country and able to support a considerable population. At the Zered we reach the Palestinian boundary. South of it lies the land of Edom, extending almost to the latitude of the Gulf of Aqabah. In Graeco-Roman times the district was called Gebalene and the name still clings to it in Arabic dress as *ej Jibāl*. The country of mountains west of the city of *Ma'ān*, the *Jebel esh Shera'*, is the Biblical "Mount Seir."

Western Palestine

We must now turn our attention to the region west of the great Jordan trough. The mountainous country, the real heart of Palestine, commands the chief interest. If Abraham had followed the invitation to pass through the land to its length (GEN. 13:17), we might imagine him as beginning a tour of inspection in the north at the valley of the Leontes.

Galilee and the Plain of Esdraelon

The region extending south from the valley of the Leontes is known as Galilee. The name goes back to Hebrew *gālīl* and means "circle." The fuller form, "Galilee of the nations" (ISA. 9:1), suggests that it was an area ringed by heathen peoples. When one remembers the Canaanite cities of the Plain of Esdraelon, as well as those in the plain of Acre, in Phoenicia and in the Mount Hermon area, this designation seems appropriate.

The land inclining northward toward Syria and Phoenicia is "upper Galilee," while that sloping toward the Plain of Esdraelon is "lower Galilee." There are high mountains in Galilee, with the supreme elevation reached by a summit of 3934 feet; its ancient name is not reported, but today it is *Jebel Jermak*. The towns on the north side of the Plain of Esdraelon belonged to Galilee and the inhabitants doubtless cultivated adjacent parts of the plain.

On the east, Galilee slopes off abruptly to the Jordan in the extreme north, but then more gently to the plain round Lake Semechonitis. In lower Galilee several perennial brooks lead into the area of the Lake of Galilee, while Mount Tabor forms, as it were, a southeastern corner outpost, commanding a marvelous view over the region round about. On its western inclines Galilee proved less attractive for settlement.

The Plain of Esdraelon was an area of great importance. The name is a Greek reproduction of Hebrew Jezreel; the fact that the kings of Israel were fond of sojourning at the city of that name must have given the name to the plain—perhaps first only a portion of it, for Jezreel itself was not a powerful city. Through the plain flows the Kishon stream, first westerly and then deflected northward by the great Carmel range to reach the Mediterranean Sea near Haifa. But the Kishon was hardly a barrier or dividing line, and the plain was therefore usually considered a part of Samaria, though in Roman times, when the power of individual cities meant less, it may have been neutral ground (page 390). The plain is very fertile and hence could support the population of a number of important ancient towns, which lay on the higher land adjoining it. But it was also swampy, since the drainage was none too good, and therefore malarial. Toward the southeast the plain terminates in the valley of "Goliath's stream" (the *Nahr Jālūd*), which drops off gently to the Ghor. Since the plain is only about two hundred feet above sea level and the town of *Bēsān* which lies on a terrace above the Ghor, only 322 feet below sea level, this constitutes the easiest descent to the Jordan. It was, indeed, the predestined highroad for those coming from Egypt or from central Palestine and bound for Gilead and Damascus. Over this road went much commerce, on which toll could be levied by the local rulers in times when there was no centralized government of the land. On the high tableland east of the Jordan, routes coming from Acco across Galilee merged with it. One of these is the "road of the Hauranians" (*darb el Ḥawārneh*).

Hills and Valleys of Samaria

The central section of western Palestine is called Samaria. It is less rugged than Galilee, and is a country of pleasant hills and valleys. A sharp division between northern and southern Samaria is formed by the pass between Mount Ebal and Mount Gerizim. As seen from the heights of Gilead, this is the only break in the Samarian skyline.

South of the Carmel range there are several watersheds. The most traveled road from Beth-shean to the coast goes through the plain of Dothan and the valley leading down from it which feeds a river that enters the sea south of Caesarea. It was the road used by the Ishmaelites to whom Joseph was sold by his treacherous brethren. The second watershed sends a valley down from the plain of Shechem. It feeds a stream called Alexander's River (*Nahr Iskanderūne*), which reaches the sea a few miles south of the other.

The plain between Mount Ebal and Mount Gerizim is a particularly central location and the ideal point from which to govern a united Palestine. From it the roads radiated in all main directions—not only to the coast but to Galilee, to the Jordan Valley, to Bethel and Jerusalem. It seems to have had a great importance in the Amarna Age (*c.* 1500 B.C.). But the plain of Shechem is narrow and its queen city had no strong defensive location. For this reason it did not suit the kings of Israel as a capital.

The natural boundary of Samaria, regardless of the variable political boundary, may be drawn in the neighborhood of modern Ramallah. Here the headwaters of the *Wadi el Qelt*, flowing toward the Jordan, and those of the valley system flowing toward Jaffa (the *Wadi Qāna*) come so close to each other that there is only a narrow span of a couple of miles between the watersheds. Near Ramallah, furthermore, is a crest from which the land slopes off southward. Hereabouts one stands at the old tribal boundary between Ephraim and Benjamin.

Judaea and Its Wilderness

The third main segment of the high country is Judaea. As used for geographical purposes it includes the territory of the tribe of

Benjamin. Important roads traversed the Benjaminite district. Eastward one might go to Jericho via Michmash or the *Wadi el Qelt.* Travel to the coast, even from Jerusalem, went via Beth-horon, especially if the objective was Jaffa or Caesarea or points north; the grade was better than that of the routes followed by railroad and highway of today.

The Benjaminite part of Judaea represents a high plateau culminating in the mountain sacred to the memory of Samuel (*Nebi Samwīl,* 2385 feet high). The Jerusalem area represents a depression, south of which the ground begins a fresh rise that carries up from there for more than a thousand feet to the heights north of Hebron (3370 feet).

On the west Judaea inclines gently to the maritime region. A number of routes to the southern coast, forming gateways both for attackers and defenders, lay here. Important was the one through the valley of Rephaim, west of Jerusalem, down to Kiriath-jearim and Beth-shemesh (the *Wadi eṣ Ṣarār*). From the Beth-zur area another road led to the coast past Adullam and Socoh (via the *Wadi es Samt*), while from Hebron there was the valley that led to *Maresha,* the Eleutheropolis of Roman times.

In the east, Judaea drops off very sharply in three successive steps or terraces to the Dead Sea. This area is called "the Wilderness of Judah" in the Old Testament. The word "wilderness" is a bit misleading. For us a wilderness is a country of forests. Actually, this is a region of bare rock. Leaving the top of the Mount of Olives east of Jerusalem or the field of the shepherds east of Bethlehem, one enters this desolate zone. A rolling country, treeless and waterless, slopes downward, and as the descent becomes more sharp develops gorges and canyons, cut into the soft sedimentary formations by torrents of rainwater in ages past. At the east end of the valley of Hinnom, which skirts Jerusalem on the south, a gorge (the *Wadi en Nār*) leads off immediately

into this wilderness. According to Talmudic sources this was the route taken when the scapegoat was led out into this seemingly accursed land and consigned to Azazel (LEV. 16:8, 10); it was probably also the attempted escape route of King Zedekiah (see page 316). About five miles from the city the wadi veers off, forcing the road to take to a ridge and cross the height of the *Jebel el Munṭār,* which provides a marvellous view over the Judaean wilderness. From it one descends to the "little plain" (*el Ibqē'a*) and can head for the lower Jordan crossings. The plain has only recently been examined archaeologically by Frank M. Cross and J. T. Milik (in 1955) and found to have had old Hebrew towns. Leaving it one crosses the *Wadi Qumrān,* which leads down to the scrolls caves and the Qumran settlement.

The Southern Border and Beyond

From Hebron the land to the south soon begins to slope off. At Beersheba the altitude is but 500 feet. The region was part of Idumaea in New Testament times, because the Edomites had occupied it after the fall of Jerusalem in 586 B.C. Beersheba is most naturally taken as the southernmost town of Palestine. A dry stream-bed that begins here and goes down toward Gaza (the *Wadi Ghazzeh*), appropriately marks the boundary line. From Beersheba east to the central rift there is no clear line of demarcation. But if one keeps in this latitude and crosses the rift, one meets the deep valley that terminates eastern Palestine—the *Wadi el Ḥesā,* or Valley of Zered. This makes Palestine's general border sufficiently distinct.

The region between the valley of Gaza and the next major valley to the south of it, "the brook of Egypt" (the *Wadi el 'Arīsh*), is a sort of no man's land between Palestine and Egypt. It has always been a scene of strife, for a strong Egypt felt determined to control the approaches to Palestine, and a strong Palestine (or power holding it) felt inclined to carry its sway to the very door of Africa. In the clash between Egypt and the Israel state of today, the age-old contest has been renewed. The region was included in the Negeb or "south land" in the Old Testament (Negev in Jewish and newspaper spelling). It was sparsely populated in those times, but after greater security was established by the Nabataeans and the Romans, it had a surprising development. Explorers have found here ruins of whole cities, the existence of which was made possible by the extensive use of facilities to store and utilize rain water. There were Roman roads at various points, as well as forts, some of which are still standing. A great system of fortifications (called *limes*), running from Aqabah to Palmyra and the Euphrates, and thence up the Khabur River and eastward to Mosul, kept the desert tribesmen from invading the region west of it and provided peace and security until the Islamic conquest of the seventh century A.D.

Up the Coast from Gaza

If Abraham had decided to start at Gaza and walk north through the coastal plain, he would have found himself straightway in what we call "Philistaea"—the area of the Philistine cities. In his time they must still have been inhabited by Canaanites. The coastal strip here is about twelve and a half miles wide, but narrows as one goes north, being only about two miles wide at Caesarea. The area around Gaza in the extreme south is a garden spot, in sight of the open sea and with a wealth of springs, olive orchards, fruit trees, and big scyamore trees, up which the grape vines climb. Down to Hellenistic times, Gaza was the terminus of the great trade route from South Arabia to the Mediterranean. No wonder then that it was one of the most important cities of the Levant! Proceeding northward the patriarch would have passed through the rolling, treeless but cultivated plain that is barred off from the sea in the west by a great zone of sand dunes rising to a height of nearly 150

feet, and paralleled by a row of low hills. Between the nine hundred foot wall of the Judaean mountain country and the plain is a foothills zone, which is called the *Shephēlāh* or "lowland" in the Old Testament. It extends north from the latitude of Beersheba to that of Jerusalem.

In his further perambulation Abraham would have passed through territory belonging to Ashkelon, which lay beyond the dunes on the coast, and would then have come to Ashdod. The next lap of the journey would have brought him to the "Reuben's River" (*Nahr Rubīn*) and the neighborhood of the Philistine city of Ekron, where Philistaea reaches its natural terminus.

The district of Lod or Lydda (*Ludd*) to the north, a fertile garden region, was readily accessible from Jerusalem, and the kings of Judah were thus able to exercise power there or to prevent the Philistines from controlling it for long. The Hebrews seem to have been barred from the coastal city of Japho (*Jaffa*), however, which was Canaanitic, and generally under the control of the seafaring Phoenicians (cf. 2 CHRON. 2:16). Only in Maccabean days were the Jews able to establish themselves here.

From the latitude of Jaffa northward Abraham would have entered the Plain of Sharon, which extends as far as the *Nahr ez Zerqā* or "Blue River" (not to be confused with a stream of the same name in Transjordan, the Jabbok), that comes to the coast south of Dor. This region was largely wooded in ancient times. Its forest constituted "the majesty of Sharon" which the pro-

1.6 *Acco, the Acre of the Crusades.* (*Keren Hayesod*)

1.7 *The White Promontory—part of the Tyrian Ladder.* (*Matson Photo Service*)

phetic writer sees turned into a desert (Is. 33:19; 35:2). The former passage implies that Sharon served of old as pasture for flocks or herds: in other words, that Israelites sent their livestock down there from the high country when vegetation grew scarce. For us Sharon is particularly associated with the Rose of Sharon (SOL. 2:1).

The flower referred to, however, is not our shrub of that name, but most probably a fragrant narcissus variety which grows early and in great profusion in this area. But there were also numerous swampy districts in Sharon, since the waters coming down from the hill-country had trouble getting through the dunes to the sea. Today the forests are gone. North of Dor the plain narrows greatly, and seems to have had no important settlements.

The coastal strip is interrupted by the Carmel range, which juts into the sea. Beyond the mountain is the Bay of Acre. Here the Kishon stream comes down to the sea from the Plain of Esdraelon. Farther to the north one comes to a shallow creek, across which lies 'Akkā, successor to Biblical Acco, the Acre of Crusader fame. Its function as port city has now been usurped by Haifa. The plain of Acre contains a number of important tells, and was a populous, well-cultivated region in early times.

As one continues north from here, the Galilean mountains are seen to slope off sharply to the plain. Soon a mountain barrier terminating in a promontory is thrust into the path of the traveler. After crossing

this barrier one comes to another spur of this same range ending in what is called "the white promontory" (*Rās el Abyaḍ*), because of the white rock of which it consists. It is skirted on the ocean side by means of a track distinguished by steps hewn into the rock. This is part of the "Tyrian ladder" over which kings and captains have led their hosts in endless single files since the dawn of history. In the narrow coastal strip that begins north of this point lies ancient Tyre. Though still geographically within Palestine, one has now entered territory inhabited by the Phoenicians and so included in Phoenicia. Not far to the north of Tyre the Leontes River comes down from the east and therewith the indicated boundary of Palestine, though not that of Phoenicia, is reached.

The Background in Nature

To understand a country one must consider how it was made and of what it is made. The drawing on the next page shows a cross section of Palestine and gives some essentials of its geological structure and history. (1) The upper layers of the earth's crust in this area are sedimentary deposits from the Cretaceous period, which preceded the Tertiary or Diluvial period, and saw the appearance of birds and mammals. At the bottom lies Nubian sandstone; above that Turonic; then Cenomanic and finally Senonite. (2) Next the land was heaved high up out of the water some five thousand to six thousand feet. Longitudinal cracks developed in this

1.8 *Leontes River Valley and Palestine border from the north with view of Belfort, Crusader castle ruins.* (*Institut Francais d'Archéologie, Beyrouth, Liban*)

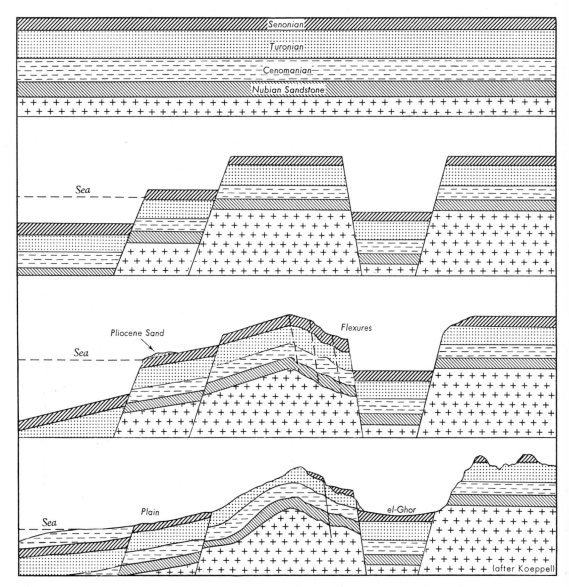

THE BASIC GEOLOGICAL DEVELOPMENT OF PALESTINE

mass and segments of it broke off and dropped down. One piece in the extreme west fell beneath sea level, while an adjoining piece fell to near sea level, thus forming what is now the coastal strip of Palestine. The central mass remained high, but a wide segment sank down in the middle, thus forming the great rift or trough of the Jordan Valley. (3) An arching of the segments west of the trough took place, giving those that had fallen a tilt, while the central block developed flexures on its eastern side and became buckled. Pliocene sands were heaped up on the maritime-plain segment. (4) Erosion then went to work on the elevated blocks, creating the profile of the land as we see it today.

We cannot follow the story of Palestine's geological history further. Only one other development needs to be mentioned here—the eruption of volcanoes, particularly in northern Transjordan, where, as already noted, their craters are still found. This eruption flooded certain areas with a coating of lava and threw bars of volcanic rock across the Jordan Valley forming the two upper lakes. But generally speaking the mountains of Palestine are a high tableland of sedimentary rock serried by erosion.

It was portentous that Palestine's crust was composed of such material. Limestone is readily penetrated by water, and so the rain seeps away quickly, instead of being retained near the surface, as would be the case were the rock of the granite type. The water creates subterranean channels, and has hollowed out most of the caves in which the land is honeycombed, including those where the Dead Sea Scrolls were found.

From Forest to Desert

Ever since climatic conditions have been the same as they are now, Palestine could be divided into three zones—forest, desert and steppe. Everything that is not desert or steppe was forested when the first neolithic men put in an appearance thereabouts. Looking at Palestine today it is hard to believe that all those bare and rocky hills once had a forest covering. The botanist tells us that the plants growing in Palestine, except in steppe and desert areas, reveal that this is by nature forest zone. The matter is governed very simply by the amount of rainfall. Where there is more than twelve to fourteen inches annual precipitation, one has forest zone, and where there is less than eight inches one has desert zone, while in between one has steppe.

The map on this page shows the basic nature of Palestine. On it we see a strip of steppe girdling all but the north border and invading the central rift to the north end of the Ghor. Each of the three zones mentioned has its own type of vegetation. The Palestinian forests, of which only miserable remnants remain, must have consisted of the evergreen oak that flourished especially in the coastal plain, the deciduous oak and to a

lesser degree the Aleppo-pines. The latter originally formed dense woods without underbrush, unsuitable even for pasturage. The present macchia–bushes are dwarf descendants of the old forests of evergreen oak. The large expanses of shining, white rock visible in Palestine are largely denuded areas, from which, after the trees were felled or burned, the soil has been washed away leaving the rock exposed. The flowers that grow in profusion out of the crevices in springtime—the anemones, ranunculi, alpine violets, asphodel, iris, and orchids—are all flora typical of a forest climate with abundant winter rainfall. The raising of sheep and goats in these areas has prevented the forest from coming back, and where some was still left around 1900, as in east Jordan, the axe has largely destroyed it. Israel and Hashemite Jordan both are doing something about reforestation.

Desert and Steppe

But a further glance at the map will show

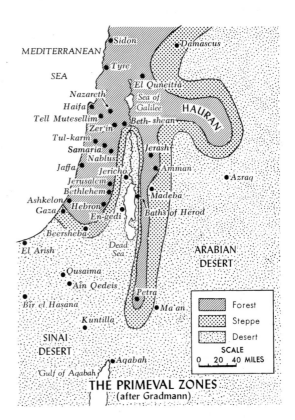

THE PRIMEVAL ZONES
(after Gradmann)

that Palestine is enveloped by a desert climate. This comes from the south and invades the Dead Sea area and the Jordan rift, including the slopes descending into it on the west, as far as Beth-shean. And of course it prevails out beyond the fertile strip of eastern Transjordan, where, however, the Hauran creates a large outward bulge in the line.

The desert is not just sand. The ground is bare only in the salt districts, but otherwise has a certain amount of vegetation—from one-twentieth to one-half of the surface being covered with it. Perhaps the desert has changed the least in the course of the ages; and yet here, too, there may be less vegetation than would naturally be the case were it not for human beings who use brush for fire and whose camels devour whole bushes. The important earmark of the desert climate is the occurrence of characteristic vegetation.

A desert may contain oases or semi-oases, depending on the occurrence of underground springs. The popular notion of an oasis is that of a little island with a few palm trees in a sea of sand. But whole regions take on an oasis-like character when they produce certain flowers or shrubs. Thus in the desert region around the Dead Sea and in the *Wadi el 'Arabah,* or in the desert of Sinai, one strikes districts where tamarisks, acacias, and the thorny zizyphus grow, and these districts, too, are to be classified as oases. Engedi, on the western side of the Dead Sea, is of this nature, and flora typical of the Sudan are still to be found there. From the botanist's angle, the "jungle of the Jordan" is likewise to be regarded as an oasis.

But between the desert and the agricultural lands is a highly important belt, the steppe. A steppe is a wide expanse which cannot support forest but has some vegetation composed of grasses, bushes, and even an occasional tree covering about half the ground. Often the original steppe-nature of an area is not immediately discernible to the eye, for with the help of cisterns and irrigation, cultivation can invade this zone. The

occurrence of certain annual plants including those ancestral to our wheat and barley, is no sure criterion, for these plants can also grow in both the desert and the crop lands. But as one really strikes the latter one finds wheat fields and at the same time the rounded bushes of the Thorny Burnet, which is one of the commonest plants in the agricultural area and is much utilized for fuel. And at sight of the first olive orchards one can feel certain of having left the steppes and of having entered the zone of cultivation.

The earliest settlements of Neolithic man in Palestine were in steppe or oasis districts where there were no forests to clear. But by the time of Israel's beginnings the forests that once covered much of the land had long been invaded, and cities had grown up in the more attractive mountain valleys of the uplands east and west of the Jordan, as well as in the coastal plain. Yet there were some woodlands left in those days, even in western Palestine, and these probably played an important role in providing the Hebrew invaders with situations for new settlements.

Weather and Climate

The climate of Palestine is that of the Mediterranean in general. Lying between 31° and 35° 15 north latitude it belongs to the subtropical zone. The sun is up for never less than ten hours or more than fourteen hours of each day. The temperature on the hottest days seldom exceeds 90°F, except in the Jordan Valley where 103°F is not unusual; the coldest days rarely reach freezing; 46°F is the mean temperature for February, the coldest month. The average annual mean temperature is 62–68°F.

Palestine is situated at a point over which ocean climate and desert climate struggle for the mastery. It lies between two zones of air currents—that of the winds of passage in the south and that of the variable winds in the north. In summer the former prevail, with an attending steadiness of barometric pressure; at this time the winds are chiefly from

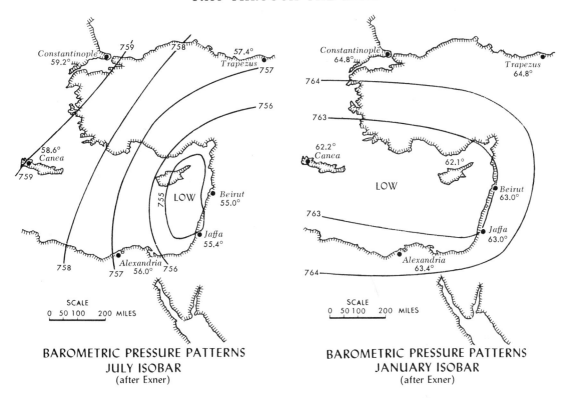

BAROMETRIC PRESSURE PATTERNS
JULY ISOBAR
(after Exner)

BAROMETRIC PRESSURE PATTERNS
JANUARY ISOBAR
(after Exner)

the northwest or west. In winter southern Palestine has mostly west wind, but changing often to south and southeast. In the transitional periods from winter to summer or vice versa, east winds are common.

The physiography of the land has a great effect on both the wind and on the precipitation. The moisture-laden west wind from the ocean brings no showers in summer, since the mountains do not rise high enough to carry these winds up to a level where they would clash with cooler air and cause rainfall. In winter, however, the warmer winds from the sea become chilled as they strike the mountains, and so produce rain over western Palestine. In sliding off into the Jordan Valley these winds can take on great velocity, thus producing such dangerous situations as that which befell the Disciples of Jesus, when they were out in a boat with him on the Lake of Galilee (MARK 4:37). As the winds descend into the Jordan Valley south of that lake, they are warmed and absorb what little moisture they find there, particularly in its deeper

and hotter portion. In rising anew to the heights of the Transjordan tableland, they spill this freshly acquired moisture as rain on the eastern part of the plateau, thus providing that region with verdant uplands and with streams flowing into the Ghor.

It may be seen from this that nature has endowed Palestine with two seasons—a rainy one and a dry one. If we think of summer as the period of heat, and of winter as the period of cold that is not the way the Palestinian looks at it. From the middle of May to the middle of October is the dry season; June through August are completely devoid of precipitation and all the vegetation withers, making the land seem an arid one. When October arrives, Palestinians long for the coming of "early rain," so often mentioned in the Bible. This merely means an advance installment of rain that will soften the hard, sun-baked ground and make it possible for the farmer to do his plowing and sowing in November before the protracted rains come. The rainy season starts in

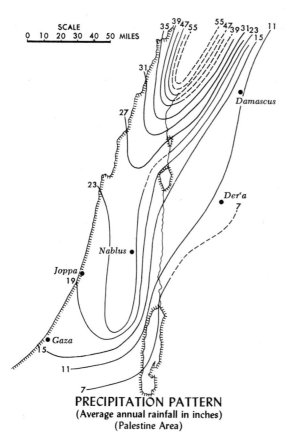

SCALE
0 10 20 30 40 50 MILES

Damascus

Der'a
7

Nablus

Joppa
19

Gaza
15

11

7

PRECIPITATION PATTERN
(Average annual rainfall in inches)
(Palestine Area)

but fortunately does not occur frequently, for heavy snow readily causes the flimsy roofs to cave in over people's heads and creates big problems in the feeding of livestock. But the snow melts quickly and lingers only on Mount Hermon and the Lebanon, which are outside of Palestine proper.

Dew is particularly abundant in western Palestine in summer. It is a life saver to the land, and so it becomes a symbol of God's grace and mercy. It is dropped by moisture-laden air, which is carried up in the night from the sea to the higher levels of the hills and mountains. The author of Psalm 133 thinks of the dew as coming down from Hermon upon the mountains of Zion. The story of Gideon's fleece vividly illustrates the drenching nature of the dew (JUDG. 6:37-40). After the fall equinox it may come down as a regular drizzle out of a clear starry sky. But after the moisture has been spilled, the air passes eastward dehydrated. In the southern Ghor no dew ever falls.

The humidity is relatively greatest in Palestine in the summer season in spite of the drought then prevailing; the lowest humidity is seen in the transitional periods, April-May and September–October (10 per cent less). The latter is the period when a much dreaded wind, the sirocco (an Italianized Arabic word meaning the "easterner") brings dry, hot, dust-laden air from the desert. This wind absorbs what little moisture there is, so that all vegetation wilts.

Beulah Land

The love of the Jews for their land is abundantly revealed in the pages of the Old Testament. It was to be called Beulah "married," for "as the bridegroom rejoiceth over the bride, so shall thy God rejoice over thee" (Is. 62:4-5). When we consider the role this country has played in the history of mankind and the manner in which it has touched everyone's spiritual existence through the pages of Holy Writ, we think of it fondly as though it were our ancestral home.

December and extends through February (some fifty-seven days of rain in Jerusalem!).

The arrival of the winter rains may be very sudden and may be heralded by a thunderstorm, as in the instance related in the story of Elijah on Mount Carmel (1 KINGS 18:41 f.). When Jesus speaks of the house built on sand that collapsed (MATT. 7:27), he was giving a good description of a Palestinian rainstorm.

The amount of actual rainfall in the most favored areas of Palestine is not much less than in the eastern United States or in western Europe. At Jaffa the annual precipitation is generally about twenty inches; at Haifa, twenty-four to twenty-eight; in the Jordan Valley eighteen inches except in the southern area, around Jericho, where it is only eight to twelve inches.

Of considerable concern is the occurrence of a snow storm. It can take place in January,

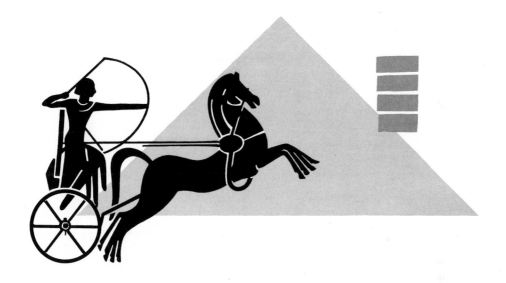

THE ANCIENT HEBREW TRADITION

The DESIGN on the preceding page shows an Egyptian pyramid, a horse and chariot of the period of Seti I or Ramses II, and bricks from an Egyptian relief showing brick-making as it was supposedly done by the Hebrews when they were in Egypt.

TOP, *the stela of Idrimi, king of Alalakh in Syria. (British Museum, with permission of Sir Leonard Woolley)* BOTTOM, *goddess and two princes of Ugarit (Ras esh Shamra). Phoenician king of Ugarit smiting foe. King and queen of Ugarit. (C. F. Schaeffer, Mission Archéologique Francaise, copyrighted)*

CHAPTER III

IN THE BEGINNING

When Washington Irving wrote his humorous Knickerbocker's *History of New York* he opened it with a preliminary section on "The Creation and Population of the World." He was parodying ancient authors, who followed this procedure in relating the history of their own city or nation. Thus Berossus, a Graeco-Babylonian writer of the days of Alexander the Great, began his story of his country's past with the "Creation of the World," "The Kings before the Flood," "The Flood," and "The Kings after the Flood." So, too, several of the Hebrew writers, whose originally separate accounts were used by the compiler of Genesis, had started their histories. They began at the very beginning of things.

"As It Was in the Beginning"

For the keynoter, the compiler selected the youngest of these writers, putting his account of Creation (Gen. 1:1–2:4) first.

His idea of the structure of the world ("cosmology") invites comparison with that of the Babylonian priests The drawing on page 42 shows the latter. The Jew does not think of the earth as a "world-mountain," or speak of the seven stories of Heaven. He does not mention the nether world, let alone its seven stories. But he thinks of the firmament as having been reared in the midst of the waters, so that there were waters above (a heavenly ocean) and waters below (a nether ocean). Out of the latter God had then raised the dry land, which was ringed about by waters like an island. By special acts of creation, distributed into six working days, the phenomena of nature and the living creatures were called into being through the mere word of the one and only God. Under the benison of a celestial Sabbath, prototype of the weekly rest day that assumed such importance in the Exile and that has been perpetuated in our own

BABYLONIAN WORLD VIEW
(after Meissner)

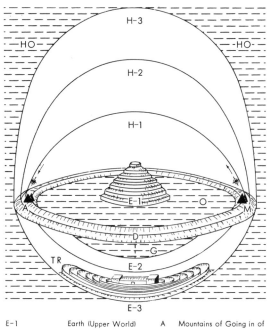

E-1	Earth (Upper World)	A	Mountains of Going in of
E-2 E-3	Earth (Nether-World)		the Sun
H-1 H-2 H-3	Heavens	M	Mountains of Going forth
HO	Heavenly Ocean		of the Sun
O	Terrestrial Ocean	D	Embankment
G	Bottom of Ocean	TR	Nether-world palace and
			its seven walls

rest day, the life of the world had been launched.

As we pass through this massive portal into Biblical history we immediately encounter a story written by a writer of an earlier age (GEN. 2:4 f.). He had likewise begun with the creation of the world, but had hurried over that matter to other things of greater concern to the people of his time. His brief remarks show that he thought of the earth as having been a desert waste at first. The LORD had brought fertility about by means of a primeval mist or ebullition of water (the exact nuance of the word cannot be determined with certainty). The LORD had then formed man of clay and infused the breath of life into this model.

"O Paradise, O Paradise!"

This older writer was quite interested in geography in speaking of the beginnings of

humanity and of its earliest home, and develops a sort of world map for his readers. This writer's picture of the world is shown on this page. His basic idea is that there are four world rivers, which fan out from the single river of Paradise. Since two of them are named with historically established names, the Hiddekel and the Pherath (the Babylonian-Assyrian names for the Tigris and the Euphrates), he must have sought Paradise in that mysterious and fearful northland of Armenia. If the name Eden is used for the country in which Paradise lies, this is probably because a district called Eden (AMOS 1:5) blocked the way to it; that name was extended to cover the region beyond, a thing that also happens with other geographical names (e.g., Shinar, page 53). Later in the story Eden is used simply as the name of the garden of God. The names of the rivers Gihon and Pishon, which form a rhymed pair, are not, however, names of actual geography, but rather designations given by the writer to these remote waters whose foreign names he may have heard and considered too uncouth or strange. When he speaks of Havilah (page 48) it seems quite obvious that here, too, he is using the name of a nearer region in place of one far beyond, and is thinking of Yemen. Cush is the regular name of Nubia, but pos-

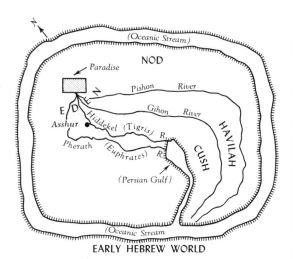

EARLY HEBREW WORLD

sibly is used here by extension for Ethiopia.

In this connection the map (page 42) which sets forth this geography deserves comparison with a Babylonian world map (see this page). This map is a Neo-Babylonian copy of a much older map. It dwells on the Tigris-Euphrates countries and on points north, and ignores Syria and Egypt. The city of Babylon, bisected by the broad band of the Euphrates, is the very hub of the world. Circles on the map are cartouches for the names of cities or districts. Several are left blank, perhaps because the tablet from which this copy was made by the ancient scribe had been damaged, so that the names were lost or illegible. Bit Yakin is prominent near the mouth of the river, a principality whose ruling house in the eighth century got control at times of the city of Babylon (page 299). Possibly the unnamed island-town was Dilmun (or Bahrain Island). Upstream Dēr is mentioned, probably identical with Akkad. Khabban or Bit Khabban is also named, but its exact location is not yet known and references to it are scarce in the Babylonian texts. Assyria is named, too, but the Tigris River ignored. Around the disk-like earth runs the oceanic stream ("the Bitter River"), and a bayou from it runs up at an angle to the Euphrates. The six triangles extending out from the Bitter waters lead over to islands beyond the oceanic stream. The map of Genesis 2:10 f. has the broader horizon, though here, too, there is complete silence about the west. The interest in regions to the east and south, however, is particularly noteworthy.

The Land of Nod

Man, expelled from the paradise, departed eastward, but still lived in the area for which the concept Eden is used. Cherubim and "a flaming sword which turned every way" were put at the eastern entrance of the garden to prevent any attempt to return.

The first children of the first human pair were Cain and Abel. Cain, after committing the crime of slaying his brother, was driven out "from before the face of the LORD" and dwelt in the "land of Nod." That name is an appellative, meaning "land of wandering." In the light of the connection one might look for that land in Kurdistan or Media. However, the Cain story taken by itself belongs in the south Palestinian scene, for Cain is the ancestor of the tribe of Cain (NUM. 24:22). The name has recently been vindicated as a personal name, too, in the inscription of a North Arabian king (page 334). Nod, therefore, may have been a term for Cain's country. One may compare the "Wilderness of the Wandering" (*Bādaiet et Tīh*), which is used by the Arabs for the region south of the Negeb. The same area could once have been called the "land of Nod." The Genesis writer, recognizing its appellative nature, held it to be an appropriate designation, too, for the vast region "east of Eden," through which came the innumerable migrations of early humanity.

The ancestral parents living in the Eden territory found a replacement for their son Abel in Seth (GEN. 4:25). With him begins the line of the "antediluvian" patriarchs (i.e., the ones before the Flood), who,

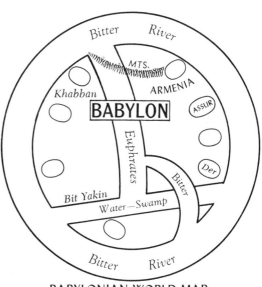

BABYLONIAN WORLD MAP

though long-lived, are very much the juniors of their Babylonian colleagues, the Kings before the Flood. But the Sethite line, too, is drawn into evil ways; a violent breed of supermen emerges from them (GEN. 6:1 f.), causing bloodshed and terror on the earth. God, therefore, determines to send a deluge to destroy humanity, sparing only a single pious man and his family.

The Land of the Flood

In the Biblical flood story it is not stated where Noah lived. The discovery in the royal library of Nineveh of an epic containing a story of the Deluge startled the world, when announced by the British Assyriologist George Smith in 1876. For it revealed that the tradition of the Flood also existed in lower Babylonia. The flood hero of the Babylonian epic dwells in Shuruppak, of which it is said "that the city was old," when the disaster came. Its site has been identified as *Fāra,* a rambling mound five-sixths of a mile long and two-thirds of a mile wide, where Sumerian tablets in archaic writing have beeen found. The place was destroyed very early and plays no role in Babylonian history. The old Sumerian name of the flood hero was *Zi-ū-sud-ra,* "life unto distant days," and was evidently conferred on him in retrospect because he had attained immortality like the Biblical Enoch (GEN. 5:24). The aforementioned Berossus transcribed the name in Greek letters as Xisouthros. In the classic Semitic-Babylonian version, however, the hero's name is Ut-napishtim, while in the Biblical version, which presumably is connected with old Canaanite or Amorite tradition, the name Noah was substituted. This name, being derived from the root meaning "to rest," must also have suggested some aspect of the flood hero's life or fate—possibly only his (and the ark's) "resting" or grounding (GEN. 8:4).

Sumer or lower Babylonia is indeed the most natural and appropriate setting for a flood. For here torrential rains and the freshets of rivers descending from the great mountains often must have created dire peril for the inhabitants of the alluvial plain. The occurrence of a tidal inundation from the Persian Gulf was likewise within the realm of possibility. Sir Leonard Woolley in his excavations at Ur (page 55) found what he believed to be material evidence of a great river flood that had piled silt over the town. While some uncertainty attaches to this claim, the Babylonian flood story is evidence enough of the terror of the waters back in those primitive times, when men had not yet learned how to harness them and diffuse their impact.

The antiquity of the epic is made vivid by the simple life it mirrors. Men were dwelling in reed houses such as are still made today of giant reeds by the Marsh-Arabs of the region at the mouth of the Tigris River. For when the God Ea desires to warn the Babylonian Noah of the decision of the gods to send a flood, he addresses the reed house in which he dwells:

Reed-house! Reed-house! Wall! Wall!
Reed-house, hear; and wall, give attention!
Man of Shuruppak, son of Ubara-Tutu,
Fashion a structure, build a ship!
Leave possessions, seek life!

If the flood was a river inundation, or even a tidal wave from the Persian Gulf, which in ancient times extended much farther inland than is the case now, one may imagine the ark of the earliest Sumerian versions as having landed on some topographic eminence, or foothill of the mountain country to the east. But in the succeeding versions of the epic the horizons became ever greater.

Ararat

In the Ninevite version the ark lands on Mount Niṣir (see Color Map III), which can be localized because of the campaigns that Assyrian kings carried on in its vicinity. It is the Grandfather Omar Mountain (*Pir*

Omar Gudrun), which lies in the mountainous country north of the Babylonian plain. "Its remarkably shaped top, especially when snow-capped," says Ephraim Speiser, "attracts the eye from a great distance. Often visible for more than one hundred miles it was to the Babylonians the most natural place to perch their ark upon." In the version of Berossus the ark lands in Gordyene (Kurdistan). In the younger of the interwoven Biblical versions the scene of the landing of the ark is placed on "one of the mountains of Ararat." Ararat was the name the Assyrians had used since the ninth century B.C. for an important state in Armenia, though they vocalized it differently as *Urartu*. The capital, named *Ṭuspa, Ṭurushpa,* lay at Lake Van. Here rock-carved cuneiform inscriptions in the Urartaean language tell us of the old kings of Ararat. Their people were the Khaldians (not to be confused with Chaldeans), who were later succeeded by the Armenians. For Christian tradition which naturally was influenced by the Armenian church, Ararat has, however, become the name of a single mountain.

Mount Ararat, called the *Koh-i-Nu* or "Mountain of Noah" by the Kurds, is the culminating point of the Armenian plateau. It rears up its head in grandeur to an elevation of seventeen thousand feet from the Plain of Aras (itself nearly three thousand feet above sea level). There are few mountains in the world rising from such a low base to such dizzy heights. It has two peaks, and on the lesser one three realms corner— the Soviet Union, Turkey and Iran. The higher peak, of course, is that on which the ark supposedly landed.

A Small Horizon

The Book of Genesis does not say where Noah and his family sojourned after the flood. In a narrative going back to a very early storyteller (GEN. 9:19–27) he is described as the discoverer of wine-growing. The scene of his sojourning must therefore have been in the zone where raising of grapes is carried on (e.g., Syria). With this westerly home of humanity the statement of Genesis 11:2, that an eastward journey brought men to Babylonia, is in accord. In the story of Noah the Vintager his three sons are Shem, Japheth and [Ham the father of] Canaan. The bracketed words were added by the compiler of the present Book of Genesis in order to reconcile this old material with younger accounts which substituted Ham for Canaan. That change made it possible to list additional peoples under the third son's name in Genesis 10.

Shem, Japheth, and Canaan, as originally viewed in this episode, however, are ancestors in a very limited sphere only; the broader panorama of the Table of Nations (GEN. 10) is not yet in view. Indeed, the scene is purely Syrian and Palestinian. The three sons of Noah represent different peoples of the time when the story was composed.

The first and leading group is called Shem, "name." The designation is evidently one of pride, not the actual name of a nation or tribe. Another group is called Japheth, and is welcomed as co-operating with Shem in the subjugation of the following third group. This name, too, is hardly a national or tribal name but is chosen to cover various elements. The third group is called Canaan. This definitely identifies the group meant—the early inhabitants of Phoenicia and Palestine. Since Canaan is destined to become a slave to his brethren, the story reflects the subjection of the old Canaanite population of Palestine to slave status by newcomers Shem and Japheth. "Shem" is thus the conquering group of nomadic peoples ("tents of Shem"), the Hebrews and related tribes, which overcame the Canaanites. Japheth, name of an ancient hero who appears as *Iapetos* in Greek genealogies of the gods, must then be a name for allies of a very different stock, who are regarded as guests in the general territory claimed for Shem. We know too little about what happened in the early days to be sure of who they were. Some Cretan-Mycenaean

45

2.1 *Assyrian King Ashurbanipal bringing a libation after the hunt.* (*British Museum*)

groups may have co-operated with the Israelites in warring on the Canaanites. Or the reference might have been to the sea peoples who came down the coast in the days of Pharaoh Ramses III (see page 131). It is only a hint of a forgotten history.

The First Empire Builder

Another intriguing story of early humanity is found in the Table of Nations, where the mention of Cush suggests it. It is about Nimrod the Cushite, founder of Babylonian and Assyrian cities and a great hunter.

The name and identity of Nimrod have been matters of much speculation. Some scholars think the name is Libyan, for it is seemingly found in that quarter, as revealed by Egyptian texts. Others would derive the name from the god Nimurta or Ninurta, patron of war and of the chase among the Assyrians. The figure of the ancient worthy certainly stood vividly before the mind of Palestinians, and presumably of Syrians, as representative of Assyria, for Asshur is "the land of Nimrod" (Mic. 5:6). When Greek writers speak of Ninos, who built Nineveh, they probably had heard of Nimrod and just changed the name to connect it with the famous capital. On the ancient Near Eastern cylinder-seals the figure of a hero fighting a monster or a lion is extremely common.

It also appears in impressive form in Assyrian sculpture. Scholars believe the portrayal to be that of Gilgamesh, hero of the famous Babylonian epic that contains the flood story as related to him by his ancestor Ut-Napishtim. Just as the name of the flood hero was changed to Noah in the passage of the tradition to the west, so that of Gilgamesh may have been changed to Nimrod.

The story of Nimrod is meaningful in several respects. That the beginning of his kingdom was in Babylonia and that from there he went to Assyria, accurately reflects the fact that the Assyrian civilization was of Babylonian origin; and that he was a great builder and hunter typifies two leading characteristics of the eastern monarchs as such. Tiglathpileser I (1100 B.C.) well illustrates for us what it means to be a "mighty hunter before the LORD." A servant goes *before* his master in executing his commands, and hence a king, too, goes before God as his servant. At the command of his god, says Tiglathpileser, he killed four wild bulls on the Syrian border and ten elephants in the Haran area; at the command of his god he killed 120 lions, hunting on foot, and 800 from his chariot. Figure 2.1 shows a later ruler paying homage to his god over the bodies of slain lions. Hunting was not a mere sport, but part of royalty's obligations.

Of course, no one ruler built all the cities Nimrod is said to have built. It is apparent, therefore, that he is more of a symbolic figure than anything else. The mention of Babel, Erech, and Accad (*Akkad*) ties together three of the most famous of cities of the early Babylonian history. As the star of imperialism takes its westward way Nineveh and Calah in Assyria stand vividly before the author's mind—cities of which we will hear more at later occasions. Three city names are still problematic: that of the fourth Babylonian city, and those of two Assyrian cities (cf. Table, page 49). Only older manuscripts, like the Dead Sea Scrolls, can bring the solution of the difficulties posed by these names.

A Changing International Scene

The early Hebrew story about Shem, Japheth, and Canaan (GEN. 9:20–27) had, as we have seen, a very limited world horizon. Later a writer was stimulated by it and utilized its basic idea, merely broadening the scope to include all peoples and tribes that meanwhile had come into the Hebrew field of vision. In doing this he changed the name of Noah's youngest son from the too specific Canaan to the more general Ham. Additions were later made to his new list. The youngest of the Pentateuchal writers, writing in the Persian era when there had been a great deal of additional change in the world picture, set up a fresh list, but adhered to the same system of Shem, Ham, and Japheth. Finally the compiler joined these parallel materials together, sacrificing parts of each and giving us Genesis 10 in the form in which we now have it (see Table of Nations, pages 48–51 and Color Map IV). The result, of course, is that we have no list of any one time completely.

By virtue of the authoritative position held by the Bible in the seventeenth and eighteenth centuries of our era, the triple classification of humanity as descendants of Shem, Ham, and Japheth had a considerable influence on anthropology and linguistics. One still hears men speak of "Semitic" (for Shemitic) and "Hamitic" peoples and languages, though in a manner not identical with the Biblical writer's idea of who was a Semite and who was a Hamite. "Japhethitic" is nowadays used only for a group of languages spoken in the Caucasus. The great division that comprises English and so many other tongues is called Indo-Germanic instead. This system of Indo-Germanic, Semitic, and Hamitic languages is serviceable where one takes a purely "western standpoint," but is inadequate from a world-wide point of view, since it provides no place for the far-eastern and other languages.

It is noteworthy that the sons of Japheth are put first in the list, as least important to the readers for whom this was written. They had played only a slight role in Hebrew history; the co-operation they had given in the very earliest days in the subjugation of the Canaanites, as reflected in Genesis 9:27, was later forgotten. Israel had had much more contact with the sons of Ham, who therefore come second in the ascending scale. The climactic position, of course, is appropriately reserved for the sons of Shem, since the Israelites are considered a member of that family of peoples and since the objective is to lead over to their national ancestors.

A surprising number of the names in this Table of Nations have been reliably identified, thanks partly to classical sources and partly to the ancient inscriptions which tell us so much about the world in which Israel lived. This contemporary evidence has also enabled us to see how such names could sometimes be wrongly vocalized by the Hebrew tradition, which supplied the purely consonantal text with vowel signs. Thus Gomer should have been Gemer, Meshech should have been Moshech, and Togarma should have been Tegarama according to the evidence of the Assyrian inscriptions.

Roughly speaking, the Japhethites occupied Armenia, much of Asia Minor, Greece,

Names reported by youngest author in CAPITALS; those of older source in Roman; supplements to older source in *italics*. See Color Map IV.

I. JAPHETH. The northern and western peoples.
  A. GOMER. The Cimmerians; a Scythian people; at time of the youngest writer in Crimaea. Earlier in Asia Minor. Called *Gimirrai* in Assyrian texts.
    1. ASHKENAZ. The Saka or Scythians. Wide-spread people. Assyrians call them *Ashguzai, Ishkuzai*. At time of this writer the groups in north of the Pamir? (Cf. also Color Map IV.)
    2. RIPHATH. Name not yet found in inscriptions. Connection with Riphaean Mountains, which Greeks held lay in far north? Josephus: Paphlagonians, but without further explanation.
    3. TOGARMAH. *Tegarama* in Hittite inscriptions, *Tilgarimmu* in Assyrian texts. City and principality in E. Cappadocia.
  B. MAGOG. Judaean term for northern peoples of nomadic sort, like Assyrian term *Umman-Manda*? Name coined by Ezekiel (38:2, 39:6)?
  C. MADAI. The Medes; region round *Hamadan* in Iran.
  D. JAVAN. The Ionians. Name for eastern Greeks of Greece and western Asia Minor in general.
    1. ELISHA. Many comparisons possible, but all uncertain. Probably term for western Greeks of Sicily and southern Italy. Elis on the northwest coast of the Peloponnesos may have provided the name, which then was extended to points lying farther to the west. Josephus: Aeolis, or Aeolian Greeks.
    2. TARSHISH. Sardinia? or Tartessus in Spain?
    3. KITTIM. Originally people of Kition (Cyprus, named after its then dominant city); here, perhaps, islands of sea in general. Later used for Romans.
    4. DODANIM. Text not too certain in case of this word. In Greek translation and in 1 Chronicles 1:7 spelled RODANIM; inhabitants of island of Rhodes and nearby coast? Other possibility: miswriting for *Danunim*(?)—people in Cilicia, mentioned by Phoenician inscription from *Karatepe*.
  E. TUBAL. Vocalized thus under influence of Tubal (GEN. 4:22); originally *Tabal; Tabali* in Assyrian texts. In Asia Minor, *Kayseri* area.
  F. MESHECH. Assyrian *Mushki;* Greek *Moschi*. Are joined with *Tabali* in inscriptions in same way. In eastern Phrygia.
  G. TIRAS. Probably the Tyrsenians of classical tradition; *Turusha* of Egyptian texts of earlier age. In northwest Lydia.
II. HAM. Peoples of African origin, or belonging to that sphere in some way.
  A. CUSH. Nubia—region south of First Cataract of Nile. Called *Meluḫḫa* by Assyrians. Misnamed Ethiopia by the Greeks. Cush held ancestral to
    1. SEBA. Differentiated from Sheba by spelling. Classical geographers mention a city named Saba on African coast of Red Sea.
    2. HAVILAH. Area in central Arabia. Cf. list page 51 and page 69.
    3. SABTA. Sabata of Greek geographers, *Shabwat* of South-Arabian inscriptions. Capital of Hadramaut, the region on southeast coast of Arabia.
    4. RAAMAH. Greek Bible: Regma. *Rajmat* in the *Nejrān* which is a

region west of the great sand desert *Rub᷅ el Khali.*

     a) SHEBA. Land of the Sabaeans in Yemen. Capital Marib near *Ṣan᷅a* (see page 222).

     b) DEDAN. Oasis *el 'Ela* in Midian.

5. SABTECA. Uncertain. Name corresponds to that of Egyptian Pharaoh *Shabataḳa* of *c.* 700 B.C. City or colony founded by him? Some seek it south of Sabta at *Shabaḳa* or *Shubaiḳa?*

> Nimrod (personal rather than geographical name). Founder of the following Babylonian and Assyrian cities:
>
> Babel. Leading position reflects importance of this city since Hammurabi, *c.* 1700 B.C. Not important earlier.
>
> Erech. Babylonian: *Uruḳ* (today ruins of *Warḳa*). *Epic of Gilgamesh* glorifies a legendary king of this largest and perhaps most ancient of Babylonian cities.
>
> Accad (Akkad). Not certainly identified yet, but probably the one later called *Dēr,* which lay 16 miles southwest of Bagdad. Akkad was the seat of the first Semitic empire and of a great culture under its kings Sargon and Naram-Sin. After it all northern Babylonia was called Akkad.
>
> Calneh. (R.S.V. "all of them"). Calneh was in Syria (AMOS 6:2); written Calno in Isaiah 10:9; and so name must be miswritten or thoughtlessly supplied in Genesis 10:10 by an editor in filling gap in manuscript (see page 305).
>
> Nineveh. Old city, but only put first among Assyrian cities because of its mighty role, which began in the 8th century B.C. See page 310. The original Assyrian capital was Asshur (*Qal᷅at Sherqāṭ*), and its omission here is surprising. On it see page 267.
>
> Rehoboth Ir. Could not be exact name of an Assyrian city, for these are Hebrew words meaning "spacious places of a city," or "spacious places [city]." Cf. "Rehoboth by the river," R.S.V. "Rehoboth on the Euphrates," (GEN. 36:37). An appellation for Asshur?
>
> Calah. Assyrian *Kalḳhu,* today *Nimrūd.* Scene of early as well as recent excavations (see page 267).
>
> Resen. No such city between Nineveh and Calah is known; town fitting description is *Khalṣu* (today, *Selemiyeh*). Name an error for *Isana?* That city lay between Nineveh and Calah in a certain sense, but farther back from the Tigris. The words "The same is the great city" must apply to Nineveh (cf. JON. 3:3), and are thus slightly misplaced.

B. MIZRAIM. Egypt, including land almost up to Gaza. Ancestral to

  1. *Ludim.* North African group. Offshoot of III-D?

  2. *Anamim.* Uncertain, but north-African; perhaps Cyrene.

  3. *Lehabim.* Variant Lubim (Dan. 11:43); Lybians of the Marmarica.

  4. *Naphtuhim.* Uncertain. Name misspelled? *Pato-meḥ,* name of Delta region (with article)? People of "lower" or northern Egypt.

  5. *Pathrusim.* People of Pathros (Jer. 44:15 f.), later name of southern Egypt (Patures).

  6. *Casluhim.* Name uncertain; Greek translation has *Chasmonim,* which may be a mispelled Nasmonim, and then must mean the

Nasamones, who according to Greek reports lived on Gulf of Sidra.

    a) *Philistines.* Amos 9:7 brings them from Caphtor. The latter then the second lap of their migration?

7. Caphtorim. The people of Crete. Late Egyptian *Kaptara.*

C. PUT. The *Puṭaya* of the Old Persian inscriptions; late name for North African district adjacent to Delta of Nile.

D. CANAAN. Here used of Phoenicians and Canaanites of Syria and Palestine.

    1. Sidon. Famous Phoenician city; Tyre evidently included in its area here, since not mentioned.

    2. Heth. Here the North Syrian Hittite principalities using the old hieroglyphic writing, like Carchemish, Malatia, etc.

    3–6 *Jebusites, Amorites, Girgashites, Hivites.* Peoples of Palestine. Added in this connection on basis of historical narratives?

    7. *Arkites.* People of Phoenician city of *Arqa* (*Tell Arqā*), 12½ miles north of Tripolis (*Tarablus*).

    8. *Sinites.* People of Phoenician city of Shiannu (so Assyrian texts).

    9. *Arvadites.* People of Phoenician city Arvad, Aradus (*Ruād*).

    10. *Zemarites.* People of Assyrian texts mention *Ṣumur* and *Ṣimirra* (the same or two different cities?). Location on Phoenician coast not definitely established as yet.

    11. *Hamathites.* People of city on Orontes river in Syria (today *Ḥamā*).

III. SHEM. Peoples thrust in between Japhethites and Hamites.

A. ELAM. Region around Susa. Language non-Semitic, according to our way of thinking, but still important in Persian times, as shown by Darius' I *Behistūn* inscription, where Old Persian text is accompanied by Elamite and Babylonian translations.

B. ASSHUR. Assyria; late usage includes Syria (shortened form of "Assyria").

C. ARPACHSHAD. Name not yet found in inscriptions. Perhaps originally two words like Ur Kasdim (Ur of the Chaldees, GEN. 11:28); "Arap of Chesed" (Hebrew *Kesed,* singular of *Kasdīm,* GEN. 22:22). Arrapa late pronunciation of *Arrapkha* (today *Kerkuk*), under influence of Elamite language; Arrapa in Ptolemy's Geography.

    1. *Shelah* (A.V. Salah). Introduced here from Genesis 11:12; personal rather than geographical name? (cf. Methuselah).

        a) Eber. In older source (verse 21) son of Shem. A name that may or may not hang together with the *'Ibrīyīm*-Hebrews (see page 97). We take it as short for *Eber-hannahar,* "the region on the other side of the river" (1 Kings 4:24 A.V.), a rendering of the Assyrian and later Persian designation for Syria and Palestine.

            (1) Peleg. Region east of Khabur river mouth where a canal *nār Palgā* is mentioned by the Assyrian king Tukulti-Ninurta II (ninth century B.C.). Later geographers, too, have a *Phaliga* here. According to youngest source (GEN. 11:18 f.) Peleg's line leads to Abraham, but list of Genesis 10 was abridged at this point because of Genesis 22:20 f. and 25:13 f., which contained many of the same names.

It will be useful to put the names of Gen. 11:18 f. following Peleg's here.

REU. Probably short form of REUEL. To be identified with city of *Raḵhīlu* "in the midst of the Euphrates" in *Suḵhu* area?

SERUG. Assyrian texts mention *Sarugi* and *Naḵhiri* as two cities of Harran district. Sarugi's name survives in *Serūj*.

NAHOR. Appears as *Naḵhuru* already in Mari texts of second millennium B.C. Later *Naḵhiri*. Site unknown.

TERAH. Old city name of Harran district, *Til Turaḵhi* in Assyrian texts.

(2) Joktan (parallel: Jokshan, Gen. 25:2). Tribal and personal name. A list of the descendants of Joktan is given in v. 26 f., reflecting the growing interest in South Arabia in the late period.

    (*a*) *Almodad*. Cf. use of word *Maudad* in South Arabia. Applied to Gebanites by Minaeans.

    (*b*) *Sheleph*. Between Sheba and Hadramaut, where Ptolemy put the *Salipeni*.

    (*c*) *Hazarmaveth*. Hadramaut, the frankincense country, northeast of Aden. Hebrew vocalization artificial (*maveth* = death).

    (*d*) *Jerah*. Unknown. Misspelled? Cf. *Yaḥar* a district east of *Jebel Isbīl* and belonging to Hadramaut in Ptolemy's time.

    (*e*) *Uzal*. cf. *Azal, Izal,* allegedly old name of Ṣanʿa? But cf. also *Azalli* of Assyrian texts, which must be sought much farther north.

    (*f*) *Diḵlah*. "Date-palm," cf. *Naḵhla* (same meaning) s. of Mecca? Others identify it with North Arabian *Jauf*.

    (*g*) *Obal*. cf. *ʿObal,* east of *Hodeida*.

    (*h*) *Abimael*. Personal name like Abiel with infixed *m*, common in ancient South Arabian dialects.

    (*i*) *Sheba*. Already under Ham, verse 7.

    (*j*) *Ophir*. Added here because of historical narratives? cf. page 222.

    (*k*) *Havilah*. Already under Ham, verse 7.

    (*l*) *Jobab*. Uncertain. cf. Ptolemy's *Iobaritai* in eastern S. Arabia. For phonetic change cf. *Jerīb* < *Jerīr*.

D.   LUD. The Lydian realm conquered by Cyrus.

E.   ARAM. Aramaic-speaking areas.

    1. UZ. Distinct from Edomite Uz (Gen. 36:28; Lam. 4:21), but identical with first-born of Nahor, Gen. 22:20. Hauran region?

    2. HUL. *Leja* region? Cf. Assyrian *Khulḵhulite,* today *Khulḵhuleh.* Or *Ḥuleh* area? See page 26. Josephus takes Hul to be Armenia.

    3. GETHER. Uncertain. Josephus: Bactria!

    4. MASH. Uncertain. Carchemish (Fortress of *Mish*)? Or Mons Masius (*Tūr ʿAbdīn*) in upper Tigris area? Josephus takes it to be district of Mesene (capital *Charax Spasini*) at mouth of Euphrates.

and the Mediterranean isles. The Hamites may be described as those peoples that belonged to the former Egyptian sphere of influence, including Cushites, North Africans, some peoples of Yemen, and the Canaanites of Syria-Palestine. The inhabitants of Yemen were evidently not considered Hamites by the earlier strand in Genesis 10, for some of the same names reappear among the sons of Shem in verses 26–29. But relations between South Arabia and Africa were always close, and so the classification of them as Hamites is understandable. The Canaanites, both of Palestine and the Phoenician coast, were so Egyptianized in cultural respects after ages of political and commercial domination by Egypt that it seemed fitting to group them with Egyptians and Cushites.

In the case of the Canaanites, an important statement about their distribution has been preserved.

"And the territory of the Canaanites extended from Sidon, in the direction of Gerar, as far as Gaza, and in the direction of Sodom, Gomorra, Admah and Zeboim as far as Lasha." (GEN. 10:19 R.S.V.)

The present text probably combines several variant manuscript readings. Sidon to Gerar is lucid enough; the location of Gerar will engage us in the patriarchal stories (page 80). It was, indeed, not far from the better known Gaza, which lay in the extreme south of the coastal plain near the sea. From Gerar or Gaza, then, the line is taken eastward to Lasha. The localization of that place as near "Sodom and Gomorrah" (page 71) suggests that a point close to the southern end of the Dead Sea is meant. Jewish sources, followed by Jerome, connect it with the later Callirrhoë, noted for its warm springs: some modern scholars hold it to be a misspelling of Bela, the archaic name of Zoar (GEN. 14:2). The delimitation of Canaanite territory breaks off rather abruptly at that point; one would expect the territorial line to be taken up the Jordan Valley to Mount Hermon and then back to Sidon.

The sons of Shem comprised virtually all the rest of the peoples of western Asia, notably the Assyrians, the Aramaeans, Israelites and Arabs. The inclusion among them of the Elamites, whom we would consider non-Semitic, is no doubt due to their having been conquered by the Assyrians and overrun by Semitic-speaking tribes in the late period. But one is surprised to find the Lydians, too, put in the Semitic family. The most obscure member of the Semitic peoples is Arpachshad. It is from this son of Shem that the lineage of Israel is derived (GEN. 11:10 f.). Arpachshad's son Eber, ancestor of all the "sons of Eber," also has a name that has caused much discussion. On both see the Table of Nations, pages 48–51. There are two branches of Eberites—one descending from Peleg, the other from Joktan. The former leads over to Abraham; the latter group comprises the Arabian peoples.

There is a surprising amount of detail about the sons of Joktan in the older version of the list, but most of these names were added to it by a later hand. An intriguing remark by the older writer himself, however, concludes the Joktan list. He says, "Their dwelling was from Mesha, as thou goest unto Sephar, a mount of the east" (GEN. 10:30). The question is: Which is the nearer and which the farther of these places. The list in its present form contains Sheba and Hazarmaveth, names putting distant Yemen in the sphere of Joktan. However, it is by no means certain that the older writer in penning these lines extended the Joktan group so far, for he put Sheba among the descendants of Ham (verse 7). In the analogous description "from Havilah to Shur" (GEN. 25:18), furthermore, the farther point is mentioned before the nearer, and so Sephar may actually have been closer. Whether it was a definite mountain or a whole mountain area like the *Jebel Haurān* is hard to say. The word "east" is not the natural one for south Arabia in any case, but applies rather to the region east of Palestine and southern Syria. Mesha is spelled the same way as Massa, mentioned with Tema in Genesis 25:14–15. The Assyrian king Tiglathpileser III in one of his inscriptions also mentions *Mas'u* and *Tem'u* together. If Tema is the *Teima* of today then the farthest point of the Joktan tribe was originally in the region south of the present Tebuk.

The world-stage has thus been set with this array of peoples, according to Biblical authors. "By these were the nations divided in the earth after the flood," says one of them (GEN. 10:32). The great travail of human history could begin.

The Tower of Babel

One of the most charming of the ancient Hebrew traditions is that about Babylon and its mighty tower (GEN. 11:1–10). It tells of the first migration of human history. The journey was not "from the east" (A.V.) or "in the east" (R.S.V.), but in an easterly direction. The assumption is that humanity had increased in Mesopotamia or Armenia and traveled down to the plain in Shinar and settled there. Archaeologists have only recently found out that the earliest villages lay in the Kurdish foothills of Mesopotamia, at *Kārim-Shāhir,* at *Palegawra,* and at *Jarmo* (Color Map XXI); here men came out of the caves and began to live in towns about 6000 B.C. As the changing climate began to dry out the vast swamps of the river valleys, the fertility of these lands attracted "the man with the hoe" to settle in those lower regions.

The name Shinar is the regular name for Babylonia in the Old Testament. It is probably derived from a city and principality that enjoyed a temporary prominence in Mesopotamia in the fourteenth century B.C. and that is called *Shankhar* in the Tell el Amarna letters. Somehow its name came to represent the regions beyond (cf. Eden and Havilah for a similar situation). In these same times the name used for Babylonia in that country itself was Kar-Duniash, the last word being the name of a Cassite god.

The clay available in this plains country led to the discovery of brickmaking and made possible heretofore unimagined developments in building. The most significant and impressive type of structure built in Babylonia was the *ziggurat,* or tower. The first one constructed here is thought to have been built at Babel, and to have been regarded by the LORD with disfavor; human beings were proposing to invade the celestial territory! To stop this self-aggrandizement of men, the LORD confused their speech so that they could no longer understand each other. Hence there are many languages instead of the one language of an earlier day—a state of affairs preventing co-operation and achievement! Thus the old narrator reasoned.

According to our present way of thinking the inventors of the ziggurat were not the people who came down from Mesopotamia, but rather the Sumerians who came into Babylonia from Iran. They first built these towers not out of pride but for other reasons. A practical consideration such as a refuge from floodwaters may have had something to do with it, though most scholars stress the idea that these are artificial mountains, raised up for the mountain-gods whom the Sumerians had worshipped in their original homes. On the top of such a tower, which always stood adjacent to the temple court, there was a chamber for the deity.

The Hebrew narrator believed that Babel was the first of cities—a view also found in Genesis 10:10, when it is put at the head of those built by Nimrod. But this is not substantiated by archaeology. It was probably the vast impression that Babylon's long predominance in Babylonia had made on the mind that led people to think of it as so old. This is a tribute to the mighty achievements of Hammurabi, who raised this inconsiderable city to greatness and to the Cassite

Dynasty which ruled Babylonia for 576 years. But in historical terms Babylon was a latecomer compared to a city like Erech.

The storyteller's Hebrew explanation of the name Babel as due to the "confusion of tongues" is a good example of a popular etymology: the name is actually Babylonian and is composed of the two words *Bab-ili* meaning "gate of god." The name is rarely spelled out in Babylonian writing, but written with the Sumerian words *ka-dingir-ra,* "gate of god." Babylon and its tower are symbols of man's striving. The temple-tower (ziggurat) was as typical of the Babylonian scene as the church spire has been of the European.

The lofty *Birs Nimrūd,* the ruins of which are visible far across the plains, was long believed to be the Tower of Babel. Since the site of Babylon was known because of the mound *Bābil,* near modern Hillah, it had to be supposed that the city covered a very large area. But after scholars learned to read and understand the Babylonian writing it was shown that *Birs Nimrūd* was the tower of the city of Borsippa. The tower meant by the Biblical story was, of course, that of Babylon itself. This tower, frequently rebuilt and renewed by the Babylonian kings, was called in Sumerian *E-temen-an-ki,* "House of the Foundation of Heaven and Earth," and the temple in which it stood was called *E-sag-ila,* "House that Lifts up the Head." The tower was leveled to the ground by Alexander the Great, who planned to rebuild it in surpassing glory but who died before he could do so. In the excavations carried on at Babylon by the German Oriental Society, 1899–1918, the site where it stood was determined.

Hebrew Origins

In the period of their migrations, primitive peoples are too much engaged in a struggle for existence and too ignorant withal to preserve for very long any knowledge of their former homes. By the time interest in that matter is awakened, the facts are lost and it becomes necessary for the peoples themselves to resort to hypotheses. Greeks, Romans, Celts, Teutons, Slav—wherever one turns there is always a complete blackout at the beginning, which, in some cases, as with Greeks and Romans, legend and speculation seek to illumine. Things were much the same with Israel. One of the earlier Pentateuchal writers derived the Hebrew ancestry from Peleg, son of Eber, son of Shem. The youngest writer developed the matter a bit further and allowing 290 years from the flood to Abraham (GEN. 11:10 f.), provided a chronology. On the names, see the Table of Nations, pages 48–51.

The Hebrew tradition tells nothing of the rise and fall of empires that took place between the time when civilization began in the Tigris-Euphrates Valley and the migration of the first Hebrew tribesmen to Palestine. The Table of Early Civilization on pages 58–61, based on what a century of Oriental research has revealed of those forgotten events, gives an inkling of a gigantic process, to which fresh discovery is almost daily adding new knowledge.

The Migration of Terah

The genealogy of the sons of Shem passes over into narrative after Terah's sons Abraham (who is called Abram until Genesis 17:5 in the Biblical text), Nahor, and Haran have been named. We have seen in the Table of Nations, pages 48–51, that some of the personal names in the lists are at the same time geographic names. That of Nahor is a case in point, and the very same thing is true of Haran, whose name (written with a soft *h*) is only artificially differentiated from the name of Terah's city (GEN. 11:32). The name Nahor, we note, appears twice: once as that of Terah's father (so the youngest author in Genesis 11:24) and again as that of Terah's son (so the early source that contained Genesis 11:28-30). The name Abram (of which Abraham is only a distended form), however, is a true personal

2.2 *Ur excavation scene.* (*Matson Photo Service*)

name. Its meaning depends on whether it is to be linked with some very similar Assyro-Babylonian names or with "Canaanitic" names. In the latter case, it is virtually the same as the name *Abiram* (cf. 1 Kings 16:34).

Where the migration account begins in Genesis 11:31 f., we find Terah in the territory of Ur of the Chaldees or Chaldeans. Since all the family names point to Mesopotamia we may imagine Terah and his sons as nomads, who had previously traveled to Chaldea from their northern home before the story of their further migrations opens. Such a southward movement of tribesmen from Mesopotamia to Babylonia takes place annually to this day. Mesopotamian winters are hard, and so the Bedouin go down to pasture their flocks in the Babylonian area during that season, ranging as far as the *Shaṭṭ el Ḥai*.

In times when there was no strong government these nomads were wont to rob the farming population en route or levy on it at will.

Ur was rediscovered by J. E. Taylor, British vice-consul at Basrah, who carried on some exploratory excavations at *el Muqayyar* in 1854 at the request of Sir Henry Rawlinson. The place was difficult of access, for the Euphrates on which it once lay has shifted its course, and the ruins now lie out in the desert. It was a thrilling event when Rawlinson, after deciphering an inscription from there, could announce that the Biblical Ur of the Chaldees had been found! Large-scale excavations were carried on here under Leonard Woolley in 1922–34 on behalf of the British Museum and the University of Pennsylvania, and important new knowledge was gained about this old city of the Sumerians. The most spectacular finds, however, such as those made in the royal cemetery where early kings were buried with a whole retinue of attendants in regular "death-pits," or those made at *el 'Obeid,* a small mound near Ur, all belong to *c.* 2500 B.C., a time long before Abraham. But Ur had a second great period of flowering under its Third Dynasty (*c.* 2000 B.C.). How far its influence extended may be seen from the fact that the cuneiform script adopted by the Hittite kings in Cappadocia is the writing of the Third Dynasty of Ur! One of its great rulers was Ur-Nammu, who may, perhaps, be the creator of the stage-type of temple-tower, and who set up a law code of which a fragment was recently found at another great Sumerian city of his realm, Nippur. A partially preserved sculptured panel from Ur shows the king receiving and executing the command of the moon-god to build him a temple. To it belonged the tower the patriarchs might have seen, if they got to the vicinity of the Sumerian metropolis. But it betrays the relatively late time in which the Biblical writer, who speaks of Ur, lived, when he calls the city "Ur of the Chaldees" or Chaldeans. It was not until the seventh century B.C. that the Chaldeans, an Aramaic tribe, got hold of the Ur district.

The Terah clan was certainly only a sojourner in the Ur vicinity, lingering there by treaty or agreement with the local authority. Their sheep or goats would not have been permitted to invade those well-irrigated, fertile lands on which the life of Ur depended. From afar these shepherds, however, could see the mighty ziggurat or tower of the city—today the best-preserved ziggurat of Baby-

2.3. *Ur, the ziggurat as seen from the northwest. (Matson Photo Service)*

lonia—like a great landmark (cf. GEN. 11:4), and it may have made them feel at home that the god Nannar or Sin, the moon-god who was so prominently worshipped at Haran, was revered there also. But the Sumerian psalms that the Ur priests sang to this god, one of which has been preserved, would have sounded strange and incomprehensible to their ears if they had been permitted to attend a festival at the temple.

The death of the son Haran in the Ur neighborhood provided an impetus to leave this region. It may have been time to move on in any case, if Terah's journey is typical of the return movement of the Bedouin. This takes place in late winter, for in the spring and summer the floodwaters would make migration impossible. In years when the winters are cold and when early vegetation is sparse, the Bedouin may lose a great part of their herds on such a return journey.

Terah is said to have started his renewed trek with a more distant objective in mind— to go to the land of Canaan. At Ur he could have met other tribesmen from inner Arabia and heard from them of favorable conditions of livelihood existing in Palestine. But since he goes to Haran, we may imagine him as taking the familiar migration route back to the home area. Perhaps his herds had not crossed the Euphrates at all to the southern shore on which Ur lay, for the river was certainly a formidable obstacle. In returning he would have gone up the west side of the Tigris (see Color Map III). We may imagine him as passing mighty Asshur, the capital of Assyria, and eighty miles beyond he would have seen Nineveh across the river, a city of yet lesser consequence, but destined to become the seat of an empire that was to trample his descendants under its feet. Leaving the Tigris, Terah would have taken the westward track to Nisibis, and crossing the headwaters of the Khabur River would soon have come to Haran on the upper *Balikh* River, another tributary of the Euphrates.

The general location of Haran has never been lost sight of, for the name *Kharrān* has clung to a town there to this day. The name meant "road" in the Assyrian tongue, and is suggestive of the fact that the city was situated on a highway from Babylonia to the west. Its temple was dedicated to the moon-god Sin. The remains most in evidence there now are of Islamic times—a gigantic ruin-field, with a castle and mosque— but there is a great mound at the site that may well cover the acropolis of a much more ancient period. The difficulties facing the excavator here, however, are great. A British expedition under Seton Lloyd which surveyed the possibilities in 1950, made an exploratory dig instead at a site called *Sultān Tepe,* some distance away, near the town of *Yarimtsa,* where a monumental building of Assyrian days had been located. Tablets found there show that another temple dedicated to Sin of Haran stood on this mound, and that it had a seventh-century library, arranged much like that of King Ashurbanipal at Nineveh and including classic Assyrian religious texts.

In 1952, however, D. S. Rice made a short dig at the great mosque of Haran, and continued it with surprising success in 1956 in the East, West and North gateways. Inscribed stelas of Nabonidus, the last king of Babylon (see page 324), were found in the first two, while in the third a stela giving the full text of the so-called "Inscription of Nabonidus' mother," including an account of her burial at the age of 104 years, was discovered. It thus seems certain that the moon-temple of Haran lay at the site occupied by the mosque. We here stand on the spot to which Joshua refers when he says to the assembled tribes that their fathers lived of old beyond the river and served other gods. (JOSH. 24:2). First among these gods was Sin of Haran. It was near here that the divine revelation calling Abraham to a land of promise was given. Truly at Haran one stands at the source of the River of Life.

TABLE OF EARLY CIVILIZATION

3200 B.C.   Early Dynastic Period begins. Erech great center.

2800 B.C.   Archaic Sumerian writing on clay begun.

2600 B.C.   Mesilim, king of Kish; first royal inscription.

2500 B.C.   First Dynasty of Ur. Royal tombs. Inscription of second king (A-an-ni-pad-da son of Mesannipadda). Ensis (lesser kings) of Lagash.

2450 B.C.   Eannatum I conquers part of Babylonia.

2400 B.C.   Entemena; silver vase.

2370 B.C.   Urukagina. First social reformer. Lagash destroyed by king of Umma, Lugal-zaggisi.

2330 B.C.   Third Dynasty of Erech. Lugal-zaggisi gets control of city and founds empire. His votive inscription from Nippur.

2350–2150 B.C.   Dynasty of Akkad. Dominance of Semites over Sumerians. Sargon I takes over Lugal-zaggisi's realm. Sumerian writing adopted for Semitic Babylonian tongue. Expedition to Asia Minor. Sargon legends. Great culture.

2267 B.C.   Naram-Sin, grandson of Sargon, campaigns in north. His stela of victory. Decline of power under subsequent rulers.

2150–2050 B.C.   Dynasty of Gutium; foreign dominion by people from northern mountains. Decline of culture. Deliverance by Fifth Dynasty of Erech (Utu-hegal).

2050–1950 B.C.   Third Dynasty of Ur. Last flowering of Sumerian Culture. Rule extended over Subartu (Assyria). Ur-Nammu defeats Lagash, chief rival. His law code. His building of temple and his sculpture. Shulgi. Era of great commerce; "Ur-dynasty tablets."

1975 B.C.   Amorite migration strikes Babylonia. Last king of Ur, Ibbi-Sin a Semite.

1950–1698 B.C.   Dynasties of Isin and Larsa. Divided rule.

1875 B.C.   Lipit-Ishtar of Isin and his law code.

1770 B.C.   Larsa falls under domination of Elam (Kudur-Mabug). Warad-Sin king of Larsa.

EGYPT

Before 2850 B.C.	Kingdoms of North and South, red crown and white crown.
2850–2052 B.C.	Old Kingdom; Dynasties I-VIII.
2850 B.C.	Menes, founder of First Dynasty; royal tombs at Abydos.
2650 B.C.	Third Dynasty begins. Pharaoh Zoser builds Pyramid at Sakkara.
2650–2480 B.C.	Cheops, Chephren and Mykerinos; Pyramids of Gizeh.
2480–2350 B.C.	Sahure, Niuserre; Pyramids of Abusir. Golden age of Art.
2350–2190 B.C.	VI Dynasty. Teti; Pepi I (campaigns to Sinai and Palestine to Mt. Carmel). Pyramids of Sakkara.
2190–2052 B.C.	First Intermediate Period. VII-VIII Dynasties. Akhthoes of Heracleopolis. Beginnings of Egyptian literature.
2052–1778 B.C.	Middle Kingdom. Dynasties IX-XII.
2052–1991 B.C.	XI Dynasty. Mentuhotep of Thebes. Renewal of power.
1991–1792 B.C.	XII Dynasty. Time of great power. Amenemhet I-IV; Sesostris I-III; Tale of Sinuhe. Sesostris III campaigns in Palestine (Shechem).
1778–1610 B.C.	Second Intermediate Period; Dynasties XIII-XVI.

WESTERN ASIA

1758–1698 B.C.	Rim-Sin, brother of Warad-Sin, King of Larsa. Conquers Isin and unites Babylonia. Mari, Amorite city west of Babylonia, rules western regions, but tributary to Rim-Sin. King Iahdun-lim's soldiers reach Mediterranean. Terqa, nearby city destroyed. Shamshi-Adad I, escaped member of royal family of Terqa, gets control of city of Asshur.
1749–1717 B.C.	Assyrian realm of Shamshi-Adad I; conquers Mari and makes son governor. His correspondence. Decline of kingdom under his son. Mari Dynasty regains throne and power, Zimri-lim of Mari and his famous palace. Relations to western kingdoms—Yamkhad, with capital Khalab (Aleppo), Mukish, with capital at Alalakh in the plain of Antioch.
1831–1530 B.C.	First Dynasty of Babylon. Mesopotamia and Syria invaded by Hurrians, northern people.
1698 B.C.	Hammurabi, 6th King of First Dynasty of Babylon conquers Rim-Sin of Larsa. Destroys Mari when it rebels. His laws and letters. New era of civilization. Sea-land dynasty near Persian Gulf. Hittite kingdom in Cappadocia.
1530 B.C.	Hittites under Murshilish I overthrow First Dynasty of Babylon.
1500–1150 B.C.	Cassite Dynasty at city of Babylon; line of 36 kings, Babylonia sinks to level of second-rate power. Dur-Kurigalzu founded by King Kurigalzu I.
1500 B.C.	Shuttarna I of Mitanni regains paternal throne.
1490 B.C.	Idrimi, of Alalakh in Syria, is recognized by Hurrian overlord. Raids Hittite country. His unique stela.
1470 B.C.	Shaushatar of Mitanni. Age of the Nuzi-tablets.
1450 B.C.	Sea-land dynasty ends; last king Ea-gamil. Renewed rise of the Hittite empire.
1390 B.C.	Tushratta of Mitanni.
1380 B.C.	Shuppiluliuma II, king of the Hittites.

1778–1700 B.C.	XIII Dynasty; decline of kingdom.
1670–1570 B.C.	Hyksos period. Dynasties XV-XVI.
1610–715 B.C.	New Kingdom; Dynasties XVII-XXIV.
1610–1570 B.C.	XVII Dynasty.
1570–1545 B.C.	XVIII Dynasty. Amosis; liberator from Hyksos rule.
1545–1524 B.C.	Amenophis I. Campaign to Naharina.
1524–1502 B.C.	Thutmosis I and II.
1502–1448 B.C.	Thutmosis III.
1501–1480 B.C.	Queen Hatshepsut exercises sway; Punt expeditions.
1480 B.C.	Thutmosis, after seizing power, begins expeditions to Asia. Battle of Megiddo. Conquest of Syria and Naharina.
1448–1422 B.C.	Amenophis II. Zenith of power. Asiatic campaigns; deportations of Asiatics to Egypt.
1422–1413 B.C.	Thutmosis IV. Campaign to Naharina. Marriage to Mitanni princess, daughter of Artatama.
1413–1377 B.C.	Amenophis III; First Amarna letters.

CHAPTER IV

WANDERINGS OF ABRAHAM

TERAH was unable to carry out his purpose to go on to the land of Canaan. The youngest Genesis author states laconically "and Terah died in Haran" (GEN. 11:32). But Abraham, divinely called to carry out his father's purpose, folded up his tents and went.

To God's Country

The route Abraham took is not given, for the items next related concern only his visits to certain Palestinian localities after his arrival there. No doubt he and his family went westward from Haran and crossed the Euphrates near *Til Barṣip,* later an important city of the Aramaeans, which Shalmaneser III (859–824 B.C.) then captured and renamed Kar-Shalmaneser, and which lay at *Tell Aḥmar* (fig. 2.3) near Carchemish. We

can imagine the tribesmen accomplishing the river crossing with inflated goatskins, in the manner illustrated on some Assyrian reliefs, and still in use today. The animals had to swim, and can be imagined as reluctant.

If Abraham had emigrated in the spring of the year, the natural time to go, the flocks could have grazed all the way along the Syrian steppes from *Aleppo* to the region of Damascus. Keeping east of that city he would soon have come to the *Jaulān* and the tracks to the Jordan crossings.

There is no clear indication of the point at which Abraham passed over the Jordan River into western Palestine. The story merely relates that Abraham passed through the land to the place of Shechem, to the plain, or oak, of Moreh (GEN. 12:6 f.).

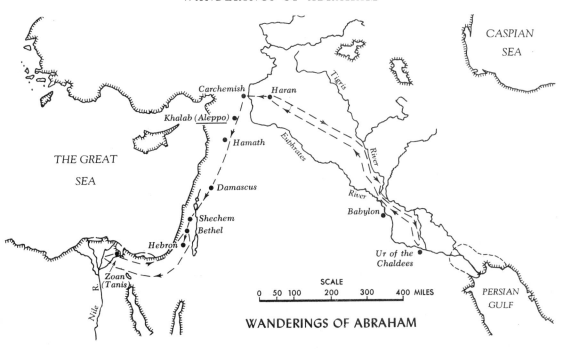

WANDERINGS OF ABRAHAM

The name "Canaan" was restricted to western Palestine (cf. GEN. 10:19). Abraham's "passing through it" suggests that he did not come up directly from across the Jordan to Shechem, but that he had forded the river farther north, perhaps where the "road of the Hauranians" crosses it (see page 30), below the Lake of Galilee. A temporary objective, then, is reached by Abraham at Shechem.

"The place" of Shechem where we now find him is its "holy place." Here stood "the oak of Moreh" (DEUT. 11:30, "the oaks"). The name Moreh means "soothsayer," and suggests that a member of that craft had once carried on his work there. An editor apologetically adds the remark "the Canaanites were then in the land." But the storyteller does not mention the heathen sanctity of the spot. He relates that the LORD appeared here to Abraham, confirming the fact that the patriarch had now reached the destination to which he had been called (GEN. 12:2), and that Abraham thereupon built an altar and brought the first sacrifice ever offered there. This reflects the great importance of the Shechem sanctuary.

Ancient Shechem was situated at the mound of *Balāṭah*, east of modern *Nāblus*, near the entrance to the valley (cf. further page 85 and sketch map on this page). We can only guess where "the [holy] place" and the oak of Moreh lay. The wording suggests that they were outside of the town, perhaps at the foot of Mount Gerizim.

But a more southerly Ephraimite neighborhood, too, claimed possession of a holy place founded by Abraham—Bethel (GEN. 12:8). Abraham, we must assume, traveled down the main track that led from Shechem to Jerusalem. Nature has dictated its course. To

2.4 Til Barṣip, *where Tiglathpileser III had a castle, and where Assyrian armies often crossed the Euphrates. (Courtesy Maurice Dunand)*

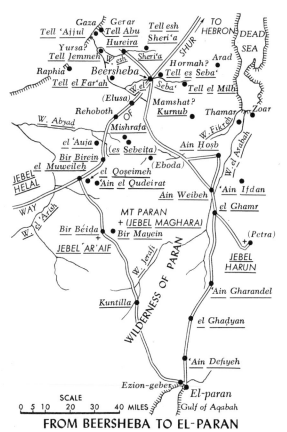

FROM BEERSHEBA TO EL-PARAN

the regular road of easiest travel. While we are not told where he tented we may assume that the region round Beersheba, where we subsequently find him, is meant.

A Round Trip to Egypt

The Negeb is very much in the sphere of Egypt. This is illustrated by the continuation of the Abraham story (GEN. 12:10). Just as the sons of Jacob later turned toward Egypt in days of famine so the ancestor Abraham, too, was reported to have done. From the Beersheba area the patriarch would probably have gone southward on the "way of Shur" (see page 69). But the account of his journey and of his stay in the land of the Nile is lacking in concrete geographical or historical information. We are left in the dark, too, as to the identity of the Pharaoh with whom he made contact or the location of his capital.

Since the narrator now has further materials to relate that are localized at Bethel, he brings Abraham back to that place again.

Lot's Choice

The thirteenth chapter of Genesis gives us a vivid picture of ancient tribal life. Abraham and Lot could only roam about in the uncultivated portions of the country. Even then they could not have had as much independence as the reader of the narratives might think. Studies of Bedouin tribal life in recent times have shed much light on such matters. Agreements had to be made with local authorities, for the citizenry of the country would certainly not have permitted the nomads and their flocks to rove at will. With the passing of time, however, the growth of the herds of the two typical clans here mentioned, and the increase of the clans themselves, bring about a rivalry between them for the grazing grounds. Any given section, one can readily realize, can sustain only a certain number of sheep and goats. The narrative simplifies this picture to more vivid personal terms—it tells of Abraham

the left of this road stood Bethel (*Beitin*), then called Luz (cf. page 148). But the patriarch did not enter this Canaanite city; he tented between it and Ai. The latter place, of which we shall hear more when we discuss the story of Joshua (see page 136), lay to the east of Luz (at *el-Tell*); if Abraham pitched his tent between these two points where one had a view over the Jordan valley (GEN. 13:10), then the logical spot was at *el Burj* (Burg, a name of Crusader origin). The excavations in 1957 by J. L. Kelso disappointed those who hoped to find the temple of Jeroboam I at this site. A sixth-century church stood here, no doubt honoring Abraham.

But the storyteller also has traditions reporting a presence of Abraham in the extreme south country, called the *Negeb* in the Hebrew, where the tribe of Simeon later dwelt. Accordingly he describes him as going there (GEN. 12:9). No doubt we must imagine the patriarch as continuing down

2.5 *The Ghor country above Jericho looking toward the mountains of Ephraim in the northwest. (Keren Hayesod)*

and Lot's finding the land unable to support both of them and their flocks. Abraham suggested they part company and gave Lot the choice of going right or left. The "right" is regularly the south (as one faces east in the act of "orientation") and the left, north. In the district where they are said to have been, the view is chiefly to the east. Lot was attracted by the sight of the "plain of the Jordan." The latter phrase used literally means "the circle of the Jordan" (Hebrew, *kikkar hayyardēn*), and is a term employed to describe the Ghor terrace on which the cities of the Jordan country are situated. We know since Albright's explorations (1926) that this was a well-populated area in the Bronze Age. The son of Abraham's brother thus foolishly relinquished the whole land of Canaan, the promised land in which he might have had a share, to Abraham, and therewith removed himself from the pale of the destiny reserved for that land!

In the Ghor, Lot lived as a tent dweller and migrated south in the winter season as far as Sodom. The writer of this narrative believed that the Jordan Valley prior to the destruction of Sodom and Gomorrah was a garden spot clear down to Zoar. If he thought that these cities lay south of the Dead Sea

(page 71), he may have supposed that a verdant region once existed where those brackish waters now create a scene of desolation. Certainly writers of a later day like Josephus and Pliny are lavish in their praise of the Jordan Valley from Jericho northward. In the time of the Bronze Age cities, cultivation will likewise have been intensive here. In any case our passage reflects the amount of irrigation that must have been carried on here in Israelite times.

After Lot had departed, Abraham was assured by the LORD of the possession of the whole of western Palestine, and was invited to take it over symbolically by journeying through its length and its breadth. Instead of doing so, however, he merely goes a day's journey southward. The narrator thereby brings him to the scene of the next major incidents which are localized in that area.

In journeying from Bethel to Hebron, the patriarch had to go by the same route along the divide which is followed by the road of today. It was ten miles to Jerusalem, five from there to Bethlehem and thirteen more to his destination. The reference to the "plain" or "oak" of Mamre, under which he tented and built an altar, is followed by the clause "which is in Hebron" (GEN. 13:18). The

2.6 Rāmet el Khalīl. (*Courtesy American Geographical Society*)

words are best taken as referring to Mamre, not to the oak or oaks (so the divergent reading followed by R.S.V.). If Mamre is in Hebron, that need merely mean in the township, and does not rule out the traditional Mamre which lies two miles north of that city. The latter is today named *el Khalīl,* "the friend" of God (i.e., Abraham).

Abraham as Military Leader

The Dead Sea Scroll that is written in Aramaic and that was opened early in 1956 at the Hebrew University has a passage elaborating on the fourteenth chapter of Genesis and containing many new geographical names. Such late elaborations of Biblical narratives, however, show chiefly how Jews of the time of Christ thought about their ancient records and sought to bring their geography up to date for their contemporaries. Nevertheless this material gives Genesis 14 a new timeliness for the modern reader.

Few chapters of the Old Testament have had so much written about them. The urge to restudy it arises from the fact that this is the sole point at which a synchronism establishing the date of Abraham could conceivably be found. For here are mentioned a number of Oriental kings. The decipherment of innumerable cuneiform texts in a variety of languages is continually providing us with new king-names, stories of campaigns, etc. A whole book could be written on the different combinations that have been made between the kings of Genesis and those

of the inscriptions—all of them premature and discarded in short order. The four rulers named in the Bible are kings of Shinar, Ellasar, Elam, and of the Nations (Goiim). Shinar is Babylonia in the Old Testament; yet some would evade this and revert in this instance to that earlier use of the name evidenced by the Tell el Amarna letters (page 53). It was widely believed formerly that Ellasar is to be linked with the Babylonian city of Larsa, but this is largely abandoned now since it takes no heed of the prefixed syllable. Elam is the only unquestioned entity; it is the country east of the mouth of the Tigris. The allusion to the Nations is particularly mysterious; this could refer to northern mountain peoples or less probably to the sea-peoples who settled along the coast of Palestine (cf. Harosheth-hagoiim, JUDG. 4:2 R.S.V.)

No constellation of rulers can be identified as yet with the kings named here. The situation presupposes the dominance of Chedorlaomer of Elam in this coalition. Unhappily the Elamite king-list is as yet very imperfectly known, though this will be remedied in time, as more and more Elamite documents are studied and published. The French excavations under Ghirshman at the Elamite city of Dur-Untash (*Zogha-Gambil*) may be expected to provide fresh information. Tidal corresponds to a good name—*Tudkhalia*—which was borne by a Hittite king who lived early in the sixteenth century B.C. and by two others who lived in the fifteenth century B.C. Those certain enough of this equation can consider regarding "Goiim" an error for "Khittim" (Hittites). The name Arioch receives some fresh light from letters to King Zimri-lim of Mari (1700 B.C.), which mention an *Arriyuk,* evidently a vassal, who calls himself that ruler's "son." The name Amraphel has been most often connected with that of Hammurabi (Khammurapi), under the supposition of some slight corruption of the name. If one holds the identification of Shinar and Babylonia to be unshakable then there is, indeed, no king-name in the list of the Babylonian rulers as comparable as that. It would then be a case of a wearing down of a name in long transmission or of corruption by copyists of Biblical manuscripts. A dominion of Elam over Babylonia under a king Kudur-Mabug existed before the time of Hammurabi. The ruler of the Larsa Dynasty whom Hammurabi overthrew, Rim-Sin, was a son and appointee of that king of Elam. But all further speculation is unprofitable until the history of Hammurabi's time is better known.

Chedorlaomer and his vassal kings are said to have made war on the kings of Sodom and Gomorrah and allied cities. Until very recently that seemed hard to understand, but the discovery that copper mining was anciently carried on in the region between the Dead Sea and the Gulf of Aqabah (page 221) has put a new face on the matter. Babylonian and Elamite rulers in particular had a problem on their hands to obtain metals, as well as wood. If Sodom and Gomorrah lay southeast of the Dead Sea these towns could well have controlled the mines of *el 'Arabah,* so that an expedition from Mesopotamia to seize the mines would in popular reporting assume the form of a campaign against these places.

The invaders came through Gilead to Moab and Edom. Recent explorations by Glueck have established that there was a line of Bronze Age cities running down through this region. Several such are mentioned as being. subjected (GEN. 14:5–6). The places referred to can be identified with considerable certainty. Ashtaroth-karnaim, treated as one name, was actually two sister towns, Ashtaroth and Karnaim. The latter lay at *Sheikh Sa'ad,* and has a fine tell, at which the Czech scholar Hrozny carried on some excavations in 1924. Ashtaroth lay about three miles to the south, where a mound with Bronze and Iron Age sherds still bears the name *Tell 'Ashtarah.* The name Ham is preserved to this day in *Hâm, near Irbid.*

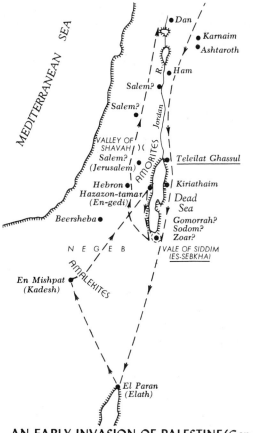

AN EARLY INVASION OF PALESTINE (Gen. 14)

The ancient circular tell with both Bronze and Iron Age walls lies southeast of the present village, overlooking a small wadi, a branch of the *Wadi el 'Arab* that enters the Jordan near Beth-shean. The next lap in the southward march brought the kings to "Shaveh-kiriathaim." No doubt this ought to be translated "plain of Kiriathaim." The implication may be that only some villages, not the city Kiriathaim itself, submitted. The latter was a Moabite city which is mentioned in Numbers 32:37. Going on through Moab they come to "Mount Seir," or Edom. El-paran, which they then reach, is a fuller name for Elath or Aila, on the Gulf of Aqabah. It describes it as being at the time under the control of a city named Paran.

From the Gulf of Aqabah the invaders took a course that led them northwest into the Negeb area. En-mishpat is explained as identical with Kadesh which lay southeast of Beersheba, here described as in or near the Amalekite country (cf. page 117). The final objective mentioned is Hazazon-tamar, said to be in "Amorite" territory, though that word is here merely another word for "Canaanites." This town is identified with En-gedi in 2 Chronicles 20:2, but that may be an approximate localization. The name *"Hazazon"* survives to this day in *Wadi el Ḥaṣāṣa,* close to the oasis of En-gedi (*Ain Jidī*). Neither townsite has as yet been satisfactorily located; it seems unlikely that they were more than villages.

A battle took place between the invaders and the local kinglets in the "Valley of Siddim." The troops from the east must thus have turned south from En-gedi and kept along the shore of the sea. "Vale of Siddim" is apparently a name for the district at the south end of the Dead Sea. It is described as full of slime pits (r.s.v. bitumen pits), which proved disastrous for the fleeing defenders. We have previously noted that the Dead Sea at times spews up some bitumen or asphalt. Whether there originally were asphalt pits or wells to the south of it is not yet known. But Glueck happened on lumps of asphalt on the shore south of En-gedi in 1953, and describes it as a wonderfully lucky find which might not have been made a day earlier or later. In the last century alone the waters have risen six and one-half feet or more, so that the southern Dead Sea basin has been enlarged by one-third and considerable land has been put under water.

An escapee from the battle in the Vale of Siddim comes to Mamre and brings Abraham the news of Lot's capture. The local Amorite clans Aner, Eshcol, and Mamre (the last two clearly being local rather than personal names) are mobilized by Abraham, who here is called "the Hebrew" (*'Ibrī*), along with his own retainers. With a total of 318 men he starts in pursuit of Lot's captors.

The homeward route supposedly taken by the eastern kings is not expressly stated.

Abraham is said to have surprised and defeated the foe north of Dan. From this point the pursuit carried "to Hobah north of Damascus." A place of this name (*Ḥōbā*) still survives on the road to Palmyra. The Aramaic scroll has Helbon (cf. Ezek. 27:18) for Hobah; the name survives at *Ḥelbūn,* fifteen miles north of Damascus.

On his return from the campaign Abraham is received by the king of Sodom in the "Valley of Shaveh." This is explained as "the king's valley." There later stood the monument of Absalom (2 Sam. 18:18). Josephus puts this two stadia (*c.* 400 yards) from the city. In the scroll version, the king's valley is equated with the Vale of Beth-haccerem (Jer. 6:1; Neh. 3:14). This makes it highly probable that Beth-haccerem is the city that stood near the present *Ramat Raḥel* south of Jerusalem (page 340). Salem, whose king Melchizedek brought out bread and wine to Abraham, is Jerusalem (Ps. 76:2). That name could thus be shortened to Salem, at least in poetry.

In the Aramaic scroll, Arioch is king of *Kptk* (Cappadocia, the old Hittite land), while Tidal is called "king of nations who was between the Rivers," i.e., Mesopotamia. Amraphel is called king of Babel. The "way of the wilderness" which they take apparently means "the king's highway" of Numbers 20:17 (see page 119).

The Promised Land

The covenant ceremony described in Genesis 15 is not directly localized, but is probably imagined as having taken place at Mamre (Gen. 13:18). The covenant promise awards to Abraham's descendants the land "from the river of Egypt to the great river, the river Euphrates." The northern orientation is quite marked here. Before the writer's mind the Euphrates stands as "the great river." The river of Egypt can only be the Pelusiac mouth of the Nile, not the mighty Nile itself prior to its division into many arms. This southern boundary implies a surprising extension of the promised land. Ordinarily the southern border of Palestine is put at the "brook of Egypt" (the *Wadi el 'Arīsh*). Possibly a faintly written "brook" was misread as "river" in some Hebrew manuscript. In the covenant ceremony, on which we may not dwell here, the smoking furnace (GEN. 15:17) is possibly a symbol of Mount Horeb or Sinai. The allusion to the 400-year bondage in Egypt (GEN. 15:13) is an interesting and important chronological item, but causes historical difficulties (see page 95 f.). Numbers, furthermore, were originally written with numerals and were readily subject to corruption or editorial change. A very comprehensive list of the peoples, including Kenites, Kenizzites, and Kadmonites, inhabiting the land of Palestine before Israel is given in this connection (GEN. 15:19–21).

The youngest writer of Genesis has given his own version of the covenant with Abraham in Genesis 17. But he is far more concerned with ritual than with what territory Israel is to possess. The institution of circumcision and its significance are paramount in his narrative of the occasion.

2.7 *On the way to Shur, a road Abraham may have taken; passing* 'Abdeh. (*Courtesy Archaeological Department, Hebrew University*)

Hagar

Slavery and concubinage were accepted things in Abraham's world, and the poignant story of Hagar gives an inkling of some of their tragic aspects. As in the case of so many other figures of the early Hebrew story the personal name is more than just the name of the person, and has geographical or tribal associations. This was still understood by Paul, when he notes that "Agar" is the Arabian name of Sinai (GAL. 4:25). It is not clear where Paul thought Sinai lay; but Strabo speaks of drawing a line from Petra to Babylon which would bisect the regions of the Nabataeans, Chauloteans (Havilah), and Agraeans. The last-named people, who appear as the Hagrites in 1 Chronicles 5:19, may well have furnished the name for Hagar. Indeed, *el Ḥejr,* an important Arabian road junction, may preserve the name

of the Hagrites. Their earlier habitat may have been more westerly. That Hagar is "Egyptian" suggests residence in the north Sinaitic area.

Abused by the jealous Sarah, the pregnant Hagar fled. The angel of the LORD found her by a fountain of water in the wilderness, the fountain on the way to Shur (GEN. 16:7). Shur is believed to be the Hebrew term for the Egyptian defense line of the isthmus of Suez, though that word, which means "wall," does not quite accurately describe these defenses. According to the French Egyptologist Clédat, who explored the region, they seem to have consisted rather of disconnected fortified posts. However that may be, the way to Shur is probably the ancient transport route to Egypt from Beersheba, named *Darb el Shur* by Woolley and Lawrence, and going via *Khalaṣa, Ruḥeibeh, Bīr Bīrein, Muweilleḥ* to the south (see map on page 64). In this parched land Hagar was nigh unto death, but through an angel's intervention discovered a spring or well which she called "Beer-lahai-roi." Its location is given as "between Kadesh and Bered." The point Kadesh is probably a fixed one (see page 117), but Bered remains uncertain. The name, meaning "coldness," suggests a place where there

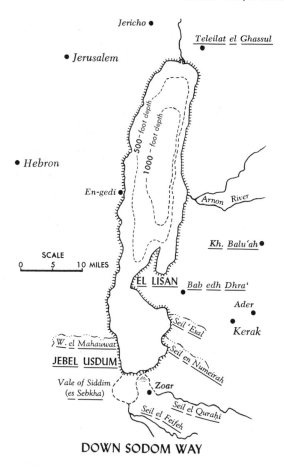

DOWN SODOM WAY

attained a great significance for the Jews in later times. A great oak, believed to be the very tree under which Abraham had spread the repast for his celestial visitors, was of course the most holy thing to be found there. There was also a cistern which was revered as the work of Abraham. The lower masonry of the massive quadrangle that the visitor to *Rāmet el Khalīl* sees today is made of masonry like that used by King Herod, the largest block seventeen feet long, and shows that this was regarded as Mamre before the time of Christ. Whether it is the true site meant by the Genesis authors is, however, a question (cf. page 77).

After the repast, Abraham accompanied his three visitors to a point from which one could look forth over the Sodom area—the same point, no doubt, to which he then returned later and saw the smoke coming up from the destroyed place (GEN. 19:28 f.). If Mamre is *Rāmet el Khalīl,* the present *Beni Na'īm,* where of old stood a Jewish village named *Kephar Barīkha,* "the village of the Blessed One" (i.e., Abraham), is indeed an appropriate spot to localize this event.

was cold water. Various places with Iron Age I remains found in this area will have to provide the clues for Bered and Beerlahairoi. Knowledge of this region has been greatly increased by the Louis Rabinowitz expedition under Glueck to the Negeb.

The Oaks of Mamre

Abraham, as we have heard, lived in a tent under the oak of Mamre (GEN. 13:18). Here, according to Genesis 18, he received three mysterious visitors, who, after he had shown them exemplary Oriental hospitality, prophesied to him that he was to have a lawful son and heir. Behind this narrative connection one discerns an independent local story explaining why Mamre was a sacred place.

The site of Abraham's dwelling, associated with the very origins of Israel by this tale,

The Cities of the Plain

While Lot has been described as a nomad (GEN. 13:12) we find him passing over to settled existence and sojourning in Sodom in Genesis 19. The story of the iniquity of the Sodomites and of the punishment that befell them, as well as of Lot's escape, needs no retelling.

An air of mystery hovers over the location of the cities of the plain. Some have sought them north of the Dead Sea, and this idea received fresh nourishment when the Jesuits, under Alexis Mallon, dug at the mounds of *Teleilāt el Ghassūl* and found remains of a phase of chalcolithic culture (see page 23) of the fourth millennium B.C., which is therefore labeled as Ghassulian by scholars. However, the names Sodom and Zoar lingered in the area south of the Dead Sea into late Roman times, and in view of the general tenacity of local tradition in Palestine, it seems highly probable that that is where those towns lay. If the oldest author asserts (GEN. 13:10) that the Jordan plain was of old a garden of the LORD all the way to Zoar, this seems to imply that he regarded the Dead Sea as nonexistent in those early days, or at least as not having been as desolate as now. The remark that the vale of Siddim is to be identified with the Dead Sea (GEN. 14:3) lent weight to the belief that this vale had been submerged beneath the waters. The narrative of the destruction of the cities, however, says nothing at all about the drowning of lands or of the cities, although that idea is found already in writings of Hellenistic-Roman times.

Recent writers of the highest competence have been willing to assume that Sodom and Gomorrah lay by the Dead Sea shore and that they were submerged by the rise of the waters. However, the land suitable for agriculture was precious in a country like Palestine, and was reserved for that purpose. One must therefore look for the sites of Sodom, Gomorrah, and Zoar on higher ground and back from the lake. Their destruction would then have to be due to other agencies than the waters of the Dead Sea.

The names of the cities are certainly not invented. Sodom and Zoar, furthermore, still occur as names of inhabited places south of the Dead Sea area in the fourth century A.D., and the former name clings to the *Jebel Sudum,* as local natives called it, or *Jebel Usdum,* as it has become known since Robinson to this day. These Christian towns may not have stood on the identical sites of the ancient ones, but they presumably were close to them to preserve the old names. All indications point to their having lain near the southern end of the Dead Sea.

It seemingly follows from Genesis 10:19, 14:2, 8 and Deuteronomy 29:23 that Admah and Zeboim were believed to have been adjacent to Sodom and Gomorrah. But it is possible that they are a parallel pair and lay

2.8 Jebel Usdum, *seen from the Dead Sea.* (*Courtesy American Geographical Society*)

elsewhere, perhaps in the Jordan Valley east of the Benjamite country (HOS. 11:8), where there is a valley of Zeboim (1 SAM. 13:18).

If one looks at the area on the south end of the Dead Sea, one notes first of all that on the west side there is no suitable location for any habitations, because the brooks that enter in here near the Jebel *Usdum* are salty.

Far different, however, is the situation on the eastern side of the south end of the Dead Sea. Here there is a plain extending south along the shore from the *Lisān* to the end of the lake. Travelers stress the luxurious growth of the vegetation in this area. Robinson compared it to the oasis of Jericho and Tristram (1865) even speaks of riding through rich groves "revealing the tropical verdure and the swarming ornithology of its labyrinths." Five sweet-water brooks coming down separate ravines are responsible for this fertility. Some find this significant for the five towns of the story, assigning one to each. The *Seil el Qurāḥi* is beyond doubt the finest of all and the leading town, Sodom, may have lain near it. On one of the hills bordering the *Seil el Feifeh,* a site of considerable importance has been spotted from an airplane. A very ancient settlement at *Bāb ed Dhra ',* five miles inland on the road from *Lisān* to *Kerak,* has been visited and studied. It was a place to which the people of the plain went up for religious celebrations, especially at the time of the summer heat. But only further exploration and some excavation can shed light on the old cities of this neighborhood.

How were Sodom and Gomorrah thought to have been destroyed in the account of that event? The words of the final recapitulation (GEN. 19:29) at first glance suggest an earthquake.

The same word "overthrow" is used in the case of destruction of a city by human hands (2 SAM. 10:3). In the narrative itself the agency of destruction is described as having been through "brimstone and fire from the LORD out of heaven" (GEN. 19:24). That suggests volcanic phenomena, such as swallowed up Pompeii. But geologists tell us that the most recent volcanic activity in that area took place ages before Abraham's time. The details of such an old Hebrew story can hardly be pressed. One item, however, is interesting in that it suggests observation of a phenomenon from the vantage point of the Judaean plateau: viz., that Abraham looking toward the cities of the plain the next morning "beheld, and lo, the smoke of the country went up as the smoke of a furnace" (GEN. 19:27–28).

The furnace comparison suggests a smelting furnace. It is worthy of note that on the hill of *Sheikh Īsa* in the *Ghōr es Safi,* close to where Sodom and Gomorrah must have lain, there has been found slag belonging to such a smelting furnace. Many more such furnaces existed farther south in the Arabah, and the inhabitants of *Beni Na'im* and other places with a view in that direction may often have seen the smoke hanging over the southern end of the Dead Sea. The observation may have suggested the comparison with the aftermath of the destruction of the cities of Sodom and Gomorrah.

Ammonites and Moabites

In the country east of the Dead Sea there dwelt the Moabites, and farther north and east were the Ammonites. The Israelites had only a foothold in this eastern territory, and their colonists had to fight for their very existence against these hostile neighbors. At the same time, however, these Ammonites and Moabites spoke a language identical with that of the Israelites, and the latter could not help realizing that these people were closely related. The common ancestor of Ammon and Moab was said to have been Lot, who lived in a cave after his escape from Sodom.

Abraham in the Negeb

The Hebrew narrators have also collected some Abraham stories from the Negeb. The younger source tells of Abraham's going there from Mamre. Abraham is said to have dwelt first between Kadesh and Shur. We may infer from Genesis 16:14 that Beerlahairoi is meant (see page 69). In the course of further wanderings he also sojourned in the district belonging to the city of Gerar. Genesis 10:19 already revealed that Gerar was not far from Gaza.

Here at Gerar, according to the younger narrator, King Abimelech had Sarah made a lady of his harem (GEN. 20:2–14). The story is much like that told of Pharaoh in Genesis 12:10 f. and has a further near-parallel in Genesis 26:7 f. The birth of Isaac, too, is connected with the Negeb sojourn in the first eight verses in chapter 21 (contrast GEN. 18:10, which would localize that event at Mamre). This is doubtless because Isaac was particularly at home in the Beersheba area. Here, finally, in Genesis 21:8–21, is also put an older story of Hagar than that which was given in Genesis 16:7–14.

Call His Name Ishmael

The Hebrews recognized a kinship between themselves and certain desert tribes of North Arabia. These tribes are listed for us in Genesis 25:12–18 (see the table on pages 73–74). But tradition held that an ancestral tribe called Ishmael had originally lived in

Peoples Related to Israel

I. The Descendants of Nahor. Genesis 22:20-24.
   A. Milcah-sons.
      1. Uz; cf. already in Genesis 10:23 as first-born of Aram.
      2. Buz. Jeremiah 25:23 in Arab group, with Dedan and Tema. cf. also Elihu the Buzite, Job 32:2. Oasis of *el Ḥigr?* Or *Bāzu* of Assyrian texts, on Arabian northeast coast?
      3. Kemuel "father of Aram." But cf. Genesis 10:22, where Aram is son of Shem. An Aramaean ancestor, as Abraham or Jacob were for Israel?
      4. Chesed. Ancestor of the "Chaldeans" (in the Babylonian language *Kaldu < Kashdu*). At time of this author not yet in lower Babylonia, but in Arabia south of it? Cf. also Job 1:17, 2 Kings 24:2.
      5. Hazo. Assyrian campaign to *Khazū,* beyond *Bāzu.* Cf. *Ḥazwa* in Central Arabia.
      6. Pildash. Unknown.
      7. Jidlaph. Unknown.
      8. Bethuel. Personal name like Kemuel. In narratives father of Laban (Genesis 22:22, 24:15).
   B. Reumah-sons. Less pure strain (from concubine).
      1. Tebah. City name in Syria (2 Sam. 8:8, text corrected with Greek version; Hebrew has Betah). *Tubiḵhi* in el Amarna letters; mentioned also in Palestine list of Thutmosis III.
      2. Gaham. Unknown.
      3. Tahash. City in Syria. *Taḵhshi* in Amarna texts; mentioned also in Egyptian inscriptions. To be sought south or southeast of Kadesh (*Tell Nebi Mind*).
      4. Maacah, or Beth Maacah; Aram-maacah in 1 Chronicles 19:6. At foot of Mount Hermon, north of Geshur, 2 Samuel 10:6, 8.

II. The Descendants of Keturah, Genesis 25:1-6.
   1. Zimran. Unknown.
   2. Jokshan. cf. Joktan, Genesis 10:28.
      a) Sheba. Cf. Table of Nations.
      b) Dedan. Cf. Table of Nations.
         (1) Ashurim. Ashur of South Arabian inscriptions?
         (2) Letushim. Unknown.
         (3) Leummim. In Edomite sphere? (cf. Genesis 25:23 Heb.)
   3. Medan. Uncertain. *Badanaean* city (with change of *b* to *m*) mentioned by Assyrians? Then in *Hejāz,* southeast of Dedan.
   4. Midian. Cf. page 100.
      a) Ephah. cf. Isaiah 60:6. *Khayāpa* in inscriptions of Sargon of Assyria. Today *Ghwafa* in *Ḥesma* territory, east of Gulf of Aqabah.
      b) Epher. Cf. *Eperu* or *Apuriu* (= *Khapiri?*) of Egyptian inscriptions; in Negeb or Sinai area?
      c) Hanoch. (= Enoch, city named for son of Cain, Genesis 4:17; in *el ʿArabah?*
      d) Abida. *Ibadidi* in inscriptions of Sargon II?
      e) Shuah. Home of Bildad the Shuhite, Job 1:11. In North Arabia? Name also that of district on Euphrates (*Suḵhu*).

III. The Descendants of Ishmael (Genesis 25:13-18).
    A. Nebaioth. Cf. Isaiah 60:7. Assyrian campaign to *Nabaiate,* "whose place is far away." In southern part of *Wadi Sirḥan?*
    B. Kedar. Assyrians: *Qidri.* On inscription of a king of Kedar see pages 334 and 335. South of Nabataeans (later inhabitants of Edom), according to Pliny.
    C. Adbeel. Assyrians: *Idiba'il;* tribe subdued and resettled near Ashkelon in Philistaea by Tiglathpileser III.
    D. Mibsam. Unknown.
    E. Mishma. In 1 Chronicles 4:25 among Simeonite clans; their Arab origin forgotten; then probably among the *Idiba'i l* settled by Tiglathpileser. But here still in Arabian home. *Jebel Misma* east of *Wadi Sirḥan* may preserve name.
    F. Dumah. Oasis *Dumat el Jandal,* 250 miles east of Petra. Called *Adumu* by Assyrians.
    G. Massa. Cf. above page 53.
    H. Hadad. Error for Harar? Cf. Assyrian *Khurarina,* perhaps *el Hawārīn.*
    I. Tema. Oasis of *Teima?* Cf. Jeremiah 25:23, Isaiah 21:13. The place where Nabonidus, king of Babylon, spent seven years, according to Babylonian text (cf. page 325).
    J. Jetur. Cf. under K.
    K. Naphish. In 1 Chronicles 5:19, where Nodab is added to them they are adversaries of Transjordanic Hebrew tribes (in late view). Jetur pushed north later and gave name to Ituraea (cf. page 354). Here still farther southeast than in 1 Chronicles?
    L. Kedemah (cf. 1 Chronicles 1:31). Differentiated from Kedem?
IV. The Edomite Kings and their Cities (Genesis 36).
    A. Bela. Capital: Dinhabah. Eusebius would connect with place called *Dannaba,* seven Roman miles from Heshbon. If right, that would suggest a Moabite domination.
    B. Jobab son of Zerah of Bozrah. The latter name survives in *Buṣeirah* ("little Bozrah"), in the high country east of Petra.
    C. Husham of the land of the Temanites. Eusebius knew a village of *Taiman* 15 miles from Petra. Perhaps *et Twāneh,* a large site with Iron Age sherds, five hours walk north of Petra? Glueck found an important Iron Age site near Petra at *Tawīlān,* holding that to be Teman.
    D. Hadad son of Bedad "who smote Midian in the field of Moab"; Awith his city. Musil held latter name survives in *Jebel el Ghuweitheh,* a mountain south of the Arnon. Like No. 1, really a Moabite? Midianite battle suggests time of Gideon.
    E. Samlah of Masrekah. Locality in eastern Edom? Musil mentions cone-shaped mountain *el Meshariq* in the *Hejāz,* close to southern border of Edom.
    F. Saul of Rehoboth by the River (R.S.V. Euphrates). The place meant in Gen. 10:11? Eusebius knew a Rehoboth in Edom; name preserved in *Seil er Rhāb* southeast of southern end of Dead Sea (Musil)?
    G. Baal-hanan son of Achbor. No place given.
    H. Hadar. City Pau (R.S.V. Pagu). Error for Peor (so Greek translation)? Musil would find name Pau lingering at *Wadi Fā'i* west of the el *'Arabah,* near *Kurnub.* Mention of queen and her family suggests she played important role.

the Negeb. According to Genesis 21:8–21 the slave girl Hagar was sent forth by Abraham along with the little boy she had borne him. She wandered about in "the wilderness of Beersheba." The well of water, which she discovered when God opened her eyes, saved her life and that of Ishmael. The name of the well is not given—probably because it was already presented in the other version.

A brief report of Ishmael's and hence of the Ishmaelites' skill in archery and a hint of his original habitat are then offered.

> "And he dwelt in the wilderness of Paran: and his mother took him a wife out of the land of Egypt." (GEN. 21:21 A.V.)
>
> *"He lived in the wilderness of Paran; and his mother took a wife for him from the land of Egypt."* (GEN. 21:21 R.S.V.)

The Egyptians at times employed archers from northern Sinai as mercenaries; their inscriptions, however, do not deign to name tribes of these "miserable Asiatics." They call the Bedouin *Shasu.*" The intermarriage of Ishmaelites with Egyptians is understandable in view of the proximity of their territory to Egypt. The wilderness of Paran is given as the original home of the Ishmaelites. El-paran (GEN. 14:6) suggests that Paran extended to Aqabah (see further page 116).

How Beersheba Got Its Name

The narrative of Hagar's expulsion presupposed Abraham's living in the vicinity of Beersheba. We now learn that Abimelech of Gerar visited Abraham in this locality, realizing with prophetic foresight that he was going to have Abraham's descendants for neighbors (GEN. 21:23 f.). The Canaanite king of Gerar was quite anxious, like the Gibeonites of Joshua 9, to have some sort of treaty of protection that would safeguard his descendants from Hebrew encroachment. Originally the thing may have been the other way around. The tenting Hebrew clansmen would have sought an agreement from the

Canaanite king permitting their grazing in this area in return for certain concessions on their part.

In connection with the event as it is related here, the legal rights to a well, which Abraham's men allegedly had dug but which the Gerarites had seized, play a role; in the covenant ceremony seven ewe lambs were set apart by Abraham and handed over to Abimelech. The narrator adds, "wherefore he called that place Beersheba; because there they sware both of them." (GEN. 21:31). He could thus interpret Beersheba as "well of the oath," but this is philologically less likely than the alternative explanation "well of the seven," at which the "seven lambs" may hint. But both explanations are instances of popular etymology. The town, like most others supposedly getting their names because of what the patriarchs did there, was doubtless in existence long before Abraham tented in its vicinity, and the "seven" after whom it was named will have been clans or spirits.

The general location of Beersheba is known, for the name survives to this day as *Bir-es-seba'*. Whether the ancient town stood on the site of the present settlement currently being built up as an Israeli center is a moot question. The remains there seem to be exclusively late Roman and Byzantine. There is a *Tell es Seba'* (also called *Tell el Mshāsh*) three miles east of the present Beersheba which has a good claim to be regarded as the town the patriarchs knew, though only excavations could determine whether it was inhabited in the Late Bronze Age. Some scholars, however, hold that this was a different city (see page 118). Round about Beersheba recent explorations have discovered the existence of chalcolithic settlements.

The Sacrifice of Isaac

Of all the stories to come down from ancient Israel that of the sacrifice of Isaac is one of those that have stirred humanity most. The text of the passage states:

"And he said, Take now thy son . . . and get thee into the land of Moriah; and offer him there . . . upon one of the mountains which I will tell thee of." (GEN. 22:2 A.V.)

"He said, 'Take your son . . . and go to the land of Moriah, and offer him there . . . upon one of the mountains of which I shall tell you.'" (GEN. 22:2 R.S.V.)

The name Moriah, declared in 2 Chronicles 3:1 to be that of the mountain on which Solomon built the temple, cannot be relied on very heavily; the ancient Greek translation, the Septuagint, does not support it, but has "the high country," while the old Syriac translator reads "the land of the Amorites." Again, one is curious to learn if a Dead Sea scrolls fragment lends any help. As we shall see, Jerusalem can hardly be the objective intended by the original writer, much less Shechem, as asserted by the Samaritans.

The place from which Abraham started out was presumably Beersheba, for there the same source that gives us this narrative left him in chapter 21. From that point, then, the patriarch traveled north into the ascending mountain country, doubtless via the road to Hebron. On the third day he "lifted up his eyes and saw the place afar off." That third day reference need not be taken too literally; it is an element of narrative style and suggests a journey of some distance. However, it may be of interest to note that Robinson in 1838 found it a twelve-hour trip with camels from Beersheba to Hebron, while from Hebron to Jerusalem took eight and a half hours more. A pedestrian carrying fire, with a carefully nursed flame, and accompanied by a boy, a donkey, and a manservant might well have taken until early on the third day to get to the Hebron area. To reach Jerusalem by that time and under such circumstances would have been difficult. Furthermore one cannot see the Temple Hill of Jerusalem from afar in coming to it from the south, as this story requires.

Since this is no doubt originally an old tale of how a certain sacred high place was first consecrated, the mountain is imagined as a wild place where there was a thicket, in which Abraham, after being told not to sacrifice his son, finds a ram (?) caught by the horns. A suitable sacrifice was thus divinely provided. The crucial words "The LORD will provide" (*Jehovah Jireh*) hinting at or giving the name of the sacred place are then uttered by Abraham. An ingenious suggestion has been put forward that the words hint at the name of Jeruel which lay on the edge of the wilderness of Judah (2 CHRON. 20:16). However, the words could be the name of a hilltop sanctuary in the Hebron area. The "high country" of the Septuagint would agree well with that, for the Hebron district marks the crest of this region. Perhaps the *Rāmet el Khalīl,* which later became identified with Mamre (cf. page 77), was originally meant.

The Tomb of the Patriarchs

The death of Sarah forced Abraham to find a family burial place. As an alien in the land he owned no real estate, for the Oriental was loath to part with his property. In the Near East burial took place on the day of death, so the arrangements had to be quickly made. His predicament was recognized and human consideration for it expresses itself in high courtesy. The late narrator, who gives us the account, thinks of Abraham as living at Mamre rather than Beersheba. He uses the older name for nearby Hebron, Kiriath-arba, i.e., "city of the four" (villages, clans, gods, wells?). Abraham was forced to deal with the people of this nearby city, who here are named "Hittites." While it is not impossible that there was an old upper stratum of Hittites in the community, for there were many groups and offshoots of groups in antiquity that migrated as did the Beerothites or the Danites (2 SAM. 4:3; JUDG. 18), it seems more probable that that should not be stressed here. This youngest author

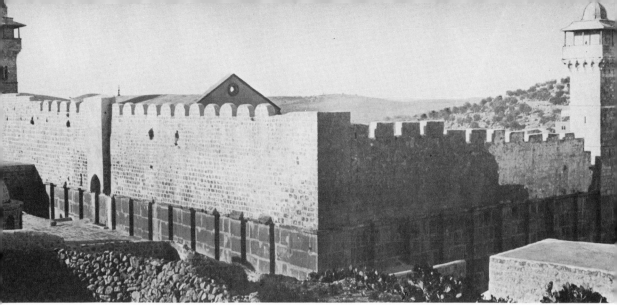

2.9 *A Hebron mosque at the patriarchal tombs. (J. Lane Miller)*

just uses "Hittites" for the pre-Israelite population in general. The usage has precedent in Assyrian royal inscriptions which sometimes refer to the West as "Khatti-" or "Hittite-" land. In Genesis 14:13 the inhabitants of Hebron were described as "Amorites"; in Judges 1:10 they are called "Canaanites."

Abraham asked the leading citizens of Hebron, whom he found assembled in the gateway, to persuade a certain property owner named Ephron to sell him a certain cave as a tomb. The deal was made after typically Oriental negotiations, in which the sale of the field, at one end of which the cave is situated, was joined to that of the cave in high courtesy. The words of Genesis 23:17-18 recording the sale read almost like a legal deed that seeks to leave no loopholes. It is the description of the locality, however, with which we are concerned here.

Tradition has long since settled matters to the satisfaction of its followers. The burial place of the patriarch is at *el Khalîl,* where there is a sacred enclosure or *Ḥarām* of sixty-five by thirty-seven yards. Like the enclosure at Mamre it, too, exhibits courses of the same huge blocks of stone that are characteristic of Herodian masonry still visible at Jerusalem (see page 399). Since the days of the Crusades few non-Mohammedans have entered the supposed tomb of the patriarchs, for Moslem fanaticism keeps all others out. Several members of European royalty and a British army officer, who went in in the confusion of 1918, are the only ones to have enjoyed this distinction. All reports agree that there is a real cave there and there is a high probability that it is the one the storyteller of Genesis 23 had in mind. Indeed, it may be regarded as the fixed point in all discussions about Hebron.

One should note that in the precise Biblical statement cited above, the field is *in Machpelah,* just as the garden of Genesis 2:8 was *in Eden;* if the cave itself is later called Machpelah, this is speaking inexactly, just as it is when the garden is called Eden. If the field was "before Mamre" (GEN. 23:19, then in which direction from Mamre did it lie? The word "before" may frequently be rendered "east of," but if that is done here then the description does not fit the two supposed holy places. It must be pointed out, however, that "before" in the Hebrew specifications of this nature sometimes only means "over against" or "near." If the field of Machpelah actually lay "over against" Mamre, then Mamre should be sought on the western side of the valley opposite the cave.

But what of Hebron itself? In the story of

HEBRON AND VICINITY

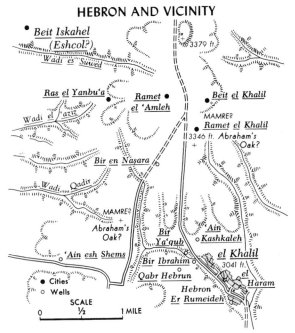

the spies sent out by Israel we learn incidentally that Hebron was built seven years before Zoan (Tanis) in Egypt (NUM. 13:22). This very astonishing piece of chronological information suggests that it was an important point for the Hyksos, prior to their invading Egypt and making Tanis (then called Avaris) their capital. One would thus look for some visible evidence of a rather strong city. The fact that David began his career as a sovereign there (2 SAM. 2:11) also suggests that it was a place of real consequence. Yet it has not been possible thus far to determine definitely where Hebron was situated. Since a city of those days needed a good defensive position and water, Hebron ought to have lain on the hill of *Rumeideh*

on the south side of the valley. This hill is really a projection of the high, rocky country that lies beyond it. A good spring exists at its foot. A remark in Genesis 23:19 that was added by some editor actually asserts the identity of Mamre and Hebron. But since Hebron's old name was Kiriath-arba and not Mamre, the identity cannot be regarded as absolute. It seems likely that the localization of Mamre has been shifted a number of times, owing to the desirability of associating it with a great oak tree. There was such a one at *Rāmet el Khalīl* in the time of Christ, and long afterward. It probably drew the localization of Mamre to that point. In recent times a great oak near the Russian hospice west of *el Khalīl* was pronounced the oak of Abraham.

In the cave thus obtained Abraham buried Sarah. Later he himself also was laid to rest in it (GEN. 25:9), as were Isaac and Rebecca (GEN. 49:31), and Jacob and Leah (GEN. 50:13), according to the youngest Pentateuchal writer.

One can easily realize that the spot where all the patriarchs were thought to have been buried was immensely important to the Jews. When this story was written they no longer had possession of Hebron; it had fallen into the hands of the Edomites (cf. EZEK. 36:5). The story was written in such detail for a definite purpose. The writer is bent on proving that Israel's ancestor bought the burial place of the patriarchs from the earlier population, and that his descendants, therefore, have a title to it that cannot be taken away by the Edomites under a law of angary.

CHAPTER V

THE TENTS OF ISAAC
AND THE STAR OF JACOB

THE INIMITABLE story of how Abraham's faithful servant journeyed to the homeland with a ten-camel caravan to obtain a wife of pure stock for his master's son Isaac (GEN. 24) is one of the best-known and best-loved Biblical narratives. According to Genesis 11:31, Haran was the home of Abraham, but no general geographical name was used in that passage.

At the City of Nahor

There is no light on the starting point or course of the servant's journey. The reader is taken straightway to the objective: the city of Nahor. For the Biblical storyteller this is the unnamed city where a man named Nahor lived. But we have already seen (see page 51) that Nahor was also and first of all the name of a city in the Haran area.

Abraham's servant stopped at the well where the women and girls of the town must fetch water with their earthenware jars.

Here, then, he encountered Rebecca, who, after appropriate negotiations with her family, consented to become Isaac's bride. She returned with the servant to the land of Canaan, accompanied by her nurse. The closing scene of the narrative describes the meeting of bride and groom.

"And Isaac came from the way of the well Lahairoi; for he dwelt in the south country.

And Isaac went out to meditate in the field at the eventide; and he lifted up his eyes, and saw, and, behold, the camels were coming." (GEN. 24:62–63 A.V.)

"Now Isaac had come from Beer-lahai-roi, and was dwelling in the Negeb. And Isaac went out to meditate in the field in the evening; and he lifted up his eyes and looked, and behold, there were camels coming." (GEN. 24:62–63 R.S.V.)

79

2.10 Tell *and* Wadi esh Sheri'a, *a possible site of Gerar. Railroad line and bridge. (Bavarian State Archives)*

The first sentence must probably be understood to mean that Isaac had *gone to* Beerlahairoi, for there we later find him living (GEN. 25:11). It was near this well, then, that he went out in the eventide *to walk* (so the Hebrew). The localization reveals the origin of the tradition in the area south of Beersheba, rather than in that of Hebron.

The High Places of Isaac

In later times the Israelites of the tribe of Simeon who lived in the Negeb revered Isaac as their ancestor. But so also did some northern tribes. When the prophet Amos went up to prophesy to Israel, he makes allusion to the "high places of Isaac," and the priest Amaziah even calls Israel "the house of Isaac" (AMOS 7:16). Pilgrimages were undertaken to Beersheba (AMOS 5:5, 8:14), which evidently was a holy place to Israel chiefly because reminiscences of Isaac were so prominently associated with it.

Not very far from Beersheba was Beerlahairoi. This must have been a second holy place visited by northern pilgrims to this area, for it also had important associations with Isaac (GEN. 25:11). It was here that Isaac prayed for his still childless wife, and that the worried Rebecca made inquiry of the oracle (GEN. 25:21 f.). In this vicinity Esau and Jacob were born. From here Esau, a "man of the field," or plainsman, went

hunting, seeking to take the fleet gazelle, or the oryx antelope, while Jacob tended the flocks. The Ishmaelites, too, held Beerlahairoi in reverence (GEN. 16:14-15).

But there were also reminiscences of Isaac in an area west of Beersheba—in the territory of Gerar. A famine is said to have caused him to go there.

Just where Gerar was situated is still uncertain and depends on how one locates other towns in this general area and fixes the boundary of Simeon, which is not given in Joshua 19:1-9, where the tribe's towns are listed. Nor is it mentioned among the Negeb towns that include Beersheba (JOSH. 15:28). In late Roman times there was a district *Geraritiké,* evidently so named because it was composed primarily of the old Gerar territory, and at that time Beersheba was included in it. *Tell Jemmeh,* an important mound south of Gaza, which was partly excavated by Sir Flinders Petrie in 1927, was identified by him with Gerar. Some scholars doubted that Simeonite territory extended so far and favored *Tell esh Sherī'a* northwest of Beersheba. According to a 1961 report, however, Israeli archaeologists have found that a mound not far from there, on the road from Beersheba to Gaza, *Tell abu Hureira,* with preHyksos remains, has greater importance than either of these two tells, and merits equation with Gerar.

Isaac is described as living in the city itself —an interesting example of the transition from nomadism to semi-nomadism. He resided right near the palace of Abimelech, the local king. His departure being requested by the jealous townsmen, who anachronistically are called "Philistines," Isaac went forth to "the valley of Gerar," in other words farther up the particular wadi on which the city lay. Here his shepherds dug two wells, the ownership of which was speedily contested by the shepherds of Gerar. The names of these wells, Esek ("contention") and Sitnah ("quarrel"), seemed suggestive to the narrator of the feuding that went on between the nomads and the city shepherds. A *Wadi Shuṭneh*, three miles north of *Ruḥeibeh*, may preserve the name of Sitnah, according to Robinson. Isaac then moved on beyond the pasture area of Gerar and dug a new well which he called Rehoboth, "roomy place" (cf. the Mesopotamian city, GEN. 10:11). This is clearly a town name rather than that of a well, and it is held to have survived in the important site of *er Ruḥeibeh,* just mentioned. The place lies in a small valley forming a separate entity between *Wadi Ghazzeh* and *Wadi el ʻArīsh.* It is on the important route from Beersheba to Egypt, on which Hagar had fled and near which Abraham had tented (GEN. 16:7, 20:1). There is an old well, three hundred feet deep, in the valley near the town. While nothing

pre-Nabataean has been found on the surface of the site, the possibility of more ancient occupation is conceded by archaeologists.

Isaac (in an item drawn from the older narrative) then moved back from the Gerar district to Beersheba (GEN. 26:32–33). The story implies that he is the discoverer of its well. It was found shortly after Abimelech of Gerar visited him in order to make a covenant with him. Isaac gave the well the name *Shibah* in commemoration of this ceremony. It is here interpreted as "(well of) the oath." From this, one must infer, came the town name Beersheba. As we have seen, a different etymology for the town name was offered by younger tradition in Genesis 21: 25–34, which has attributed the incident to the more illustrious figure of Abraham.

The Wanderings of Jacob

Isaac had two sons, Jacob and Esau. The two become representatives of the two nations held to have sprung from them: Israel and Edom. But Jacob's name was a genuine personal name. It appears as that of a Hyksos ruler (*Yʻqb-Ḥr*) around 1600 B.C., and occurs as the name of a clan-held town *Yaʻqob-el,* "may God protect" (the full form, no doubt, of Jacob's name), in the Palestine list of Pharaoh Thutmosis III (*c.* 1480 B.C.). Recently it has even turned up in a tablet of the late eighteenth century B.C. found at Chagar Bazar in Mesopotamia, as *Ya-aʼ (AKH)-qu-ub-ilu.* It is possible that Jacob was a more important figure than the simple patriarchal story would lead one to suppose; the remark about his capture of Shechem (see page 87) points in that direction.

While Jacob is Israel and Esau is Edom, that does not mean that every element in the stories about them can be explained on such a basis. To all intents and purposes we have here tales about human individuals. But an underlying substratum of national history is mirrored in the basic idea that Esau (Edom)

was outstripped by Jacob (Israel). Edom, it was held, was the elder people and, therefore, should have had the more glorious history. Several parallel explanations are offered why it did not happen that way: 1) God willed it so, and predicted it even before the ancestral brothers were born (GEN. 25:23); 2) Esau sold his birthright (GEN. 25:29–34); 3) Jacob rather than Esau obtained the history-moulding blessing of the dying Isaac (GEN. 27:27 f.).

The third of these explanations had dramatic possibilities. The man cheated becomes an enemy, and thus is set up the rivalry of the brothers, which reflects the enmity between the Israelites and Edomites. But here the national backgrounds fade and the personal history of two individuals comes into focus. To escape the wrath of Esau, Jacob, at his mother's suggestion, fled to her brother Laban in distant Haran.

The youngest Pentateuchal storyteller, however, being of a more solemn attitude of mind, portrayed this personal history differently. He sees the patriarchs as saintly personages and so leaves out all incidents that reflect unfavorably on their characters. He therefore explains Jacob's going to Haran in another way. Rebecca, he alleges, was dissatisfied with the wives Esau had taken from the "Hittite" population (see page 77). She induced Isaac to send their son Jacob to Paddan-aram to her brother's home, where it was hoped he would find a wife of pure stock (GEN. 27:46 f.). That was the reason for Jacob's departure!

The more detailed earlier narrative thinks of Jacob as starting off from Beersheba (GEN. 28:10). It mentions only one stop on the way—that at Bethel. But this could certainly not have been the first night's resting place for a traveler who had left Beersheba in the morning (cf. page 76); that shows that the Bethel story is really an independent local narrative. Tradition asserted that Jacob had rested his head on a stone slab, and had had a dream in which he saw a ladder or staircase leading to heaven and the angels ascending and descending. This dream induced the patriarch to conclude that here was the gate of heaven, so he raised up the stone on which he had slept and anointed it and vowed that in the event of his safe return this place should become in the future a "house of God" (i.e., that a regular sanctuary and cult should be established here). In the Abraham narratives it was that patriarch who raised the first altar at Bethel and thus hallowed the site (GEN. 12:8, 13:4), another instance of transfer of an achievement from a lesser to a greater personage, for Jacob is more firmly rooted here than Abraham. "Bethel" means "house of God." But the phrase was also used for the sacred stone pillar. Such an object stood in the Israelite sanctuary of Bethel, and is doubtless the real reason for the name of the city.

The sacred stone of Bethel can hardly be one of the monolithic type (fig. 2.11), but must rather have been flat and thin, somewhat like the gravestones one sees in old American cemeteries, for no one can be

2.11 *Menhir at Ader in Moab; a sacred pillar of great size.* (*Courtesy Nelson Glueck*)

imagined as sleeping with his head resting on a prostrate monolith. The recent Hebrew University excavations at Hazor have produced flat, sacred slabs of this sort. One may be in doubt as to whether the pillar Jacob is said to have raised stood in a shrine near the city (see page 64), or whether the storyteller is thinking of one that stood in the city temple, like the main pillar at Shechem (page 160). In the latter case, the story of Jacob's erecting it would represent an attempt by the Hebrew successors of the Canaanites of Bethel to connect the pillar with their own ancestor. The main temple was certainly within the city. It was there that Amos was ordered to leave (AM. 7:10 ff.).

How Jacob went from Bethel to Aram-naharaim (cf. GEN. 24:10) is not related in detail. The narrative speaks of his coming to "the land of the people of the east," literally, "the sons of *Qedem*" (GEN. 29:1). It is rather surprising to find that term used for the Haran area, for it applies properly to eastern Syria and the regions east of eastern Palestine (page 153). But Mesopotamia has always been open to invasion of people from north Arabia, and that was very much the case at the time when the Aramaeans gained control here. In a later narrative about Laban, we will find him ranging all the way from Haran to Gilead.

Another well scene, evidently a much-loved theme for the ancient reader, brings the fugitive into contact with the people of the region to which he had fled. The well is said to have been covered with a heavy stone, a custom that still exists, as noted by Palmer in describing a place south of the *et Tīh* plateau in the Sinaitic region. In the Genesis story the stone was so heavy that it took a number of men to move it. The shepherds told Jacob they were from Haran, previously mentioned as the home of Laban (GEN. 27:43). As Jacob asked about him, Laban's daughter Rachel appeared in the role of shepherdess. Thus Jacob had reached his objective at or near Haran, and another famous and much-loved Biblical romance that the reader must read for himself gets under way.

Jacob's life at Haran mirrors the nomadic existence in a vivid manner. Laws and customs presupposed show affinity with those in old Mesopotamian texts from Nuzi (*Yorghan Tepe* near *Kerkuk*) unearthed by a Harvard and American School's expedition 1925–31.

Jacob's Flight to Gilead

In the end Jacob decided to return to Palestine. The younger storyteller attributes this decision to a dream-oracle of the god of Bethel (GEN. 31:13). But the hero could extricate himself from the control of his father-in-law only by flight. He chose an occasion when Laban was away engaged in sheep-shearing, so that it would be several days before he found out about his son-in-law's departure. He crossed the Euphrates River (GEN. 31:21), though we do not learn how this was accomplished (cf. page 62). His objective was Gilead, and since this was spring of the year, we may imagine him as moving on across the steppes. The Anti-Lebanon Mountain range loomed to the west as a great landmark and pointed toward his native land. Ever southward went the course through the *Jaulān* to Gilead. We may imagine him as keeping on the high ground and crossing the Jabbok rather far upstream.

"Laban the Aramaean," learning that Jacob had quit him, pursued him and caught up with him on Mount Gilead. The name of this mountainous district is doubtless derived from that of the city Gilead (JUDG. 10:17, Hos. 12:11), and the latter probably lay at *Khirbet Jel'ad*. The mountain area thereabouts, too, continues the name, for it is called

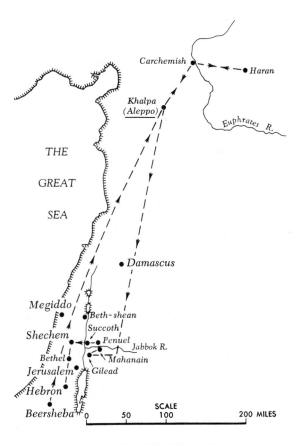

WANDERINGS OF JACOB

Jebel Jel'ad, "Mount Gilead." It lies some distance south of the river Jabbok and extends in an east-west direction. The name Gilead, however, is often used to include part of the *'Ajlūn,* the region north of the Jabbok, and so some scholars seek the places mentioned in this narrative in that area. As will appear, that supposition, too, has its difficulties.

In the negotiations that then took place between Jacob and Laban there is veiled allusion to the names of several Gileadite cities. According to the oldest strand of the story, the two men made a mound or cairn of stones and held a meal beside it. Laban invoked the cairn as a witness, for which reason it is called *gal'ēd* ("mound of witness")—obviously a pun on the name "Gilead." An editor held that Laban the Aramaean must have spoken Aramaic and so adds that Laban for his part called it Jegar Sahadutha (GEN. 31:47). It is obvious that Laban and Jacob here represented the Aramaean and Israelite peoples. Evidently the place where the treaty was made once marked the frontier between the two nationalities.

If one will take the *Jebel Jel'ad* as the mountain referred to in this narrative, the cairn marking the Hebrew-Aramaean boundary by Jacob must be a definite spot on this range. The allusion to a pillar named Mizpah (GEN. 31:45, 49), too, has local significance. It was probably a sacred place at which the treaty-making was held to have been carried out. We hear of a Mizpah in Gilead as an important town and sanctuary in the time of the Judges (JUDG. 10:17, 11:11, 29, 34). At a much later date a prophet addresses a rebuke to those who have been a snare at Mizpah, probably meaning this same place; he implies that they have brought misfortune on Gilead by their counsels and actions (HOS. 5:1). Mizpah probably lay close to the city of Gilead. *Rēshūni,* northwest of *Khirbet Jel'ad,* has been suggested for Mizpah, but others would seek it in north Gilead.

Pressure of Aramaean tribes against the Gilead area, such as this story presupposes, probably reflects the situation prevailing in the ninth to eighth centuries B.C. A penetration of the country south of the Jabbok by an isolated group led to a treaty of amity.

The Last Lap of Jacob's Journey

After the treaty with Laban, Jacob, according to the younger version of the events, journeyed to Mahanaim (GEN. 32:1–2). At this place he encountered angels of God and ejaculated, "This is God's host," literally, "This is the encampment of God('s host)." The inference is that it was Jacob who named the place Mahanaim, "the encampment." The earlier narrator, too, must have had Jacob go to Mahanaim, for he likewise hints at an explanation of that name in his account (GEN. 32:3–13). Jacob was afraid when he heard of Esau's coming, and divided his retinue into two bands or companies (hence Mahanaim interpreted as "two camps"). Now Mahanaim was important enough to serve as capital for Saul's successor as well as for David during Absalom's rebellion (2 SAM. 2:8; 17:24). It must thus have been a fortified city in a strategic location. Its identification is a matter of historical importance.

Apparently it was some distance from Mahanaim to the Jabbok. Jacob strategically divided his possessions into two detachments and led them toward that river valley. We next find him at the ford. After instructing his family and herds to go to the other side of the stream, he spent the night alone on the hither side. Here he had the nocturnal encounter with a supernatural opponent. The spot where this took place thus also lay on the hither side of the stream. On the following morning Jacob called the place Penuel ("God's countenance"), and that, then, is how the city which lay there got its name. The question is: From which direction did Jacob approach the river, from the north or from the south?

If one connects Mount Gilead with the *Jebel Jel'ad,* then Jacob must have come from the south. He could have proceeded to a crossing at which lay a city of some consequence. There are two mounds there—"the tells of gold" (*Tulūl edh Dhahab*)—one on the left side of the Jabbok and one on the right side. The river makes a sharp loop around the one on the right side, which is the larger and is situated on a natural hilltop, but the one on the left bank, *Tell Dhahab el Gharbīyeh,* "the Western," also lying on an eminence is the older, Iron Age site. It may well represent the city of Penuel, as first suggested long ago by an American explorer of Transjordan, Selah Merrill. The place probably owed its name to the hill on the opposite side, *Tell Dhahab esh sharqīyeh* "the eastern," which is virtually a promontory; for we note that there was a promontory on the coast of Syria which was also called Penuel (*Theouprosopon* in Greek, today *Rās Shaqqā*). Mahanaim should then be sought between the *Jebel Jel'ad* and the Jabbok. On its location see page 206.

Jacob, so the story goes, next meets Esau. The encounter is not localized, but from the connection one would imagine it to have occurred at the edge of the Ghor. Dramatic necessity, however, rather than local tradition governs the mention of this item and so one must not look for a localization.

Jacob next comes to Succoth. This again is a local report, for the naming of the place is attributed to the patriarch. Succoth is generally sought at the site of *Tell Deir'allā,* north of the lower Jabbok. It should be noted that Succoth so located could be reached only by crossing the Jabbok from the south and proceeding in a northerly direction. Had Jacob crossed from the north, proceeding south, he would not have gone by *Tell Deir'allā.*

Jacob's Arrival at Shechem

Rather strangely, nothing is said about crossing the Jordan or the ascent to the mountains. The travel objective of Jacob is Shechem (GEN. 33:18), just as it had been

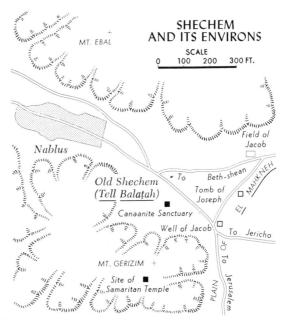

that of Abraham (GEN. 12:6). Jacob, encamped before the city, the location of which at *Tell Balātah* was already mentioned (see page 63). It is as though this were to be his definite abode.

Jacob, we are told, purchased the field on which he camped from the "children of Hamor" (cf. JOSH. 24:32), a Canaanite clan that ruled Shechem, much as the clan of Qureish ruled the Mekka of Mohammed. This purchase is in a certain sense parallel to Abraham's purchase of the field (and cave) at Mamre. It is as though Israel's right to a certain piece of ground in the area were to be established. Jacob's purchase price of one hundred kesitah is mentioned. Here, then, he erected an altar (originally no doubt a pillar, for altars are not usually "erected") and called it *El Elohe Yisrael.* The name is confessional: "El (God) is the god of Israel." It is an identification of the god of the Israelites with El. The latter has become simply a short word for God in Hebrew, but is chiefly used in poetry; the common prose word for God was *Elohim* (plural of *Eloah*). Originally, however, El was the name of a deity, as the early north Canaanite epics from Ugarit (*Rās-esh-Shamrā*) in

2.12 *Shechem as Jacob may have seen it. (after G. Welter)*

Syria taught us. The sacred pillar at Shechem was doubtless much older than the Hebrew writer knows and was dedicated to that deity. The Hebrews, represented by Jacob, rechristened it "El is the god of Israel" (i.e., El is Yahweh). Identification of one god with another is a mode of absorption and conquest very common in the religious process.

It would be interesting to know just where the pillar stood. The sanctuary of which it formed the core is not necessarily identical with that which lay at the oak of Moreh (GEN. 12:6, DEUT. 11:30). There were apt to be several shrines in such a locality. Perhaps the pillar was not far from "the well of Jacob" and "the grave of Joseph" (cf. page 143). The latter may be the true site of the ancient holy place here referred to. On an old Canaanite shrine discovered by Welter on the slope of Mount Gerizim see page 159.

Simeon and Levi Bring Jacob into Disrepute

The sojourn of Jacob at Shechem (Genesis 34) illustrates how the relations between a Canaanite city and the nomads were sometimes adjusted, and how treachery on the part of the nomads could even lead to the seizure of a city. The citizenry of such a fortified city might easily have driven off these Bedouin, but to do so was to invite harassment of agriculture, commerce, and travel, and so it was cheaper to come to an agreement regulating mutual relations. One thing always much desired in such an old city was young girls for the harems of the rich. Intermarriage was therefore an impor-

tant part of such agreements. The seduction of Jacob's daughter Dinah by a young aristocrat of Shechem provides a tense situation in which the nomads can dictate terms.

The name Shechem as a personal name is artificial, for it is a geographical name. The word signified "shoulder"; the place probably got its name from the fact that it was situated at the foot of Mount Gerizim, which must be the "shoulder" that is meant. Simeon and Levi are obviously imagined as tribes here rather than as individual sons of a man named Jacob, for they are able to muster a considerable number of fighting men.

The terms imposed on the Shechemites involved circumcision. Contrary to the impression here given, however, circumcision was practiced by the Canaanites; the Philistines are the notoriously uncircumcised group. One may, of course, suppose that there was a foreign non-Semitic element in Shechem which had not accepted this custom, and that these were the people primarily affected. In the Amarna Age a man named Labaya resided at Shechem, and his name gives indication that a Hurrian element controlled the city. Simeon and Levi, treacherously taking advantage of the post-operative incapacity of the men of Shechem, attack the unsuspecting city with the sword, killing all male inhabitants and carrying off women and children as well as spoils. Jacob allegedly disapproved of the act of the two sons and complains that they have imperiled his safety. The blessing of Jacob (GEN. 49:5-7) reveals knowledge of an unlocalized story somewhat like this.

Shechem was one of the most powerful Canaanite cities of Palestine in patriarchal times. The excavations carried on there by Sellin revealed that in the seventeenth to sixteenth centuries B.C., it had sloping walls reaching a height of thirty-three feet. It is improbable that a nomad family could have seized it or dealt with it as here described. Nor can one build on these items any sure knowledge of Levi's having been a tribe or of Simeon's early sojourn in the center of the land. Levi, so far as is known, was never anything but a guild of priests and Simeon lived in the Negeb. Some scholars think that the story reflects the capture of Shechem (cf. Judges 9) and has been secondarily connected with Simeon and Levi in order to explain their failure to achieve prosperity. The fact that the Levites had no tribal territory and that the Simeonites were absorbed by Judah or scattered could be readily interpreted as due to divine retribution. A very different story about the Israelite capture of Shechem is reflected in later words of Jacob, spoken in bequeathing this locality to Joseph. According to it Jacob took Shechem out of the hand of the Amorite with his sword and bow (GEN. 48:22). In both of the stories we have old echoes of the fall of this important city.

The Journey from Shechem to Bethel

After sojourning for some time in the Shechem area Jacob receives a divine command to go to Bethel and to fulfill there the vows he had made of building an altar to the LORD (GEN. 35:1–7). Before starting he commands his family and all that were with him—presumably slaves and others who had attached themselves to his group—to deliver up all "foreign gods" (clay figurines portraying deities), to purify themselves and to put on fresh garments. Not only are the "gods" delivered up to Jacob but also the earrings, the idolatrous significance of which is thereby hinted at. Jacob then buried these objects under the "oak which was by Shechem." This doubtless means the same tree that a different tradition connected with Abraham (GEN. 12:6). Thereupon they all journeyed to Bethel by the road the traveler must take to this very day.

This narrative is more than just the reporting of an ancient incident in the private life of Jacob and his family. At the very same place, Joshua similarly requests the Hebrew tribes to put away foreign gods (JOSH. 24:14–

28). The episode is understood only when seen as a ritual act, regularly repeated at this spot. The Genesis passage reveals something not divulged in Joshua 24, namely, that a pilgrimage or religious procession from Shechem to Bethel followed the ceremonies under the oak. We may recall here that later on Jeroboam I resided at Shechem and that he established the official southern temple for the Hebrew tribes at Bethel (1 KINGS, 12:25, 29). An annual commemoration of this act by the Shechemites, to maintain the idea that Bethel was a sanctuary founded by them, would be natural. Burial of the idols under the oak may reflect the fact that the new worship inaugurated by Jeroboam I was ruthlessly promulgated and that the people of Shechem (notably the surviving Canaanite elements) were at that time forced to put aside their idols.

According to the narrative of previous events Jacob had erected a pillar at Bethel and had given the place its name (GEN. 28:18–19), but now an altar is provided. He thereupon calls the altar *El-bethel* (GEN. 35:7). This is another confessional formulation like El-Elohe-Israel in Genesis 33:20, and probably means "El is Bethel." If so, it is a case of identifying the two gods El and Bethel. This is an early occurrence of the god Bethel, whom we meet in Phoenicia, Palestine, and in the Aramaic-speaking Elephantine colony in Egypt of the fifth century B.C. He is evidently a personification of the sacred pillar. The altar here attributed to Jacob is probably identical with the one previously attributed to Abraham (GEN. 12:8).

The Oak of Weeping

In the Bethel area is localized the incident of the death of Rebecca's nurse Deborah. She is buried below Bethel under the oak that was called *Allon-bacuth*, "oak of weeping." That oak must have gotten its name from some Canaanite religious celebration, involving weeping or lamenting, such as is referred to in Zechariah 12:11. The

Hebrews gave the name a new and harmless explanation, connecting it with the incident of the death of a woman of the patriarchal household. The localization "below Bethel" probably means the valley to the east of *Beitīn* (*Wadi eṭ Ṭaḥūneh*). In this area, and near the road leading up past *Burj Beitīn* to the north-south highway may have stood the "oak of weeping." Perhaps the pillar erected by Jacob stood near it (GEN. 35:14).

According to the youngest writer the name Israel was conferred on Jacob at Bethel, not at Penuel as the earlier version has it (GEN. 32:28). It was on this occasion, he claims, that Jacob gave the place its name (GEN. 35:9–13, 15).

The Tomb of Rachel

Jacob reminiscences, however, existed at other places and the only way of getting them into the narrative was to have the patriarch journey there. A figure of importance in the stories about Jacob is Rachel, mother of Joseph and Benjamin. We must bear in mind that these two tribes (the former subdividing into Ephraim and Manasseh) constituted the very core of the Israelite state. Their ancestral mother is thus of great interest to them (cf. JER. 31:15).

The narrative of the younger storyteller reports Rachel's death in connection with the birth of Benjamin and localizes the event on "the way to Ephrath" (GEN. 35:19). She was buried by the roadside and Jacob erected a pillar on her grave, which has the name "the pillar of the tomb of Rachel." In the present text Ephrath is accompanied by an explanatory remark "that is Bethlehem" (so also in GEN. 48:7) to clarify the location for the reader.

That the tomb of Rachel was originally shown in Benjamin rather than in Judah is proven by the reference to "Rachel's sepulchre in the border of Benjamin at Zelzah" (1 SAM. 10:2). There may have been an Ephrath or a town of somewhat similar name in this area, too. After the fall of the northern

kingdom, Judaeans evidently found it desirable to localize the site of Rachel's tomb near the place where they believed all the patriarchs to be buried. Tradition hails a cupola-topped, fifteenth-century A.D. structure on the roadside from Jerusalem to Bethlehem as "tomb of Rachel." It is particularly revered by Jews who go there on certain days to ask Rachel's intercession. In the time of the sixth-century pilgrim Arculf, the grave was already marked by a monument of some sort, which he calls a "pyramid." That probably means a pyramid-topped mausoleum, for these were frequently constructed in Roman times.

Migdal Eder

Another local story connected with Jacob was reported in the older source. It was attached to a place called tower of Eder or Migdal Eder (GEN. 35:21–22). The story which concerned Reuben, Jacob's eldest son, was of such a scandalous nature that it is reported only in brief. Since Reuben is a tribe and since Bilhah is the mother of the tribes Dan and Naphthali there is an element of tribal history involved. The incident is also referred to in the Blessing of Jacob (GEN. 49:4). The preceding praise of Reuben in Genesis 49:3, however, is so glowing that the harsh words were probably added after Reuben's decline, for the Hebrews required an explanation of the tribe's fate in terms of the divine justice. Possibly Reuben originally tented in this region, but had to migrate (like Dan, JUDG. 18:1 f.).

The Passing of Isaac

The youngest Pentateuchal author now takes up the story (GEN. 35:22–29) and, after giving a summary list of the children of Jacob, reports his arrival at Kiriath-arba (Hebron), where, he believes, Isaac sojourned all his days. The death of Isaac follows this homecoming. Esau, who in divergence from the older version (cf. GEN. 32:3) is imagined as living at home, and

Jacob dutifully attend to the solemnities. For this author has omitted any reference to strained relations. Evidently the compiler had no report from an older source describing the homecoming of Jacob—and the passing of Isaac in a manner more satisfying to the sentiments—or, if he did, he chose to drop it.

The Edomites

After the death of Isaac, according to the youngest narrator, it became necessary for Esau and Jacob to go separate ways, for there was not enough pasturage for the flocks of both (GEN. 36:6–7). Esau, therefore, departed for Mount Seir (see page 29) and the Edomites that dwell there are his descendants, just as the Israelites are the descendants of Jacob.

Chapter 36 of Genesis lists the following important information about the Edomites: 1) the tribes that could claim descent from Esau; 2) the "dukes" or chiefs of the sons of Esau, i.e., probably the centers furnishing a thousand-man unit for the Edomite army; 3) the tribes of the pre-Edomite inhabitants who are called Horites; 4) the Edomite kings who had reigned before Israel had a king.

Much light has now been shed on the Edomite names in these lists from inscriptions gathered in recent years, notably through the explorations of the Fathers Jaussen and Savignac.

The allusion to the Horites (GEN. 36:20 f., cf. 14:6) requires brief attention. We are told in Deuteronomy 2:12, 22 that they were an earlier population whom the Edomites dispossessed. The name was formerly thought to mean "cave dwellers," but the Egyptian inscriptions provided a name *Kharu*, which was used for southern Syria, and this was found comparable to the name Horites. Since the decipherment of the Hittite inscriptions, the *Khurri* (from whom the Egyptian name was doubtless derived) have become well known as an element in Mesopotamia and Armenia in the sixteenth and seventeenth centuries B.C. The Mitannians belong to this group, and a Hurrian grammar has even been written in recent years. According to the laws of the Hebrew language *Khurri* would become *Khōrīm-Horites,* and so the equation is perfect. That some Hurrian group got down as far as Edom and held control there for a time need not be doubted. It is easier to believe than the suggestion that Horites is an error for Hivites, in three different connections. In the period of migrations, splinter groups often push very far in their desperate search for a place to settle. Such groups bring little with them that is distinctive and that could be found archaeologically.

The survey of Edom carried on by Nelson Glueck in 1936–38 has shown that the early agricultural civilization in this region, as in Moab and points farther north, was wiped out about 1900–1750 B.C. This was the time of the Amorite migration, and it seems reasonable to believe that the Amorites were the agent of destruction. There is no mention of Edomite places in the Amarna letters of the fourteenth century. About 1300 B.C., however, so Glueck discovered, a new agricultural civilization arose in Edom. Its founders could have been the Horites, who then were soon succeeded by the Edomites. For Moab we even seem to have a trace of a ruling caste of western origin at about this same time in the stele of *Balū'a* (see page 120).

Some general interest attaches, also, to the list of the kings who reigned in Edom before any king reigned over the Israelites (GEN. 36:31–39). Since David conquered Edom, thus terminating the Edomite monarchy for a time (I SAM. 8:13–14), this probably meant that the last name is that of the king de-

89

throned by him. There are eight kings and if one allows an average of twenty years the list would shove the beginnings of the Edomite monarchy back 160 years. The monarchy of the Edomites cannot have been hereditary, for the kings come from different places (see the table, Side Glances at Peoples Related to Israel, on pages 73–74).

Joseph and His Brethren

We hear little in the narratives preceding the Joseph-cycle concerning the various sons of Jacob. And that little is not very much to the credit of the individuals thus singled out. In Genesis 34, Simeon and Levi came in for attention in connection with the role they are held to have played in the Shechem area. In Genesis 35:21–22 there was some notice of Reuben. Genesis 38 now gives us information about Judah. The strange position of this narrative after the first installment of the Joseph stories is due to the fact that in chapter 37 Judah is with his brethren; hence the compiler was not able to introduce it sooner. We will take it up first before turning to Joseph.

There are indications that the tribe of Judah had an early history apart from the other tribes. Indeed, these others were inclined to claim that Judah did not belong to "Israel" at all. The story of Genesis 38 lends some substance to this by what it tells of the personal life of the ancestor. Judah, we are told, left his brethren and entered into an alliance with Hirah of Adullam. It would not be surprising if it turned out some day that Hirah was the name of an actual king of this Canaanite city, which lay in the Shephelah, or hill country, bordering the Philistaean plain. The name of Adullam survives to this day in an Arabicised form (*'Id el mīyeh*). The Adullam of antiquity did not lie exactly at that village, but rather to the south of it on a site situated on a nearby hill (*Khirbet Sheikh Madhkūr*), where sherds of the Middle Bronze Age confirm the existence of a city of patriarchal times. An important highway passed through here. Travelers going from Hebron to Jaffa, or from Jerusalem to Gaza, would be attracted to it. King Rehoboam later found it worth while to fortify this city (2 CHRON. 11:7).

As already seen in considering Genesis 34, such alliances between the nomads and the city dwellers always involved intermarriage. So it is not surprising to learn that Judah married a Canaanite wife. The sons of that union were thus half-Canaanitic. Since they represent Judaean clans the story admits that these clans had a large admixture of Canaanite blood. The third of the sons was born at Kezib, a town the name of which hints at lying or deception, and was probably given first to a nearby spring because once upon a time it failed its inhabitants. It seemed significant to the author to have Sela born there, Sela being the son about whom Judah later deceived his daughter-in-law. It is very possible that the name Kezib survives in the fountain called *'Ain el Kadhāb* in the vicinity of *Beit Nettif*.

A joint trip which Judah takes with Hirah brings him past Enaim, the home of his neglected daughter-in-law, Tamar. Hirah was going up to Timnah to inspect the activity of his sheepshearers. It is a question whether the Timnah meant here is the one of the Samson story (JUDG. 14:1), which lies rather far to the north outside of Adullam's natural bailiwick. A more southerly Timnah is mentioned along with a Gibeáh in Joshua 15:57. East of *Beit Nettif* on a ridge extending up toward the Judaean hill country there is a site which suits the requirements and preserves the name in a slightly modified spelling (*Tibneh*). Enaim then must have lain down lower on the ridge. It is elsewhere spelled Enam (JOSH. 15:34), and the name in either form suggests the existence of a spring. Tamar, apprised of Judah's coming, sets a trap for him by assuming a harlot's guise, and thus obtains from him heirs to her first husband's property.

The Tamar episode has the purpose of explaining the origin of two new Judaean clans that came up after two other clans, Ger and Onan, had become extinct.

Jacob's Sons Go to Egypt

The belief that Israel had come up out of Egypt played a large role in the national religion. Tradition held that Israel's ancestors had previously gone down from Palestine to the land of the Nile and that the family had increased there in the course of time and become a people. Beginning with Genesis 37 we have an account of how the Egyptian sojourn came about. The ancient storytellers linked this emigration with a famine that forced the sons of Jacob to go down to this great food-producing region. Their obtaining permission to settle there was held to be due to the fact that one of them had attained a prominent position at the Egyptian court.

The personal fortunes of this young man, who is given the name of the ancestor of an early Hebrew tribe, Joseph, thus were of great interest. How did it happen that he went down to Egypt ahead of the rest of the family and how did he become so important a personage? These are some of the questions tradition sought to answer. The story of Joseph has an emotional effect on almost everyone to whose attention it is brought; it has become one of the world's best-loved stories. It is an unexcelled example of a piece of writing conveying a religious and moral lesson without creating boredom or dissatisfaction on the part of the reader.

The geographical background of the Joseph stories, which alone concerns us here, is not very prominently developed. It is particularly hazy so far as Egypt is concerned. The most definite information conveyed in

them concerns localities in Palestine that are mentioned at the beginning and at the end of these narratives.

The Young Joseph's Errand and Fate

Joseph, the spoiled young son of Jacob, is sent by his father to Shechem to find out how his brothers and the flocks they are pasturing are faring (GEN. 37:14). The allusion to Hebron as starting point of Joseph's journey was probably added by an editor, who was thinking of Genesis 35:27, where the youngest narrator had brought Jacob to that destination. It is altogether unlikely, however, that Jacob's flocks would have ranged as far north from there as to Shechem. The original presupposition of the story must have been that Jacob lived in the vicinity of Bethel, to which place the writer who relates this narrative had last brought him (GEN. 35:1). It was probably summer and difficult to find grass, so that it was necessary for the shepherds to go beyond their usual pasture area. From Bethel to Shechem was a reasonable distance for them to wander, and for a youth like Joseph to be sent on an errand.

But Joseph failed to find his brethren at Shechem; the grazing must have been exhausted thereabouts, too. A man whom Joseph met in the countryside told him that his brothers had gone on to Dothan. This was a considerable distance farther to the north, but the adventurous youth followed them to that place. No doubt he was directed to take the west road that led from the plain of Shechem past the hill on which Samaria was later to be built, to En-gannim (*Jenīn*). It crossed the plain of Dothan west of the city and rejoined the more easterly direct road from Shechem to *Jenīn* at Ibleam. Dothan, though not often mentioned in the Old Testament, occurs in the Palestine list of Pharaoh Thutmosis III. It must have been an important city in Patriarchal times, for the mound containing its ruins and bearing its name (*Tell Dothā*) is a large one and

2.13 Tell Dothā. (*Matson Photo Service*)

near it is an excellent well (fig. 2.13). Excavations have been conducted there since the spring of 1953 by a Wheaton College expedition under Joseph P. Free and have shown that the city had eleven strata and an over-all depth of thirty feet, and that occupation ran from Early Bronze to Iron Age II. But the brethren of Joseph certainly could not have pastured their flock under the very noses of the inhabitants of Dothan. The meeting place of Joseph and his brethren, therefore, cannot have been close by the city. They must have been on the northern side of the plain, near the road that forked off to the left from the Shechem–En-gannim route and ran westward to the coast. For after the brethren had decided to deal treacherously with Joseph, they saw a caravan of Ishmaelites coming. which was bound for Egypt (GEN. 37:25). This caravan must have crossed the Jordan near *Bēsān*. It had evidently come from inner Arabia via the *Wadi Sirhān*. The burdens it was taking to Egypt consisted of gum, balm, and myrrh—South Arabian products much in demand for the manufacture of cosmetics. The younger of two versions combined by the compiler speaks of Midianites instead of Ishmaelites and attributes to Reuben rather than to Judah a desire to save Joseph.·

Joseph in Egypt

The narrative about Joseph's life in Egypt is strikingly vague in two respects: there is no mention of the city to which he was brought or of the name of the Pharaoh into whose service he was drawn. The omission of this most essential information shows that the stories were written long after the events they relate. Speculation takes free rein here in the search for a suitable Pharaoh. The scene differs according to the time in which one places the events. The four possibilities are 1) the Hyksos age; 2) the early Eighteenth Dynasty; 3) the Amarna Age; and 4) the Ramessid period. If one goes as far back as the Hyksos age, then Avaris was the capital and the scene of Joseph's life at court. Avaris is believed to be identical with Tanis, the home also of the Ramessids. If one puts Joseph under the Pharaohs of the Eighteenth Dynasty or under the Ramessids, then Thebes would be the place to which Joseph was brought. If one holds to the theory that Joseph came to Egypt in the reign of Akhnaton (*c.* 1370 B.C.) he might have come to the new capital built by. that heretic king halfway between Memphis in the north and Thebes in the south at *el Amarna*.

Perhaps a straw in the wind as to the locale in which Joseph lived and labored is afforded by the reference to his marriage.

"And he [Pharaoh] gave him to wife Asenath the daughter of Potipherah, priest of On." (GEN. 41:45 A.V.)

"...*and he gave him in marriage Asenath, the daughter of Potiphera priest of On.*" (GEN. 41:45 R.S.V.)

"On of Egypt," as a Phoenician inscription calls the city, was in northern or lower Egypt and on the eastern side of the Nile, a little to the north of Memphis (see Color Map III). The Greeks called it Heliopolis, "City of the Sun" and the Semites could, on occasion, call it Beth-shemesh (JER. 43:13). The act of Pharaoh in giving Joseph the daughter of a priest of On suggests a special interest on the part of the sovereign in the god of that city. That provides a slight reason for identifying the Pharaoh in question with Akhnaton who made the sun-god Re-Harakhte of Heliopolis his god, calling him Aton. But if the mention of the land Rameses in Genesis 47:11 were not an anachronism, a later juncture would be indicated (cf. page 96 f.).

Jacob's Journey

We need not follow in detail the story of what Joseph did or experienced in Egypt, for geography plays only a small role in what is related. After he has revealed his identity to his brothers he bids them bring his aged father and their families to Egypt. A whole caravan is dispatched with wagons, ten asses bearing gifts, and ten she-asses bearing food. The antiquity of this material is shown by the lack of mention of camels, which only began to be widely used in the twelfth century B.C. The arrival of the caravan has the effect of convincing Jacob that his son Joseph is, indeed, alive and persuades him of the feasibility of the journey (GEN. 45:17–28).

It is not clear where Jacob is imagined as residing. Presumably the earliest narrative had him in the neighborhood of Bethel. Quite in accord with the close link between the Israelites of the Negeb and those of the center of the land (see page 80), a stop is made at Beersheba before crossing the "brook of Egypt" into Egyptian territory in order to consult the oracle of the God of Isaac (GEN. 46:1 f.). A fresh start is then made with Jacob, the women, and the children riding in the wagons. The youngest Pentateuchal author gives the number of the

travelers as sixty-six and meticulously supplies the names of all the children (GEN. 46:8–27); these include names of clans and towns known in the later period.

Joseph, apprised of his father's arrival in Goshen, goes up there in his chariot to meet him (GEN. 46:29). The Septuagint text even mentions the place of their meeting —Heroonpolis (cf. page 104). This district is imagined as the ideal place for shepherds such as they to stay, and Joseph instructs his brethren to make it plain to Pharaoh that they are shepherds, in order that he may assign them to this territory. The other version, however, speaks instead of the land of Rameses (GEN. 47:11). This is only artificially differentiated from the city of Raamses (EXOD. 1:11) and means the district in which the latter lay.

The location of the land of Goshen is known. The old Greek Bible translation calls it "Gesem of Arabia" and thus shows that Egyptian Jews of the Hellenistic period identified it with a part of the later Egyptian nome of "Arabia," the capital of which was Phacusa (today *Faqūs*). In the times of which we are speaking the district was called *Gsm* and its capital was *Pi-Sopd (Pi-shapti* in Assyrian inscriptions), meaning "House of the god Sopd"; the latter name still survives in the present name of the site (*Saft el Ḥenneh*). Generally speaking, the area west and south of the Isthmus of Suez is meant. If Joseph lived at Heliopolis he would have had a journey of several days by horse-drawn chariot to meet his father. From the land of Rameses he would not have had so great a journey, for that city was not very far from Heroonpolis (see page 99).

The shepherd's life is the same from age to age, and so the existence of these nomads in the region west of Suez can command little interest. The story begins to move again only with the death of Jacob. The latter, in his last illness, adopts and blesses Joseph's two sons, personifications of the tribes that replaced the earlier tribe of Joseph (Genesis

48). The blessing provides the reader with an explanation of why the younger Ephraim became more important than the elder Manasseh. Thereupon Jacob pronounces a blessing over each of the twelve sons, including Joseph (Genesis 49). The poetic stanzas, like those of the Blessing of Moses (Deuteronomy 33) and the Song of Deborah (Judges 5), are among the most important sources for the earliest history of the tribes.

Requiem

Jacob's death now followed. The earlier writer tells of the mourning that took place; of how Jacob was embalmed in the Egyptian manner; of Joseph's request, mediated to Pharaoh by courtiers, for a leave of absence to bury his father in Palestine; of the journey undertaken thither by Jacob's sons, who left their families behind them on this occasion; and of the impressive retinue of Egyptians that went along to honor the father of the great Joseph. Very oddly, however, we find the funeral caravan in an unexpected place in the end—at the threshing floor of Atad, then called Abel-mizraim (GEN. 50:10–11). One must assume that, according to this older storyteller, Jacob was buried in Transjordan, but it is not clear that it was at Abel-mizraim. Perhaps the latter was only a stop en route, mentioned because of its intriguing name associating it with Egypt (Mizraim) or the Egyptians. The threshing floor of Atad "the thorn-bush") was presumably the old name of the site on which the sanctuary of Abel-

mizraim stood, just as "the threshing floor of Arauna" was the site of the sanctuary of Jerusalem. (2 SAM. 24:18).

The explanation of the name Abel-mizraim as "mourning of the Egyptians" is a case of a popular etymology. It is made possible by the fact that in the unvocalized Hebrew writing of those times the first word could just as well be read *ebel*, meaning "mourning," as Abel. The latter word, in all place names of which it is an element, means a brook of running water, or a vale through which such a brook runs. Probably Abel-mizraim is only another name for Abel-shittim, "the Abel of the accacia trees" (on this city, see page 124). Perhaps at some time in the remote past it was Egyptian crown property, or the seat of an Egyptian garrison. Hebrew tradition knew nothing of the history of Palestine and of how the Eighteenth Dynasty pharaohs had controlled the land, and so provided an elucidation of its own for this name, connecting it with "the mourning of the Egyptians," at the time when Jacob's funeral cortege stopped there. A wailing or mourning ceremony that was carried on annually at Abel (cf. ZECH. 12:11; JUDG. 11:38) may have suggested the idea.

Where the oldest tradition put Jacob's burial is uncertain—but no doubt it was in the northern kingdom. This would naturally be quite unsatisfactory to the Jewish readers of the youngest author's time. His version put the burial in the Machpelah cave at Hebron (GEN. 49:28–33; 50:12–13).

CHAPTER VI

FROM EGYPT TO THE HOLY MOUNT

THE ANCIENT Hebrew tradition assumes a long residence of the Hebrew tribes in Egypt, and their increase there to a numerous people. A change of dynasty as well as of policy toward these people is reported in the words

> "Now there arose up a new king over Egypt, which knew not Joseph." (EXOD. I;8 A.V.)

> *"Now there arose a new king over Egypt, who did not know Joseph."* (EX. I:8 R.S.V.)

The existence of shepherds and of farmers in ancient days went on monotonously, and the passing of time was marked chiefly by the succession of generations. But out in the great world of the cities, events were going on and a history was being made, of which we have a considerable knowledge—though with many gaps—thanks to all that has been gleaned from inscriptions in many tongues which have been recovered and deciphered by nineteenth- and twentieth-century scholarship.

What was the duration of the stay of Israel in Egypt, and when did the Exodus take place? Josephus in his great apologetic treatise "Against Apion," an anti-Semitic agitator, connected the Hebrew Exodus with the expulsion of the Hyksos, around 1570 B.C. But that is much too early. The so-called "Biblical chronology" asserts that 480 years elapsed between the Exodus and the building of Solomon's temple (I KINGS 6:1). If we accept a figure of 955 B.C.

95

2.14 *Capital in form of head of goddess Hathor at Deir el Bahari in Egypt. (Courtesy Julien Bryan)*

for the fourth year of Solomon's reign we obtain a figure of 1439 B.C. for the Exodus, which would put the event in the reign of Amenophis II (1448–1422 B.C.), according to rather well-established Egyptian chronology for this era. But archaeological and historical considerations, as we shall see, give strong reason to believe that the Hebrew tribes entered their promised land about the middle of the thirteenth century B.C., or even a little later. The world historical background accordingly is provided by the great events of the period just preceding.

The World Historical Background

In Babylonia the great Hammurabi Dynasty had come to an end about 1530 B.C., according to the currently widely-favored low chronology. The Khatti or Hittites of Asia Minor had invaded Syria and from that vantage point had raided Babylon. The land of Shinar now fell under the sway of an invading northern people, the Cassites, and its kings for several centuries bear Cassite names. An Assyrian state continued to exist, but Mesopotamia as a whole was under a northern people called the *Khurri,* or Hurrians, no doubt identical with the Horites, of whom the Old Testament still has knowledge (see page 89). There were several Hurrian states in the north, the most important being that of Mitanni,

in which an aristocracy of Aryans got control. The Hittites had similarly fallen under an aristocracy of Indo-European origin, and powerful rulers arose out of their midst. The minor kingdoms in Syria, such as Carchemish on the Euphrates, Khalpa (Aleppo), Mukish with its capital Alalakh in the plain of Antioch, and Ugarit on the Phoenician coast near Latakieh, had to accept the overlordship of the Hittites. The days were over when Egypt could dominate Syria and Mesopotamia. Palestine, however, and some Phoenician cities, remained under Egyptian control.

Amenophis III (1413–1377 B.C.) represents a high water-mark of Egyptian civilization. He is the king who is represented in the famed seated colossi of Memnon at Luxor. Under his son Amenophis IV or Akhnaton (1377–1345 B.C.), however, Egypt's grip on Palestine weakened. Amenophis IV is one of the most interesting of the Pharaohs, since he was a great heretic; he broke away from the god Amon of Thebes and revered the solar divinity Rē, so prominently worshipped at Heliopolis, but calling him Aton. The idea that Moses lived at this time and was influenced by the noble monotheism of Amenophis IV naturally has an attraction for various scholars. Akhnaton established for himself a new

2.15 *Ancient Ugarit (Ras esh Shamra). (Courtesy Institut Francais d'Archéologie, Beyrouth, Liban)*

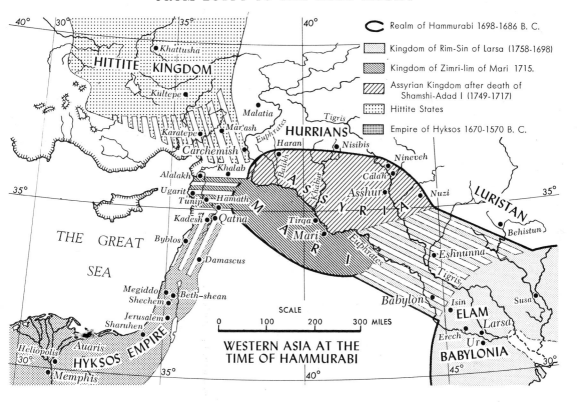

WESTERN ASIA AT THE
TIME OF HAMMURABI

Realm of Hammurabi 1698-1686 B.C.

Kingdom of Rim-Sin of Larsa (1758-1698)

Kingdom of Zimri-lim of Mari 1715.

Assyrian Kingdom after death of
Shamshi-Adad I (1749-1717)

Hittite States

Empire of Hyksos 1670-1570 B.C.

capital, the remains of which have been excavated at *Tell el Amarna* by German and British archaeologists. Attention was first called to the site by the discovery there in 1887 of the famous *Tell el Amarna* tablets, which are archives of Akhnaton written in the cuneiform script, mostly in the Babylonian language. They were letters from Asiatic princes to the Pharaohs giving vivid insight into relations of Egypt with foreign powers as well as to its vassals and into the relations among the vassals themselves. A few additional letters of this archive came to light in 1922 and 1934. Many of the tablets, among them some from Abdi-Khepa, king of Jerusalem, complained of danger to the various cities from the *Khabiri* or *Khapiri* (Babylonian writing using the same sign for *bi* or *pi*). Like the Hyksos of a previous era these have been the subject of an immense amount of unprofitable speculation on the part of those who would in some way connect their name with the Hebrews.

Akhnaton was followed by Tutankh-aton (1358–1349 B.C.), who could hold power only by an abject surrender to the priesthood of Thebes and by giving up the capital at Amarna. Symbolic of this change of policy was his change of name to Tutankhamen. The discovery of his tomb in 1922 by Howard Carter was a sensational

2.16 *Memnon Colossi. (Courtesy Julien Bryan)*

2.17 *Stela showing the Hittite king bringing his daughter to wed Ramses II. (Oriental Institute, University of Chicago)*

event in the annals of archaeology. "Tut's" successor was an Amarna courtier named Ḥui (1349–1345 B.C.). He was to be the last ruler of the great Eighteenth Dynasty.

The Nineteenth Dynasty (1345–1200 B.C.) again saw a series of great rulers. Its founder was Harmhab (1345–1318 B.C.). He was followed by Ramses I (1318–1317 B.C.), not a relative of Harmhab, but from Avaris in the Delta. From Ramses I were descended the men who ruled Egypt for the next century. His son Seti I (1317–1301 B.C.) again re-established Egyptian authority in Asia. Stelas of Seti found at *Beth-shean* bear tribute to his control of Palestine.

Ramses II (1301–1234 B.C.) had a long and eventful reign. In his time occurred the great wars with the Hittites, who threatened Egypt's hold on Palestine and the Phoenician coast. We have rich information about a great battle at Kadesh on the Orontes River in Syria, fought in 1296 B.C. Ramses seems to have had a narrow escape from being surrounded at that occasion. The long period of the Hittite wars ended with a treaty between Ramses and the Hittite king, Hattushil III. In 1267 B.C. the Hittite king brought his daughter to Egypt to wed Ramses. The incident is commemorated in various stelas, including one near the entrance of the great rock temple of Abu Simbel in Nubia.

The Oppression and the Mission of Moses

The Old Testament narrative reports that the Israelites built (or rebuilt) for the Pharaoh who oppressed them the "treasure cities," or better "store cities," of Pithom and Raamses (EXOD. 1:11). The great need evidently was for facilities for the storage of grain for the Egyptian army and for export. The name of the second city, Raamses (Rameses), hangs together with that of the Pharaohs called Ramses (as we prefer to spell the name), who ruled from 1318–1090 B.C. (the Nineteenth and

Twentieth Dynasties). We know from Egyptian sources that Ramses II built a city bearing his name. He therefore may be regarded as the Pharaoh of the oppression. Those who favor an earlier date can, of course, consider the reference to the city of Raamses an anachronism (cf. GEN. 47:11).

The city of Raamses was not just a "store city," as the later Hebrew tradition thinks, but the royal capital, the full name of which was "House of Ramses Great of Victories." This Pharaoh, who was engaged in fighting great wars with the Hittites, felt that a capital near the border area was needed. It was difficult to keep a firm hand on the Asiatic possessions from places far up the Nile like Memphis or Thebes. Several poems, in praise of this city that Ramses built for himself, have been preserved in Egyptian papyri.

There has been much debate as to the location of this city of Raamses. Excavations carried on by a French expedition under Pierre Montet at *Ṣān el Ḥagar*, near *Lake Menzaleh* have led the excavator and other Egyptologists to believe that the city which lay here was not only Tanis (Biblical Zoan), residence of the Twenty-first Dynasty kings, admittedly the case, but also the Hyksos capital Avaris and finally the city of Raamses. If that be true, it underwent two changes of name, with the first outlasting all the others (Tanis-*Ṣān*). This much is clear that Tanis was at the height of its prosperity under Ramses II. Some scholars of great repute are not convinced yet, however, that Tanis is the city of Raamses, and seek the latter at *Qanṭîr* near *Fāqūs*. Only the discovery of actual inscriptions at the sites themselves can finally clinch the matter. In any case, Raamses was in this delta area, not far from the land of Goshen, or *Wadi Ṭûmîlât*.

The other city built by the Israelites was Pithom. We know that this city was called Heroonpolis in Greek times. According to a Roman milestone found at *Tell el Mash-*

khûta (which long but erroneously was identified with Pithom after the excavations carried on there by Naville in 1883), Heroonpolis lay eight miles east of this point on the road to Klysma (Suez). This has rendered quite certain the identification of Pithom with the important *Tell el Erṭâbeh*. Some day, when that site has been excavated, we will know more about the city built by the Israelites.

Birth and Youth of Moses

A much-beloved Old Testament story told of the cruel slaying of the male progeny of the Hebrews, and of the babe that was "exposed" in the bulrushes on the banks of the Nile in a box made of reeds, only to be found by Pharaoh's daughter and adopted as her son (EXOD. 2:1-11).

The story does not mention the name of this princess any more than it does that of her royal father. Moses' name allegedly was conferred on him by his foster-mother and seemingly is explained with a popular etymology, based on the Hebrew verb *māshāh,* as meaning: "I drew him out of the water." However, if the name were Hebrew it would mean "drawer of water"; if it was Egyptian, as it would have to be if given to him by an Egyptian, then a connection with Egyptian *mesu,* "child," which appears in Greek form as Mosis in king-names like Thutmosis (child of the god Thot), seems to be the most probable explanation.

Escape of Moses

Moses, grown to manhood, did not forget his origin, but retained his interest in the cause of his oppressed people. He slew an Egyptian overseer for mistreating a Hebrew workingman. This brought about his flight (EXOD. 2:11 f.), and a whole sequence of events leading to the Exodus.

The escape of Moses from Egypt receives no further description. An interesting parallel to his flight is provided by the story of an Egyptian named Sinuhe, who lived under Amenemhet I (twentieth century) and under his son Sesostris I.

Moses in Midian

The Biblical storytellers do not often go into details on itineraries (cf. GEN. 12:5, etc.). In the case of Moses we hear only that he went to the land of the Midianites (EXOD. 2:15) and not a word of how he got there. Where is that land?

We have already heard that "Midian" was considered a son of Keturah and that Abraham sent these out "unto the east country" (GEN. 26:1–6), the region east of eastern Palestine. We must not take "east" too much according to the compass, however, for it embraces the Arabian regions. One might thus infer that Moses took the so-called pilgrim route from Egypt to Aqabah and went beyond the *el 'Arabah*—the depression extending down from the Dead Sea to the Gulf of Aqabah on the Red Sea. The ancient geographers know a city of Madian, or Madiam, in Arabia, which is believed to have lain at *el Bed'*, east of this gulf. It had a harbor on the coast but was actually twenty-six miles inland. Both Josephus and Eusebius connect the Midian of Moses with this Madian. The distance from the Isthmus of Suez to Aqabah is about two hundred miles; thence to Madian is about seventy-eight miles.

The land of Midian would have extended to the southern boundary of Edom. Such a localization of it agrees well with the fact that in the Old Testament narratives in which the Midianites occur, they are passing through Transjordan; for that region was easily subject to invasion from Arabs living to the east and south of it (cf. page 126 f.).

That Moses could have gone to Midian proper must be conceded. Nevertheless, the possibility that a Hebrew writer, with only a vague idea of geography, might have included southern Sinai in Midian cannot be dismissed, for this group of mountains lies just across the gulf from that region. Nor

was it absolutely necessary for a fugitive from Egypt to go east of the *el 'Arabah*. The traveler Seetzen in 1807 found tribesmen in the wilderness north of Sinai who considered themselves independent of Egypt, and a man sufficiently hardy to stand their miserable existence could no doubt have taken refuge with them. The priest of Midian, Jethro, of course, must have been priest of a definite sanctuary.

Moses at the Holy Mount

One of the most impressive tales of the Old Testament is that of the third chapter of Exodus, describing how Moses received the revelation from "him that dwelt in the bush" (DEUT. 33:16), commissioning him to lead Israel out of Egypt. He came to the place where the deity dwelt, accidentally, as it were, in keeping the flock of his father-in-law. It happened when he led the flock to the backside of the desert, and came to a mountain (EXOD. 3:1). There is no clear-cut direction here, since the starting point, the home of Jethro, is itself left in obscurity. The Revised Standard Version's "to the west side of the wilderness" is too specific. The phraseology need mean no more than that Moses went farther than usual into the wilderness area.

The name of the holy mountain is given as Horeb. There is a strange variation on this matter in the Pentateuch since in other passages the mountain is called Sinai. A given single writer would naturally have stuck to one name. Modern Old Testament scholarship explains this diversity as due to the fact that the narratives were compiled from several different writers. The older one uses the name Sinai, and therein is followed by the latest source. But the younger of the two early writers uses Horeb and therein is followed also by the Book of Deuteronomy. Horeb seems to reflect the usage of the inhabitants of the Kingdom of Israel (cf. 1 KINGS 19), while the people of Judah preferred Sinai.

It will be apparent that no indications clear enough to locate either Midian or the Holy Mount are given in the story of Moses. It remains to be seen whether the story of the Exodus itself sheds any better light on this problem.

How Moses returned to Egypt and all the wonder-working he did there require no repetition. In the end Pharaoh was forced to let the Lord's people go.

Preliminary Considerations

Certain happenings can attain a vast importance for the consciousness of a people when they are seen from a later perspective and happen to be made the subject of annual commemoration. We have an example of that in the way in which the landing of the Pilgrim Fathers has assumed a national significance for us through our Thanksgiving festival. In pre-Civil War days that event had no such prominence. The Exodus attained its place before the mind of the Hebrew people in a similar manner, namely through the Passover festival, for which it provided the explanatory background (Exod. 12:21 f.; Deut. 16:1 f.). There is no way of establishing how far back this connection between event and festival actually goes. What we have before us in our narratives is the fully developed product: the sacred lesson for the holy festival. But we can see in these narratives a gradual building up of the scope of the event.

The youngest of the Pentateuchal writers thinks of the Israel that went forth from Egypt in terms of a full-blown people of 600,000 men, perhaps taking old census figures of Israel-Judah as a basis for his numbers (Exod. 12:37 f.). But any exodus of human beings from Egypt would be practicable only with small numbers. A large-scale movement of this sort inevitably would lead to utter disaster.

A realistic idea of what even a normal seasonal migration of Bedouin means is given by an experienced observer of desert life, the Czech explorer Alois Musil. He notes that if today a tribe numbering five thousand families migrates with its flock, it forms a column at least twelve miles wide and three miles deep. The wider the line is, the more pasture the flocks will find, but the greater also the risk of groups lagging and getting cut off by enemies. The deeper the line is the less pasture for the flocks in the rear and the greater the confusion. If the Hebrews had migrated in March, as the old stories assume, and if (a big *if*) there had been an abundance of rain that winter, they would have found rain pools in the various wadies and could have watered their flocks and filled their goatskin water bags. Where they had to depend on water bags or cisterns, the job of watering flocks and filling water bags would have been an arduous one. It will be obvious from such considerations that the smaller one imagines the migrating group of Hebrews to have been, the more feasible would be such a migration.

Our concern here is chiefly with the geography of the Exodus narratives. The nature of this reporting is such that various constructions can be put upon it. There are serious gaps in the narratives, creating uncertainties. It is noteworthy that in the Book of Deuteronomy where Moses describes the travels from Sinai to the Plains of Moab (Deut. 1:19 f.), he omits a description of the journey from Egypt to Sinai. The author of the itinerary in Numbers 33, furthermore, in mentioning the stations from Egypt to Sinai (verses 1–15) merely recounts the names given in the compilation of the older and younger narratives of Exodus 13–19, that he had before him. Each of these two narratives may or may not have had a sensible itinerary, but in combined form they give no recognizable route.

The idea which the compiler followed, and which Deuteronomy also presupposes, that the entire body of fugitives first went to the Mountain of God, is thus not as certain as it would seem at first glance. As we shall see there are weighty reasons for believing that the first objective was Kadesh-barnea in the Negeb area south of Palestine. But we will note in advance that in every attempt to work out a route for the Exodus, one tradition or another furnishes an obstacle that has to be set aside. We have before us, it would seem, a body of materials of diverse origin which have been pressed into a connection by editors, who themselves were unable to solve the historical problems the materials posed. The individual stories, therefore, are the primary thing, and the first task is to understand them by themselves, and not to construe them or violate their meaning by bending them to fit the sequence of some preconceived route.

Geography of the Crucial Area

If one looks at a map of Egypt showing the fertile and arid lands, one will note that there are two separate fertile districts which reach out from the delta country, like the claws of a pair of pliers, in the direction of the northern part of the Suez Canal. The northern claw points toward the Balah Lakes and the famous canal crossing of el Kantara. The southern claw is the *Wadi Ṭūmīlāt* and extends from *Zagāzīg* to *Ismai-līeh* on Lake *Timsaḥ*. From Lake *Timsaḥ* the Suez Canal is cut through higher ground to the Bitter Lakes and thence again through dry land to the Red Sea which it reaches at Suez. The total length of the Isthmus of Suez is seventy-two miles.

The present-day situation along the Isthmus of Suez, however, is not quite the same as it was in the days of Moses. In the first place there was at that time a branch of the Nile which flowed from the vicinity of *Zagāzīg* to the Mediterranean at Pelusium and is called by classical geographers the Pelusiac arm of the Nile. In the second place a canal had been built (perhaps by Seti I, 1317–1301 B.C.), which left this Pelusiac arm of the Nile at Bubastis (*Tell Basṭa* a mile or two southeast of *Zagāzīg*) and was carried through the *Wadi Ṭūmīlāt* past Pithom-Heroonpolis (*Tell el Erṭābeh*) to the Bitter Lakes. The channel of the ancient canal is still traceable in parts of the *Wadi Ṭūmīlāt*. Ships thus could ascend the Pelusiac arm of the Nile to Bubastis and then sail along the canal to Heroonpolis and the Bitter Lakes. It is a moot question whether the Pharaohs had a waterway from these lakes to the Red Sea. But we know that a canal was constructed by Darius I (521–485 B.C.), who set up along its course stelas with inscriptions celebrating the event, and recording that it was now possible to sail to Persia by water. One inscribed monument of Darius was even found a half mile from *Tell el Mashkhūta* at the fresh-water canal. Ptolemy II Philadelphus (*c.* 285 B.C.) seems to have renewed the canal and at its junction with the Red Sea built a city named Arsinoë, opposite *Klysma* (see Peutinger's Table, page 22).

The Crossing of the Sea

The younger of the early narrative strands introduced its account of the Exodus by pointing out that God did not lead the people by the way of the land of the Philistines, although that was near, but by the way of the wilderness of the Red Sea (Exod. 13:17–18). That presupposes a start-ing point in the north and that the objective was Palestine. The writer knew that there were formidable cities in the coastal plain blocking this road to the Promised Land, and that they would resist any invaders. That to him explained why the Israelites did not take that regular road. To speak of it as the "way of the land of the Philistines" was, of course, an anachronism, for the Philistines did not get there until later (see page 132).

The highroad from Egypt to Palestine was one over which the Egyptian armies had traveled many times, long before the Hebrews existed. Some of the Pharaohs have given detailed itineraries of it. The starting point in the old days was a border fortress the name of which, *Tr,* was later written Sile (or the like) in Roman and Byzantine sources. According to a Roman itinerary, Sile was twenty-four miles from Pelusium, in the region of el Kantara, probably at *Tell abu Seifeh* (see Color Map III).

At a later age the road to Palestine started a little farther to the north, from Pelusium, where the Pelusiac arm of the Nile ended. The ruins of Pelusium are identified as *Tell el Farāma.* The road starting from Pelusium met the road starting from Sile, though there was also a branch road that went to the left along the Mediterranean shore rather than inland, as did the usual route.

From el Kantara to Raphia in southern Palestine is a distance of 117 miles. Thutmosis III in the Asiatic campaign of the twenty-third year of his reign took ten days to go from Sile to Gaza; Alexander the Great and his troops covered the distance in seven days; Ptolemy IV and the Roman, Titus, required only five days. The way leads through drifting sand, with which the wind from the sea has covered the region. There are no brooks or springs. Even "the brook of Egypt" (the *Wadi el 'Arīsh*) is described by the Assyrian King Esarhaddon as "a place where there is no stream." At the northern boundary of these arid lands, there lay a town the Assyrians call Arza and which the Greeks later named Rhinocorura. In Greek times it was a sort of Egyptian penal colony, where people whose noses were cut off in punishment for some offense were settled—hence its Greek name.

The reliefs of Seti I and Papyrus Anastasi I show that there was a series of eight stations or forts along the way. Lack of water was characteristic of this route. Water brought from Egypt in wine crocks was stored at places along the way for official or military use.

This route, then, the Israelites did not take, but rather another. Here difficulties confront the reader. One cannot be sure that the statement about this alternate route has come down in its original form. It may be a combination of two accounts, one of which said "he led the people round by the way of the wilderness" and the other (he led them) "the way of the Red Sea" (EXOD. 13:18). Two entirely different routes might have been meant thereby. As it stands, the text suggests a passage through arid country to the Red Sea, and so in effect the way to the latter. What, we must ask, is meant by the Red Sea?

The Red Sea

The Hebrew term *"yam sūf,"* translated as "Red Sea" in our Bible translations, is believed to mean "Sea of Reeds." Where the name is most definitely identifiable it refers to the Gulf of Aqabah (cf. 1 KINGS 9:26). Its extension to other parts of the Red Sea is thus possible, but rests entirely on the assumption that that sea is meant in the Exodus narratives. The name "Sea of Reeds" is puzzling, however, even for the Gulf of Aqabah, because no reeds are to be found there, any more than they are found in the Gulf of Suez. There is a possibility that the term applied originally to the lakes on the Isthmus of Suez, and was secondarily extended to the Red Sea. This possibility creates the opportunity for making the Israelite crossing of the Red Sea a crossing at some point farther north. The only passage shedding any light on the phrase "Red Sea"—that referring to the locusts as being cast into the Red Sea by a west wind (EXOD. 10:19)—is not particularly helpful, for, while "all the land of Egypt" is mentioned in that connection, it is doubtful whether the writer thought of anything more than the delta region. As a glance at the map will show, the lake region of the isthmus or the Nile estuary would fit better for a drowning of the locusts than the Gulf of Suez.

The Old Testament Tradition

A recapitulation of the first leg of the route is given in Numbers 33:5–8, but is merely based on the narratives of Exodus 13–14. The stations are: "Raamses, Succoth, Etham "on the edge of the wilderness"; then a change of direction and arrival at Pi-hahiroth "before Baal-zephon," with encampment before Migdol. Since the Hebrews then depart "from before Pi-hahiroth," Migdol is evidently just another name of that place. The sea crossing follows next, and so the arrival at a body of water within a day's journey from Pi-hahiroth is presupposed.

The Theory of a Southern Crossing

The ancient theory of the crossing of the Israelites was more or less dictated by the road connection from Egypt to 'Aqabah which is so excellently shown on Peutinger's Table (page 22). It implied the belief that the Hebrews had started from the neighborhood of Memphis. The theory was already held by Josephus, who must have gotten it from Egyptian Jews; he says they started from "Letopolis, a place at that time deserted, but where Babylon was built afterwards, when Cambyses laid Egypt waste." Letopolis, or Babylon, lay on the site of what is now called "Old-Cairo."

The modern scholar, however, no longer clings to the idea of a start from Memphis. Knowing as he does that the Hebrews were at points farther to the north he will prefer to think of them as coming from the vicinity of Heroonpolis. But that does not necessarily deter him from assuming a sea crossing near Suez. Indeed, such a view has

had prominent defenders in very recent times. Some have held that the Egyptian pursuers were caught on one of the big sandy flats that exist east of Suez after the Israelites had successfully crossed, and that an incoming tide, driven by an east wind, overwhelmed them. The tradition, however, states that the east wind drove the waters *back,* not *in* (EXOD. 14:21), and it is difficult to see how an east wind could do that at this point. Those with a realistic knowledge of these parts discount any effect of a wind on the sea level hereabouts.

A time-honored assumption is the one shared by St. Etheria (540 A.D.) that the Red Sea in Moses' time extended all the way to the Bitter Lakes—notably at high tide—and that the crossing then took place between gulf and lakes. But this assumption is geologically untenable. The discovery of an Egyptian settlement on the coast of the Sinai Peninsula near *Abu Zeneimeh* (cf. page 111) has shown that the water level has not risen more than three to six feet, if at all, in thirty-five hundred years, and the same thing was previously observed on the Gulf of Aqabah at *Tell el Kheleifeh*.

The Theory of a Central Crossing

The theory of a central crossing has enjoyed more favor on the part of modern scholars than that of a southern crossing. Many connect Succoth, the second station of Numbers 33:5, with Egyptian Theku, which, as is now known, lay at *Tell el Mashkhūta,* "the hill of the image," so named after a monument found there but now resting on the lawn of the gardens in Ismailieh. Theku lay eight miles from the city of Pithom or Heroonpolis (*Tell el Ertābeh*). This, of course, takes one into the other area of fertile land, in what we have called the lower claw of the pliers, reaching to the Suez Canal—the *Wadi Ṭūmīlāt.* If the Hebrews had gone from Raamses (whether that be at *Sān* or at *Qanṭir*) to Succoth, they would have had to cross the

Pelusiac arm of the Nile and continued to Ismailieh, there crossing the Suez Canal line at what is now the northern end of the Crocodile Lake (Lake *Timsaḥ*). There are, of course, difficulties. That the name "Sea of Reeds" originally applied to the lakes of the isthmus is quite possible, but the oldest version's allusion to a strong east wind's causing the sea to go back (EXOD. 14:21), which contrasts markedly with the youngest author's view of the happening (EXOD. 14:16, 26), finds no explanation here, either; for in the opinion of those familiar with the area, the strongest gale would only lower the water level a few inches on the windward side, but no great expanse of sand or mud would be exposed.

The Theory of a Northern Crossing

Scholarly interest, however, has swung to another theory, thanks to the discoveries of Pierre Montet at Tanis, held by him to be the city of Raamses, and due to the fact that some of the places mentioned in the Biblical record can now be located in the north. This theory (first put forward in 1858) would identify the Sea of Reeds with Lake Sirbonis and imagines the Israelites as making their escape in the extreme north and as passing over the narrow spit of land between that lake and the sea. This is an area that saw some military disasters in Hellenistic times as reported by classical authors, and there is reason to believe that similar events occurred there in earlier ages.

That theory, it would seem, involves giving up the identification of Succoth with Theku (*Tell el Mashkhūta*), which only has plausibility anyway within the scope of a possible exodus from the *Wadi Ṭūmīlāt*.

In connection with considering a northern escape route, it may be of interest to cite the itinerary of the Roman general Titus, who took that road to Palestine in 68 A.D. His start was from Alexandria whence he went to a "small place called Tanis," which, as already mentioned, is probably the site also of Raamses. Departing thence

> his second station was Heracleopolis and his third Pelusium; he then refreshed his army at that place for two days and on the third passed over the desert and pitched his camp at the temple of Zeus Kasios, and on the next day at Ostrakine. This station had no water, but the people of the country make use of water brought from other places. After this he rested at Rhinocorura, and from thence he went to Raphia, which was his fourth station. This city is the beginning of Syria. For his fifth station he pitched his camp at Gaza, . . .

Titus thus went through a desert from Pelusium and then up the narrow spit of land between Lake Sirbonis and the sea. He did that, no doubt, because he could provision his army more easily with the aid of ships standing off shore than to take a baggage train and have it struggle through the sand of the inland road, the regular "way of the land of the Philistines."

Some scholars think that the Hebrews after leaving Raamses took the same Mediterranean shore route as did Titus. At least two of the place names of the Old Testament narratives fall into line under such a supposition. The first is Migdol, which is named as the northernmost point of Egypt in the Old Testament (JER. 44:1; 46:14; EZEK. 29:10; 30:6), and which is identified with *Tell el Ḥēr,* for which an old itinerary has *Magdolo.* The modern name could suggest a connection with Pi-hahiroth as well. The second identifiable place is Baal-zephon, by the sea, where the Israelites encamped; for Baal Zephon, or better Zaphon, "Lord of the North," is the Semitic name of the God Zeus Kasios, who had a sanctuary along this shore on a knoll that the ancient geographers always refer to as *Mons Casius.* This mount probably is *Rās Qaṣrūn* near *el Gals.* The temple on it evi-

2.18 Mons Casius *in Phoenicia.* (*Courtesy Maurice Dunand*)

dently was founded by Phoenician navigators and served the sailors who sailed between Phoenicia and Egypt as a point opposite which they could offer up prayers to their patron deity. The real *Mons Casius* and great sanctuary of the god Baal Zaphon lay in Phoenicia on the high peak south of the mouth of the Orontes River in Syria. In view of the mention of the proximity of Baal-zephon to the sea, we regard this identification of it with the place at Lake Sirbonis as convincing, though some scholars would put it at Tahpanhes, the place later called Daphne, for at that place there was also a sanctuary of the god Baal Zaphon, which has been excavated by Jean Clédat. In a Phoenician papyrus reference is made to "the god Baal Zephon and all the gods of Tahpanhes." But Tahpanhes has its own name, while the Zeus Kasios place has none but Baal-zephon and lies by the sea. To put Baal-zephon at Daphne, furthermore, would not suit the identification of Migdol already proposed. One might more suitably put it at Pelusium, where Clédat also was able to establish the existence of a Baal Zaphon sanctuary.

Given the supposition of this route where could Succoth have lain? It is attractive to think of Succoth as either at or near *Mohammedîyeh*. Later sources speak of a Skenna (Scenae)—a Greek word synonymous with Hebrew Succoth—in this area. However, the first station after Raamses-Tanis, as shown by comparison with Titus' march, ought still to have lain west of the

Pelusiac arm of the Nile, for Titus stopped at Heracleopolis (Parva) and the following day at Pelusium. The Egyptian name of Heracleopolis is reproduced by Greeks as Seothres, with which the name Succoth can hardly be linked. For Etham, too, there are only arbitrary identifications. Under the theory of an escape via the Pelusium area, therefore, there are still gaps in the sequence of stations, to say nothing of the question of how and where the Pelusiac arm of the Nile could be crossed.

But this theory of a seashore escape route does make plausible to some degree the disaster that is said to have befallen the Egyptians and the escape of the Hebrews. The route skirts the outside of the lake called Sirbonis by the Greeks, and now called Lake *Bardawîl* (corruption of the name of Baldwin, the Crusader king). On certain portions of this lake there are big areas of rushes, so that the name "Sea of Reeds" would be an appropriate designation. The lake is forty-five miles long and thirteen miles wide. Major C. S. Jarvis, one-time governor of Sinai, describes it as an enormous clay pan about six to ten feet below the level of the Mediterranean Sea, and separated from the sea by a very narrow strip of sand, one to three hundred yards in width. The normal condition of the lake, he says, is that of a vast salt-encrusted pan.

In short, one can imagine the Egyptians being overtaken by disaster here when the sea broke through into the lake area, if one supposes that the pursuers took a short cut through el Kantara and *Qaṭîeh* and across the clay pan to head the Israelites off, or were caught in a breakthrough of waters, when pursuing them along the narrow spit between lake and sea. According to Jarvis a strong east wind causes a heavy sea on the coast of Sinai—a much bigger one than a northerly or northwesterly gale. This causes the waves to break through the narrow spit of sand at a half-dozen places and in a short time floods the whole salt-pan of Lake Bardawil to a depth of five or six feet. An event of this sort, which occurs several times every year, accounts, in Jarvis' opinion, for the drowning of the Egyptians (EXOD. 14:23 f.).

Speculations of this sort are intriguing, of course, but can lead to no definite result. As a master-plan theory, the seashore route is unsatisfactory in that in the last analysis it feeds into "the way of the land of the Philistines," which the Hebrews were not supposed to take. One may grant, however, that the definite localization of Migdol and Baal-zephon in this area does point to the fact that reminiscences of travel by this route to and from Egypt have entered into the Exodus narrative.

From the Sea Crossing to Sinai

According to the older Pentateuchal source the Israelites went into the Wilderness of Shur after the sea crossing (EXOD. 14:22). We have already heard of this wilderness as north of the Isthmus of Suez (page 69). The youngest source substitutes "Wilderness of Etham" (NUM. 33:8). We need not enter into the various possible explanations of the name Etham, but will content ourselves with the view of the Biblical writer who substituted it for Shur.

The next station of Exodus 15:23 is Marah. According to Jarvis, the Israelites, after reaching the end of Lake Sirbonis, then turned southwards in search of water and found the wells at *Mazār*, "which are undoubtedly bitter"—so bad in fact that even railroad engines cannot use their water. If the Hebrews next camped at Elim (EXOD. 15:27), we are assured that this is probably the present *Masā'id,* where they would have found plenty of water and some palm trees. The encampment by the sea (NUM. 33:10) is then construed as on the Mediterranean.

This is not very convincing, however, since it requires aberrations from a straight course. But perhaps Marah and Elim should not trouble us too much. The incidents in which they are mentioned may be floating materials, attached to places of which the story tellers had no clear knowledge.

Definitely at home, however, in the region along this shore is the story that a divinely sent wind brought quails from the sea, and let them fall by the camp (NUM. 11:31).

We have in these words an accurate description of what happens when the seasonal migration of quail occurs—unfortunately for verisimilitude, however, in autumn, not in spring. The sea meant can only be the Mediterranean. The neighborhood of *El Masā'id* is the best spot on the coast for quail. They arrive usually at dawn, flying low and dropping exhausted on the shore. They rest there and then fly southwards, not alighting again anywhere in the Sinai Peninsula. They are caught by the thousands in nets nowadays by the natives of *el 'Arīsh* and sold to European markets.

No serious attempt has been made to place the stations Dophka and Alush (NUM. 33:13) under this theory of an Exodus via the Mediterranean shore. The Wilderness of Sin preceding them, however, could well stand for a wilderness considered as belonging to the bailiwick of Pelusium, the Egyptian name of which was Sin (cf. EZEK. 30:15 f.), though reference to it would fit better had it occurred sooner.

As for Rephidim, the next station mentioned, it belongs to the Kadesh area in the older version of the Exodus story, owing to the phrases "chiding" or "finding fault" with Moses, and "tempting" or "putting the LORD to proof" (EXOD. 17:2, 7), which are allusions to Massah and Meribah, places of the Kadesh-barnea neighborhood. And, indeed, the incident is related again in that scene (NUM. 20:7 f.). Confusion has been wrought through combination of the older version with the younger version which put the "water from the rock" incident in the Horeb neighborhood (EXOD. 17:3–6). The occurrence of the same thing in places seemingly far apart gave rise to the legend of the rock that followed the migrating Hebrews, of which Paul made figurative use (1 COR. 10:4).

Obviously, the Rephidim incident would most probably have happened in a limestone region like that around Kadesh-barnea, not in a granite rock area like that around the traditional Mount Sinai. Major C. S. Jarvis describes how a petty officer by accident struck water from limestone rock in this area. The battle with the Amalekites, which is closely associated with Rephidim, also points to the Kadesh area, for the Amalekite country is the region immediately south of Palestine (cf. page 182). There is no proof of the Amalekites ranging into southern Sinai, much less into Arabia.

Northern Sinais

If one assumes that Israel went first to Kadesh-barnea and puts the Rephidim episode in that neighborhood, then the "wilderness of Sinai" as the next stop (EXOD. 19:2) is a bit perplexing, in view of the fact that one already has wildernesses contiguous to Kadesh-barnea—that of Zin (NUM. 13:21, 26) and that of Paran (cf. page 116). One would have to confine this new wilderness to the environs of the mountain taken to be Mount Sinai.

Here Jarvis can recommend as his Sinai the *Jebel Helāl,* which rises to a height of 2920 feet. It stands in the midst of a plain, and thus looms up as a most impressive landmark. It has the advantage of being the mountain nearest to Kadesh.

One is not limited to the mountains west of Kadesh, however. Mount Sinai could just as well have been a mountain lying to the east or south of Kadesh. Here the *Jebel 'Arā'if* in the latter direction has enjoyed prominent sponsorship as possible Sinai. It is

a blue-black pyramid with innumerable towers and turrets, and only a few hours distant from a route that leads to Aqabah.

If one assumes a departure from Egypt beginning at Lake *Timsaḥ* and a subsequent northward journey from there, one can still regard the Kadesh-barnea area as the objective. This makes it possible to think of the Holy Mount as lying even closer to Egypt and to bring it within range of the original objective announced by Moses in the oldest version of events: To go three days into the desert to sacrifice to God (EXOD. 3:18; 5:3). It also would agree with the idea of the youngest version that Aaron went forth to meet the returning Moses at the Holy Mount (EXOD. 4:27)—which certainly does not suggest a remote journey! If Israel is said to have wandered about in the Wilderness of Shur (EXOD. 15:22), that also points to the area of which we are speaking, for as we have seen this district lay contiguous to Egypt (see page 69). There are several mountains that could be reached in three days from the Egyptian border. Thus the old route going north from Ismailieh brings one past the *Jebel Maghāra* (2420 feet) or the more monumental *Jebel Yeleq* (3566 feet), with its huge mass of yellow rock. Either would make an appropriate Sinai, if one be willing to forego identifications for the stations Marah and Elim. The region was not as bare in antiquity as at present, but was covered with scrub and full of game; nomads could eke out a living.

An Arabian Sinai

But strong reasons can also be adduced for supposing that the Israelites went to Arabia. We have already seen that the real land of Midian lay there. Furthermore, since the *yam sūf,* or "Sea of Reeds," of the Old Testament in all really historical passages is the Gulf of Aqabah, there is strong reason to insist that it means that in the Exodus story.

The notion of a journey to the Arabian quarter does not fit very well with an escape via the Mediterranean shore route. Nevertheless, such a detour cannot be said to be impossible, since a track runs from *el 'Arīsh* past the neighborhood of Kadesh to Aqabah, a distance of 165 miles. An Arabian journey is better suited, however, to a departure from Ismailieh or from Suez by the route used in more modern times by pilgrims from Egypt to Mecca. The distance from Suez via *en Nakhl* to Aqabah is about two hundred miles. The last part of the way, in which the roads from Suez and *el 'Arīsh* become merged, involves a steep descent from the high plateau region to the Gulf of Aqabah, but provides marvelous views of the deep blue gulf with the grove of date palms near the settlement at its head.

The explorer Alois Musil, who favors that route for the Exodus, does not try to locate Marah (which could arbitrarily be put at *en Nakl* or *Themed*), but identifies Elim with the El-paran of Genesis 14:6 (otherwise called Elath, 1 KINGS 9:26; 2 KINGS 14:22), the Aila of later ages and *Haila* on Peutinger's Table. Palm trees and springs are typical of that place; in fact, water may be obtained wherever one chooses to dig two to six feet below the surface. Close by lay the later Eziongeber.

Since the Hebrews got to Aqabah at some point, the idea that the Holy Mount lay somewhere east or south of there has had its attraction. The idea gains its greatest force from the fact that the area is the true "land of Midian" (EXOD. 2:15; cf. page 100). Both Josephus and Eusebius did not waver on this, but imagined Moses as having gone there. Paul, too, thinks of Sinai as being in Arabia (GAL. 4:25), asserting its name to be Hagar, and thus evidently seeking it in the territory of the Hagrites of 1 Chronicles 5:19 f.

An important argument put forward in favor of the idea of an Arabian Sinai is based on the so-called "volcanic" phenomena that seem to enter into the description of Sinai (EXOD. 19:16–19). The pillar of cloud and fire that led the Israelites (EXOD. 13:21–22) is also held to be connected with a volcano;

of course it is conceded that it would not have been visible on departure from Egypt. But the advocates of the theory say it could have been seen from the high plateau before descending to Aqabah.

The view that Sinai or Horeb must have been a volcano was first advanced by Charles T. Beke, English geographer, who set out in 1874 to investigate the matter and came to the conclusion that since there were no volcanoes in the Sinaitic Peninsula, the mountain of the Law must have lain east of Aqabah. In more recent times the Czech explorer Alois Musil has suggested Arabian localization, not so much because of the volcanic phenomena, as because of his belief that here lay the real land of Midian.

He finds a counterpart to Rephidim, in *er-Rafīd*, a basin about sixty miles south of Aqabah and eighteen miles northwest of *el Bed'*, the ancient city of Madian or Midian. The Wilderness of Sin, according to him, denotes the mountain range east of Aqabah. He imagines the real home of Jethro as having been in the oasis of *el 'Ajnūna*, thirty miles south of *el Bed'*, and the main camp of the Israelites about eighteen miles north of the latter oasis near the *she'īb*, or ravine of *el Khrōb*, in which he thinks the name *Horeb* (Hebrew, *Khōrēb*) has survived. The isolated peak of *el Zihed*, which resembles a kneeling camel, rises above the entrance to this narrow valley. But Musil gives no indication that it is considered a holy mountain. In that respect an earlier suggestion of his had an advantage, and some adherents of an Arabian Sinai prefer it. On the southern boundary of the remarkable white-rock plain of *el Ḥismeh*, one hundred and twenty miles away, is a great lava field (*Ḥarra er Raḥa*), extending eighty miles to the southeast. Between it and another similar volcanic group to the south, there is a green plain called the "watering place" (*el Jāw*), and nearby are various sacred places and supposed sites of the history of Moses. On the eastern side of the great table mountain of *Thadra* is the black volcanic cone of *el Bedr,* which is re-garded as a holy mountain, since it once vomited fire, killing many Bedouin and their flocks; the present natives do not even allow their animals to go near it (cf. Exod. 19:23). Southeast of the *Thadra* is a volcano called *el 'Aṣī,* in which are "the caves of the serv-ants of Moses," where they allegedly stayed while their master was speaking with God. Another holy place hereabouts is called *el Manḥal,* and on it are twelve stones known as *el Madhbaḥ,* or "place of sacrifice" (cf. Exod. 24:4), where the Bedouin still offer sacrifices.

Further support for the view that *Horeb* was somewhere in Midian has recently been adduced on the basis of a study of the list of stations offered in Numbers 33:17 f. While the first part of the list (verses 1–16) fol-lowed the narratives of Exodus (except for Dophka and Alush), it was argued that the remainder (except for verses 36–42 which are again based on the narratives) gives the sta-tions along the route from an Arabian Sinai to the plains of Moab. Such a list could have been set up—and no doubt then in reverse order—for the benefit of pilgrims who wanted to go to Sinai.

The suggestion is intriguing. While we hear nothing of pilgrimages to Sinai we can assume that the idea had a very great attrac-tion. Distance is no obstacle in pilgrimage, as the journeys of the Moslems to Mecca illustrate. Judaeans, who localized the dwell-ing place of the Lord on Mount Zion, may not have favored such pilgrimage, but Is-raelites hardly shared that belief and may well have encouraged a Horeb pilgrimage. Notably those Israelites dwelling east of the Jordan would have been tempted to go there. At least one individual from that quarter is reported to have made such a pilgrimage—the Prophet Elijah (1 Kings 19).

The only definitely fixed point in the itinerary of Numbers 33:17 f., however, is Ezion-geber, which, as we already know from 1 Kings, lay on the Gulf of Aqabah.

For all the points mentioned between Mount Sinai and Ezion-geber (verses 16–35), there is only one other suggested identifica-tion in the Arabian quarter that we can refer to here, that of Haradah, which can be linked with an *el Kharada* about thirty miles southwest of the north end of the Gulf of Aqabah. But such isolated occur-rences of similar names cannot carry much weight.

Nevertheless, a Midianite Sinai is worth considering, since under such an assumption no stretching of the concept "Midian" is necessary, and since the poetic passages men-tioned on page 116 fall into line with a com-ing.of the Lord from that quarter. But in that case one might look for Sinai nearer to Edom. There has long been a theory in the field, which would put Mount Sinai at Petra, on the high Edomite crags above the *Wadi el 'Arabah,* and not far from the tradi-tional Mount Hor. However, since there are no indications of Late Bronze or Early Iron Age worship at Petra, the locality would hardly seem suitable. And the same thing applies to *Jebel et Tannūr,* on the top of which Glueck unearthed a later Nabataean sanctuary, but found nothing earlier.

To the Traditional Sinai

After roaming so far in various directions the baffled searcher for Sinai will be ready to try out the route of the early Christian pilgrims or of travelers like Robinson and Palmer. The best and most natural route to the traditional Sinai goes to the Gulf of Suez, and then eastward into the mountains. The time involved in the three days' journey to Marah (Exod. 15:22) suggested its identi-fication with the well of *'Ain Ḥawwārah,* about fifteen hours from Suez, or else with the *Wadi Gharandel* two hours to the south of the former place, though these identifica-tions were open to the criticism that they contradicted Exodus 15:23. According to that passage Marah was the first water to which the Israelites came, while if they had traveled in the assumed direction the springs of *'Ayūn Mūsa* would have been reached previously. Those favoring the idea of a crossing of the Hebrews in the Ismailieh area but holding the traditional Sinai to be their objective, imagine them as traveling on a road like the one that at present leads from Ismailieh to the Gulf of Suez. They then can put Marah at *'Ayūn Mūsa* and Elim at the oasis of *Wadi Gharandel*.

The ancient and modern pilgrims took the plain of *el Merkḥāh* which is about twelve miles long and five miles wide, to be the Wilderness of Sin (not to be confused with that of Sinai or that of Zin), though there was no basis in any existing nomenclature for such an identification. For the encampment by the sea, mentioned in Numbers 33:10, the vicinity of *Rās abū Zeneimeh* on the Gulf of Suez, now headquarters for companies engaged in manganese mining, naturally suggested itself. About five miles south of that point a small Egyptian settlement of *c.* 1500 B.C. was discovered in 1947 by a University of California African expedition under Wendell Phillips. The place, already abandoned in the days of the Exodus (if that occurred in the thirteenth century B.C.), could have been the site of the Hebrew encampment.

Serābīṭ, which some have sought to identify with the Dophka of Numbers 33:12, lies a five hours' trip into the mountains east of the *el Merkḥāh* Plain. Old Egyptian inscriptions were noticed there already by Niebuhr in 1761 and Robinson in 1838, though these travelers still had no idea that this settlement was a mining colony. In 1905, however, Sir Flinders Petrie cleared the ruins of what proved to be an Egyptian temple of the goddess Hathor, built in front of a cave which was the original holy place. He was able to show that in the third and second millennia B.C. the Pharaohs had carried on mining operations there. Included in Petrie's discoveries were eleven inscriptions on objects and rock-cut tablets. They were in an alphabetic script,

2.19 Jebel et Tannūr. (*Courtesy Nelson Glueck*)

the signs of which strongly resembled Egyptian hieroglyphics. Petrie, as is now clear, dated them rightly in the time of Thutmosis III (1502–1448 B.C.). The Sinai script is the earliest known antecedent of the Phoenician and Hebrew alphabet.

Better routes from the *el Merkḥāh* Plain to the great mountains in the apex of the Sinaitic Peninsula, composed of summits rising over five thousand feet and known as a group to the Arabs as the *Jebel eṭ Ṭūr,* could be taken either via the *Wadi Feirān* or via the *Wadi Shellāl*. The name of *Wadi Feirān* certainly hangs together with Paran, and in Byzantine times there was a city of Pharan here, which was even the seat of a bishopric. However, there is some reason to believe that the city of Pharan got its name as a result of Christian speculation about the Exodus tradition, and that Paran originally belongs in a more northerly setting. For those living at this Christian Pharan it must have been an attractive idea to identify Mount Sinai with the great *Jebel Serbāl*. But the main line of old Christian tradition as attested to by the pilgrimage of Silvia (*c.* 400 A.D.), and accepted by the advisers of the Emperor Justinian (527–565 A.D.), when he established the Sinaitic monastery, held that the *Jebel Mūsa,* or mountain of Moses, was the real Sinai.

If one goes by way of *Wadi Shellāl* one comes to the famous *Wadi Mokatteb,* which is about six miles long and two miles wide; here numerous stone blocks that have tumbled down from the mountain sides display crude inscriptions—so-called graffiti—in Nabataean, Greek and Coptic. They testify to the amount of travel and pilgrimage that has gone through here. However, according to Palmer, this route was hardly in use in the Biblical period.

Robinson reasons that the Israelites probably approached Sinai by the *Wadi Feirān,* as Palmer also supposes, and entered the plain of *er Raḥa* (of which more will be said presently) by the upper part of the *Wadi esh Sheikh.* The three stations Dophkah, Alush, and Rephidim (NUM. 33:12–15) he holds equivalent to four days' journey; by camel travel he found it to be twenty-six to twenty-eight hours. While he had no identifications for Dophkah and Alush he sought Rephidim in the *Wadi esh Sheikh,* an hour below the spring called *es Suweirah* and about five hours from the plain of *er Raḥa* in a defile, in which tradition points out a "Seat of Moses."

E. H. Palmer, on the other hand, who explored this region with the British Ordnance Survey of 1868–69, seeks Dophkah and Alush somewhere in the coastal plain and imagines the Rephidim events as having occurred in the *Wadi Feirān.* But it is useless to seek Rephidim in southern Sinai, for the Rephidim reminiscences belong in the vicinity of Kadesh-barnea, as we have seen (see page 108).

The Mountain of Moses

Robinson's attention and interest were fixed on the northern end of the ridge, which rises majestically over the plain of *er Raḥa* and which is called the *Rās Ṣafṣafeh* by the Arabs. The plain of *er Raḥa,* which is two miles long and one-third to two-thirds of a mile wide and provides one square mile of space, seemed to him the ideal location for the Hebrew encampment, and for setting bounds around the mountain (EXOD. 19:12). If the space seemed a bit small for the Biblical host which Robinson (even though he must have regarded the traditional figures as incorrectly handed down) still imagined as very large, the *Wadi esh Sheikh,* coming

into it from the right, provided additional elbow room. He points out that no such favorable situation exists in the area of the culminating summit of the ridge, the *Jebel Mūsa,* three miles farther south.

The cliff of *Rās Ṣafṣafeh* rises some five hundred feet above the plain, and the distance to the summit, which can only be reached by a detour up a steep ravine, is more than half a mile. Robinson felt rewarded for his exertions in climbing it by seeing the plain spread out before him, with the adjacent wadies and mountains. Palmer, who concurred in the belief that this was the scene of the Biblical events, notes that a ravine called "Jethro's path" (*Sikket Shu'eib*), near the northeast end of the range is the easiest path to the summit. Descending here Moses and Joshua could have heard, but would not have seen, what was going on in the camp in the plain of *er Raḥa* (EXOD. 32:15 f.).

The *Jebel Mūsa,* up whose rock-cut stairs the feet of innumerable pilgrims have climbed, was disappointing to Robinson. Its view is limited by nearby higher peaks on the east, south, and west. It is only toward the north that one has a view over the ridge that ends in *Rās Ṣafṣafeh* and over the distant landscape. One cannot see *Jebel Serbāl,* or the Gulf of Suez or the regions to the west. A small portion of the Gulf of Aqabah with the island of *Tīrān* lying in it can be seen, however, in the south. Robinson saw no reason to suppose that Moses had anything to do with *Jebel Mūsa.* It is three miles from the plain of *er Raḥa,* no part of which is visible from it, and there is no spot nearby where the people could be imagined as assembled. He derived great satisfaction, however, from the ascent of Mount St. Catharine (*Jebel Katerīn*), the view from which is obstructed only by the spire of "Mount Shaumer" (*Jebel Umm Shomer*) toward the south; for from it, the Gulf of Suez and Africa, and the Gulf of Aqabah and Arabia were unveiled before the eager eye. However, contrary to the view of such a traveler as Ulrich Seetzen, Robinson felt certain that the *Jebel Katerīn* had no serious claim for identification with Sinai.

If one is willing to make a far more radical reduction than Robinson and Palmer did in the numbers involved in the Hebrew wanderings, then the objections to *Jebel Mūsa* would fall to the ground. One will then have no special need for the plain of *er Raḥa,* on which those scholars relied so much, but could revert again to the smaller and more elevated plain beneath the highest part of the *Jebel Mūsa* as the scene of the events connected with the lawgiving. For there is a weightier consideration—namely that the mountain of God must have been known as such before Moses (EXOD. 3:1). Holy places have a continuity through long ages, and there is no evidence that the *Rās Ṣafṣafeh* was ever regarded as such a one. That does not speak well for it. That the more southerly, greater height of the range, the *Jebel Mūsa,* was identified with Sinai suggests that it had already enjoyed special sanctity in pre-Christian times. The mere fact that its view lies open to the distant *et Tīh,* could well suggest to those who saw it from some northerly vantage point, or knew of its existence in that mysterious pocket, that it was, indeed, the Holy Mount. Robinson's characterization of *Rās Ṣafṣafeh* applies even better to *Jebel Mūsa:*

> This adytum in the midst of the great circular granite region, with only a single feasible entrance; a secret holy place shut out from the world amid lone and desolate mountains.

Final Observations on the Exodus

There is at present no way in which certainty can be obtained as to the route taken by a Hebrew group that was the bearer of the Exodus tradition and contributed it to the earliest recollections of the nation. The parallel accounts have been combined and important elements of each sacrificed in the compilation. But even if we had them intact and could separate them successfully, it

2.20 *Where Edward Robinson thought the law was given. Seen from the top of his Sinai (Ras Ṣafṣafeh). (Matson Photo Service)*

seems doubtful that they would have geographical knowledge of a realistic sort. The scenes of the events were too distant. Before the oldest narrator did his work there were probably only loose anecdotes and episodes which he strung together in a sequence. Some of these came from widely different areas and from diverse groups. The younger narrators followed suit with variations based on materials and viewpoints gathered in other quarters.

Under the circumstances only a hypothesis can be a light to one's feet in this labyrinth. The best hypothesis will be one that sticks close to the most assured facts: the sojourn of a Hebrew group at Kadesh and the occurrence of identifiable place names in the Pelusium area. It seems reasonable to suppose that a delegation or small tribal group should have gone from Kadesh to some distant mountain to enter into a covenant with the LORD, who had revealed himself to their leader. We can conceive of no more probable goal than that lying south of the fearful wilderness of the *et Tīh,* where loomed the shining, mysterious sentinels, which the ancient mind must have regarded with absolute awe. Here was the appropriate home for a deity destined to be understood in later times as the one and only God.

CHAPTER VII

THE WILDERNESS SOJOURN

IF ONE ACCEPTS the traditional Sinai as the mountain of the Law and wishes to suppose that a migrating group of Israelites went there via the traditional route, then where did they go from there? There were only three things to do: 1) go back to Suez (which can be eliminated as improbable); 2) go to Aqabah; 3) go north or northeast across the *et Tīh*.

The regular route from the Sinaitic convent to Aqabah was traveled in part by Burckhardt in 1815. He noted that on the way there was an *'Ain Ḥudherah* and that this name corresponded to the Hazeroth, the second station after the departure from Sinai (NUM. 33:17). Robinson, who made the six-day trip from the convent to Aqabah in 1838, took eighteen hours to get to *'Ain Ḥudherah*

by camel, and, assuming each station to be another night's stop, found the identification quite in accord with the requirements. Indeed, he held that if it were correct, it would settle the route of the Israelites after leaving Sinai. In that respect he was over-optimistic, for Hazeroth only means "corrals" or "courts," and such a name could occur almost anywhere. Robinson believed that the only possible course for the Israelites from there would have been the one he then took, which led him to the Gulf of Aqabah (via the *Wadi Ghāzaleh*) and then up the coast to its head.

Robinson erred in this assumption. From *'Ain Ḥudherah* it is also possible to go north. H. E. Palmer took that route in connection with the Ordnance Survey of 1869. From

'Ain Ḥudherah they kept northeast and crossed the divide of a fine, broad valley (*Wadi Elthi*), and then came into another large valley (*Wadi el 'Ain*) at the foot of a mountain named *Jebel 'Arādeh*. That name Palmer connected with the Biblical Haradah (NUM. 33:24). Journeying up the winding valley they came in the end to the great drop-off of the northern high-plateau country, the *Jebel et Tīh* (hereabouts called *Jebel el Ejmeh*). Through a hitherto unknown pass (*Naqb el Mīrād*), they ascended the mountain range. Once the height was attained the view to the north over the plateau region was the most desolate and monotonous Palmer had ever seen. But a marvelous view was to be had toward the south. Beneath them was the strip of low sandstone hills that forms an interval between the *et Tīh* and the granite mountains of the great Sinaitic group. Yonder lay in all their grandeur the *Jebels Feirān, Kāterīn, Serbāl,* and others. The southern rim of the range on which they stood could also be observed from the vantage point chosen. Leaving that grand prospect, the surveyors turned northward and passed through an area of yellow limestone hills. After a day's march this changed to a wide plain of white gravel and coarse black sand. Finally they saw a series of white elevations that looked like tents (*el Kheimatein*). Behind these in the northwest rose the distant summit of the *Jebel Yeleq* (see page 108). They were lost here until they found a new local Arab guide, with whose aid they reached *en Naḳhl,* at that time a fort on the pilgrims' road from Suez to Aqabah. Their need for Arab guidance in these journeys reminds one of how the Israelites on leaving Sinai got Hobab to serve as "eye" for them (NUM. 10:31). Musil, the Czech explorer, notes that among the Bedouin today the scout of a war party is still called its eye (*'ayin*), but that a different term (*qallaṭ*) is used for the scout of a migrating tribe. He would infer from this that the Israelites constituted a warlike expedition.

Palmer's route took the most easterly pass through the *et Tīh* and illustrated the fact that a Hebrew group leaving Sinai could have chosen such a course. There are also several westerly passes, notably the *Naqb el Emreikheh,* which would have been the natural course for a Hebrew delegation going from Kadesh to Mount Sinai. The traveler Seetzen took this route in journeying from Hebron to Sinai in 1807. Passing through desolate wastes he crossed the Suez-Aqabah pilgrim road on April 4. On April 7, he came to the descent from the *Jebel et Tīh*. He notes the sandy plain that follows the foot of this range. Proceeding along the base of the *Jebel Dhallāl* he came on April 9 to heights from which *Jebel Feirān* and *Jebel Serbāl* were to be seen. Finally on that same day, the great moment arrived when he had the entire Sinaitic mountain group before him tinged in a deep blue color. Never had he seen a mountain region more beautiful. He noted that *Jebels Mūsa* and *Kāterīn,* showing as central point from here, stood out above all the rest.

In the light of such a journey which an Israelite group, too, may have made, whether in the same direction or in the reverse one, the statement of Deuteronomy 1:2 seems significant:

> "There are eleven days' journey from Horeb by the way of mount Seir unto Kadesh-barnea." (DEUT. 1:2 A.V.)

> *"It is eleven days' journey from Horeb by the way of Mount Seir to Kadesh-barnea."* (DEUT. 1:2 R.S.V.)

The *direct* trip from the traditional Sinai to the neighborhood of Kadesh suits that specification very well, for Seetzen's journey took about the same time. Some difficulty, however, is caused by the qualification that the journey is "by way of Mount Seir." If Mount Seir in this verse had its usual meaning of the high Edomite country northeast of the Gulf of Aqabah, then a journey from *Jebel*

Mūsa to Kadesh by that route would involve useless and arduous ascents, and could not be accomplished in the stated time. Nor would the latter suffice if the words "by way of Mount Seir" merely meant going up the *el 'Arabah,* at the foot of the Edomite mountains. One explanation of this difficulty is to suppose that "Mount Seir" is used here in an imprecise manner. After the Edomites were driven out of their homeland, the term "Mount Seir" and "Edom" seem to have been occasionally applied to the Negeb region west of the *el 'Arabah* (cf. Deut. 1:44; Josh. 11:17; 12:7; 1 Chron. 4:42-43). This may also be the case in the passage quoted above. Possibly the same explanation applies to certain poetic passages which speak of the coming of the Lord via Edom or Seir (Judg. 5:4-5; Hab. 3:3; Deut. 33:2).

Paran

The youngest of the Pentateuchal narrators in speaking of the departure from Sinai describes the cloud as preceding the host and settling in the "wilderness of Paran" (Num. 10:12; in 12:16 the allusion is probably secondary). The next objective after that in this version of the events is the Wilderness of Zin and Kadesh (Num. 20:1, 22). The same writer apparently thinks of the Paran Wilderness as extending to the latter place (Num. 13:3), while the Deuteronomist speaks of Mount Paran (Deut. 33:2).

Some maps put a *Jebel Fārān,* the name of which would correspond exactly to Mount Paran, seven miles southeast of the *Jebel Maqrāh.* Unhappily, it was never reported just how this name was ascertained, and an explorer like Musil could not confirm it.

If in Deuteronomy 33:2 the Lord comes from Sinai to Seir and from Seir to Paran and from Paran to Kadesh, that would be attributing to him a rather zigzag course, if Seir be taken as east of the Arabah and Sinai as the *Jebel Mūsa,* and Paran as west of *'Aqabah.* One must, in order to get a proper progression, either locate Sinai east

or south of Seir proper or assume that we have here the late use of Seir (cf. above).

Somewhere within a radius starting from Paran was originally put the scene of the Deuteronomist's Mosaic preachments. They are said to have been uttered beyond the Jordan in the wilderness, in the plain over against Suph, between Paran and Tophel, Laban, Hazeroth, and Dizahab. (Deut. 1:1). The text seems overloaded, probably because readings of divergent manuscripts were combined. The words "beyond the Jordan" clash with "in the wilderness," and the latter with "in the plain," if that here has its usual sense of the *el Ghōr* plain, though if the *el 'Arabah* proper be meant there is no disharmony between the last two. Also overloaded is the description of the more precise point. To say Suph (which the r.s.v. has, the a.v. has "Red sea") lay between Paran and Tophel makes sense if Tophel can be connected with *eṭ Ṭafīleh,* an important place in the Edomite country. Suph would then probably be a spot in the *el 'Arabah,* and if it gets its name from *sūf* (reeds), one might think of it as on the edge of the swampy area in which the *el Ghōr* terminates. Another text or recension seems to have located the place of the preachments north of the Dead Sea and east of the lower Jordan in the Moab plains. A third localization seems presupposed by Laban, Hazeroth and Dizahab. A recently published inscription of the Assyrian King Sargon (721-705 b.c.) speaks of "the sheikh of the city of Laban," evidently a town in the vicinity of Raphia. Hazeroth is the fourth station from Sinai (Num. 33:17). It is impossible with present means to clarify the variant setting to which these names pointed.

To Kadesh

There is no mention of a detour to Aqabah in Deuteronomy 1:6-7. The Israelites, according to the Deuteronomist, were commanded to go from Horeb—wherever that may have lain—straightway to the "hill country of the Amorites," i.e., the region that rises north of Beersheba and constitutes the mountainous area later inhabited by Judah and Israel. In the journey from Horeb the Israelites are said to have passed through a "great and terrible wilderness" and to have arrived at Kadesh-barnea (DEUT. 1:19).

The location of Kadesh is naturally of considerable interest. If Israel had an extended sojourn in the wilderness, most of it will have been spent there (cf. DEUT. 1:46). The name, which it shares with a city in Galilee and a greater one in Syria, marks it as a holy place—originally, of course, of some pagan cult. Its association with lawgiving or juridical matters is vindicated by the appellation En-mishpat (GEN. 14:7), "Spring of Judgment." It is sometimes called Kadesh-barnea (DEUT. 1:19; 2:14; JOSH. 15:3). It lay south of the Amorite mountain country (DEUT. 1:20), east of Gerar (GEN. 20:1), and at the southern extremity of the region reported to have been conquered by Joshua (JOSH. 10:41). More precisely, it lay on the southern boundary line of Judah which extended from the southern end of the Dead Sea and the ascent of Akrabbim in the east to the brook of Egypt in the west. The indicated course would be up the *Wadi Fikreh,* and the ascent of Akrabbim is probably the pass called the *Naqb eṣ Ṣafa.* If Kadesh is said to be on the border of Edomite territory (NUM. 20:16), that must have been written at a time when Edom's control extended across the *el 'Arabah* into the Negeb. According to Numbers 20:1 f., Kadesh is in or close to the Wilderness of Zin (*Ṣin*). That wilderness is apparently named after a town or settlement Zin which lay between the ascent of Akrabbim and Kadesh (JOSH. 15:1; NUM. 34:3), but has not been successfully placed.

Kadesh thus lay in the *el 'Arīsh*-Raphia-*Qoṣeimeh* triangle, which, indeed, is the only district in the whole Sinaitic region in which a nomad group of any size could have existed for any length of time. The survey of the Israeli Negeb by Nelson Glueck, carried on indefatigably every summer since 1951, has established the fact that there was considerable occupation of this region in the Middle Bronze period and again in Iron Age II, and thereafter in Nabataean and late Roman times. The absence of indications of Late Bronze and Early Iron settlements shows that a favorable situation existed for the migrating Hebrew tribes to move into the vacuum. It also confirms the belief of the Old Testament sources that they did not stay long in this area but moved on to conquer the more attractive regions.

A place called *'Ain Qedeis* was discovered in the appropriate area in 1842 by J. Rowlands, who lost his life at the hands of the Bedouin. It was rediscovered by H. C. Trumbull who publicized it in 1884. At nearby *'Ain el Qudeirāt,* which is a far more copious spring, lies a mound representing a settlement with Iron Age sherds. According to Glueck, this is the chief Iron Age site in the whole area. The peculiar combination-name Kadesh-barnea, according to Albright, represents twin towns, as does that of Ashtaroth-karnaim (see page 67; cf. GEN. 14:5). Barnea then must have been at the greater spring and Kadesh at *'Ain Qedeis.*

Localities at or near Kadesh are also referred to in the narratives. Here must be sought the localities of Massa, Meribah, and Rephidim. In the older source (NUM. 20:3) we hear that the people *contended* with Moses concerning a lack of water, whereupon Moses smote the rock so that water came forth, and so they were called the waters of Meribah ("contention"). In another version of the same material (EXOD. 17:1–7) the incident is (artificially?) placed at Rephidim and not only construed as *contention* (Revised Standard Version: fault-finding) with Moses, but as putting God to proof, wherefore the place was called Massah ("proof") and Meribah ("contention"). In the early saying about Levi (DEUT. 33:8), the LORD does prove and contend.

Still other things happened at Kadesh.

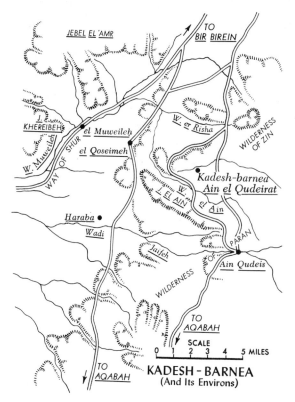

KADESH - BARNEA
(And Its Environs)

opponents and says that they scattered the Israelites *in Seir* as far as Hormah (DEUT. 1:44). Seir here has the late usage already mentioned before. Hormah is a place in the Negeb (JOSH. 15:30), that prior to the destruction, at which its name hints, was called Zephath (JUDG. 1:17). How little one can depend on this part of the reporting about the wanderings is, however, illustrated by the older, very different version of what happened at "Hormah" which is put after the youngest author's account of the death of Aaron (NUM. 21:1 f.). The version referred to speaks of Canaanites, rather than Amorites, as living in the Negeb (DEUT. 1:44). They hear of Israel's coming via the way of Atharim (the way of the spies, A.V.) and inflict a defeat on them. A mighty vow of Israel, however, brings divine favor and victory. The cities of the Canaanites are then captured and destroyed and the leading ruined site ever after was called "Hormah." This narrative clearly belongs to an invasion account of Judaea from the south, and thus fits ill with the general connection in which it is now found. "Hormah" is probably to be sought in *Tell el Mshāsh,* east of Beersheba, or still farther to the east at *Tell el Milḥ.*

Journey to Mount Hor

The youngest Pentateuchal narrator, after describing the discord over the spies, takes the Israelites to the Wilderness of Zin and Kadesh (NUM. 20:1). Here this author has introduced a journey to Mount Hor, as the first step in the departure from Kadesh (NUM. 20:22–29; 33:37). The older storytellers did not have this (in Numbers 21:4, it has been editorially added), and the Deuteronomist does not mention it in his résumé.

Mount Hor is said to be on the boundary of Edom (NUM. 20:23). Josephus puts the mountain at Petra.

Southwest of Petra is a height now called *Nebi Harūn,* or "Prophet Aaron," on the summit of which is the supposed tomb of Aaron (complete with a sarcophagus!).

Moses' sister Miriam died and was buried there (NUM. 20:1). In the Deuteronomic version of events the spies were sent forth from Kadesh (DEUT. 1:22 f.). They came to Hebron and to the vale of Eshcol ("grapes") to the north of it, and carried back a sample of the grapes growing there. The name Eshcol still seems to linger in the village of *Beit (Is)ḳāhel.* The youngest source has the spies start out from the Wilderness of Paran (NUM. 13:3, 21).

On the return of the spies, the Israelites at first were discontented over the formidable Canaanite defenses reported to them. According to the older versions (NUM. 14:25) the LORD thereupon commanded them to turn about and take the road to the Red Sea (Gulf of Aqabah). However, instead of obeying the LORD, the Israelites wilfully attempted an invasion of the mountains of southern Palestine. The Amalekites and Canaanites thereupon came forth and defeated them and scattered them as far as Hormah. A late parallel account makes the Amorites their

2.21 Naqb Shtār *on the Edomite frontier looking toward Midian.*
(*Courtesy Nelson Glueck*)

Actually this tomb is a rebuilt Christian church of the days of the Emperor Justinian (527–565 A.D.). Because of this incident of the death of Aaron and its Jewish localization, it has been suggested that Kadesh, which in the earlier source is also put on the boundary of Edom (NUM. 20:16), should be sought at Petra instead of south of Beersheba. But that runs contrary to the clues for the location of Kadesh, considered before, and receives no archaeological confirmation at Petra, where the holy places are of Nabataean origin. The course described in Numbers 33:37 and 41 f. (disregarding the misplaced reference of verse 40 to the Hormah incident), is not unfavorable to the traditional identification of Mount Hor.

The earlier sources may not have mentioned Mount Hor at all, for the allusion now found in the text of the younger author (NUM. 21:41) is considered an editorial addition. The Deuteronomic writer puts Aaron's death at Mosera (DEUT. 10:6), which is evidently the Moseroth of the late itinerary (NUM. 33:30) and which lay somewhere between Sinai and Ezion-geber ('Aqabah).

Israel and Edom

According to the older writer, Moses, before leaving Kadesh, sent an embassy to the king of Edom, with a request for permission to go through his land (NUM. 20:14 f.). Moses offered to take the "king's highway" and promised that his people would touch nothing en route. This "king's highway" through Edom is evidently the one that the Romans later developed and which in turn became "the Sultan's road" and today is "the road of the Emir." It is a north-south artery, along the course of which lie the ruins of numerous Bronze Age cities of the 23rd–20th centuries B.C. The route is thus of great antiquity. The kings from the east must have traveled it with their army in Abraham's time (GEN. 14:6), but it is more probably named after some Bronze Age monarch.

The purpose of Moses, as envisioned here, was apparently to enter Edom from the south. It is really not quite clear why he should have to go to 'Aqabah at all; perhaps this journey has the function of joining together divergent traditions of the events, one of which led the Israelites directly across the el 'Arabah from Kadesh into Moab, while the other had brought them from Sinai to 'Aqabah, and had no room for any sojourn at Kadesh. The latter tradition evidently did not mention the sending of messengers to the king of Edom, but put a negotiation with the Edomites at their southern frontier.

The explorations of Glueck have shown that the southern border of Edom was strongly fortified. Coming from 'Aqabah one ascends to the Edomite country by the *Naqb Shtār,* a steep pass. Here stood an Edomite fortress (*Khirbet Naqb Shtār*),

2.22 *Stela of Balū'a, dating from the thirteenth to eleventh centuries,* B.C. (*George Horsfield through Nelson Glueck*)

which originally had towers and buttresses, but which is now a jumbled ruin. Northeast of it, less than two miles away, is another fortress (*Khirbet Shedēyid*). As Iron Age sherds are found in both places, one can visualize here the Edomite refusal of passage, backed by enough armed might to be deterrent, for migrating people do not detour out of courtesy.

The archaeological history of Edom has been clarified by Glueck's surveys, carried on for the American School of Oriental Research. There was an Early Bronze Age civilization in this region (as also in Moab and points farther north). It was destroyed about the end of the twentieth century B.C., and the area remained without sedentary occupation until the beginning of the thirteenth century B.C. It is apparent, therefore, that if the Edomites and Moabites were actually settled in their land before the Exodus of Israel, they cannot have been there very long as yet.

Their path barred, the Israelites were compelled to take a different course, according to the older sources, going around Edom on the south (NUM. 21:4). The same thing is meant by the Deuteronomist.

"And when we passed by from our brethren the children of Esau, which dwelt in Seir, through the way of the plain from Elath, and from Ezion-gaber, we turned and passed by the way of the wilderness of Moab." (DEUT. 2:8 A.V.)

"So we went on, away from our brethren the sons of Esau who live in Seir, away from the Arabah road from Elath and Ezion-geber.

And we turned and went in the direction of the wilderness of Moab." (DEUT. 2:8 R.S.V.)

Jephthah, too, presupposes this route when he says that the Israelites on leaving Kadesh went around Edom and Moab on the east and encamped on the other side of the Arnon (JUDG. 11:18).

In his explorations in Moab, Glueck was able to establish the location of the eastern boundary of the old Moabite kingdom. It is marked by a line of border fortresses of Iron Age I–II, which were in sight of each other on the top of a range of hills west of a long valley (*Wadi Fejj el 'Aseiḳer*), which he holds may have been the passageway of the Israelites in their migration. The existence of these fortresses certainly helps to explain the impracticability of attacking Moab on the east.

The individual points touched upon in the account of the older source are not preserved. The younger narrator (NUM. 21:10 f.) gives Oboth, Iye-abarim and the Brook of Zered. After that the Israelites reach the Arnon, where they encamp in the wilderness that extends out from the border of the Amorites, i.e., the Amorite principality, which these writers believe existed in Moses' time in northern Moab. In this connection is quoted a snatch of old poetry which refers to the valleys of the Arnon, and the slope of the valleys extending to the seat of Ar, and leaning to the border of Moab (NUM. 21:14–15). The passage mirrors the Hebrew claim that the Arnon is the northern border of Moab (as also argued by Jephthah, JUDG. 11:18). The name Ar is usually linked with the later Areopolis, which Eusebius says was also called "Rabbath Moab." The latter name, it has been held, may survive at *Qaṣr er Rabbah,* twelve miles south of the Arnon. The surface remains there, however, according to Glueck, are only Nabataean and the identification does not do justice to the description of Ar as a border town.

The next five stops in the younger source lead to the end of the journey. The initial three, Beer, where the incident of the Song of the Well is placed (Num. 21:16–18), Mattanah, and Nahaliel cannot as yet be identified. Bamoth is no doubt identical with Bamoth Baal (Num. 22:41). Last comes the valley lying by Pisgah (Num. 21:20). On these two points see pages 126 and 127.

Stations after Kadesh in the List of Numbers 33

Apparently, however, the youngest of the Pentateuchal narrators did not take Israel on a detour around Edom and Moab on the east, but rather took them along the *'Arabah,* from Mount Hor up into and through Moab. While his detailed narrative has not been preserved, his list of stations in Numbers 33 reflects his idea of the route. The fact that several of the stations, which cannot be identified under the theory of a journey around Edom and Moab, appear in his list also and can be identified under his theory of a journey up the *'Arabah* with some degree of confidence speaks well for this presentation of the matter.

The early stages, according to verses 37, 41–44, are the following:

Kadesh to Mount Hor "on the edge of the land of Edom"

Zalmonah

Punon

Oboth

Iye-abarim in the territory of Moab

No journey from Kadesh to the "Red Sea" is reflected in this list; however, there had been a coming to the "Red Sea" (Ezion-geber, cf. page 221) prior to the arrival at

2.23 *Arnon Valley, showing Roman road ascending to plateau. (Courtesy Nelson Glueck)*

Kadesh (Num. 33:35–36). Zalmonah is not known, but we suspect it to be the name of a mountain, as is the case in other occurrences of this name in Ephraim and Bashan (Judg. 9:48; Ps. 68:14).

We seem to emerge on firmer ground with the next station, Punon, for the name appears in Byzantine sources (as Phaino) and survives to this day in *Feinān.* It lies on the east side of the *el 'Arabah,* where an important track leads up into Edom. According to Glueck, the area covered by the ruins of Phaino marks it as one of the few large places of this area in late Roman times. Not only some Early and Middle Bronze sherds, but also sherds of Early Iron I and II were found at this site. It was evidently an important place for the mining and smelting of copper in King Solomon's time, and one must imagine the forests that once rose on the heights of Edom to the east as providing the charcoal needed for the smelting furnaces.

Oboth has long and rightly been connected with *'Ain el Weibeh,* a place on the west side of the *el 'Arabah,* about thirty miles south of the Dead Sea. At this point a road comes down from *Kurnub* in the Negeb. It is not necessary to suppose that the Israelites zigzagged from Punon in the east to Oboth in the west and back again to the east to the next stopping place. Each place naturally had control of a certain amount of territory and that of Oboth may have extended to the east side of the valley.

With Iye-abarim, we are already across the southern boundary of Moab and up in higher country. The addition Abarim is used to differentiate this Iyim (or *'Iyyīm*) from other places of the same name (cf. JOSH. 15:29) by indicating that it lay on Abarim, the mountain range on the western side of the Transjordan plateau extending down to the border of Edom. That name combination by itself shows that the localization given in the younger source, which speaks of it as "in the wilderness east of Moab" (NUM. 21:11), is mistaken. The name of this Iye-abarim may have survived at *Khirbet 'Ayy,* two miles northeast of *Kathrabba,* which lies southwest of *el Kerak.* The Madeba mosaic, too, has an *Aia* in southwestern Moab, evidently meaning the same place.

It is strange that the valley of the Zered is not mentioned in Numbers 33, as is the case in Numbers 21:12. Actually the Zered—if that be the *Wadi el Ḥesā,* as is generally supposed—lies south of *Khirbet 'Ayy* and would have been reached first. That suggests that the entry into Moab is imagined as having been made from the vicinity of the southern end of the Dead Sea. The road evidently ascended via *Khirbet 'Ayy,* and went on to *el Kerak* and points farther north.

The Israelite Expansion in Transjordan

The account of the early narrators took the Israelites to the final objective at Mount Pisgah (NUM. 21:20). One is quite surprised, therefore, to find oneself back farther to the south again at the River Arnon in Numbers 21:21 f., and to be given the idea that the area north of that river all the way to the Jabbok belonged to an Amorite kingdom under a King Sihon. The Israelites applied for permission to cross his territory. According to a Deuteronomic version of the events, they sent word to Sihon from the Wilderness of Kedemoth (DEUT. 2:26). The latter name appears as that of a city of Moab (JOSH. 13:18; 21:37; 1 CHRON. 6:79), and the wilderness is no doubt the area to the east of it. It must be sought at the headwaters of the Arnon. Sihon took the field against them and attacked at Jahaz, a city mentioned also in the stela of King Mesha (see page 284), and placed by St. Jerome between Medeba and Dibon. The Israelites defeated Sihon and took his kingdom and all its cities up to the Ammonite border which is said to have been strongly fortified.

The belief of the narrators that these great events occurred at the time of the wilderness wanderings is shown to be altogether improbable by the verbiage used. The text states that the Israelites took all these cities and that then they dwelt in them (NUM. 21:25). That indicates a long process and continued settlement, not a mere passage through the land. Scholars have held therefore that this material has only been editorially brought into the Mosaic period, and that we actually have echoes here of an expansion of Israel across the Jordan that took place under the early kings of Israel. A poetic piece quoted from an old paean (NUM. 21:27–30) gives valuable hints of this forgotten history of national beginnings.

We must suppose that the Hebrew expansion across the Jordan had been preceded by an "Amorite" expansion, though from what base that had been undertaken is not said. Sihon, after gaining Heshbon, had also taken Ar. But Israel then conquered the territory, which (disregarding the dubious Nophah) included Heshbon, Dibon and Medeba, three of the most important places of Moab. Their locations are well known. Heshbon's

2.24 *Salecah* (Salkhad)—*outpost of King Og's Court.* (*Courtesy Institut Francais d'Archéologie, Beyrouth, Liban*)

name still survives in *Hesbān,* seven miles north of *Mādeba* on a high hill. There are remains from Roman times there, which have overlaid those of the Moabite era.

Dibon survives in *Dhībān* on the north side of the Arnon River. Later it was the Moabite capital (Is. 15:2; JER. 48:18, 22). The Moabite King Mesha who reconquered the city from the men of the Hebrew tribe of Gad declares that the Gadites had taken it in the days of King Omri. This gives us the proper frame of reference for evaluating the report concerning the cities built by the Gadites (NUM. 33:45 f. and see Color Map VI.)

The third city, Medeba, retains its ancient name to this day as *Mādeba.* The site is marked by extensive ruins, mostly of Roman times. Mesha took it from the Gadites, and it is a Moabite city in subsequent prophecy (cf. Is. 15:2). A fuller list of the Israelite cities in Moab is given in Numbers 32:3 and 32:34–38; Isaiah 15–16 and Jeremiah 48 give the whole Moabite panorama.

A small Amorite principality seems to have lain north of that of Sihon. Its center was Jazer (NUM. 21:32). It is previously described as on the boundary of Ammon (NUM. 21:24 R.S.V.). A late writer, at a time when the term Gilead was used loosely, speaks of Jazer of Gilead (1 CHRON. 26:31). Spies were sent thither by the Israelites before an attack was launched against it. The region is called a good pasturage (NUM. 32:1). According to Eusebius, Jazer lay at the eighth or tenth milestone west of Rabbath Ammon. The recovery of a milestone south of '*Ammān* has revealed the course of the Roman roads in this neighborhood and made it probable that *Tell el Yadūdeh,* an important mound with Iron Age sherds, is Jazer. It lay where the road coming from Heshbon forked, one branch going to Rabbath Ammon, the other into the desert.

At this point an expedition to the northerly region of Bashan (see page 28) is attributed to the invading Israelites. Near the city of Edrei its King Og was allegedly defeated (NUM. 21:33–35; cf. DEUT. 3:1 f.). The name of Edrei survives to this day as *Der'a.* The Iron Age city doubtless lay on the steep, well-isolated hill that marks a strong defensive position. The more detailed account of Deuteronomy (3:16 f.) speaks of sixty cities that were ruled from here, and of the district of Argob in which they lay. Og's easternmost city was Salecah (today *Ṣalkhad*). Imagination was stirred by a large iron bedstead of Og of Bashan, which later was exhibited at Rabbath Ammon, presumably as spoil of war.

The name of King Og is clearly based on tradition, and it would not be surprising if it were found some day in a cuneiform text of the Amarna Age or later. However, the arduous and protracted campaign to Bashan is not very probable in the situation in which it is related. One must suppose that it has been put here for ideological reasons: to embrace these territories in a Mosaic testament to Israel. Actually, the Israelite expansion into this area will have taken place somewhat later, and have been carried out from the west by Machir or Manasseh, the tribe claiming the region (JOSH. 13:31; NUM. 32:33). As Solomon had the territory in hand (1 KINGS 4:13), the conquest must have taken place before his time.

Last Encampments of the Israelites

It will be noted that the list of stations in Numbers 33:45 makes no reference to the conquest of an Amorite kingdom between Arnon and Jabbok or to an expedition to Bashan, but takes Israel from Iye-abarim to its objective by four further stations:

Dibon-gad (i.e., Dibon of the Gadites)
Almon-diblathaim
The Abarim mountains east of Nebo
The plains of Moab at the Jordan across from Jericho, from Beth-jeshimoth to Abel-shittim

We have spoken of Dibon already. The next name, Almon-diblathaim, is really a compound of two names—the Almon in the bailiwick of Diblathaim. The latter is once called Beth-diblathaim (JER. 48:22) and is among the places on the elevated plains (*mīshōr*) of the Moabite country. The Moabite King Mesha mentions it in his inscription between Medeba and Beth-baal-meon. The latter place is to be sought at *Ma'īn* and, since there are not many Iron Age sites between that point and Medeba, *Khirbet et Teim,* a mile and a half southwest of Medeba has been suggested for Beth-diblathaim, and *'Ain ed Dīb* for Almon. Abarim mountains (in NUM. 27:12; DEUT. 32:49 less exactly as "Mount Abarim") as previously stated, is the general name of the range that rises about six hundred feet on the west above the high plateau country of Moab, but then descends several thousand feet to the Dead Sea. It is called *esh Shefa* by the Arabs.

The final point mentioned is that of the "plains of Moab." The term is used for the plains between the Jordan River, and the Moabite mountain country from the Dead Sea up to the valley on which Beth-nimrah (NUM. 32:36) was situated (*Wadi Nimrīn*). The name bears testimony to the fact that at one time this was part of the kingdom of Moab (see page 150).

A little more than four miles south of old Beth-nimrah, which lay at *Tell Bleibil,* according to Glueck's survey, is *Tell el Kefrein,* situated on a cone-shaped hill guarding the *Wadi Kefrein* and commanding a splendid view of the plain, which in this vicinity is intensely cultivated. Numerous Iron I and II sherds are found on the top and slopes of the hill. It was certainly an important, if small, fortress of Biblical times, controlling an important track to the hills behind it and owning the nearby rich garden lands. It has generally been identified with Abel-shittim. But Glueck's explorations in this area have called attention to a more heavily occupied Iron Age I and II (and Early Bronze I) site, higher up on the same brook, namely *Tell-el-Ḥammām,* near the base of the hills rising steeply toward Moab. On it are the remains of a large and strongly built fortress; the lines of the outer fortification wall that once completely enclosed it and traces of a glacis can still be discerned. At both ends there were massive towers. This, indeed, must be Abel-shittim, which got its name from its situation at a brook (*ābēl*) by some accacia trees (Hebrew *shittīm*).

In the vicinity of *Wadi el 'Azeimeh* lay the Beth-jeshimoth of the narrative of Numbers 33:49. The name clearly survives in *Khirbet Sweimeh* on the north side of *Wadi el 'Azeimeh,* but since no sherds of pre-Roman origin are to be found there, this must again mark a later phase in the history of the settlement. The Biblical city evidently lay a mile and three-quarters higher up the wadi at *Tell el 'Azeimeh.* The tell guards an important track up to Madeba. It had the additional advantage of a strong spring close at hand. The tell is described as lying on an "oval bench," from which the land falls away sharply. A fine view is had over the plain which descends from here in easy stages to the Dead Sea. There is a good-sized rectangular area which is enclosed by a fortification wall. Among the sherds found, those of Iron Age I–II were the most numerous. It seems to be the only possible site in the area at which to locate Beth-jeshimoth. We may note in passing that about five miles to the west is *Teleilāt Ghassūl,* where the Jesuit fathers in 1929–1938 first laid bare the life that was lived here in Chalcolithic times, twenty-five hundred years before Israel came to this neighborhood.

This then was the area in which the Israelites were to have encamped according to Numbers 22:1, 25:1, 33:48. Some perplexity is caused by the fact that another line of tradition stressed a place called Beth-peor, in the valley opposite which Israel is said to have stayed (DEUT. 3:29). With that vicinity, furthermore, there is associated an incident in one of the most delightful and impressive Old Testament narratives—the story of Balaam (NUM. 22:2–24:25).

The Scenes of the Balaam Narrative

The Moabite King Balak, around whose country Israel had passed, according to the older storytellers, is greatly concerned about the Israelite migration. He sends for the seer Balaam to come and curse Israel. That, of course, presupposes a belief not only in the potency of magic utterance in general, but of magic utterance by professional wizards in particular. It also illustrates the celebrity that was attained by some wizards that Balaam was summoned all the way from "Pethor which is by the river" (NUM. 22:5) or in "Aram Naharaim" (DEUT. 23:4, so the Hebrew; A.V. and R.S.V., Mesopotamia). This town of Pethor was otherwise unknown, until its existence was confirmed by the cuneiform inscriptions. The name, however, has been falsely vocalized by the Jewish tradition, for it appears in the inscriptions

2.25 *Head of Moabite king from* el Medeiyineh. (*Courtesy Nelson Glueck*)

of Shalmaneser III as *Pitru.* That name, furthermore, was only used for it by the people of Syria ("the Hittites"); its inhabitants had another name for it in Shalmaneser's day. It lay at the junction of the Sajur River, which rises in Syria and flows eastward, and the Euphrates. According to his poetic utterances, Balaam came from "Aram" and "the mountains of the East" (NUM. 23:7). These areas were certainly stages in his trip—the mountains being the more easterly, namely the range from the Hauran to the Euphrates, while Aram is the nearer territory that was controlled by Damascus in the Biblical writer's day.

Balak, in Oriental courtesy, goes forth to receive the great seer at "the city of Moab" on the Arnon boundary (NUM. 22:36 R.S.V.). There is no "city of Moab"; the suggested correction "Ar of Moab" agrees with Numbers 21:15 (cf. page 120). From the Arnon they go to Kiriath-huzoth, "the city of streets" (NUM. 22:39), but there is no clue as to where that place lay. Since the younger source, which gives the main narrative about Balaam, cuts in at this point it remains uncertain how the earlier story continued.

Wherever it was that Balak was staying, according to the younger source, he took Balaam up to Bamoth-baal. This is probably the high place of the city listed by that name in Joshua 13:17, but called Bamoth for short

125

in Numbers 21:19 f. The Beth-bamoth mentioned in the inscription of the Moabite King Mesha must mean the same town. Musil suggested identifying Bamoth-baal with the hill of *el Qweizīyeh,* lying to the west of a road that crosses the ridge road (the *darb esh-Shefa*); from that eminence one can look down through the valley into a part of the plains of Moab, and see the waste lands on the west side of the *Rās Ṣīyāghah;* toward the north one sees the southern slopes of Mount Nebo. The height is considered a holy place by the natives and numerous dolmens are found there. On the other side of the road and of the wadi below it is the only townsite hereabouts, *el Muḥayyiṭ,* and hence the probable site of the town of Nebo. Eusebius puts the town eight Roman miles west (which can include southwest) of Heshbon, while Peter the Iberian says it lay on the south side of Mount Nebo. These descriptions seem to suit the identification. It was a Reubenite city (NUM. 32:3, 38), the population of which King Mesha exterminated and from which he took away certain sacred objects of the LORD. We find it later among the cities of Moab (Is. 15:2; JER. 48:1). Its position was strong and there are traces of ancient walls as well as plenty of Iron Age II sherds there. It is not impossible that in the younger source this Nebo was Balak's town, from which he would have taken Balaam to the hilltop of *el Qweizīyeh,* from which he could see "the nearest of the people" (i.e., the southernmost tip of the Hebrew encampment) in the distant plain.

After Balaam, much to Balak's disgust, had blessed Israel, Balak took him to a different point, presumably one from which he would get a still better and nearer view of the Hebrew encampment.

"And he brought him into the field of Zophim, to the top of Pisgah." (NUM. 23:14 A.V.)

"And he took him to the field of Zophim, to the top of Pisgah." (NUM. 23:14 R.S.V.)

The word Zophim, however, should be translated here as "field of the watchers." There is a possibility that the name has survived in the *Ṭela 'āt eṣ Ṣafa,* which adjoins the *Nebā* district on the northeast.

The third and climactic point to which Balaam was conducted was probably one affording an even closer and better view of the encampment of Israel than its predecessors.

"And Balak brought Balaam unto the top of Peor, that looketh toward Jeshimon." (NUM. 23:28 A.V.)

"So Balak took Balaam to the top of Peor, that overlooks the desert." (NUM. 23:28 R.S.V.)

It was there, after Balak had discharged him, that Balaam then uttered his famous "Star out of Jacob" prophecy. The mountain of Peor must be close to the town of that name, which elsewhere is called by its fuller name Beth-peor (DEUT. 3:29; 4:46; 34:6), and is listed among the Reubenite cities (JOSH. 13:20). It was within easy reach of (Abel-) Shittim, since Israel there followed Baal Peor (NUM. 25:3; DEUT. 4:3)—no doubt the god of Beth-peor—and associated too intimately with Moabite women (NUM. 25:6–18). Eusebius knows of a Beth-peor near Mount Peor, six miles east of Livias (*Tell er Rāmeh*), which would indicate that it lay on the next summit north of Mount Nebo.

Events in the Plains of Moab

A younger supplement to the early source speaks of harlotry of the Israelites with Midianite women instead of Moabitesses (NUM. 25:6–18). It thus prepares the way for the account later given by the youngest source of a cruel war against the Midianites (chapter 31). The latter development seems astonishing in view of the debt of gratitude Moses owed the Midianites. The report is also strange in the light of the situation hitherto described, for the country was occupied by the Moabites. However, at the time when the youngest Pentateuchal author was writing, the Arab invasion had swamped Transjordan, and so he thinks of the inhabitants of the region as Midianites. The story of the war contains no precise geographical elements.

After giving the list of stations of the Exodus and wilderness wandering, the youngest writer introduces a description of the boundaries of Israel's promised land (NUM. 34:1–12). The Levite cities and cities of refuge are then referred to in chapter 35, but not enumerated. In a different connection, however, Moses names the three cities of refuge east of the Jordan (DEUT. 4:41–43; cf. JOSH. 20:8). The southernmost is "Bezer upon the plain" (*mīshōr*) in Reuben. It is mentioned also in the inscription of King Mesha, but there is no indication as to its location. The central one, Golan, was evidently the leading city of the *Jaulān*. Its proposed localization (at *Saḥem ej Jaulān*) lacks archaeological confirmation. On Ramoth Gilead, cf. page 281.

An odd incident mentioned in connection with events in the plains of Moab is that concerning the daughters of Zelophehad, the son of Hepher. There is more to this than the matter of private family inheritances. For the "daughters" are clans of Manasseh, or places controlled by the Manassites. Thus reference is made to Tirzah, a city of considerable importance (see page 293). Two of the clans named Noah and Hoglah have been found mentioned on the inscribed potsherds or ostraca from Samaria found by a Harvard University expedition under Reisner, 1908–11. The strange name Zelophehad itself has not yet been satisfactorily explained.

The Death of Moses

The impressive Balaam story is paralleled by the no less wonderful story of the death of Moses, who, before departing this life, sings his swan song (DEUT. 32), blesses the tribes (DEUT. 33), and then ascends to a high

vantage point and looks forth over the Jordan Valley and western Palestine. The verbiage of two sources has been combined in the narrative in Deuteronomy 34:1; the older source spoke of Moses ascending Mount Nebo, whereas the younger spoke of "the top of Pisgah that lies east of Jericho" (cf. DEUT. 3:27).

Pisgah is no real name, since it is given the definite article "the Pisgah." It means "portion" in late Hebrew and Aramaic. It cannot be regarded as certain that Mount Nebo and "the Pisgah" refer to the same spot. Conceivably, different groups of people at different times localized the vantage point at which Moses had stood somewhat differently.

Mount Nebo evidently got its name from the town of Nebo. The latter place is described as on the Abarim range (NUM. 32:47); the name presumably is short for Beth-nebo, as Peor is short for Beth-peor. The name Nebo survives to this day at *Nebā,* but is used by the Arabs to designate a piece of territory lying south of the *Rās Ṣiyāghah,* a more westerly but lower summit that is separated by a saddle from the summit the Christians call Mount Nebo. To the rear of the traditional Nebo, at a somewhat higher level, are the ruins of *el Mḥatta,* called *Sheikh Jāyel* by Musil and others. Here the holy place of Baal Peor is localized by some scholars.

From the Nebo platform is had a view that is most noteworthy and that impressed the ancient churchmen to such a degree that many regarded it as the point where Moses had his final view of the land. An objection to this could be raised if one were disposed to be very literal about Deuteronomy 3:27, since no eastward view is to be had from here. In the other three directions, however, the map of Palestine is spread out quite wonderfully. Given a clear atmosphere, one can see in the north the high mountain country of southern Gilead, and through a gap east of *es Salt* part also of the mountain country between the *'Ajlūn* and *Jerash.* In the southwest through a gap one can gaze across the Dead Sea to the oasis of En-gedi and above it see the distant mountains south of Hebron. Looking past the obstruction of the lower Nebo-spur, the *Rās Ṣiyāghah,* one sees on either side of it the northern part of the Dead Sea, and beyond it the high country of the promised land. The Jordan Valley is an open book from the Lake of Tiberias to Jericho. Says Musil in an account of his travels in Moab:

No wonder that at this glorious view the poor Bedouin may feel an irrepressible longing to journey westward across the valley into that paradisical land, where there is water a-plenty, where the rich verdure never seems to disappear, and where he believes he will find everything his heart desires.

The same urge will have been felt by the Israelites after their long sojourn in the grim wastes. The more tragic then the fate of Moses not to be permitted to enter this promised land; and we may add the sterner is the lesson conveyed by the fact that he was barred because he once had broken faith with the LORD at Kadesh (DEUT. 32:51).

But, as already mentioned, some of the sources, instead of speaking of Nebo, speak of the top of "the Pisgah." It was from that point that Balaam had last viewed the Hebrew encampment (NUM. 23:14). Musil held that the word designates a sector of the Abarim range—more particularly that part between the *Wadi 'Ayūn Mūsa* in the north and the *Seil el Kneiyēseh* in the south, and hence includes Mount Nebo. The "slopes of Pisgah" (JOSH. 12:3; DEUT. 3:17) then means the western declivities of this part of the range. One could also argue, considering the Semitic habit of thinking in terms of small units, that "the top [Hebrew *rōsh*] of the Pisgah" means rather a projecting promontory (Arabic *rās*) of a particular mountain. It is tempting to apply it to the *Rās*

Ṣiyāghah, which, as already noted, lies in front of Nebo, separated from the higher summit by a saddle. The thought gains support from the fact mentioned in Numbers 21:20 that from the top of Pisgah one looks down upon Yeshimon, i.e., the desert, of the *Ghōr el Belqā,* in which Beth-jeshimoth lies. The *Rās Ṣiyāghah* is indeed the appropriate vantage point from which to see the waste area south of the *Wadi el 'Azeimeh.*

It is not said that Moses died on the mountain, though a later hand (DEUT. 32:50) put it thus. The item about his burial is intriguing. He is said to have been interred "in a valley in the land of Moab, over against Beth-peor."

It is evidently the same valley where the Israelites are said to have remained (DEUT. 3:29) and hence the burial place was not far from the encampment. Whether the valley lying

"In the country of Moab, to the top of Pisgah, which looketh toward Jeshimon." (NUM. 21:20 A.V.)

"In the region of Moab by the top of Pisgah which looks down upon the desert." (NUM. 21:20 R.S.V.)

means the same valley is thus the question. If "the top of the Pisgah" be the *Rās Ṣiyāgha,* then the valley of Numbers 21:20 may well be that of the *'Ayūn Mūsa,* whose spring and waterfall and great cave (seventy-nine feet high, forty-five feet wide, seventy-six feet deep) with stalactites, are noteworthy and are visited by travelers willing to take the time to descend to them from Mount Nebo.

That Moses was buried in the land of innumerable dolmens, which mark the burials of men of the Stone Age, seems appropriate. The thirty days mourning for him in the plains of Moab (DEUT. 34:8) remind one of the fact that the mourning for Jacob, too, took place in this same vicinity (GEN. 50:10–11).

THE PROMISED LAND

The DESIGN on the preceding page shows a Canaanite fortress from Egyptian and Mesopotamian reliefs, a spearhead from Megiddo (Late Bronze or Early Iron Age), and figures which are tribute-bearing suppliants (Syrians) from an Egyptian relief.

TOP LEFT, *a drawing of the "Lordly Bowl." (C. F. Schaeffer, Mission Archéologique Francaise)* TOP RIGHT, *Hittite god and young king. (Oriental Institute, University of Chicago)* BOTTOM LEFT, *seal of a king of Carchemish on a cuneiform tablet found at Ras esh Shamra. (C. F. Schaeffer, Mission Archéologique Francaise, copyrighted)*

CHAPTER VIII

THE CONQUEST AND DIVISION

THE PERIOD IN WHICH the "Desert Wanderings" of Israel are in all probability to be placed is one of the most important in human history. In it began a great migration of peoples that ended an old cycle and inaugurated a new one. Greece and the Aegean world in general were overwhelmed by the Dorians and the old Mycenaean civilization came to an end. Large groups such as Achaeans, Sardinians, and Lycians seized coastal and island possessions and ranged as far as Libya. From Libya an invasion of Egypt was attempted, but was defeated by Merneptah (1234–1220 B.C.). This great Pharaoh, of whose reign relatively little is as yet known, also had to contend with some minor troubles in Palestine and Syria. He refers to them incidentally in a stela set up at Karnak to commemorate the Libyan victory. It is commonly known as the "Israel Stela," because it gives us the first historical mention of Israel in an inscription. The bronze sword of Merneptah recently found at Ugarit (*Rās esh Shamrā*) shows his influence in Syria.

Merneptah was followed by several lesser rulers with short reigns. The Nineteenth Dynasty then yielded to the Twentieth. Its founder, Seth-nakht (1200–1197 B.C.), also came from Raamses in the delta. He was succeeded by Ramses III (1197–1165 B.C.), the last great ruler of the new kingdom, for his successors, Ramses IV–XI, do not seem to have amounted to a great deal. The temple of *Medinet Habū* is his great monument. Under him occurred a new phase of migration of the sea peoples. They seem to have come from Asia Minor, where the Hittite kingdom perished about this time, and down the

Palestinian coast. Among them were the Peleset or Philistines and the Thekel. Ramses III defeated these peoples in a great battle by land and sea in the vicinity of Pelusium. His mighty efforts seem to have exhausted Egyptian strength. We may suppose that this vast cataclysm brought about economic disintegration, from which recovery of world prosperity could be only a gradual process. The Philistines were able to settle in southern Palestine, where they could occupy some cities, while the Thekel settled at Dor, on the coast south of Carmel.

The period was likewise an ideal one for new elements from the Arabian quarter to enter Palestine and establish themselves. Egyptian sovereignty was fading out. The local Canaanite kings were probably warring to create larger principalities, in which better economic conditions might prevail, but thereby were ruining each other and creating opportunities for invaders.

Nature of the Conquest Narratives

The glorious conclusion of the story of the Exodus and Wanderings saw Israel at the threshold of the land promised by the LORD to the patriarchs. Its great leader had blessed each of the tribes with words prophetic of their future and had died after seeing the land from Mount Nebo. Joshua, the son of Nun, had been appointed commander. The Book of Joshua now continues the story with a description of the Conquest (chapters 1–12) and an account of the distribution of the territories of Palestine among the tribes (chapters 13–22). Having done this the victorious leader assembles and admonishes his people's representatives and dies (chapters 23–24).

The conquest narratives of chapters 1–12 represent a religious history writing of a rather grim Old Testament spirit. The writers evidently put together what they were able to gather in their own time hundreds of years after the actual events. It is very unlikely that these materials give a complete story of what happened. The chief incidents are very much focussed on territory inhabited by the tribe of Benjamin and on southern Ephraim and concerned with places of local interest to their people. One must suspect that the narratives came from these quarters. Each tribe must have emphasized different places, where things of concern to it occurred and possibly even different invasion points. Indeed, many historians think that the confederacy of Hebrew tribes was formed only after the separate groups had completed independent migrations and that the thought of their all having come across the river near Jericho is a one-sided presentation, generalizing what had been the experience of only one tribe.

The Conquest of Jericho

The commission was given to Joshua to lead Israel on a path of conquest (JOSH. 1:1 f.). From (Abel-) Shittim (see page 124 and Color Map VI) where they were encamped two spies were sent out secretly to Jericho (JOSH. 2:1 f.), who, after the manner of spies, made contact with the local "underworld" where aid was most apt to be found. Starting from Abel-shittim the host went only as far as the Jordan, spending the night there before passing over to the other side (JOSH. 3:1 f.). A parallel account kept them at the river's bank for three days (JOSH. 3:2). The crossing took place in the harvest time or spring of the year, in which it is virtually impossible to ford the river (JOSH. 3:15). The Biblical narrative employed thinks of Israel as attended by special providences, and so a miracle like that at the Red Sea crossing takes care of the obstacle. Interest is focussed on the ark and the priest bearing it. With proper ceremony they enter the river, which thereupon is divided like the sea at the Exodus, while they stand in it, permitting the host to cross (JOSH. 3:13). But a different and seemingly a natural explanation of how it was possible to cross the Jordan is hinted at in one of the narratives used by the compiler of the present story and is included by him. According to that account the waters "stood in a heap" far up the river "at Adam the city that is beside Zarethan," while those below that point ran off to the Dead Sea, leaving the stream bed dry (JOSH. 3:16). This "standing in a heap" may refer to a damming up of the river by a natural cause, and as we shall see there is good evidence for such a possibility. The locality referred to in this remark cannot be in doubt.

The name of Adam, it seems, still survives in the ford of *ed Dāmieh* and at a rather small city mound *Tell ed Dāmieh,* which lies on a natural elevation east of the

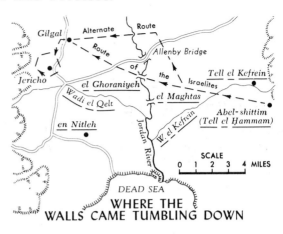

WHERE THE WALLS CAME TUMBLING DOWN

river. The *Zōr,* or depression in which the river flows, widens out here into a rich bottom land, joining with that around the mouth of the Jabbok. Adam guarded an important river crossing, with roads leading into the heart of both western and eastern Palestine. On the tell Late Bronze II and Iron I–II sherds are found, so that it was clearly a city that was inhabited in the times here referred to. But in the day of the Biblical writer it had evidently become less well known and required localization by a more familiar place, Zaretan (or Zarethan according to the R.S.V.; on its location see page 219).

In the *ed Dāmieh* locality the river skirts limestone cliffs, and it has repeatedly happened there that rocks have fallen into the river interrupting its flow. Such an occurrence took place in 1927, when the fall of a cliff one hundred and fifty feet high dammed up the Jordan for twenty-one hours.

Gilgal

In connection with the crossing two variants concerning a memorial have been combined in the present narrative (JOSH. 4:5-8). According to one version twelve stones were set up *in* the river bed at this point; according to the other version twelve stones were taken up *out* of the river and carried to the next camping place, Gilgal, which is described as "on the east border of Jericho"

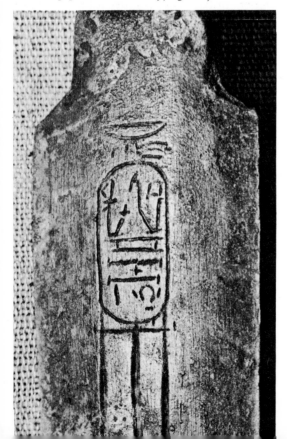

3.1 *Bronze sword of Pharaoh Merneptah from Ras esh Shamra. (Courtesy C. F. Schaeffer, Mission Archéologique Francaise, copyrighted)*

3.2 *Looking toward ancient Adam, buried in* Tell ed Dāmieh. *The mountain in the west later bore the Alexandrium* (Qarn Ṣarṭabeh). (*Courtesy Nelson Glueck*)

(JOSH. 4:19). That, of course, could mean northeast, due east or southeast, and so is not very precise.

Since the Jordan ford where the crossing was effected is not specified, the localization of Gilgal takes on a special interest, for if its site were known, the ford in line with it would have to be considered the one meant in this account.

The site first brought forward for Gilgal lies hard by a famous tamarisk tree, visible afar over the desolate plain, and called *She-jeret en Nitleh*. It was for many years the favorite localization of Gilgal. There are quite a number of *tumuli* (hillocks) there, but recent excavations by James L. Kelso have revealed nothing older than a church which existed in the fourth to ninth centuries A.D. and underwent many changes in construction. Attention has shifted since 1931 to *Khirbet el Mefjir*, northeast of old Jericho, a site more in line with the Madeba map. But excavations in 1936 by Baramki, for the Department of Antiquities, only brought to light in that mound a fine palace of the Omayyad Caliph Hisham (724–743 A.D.). However, the site is a large one and it seems highly probable that the Byzantine Gilgal and its Dodekalithon church, which Brocardus saw on his left when he came down to Jericho from the north in 1283 A.D., lay there, too. Recently, James Muilenburg in exploring and carrying on a brief dig at small ruin-sites close to *Khirbet el Mefjir* found abundant Iron Age remains, thus

lending weight to the supposition that Gilgal lay thereabouts. Like all ancient cult centers, it had a sacred story about the discovery of its sanctity. This story, however, is only partly preserved; it told of Joshua's vision of a man with a drawn sword in his hand (JOSH. 5:13–15).

If this be Gilgal, then a crossing of the Israelites coming from Abel-shittim (*Tell el Ḥammām*) might have taken place at the ford at *el Maghtās* (*el Hajleh*), or farther up stream at the ford called *el Ghoranīyeh* at the mouth of the *Wadi en Nu'eimeh*. Beyond the former ford was the town of Beth-hoglah (JOSH. 15:6; 18:19), at *'Ain Hajleh*, so there were established communications here.

The Fall of Jericho

It has long been known that an ancient city lay at *Tell es Sulṭān*, a high ruin-mound north of modern Jericho, close to the *'Ain es Sulṭān*, one of the best living springs of Palestine. Pioneer excavations were carried on here by a German expedition under E. Sellin and C. Watzinger in 1907–09. The work done there was later continued in 1930–36 under British auspices by John Garstang. Between 1952 and 1958 Kathleen Kenyon conducted seven seasons of excavation. Jericho has turned out to be earth's oldest city, as far as is known, for on bedrock was found a sanctuary that the excavator dates at 7800 B.C. One must imagine western Palestine as forested in those times, except in the *Ghor* (see pages 27, 35 f.). Jericho was a flourishing city in the Chalcolithic and Early Bronze ages, but reached its maximum development in the Middle Bronze Age. The city of that period had a glacis on which its strong walls rested. It was destroyed around 1550 B.C., apparently by the Egyptians, who at that time—in connection with the campaigns of Amenophis I (?)—destroyed many Palestinian cities. There is no trace of fresh fortifications having been constructed. Late Bronze Age occupation was very slight. What there was of it disappeared in the centuries in which the mound was unoccupied. An Israelite village was built there beginning about the tenth century, and ruins of what may have been a granary exist. Archaeology thus does not confirm the fall of a walled Jericho in the thirteenth century—the most probable time for the Hebrew invasion. Presumably the story of the fall of the city was inferred from the existence of the desolate mound and the sight of standing and collapsed portions of the great wall. It was a natural inference that the Israelites had destroyed the city. At the nearby Benjaminite sanctuary of Gilgal (1 SAM. 10:8, 11:14) the event may have been celebrated. The rebuilding of Jericho in the tenth century excellently fits the report of Hiel's rebuilding it in the time of Ahab (1 KINGS 16:34). From the Persian era of the city's life (cf. EZRA 2:34) came jar handles stamped with *Yh*, or *Yhw*, which when first found in 1908 provoked much speculation based on the supposition that this was the divine name. They were written in Aramaic script. But in 1934 it was shown by E. L. Sukenik that this was only an abridged writing for a hitherto misread inscription on jar handles which gave the name of the Persian province of Judaea: *Yhwd;* i.e., *Yehūd*.

The Conquest of Ai

According to the conquest saga of the Book of Joshua the next objective was Ai. The word simply means "the ruin mound," and is thus no name at all. Apparently the city's real name was forgotten, unless a recent theory that it was Beth-aven should prove to be acceptable. The location was already noted in connection with Abraham's altar between Bethel and Ai (GEN. 12:8). The site, strangely enough, is known as *et-Tell* to the Arabs, just as it was *hā 'Ai* to the Israelites.

First Attack on Ai

The narrative does not dwell on the route taken from Jericho to Ai by the scouts whom Joshua sent out, or of the route taken by the task force that these scouts believed capable of taking the city. The best track to Bethel is from *'Ain ed Dūq* via the *Wadi Lereid,* which, after an initial climb of fifteen hundred feet, makes the remaining seventeen hundred feet of the ascent in easier grades. From Jericho to Ai by this route is thirteen miles. It is unlikely that tradition thought of any but the easiest and best road —the one pilgrims from Bethel will naturally have taken to go to Gilgal. The task force was defeated and according to our translations chased as far as Shebarim (JOSH. 7:5). Shebarim is not a proper name, however, but merely means "quarries" or "benches of rock," and here refers to the first part of the rocky gorge (*Wadi Sneisil*) through which the force had to retreat to get back to the main valley leading down to *'Ain ed Dūq.* The men of Ai "smote them in the going down," i.e., that the losses were heaviest at the point where the declivity began and where they had to funnel into the gorge.

The Vale of Achor

The defeat was interpreted as implying divine disfavor and led to an investigation as to what had caused it. Allegedly this was determined by "lot" and produced the finding that a man named Achan belonging to the tribe of Judah had violated the order to destroy the spoils of Jericho by taking a "Babylonish garment," or "mantle from Shinar," and a bar of gold. He hid the objects under his tent. Achan is then executed.

The story of Josh. 7:24–26 explains the name of a certain valley of Achor as "valley of trouble." It is clearly attached to a valley that bore the name in the time of the author, who knew of a cairn held to be Achan's burial place. In the Copper Scroll from Qumran, listing the hiding places of treasure (page 18), one such is the cairn of Achan in the vale of Achor. The place was thus known in the first century A.D.

The vale of Achor has been diversely located, but the identification currently enjoying the most favor is that of Noth with "the little valley" (*el Buqei'ah*) which lies west of Qumran and is about four miles long and less than two miles wide. It was explored in 1955 by Cross and Milik. Three fortified Iron Age II settlements were found, perhaps established by Jehoshaphat in the ninth century B.C. and lasting to the exile. If Qumran was the City of Salt of Josh. 15:61–62, the others may be the towns mentioned before it: Middin, Secacah, and Nibshan.

The Capture of Ai

After the execution of Achan the attack on Ai is renewed. The strategist Joshua sends part of his force to a point behind the city. The road that passes Ai to go to Bethel is obscured west of the former place by a ridge of broken rocks. In these rocks, it has been held, the ambuscading group concealed itself. When the main force fled toward the gorge leading to the Jordan Valley and was pursued by the defenders of Ai, the men in ambush captured the town and set fire to it. The main force then turned against its pursuers, who were now attacked from both sides and destroyed. There was a great stone heap at the gate of Ai allegedly marking the burial place of its king.

Ai was the scene of excavations by a French expedition conducted by Madame Krause-Marquet in 1933–34. These excavations showed that it had a five-century period of occupation in the Early Bronze Age, but

that it then lay uninhabited for a thousand years. It is not surprising, therefore, that its true name was lost. A short period of renewed occupation of that site followed in Early Iron I (1200–1000 B.C.), and was presumably by Israelites. The archaeological evidence thus suggests that the story of the fall of Ai arose in local tradition, connecting this impressive ruin-mound with the Hebrew conquest. If a city hereabouts was actually taken by invaders coming from the Jordan country it might have been Bethel.

The continuation of the story introduces the account of the building of an altar on Mount Ebal and the reading of the book of the law there (Josh. 8:30–35). Since there were Canaanite cities to be captured before this point could be reached, this seems rather premature. It could, however, hang together with a tradition of a more northerly river crossing at Adam in which the objective would have been Shechem.

Canaanite Cities in Israel

The capture of Ai was only a first step. Beyond lay other city-states. Would the Hebrews have to reduce them one by one? The Book of Joshua does not tell us how some important nearby places like Bethel and Michmash and others west of them were overcome or could be bypassed. It just selects another significant incident which is of a different nature, showing how a very important city-state north of Jerusalem, with its tributary cities, made peace with Israel, and thus avoided having to fight for its life. The underlying historical fact is that these Canaanite cities were still inhabited by Canaanites in the days of these writers. This peculiar fact required an explanation and the account about the Gibeonites provides one (Josh. 9:3 f.).

Gibeon has usually been sought at *ej Jib*, eight miles north of Jerusalem on the road branching off toward the coast. The identification was proven correct through the discovery there of jar handles with the name Gibeon engraved. Excavations have been carried on there by James B. Pritchard since 1956 on behalf of the Church Divinity School of the Pacific and the University of Pennsylvania Museum. It is a sixteen-acre site, and so the city that stood here could well be described as "a great city like one of the royal cities" (JOSH. 10:2). It was surrounded by a wall ten feet thick, broadened to twenty-six feet where the towers were placed. Of its waterworks something will be said later (page 192).

Gibeon had three tributary cities, two of which we will encounter again. The third, Chephirah, survives in *Khirbet Kefireh,* an impressive hilltop location of four to five acres, southwest of *ej Jīb.* The others are:

Beeroth, the location of which is also much debated. It is usually sought at *el Bireh,* but the names are not connected in any way. A recent theory would identify it with the town that lay on *Nebi Samwīl.*

Kiriath-jearim, two miles south of Chephirah, a six-acre site on a commanding eminence, controlling the present road from Jerusalem to Jaffa (which, however, was not the main route in ancient times). The name "forest-town" suggests that this was a wooded area at one time (cf. page 175).

Defeat of the League of Kings

The surrender of Gibeon frightened and incensed other Canaanite city states to the south. Jerusalem allegedly felt threatened and with a league of others sought to bring the Gibeonites back into line (JOSH. 10:1 f.). The list of cities is not preserved in its original form. Jerusalem and Hebron have usurped the places of Debir and Libnah. We will comment only on two cities.

Jarmuth (*Khirbet el Yarmūk*), sixteen miles west of Jerusalem in a dominating position, with a view over the coastal plain and the ocean. It was a six- to eight-acre city on the road from Jerusalem.

Eglon, which probably lay at one of the first sites excavated in Palestine, *Tell el Ḥesī* which was formerly taken to be Lachish. The identification with Eglon is recommended by the fact that the name still clings to a nearby site (*Khirbet 'Ajlān*). The excavations revealed that the fortified city at *Tell el Ḥesī* dates from the Middle Bronze Age and existed until the fourteenth century B.C.

The Battle of Gibeon

When the league of kings attacked Gibeon, Joshua had to march to its aid. The Hebrew base camp apparently was at Gilgal, and so this meant an all-night march (JOSH. 10:9). The flight of the defeated foe to the coastal region was via the "Ascent of Beth-horon," so named from the point of view of those living in the lowlands. From upper Beth-horon (*Beit 'Ūr el fōqā*) the road drops off downhill to "lower Beth-horon" (*Beit 'Ūr et taḥtā*). The latter was the ancient city;

3.3 *A distant view of* ej Jīb *from the north.* (*Matson Photo Service*)

3.4 *Lower Beth-horon. (Matson Photo Service)*

the site exhibits Late Bronze Age remains and evidently covered eight to ten acres. It had a strategic position, blocking the entrance into the heart of the country from the plain, for this was the main route to Jaffa, even for Jerusalem. The descent from Upper to Lower Beth-horon was a particularly dangerous one for a defeated army, as its retreating files could be assailed from the slopes above the road. A hailstorm is said to have increased the difficulty of that day of battle for the Canaanites (though the reference to its lasting until they got to Azekah may be discounted). Joshua, in the pursuit of the defeated foe, implored the sun to stay over Gibeon behind him in the east (it was thus in the morning hours), and the moon over the vale of Aijalon ahead of him in the west. Nothing is said of Aijalon's capture, and according to Judges 1:35 it remained an Amorite city for a long time. The name still survives in *Yālo*. The modern village lies on the site of the Late Bronze Age city, which guarded the point where the Beth-horon road emerged from the hills into the lowlands. In times still earlier Aijalon stood on the prominent height above *Yālo*.

The Kings in the Cave of Makkedah

In the oldest version of the events the battle probably did not extend beyond Beth-horon. There Joshua gave up the pursuit and returned to Gilgal (JOSH. 10:15). But a younger version described the pursuit as continuing on to Azekah and Makkedah

(cf. verses 10 and 28 f.). Azekah is identical with *Tell Zakarīya,* described by Garstang as a "bold site filling a strategic position below Jarmuth, where the *Wadi es Samt* opens as it emerges from the hills." The location of Makkedah, however, still remains uncertain. A recent suggestion puts it about seven miles southeast of *Beit Jibrīn* (at *Tell Maqdūm*), which agrees well with Eusebius' eight Roman miles from Eleutheropolis.

A supplementary episode, localized near Makkedah, is given in Joshua 10:16–27. Features of local topography play such a role in the story that the latter must be regarded as explanatory of them.

The Capture of Cities of the Shephelah

A further supplement, Joshua 10:28–43, elaborates on a campaign in this general area. Its original intent was to tell how the cities of the five kings were taken; but the list varies from that given in the third verse of chapter 10, as already noted before. Joshua, in the manner later demonstrated by Assyrian warriors like Sennacherib, went to one mighty fortress of the Canaanites after the other, apparently easily taking them. The individual cities either have been mentioned or will occur in other connections.

A summary statement (JOSH. 10:41) indicates that now the whole region from Kadesh-Barnea to Gaza and "all the country of Goshen as far as Gibeon" were subdued. Goshen (cf. JOSH. 11:16), which has the same name as the region in Egypt (cf. page 93), is used as a term for the territory lying between the Judaean mountains and the Negeb.

The Conquest of Galilee

Under the leadership of the king of Hazor a fresh coalition was formed against Joshua in the extreme north of Palestine. Hazor is believed to have lain southwest of Lake Semechonitis, at the point where the road from Sidon to Beth-shean meets one leading from Megiddo to Damascus. It was a key place. The suggested site is *Tell el Qedah,* or

Tell Waqqās; it was discovered by Garstang in 1926. Excavations were conducted at this vast site during 1955–58 by Yigael Yadin and a Hebrew University expedition. The history of the city could be traced from 2700–150 B.C. Remarkable discoveries included a Canaanite temple, similar in ground plan to Solomon's. A complete destruction befell the city in the thirteenth century, no doubt the one reported in Josh. 11 :11. A gate like the Solomonic one at Megiddo was found (cf. 1 Kings 9:15). Evidence of the destruction by Tiglath-pileser (2 Kings 15:29) was also secured.

Three additional cities were in the coalition:

Madon, probably situated on the Horns of *Ḥattīn.* The ancient name has survived at *Khirbet Madin,* half a mile to the northwest of the old site, which represents a strong city, especially of Late Bronze Age times. From this famous height it dominated the area.

Shimron, in Joshua 12:20 Shimron-meron (Shemesh-meron?, cf. *Samsi-muruna* of Tiglathpileser); perhaps Marun on road from Tyre to Dan.

Achshaph. The one that is meant here is perhaps that of Joshua 19:25, and must have lain in the plain of Acre, where there are some fifteen tells showing Late Bronze Age occupation. *Tell Berweh,* at the foot of the hills and commanding a road coming down from near *Ṣāfed,* is a likely site for it.

To these cities were added the kings of the northern Palestinian hill country and of the plain south of Chinneroth, or Chinnereth. The city of Chinnereth lay on a hill called *Tell el ʿOreimeh,* "mound of the harp," overlooking the Sea of Galilee and near the later Capernaum. Excavations were conducted at this site by a Catholic group. An Egyptian stela, much broken, was found there.

Then are added the kings in the coastal plain and in the borders of Dor on the west. Dor lay on the coast, north of the village of *eṭ Ṭanṭūra* in the Mount Carmel vicinity, and was a harbor town. It played a role in Egyptian days as evidenced by the story

3.5 *Probable site of Azekah* (Tell Zakarīyeh). (*Matson Photo Service*)

of Wen Amon, and in Hellenistic times ("Dora"). To all these adversaries is added the oft recurring list of the pre-Israelitic inhabitants of Palestine (see page 69), concluding with "the Hivites under Hermon in the land of Mizpeh."

The kings of the hostile coalition encamped at "the waters of Merom." It was long taken for granted, both on account of the "waters" and on account of the seeming need for a plain where chariots could be used, that Lake Semechonitis is meant; on some maps that sheet of water even appears as Lake Merom. But Merom is just an archaic form of Meron (the Greek translation has *Maron*) and a place named *Mārūn* to this day lies west-northwest of the modern town of *Ṣāfed.* Here there is a plain, and abundant water is provided by a spring that flows down through a valley of that name (*Wadi Mārūn*) to the Lake of Galilee. These must be "the waters of Merom." The ancient city of Meron has not yet been discovered.

The Canaanites were defeated in this battle. A part of them fled westward to Sidon and to Misrephoth-maim. Sidon, here called "the great," lay on the Phoenician coast at *Ṣaidā* (see page 149). "Misrephoth of the waters" is clearly the Bronze Age site *Khirbet el Mesherifeh,* south of the "Tyrian Ladder" (page 33). Some warm springs close by the mound, which doubtless had some importance for a heathen cult, account for its peculiar name. Other Canaanite fugitives fled to the valley of Mizpeh, which was re-

3.6 *The Valley of Mizpeh?* (*A view of Ḥaṣbaya from the upper mountain side.*) (*Matson Photo Service*)

ferred to above as "land of Mizpeh" and localized "under Hermon." Such a flight might have led to Hazor and on northward to *Ḥaṣbaya,* where the lower *Wadi et Tēm* would provide a suitable "valley of Mizpeh," or else across the Jordan to *el Quneiṭrah* and to the *Baniās* vicinity, where *Qal'at eṣ Ṣubeibeh* would provide a suitable high point for a place named Mizpeh.

Retrospects

The available narratives about the conquest of Canaan have been rehearsed. The compiler of the book now brings in another review (JOSH. 11:16 f.), since the preceding one of 10:40–43 had not yet taken into con-

3.7 *Another possible location for Mizpeh:* Qala'at eṣ Ṣubeibeh, *with ruins of Crusader fortress.* (*Courtesy Institut Francais d'Archéologie, Beyrouth, Liban*)

sideration the conquest of the northern part of the country. The final statement is of interest:

> Even from the mount Halak, that goeth up to Seir, even unto Baal-gad in the valley of Lebanon under mount Hermon." (JOSH. 11:16–17 A.V.)

> . . . *from Mount Halak, that rises toward Seir, as far as Baal-gad in the valley of Lebanon below Mount Hermon."* (JOSH. 11:16–17 R.S.V.)

New in this description is the mention of the southern limit, Mount Halak, literally "the smooth mountain." In Joshua 10:41 a more westerly point, the city of Kadesh-barnea, was given as southern outpost. Mount Halak lies on the east side of the tableland, near the *'Arabah.* It was rediscovered by Musil in 1897. When exploring the inhospitable Negeb, he learned that a mountain on which he was standing was called *Jebel Ḥalāq* and that the territory west of it was composed of lands belonging to *Sbeiṭa,* where there is a ruined city of Byzantine times. The mountain is here described as "the one going up to Mt. Seir." The latter, as we have already seen, is in the Edomite country on the other side of the *'Arabah,* more particularly its southern portion, the *Jebel esh Shera.* The *Jebel Ḥalāq* is low by comparison with the lofty Edomite crags and worthy of mention only because it is the last west-Palestinian height passed on the road leading down from Beersheba into the *'Arabah* as one goes toward Seir. That the mountain itself "rises toward" Seir may be a succinct way of saying that its broad side faces in the direction of that region, which is quite true, since it runs from southwest to northeast.

The other details in Joshua 11:16–23 have either been explained already or will receive attention in connection with the first chapter of Judges (see page 146 f.).

Another comprehensive retrospect is provided in Joshua 12:1–6, by way of impressively rounding out the facts of the conquest. The most important part of it is a survey of the kings allegedly defeated by Joshua and Israel west of the Jordan (JOSH. 12:7 f.).

The Apportionment of Palestine Among the Tribes

In spite of all these conquests that are reported as having been made in Joshua's lifetime, it was plain that not all objectives had been attained. A divine revelation given to the aging leader enumerates districts not yet subjugated, and promises that the LORD himself will drive out all these people before Israel. Joshua is to proceed and make the land allotments (JOSH. 13: 1–7).

The Distribution

The chapters of the Book of Joshua dealing with the actual distribution of the country among the nine and one-half tribes contain three kinds of materials, which have been fused by the authors or editors: 1) Short items about events connected with the conquest of various territories and about Canaanitic states that remained independent; this scattered material duplicates some that is found in the first chapter of the Book of Judges. 2) A detailed account of the boundaries of the tribal territories. 3) Lists of the cities or towns in the tribal territories.

Of these materials, those dealing with the tribal boundaries were the most important to the editor of the Book of Joshua and hence are put first in most instances.

Western Palestine is pretty well covered by these descriptions, though no boundaries are given for Simeon and Dan and the northern boundaries of Asher and Naphthali are not fully preserved.

This system of the tribal boundaries has sometimes been regarded as pure theory. But more probably it represents an early state of tribal claims that was soon outdated when the monarchy arose and the tribal boundaries replaced by administrative divisions. When the separate tribes were still conscious of their importance, the boundaries between them had to be agreed upon and quarrels over them had to be settled either by force or by adjudication. A federation or alliance of tribes such as existed at the time of the Song of Deborah (Judges 5) must have implied mutual recognition of boundaries. At such a period lists of border towns could well have been set up.

In the religiously oriented Book of Joshua, quite naturally, the tribal-boundary system is divinely decreed. Joshua is commanded to apportion Palestine among the nine and one-half tribes, two and one-half having received their portion previously from Moses (JOSH. 13:7 f.). The division is to be executed by casting the lot. That idea was suggested by the custom of apportioning the agricultural lands of a town to the citizens through lottery. It was held that the same procedure was followed on a grand scale when the tribes received their portions, and the thought is that thereafter each tribe took possession of its assigned territory.

For the sake of completeness, the portions given the two and one-half tribes on the other side of the Jordan, as already related in the story of Moses, are restated in Joshua 13. But the real concern is with western Palestine. A special lot is given to Caleb the Kenizzite (GEN. 15:19), but this section really stands apart from the assignments to the nine and one-half tribes. We naturally cannot enter into the details of the boundary descriptions here, any more than one would dwell on those of the thirteen American colonies. Such matters are important, but highly technical. The general reader finds more rewarding a map-picture (see Color Map VI) showing him the results of the research undertaken by surveyors to trace old boundaries, and he cannot quite share the thrill of going over the ground with the old field-notes of long ago.

The third type of material in this part of the Book of Joshua, that of the lists of cities and towns in the tribal territories, is believed to be drawn from an older document devoted purely to that objective. The compiler of the present book then combined this information with the boundary descriptions. But the town listing is not handled uniformly. While the southern tribes—Judah (15:21–62), Benjamin (18:21–28), Simeon (19:1–8) and Dan (19:40–46)—are treated in detail, the highly important central area of Ephraim and Manasseh, is not covered at all. The information about the cities of the northern tribes—Issachar (19:17–23), Zebulun (10–16), Asher (24–31) and Naphthali (19:32–39) is meager.

There are twelve groups of places which one may designate by the best known city in each group. When the territories represented by these city and town lists are visualized on a map (see Color Map VI) we get what actually seems to have been the administrative divisions of the kingdom of Judah at the time of King Josiah (see map, page 310). Perhaps the meager listings of the northern tier were derived from a similar list set up at the time when King Josiah, at the cracking up of the Assyrian Empire, sought to expand his territory into the north. A trace of his ambition in that direction may still be seen in the report that the effect of his religious reforms extended as far as Naphthali (2 CHRON. 34:6).

After the tribal boundaries and city lists have been given, some loose ends are gathered up in materials of rather late origin. We get an account of the Cities of Refuge and the Cities of the Levites (Joshua 20, 21).

The Altar on the Other Side of the Jordan

An interesting item comes up in connection with the dismissal of the Reubenites, Gadites, and half of the Manasseh to go to their Transjordan portions (JOSH. 22:1 f.). We hear of an altar of great size set up by them on the western side of the river (in the land of Canaan!). This is considered a provocation by the other tribes. A delegation headed by the High Priest's son is sent to make complaint. The matter is peaceably settled when the Transjordan tribes explain that the altar was not built for bringing sacrifice but rather as a witness of the fidelity of the eastern tribes to the religion of the LORD. This debate must be understood in the light of the reformation of King Josiah (2 KINGS 23), which forbade such altars. This one probably stood near Adam (Hos. 6:7 R.S.V.).

Joshua's Farewell Address

A great leader of the people must pass from the scene in a manner worthy of him. The youngest of the Hexateuch sources makes Joshua, in chapter 23, assemble Israel and deliver a farewell address. In chapter 24 the Israelites are assembled all over again, but this is merely due to the fact that we now get a different version of Joshua's last act, drawn from earlier authors. The place of the gathering is Shechem. Since we subsequently, in the period of the Judges, still find the Canaanites in possession of Shechem (Judges 9), one is at a loss to see how Israel could have been assembled there. They are doubtless pictured as congregated at the open-air sanctuary outside the city. (JOSH. 24:26). There can be little doubt but that the spot referred to is the same one mentioned in the narratives of Abraham and Jacob (cf. page 86). The story duplicates Jacob's action in doing away with the foreign gods (GEN. 35:4; cf. JOSH. 24:14). The pillar that stood near the altar is reported to have been set up by Joshua and is interpreted as a "witness." This is an interesting interpretation by a later age that had progressed beyond the worship of stone pillars, but that still felt too awed by the venerable antiquity of the object to destroy it.

After thus solemnly enjoining his people Joshua, "the servant of the LORD," died.

"And they buried him in the border of his inheritance in Timnath-serah, which is in mount Ephraim, on the north side of the hill of Gaash." (JOSH. 24:30 A.V.)

"And they buried him in his own inheritance at Timnath-serah, which is in the hill country of Ephraim, north of the mountain of Gaash." (JOSH. 24:30 R.S.V.)

It seems strange that the inheritance of Joshua was so far away from the scene of his major deeds. The name is doubtless preserved in *Khirbet Tibneh,* which lies seventeen miles or more west of Shechem on the ridge between two sources of the *Nahr el 'Aujā* and on a hill which is easily accessible only from the west, as there are steep declivities on the north and east. It is described as a true tell with a beautiful contour, though not with great depth of debris. Late Bronze and Early Iron Age sherds show that it was inhabited in Joshua's time. It is regarded as a site worthy of excavation. Timnath-serah is called Timnath-heres in Judges 2:9, so evidently it was a seat of sun-worship in Canaanite days. The significance of the site rests on the fact that it controlled a road ascending a tributary valley to the south. It is thus understandable that the Seleucids fortified the place (cf. Thamnathah in I MACC. 9:50). The hilly region to the south of this town, culminating at *Beit Ello,* must be the hill of Gaash. Among David's men of valor was Hiddai of the brooks of Gaash (2 SAM. 23:30). There are numerous rock tombs opposite *Tibneh* on the south, but none of them go back to the Iron Age. In Eusebius' time a tomb of Joshua was shown in this neighborhood.

Belatedly, indeed, is reported the burial of the remains of Joseph (JOSH. 24:32) in the field which Jacob had purchased from the Shechemites (GEN. 33:19). The traditional tomb of Joseph (see map, page 85) is shown east of ancient Shechem and doubtless lay close to the holy place marked by altar, tree and stone pillar of Genesis 33:20, 35:4 and Joshua 24:25–26.

Fittingly the book concludes with the passing of the priest Eleasar who appeared prominently in it as son and successor of Aaron. Eleasar was buried at the "Gibeah of Phinehas" (his son) on Mount Ephraim. There is no clear indication anywhere in the Old Testament as to where this Gibeah lay. But Eusebius mentions a Geba five Roman miles north of Gophna (*Jifna*); since Gibeah and Geba are almost interchangeable names, this could be the Gibeah of Phinehas and it is in the required Ephraimite region. A site called *et Tell* south of *Sinjīl* is believed to fit the church father's specifications.

The great saga of the birth of a nation fades out with these memorials of personages. Viewed in its totality, it is not only a story full of marvels but a marvelous story, of a scope and depth no other national saga can equal.

CHAPTER IX

THE PERIOD OF THE JUDGES

IT WAS A NEW WORLD in which the events reported in the Book of Judges took place. The historical cataclysms lay in the past and the pattern of the future was only emerging. The peoples newly pushed to the fore in Palestine, Syria, Mesopotamia and Asia Minor were just beginning either to adapt themselves to the cultures of the earlier inhabitants or to develop some new cultural synthesis of their own. Their life apparently went on without interference from the greater powers that had previously held the stage. Of these the Hittite empire had been utterly wiped out, and the Hurrian state of Mitanni was likewise gone. Babylonia, which had so long been ruled by a Cassite Dynasty, had sunk into a weakened condition. The state of affairs there is high lighted by the fact

that in the twelfth century B.C., Elam on the east was able to flourish and develop a great culture. Its kings now wrote inscriptions in their own language and a distinctive cuneiform script. One of the kings, *Shutruknah-hunte,* carried off as spoil to Susa some of the greatest monuments of Babylonia's past, including the Stela of Naram-Sin and the Code of Hammurabi. He installed his son as ruler in Babylonia, and when the son succeeded, he brought the statues of the great deities of Babylon and Erech to Susa. His brother and successor exercised control to the very borders of Assyria.

But the Elamite sovereignty was terminated by a new dynasty that arose in Babylonia—the Second Dynasty of Isin, whose third and most important ruler was Nebuchadnezzar I (c. 1130 B.C.). It was not possible for this dynasty to flourish very prominently because, in addition to having Elam on its flank, it had Assyria for a northern neighbor of increasing consequence. Under Tiglathpileser I (1112–1074 B.C.), Assyria embarked on the path of its destiny which was to lead it to new heights far beyond any dreamed of by Shamshi-Adad I many centuries before. This new Assyria was a product of the fusion of Semites and Hurrians. Tiglathpileser had to ward off the encroachment of the migrating Aramaeans who were establishing themselves along the Euphrates and in Syria.

The mightiest nation of the past, Egypt, had sunk into an enfeebled condition after the rule of Ramses III (1197–1165 B.C.). The rulers Ramses IV–XI continued to reside in Tanis. Political power was pushed into the background by the rise of the power of the priesthood of Thebes, which established a sort of theocratic state at that city. Ramses IV (c. 1165 B.C.) was the last Pharaoh to work the mines in Sinai.

A vivid light is thrown on the impotence of proud Egypt by the story of the journey of the Theban ambassador Wen-Amon to Byblos in Phoenicia to obtain timber for the sacred barges of the god Amon. He is compelled to listen to the jibes of the prince of Byblos for coming on a Syrian vessel and without means of transporting the desired lumber. The treatment he receives would have been unthinkable in the days of Egyptian greatness.

Deliverers and Judges

Between the entry of the Israel tribes into the Promised Land and the beginning of an Israelite monarchy there was a period of consolidation. There were struggles with the unsubdued Canaanite city-states; there were invasions by new foes from the outside who took advantage of the anarchy in the land to lay hands on parts of it; there were even inter-tribal struggles and tribal-territorial

shifts. Over against Canaanite or foreign oppression there arose men with the divine gift of leadership, and who are remembered as "deliverers."

In addition to the stories of such heroes the compiler of the Book of Judges had available a list of functionaries who were called "Judges." The years of their office-holding are given with exact rather than round numbers, thus indicating excellent tradition. Perhaps because Jephthah is called a judge, but also is the subject of a "deliverer" story, the compiler of the book viewed all the rest of the deliverers "judges," and considered the period as such the Period of the Judges. Actually this is artificial. It seems probable that those specifically called "judges" had a judicial function. The institution has its counterpart in Phoenicia, where we hear of annually elected judges standing at the head of colonies like Carthage, and of judges taking the place of kings for brief terms (so in Tyre, where judges governed in 563–556 B.C.).

A chronology of sorts, totaling 411 years, follows from adding the figures of the oppressions, periods of peace, and judgeships

3.8 *Ancient Gebal or Byblos in Phoenicia, where great discoveries of old Phoenician times were made by Pierre Montet and Maurice Dunand.* (*Courtesy Institut Francais d'Archéologie, Beyrouth, Liban*)

given in various chapters of Judges. If one puts the Exodus in the thirteenth century B.C., the years must certainly be lowered. The Jephthah story estimates the period since the Transjordan tribes had occupied their territories as three hundred years (JUDG. 11:26). Even that allows more than seems probable if one dates Saul's kingship around 1000 B.C.

Review of the Conquest

Before giving us the stories of Israel's early heroes in Judges 3:7–16:31, the compiler of the book prefixes a preliminary section, of which chapter 1 is one of the most important passages in the Bible from the point of view of the historian.

Judah's Role

After the death of Joshua, the compiler of Judges reports, the Israelites had to possess themselves of their assigned territories; the battles fought under the son of Nun were in no sense yet an occupation of Palestine. They inquired of the LORD as to who was to go forth first. The oracle declared Judah should make a beginning. A battle is fought at Bezek and Adonibezek is captured, humiliated and brought to Jerusalem, apparently by Judah, thus presupposing this tribe's possession of the city. But this version of events is composed of faded memories. Adonibezek must be corrected to Adonizedek (JOSH. 10:1). Neither he nor the tribe of Judah has any business in the northerly Bezek, a place that we will encounter in the story of Saul (1 SAM. 11:8). The "negative account" of verse 21 f. says that Jerusalem was not taken by Judah. And since we know that it was captured by David (2 SAM. 5:6 f.), the story here told that the Judaeans took it and burned it apparently reflects that later event.

We next have the report in Judges that Judah then took Hebron and Debir (Kiriath-sepher). In the story of Joshua 14:6–15, however, it is Caleb, the Kenizzite who obtains Hebron as his portion, and the assumption is that he captured it. In the later view here represented, Caleb's Kenizzite origin is lost sight of and he has simply become a Judaean clan. Judah's next objective is the city of Debir, then known as Kiriath-sepher. We learn how this was taken by a clan related to or affiliated with Caleb.

> "And Caleb said, He that smiteth Kiriath-sepher, and taketh it, to him will I give Achsah my daughter to wife. . . .
>
> And she said unto him, Give me a blessing: for thou hast given me a south land; give me also springs of water. And Caleb gave her the upper springs and the nether springs." (JUDG. 1:12, 15 A.V.)

> *"And Caleb said, 'He who attacks Kiriath-sepher and takes it, I will give him Achsah my daughter as wife.' . . . She said to him, 'Give me a present; since you have set me in the land of the Negeb, give me also springs of water.' And Caleb gave her the upper springs and the lower springs."* (JUDG. 1:12, 15 R.S.V.)

The location of Debir is still uncertain. *Tell Beit Mirsim* in the Shephelah, or foothills country, one of the largest mounds of Palestine, though with less depth of debris than that of Lachish (*Tell ed Duweir*), has been urged as a likely candidate. An expedition of the American School of Oriental Research and Xenia Theological Seminary carried on methodical excavations there in 1926–1932 and clarified the history of the site in an exemplary manner. City walls and revetment are well preserved. The occupation of the place ended with the Babylonian exile. The excavators of *Tell Beit Mirsim*, W. F. Albright and M. G. Kyle, held that the springs or wells (*gullōth*) mentioned in the request of Achsah refer to certain shafts giving access to the ground water which are typical of this region. There are such wells of undoubted antiquity a mile below and two miles above *Tell Beit Mirsim,* which would excellently fit the upper and lower wells Achsah received. But others find these wells in the springs above and below the road at the *Seil ed Dilbeh,* five and three-quarter miles southwest of Hebron on the way to Beersheba, and would put Kiriath-sepher at a site to the south of it (most recently *Khirbet Rabūd*).

Not only the Kenizzites but also the Kenites were closely linked with Judah at first.

> "And the children of the Kenite, Moses' father in law, went up out of the city of palm trees with the children of Judah into the wilderness of Judah, which lieth in the south of Arad; and they went and dwelt among the people." (JUDG. 1:16 A.V.)

> *"And the descendants of the Kenite, Moses' father-in-law, went up with the people of Judah from the city of palms into the wilderness of Judah, which lies in the Negeb near Arad; and they went and settled with the people."* (JUDG. 1:16 R.S.V.)

Judah's campaign of conquest is construed as starting from the Jericho area. That may be an attempt to harmonize the course of events with the picture of the conquest given in the Book of Joshua; Judah's actual invasion route will have been from the south (cf. NUM. 21:1 f.). By the "wilderness of Arad" is meant the country near that city which lay toward the *'Arabah* at *Tell 'Arād.* But the Kenites did not stay there long—they went on southward and dwelt with "the people" (Hebrew *hā'ām*). However, this is a case where a word has been clipped at the end. The text can and must be restored to read "Amalekites" on the basis of manuscripts of the Greek version, even though the Revised Standard Version did not do this. The change is confirmed by what we hear of the Kenites later on (1 SAM. 15:6).

Next Judah co-operated with the Simeonites in the conquest and destruction of Zephath, which since that time got the name "Hormah" (JUDG. 1:17). This evidently is a different version of what was already reported in Numbers 21:3 (see page 118).

In a concluding general statement in Judges 1:19, we are told that Judah conquered the hill country but could not take the (coastal) plain, because the inhabitants had chariots. This shows that the report of the capture of Gaza, Ascalon and Ekron (verse 18), all of which lay in the plain, is unreliable; that verse probably was added in late times to furnish a ground for Jewish expansion in this direction, such as was carried out by the Maccabees. Of different quality are the statements that follow in verses 20–23. They concede that Judah could not take the cities of the plain, but was restricted to the mountains; that Caleb drove out the Anakim from Hebron and that Jerusalem, too, was not taken and that the Jebusites continued to live there until the writer's own day. Here we strike the solid rock of reliable tradition.

Judah's role in the conquest seems to have been a very inconspicuous one. Basically, the picture given in Genesis 38 of alliance and intermarriage with the Canaanites reflects this tribe's settlement. Its membership in the "Israel" confederacy was not acknowledged by the real Israel tribes.

Joseph's Expansion

The decisive act of "Joseph," the older tribal unit that subsequently divided into Ephraim and Manasseh, was the taking of Bethel, which played such an important role in Hebrew history and tradition. Bethel's location cannot be in doubt. It lay to the right of the road leading northward from Jerusalem, about eleven miles from the latter place. It occupied a spur jutting southward from a main ridge, with a spring at its foot. The name has survived with a slight phonetic change in the modern *Beitīn,* which stands on the ancient site. The city had a good defensive position; the northern approach to it was once protected by a moat. The story conceded that the Hebrews got Bethel through an act of betrayal on the part of a citizen apprehended in the fields. This individual is said to then have gone to the land of the Hittites (here=Syria) and there to have founded a city named Luz. The story-teller must have seen such a Syrian city, but no reference to it has been found as yet in the Assyrian inscriptions unless, perchance, it is the *Ullaza* of the Amarna letters. Since *Beitīn* is an inhabited town only limited opportunity for excavation exists there. Such were carried out by Albright in 1927 and 1934 and by J. L. Kelso in 1954 and 1957. Actual city life began here in the Middle Bronze Age (*c.* 2000 B.C.). In the Hyksos period (*c.* 1700 B.C.) a fine north wall, still standing to a height of ten feet, was built. A wall in the west with a tower dates from *c.* 1500 B.C. The city underwent a terrific destruction in the thirteenth century, no doubt the one which JUDGES 1:25 attributes to the Joseph tribes. This helps to fix the date of the Hebrew conquest of the region. The Israelite city that rose on the ruins was not destroyed by Nebuchadnezzar in 587 B.C., being regarded as outside the Judean territory, but was destroyed *c.* 550 B.C. and then no doubt by Nabonidus for some unknown reason. Small objects of interest found include an Astarte cylinder of *c.* 1300–1100 B.C. and a clay stamp with a South Arabian inscription, dating from *c.* 800 B.C. The former illustrates the ancient cult of Bethel; the stamp may have accompanied a shipment of incense for the Israelite temple shortly before the time of Amos.

The Negative Account

From Judges 1:27 f. we hear nothing further of conquests of tribal portions. Instead, we get a list of the cities that were *not* conquered and in the case of Dan of three that apparently were lost again. Only the northern tribes are dealt with, with omission of Issachar and the Transjordan group.

We need not linger here over the cities which Manasseh and Ephraim failed to obtain. They will occupy us in narrative connections. Very little information has, however, come down about events in Galilee, and so some comment on the cities of Asher and Naphthali may be given.

KITRON. This city is believed to have lain at *Tell el Fār*, in the southern part of the plain of Acco, which borders on Zebulun. It lies halfway between *Tell Harbaj,* the most important site hereabouts (probably the Helkath of JOSH. 19:25), and the entrance to the *Wadi el Malik* leading up into the high country. Habitation began here with Early Iron. That is not too favorable for the identification, but other sites suggested take one too far from the Zebulun border.

NAHALOL. It has been suggested that *Tell en Naḥl,* the largest and southernmost of a series of small sites in the plain, preserves the name of Nahalol. As it lies in the right area and has Late Bronze and Early Iron remains, the identification seems to be a good one.

ACCO. The cities that Asher failed to obtain are led off with Acco, which still bears the ancient name *'Akkā,* though the place has yielded its ancient importance to nearby *Ḥaifā.* It was the terminus since pre-Israelitic time of a route from the Hauran to the sea, as may be seen from the Late Bronze Age sites which lie along that route. SIDON. While the boundary of Asher is extended north to Sidon in Joshua 19:28, this seems a goal of ambition, rather than a practical possibility. On Sidon, see page 139.

AHLAB, OR HELBAH. These two names are really variants and refer to one and the same city; the second name was probably written in the margin of the manuscript and transferred to the text by a copyist. Another form of the same name is the Mehebel of Joshua 19:29 ("from the coast to," A.V.), which the Revised Standard Version corrects to Ma-

3.9 *Aerial view of Sidon* (Saidā) *in its setting.* (*Courtesy Institut Fran-cais d'Archéologie, Beyrouth, Liban*)

halab. This reconstructed form is the right one, for we hear of a city called *Maḥalliba* in the Assyrian inscriptions. The name survives in *Khirbet el Maḥālīb,* twin hills with ancient remains, lying below the mouth of the Leontes River and about four miles northeast of Tyre.

ACHZIB. Called Ekdippa in Hellenistic Roman times, Achzib lay on the road from Ptolemais (Acco) to Tyre, according to Eusebius. The name survives, clipped off at the beginning, in *ez Zīb,* eleven miles from Acco. There is a tell there with remains starting in the Early Bronze Age.

APHIK. The name is given more correctly as Aphek in Joshua 19:30. The important *Tell Kerdāneh,* which was occupied during the whole Bronze Age period and lay in the plain of Acre on the highway from Phoenicia to Egypt, has been suggested for it.

REHOB. This is no doubt a city of the Acre area, and not to be confused with several other places of the same name in other regions. There is no clear indication as to which of the tells of the plain of Acco represents it.

The general importance of this negative account of Judges 1 cannot be exaggerated.

Here we are in the real world of gradual change, rather than in the world of ambitions and dramatic happenings. We learn what the Hebrew conquest actually was like. It was a case of migratory tribes coming into Canaanite territory and being unable to conquer the powerfully fortified cities. However, the historical process worked for them. A similar situation brought on the collapse of the Asia Minor cities in the thirteenth century A.D.; it was the invasion of tribes from the east that laid them low, not by direct attack, but simply by the ruin of their economies in consequence of the disruption of commerce. We must imagine similar results flowing from the Israelite invasion of Canaan in the thirteenth century B.C. The cities instead of perishing, however, accepted domination by the invaders and paid them tribute, as they had previously paid it to the Egyptian overlords.

From Gilgal to Bochim

We have seen that the Benjaminite and southern Ephraimite tradition regarded Gilgal near Jericho as an exceedingly important place. There must have been close relations between Bethel and Gilgal. Such cultic relations are presupposed in the story of Bochim (Judg. 2:1–5), which is incompletely preserved. We hear elsewhere of a place called Bochim, "the weeping ones." There is, however, Allon-bacuth or the "oak of weeping" of Genesis 35:8 in the vicinity of Bethel. It has been suggested that this locality was Bochim, which need not be a city name, but would merely be the name of a locality where ritual weeping or wailing was carried on at certain seasons in connection with the cult of a dying and rising god of vegetation. We see here how the Hebrew religion could take over such a pagan custom and moralize it. The weeping of the people is penitential, based on a sermon uttered by the angel of the Lord. This story originally may have preceded the attack on Bethel (cf. Josh. 5:13 before the attack on Jericho).

Ehud's Daring Deed

Foreign invaders took advantage of the weakness of Palestine in this situation. A king, Cushan-Rishathaim from Aram Naharaim, or Mesopotamia, opens the series of invasions (Judg. 3:8). But the name is garbled, and if Cushan were original would point rather to Edom than Aram (the two words were sometimes confused).

The report of an oppression of Israel by a king of Moab is better attested. The tribe most affected is Benjamin, the territory of which embraced Jericho; it is not clear whether Judah already had possession of the contiguous area south of Jericho at this time. According to Judges 1:19 that tribe was up in the mountain country. Allegedly Eglon defeated Israel with the aid of Amorites and Amalekites and occupied "the city of the palms." There was probably a new settlement at or near Jericho, which called itself "city of the palms" (cf. Deut. 34:3, Judg. 1:16). It was this that Eglon took (Judg. 3:13).

The old story, like many others handed down in oral tradition, has lost some of the concrete information very much needed for

3.10 *Sculptures of the late Hittite sort at* Karatepe *in Cilicia. (Courtesy Theresa Goell, with permission of Helmuth T. Bossert)*

its understanding. Where was it that Eglon resided and that Ehud delivered the tribute? If Ehud turned back at Gilgal, did he come from across the Jordan? We have seen that Gilgal is probably to be sought northeast of Jericho; there would have been no occasion for Ehud to pass by the place if he had presented his tribute to Eglon at the "city of the palms." He obviously came from across the river. We must imagine the Moabite king as receiving his payment at a place like Abel-shittim. Certainly it would be unrealistic to suppose that Ehud had gone very far from Eglon's abode before turning back at the "sculptured stones" (A.V. quarries, Hebrew *pesīlīm*) to deliver his secret message.

After assassinating Eglon, Ehud passes the "sculptured stones" a second time and escapes to Seirah. There is no clue as to exactly where the latter place lay. It has nothing to do with Mount Seir, but must be in Ephraim —in other words, north of Ehud's native Benjaminite country, which may have been policed by Moabites. Here Ehud mobilized the Ephraimites who then occupied the Jordan fords and cut off the Moabites that were west of the river. As already noted, the term "plains of Moab" used for the area southeast of Jericho may commemorate the temporary domination of this region by the Moabites.

One extremely interesting feature of the story is its admission of the existence of sculptured stones at Gilgal. These are doubtless pre-Israelitic. The Hittite and Hurrian kings weie much in the habit of providing their shrines with sculptures. Carchemish and *Karatepe* have provided vivid illustration of that (see fig. 3.10).

Shamgar and the Philistines

The twelfth century B.C., as we have seen, marked the coming of the Philistines. They were hardly established when they attempted to expand northward and seize the approaches to Galilee. Tradition speaks of a Shamgar ben Anath who was a mighty hero in warding off their aggression. It has been suggested that Shamgar was from the city Beth-anath, which probably lay in the same plain in which the "Cana in Galilee" is to be sought (the *Sahl el Baṭṭōf*). *Deir Hanna* near *Saḥnīn* has been suggested as a suitable site. The name Shamgar is not an Israelitic name, but rather of Hurrian type. It is not clear at all that he was an Israelite. He may have been a Canaanite city king, who took the lead in resisting the Philistines. He was of recent memory, when the Song of Deborah was composed, which alludes to the total cessation of travel and commerce in the days of Shamgar (JUDG. 5:6).

The Battle of Taanach

Reassertion of Canaanite power now followed. Oppressive measures were evidently taken against the Israelites, and led to a concerted uprising on the part of a federation of tribes.

The territory that the tribe Manasseh aspired to control was ruled by a group of very strong Canaanite cities (JUDG. 1:27). These were at that juncture under the general sway of a king named Sisera, who resided at Harosheth-ha-goiim. If Sisera is described as a lieutenant of Jabin of Hazor (JUDG. 4:2), that is not supported by the poem of chapter 5. The defeat of Jabin of Hazor, moreover, was already reported in Joshua 11:1 f. However, it is quite true, according to Judges 4:10, that the starting point of the rebellion was in the territory

formerly ruled by Hazor (see page 139).

The name of the city of Sisera reminds one of the "King of the nations [*Goiim*] of Gilgal" (JOSH. 12:23). Presumably Harosheth, like Gilgal, was a place that had fallen under the control of the sea-peoples that had come down the Palestinian coast in the thirteenth century (see page 131). A city dominating the plain of Esdraelon would naturally have lain in or near that plain. The name Harosheth is believed to have survived at *el Ḥārithīyeh* near the western exit of the plain, north of the Kishon stream. However, as is so often the case, the name has wandered from the original site, for Garstang found no signs of ancient occupation at *el Ḥārithīyeh,* a village which itself had moved from the point it formerly occupied. Nearby on the north side of the Kishon River is *Tell Qassīs*, while opposite it on the southern side of the stream is *Tell ʿAmr*, guarding the fork of the roads to *Ḥaifā* and Acco. British trial soundings at *Tell ʿAmr* in 1922 showed that it is an Iron Age site, and this agrees well with the fact that Harosheth is not named among the Palestinian cities in the Egyptian sources of the Late Bronze Age. Some would identify Harosheth with the more important mound *Tell Harbaj* on a confluent of the Kishon, three miles north of *el Ḥārithīyeh,* but that site is a bit distant and was probably ancient Helkath, as already mentioned above.

According to the narrative of Judges 4 a prophetess named Deborah played a leading role in inciting rebellion. She was wont to be available for consultation under the "palm tree of Deborah" between Ramah and Bethel. It will be recalled that a Deborah, the nurse of Rebecca, died near Bethel (GEN. 35:8), and the possibility exists that one has usurped the name of the other and that the same place is meant. The location of the palm (an unusual tree for this area and so, perhaps, editorially substituted for "oak") takes one to the vicinity of *el Bīreh,* which is on the main highway to the north, between the indicated points of Ramah and Bethel.

According to the version of Judges 4, Deborah went with Barak to his home town Kedesh in Naphthali. The location of Kedesh is known, for the name has survived as *Qadas*. It lies seven miles north-northwest of ancient Hazor. There is a Bronze Age tell there, which was re-occupied in the Hellenistic period. The Israelites seem to have built a new city adjoining it on the northwest, and the modern village occupies its site. Kedesh is found in the Egyptian inscriptions. It is portrayed on the reliefs of Pharaoh Seti I as situated on a wooded height; the Pharaoh is pursuing enemies fleeing toward it, while on the towers the Amorite inhabitants are pleading for mercy. Hereabouts, then, Barak mustered the men of Naphthali and Zebulun. The force now marched on to Mount Tabor, at the edge of the plain of Esdraelon, apparently hiding on the forested summit.

By way of completing the information necessary for understanding the story that follows, the narrator notes that a Kenite named Heber tented up and down through that country, the terminus of his roving being "the oak in Zaanannim which is near Kedesh." "The oaks in Zaanannim" are mentioned in the description of the territory of Naphthali (JOSH. 19:33). There has not been sufficient archaeological exploration of the *Qadas* vicinity to permit any identification of this town. The point of this allusion evidently is that Heber was in secret league with Barak and perhaps provided him with "intelligence" from his observation post in the plain of Esdraelon. The Kenites (as their name implies) were smiths, and some of them lived a gypsy life, going from town to town in a given area to sell their services until the need was satisfied. We may note in passing, however, that this picture of the preliminary events of a mobilization at Kedesh in Galilee is not fully borne out by the paean of chapter 5; here the mobilization begins in Ephraim and has a much larger background (JUDG. 5:14 f.). The story is thus one-sidedly Galilean.

3.11 *Where Barak's force assembled? Summit of Mount Tabor, showing modern road ascending it. (Keren Hayesod)*

Sisera, receiving a report of the gathering of the Hebrew tribesmen, went out with his men and chariots up the Kishon stream. According to the poem there was a coalition of kings, naturally the kings of the various cities hereabouts. Barak and his force went forth to join battle with them. The poem identifies the battlefield more precisely than the narrative: at Taanach by the waters of Megiddo (JUDG. 5:19). Taanach's name survives at *Tell Ta'anek*, on the southern edge of the Esdraelon plain. Here Ernst Sellin excavated in 1902–03. Megiddo lay five miles northwest of there at *Tell el Mutesellim* (page 21). German excavations were conducted there by G. Schumacher in 1903–05; large-scale American ones by University of Chicago expeditions under C. Fisher and others in 1925–39. It is possible that Megiddo lay desolate and destroyed at this time. The excavations have shown that Stratum VII of Megiddo perished about 1150 B.C. while Taanach was inhabited. If the battle took place *c.* 1125 B.C., as has been suggested, this item would be clarified. We may imagine the

Israelites as having come from Tabor to Engannim and then northwest to Taanach. The "waters of Megiddo" are today called *Nahr el Lejjūn* and flow into the Kishon (*Nahr el Muqatṭaʿ*). The Israelite victory is attributed to confusion caused among the enemy by the LORD (JUDG. 4:15).

The poem speaks poetically of the stars fighting against Sisera and asserts

> "The river of Kishon swept them away,
> that ancient river, the river Kishon." (JUDG. 5:21 A.V.)

> *"The torrent Kishon swept them away, the onrushing torrent, the torrent Kishon."* (JUDG. 5:21 R.S.V.)

The imagination can take free reign here to picture what happened. A rainstorm had evidently brought on a sudden freshet in the Kishon and turned the plain to mud, hindering the operation of Canaanite chariotry. Many of the foe were slain at the edge of the stream as they retreated to their cities. Sisera, we are told, dismounted and fled on foot to extricate himself from the dangerous rout. He sought refuge in the tent of Heber the Kenite, with whom peaceful relations existed and where he could expect to be concealed. Instead, he was murdered by Heber's wife, Jael. The poem pronounces a curse upon Meroz for not coming to the aid of the Israelites (JUDG. 5:23). A curse such as this implies the will to exterminate the city and its inhabitants. It was hardly an Israelite city, for the un-co-operative Israelite groups are only chided in the poem, but rather a Canaanite city in a covenant obligation with a Hebrew tribe, probably that of Manasseh. As there is no hint of where the city lay, except that it must be imagined as having been relatively close to the scene of action so that its co-operation would have been of great value, attempts to locate it fail to carry conviction. The city is never mentioned, unless perchance in one of the Egyptian "execration texts" published in 1940. Probably the Israelites destroyed it, or else the population fled, like that of Beeroth (2 SAM. 4:3).

The Midianite Oppression

Israel had grown much stronger numerically and in many communities was no longer under Canaanite domination. But just as the Israelites had overrun Canaan, so they found themselves overrun by nomads from the interior of the Arabian desert, described as "children of the east" (*Qedem*) under the lead of the Midianites.

We have already heard of the Midianites in connection with the story of Moses. It seems likely that the narrative uses the name "Midianites" loosely for tribes such as are mentioned in Genesis 25:13-15. One must assume that they came up from the *Wadi Sirḥān* to the *Haurān* and, recognizing the weakness of western Palestine, crossed the Jordan and overran that country as well. When the land was under a strong government, such invasions at most strafed certain regions in Transjordan.

3.12 *A "lordly bowl" such as Sisera was wont to eat from (Judges 5:25). This one belonged to a king of ancient Ugarit, 500 years earlier, and is ornamented with hunting scenes. (C. F. Schaeffer, Mission Archéologique Francaise, copyrighted)*

It seems likely that the Midianite invasion of Gideon's day represented a seasonal northward movement of camel-breeding Arabian Bedouin, driven farther west than usual by drought prevailing in those years. That they were camel breeders is the presupposition of their coming, for only those possessed of this animal could migrate from inner Arabia in this way. We note that the domestication of the camel was something relatively new; it must have begun around 1100 B.C. It made possible a great growth of population in Arabia and it expanded commercial travel in that area on a scale hitherto impossible, for the ass is unable to go without water for many days like the camel.

The Ophrah of the Abiezrites

Israel was to experience its liberation from this dire calamity through a man surnamed Gideon, "the smiter," and that name is primarily used in the story. He lived at a city called the Ophrah of Abieser, evidently to distinguish it from other places of the same name, such as the more southerly one in Benjamin (JOSH. 18:23, I SAM. 13:17), which Eusebius mistakenly takes for the Ophrah of Gideon. Abieser is a clan of the tribe of Manasseh. Where its Ophrah lay is a particularly perplexing question. Some think it should be sought in that portion of Manasseh which looks towards the east. The *Wadi Fār'ah* marks the southernmost zone of Manassite settlement, and the suggestion that the Ophrah of Gideon is to be sought in this valley at *Tell el Fār'ah*, "the mound of the high ridge," is still attractive, except for the fact that leading scholars prefer to put Tirzah there (see page 269). If Ophrah lay there, the march to the well of Harod (JUDG. 7:1) becomes reasonable, as does also the particular peril of the Abiezrites; for *Tell el Fār'ah* lies at the head of a fertile valley leading down to the Jordan, and its crops must have been one of the objectives of the Midianite pillage. However, there are various other candidates for identification

with the Ophrah of the Abiezrites. Since the names Ophrah or Ephron were regularly replaced by Arabic *eṭ Ṭaiyibeh,* several places of the latter name with ancient remains at or near them have been suggested; one far out to the west near *Tul Kerm,* which may, however, lie out of bounds for the tribe of Manasseh; another southeast of Mount Tabor, which would excellently fit an allusion to an event at Tabor that comes out late in the Gideon-narratives (JUDG. 8:18). But the latter *eṭ Ṭaiyibeh* is believed to be Haphraim or Hapharaim (JOSH. 19:19) and lies in the territory of Issachar. On grounds of general suitability, rather than for any special reason, the Iron Age site of *Silet ed Ḍahr,* thirteen miles north of Shechem, has been suggested. It at any rate lies definitely in Manasseh. For the present, however, we must regretfully admit that the geographical problem of the Ophrah of Gideon is unsolved. If the solution is ever found it will be time enough to think of the local points mentioned in the narrative, such as the wine press of Gideon and the nearby altar called "The LORD is peace," which still stood in the author's day (JUDG. 6:24), or the altar of Baal and the "grove" (better Asherah, or wooden pillar) beside it (JUDG. 6:26).

Gideon's Band

The annual arrival of the camel-breeding Bedouin took place as expected.

> "Then all the Midianites and the Amalekites and the children of the east were gathered together, and went over, and pitched in the valley of Jezreel." (JUDG. 6:33 A.V.)

> *"Then all the Midianites and the Amalekites and the people of the East came together, and crossing the Jordan they encamped in the Valley of Jezreel."* (JUDG. 6:33 R.S.V.)

Thus the stage is set for mighty events. Gideon, assuming the leadership role, mobilizes Abiezer, and sends messengers to the rest of Manasseh and even to Zebulun, Naphthali and Asher. In the battle against Sisera, Asher had refrained from participation (JUDG. 5:17), but now this tribe lent its aid; the other two had already played a leading part at the earlier occasion (JUDG. 5:18), and bravely came forward once more. But Gideon's conversation with the Midianite chiefs in Judges 8:18 f., a narrative evidently by a different writer, shows that the reporting is very incomplete as to the initial events.

The Israelites having secretly congregated (presumably at Ophrah), the signal to march was given.

> "Then Jerubbaal, who is Gideon, and all the people that were with him, rose up early, and pitched beside the well of Harod: so that the host of the Midianites were on the north side of them, by the hill of Moreh, in the valley." (JUDG. 7:1 A.V.)

> *"Then Jerubbaal (that is, Gideon) and all the people who were with him rose early and encamped beside the spring of Harod; and the camp of Midian was north of them, by the hill of Moreh, in the valley."* (JUDG. 7:1 R.S.V.)

The early departure suggests that Ophrah lay a good distance from the Plain of Esdraelon. The location of the well or spring of Harod, near which the Israelites encamped, and of the hill of Moreh, at the foot of which the Midianites were encamped, then invite consideration. Since the subsequent flight of the Midianites must have gone down through the valley of the *Nahr Jalūd*, it is tempting to identify the spring of Harod as its source, the *'Ain Jalūd* ("spring of Goliath"). It is certainly a most appropriate stopping point for a war party coming from the south or southwest. Since Gideon and his men "descended" to it (Judg. 7:4, 5), their encampment was presumably on the heights above the spring. It has recently been estab-

lished by an Israeli archaeologist that a town lay there, which presumably was named Harod. Here Gideon and his men were safe from surprise and could observe the plain below as the story requires. The large size of the *'Ain Jalūd*, furthermore, makes it a particularly appropriate place for the scene described in Judges 7:5 f. Still, it is not the only possibility, for there are also springs near Jezreel (*Zer'īn*), which could have served the purpose.

The question of where the Midianite encampment lay hangs together with the location of the spring of Harod. The account places it "at the hill of Moreh, in the valley." It has been assumed that the phrase "hill of Moreh" stands for a part of a mountain, preferably a foothill, that could command an independent name. The independent part of Mount Gilboa, that is crowned by the village of *el Mezār*, has been suggested for it. The Midianites would then have been encamped near Shunem (*Solem*). However, it seems doubtful whether such a lofty height would have been called a hill (*gibeah*). No certainty can thus be obtained as to the exact site of the Midianite encampment and that, in turn, puts in doubt the proposed site of the Hebrew encampment. The nocturnal attack (JUDG. 7:19 f.) suggests that they were not far apart.

The rout of the Midianites brings in a geographical description:

> "And the host fled to Beth-shittah in Zererath, and to the border of Abelmeholah, unto Tabbath." (JUDG. 7:22 A.V.)

> *"And the army fled as far as Beth-shittah toward Zererah, as far as the border of Abel-meholah, by Tabbath."* (JUDG. 7:22 R.S.V.)

The text here seems to present duplicate statements, either as a result of the combination of two strands of narrative or of two variant readings of manuscripts. The objective first mentioned, Beth-shittah, is de-

3.13 *View of Jordan in the area of the Midianite battle. Main valley coming in from east is* Wadi Kufrinjeh. (*Bavarian State Archives*)

scribed as lying "toward Zererah," which is usually corrected to "toward Zarethan" (JOSH. 3:16; 1 KINGS 7:46; cf. further on page 219). The second statement sounds as though it were a variant taken from another manuscript or parallel account: "as far as the border of Abel-meholah by Tabbath." The question is whether the reference is to places west or east of the Jordan. In general, one may say that there were not many towns west of the Jordan below Beth-shean, for much of this area is ill-suited for agriculture, whereas east of the Jordan there were a great many towns, as was first established by the explorations carried on by William F. Albright (published in 1926), and confirmed by the archaeological survey of Glueck (published in 1951). It may be that the property of some of these towns extended across the river so that the story could mention them even where the happenings are localized west of the stream. For certainly, if any reliance can be placed on the connection of the story, many of the Bedouin were still west of the river when Gideon sent his message to the Ephraimites telling them to guard the river as far as Beth-barah (JUDG. 7:24). We will defer considering the location of Abel-meholah until later (page 278), but will note here that if a location *west* of the Jordan is to be chosen then *Tell Abu Sifrī*,

where Late Bronze and Early Iron sherds are to be found, is the most probable site. It would conform fairly well to Eusebius' statement that during his time it was called *Beth-maiela* and lay nine miles from Beth-shean. He cannot have been very sure of the identification, however, for he adds an alternate possibility—that of associating the name with an *Abel-mea*. It would seem wise to place little reliance on his assertion, since there seems to be no traditional knowledge behind it, but only speculation based on somewhat similar sounding but actually not comparable names. For Tabbath there is no equivalent name west of the river, though there is one on the east (*Rās Abū Ṭābāt*). Archaeological confirmation for an ancient site there, however, is still lacking.

The narrative places Gideon's meeting with the Ephraimites before his own crossing of the river. If they occupied the fords as far as Beth-barah, then the question is whether Beth-barah is a northern or a southern limit. Beth-barah is a shortened form of *Bēth-'abārā,* "ford-town." One might think of *Tell Abū Sidreh* which lies close to the Jordan, and guards the ford leading over to the probable site of Succoth (cf. page 85). But perhaps the *ed Dāmieh* ford is more probable, particularly if one regards *Tell el Mazār* a few miles northwest of it as Ephraimite

156

Ataroth (JOSH. 16:7). Beth-barah may then have been a village west of the ford.

The net thus spread by Gideon's directives trapped two Midianite princes, whose names are not reliably reported, but have just been inferred from the places where they were executed—the one was killed at the rock of Oreb ("the raven") and the other at the wine press of Zeeb ("the wolf"), places that naturally cannot be identified.

Gideon with his force then crossed the river in pursuit of those that had crossed here as well as above. On his way he passed Succoth and Penuel, towns evidently still in the hands of Canaanites, but bound by treaty to aid the Manassites. They refused to provide him with supplies out of fear of Midianite reprisal. Gideon swore to take vengeance on them later and continued the pursuit, which seems to have extended a great distance.

We learn that the Midianite chiefs Zebah and Zalmunna were at a place called Karkor with the remnant of all "that were left of the hosts of the children of the east."

> "And Gideon went up by the way of them that dwelt in tents on the east of Nobah and Jogbehah, and smote the host: for the host was secure.
> And Gideon the son of Joash returned from battle before the sun was up." (JUDG. 8:11, 13 A.V.)

> *"And Gideon went up by the caravan route east of Nobah and Jogbehah, and attacked the army; for the army was off its guard.*
> *Then Gideon the son of Joash returned from the battle by the ascent of Heres."* (JUDG. 8:11, 13 R.S.V.)

Nobah is reportedly the Israelite name for the city of Kenath (NUM. 32:42). We find a Kanatha later among the Hellenistic cities of the Decapolis. It was situated on the western slopes of the *Jebel Ḥaurān* (at *el Qanawāt*). The name Jogbehah survives in *Ajbehāt*, northwest of the Ammonite capital. These points are mentioned only to identify the

3.14 *Scene from an Arabian campaign of Ashurbanipal. (British Museum)*

course of the caravan route (literally "the road of the tent dwellers"). According to Musil there is a natural gateway between the southeastern spurs of the Hauran mountain range and the broken hills in which the Jabbok River originates. Through this gateway, which lies southeast of *Der'a*, the camel breeders enter the territory of the *en Nuqra* at the end of June, departing again at the end of August. The road leading through this gateway and another leading through a more northeasterly pass were and are known as "the way of the nomads." By this road the Midianites will have fled into the *Wadi Sirḥān.* Karkor, Musil holds, is thus to be sought along this great route into the heart of north Arabia, and he finds the name surviving in the wells of *Qerāqer* or *Qarqar*, 111 miles southeast of *'Ammān,* at the junction of important desert routes. The ascent of Heres he locates at *Darb el Mneqqā.* The narrative does not say, as Musil assumes, that Gideon pursued the foe as far as the ascent of Heres, but implies rather that he returned via the ascent of Heres.

Through Gideon's mighty deeds Ophrah must have attained considerable importance. And, indeed, Gideon himself must have assumed the rank of a city king like those of the Canaanitic cities of the land. His reported refusal of the crown (JUDG. 8:22–23) is due to the pragmatism of the general editing, according to which the kingship began as something new with Saul. Gideon's kingship, at least over a city or two, is implied in the story of chapter nine. We can see, furthermore, from that chapter that Gideon had acquired control of Shechem, one of the most important and strategically located Canaanite cities of the land, though how this came about has been forgotten. That he inaugurated an idolatrous cult at Ophrah by setting up an "Ephod" (probably a substitute word for an idol) made out of the Midianite spoil (JUDG. 8:24–27) stands in marked contrast to the picture of a protagonist of the Yahweh religion which is previously drawn of him (JUDG. 6:11 f., 8:23). Such things, however, flowed from the fusion of Hebrews and Canaanites in the cities where the former had gained a footing without being able to displace the older population.

Abimelech's Rise and Fall

The ninth chapter of Judges focuses the attention on Abimelech, Gideon's son by a Canaanite wife. She is called a "concubine" in derogatory manner by the storyteller, but no doubt was a daughter of the old royal house of Shechem. Gideon must have resided there a good part of the time, rather than in Ophrah. We have already noted that ancient Shechem lay east of modern Nablus, at *Tell Balâṭah*. Excavations were carried on at this important site by German expeditions in 1913, 1926, and 1934 under Sellin, Welter, and Steckeweh. The fortifications, as well as the palace and temple area, were partly explored. Since 1956 a Drew-McCormick expedition under G. Ernest Wright has been digging at Shechem. The city had its main development between 1700–1550 B.C., when it was destroyed. Other destructions took place after 1200 B.C. (the one of JUDGES 9), by the Assyrians in 724 B.C., and by John Hyrcanus in 107 B.C.

Abimelech murdered his brothers at Ophrah and was chosen king by the Schechemites.

"And all the men of Shechem gathered together, and all the house of Millo, and went, and made Abimelech king, by the plain of the pillar that was in Shechem." (JUDG. 9:6 A.V.)

"And all the citizens of Shechem came together, and all Beth-millo, and they went and made Abimelech king, by the oak of the pillar at Shechem." (JUDG. 9:6 R.S.V.)

The plain (-tree) or oak and the pillar are part of the regular equipment of the Canaanite sanctuary. The tree is no doubt the one of which we have already heard in the story of Jacob (GEN. 35:4). Near by must have stood the altar attributed to him or to Abraham (GEN. 33:20, 12:7). The Beth-millo or house of Millo is differentiated from Shechem. There was also a Millo at Jerusalem (2 SAM. 5:9; 1 KINGS 9:15). The word means a "fill" or "heaping up," and was probably applied to a platform surrounded by a wall of its own, in which stood the palace and dwellings of high officials or nobles, set off from the rest of the city. The excavations have shown that a great wall sealed off the northwestern part of the city, with temple and palace areas. The Middle Bronze Age temple had indeed been erected on a fill above an older palace. Carchemish and *Sinjirli* (ancient Sam'al) had a similar acropolis.

If the story subsequently refers to the tower of Shechem (JUDG. 9:46), this is evidently synonymous with the Beth-millo, merely stressing the powerful fortification that guarded the entrance to the acropolis.

The story of Jotham delivering his parable from the top of Mount Gerizim (JUDG. 9:7) fixes the attention on the important height south of Shechem, today called *Jebel et Ṭōr,* with an elevation of 2849 feet. Its counterpart is Mount Ebal on the north side of the city, today called *Jebel Eslamīyeh* and rising to a height of 3090 feet. Israel was to lay the blessing on Gerizim (DEUT. 11:29), or those saying it were to stand on the mountain

(Deut. 27:12). The location of the two mountains is described in Deuteronomy 11:30 in a text overloaded with a clause about the Jordan Valley and Gilgal. The original statement, however, merely defined these mountains as west of the road toward the setting sun. Mount Gerizim lay "beside the oak of Moreh," i.e., "of the soothsayer." We would say the oak stood beside the mountain—an interesting difference in psychological attitudes. The general sanctity of the vicinity was illustrated by the fact that on the slope of the most northeasterly foothill of Mount Gerizim, about three hundred yards south of *Balāṭah,* a sanctuary from the end of the Middle Bronze Age was excavated in 1926. It consisted of a court of about 30 by 30 feet, in one corner of which were the remnants of an altar. One might imagine Jotham as calling out his parable from here, for in describing him as standing on the "top" of the mountain the narrator is a bit unrealistic, since the speaker could not have been heard from there. The traditional location of the pulpit of Jotham is predicated on the supposition that Shechem lay at *Nāblus,* which as we have seen is erroneous.

Since Abimelech soon extended his power quite far—according to verse 22 he ruled over Israel three years—a flight of Jotham to a distant point seems to be required.

But opposition to Gideon's kingship arose in Shechem and a clan or group led by Gaal, son of Ebed, who came into the city (Judg. 9:26) raised the revolutionary cry in the temple at the autumnal festival. Abimelech had apparently chosen a safer dwelling place than discontented Shechem or Ophrah, where the murder of his brothers must have left its resentment. He was staying at Arumah. This place is usually sought at *el 'Örmeh,* a well-isolated hilltop seven miles southeast of old Shechem. Though the name does not correspond as exactly as one might wish, Early Iron Age sherds are found there and that fact lends some support to the identification. The narrative suggests that it was a place rather close to Shechem. Abimelech's prefect of Shechem, Zebul, was able to send him swift information and to suggest a course of prompt action. In the vivid dialogue at the city gate between Zebul and Gaal the latter says:

> "See there come people down by the middle of the land, and another company come along by the plain of Meonenim." (Judg. 9:37 a.v.)

> *"Look, men are coming down from the center of the land, and one company is coming from the direction of the Diviners' Oak."* (Judg. 9:37 r.s.v.)

The "middle" or "center" of the land are substitute expressions for the literal phrase "the navel of the land." This was a concept of wide use in antiquity, and is applied by Ezekiel to Judah's hill country (Ezek. 38:12). Thus the inhabitants of Rome regarded the forum near the golden milestone from which the roads went out into all directions, as navel of the city and of the earth. In the case of Judges 9:37, it is not quite clear what point the narrator has in mind. Two detachments were approaching from different directions, presumably from the south and from the west, if Arumah lay at the point mentioned above. The navel of the land could for instance be Mount Gerizim or a part thereof, or the "divide" in the plain of Shechem. Certainty is unobtainable. Nor can one be sure whether the "Diviner's oak" is identical with the oak of Moreh, which apparently stood at or near the foot of Mount Gerizim.

Gaal and his supporters were defeated by Abimelech's men and driven back to the gates of Shechem. They were then expelled from the city by Zebul.

Some time after Gaal's departure, revolutionary activity must have broken out again. Perhaps an important item has been lost from the narrative in the course of its transmission—the murder of Zebul, Abimelech's prefect. Mention of him was certainly in order in view of his loyalty to Abimelech. The slaying of this man would have involved not only the lower city, as was the case previously, but the acropolis. Some such event is necessary to understand the king's intervention and drastic action, involving a surprise attack on the city and its complete destruction. Mount Salmon, which Abimelech ascended to obtain brush for a fire that would destroy the fortress, is probably a part of the Ebal range, which even today has no single name, but whose separate portions have three different names. The last stand of the Shechemites was in the temple of Baal, who was called *Baʿal berīth* ("lord of a covenant," perhaps because he was guardian of a Canaanite-Hebrew agreement). This temple is undoubtedly the Late Bronze Age temple that was superimposed on the greater Middle Bronze Age one with a five-degree shift in orientation. In front of it was a forecourt in which once stood an altar, and to the rear of it, slightly to the left, was the base for a stone pillar, which was broken off when found by Sellin and which has been recovered and raised in its original place by Wright.

The revolution against Abimelech seems to have had a wider background than has been apparent thus far, for we find him next besieging the city of Thebez (JUDG. 9:50 f.). The name survives to this day in *Ṭūbaṣ*, north of *Tell el Fārʿah*, by the peaked *Rās el Aqrā*. Important roads from Dothan in the north and Shechem in the south converge here to head for Beth-shean and the Jordan Valley. The modern town must be built on the site of the ancient one, however, for nothing can be discerned of a tell there. Thebez, too, had a tower or powerfully fortified gate. Here an upper millstone, hurled by a woman, laid Abimelech low.

Two Minor Judges

A defender of Israel, the Issacharite Tola, is next given a judgeship. Oddly, he is described as living and being buried in Mount Ephraim at a place called Shamir (JUDG. 10:1–2), not to be confused with a town of the same name in Judah (JOSH. 15:48). There is no clue as to its location.

Tola is followed by Jair, a man of Transjordan described as a "Gileadite"—a designation involving a considerable northward extension of that term.

"And he had thirty sons that rode on thirty ass colts, and they had thirty cities, which are called Havoth-jair unto this day, which are in the land of Gilead.

And Jair died, and was buried in Camon." (JUDG. 10:4–5 A.V.)

"And he had thirty sons who rode on thirty asses; and they had thirty cities, called Havvoth-jair to this day, which are in the land of Gilead. And Jair died, and was buried in Kamon." (JUDG. 10:4–5 R.S.V.)

Presumably Camon was the center of the Havoth-jair, which must be imagined as villages rather than cities. Centuries later the Seleucid king Antiochus III captured a town called Kamun on his march from Pella to Gephrun (Ephron), 1 Maccabees 5:46. This is doubtless still the same town Camon, which thus lay on the road from Pahel (*Khirbet Faḥl*) across the river from Bethshean, to Beth-arbel (*Irbid*). The name is believed to survive in modern *Qamm,* some six miles west of *Irbid*.

A Hero of Transjordan

The Ammonites, who were closely related to the Moabites, and like them were cousins of the Israelites, had pushed from the desert into the vicinity of the present *ʿAmmān*, which preserves their name. But the Israelites coming from western Palestine had seized the region west, north and south of theirs barring the Ammonites from the Jordan Valley. As the Ammonites grew more powerful they tried to subjugate these eastern Israelites. According to Judges 11 an Ammonite army invaded Gilead and encamped at the city of

Gilead. The Israelites mobilized and gathered at Mizpeh. We have already discussed the location of these places in connection with the story of Jacob (see page 84). The name Mizpeh, we may note, is adjusted to the more common spelling Mizpah in the R.S.V.

The command of the Israelite forces was given to Jephthah, who previously had been expelled from Gilead and had gone to the land of Tob, where he had made a great reputation for himself as a bandit chief. In their hour of dire peril, however, the Israelites had pinned their hopes on the leadership of such a man, and had sent a delegation out to get him, offering him the permanent headship (kingship) in the event of success.

The region of Tob occurs several times in the Biblical narratives and in the Apocrypha (2 SAM. 10:6, 1 MACC. 5:13, 2 MACC. 12:17). The last-named passage gives the distance from Chasphor (*Khisfîn*) to the land of the people of Tob as seven hundred and fifty stadia or eighty-seven miles (with a variant reading of five hundred stadia, or fifty-six miles). This would take one out beyond the Hauran. The exiled chieftain consented to return, no doubt with his retinue of robbers. A compact was sealed "before the Lord" at Mizpeh (JUDG. 11:11).

Since the armies were camped close to each other at Mizpeh and Gilead (-city) respectively (JUDG. 10:17), the next step must be an offensive one by one side or the other. Jephthah launched the attack, which led to an invasion of Ammonite territory.

"And he smote them from Aroer, even till thou come to Minnith, even twenty cities, and unto the plain of the vineyards, with a very great slaughter." (JUDG. 11:33 A.V.)

"And he smote them from Aroer to the neighborhood of Minnith, twenty cities, and as far as Abel-keramim, with a very great slaughter." (JUDG. 11:33 R.S.V.)

For Abel-keramim, or the "Abel of the vineyards," Abela, six miles from Philadelphia (the later Greek name of the Ammonite capital Rabbath Ammon) and still a wine-growing village today (*Khirbet es Sûq*), suits the indicated distance. There is some doubt as to whether the Aroer here referred to can be the one near the river Arnon in the Moabite country (*'Arā'ir*). A different Aroer, some believe, is meant in Joshua 13:25. Still the matter of a second Aroer remains uncertain, for the diplomatic exchange between Jephthah and the Ammonites, which is concerned with the territory from the Arnon northward, mentions the familiar Aroer (JUDG. 11:26). As for Minnith, Eusebius connects that with a Maanith on the road from Rabbath Ammon to Heshbon, four Roman miles from the latter place; *Khirbet Hamzeh*, halfway between Heshbon and *el Yadūdeh* has been suggested as its site.

The narrative tells of the vow that Jephthah made before setting out on his campaign and of the only daughter that fell victim to the vow (JUDG. 11:30, 34 f.). She had but one request:

"Let this thing be done for me: let me alone two months, that I may go up and down upon the mountains, and bewail my virginity, I and my fellows." (JUDG. 11:37 A.V.)

"Let this thing be done for me; let me alone two months, that I may go and wander on the mountains, and bewail my virginity, I and my companions." (JUDG. 11:37 R.S.V.)

This part of the story is evidently the "historical" explanation of a very ancient ritual carried on by the Israelites at the Gileadite Mizpah. For we hear

"That the daughters of Israel went yearly to lament the daughter of Jephthah the Gileadite four days in a year." (JUDG. 11:40 A.V.)

"That the daughters of Israel went year by year to lament the daughter of Jephthah the Gileadite four days in the year." (JUDG. 11:40 R.S.V.)

Such a wandering and ritual weeping was once no doubt carried on in honor of a fertility goddess by the pre-Israelitic inhabitants of the area, but the practice was continued by Israelite girls with a revised explanation: they wept instead for the daughter of Jephthah. The allusion to "going down upon the mountains" is quite correct for from the high-plateau region where Mizpah lay, the serried valleys falling off to the Jordan are lined by ridges.

The tale of Jephthah's victory has a peculiar sequel in the strife with the Ephraimites (JUDG. 12:1–6). The Revised Standard Version has accepted the suggestion of modern scholars that the Ephraimites went to the city named Zaphon, rather than the older translation that they went "northward" (JUDG. 12:1). Zaphon is mentioned in Joshua 13:27 and is put first in the list of the clans of Gad (GEN. 46:16, NUM. 26:15). It was no doubt a Canaanite royal city that the Hebrews had annexed. In fact, we already hear of it in the fourteenth century, in one of the Amarna Letters. At that time it was the residence of a princess, "Lady of the Lions." The assumption of the narrative of Judges 12 seems to be that this is where Jephthah resided, rather than at Mizpah, as the preceding story assumed. The connection in Joshua 13:27 suggests that Zaphon was the next important place north of Succoth. It probably lay at *Tell el Qōs,* three miles from *Tell Deir'allā* (Succoth), on a hill on the north side of the *Wadi Rājib,* where that valley emerges from the mountainous country. The tell commands a view over the course of the stream to the river and over a large section of the Jordan Valley. It guarded an important road leading up to Gilead.

The Ephraimites took the success of Jephthah for a pretext to claim control over Gilead's inhabitants as former Ephraimites or Manassites. The story evidently assumes Ephraimite control over Manasseh at this time, for Zaphon is opposite Manasseh. Jephthah's becoming a powerful ruler at an important city like Zaphon, presumably also controlling Succoth, may have seemed dangerous. The Gileadites moved to the attack, Jephthah having strategically sent forces to the Jordan fords, probably those at *Abu Sidreh,* to block the Ephraimite retreat. Here the famous word Shibboleth was required as a password; the Ephraimites pronounced it Sibboleth and thereby revealed their identity. This inability to use the *sh* has persisted to this day at Nablus. The number of the slain has no doubt been exaggerated, presumably by later copyists of the text, who wanted to make the figures more impressive in an age when mass warfare was in vogue.

The brief final item on Jephthah speaks of his being buried "in his city of Gilead" (JUDG. 12:7, R.S.V., with correction of the Hebrew, which has "in the cities of Gilead"). Presumably this refers to Mizpah.

The Story of Samson

As the story of Jephthah gives us a glimpse of Hebrew life in eastern Palestine, so that of Samson takes us westward to the region bordering the maritime plain. It tells of the tribe of Dan which once lived on this dangerous frontier. The Danite hero is a less tangible figure than the Gileadite Jephthah. He is not a leader of an army, or a ruler, but an individual Rob Roy, engaged in single-handed exploits. He belongs to the realm of song and story.

In the Samson narratives we get our first glimpse of the fact that on the southwest the Hebrews were prevented from pushing their borders across the plain over which ran the great African trade route, and where the coastal cities lay, owing to the fact that a people called the Philistines had established themselves there (cf. page 132). The border strife with them was a serious matter, and the tribe of Dan bore the brunt of it in the early days.

The Scene of Manoah's Sacrifice

The story of Samson has been given a religious prelude in chapter 13 in the account of his birth. His father was Manoah, evidently the "ancestor" of the clan of "Manuhoth" or better, the Manahthites (1 CHRON. 2:52–54). His wife receives an angelic prediction that she is to bear a son who will make a beginning of delivering Israel from the Philistines and who is to be brought up as a Nazirite (NUM. 6). Manoah then receives confirmation of this and brings sacrifice on a stone out in the field (JUDG. 13:19).

Manoah lived at Zorah. The identity of the place cannot be in doubt, for its name still survives as Ṣarʿa, at the highest point of the Shephelah, or hill country. A low tell that extends beyond the modern village and crowns the ridge marks the ancient city's site. It lay to the north of a valley which led out to the coastal plain (Wadi eṣ Ṣarār), and which constitutes one of the important points of egress and ingress into the heart of the mountain country. Zorah was a Canaanite city, as evidenced by the Late Bronze sherds found there, and is already mentioned in the Amarna Letters of the fourteenth century B.C. It does not seem to have been strongly fortified, though it did control a track leading north from the plain. And this is quite understandable, since hard by, across the valley, was Beth-shemesh, a city of much greater consequence, that would scarcely have permitted rival towns nearby to develop strongholds.

The rock out in the field that became an altar and sacred place for the clan of the Manahthites of Zorah may still exist. South of the road from Zorah to Arṭūf there is a rock altar that evidently is of very ancient origin.

The angelic prediction given to Manoah and his wife came true, and the woman gave the son that was born to her the name Samson. The spirit of the LORD, we are told, began to stir him in Mahaneh-dan, between Zorah and Eshtaol. Eshtaol's name survives in Eshwaʿ, about two miles east of Zorah. The present village stands on part of the ancient site, near the head of the valley. Eshtaol was evidently not a large place, or a very old one, for the sherds found there indicate an origin in the transitional period from Bronze to Early Iron. The camp of Dan, better taken as a place name, Mahaneh-dan, then, is to be sought on the northern side of the valley between the two points. Its name suggests that there was no permanent settlement there, but only a camp site—perhaps one of those enclosures with beaten earth walls, best illustrated by the great one at Hazor, and regarded as belonging to the age of the Hyksos. There is a possibility, however, that the storyteller is misinformed as to the location of the Mahaneh-dan (cf. JUDG. 18:12). Evidently the tomb of Manoah, where Samson was subsequently to be laid away, was also between the two points (JUDG. 16:31). Thus the scene of Samson's country is made quite precise and vivid for us by the storyteller.

The Scenes of Samson's Adventures

The Danite hero ventures down to Timnah, which then was in the hands of the Philistines. It is a different Timnah than the one referred to in Genesis 38:12. It lay beyond Beth-shemesh in the direction of the coastal plain, and the name survives there to this day as Khirbet Tibneh. Near the village of today is the ancient site, where Early Iron Age sherds are to be found. It was here, then, that Samson saw the Philistine maiden he desired to wed. On the road approaching Timnah, as one came from Zorah, there were vineyards. There Samson had his encounter with the lion, and later found the honey in the lion's skeleton. This is said to have suggested the famous riddle which he offers at his marriage feast.

Samson's bride, after worming the answer to the riddle out of him, betrayed it to her Philistine relatives, thus leaving her husband in debt to pay the wager. But the hero knows how to help himself.

> "And he went down to Ashkelon, and slew thirty men of them, and took their spoil, and gave change of garments unto them which expounded the riddle." (JUDG. 14:19 A.V.)

> *"And he went down to Ashkelon and killed thirty men of the town, and took their spoil and gave the festal garments to those who had told the riddle." (JUDG. 14:19 R.S.V.)*

The mention of Ashkelon brings to the fore one of the five important cities of the Philistines. Its location cannot be in doubt, for the name '*Asqalān* has adhered to the place to this day. It lay directly on the shore of the sea. Some trial excavations were conducted there by John Garstang for the Palestine Exploration Fund in 1921–2. The vast overlying remains from the Roman period, however, make it difficult to explore the Iron Age or Bronze Age city. It lies in a garden area, rich in wells. In the Middle Bronze Age it was a powerful fortress, surrounded by a rampart of beaten earth (*terre pisée*), a peculiar kind of defensive system that was already referred to on page 163. A siege and capture of Ashkelon in the time of Ramses II (1300 B.C.) is portrayed in the temple of Amon at Karnak.

Why Samson went to distant Ashkelon (seventeen miles north of Gaza), rather than to the much nearer Ekron for his booty of festal garments, is not explained.

After Samson's wife was given to another, he revenged himself by setting fire to the grain in the Timnah vicinity. He then sought a hideout far up in the mountain country of Judah.

> "And he went down and dwelt in the top of the rock Etam." (JUDG. 15:8 A.V.)

> *"And he went down and stayed in the cleft of the rock of Etam." (JUDG. 15:8 R.S.V.)*

There was a city of that name south of Bethlehem; it lay at *Khirbet el Khōkh,* on a steep hill between the *Wadi el Khōkh* and the *Wadi Ain 'Atān* (which preserves the name). A road connected this city, which was a strong one, with the Bethlehem-Hebron highway. The place controlled the garden district of the *Wadi Artās.*

The report of Samson's hiding in Judah led to a Philistine raid on a place called Lehi. The name is given more fully as Ramath-lehi (JUDG. 15:17). It was clearly in Judaean territory. Since Ramath-lehi means "the height of the jawbone" it could have gotten its name from its physical appearance, which may have had the shape of a jawbone. The story, however, popularly connects the name with the jawbone of an ass that Samson picked up there and used as a weapon against the Philistines. A hollow place (*maktēsh*) that existed at Lehi is supposed to have been brought into being at this time, in response to Samson's despairing cry, as he was perishing from thirst.

> "But God clave an hollow place that was in the jaw, and there came water thereout; . . . wherefore he called the name thereof Enhakkore, which is in Lehi unto this day." (JUDG. 15:19 A.V.)

> *"And God split open the hollow place that is at Lehi, and there came water from it; . . . Therefore the name of it was called Enhakkore; it is at Lehi to this day." (JUDG. 15:19 R.S.V.)*

164

The story thus explains the name of the spring of Lehi with a popular etymology as "spring of him who called." Exploration has not as yet found any place suiting the description. The crater-like hollow mentioned may yet lead to an identification.

Samson and Gaza

The final chapter in the Samson cycle begins with a prank at Gaza and ends with a tragedy at the same place. To speak of Gaza is to speak of one of the most important cities of the Levant. It was the scene of memorable battles and sieges, for its location made it both the key to Egypt for an invader heading for the land of the Nile, and the key to Asia for Egyptian war lords bent on controlling Palestine and Syria. A modern town continuing the name (*Ghazzeh*) stands on the mound of the ancient city, but along the northern scarps may be discerned brick walls twenty-seven feet high, built in the Egyptian manner. Soundings were conducted at Gaza in 1923 by Phythian Adams for the Palestine Exploration Fund but merely substantiated what was already known from the literary sources, that Gaza existed in the Late Bronze Age and that it fell under Philistaean domination in the Early Iron Age. The city seems to have expanded in successive periods, but was doubtless already larger than other Palestinian cities in Old Testament times. It lies in a garden district, amply provided with water, and the valley of Gaza (*Wadi Ghazzeh*) forms the natural southern boundary of Palestine in the south.

The introduction to this episode of the Samson cycle relates that the men of Gaza lay in wait outside the city gates, expecting the hero to come forth in the morning, but that he went out at midnight instead, carrying the gates of the city with him to the mountain east of (or "over against") Hebron. The latter city was thirty-eight miles distant. But not much is gained by disregarding the reference to Hebron and identifying the mountain with the hill called *Jebel Munṭār* (285 feet high), lying east of Gaza. Carrying the gates was a superman's job, and so distances do not matter either.

Samson's final fate is prepared for him by Delilah, a Canaanite girl of whom he becomes enamored. She lived in the "vale of Sorek." This is indefinite, but the vale evidently got its name from a town. Jerome knew of a Kephar Sorek or "Village of Sorek," near Zorah. There is a *Khirbet Sūrīk,* situated where a small valley leaves the *Wadi eṣ Ṣarār* on the west, but no traces of early occupation have been found there. The old town may have lain at the head of this side-valley, where there was a small Arab hamlet until recently. "Vale of Sorek" may conceivably have been the name of that little valley only and not that of the *Wadi eṣ Ṣarār,* as is usually supposed.

It was hereabouts, in any case, whether in the larger valley or in this side pocket, that the princes of the Philistines offered Delilah their bribe of eleven hundred shekels of silver to betray Samson into their hands. The place was outside of Philistine territory, but their ability to go there and make such a deal illustrates the fluid political situation existing at the time. From here then they finally led the vanquished hero forth, shorn, blinded and chained, and brought him to Gaza. He was put in prison at hard labor, grinding grain with the hand mill composed of "pestle and mortar."

The final scene is staged in the temple of Dagon at Gaza where Samson is forced to appear for the amusement of the festive crowd. The god Dagon was not a specifically Philistine deity, but an old Semitic god. Thus the excavations at *Rās esh Shamrā* in Phoenicia brought to light a Dagon temple in that quarter, too. A peculiar kind of temple-architecture seems to be presupposed, when the building is described as collapsing over its inmates through Samson's pulling down of "two middle pillars upon which the house rested." The story assumes that people on the roof as well as those on the inside of the building could observe the antics of the captive Israelite hero. Ancient temples excavated thus far have not provided any example illustrating such a possibility.

That Samson's relatives were able to claim his body and take it to Zorah for interment is a surprising concession of the Philistines under the circumstances described.

The Migration of the Danites

The situation on the Philistine border was evidently an untenable one for the Danites of Zorah and Eshtaol. A group from there decided to emigrate, and sent out five scouts to find a new home. These scouts went through the region of Mount Ephraim, where they stopped overnight at a small settlement referred to as "the house of Micah" (Beth-micah), after the head of the local clan. A Jewish tradition of the second century sought his home in a town called Gerab. That name survives in *Khirbet Jerābeh,* which lies on the top of a ridge south of Lebonah (*el Lubbān*), a mile to the east of where the main north-south highway crosses. It is, indeed, conceivable that the Levite from Bethlehem, who had found employment with Micah, and the Danite scouts might have left the highway to go there, for we subsequently hear that one had to "turn aside thither" (JUDG. 18:15).

A fine view is had from *Khirbet Jerābeh.* Looking east over the deep *Wadi Mūsa* one sees Shiloh lying at a level three hundred feet lower. Toward the north looms Mount Gerizim and toward the west one beholds the sea. There are traces of a small ancient settlement on the north side of the hilltop, but no report is available as to the periods of occupation indicated. The "house of Micah" had its little chapel and "Ephod" (a word possibly substituted for "image") and a Levite priest, who conducted the ritual.

The Danite scouts, who received a favorable augury from the priest, then went up the headwaters of the Jordan to Laish, a

Bronze Age city already mentioned in the Palestine list of Thutmosis III.

"Then the five men departed, and came to Laish, and saw the people that were therein, how they dwelt careless, after the manner of the Zidonians, quiet and secure; . . . and they were far from the Zidonians, and had no business with any man." (JUDG. 18:7 A.V.)

"Then the five men departed, and came to Laish, and saw the people who were there, how they dwelt in security, after the manner of the Sidonians, quiet and unsuspecting, . . . and how they were far from the Sidonians and had no dealings with any one." (JUDG. 18:7 R.S.V.)

The last words "and had no business with any man" are probably to be corrected to read "and had no business with *Aram*" (so also, then, in verse 28), which lay adjacent to it. The statement about this lack of contact with the Sidonians and Aramaeans is repeated later with the added information that the city lay in the valley of Beth-rehob (JUDG. 18:28). The Beth-rehob referred to here is hardly the one of 2 Samuel 10:6 f., which lay in Transjordan, hard by the Ammonite country, or the Rehob near Beth-shean that we hear of in Egyptian inscriptions. Since the largest mound in the area, aside from that representing Laish, is *Tell en-Nāʿmeh,* it has a good claim to having been the previous mistress of the plain. It was evidently abandoned in the Late Bronze Age, as no Early Iron sherds have been found there. The tell is about half the size of Megiddo, and thus represents a place of considerable importance. Some scholars, however, would connect this mound with the Yenoam mentioned in Egyptian inscriptions and in the Amarna Letters.

The favorable report brought back by the scouts leads to the emigration of six hundred armed men with their families and possessions from Zorah and Eshtaol.

"And they went up, and pitched in Kirjath-jearim, in Judah: wherefore they called that place Mahaneh-dan unto this day: behold, it is behind Kirjath-jearim." (JUDG. 18:12 A.V.)

"And went up and encamped at Kiriath-jearim in Judah. On this account that place is called Mahaneh-dan to this day; behold, it is west of Kiriath-jearim." (JUDG. 18:12 R.S.V.)

We will hear more of Kiriath-jearim presently in connection with 1 Samuel 6–7. Going to that place from the *Wadi eṣ Ṣarār* involved a southerly detour to the next valley, in which this town lay. The fact that a site called Mahaneh-dan was shown there, too, presumably led the storyteller to infer that this was the route taken. Nothing is said of the further course of the emigrants until they are at a point where one could leave the main road to go to the village of Micah. Here the migrating group yielded to the temptation of robbing the villagers of their Ephod and inducing their priest to go along. Micah's protests were unavailing and the force he could muster too weak to resist. The Danites then continued on their way and captured the town of Laish.

The Hebrew city of Dan that subsequently stood on the site of Laish is at the very northern border of Israel, as the phrase "from Dan to Beersheba" (1 Sam. 3:29, etc.) has made vivid. Eusebius put its location at four Roman miles from Paneas, on the road to Tyre, at a source of the Jordan. This corresponds to *Tell el Qāḍi,* on the *Nahr el Leddān,* which name is probably a translation of a Hebrew "River of Dan." The Arabic name, meaning "mound of the judge," is a translation of Hebrew "Dan" ("judge"). It dominates the plain north of Lake Semechonitis, and is described as "a beautiful site with a clearly marked acropolis." It is a quadrangular mound, 600 by 500 yards, and 30 to 40 feet high, with ramparts visible all the way around except on the southwest, where the stream coming from the *'Ain Leddān* has eroded them. The eastern part of the tell is higher than the western, and probably marks the site of the ancient town. The Early Bronze stratum, according to Albright, extends nearly to the top of this sector. Garstang found ample traces of occupation down to Late Bronze times, but no Iron Age I occupation. In Early Iron II (ninth to beginning of the sixth century B.C.) there was, however, a renewed occupation. This has raised the question whether the Israelite city lay elsewhere, near at hand. Perhaps the migration of the Danite clans was a later event than the report in the Book of Judges would lead one to assume, and it was Jeroboam I who colonized the city, as well as made it a cult center (1 KINGS 12:28 f.). There is, however, the possibility that excavations at this most attractive site would produce information not revealed on the surface. The report in Joshua 19:47, where Laish is called Leshem (Lesham), seems to support the dating implied by the compiler.

Appended to the Book of Judges is a second narrative without mention of any individual "judge" (JUDG. 19–21). Since the places here referred to occur in other connections we will desist from discussing it.

The Story of Ruth

The Book of Ruth is put after the Book of Judges in the English Bible, as in the old Greek and Latin versions, and casts a mellow concluding light on that rather stark period. In its charming story we are taken from Bethlehem to the land of Moab and back again. The land of Moab is visible from Bethlehem; it lies on the other side of the Dead Sea on the top of the mountains of the *Belqā,* which really is a rather high plateau region. Traffic between Bethlehem and the land of Moab may have taken the track via the Theodosius monastery to the lower Jordan crossings. It is this route we may imagine Elimelech as traveling with his family in going to Moab. A famine in Judah led to the emigration. Much grain is raised on the high plateau of the Moabite country, and prior to the recent political division of the land, grain was still the chief product brought from that quarter to Jerusalem. The story remains vague, however, as to where in the land of Moab Naomi and her family sojourned. Presumably they would have gone to the old Reubenite settlements, where Israelites at this time may have been the dominant group. The vicinity of Heshbon might have furnished work and food.

It is in the return to Bethlehem of Elimelech's widow Naomi, with her faithful daughter-in-law Ruth, that the spotlight falls on that small city of Judah, already mentioned in Judges 19:1, and later to become the birthplace of David. The place name was not coined by Hebrews; while it may have been popularly interpreted as "house of bread" there can be no doubt but that it originally meant "House of (the god) Lehem," a deity named *Laḥmu* in Babylonian sources. It is probably mentioned already in the Tell el Amarna Letters under a different name (*Bīt Ninurta*). One would therefore expect to find Bronze Age remains at Bethlehem. In view of all the building and rebuilding that has gone on there, Bronze Age walls, if they existed, would have been convenient stone quarries and would have disappeared, as the Iron Age walls of Rehoboam (2 CHRON. 11:6) have done. Indeed, it is today impossible to locate the exact site of the town of Naomi and David, except on the most general grounds. These are the very simple ones, that it would most naturally be built on a hill, with water in convenient reach. The hillside west of the Church of the Nativity and the market place of the city are the probable site of the old town.

The gate of Bethlehem presumably lay on the south side, where there still is an approach. It was here, no doubt, that Boaz carried on his negotiations with a still closer relative (RUTH 4:1 f.). Hard by the gate was a cistern (2 SAM. 23:5), which then may have been at the *Bīr el Qāna,* which now taps the conduit that Pontius Pilate built to bring water to Jerusalem from the spring of *'Ain Ṣāliḥ,* but which before that may have been just an ordinary cistern. For Bethlehem had no natural spring, and as late as the time of St. Jerome, who lived there in the fifth century A.D., was still dependent on rain water.

The field of Boaz on which Ruth gleaned leavings of grain is shown by tradition near the village of *Beit Saḥūr.* That general area is, indeed, the probable locale.

It is important that a good wind should be blowing at threshing time, and one may even resort to the nocturnal hours for the purpose, as Boaz did (RUTH 3:2), in order to avail oneself of the breeze that regularly develops at that time. An evening repast, therefore, was partaken of at the threshing floor, and the flagon of wine was not wanting at this occasion. The contented farmer might then lie down to sleep at the end of the heap of grain (RUTH 3:6). It was there that Ruth, coached by her mother-in-law, appealed to him to take over the Levirate responsibility (RUTH 3:9), which most men were anxious to avoid (RUTH 4:6), and touched his heart with her devotion to the dead. But Boaz' willingness to "spread his skirt over his handmaid" (RUTH 3:9) is also recognized as high virtue and receives public acclaim.

The prophecy Micah 5:2 f. hails "Bethlehem Ephrathah," described as little among the thousands (i.e., clans) of Judah, as birthplace of the Messiah. Ephrathah, or better Ephrath, was the district in which Bethlehem lay (1 SAM. 17:12; 1 CHRON. 2:19, 51). In the story of Jesus, as given by Matthew and Luke, the prophecy is described as fulfilled.

THE GREAT KINGS

The DESIGN on the preceding page shows a Phoenician ship and logs from Assyrian reliefs, and cedar tree from Persepolis relief.

TOP, *plaque with inscription about King Azariah* (*see page 295*). (*E. L. Sukenik*) RIGHT, *King Ashur-nasir-pal of Assyria; top panel of the stela from Nimrūd* (*see page 267*). (*British School of Archaeology in Iraq*) BOTTOM, *the mound of ancient Hamath in the midst of the modern city of Ḥamā.* (*Institut d'Archéologie Francaise*)

CHAPTER X

SAUL FORMS A HEBREW NATION

THE FORMATION of an Israelite state out of a loose federation of tribes was a momentous event in Hebrew history. The Hebrews were goaded to this step by the dire necessity of defending themselves against encroachment on the part of other neighboring peoples who, like themselves, were only newcomers to Palestine but were seeking to expand their territories or sovereignties. Philistines in the west and Ammonites and Moabites in the east were leading opponents. The gravest menace came from the Philistine quarter.

World Historical Background

All these little peoples were able to develop power and carry on strife because of the extreme weakness of Egypt at this particular time, and because the old northern powers, the Hittites and Hurrians, had not yet found a successor. The Assyrians had fallen back from the high-water mark reached under Tukulti Ninurta I, and had lost their grip on Babylonia. The latter country was invaded and plundered by the Elamite ruler Shutruk-Nakhunte (c. 1160 B.C.). Soon afterward the Cassite Dynasty came to an end and a new native dynasty began, of which Nebuchadnezzar I (c. 1130–1110 B.C.) was the most important ruler. With Tiglath-pileser I (1112–1074 B.C.), however, Assyria resumed its rise. He was the first Assyrian king so far as is known to reach the Mediterranean. Under his successors the kingdom weakened again. In this period fresh hordes of Aramaeans penetrated into Mesopotamia and Syria and began to set up Aramaean kingdoms. The one destined to be of the greatest significance for Israel was "Aram Damascus," though at first a more northerly principality, Aram-zobah, seems to have held the leadership over this people. A little later we find this kingdom very much in the horizon of King David of Israel.

The Egyptian picture represents a period of weakness and stagnation in the land of the Nile. It was as though with Ramses III the last efforts had been expended. The next succeeding Ramessid rulers, Ramses IV–XI (1165–1085 B.C.), though governing from the city of Raamses, do not seem to have exerted any influence on Palestinian affairs. At this time the power of the priesthood of the god Amon of Thebes increased greatly, and the high priest of that city became in effect a ruler of upper Egypt. Indeed, with the fall of the Twentieth Dynasty, two kingdoms came again into being—the northern under Smendes residing at Tanis (as the Raamses city was now called) and the southern under Herihor at Thebes. In view of such weakness the peoples of Palestine could become stronger and in fact attain a degree of independence not experienced in that quarter since the early second millennium B.C.

The Ephraimite Supremacy

The most powerful tribe of the Israelite Federation at first was Joseph, which fell into two segments, Machir, subsequently called Manasseh, and Ephraim. The latter seems to have had the greater influence at first and so far as we know was a sort of theocratic state under a high priest of the LORD. An old relic of the desert sojourn, the Ark of the Covenant, was a particularly sacred object in its possession and a valuable symbol behind which to rally the affiliated Israel tribes. Some stories of the period of the Ephraimite supremacy have come down in the opening chapters of the first Book of Samuel. They are written from the point of view of interest in a particular figure of religious history, the seer or prophet Samuel, who is regarded as having played a role in connection with the origin of the Benjaminite monarchy.

From Ramah to Shiloh

The story of Samuel begins at a place called Ramathaim in the hill country of Ephraim. The -zophim attached to the name is an error for *Zuphi* (a Zuphite), a man from the district of Zuph. The name Ramathaim is subsequently given in shorter and more customary form as Ramah (1 SAM. 1:19, etc.). Where this Ramah was situated is not made clear anywhere, but one would expect it to have lain somewhere within the radius of towns for which Shiloh was the natural religious and political center. We are more fortunate, however, in the case of Shiloh. Its modern successor, *Khirbet Seilūn,* is situated on a hill and according to Garstang "in a passage through higher ground, by which it is almost enclosed." The excavations of a Danish expedition under H. Kjaer and A. Schmidt in 1926–29 revealed that the city was inhabited in the Middle Bronze Age, but apparently not in the Late Bronze Age, the period of the patriarchs. It was built up again in the Early Iron Age, or at the beginning of Israel's history, and provided with a new wall. The building in which the Ark was housed probably lay south of the city, where Christian and Moslem religious edifices of later times were reared. One cannot hope, therefore, to find vestiges of the old Hebrew temple of Shiloh. The imagination can visualize a Canaanite type of temple standing on this spot. It was here that Elkanah brought sacrifice and that Hannah prayed and received the oracle from

Eli; that the boy Samuel served and had his early religious experiences; that Eli's sons scandalized the pious pilgrims by their irreverence; and that Eli met his death.

The Philistine War

According to the narrative of 1 Samuel 4, Samuel (acting on behalf of Eli?) summoned Israel to resist the Philistines, when they mobilized on the Ephraimite border. They had encamped at Aphek, which doubtless is the place of that name referred to in Joshua 12:18 and 1 Samuel 29:1. It lay at one of the critical invasion points, where roads lead up from the coastal plain into the mountain country. Josephus mentions a "tower of Aphek" near Antipatris (Acts 23:31)—a city built by Herod and named after his father. The latter city stood on the site of Pegai, the name of which means "springs" and which is to be sought at *Rās el 'Ain,* the source of the *'Aujah* River. On the western scarp of the tell, on which stands a ruin of a mediaeval castle, Albright was able to find an exposed stratum with Early Iron, Late Bronze, and Middle Bronze remains. There can be little doubt, therefore, that ancient Aphek is to be located here. Its antiquity is attested to by its occurrence in the Palestine list of Pharaoh Thutmosis III, *c.* 1500 B.C. Josephus' "Tower of Aphek" may have lain at *Mejdel Yāba,* a high site close by, suitable for a lookout, with a fine view of the country from Mount Carmel to Lydda and out through the *el Aujah* Valley to the sea. This is probably the Ebenezer, where the Israelites faced their foes. Southeast of *Mejdel Yāba* is level land, which then rises gently to the higher ground that marks the western edge of the Shephelah or foothills country. That level area could very well represent the battlefield.

The Israelites were worsted in the initial engagement, but not routed; for they sent to Shiloh for the Ark of the Covenant. The renewal of the battle only brought on a disastrous defeat; the Ark was captured, Eli's sons were slain, and Eli himself died when the news was borne to Shiloh by a runner.

Fortunes of the Ark

The military and political consequences of the Israelite defeat are not described in the story of 1 Samuel, but it is certain that a Philistine invasion of Ephraim followed, and that Shiloh and its temple were captured and destroyed. That destruction is referred to in the Book of Jeremiah, as an example of what the Lord may do to Jerusalem and its temple (Jer. 26:6, 9; 7:12, 14). This is an instructive example of how things can be omitted or forgotten in historical accounts. The narrative of 1 Samuel is absorbed entirely with the terrible havoc the captured Ark wrought in three of the five major cities of the Philistines to which it was taken. That made much more pleasant reading than what the Philistines did to the region of Mount Ephraim.

Ashdod is the first city on the list. The name survives to this day at the village of *Esdūd,* about three miles from the coast, a little south of the latitude of Jerusalem. In the Hyksos period Ashdod was already a city-state of consequence, but it played its most important role in Assyrian days, becoming the provincial capital of Philistaea. The Graeco-Roman harbor Azotus (*Minet Esdūd*) shows no traces of having been settled in the period with which we are now dealing. In Roman times the situation was reversed; the Madeba map shows Ashdod as an insignificant town, but gives the seaport, Azotus, considerable importance. Garstang speaks of the sand dunes having "already almost obliterated the ancient site of Ashdod." It lay on the western part of the hill, where abundant Early Iron Age sherds are to be found. Some day excavations may bring to light the remains of the Dagon temple, in which the statue of the pagan god fell before the Ark of the Lord. However, Ashdod soon wearied of the Ark and sent it away. The Ark of the Covenant was then taken to Gath.

The location of the second city, Gath, is still in dispute. *Tell es Ṣāfi,* a mound on a hill in the Shephelah, was for a long time believed to be this site, but it lies in an area which usually was in Israelite hands and has lately been taken by some to be Libnah. Philistine Gath must rather have lain south of Ekron, and some distance from it, as required by the present narrative, which speaks of the territory "from Ekron even unto Gath" (1 SAM. 7:14). Eusebius puts it five miles north of Eleutheropolis (*Beit Jibrīn*) for those going to Lydda (*Lidd*). No important mound in that area fits this description, and the Church Father may have been misled by a village existing in his day bearing for a name the common word *gath* "wine press." Jerome, commenting on Micah 1:10, notes that Gath was still a place of importance on the road from Eleutheropolis to Gaza. He thus sought it west, not north, of *Beit Jibrīn*. This road, little traveled because of the deep dry streambeds that must be crossed, passes *Tell el Menshīyeh,* a landmark in this part of Philistaea, rising two hundred feet above the plain and crowned by a *weli*. While mostly a natural hill, the tell is surmounted by an ancient mound, and the sides give the impression of having been artificially scarped. The name Gath would have been quite appropriate for a city on a natural hill suitable for the making of rock-hewn wine presses. Though no Bronze or Iron Age sherds have been found there, some exploratory digging would probably bring them to light. The matter of the location of Gath becomes important in connection with the Philistine line of retreat in 1 Samuel 17:52.

From Gath the Ark was then taken to Ekron. The name, as Robinson saw, survives in *'Āqir,* a town on the lower course of the *Wadi es Ṣarār*. A study of the boundary line of Judah in Joshua 15:11 recommends acceptance of its location there, rather than at the tell of *Qatrā* which some authorities have favored. As a modern town covers the site of

'Āqir, it is naturally difficult to find any trace thereabouts of this Philistine city, which later played an important role in Philistaea at the time of the Judaean King Hezekiah. The Assyrians write its name *Amqarruna*.

Finding out that the Ark brought them much misfortune, the Philistines sent it off on an ox-drawn cart, with pacifying gifts, leaving the destination open to higher guidance. The oxen headed for the Hebrew country and came first to Beth-shemesh, which no doubt was inhabited chiefly by Canaanites. We have already noted that this city lay near Zorah, the home of Samson, on the southern side of the *Wadi es Ṣarār.* The name has survived in *'Ain Shems,* but the ancient town stood on nearby *Tell er Rumeileh.* Excavations were conducted there in 1911–12 by the Palestine Exploration Fund, under Duncan Mackenzie, and again in 1928–33 by a Haverford College expedition under Elihu Grant. Beth-shemesh (called Ir-shemesh in Joshua 19:41 and probably Har-heres in Judges 1:35) had its heyday in the fifteenth century B.C., at which time it had a great wall and a remarkable south gate. At the beginning of the Iron Age the walls were repaired. Quantities of Philistine pottery found there suggest that the city was in Philistine hands for some time. The narrative we are dealing with, however, presupposes that it was in the Hebrew sphere. Nothing is said about bringing the Ark into the city. The great stone in the field of Joshua, where the Ark was deposited (1 SAM. 6:14 f.) and where sacrifice was brought to the LORD, evidently gives hint of an Israelite sanctuary, where the Israelite element of Beth-shemesh was wont to worship. The storyteller even has Levites on hand to tend to the Ark.

"Even unto the great stone of Abel, whereon they set down the ark of the LORD: which stone remaineth unto this day in the field of Joshua, the Beth-shemite." (1 SAM. 6:18 A.V.)

"The great stone, beside which they set down the ark of the LORD, is a witness to this day in the field of Joshua of Beth-shemesh." (1 SAM. 6:18 R.S.V.)

A sacred stone, whether pillar or altar, in the field near Beth-shemesh is thus explained as a "witness" stone by the narrator. Actually, such a stone will have been the object of veneration since time immemorial. Northeast of the old townsite is a *weli* dedicated to the hero Samson, and below it a small height with a rocky top; it has been suggested that this was the site of the Hebrew sanctuary meant in the story.

Beth-shemesh, too, suffered misfortune from the presence of the Ark, and desired to be rid of it. Word was sent to Kiriath-jearim inviting its inhabitants to come and get the sacred object.

> "And the men of Kirjath-jearim came, and fetched up the ark of the LORD, and brought it into the house of Abinadab in the hill." (1 SAM. 7:1 A.V.)

> *"And the men of Kiriath-jearim came and took up the ark of the LORD, and brought it to the house of Abinadab on the hill."* (1 SAM. 7:1 R.S.V.)

The town of Kiriath-jearim lay on the boundary between Judah and Benjamin (JOSH. 15:9; cf. 18:14–15). It is identified with Baalah by an editor in the former passage, but that may be an approximate localization; a change of name on the part of the town is improbable, since all *Kiriath* names known are pre-Israelite. We have already had occasion to note that the Danites had camped in that vicinity (JUDG. 18:12). Eusebius puts Kiriath-jearim at nine (or ten) miles from Jerusalem on the road to Lydda. This takes one to *Qaryet el Inab* or *Abu Ghōsh* along the modern Jerusalem-Jaffa road, just beyond the fourteenth kilometer mark. The identification is supported by various pilgrim texts. The hill on which *Abu Ghōsh* lies exhibits

no ancient potsherds or other vestiges of antiquity. Just beyond to the west, however, lies *Deir el-Azhar* on a hill dominating the road. Here there is a mound representing an ancient city of five to six acres, with debris of a depth of over twelve feet on the summit. Late Bronze and Early Iron sherds are to be found there and lower down there are numerous rock tombs. The city ramparts, however, are not discernible on the surface. The ruins of a large Byzantine basilica with a central nave, two rows of pillars, and a deep apse indicate that the site was held to be of Biblical importance. *Deir el-Azhar* has rightly been identified with Kiriath-jearim. We must then imagine "the house of Abinadab in the hill" to have been in the acropolis of the town. A cult of the Ark was carried on here, until David brought the sacred object to Jerusalem to attract the support of the Ephraimites (2 SAM. 6:2 f.).

Another Philistine War

The story of 1 Samuel 7:2–17 attributes the liberation from the Philistines to Samuel's initiative. This material, therefore, in a sense anticipates and duplicates the liberation effected by Saul, chosen by the LORD to lead Israel to that goal (1 SAM. 9). We have here a "theological" rather than a "national" version of this liberation. The narrative states that a religious assembly was held at Mizpeh (cf. page 161). The Philistines hearing of the Hebrew preparations sent their army, which arrived as Samuel was sacrificing. The LORD dispelled them with thunder. The Hebrews only had to take up the pursuit of a foe already routed.

> "And the men of Israel went out of Mizpeh, and pursued the Philistines, and smote them, until they came under Beth-car.
> Then Samuel took a stone, and set it between Mizpeh and Shen, and called the name of it Eben-ezer, saying, Hitherto hath the LORD helped us." (1 SAM. 7:11–12 A.V.)

"And the men of Israel went out of Mizpah and pursued the Philistines, and smote them, as far as below Beth-car.

Then Samuel took a stone and set it up between Mizpah and Jeshanah, and called its name Ebenezer; for he said, 'Hitherto the Lord *has helped us.'"* (1 Sam. 7:11–12 R.S.V.)

Mizpah lay north of Jerusalem (see page 271 and 317). The name Beth-car is none too certain. It can have no connection with the place of that name once mentioned along with Tekoa (2 Chron. 11:6) and which is perhaps a misspelled Beth-haccerem (cf. Jer. 6:1). A more westerly point must be meant, in view of the pursuit here chronicled. For the localization of the Ebenezer, the Hebrew text has "between Mizpah and Shen." The R.S.V. changes Shen to Jeshanah, a place that lay north of Bethel (2 Chron. 13:19) and has been located at *Burj el Isāneh*. The spacious hilltop bears Arab and Byzantine remains, but on the east side of the ridge, somewhat below the summit area, Albright found traces of an Israelite town.

It must be said, however, that "between Mizpah and Jeshanah" is a rather broad localization for the stone Ebenezer raised by Samuel. Since Bethel lay nearer to Jeshanah than Mizpah, it ought to have been one of the two points named. The correction "Jeshanah," therefore, becomes doubtful. The main fact that is discernible behind this late story is that at a certain point on the north-south highway there was a stone pillar called Ebenezer, which was not destroyed in the Deuteronomic reformation. The present narrative really provides an explanation of why it was not destroyed: it was not an idolatrous object but a memorial stone, raised by Samuel in commemoration of a victory over the Philistines. A different "Ebenezer" was already mentioned in an earlier narrative (1 Sam. 4:1). While there is no direct mention of a stone in that connection, the name implies its existence. Perhaps we have in 1 Samuel 7:12 a case of the transfer of a place to a more convenient point. (An interesting comparison can be made with the relocation of Rachel's tomb, see page 88.)

Saul's Kingship

There were various traditions about how Saul came to be the first king of a united Israel. One quite early account appears in 1 Samuel 9:1—10:16, although its conclusion has been sacrificed by the editor. Here is storytelling that has the freshness of a dewy morning. The writer is deeply imbued with the role of Saul.

How Saul Gained the Crown

A man named Kish of Gibeah of Benjamin (see page 178), had lost some asses and his tall, handsome son Saul and a servant set out to look for them.

"And he passed through mount Ephraim, and passed through the land of Shalisha, but they found them not: then they passed through the land of Shalim,

and there they were not: and he passed through the land of the Benjaminites, but they found them not.

And when they were come to the land of Zuph, Saul said to his servant that was with him, Come, and let us return." (1 Sam. 9:4–5 A.V.)

"And they passed through the hill country of Ephraim and passed through the land of Shalisha, but they did not find them. And they passed through the land of Shaalim, but they were not there. Then they passed through the land of Benjamin, but did not find them.

When they came to the land of Zuph, Saul said to his servant who was with him, 'Come, let us go back.'" (1 Sam. 9:4–5 R.S.V.)

Unless one is willing to accept the theory that the text has gotten disarranged and that "Mount Ephraim" and "land of the Benjaminites" should be made to change places, the land of Shalisha must be in Ephraim. It is no doubt identical with Baal-shalisha (2 KINGS 4:42). The "land," of course, is only the district of which the town is the center. The Palestine survey found a place called *Kufr Thilth,* a name quite comparable to Shalisha; it lies in the west at the foot of the mountains. The land of Shalim, or Shaalim (R.S.V.), should perhaps be vocalized *Shualim* and then may be identical with the land of Shual (1 SAM. 13:17). The allusion to "passing through the land of the Benjaminites" is problematic, because the next area they come to, the "land of Zuph," is in Ephraim. Zuph is the district in which Ramathaim or Ramah, the home of Samuel, lay.

Ramah is not mentioned by name at all in this story. The servant merely calls Saul's attention to the fact that they are now in the close vicinity of a town where there is a seer of note, whom people can consult in connection with their problems.

To get to the town they had to go up a hill, at the foot of which lay a well or spring. From maidens who were coming down to draw water, Saul learned that the seer had just gotten back from a tour and was expected to bless a sacrifice on this very day. The city was walled and had a gateway in which Saul encountered Samuel as he was about to go up to the high place, which thus lay at a more elevated point. He was invited to attend the religious celebration, where he immediately became the guest of honor at a sacrificial meal prepared in anticipation of his coming.

The ancient Church Father Eusebius located Ramah at *Rentīs,* holding it to be identical with the place called Arimathia in the New Testament. Many leading scholars are disposed to yield to his authority in the matter, while admitting that the require-

4.1 *Gibeah of Benjamin or Gibeah of Saul* (Tell el Fūl). (*Matson Photo Service*)

ments of the narrative, viz., that the city lay on a hillside with its high place still farther up, are not met by this identification.

After the feast at the high place Saul spent the night on the roof of Samuel's house. He was awakened by the seer in the early morning and escorted to the limits of the city's territory. The servant was sent on ahead, since Samuel wished to speak privately with Saul. Samuel then anointed Saul king of Israel. He predicted certain things that would happen on Saul's journey home, which would convince him of the seer's supernatural knowledge.

"... thou shalt find two men by Rachel's sepulchre in the border of Benjamin at Zelzah; ...

thou shalt come to the plain of Tabor, and there shall meet thee three men going up to God to Beth-el, ...

After that thou shalt come to the hill of God, where is the garrison of the Philistines." (1 SAM. 10:2–5 A.V.)

"... *you will meet two men by Rachel's tomb in the territory of Benjamin at Zelzah. ... Then you shall go on from there further and come to the oak of Tabor; three men going up to God at Bethel will meet you there. ... After that you shall come to Gibeathelohim, where there is a garrison of the Philistines."* (1 SAM. 10:2–5 R.S.V.)

The tomb of Rachel thus was shown on the Ephraimite-Benjaminite border in the days of this writer, and that no doubt was still

4.2 *The Ramah of Benjamin* (Er Rām). (*Matson Photo Service*)

the case in Jeremiah's time (JER. 31:15). The point where the boundary between Ephraim and Benjamin crossed the north-south highway, therefore, takes on considerable importance. The question hinges largely on the description of the line in Joshua 18:13. It seems probable that the line passed over just south of *el Bīreh.*

The name Zelzah which occurs in the narrative is otherwise unknown and may have been merely a village name. The tomb of Rachel was shown there in these early days.

The next point where an incident is to take place is the "plain [-tree] of Tabor," or "oak of Tabor," which, therefore, lay between the tomb of Rachel and Gibeah. It must, however, still be some distance from Gibeah, because there would not have been much sense in giving Saul victuals when he was on the point of reaching his home town. We never hear of this oak again, but the Baal-tamar of Judges 20:33 must have been in the same vicinity. One may seek it north of the point where a branch road turns off eastward to the Benjaminite Ramah (*er Rām*).

The last point mentioned in Samuel's prediction is the "hill of God" or better Gibeath-elohim. It is called Gibeah in Judges 20:10 and is evidently Saul's city, where everyone knew him. There is thus good reason to believe that this is another name for the Gibeah of Saul, which lay at *Tell el Fūl. Tell el Fūl,* "the mound of the bean," is three

and a half miles north of Jerusalem. Excavations were conducted there by the American School of Oriental Research under William F. Albright in 1922–23 and 1933. A citadel built about 1200 B.C. with double wall, casemates and bastions was found to have existed there, but was destroyed and then rebuilt in the eleventh century B.C. The excavator would connect the archaeological evidence with the destruction of Gibeah reported in Judges 20 and attributes the renewed building up of the fortress to Saul.

The story of Judges 20–21 has been invoked to show that the Gibeah of Saul could not have been described as "Gibeah of God," but that is a late, anti-Benjaminite narrative and cannot be of any help in this connection.

The final point in the instructions given to Saul was that he should go to Gilgal, whither Samuel then would also come. This, of course, is the holy place of the Benjaminites, near Jericho mentioned before. There the decisive public act—the crowning of Saul—was no doubt to take place. Unfortunately, the ancient narrative breaks off in 1 Samuel 10:16 with mention of Saul's discreet silence about his interview with the seer.

Instead of an account of the happenings at Gilgal we get a late story in chapter 10, which speaks of a national assembly convoked by Samuel at Mizpah, and an account of how Saul was chosen king there by lot. This was really superfluous, if he was already divinely elected and anointed by Samuel, as related in chapter 9, and shows that we have here a parallel version of the events.

Saul Delivers Jabesh

A third version of how Saul became king, 1 Samuel 11, connects that event with his assuming the leadership on his own initiative, much as Gideon did in the version of Judges 6:33 f.

The people of Jabesh in Gilead, on the other side of the Jordan, were hard pressed by the Ammonites who had invaded the

Israelite territory. Humiliating conditions were imposed in the event of surrender; the alternative was to die fighting. Confident of the weakness of Israel, the Ammonite king consented to give them seven days' grace to obtain help. When the messengers bearing the news came to Gibeah in Benjamin to appeal for aid in their peril, Saul, the son of Kish, took steps to mobilize a force that would go to the relief of Jabesh. The suggested gathering point was at Bezek. This was in Manasseh and of course implies that the Manassites willingly co-operated.

Bezek's name survives to this day in *Khirbet Ibzīk*. The mountain peak *Rās Ibzīk*, rising to the west of it, overlooks the site. The town guarded the entrance to a ravine leading down into the Jordan country (*Wadi el Khashneh*). Across the river from the point where this ravine opens into the *el Ghōr* is an incoming eastern brook ravine on which, as we shall see shortly, Jabesh lay. Bezek was thus the natural jumping off place for an expedition to Jabesh. The important thing, of course, was to surprise the foe, and the emissaries from Jabesh were no doubt advised how to aid in the matter. They left with the assurance that an attempt to save them would materialize by noon of the next day. We must imagine that they brought the message to Jabesh that same afternoon, presumably on the sixth day of the seven-day truce. Meanwhile, fighting men from various places in Benjamin and Ephraim had to be summoned.

Since we find Saul near Jabesh before daybreak, we must assume that the march thither from Bezek was carried out under the cover of darkness—in itself no small feat. Perhaps the first part of the journey was undertaken before darkness fell. From Bezek to the eastern side of the *el Ghōr* and the entrance of the wadi leading up to Gilead was about twelve and a half miles.

The valley on the east side is today called the *Wadi ez Zqēyiq,* and has still another name in the narrow gorge above. Higher up

4.3 *Looking north at Jabesh in Gilead* (Tell el Maqlūb). (*Courtesy Nelson Glueck*)

where the valley broadens out it is called *Wadi Yābis*. It seems strange to us that a stream valley should have such shifts of name in different sectors, but this is very common in Palestine. Nelson Glueck, to whose pioneering archaeological survey of this area we are so greatly indebted, made out a strong case for seeking the city of Jabesh at the joint site of *Tell el Meqbereh* and *Tell Abu Kharaz,* which he first saw and ascertained the name of in 1942. But Jabesh is most apt to have lain in the vicinity of the sector of the valley that is still called *Wadi Yābis*. There is a site there which can well be identified with the old city—*Tell el Maqlūb*. It lies above a little valley that is a mile and a half long and a little more than half a mile wide at its widest point. The identification tallies with the statement of Eusebius that "Iabis" was six Roman miles from Pella (*Khirbet Faḥil*) on the road to Gerasa (*Jerash*). Most of the milestones of the Roman road of Eusebius' day (1, 3, 4, 5, 8, 9, 10) are still there. The missing sixth milestone must have lain about one-half mile west-northwest of *Tell el Maqlūb*. There are well cultivated garden lands at the foot of this hill. There are also orchards and extensive vineyards in the vicinity. *Tell el Maqlūb* reveals fortifications which could be of Iron Age vintage, and sherds dating from Early Bronze to Roman times are found there.

The concentric attack of three Israelite detachments on the Ammonite camp was successful. The foe was routed and the attack

4.4 *Geba in Benjamin* (Jeba'). (*Matson Photo Service*)

was kept up till the heat of the day, by which time the warriors were too fatigued to continue the pursuit. So Saul made good his promise to the Gileadite city. According to this particular narrative, it was the victory thus won that led to a widespread acknowledgment of his authority and to his being made king over Israel and Judah at Gilgal, therein no doubt paralleling the other early story (as hinted in 1 SAM. 10:8). This is clearly the most realistic account of how Saul became king. But it is not easy to reconcile with the supposition of an existing Philistine domination presupposed in 1 Samuel 10:5; 13:3 f. It should be noted that the very brief summary of Saul's wars in 1 Samuel 14:47 f. puts the war against the Ammonites *after* his attainment of the kingship.

The Uprising Against the Philistines

The sequel to acceptance of Saul's leadership—at first perhaps only by Benjamin—was his raising of a military force. It naturally had weapons, though a later writer whose primary purpose was to give glory to the deity, told the story in such a way as to leave all but Saul and Jonathan unarmed (1 SAM. 13:22).

No doubt the recruiting was done as secretly as possible. The signal of outright revolt was given by Saul's son, Jonathan. In the present text Geba is mentioned as the place where this occurred; but the name Gibeah is sometimes confused with Geba, and that is the case here. A comparison with

1 Samuel 10:5 shows that the place meant is the same one which is called Gibeath-elohim in that connection. We have seen that according to the itinerary presupposed the latter name must refer to Saul's Gibeah.

What it was that Jonathan did is debatable. The Revised Standard Version renders "he defeated the garrison of the Philistines," but the word translated "garrison" more probably means "pillar" or "governor"; if it means "pillar," Jonathan would have knocked down a war monument raised by the Philistines in Gibeah; if it means "governor," he would have assassinated the Philistine prefect at Gibeah. The latter is the most likely interpretation.

Whatever the act, a Philistine military force now was sent against Saul. We learn that Saul and his force (including Jonathan, and hence diverging from 1 SAM. 13:2) had established headquarters at Geba in Benjamin. The name still survives in *Jeba'*, which lies east of the Benjaminite Ramah (*er Rām*), and so northwest of Saul's Gibeah. The modern village stands on a considerable mound. It was strongly fortified in the days of the later kings of Judah (1 KINGS 15:22; 2 KINGS 23:8), and may already have been a walled town at this time (cf. 1 SAM. 14:16). The Philistine base of operations was at Michmash (1 SAM. 13:16). The name of the place survives in *Mukhmās* west of the Benjaminite Ramah.

"And the spoilers came out of the camp of the Philistines in three companies: one company turned unto the way that leadeth to Ophrah, unto the land of Shual:

And another company turned the way to Beth-horon: and another company turned to the way of the border that looketh to the valley of Zeboim toward the wilderness." (1 SAM. 13:17-18 A.V.)

"And raiders came out of the camp of the Philistines in three companies; one company turned toward Ophrah, to the land of Shual, another company turned toward

Beth-horon, and another company turned toward the border that looks down upon the valley of Zeboim toward the wilderness." (I SAM. 13:17–18 R.S.V.)

We have already seen that an Ophrah—though scarcely that of Gideon—lay at *eṭ Ṭaiyibeh* east of Bethel (see page 154). If a detachment was sent *west* toward Beth-horon the Philistines can hardly have come from that direction. This might suggest that their original base was farther to the north, perhaps at Beth-shean (I SAM. 31:10). The third detachment went to "the border," or better, as recommended by the Greek translation, to "the hill," that looks down on the valley of hyenas (Hebrew *zebō'îm*) toward the wilderness. The *Rās eṭ Ṭawīl*, the highest and most distinctive summit between Michmash and Jericho, with a fine view toward the south, may be the hill meant.

The name "valley of Zeboim" still abides in this area in the *Wadi abu Ḍbā'* which enters the *Wadi el Qelt* below the *Wadi eṣ Ṣewēnīt*. The Philistine detachments sent out seem to have been foraging parties robbing the herds and harvesting the grain. An outpost was put at the crossing (pass, R.S.V.) over the depression south of the Michmash. This had both an offensive and a defensive value—it could lead to an invasion of the Hebrew-held territory to the south and block the way for a Hebrew attack on the Philistines.

4.5 *Michmash* (Mukhmās). (*Matson Photo Service*)

The position of Saul and his force is also given in the narrative.

"And Saul tarried in the uttermost part of Gibeah under a pomegranate tree which is in Migron." (I SAM. 14:2 A.V.)

"Saul was staying in the outskirts of Gibeah under the pomegranate tree which is at Migron." (I SAM. 14:2 R.S.V.)

However, the name Gibeah must be an error here for Geba. It was that town (not Gibeah) that lay in the sphere of the happenings that follow. While Geba's site is known, that of Migron is less certain. It is mentioned again in Isaiah's prophetic description of the onset of the Assyrian king against Jerusalem. He imagines him as coming to this very pass (Is. 10:28–29). The statement that the point where Saul stayed was on the outskirts of Geba can well refer to the extreme limits of the town lands (cf. JOSH. 4:19, of Gilgal at the east border of Jericho). If Saul was stationed as far north as *Tell Miriam*, his ability to take immediate advantage of the situation created by Jonathan would be far more understandable than if Migron lay close to Geba. The identification of Migron with *Tell Miriam* is thus highly plausible.

The spotlight of the chapter falls on the exploit of Jonathan and his armor-bearer. It seems likely that a hero-worshipping age, in recounting the exploit, has lost sight of the fact that Jonathan had a commando force with him at the time. The young warrior evidently decided to cross the valley considerably lower down, and make a penetration into Philistine-held territory (I SAM. 14:4–5).

Accepting the challenge of the Philistine sentries, who may have been spread out along the ridge, Jonathan clambered up the ledge and gained the top. Presumably the Philistines, as dwellers of the plain, were not quite aware of the climbing ability of the Hebrew mountaineers and were taken by surprise when Jonathan (and his men) bore down on them. Confusion was caused by this attack from an unexpected quarter. The whole Philistine camp was soon alarmed.

> "And the watchmen of Saul in Gibeah of Benjamin looked: and, behold, the multitude melted away, and they went on beating down one another." (1 SAM. 14:16 A.V.)

> *"And the watchmen of Saul in Gibeah of Benjamin looked; and behold, the multitude was surging hither and thither."* (1 SAM. 14:16 R.S.V.)

If Gibeah of Saul is referred to here, this must be an error on the part of some ancient editor, or copyist, for, as we have seen, Saul was at or near *Geba*. From the towers of the latter place, but not from Gibeah of Saul, the watchmen could have observed what went on at Michmash. If a signaling system was used from Geba to give information to a force stationed in such an advanced position as *Tell Miriam,* the events become quite understandable. Taking immediate advantage of the distraction caused by Jonathan's raid, Saul and his men, so we must suppose, attacked and routed the whole Philistine camp at Michmash. The battle is said to have passed beyond Beth-aven, i.e., Bethel or Ai (1 SAM. 14:23). That suggests that the Philistines fled northward toward a base lying in that direction.

At this point the story of the battle would have seemed originally to have reached a conclusion. In what follows, another source has perhaps been utilized. The pursuit, instead of going to Bethel, goes from Michmash to Aijalon (1 SAM. 14:31). This would necessitate a turning off to the left south of "Bethaven" to strike the road that leads (via the present *Ramallah*) to Beth-horon. At the latter place this road joined the more southerly one coming from Gibeon (JOSH. 10:10). But there is no realistic geographical detail in this story. Where the wood was in which Jonathan dipped his spear into honey, and

where the altar stood that Saul raised, are not stated.

The liberation from the Philistine oppression did not mean the end of war with the Philistines (1 SAM. 14:52). Saul evidently set up and organized a Hebrew kingdom— an achievement that we wish might have been given more specific reporting. He seems to have been recognized as king by the Judaean clans, for we soon find him operating in their territory. He is said to have fought victorious wars with Moab, Ammon, Edom, Zobah, and Amalek (1 SAM. 14: 47-48). Of the Ammonite war, we have already heard the report by a source that put it before Saul's attainment of the crown (1 SAM. 11). The Amalekite war is related in the present connection (1 SAM. 15) and is the occasion of Samuel's break with Saul.

The Amalekite Campaign

It was perhaps as protector of the tribe of Simeon that Saul had to concern himself with the Amalekites, referred to as "those who plundered Israel"—not Judah! The narrative gives Samuel a leading role and has a priestly-prophetic viewpoint. One cannot believe that so vast a number of soldiers as is said to have participated was mentioned by the original author; the figure is no doubt due, as so often, to later revision. At Geba a three thousand man force was under Saul's command (1 SAM. 13:2). A similar modest force is certainly indicated for a campaign against the Amalekites in the wastes of the Negeb.

Saul mustered his force at Telaim (mentioned as Telem, JOSH. 15:24), and the same name should also be read in 1 Samuel 27:8 (instead of "from of old"). This place has not been successfully identified, as yet. Since it is mentioned right after Ziph in the reference cited, one can at least say in what general area it is to be sought; for the name Ziph survives at *Tell Zīph* southeast of Hebron.

Saul is mindful of the old link of Israel with the Kenites, who at a slightly earlier time, had left the region south of Arad and had attached themselves to the Amalekites (JUDG. 1:16, according to a text correction based on the Greek version, cf. page 147). The Kenites are given a safe conduct out of the enemy territory. Nothing is said of a capture of the Amalekite city. If Saul defeated them "from Havilah to Shur" this does not mean that the Hebrew force marched to inner Arabia where Havilah is to be sought; it merely means that the power of the Amalekites which extended from Havilah to Shur, i.e., from the *Nejd* to Suez, collapsed. They must have controlled the South Arabian trade route at this time, much as the Nabataeans did in more advanced times.

In connection with the return of Saul from the campaign, the town of Carmel is the first point reached. Of this city, which also lies south of Hebron and well to the south of Ziph, something more will be said later (see page 187). Saul set up a pillar there, perhaps bearing an inscription boasting of the success of his campaign. Here, too, is put an ominous event—the break between him and the prophet Samuel.

David and Goliath

As Saul's reign progressed one of his leading commanders, David son of Jesse from Bethlehem of Judah, came to be recognized as a rising young man. There were several stories about how he had come to the fore. The best known, and the only one requiring comment here, is that which tells how he performed a mighty feat of valor when a mere stripling. The stage for it is set by a Philistine war.

"Now the Philistines . . . pitched between Shochoh and Azekah, in Ephes-dammim.

And Saul and the men of Israel . . . pitched by the valley of Elah . . .

and there was a valley between them." (1 SAM. 17:1-3 A.V.)

"*Now the Philistines . . . encamped between Socoh and Azekah, in Ephes-dammim. And Saul and the men of Israel . . . encamped in the valley of Elah . . . with a valley between them.*" (1 SAM. 17:1-3 R.S.V.)

The locality meant cannot be in doubt, for we have a fixed point in Socoh, or Shocoh, the name of which survives to this day in *el Shuwēke*. Ancient Socoh lay to the west of the modern village on the last eminence of the same ridge (*Khirbet 'Abbād*). Early Iron Age sherds are found there and remains of ancient walls of Israelite days can be traced. Socoh had an ideal position for controlling the valley below (the *Wadi eṣ Ṣūr*) shortly before it widens out into the *Wadi es Samṭ* (or "Valley of Accacias"). The other point, Azekah, has already been mentioned (see page 138); we have seen that it is probably identical with the bold site *Tell Zakarīyeh*.

Between these two places, then, the Philistines were encamped, perhaps on a height west of the road coming from *Tell eṣ Ṣāfi* (Libnah?). Their purpose must have been to force their way up to *Beit Nettīf* and into Judah. It was the task of the defenders of Judaean territory to block this plan, and one may suppose them to have been encamped on the heights of *Beit Nettīf,* guarding the road up into the high country. The Israelite camp is said to have extended down into the valley of Elah ("the terebinth"), probably so-named for a single tree that stood there. This apparently refers to the *Wadi eṣ Ṣūr*.

How the youthful David came to visit his brothers and how he volunteered to fight the "giant" Philistine challenger is too memorable to need retelling. The only item requiring our attention is the brook from which he picked up stones to use in his sling, the first shot laying low the braggard Philistine. The brook must be the dry streambed of the *Wadi eṣ Ṣūr*.

David's victory over Goliath is followed by an attack of the Israelite forces on the

Philistines and a pursuit to the very gates of the cities Gath and Ekron (see page 174). The lateness of this story is shown by the assumption that David took the head of Goliath to Jerusalem, a city that was not yet subject to the Hebrews (2 SAM. 5:6 f.). The narrative has nevertheless preserved a vivid picture of a battle in a scene that doubtless saw more than one occasion of this sort.

David's Life at Court and His Flight

However it may have come about, David became a courtier of Saul and an officer of high rank in his army. While he was snubbed by Saul, when the latter gave the daughter promised David to a man from (Abel-)Meholah (see page 278), he received in marriage another daughter named Michal. He became a popular figure and this aroused the aging Saul's jealousy. David was forced to flee several times from the court to save his life. According to one reported incident he took refuge with Samuel in "Naioth in Ramah" (1 SAM. 19:19). Naioth is hardly a proper name, however, but must be a designation of a certain building or area (e.g., a prophet's "monastery") in Ramah. The story describes Saul as going there and gives a fresh version of how he was seized with prophetic enthusiasm (cf. 1 SAM. 10:10 f.). It has some local knowledge of Ramah when it speaks of his arrival. The uncertainty as to the location of Ramah does not permit further elucidation of the topography.

A more decisive departure is taken after conference with Jonathan and a final meeting with him in the fields near the Gibeah of Saul. Warned that Saul's intentions were definitely hostile, David went to Nob where the priest Ahimelech gave him holy bread.

Nob must have been an important sanctuary for the Benjaminites; it was probably Saul's official temple. Here was the sword of Goliath and an "Ephod." Where the town lay, whose priests soon were to suffer a bitter penalty for giving aid to David, is an interesting question.

4.6 *Thus may David have played the harp before Saul. A Meggido Ivory. (Courtesy The Oriental Institute, University of Chicago)*

The low hill of *Qu'meh,* a mile to the north of Mount Scopus and on the divide between the Dead Sea and the Mediterranean, is especially recommended as the site of Nob. It has the advantage of lying closer to the Gibeah of Saul than Mount Scopus. To the south of *el Qu'meh,* the Assyrian host advancing from Geba would first have come in view of the western hill of Jerusalem. Neither of these places show traces of Israelite antiquity, but ages of weathering and denudation well could have destroyed the shallow remains that can be expected to have been left of Iron Age villages on this rocky terrain.

David in Exile

David's flight from Nob took him to Philistaea. At Gath (cf. page 174) he was received with suspicion and found it advisable to simulate insanity. Betaking himself thence he sought safety in his native Judah. The fortress of Adullam provided him with a haven of refuge. In Judah David could count on tribal sympathy over against Saul and his Benjaminite governing clique.

Adullam's site cannot be in doubt. It lay at *Khirbet esh Sheikh Madhkūr,* on a hill west of the valley that leads down to the scene of the David-Goliath encounter (*Wadi es Sūr*). More specifically, it lies on the north end of a narrow ridge between the main valley and a side valley. On the northern side, which provides the main approach to this small but strong town, near the foot of the hill, there is a fine well with spring water and near it are a great many stone watering troughs. This well is called *Bīr 'Īd el Mīyeh* and preserves the ancient name of Adullam in Arabicised form. Adullam was, indeed, a "fortress" of some strength. Nevertheless, David, though he brought his family to this place from Bethlehem, did not feel too secure here and so negotiated with the king of the Moabites to give asylum to his parents.

The Moabite ruler is said to have resided at Mizpeh, but there is no clue to the location of this city. Perhaps the name is only another designation for Kir Hareseth (2 KINGS 3:25), an outstanding observation point and the natural Moabite capital (see page 284).

But David decided not to remain in Adullam. On the advice of a prophet named Gad, he went farther up into Judah and came to the "forest of Hereth" (1 SAM. 22:5), doubtless named after a town Hereth that lay in this locality. The forests of ancient Palestine were chiefly on the western inclines. One may surmise, therefore, that Hereth was in the mountain country southwest of Adullam. At any rate, it was near enough to Keilah that David could be tempted to intervene when the Philistines laid siege to that city and were plundering the threshing floors.

The location of Keilah ("the spur") is also known, for the name survives in *Khirbet Qīlah,* on the east side of the *Wadi eṣ Ṣūr.* It lay on a hill between two valleys that come down to the wadi. This hill is separated from the ridge of which it is a projection by a drop of forty-five feet. On the remaining three sides it falls off steeply. The fairly level top is 200 yards long by 115 yards wide. Near the foot of the hill on the north is a well with good spring water. Keilah was thus a much larger fortress than Adullam; it is mentioned in the Tell el Amarna letters.

David now had obtained a priest in the person of the fugitive Abiathar, who alone of the priests of Nob had escaped Saul's vengeance, and had brought the "Ephod" (probably the garment for a divine statue). The oracle, obtained through the priest before the Ephod, recommended David to go to the aid of the beleaguered Keilah. Though his men were reluctant to obey, they were promised success and so the action was undertaken. The Philistine siege was broken and David took residence for a while in Keilah. However, word soon reached him that Saul was preparing to trap him there. Fearing that in a showdown the Canaanitic inhabitants would deliver him up, David quit this fortress city and again took up a roving existence. It was in this period of poverty and distress that David's friend Jonathan secretly sought him out and encouraged him.

But the news of David's whereabouts was soon carried to Saul by the Ziphites.

> "Then came up the Ziphites to Saul to Gibeah, saying, Doth not David hide himself with us in strong holds in the wood, in the hill of Ha-chilah, which is on the south of Jeshimon?" (1 SAM. 23:19 A.V.)

> *"Then the Ziphites went up to Saul at Gibeah, saying, 'Does not David hide among us in the strongholds at Horesh, on the hill of Hachilah, which is south of Jeshimon?'"* (1 SAM. 23:19 R.S.V.)

Ziph is undoubtedly to be sought at *Tell Zīf,* lying on an eminence that rises about a hundred feet above the plain, some five miles south of Hebron, and must anciently have dominated this whole area. Ziph is mentioned on royal Judean jar handles and perhaps was crown property. Sherds of 1050–587 B.C. were found there in 1962. A *Khirbet Khoreisa* that could be identical with Horesh lies some two miles south of Ziph. But it is possible that the reference to Horesh is misplaced and that this town is to be sought near Keilah (at *Kharās* some three miles east

4.7 *Looking back to the high country of Judah from Masada. (Department of Archaeology, Hebrew University and Louis M. Rabinowitz)*

of Keilah). As a more precise statement about the hill of Hachilah appears in a parallel version of this incident (1 SAM. 26:3), we will defer comment on it until later. Instead of a pursuit in that area, the sequel tells us about one in the Maon district.

"But David and his men were in the wilderness of Maon, in the plain on the south of Jeshimon." (1 SAM. 23:24 A.V.)

"Now David and his men were in the wilderness of Maon, in the Arabah to the south of Jeshimon." (1 SAM. 23:24 R.S.V.)

Maon, a later district capital (JOSH. 15:55–57), lay a short distance south of Ziph, at *Tell Ma'in*, which preserves the ancient name. East of it are extensive wastelands, which could well be called "the wilderness of Maon." Jeshimon was previously encountered in connection with the view from Pisgah or Peor (NUM. 21:20; 23:28). It there seemed to mean the desert at the northeast end of the Dead Sea. Here, however, Jeshimon must mean a desert area west of the Dead Sea. The words "in the plain" do not fit very well if given the usual meaning of Jordan Valley (*el Ghōr*). Perhaps the author

uses it for the region around *Masada,* which could well be described as south of the Maon desert and where there is quite a long stretch of plain. The story goes on to speak about a rock (or crag), which ever after was known as Sela-hammahlakoth (1 SAM. 23:25, 28). The Revised Standard Version translates the phrase "the Rock of Escape," but it literally means "the rock of the ways." It seems likely that the rock got its name from paths ascending it from several angles. The possibility that the great crag of Masada itself, where Herod later built his fortress, is meant seems to us an attractive one. For this is a great place and merited a name. The ways up it need only to have been improved, not created by Herod. Others would seek the rock four miles southeast of Ziph.

Further Incidents of David's Fugitive Life

Another story about David's wandering life came from En-gedi, "the spring of the kid," an oasis on the western side of the Dead Sea, the ancient name of which survives to this day as *'Ain Jidi.* A snatch from the Song of Songs shows that it was a vineyard district in olden times (SOL. 1:14). There was evidently a town or village of that name (JOSH. 15:62) which is identified with Hazazon-tamar (GEN. 14:7). But that may only be an approximate localization (see page 68). There are various small ruin mounds in this neighborhood, though no Iron Age or Bronze Age sherds have been found at them. The late Roman En-gedi lay at *Tell ej-Jurn,* a round hill south of the spring, for it is a single spring on a terrace several hundred feet above the Dead Sea that creates the oasis, though in different ages the water was utilized by means of aqueducts in different parts of the basin, in rotating cultivation. One may suspect that David drank more than once from the spring of En-gedi, but his place of sojourn was near the steep and perilous track that leads down for a thousand feet to the spring. It was hereabouts that Saul sought again to apprehend him and once more a specific area plays a role in the events (1 SAM. 24:1 f.). The story presupposes ledges of the sort on which ibexes like to find a secure point of vantage and hence bearing the name "the Wild-goats' Rocks." At their foot was a deep cave, in front of which there was a sheepfold, no doubt made of a wall of rough field stones. One can hardly expect to find the exact locality described in a story of this sort. However, a few caves do exist near En-gedi, notably "the Cave of the Christians."

According to the Biblical story David was hidden in the cave when Saul entered it. He cut off "the skirt of Saul's robe" and later confronted the king with it, proving to him that he had spared his life. After Saul had desisted from further pursuit, David and his men "went up to the stronghold," i.e., perhaps one situated in the wild-goats' rocks; several strongholds in the En-gedi vicinity were referred to in 1 Samuel 23:29.

We next hear of David's going down to the Wilderness of Paran (1 SAM. 25:1) immediately after the death and burial of Samuel. That wilderness lay south of Kadesh Barnea (see page 116). No reason is given for the transfer, nor is any happening reported, and so this seems to be a stray, disconnected item about David's migratory days. The compiler evidently was not clear about the location of the Wilderness of Paran, for he continues with a story about a man of Maon. It relates how David "levied" on the wealthier citizens of this general area in order to "protect" them, and how one man named Nabal, who would not pay for such protection, was saved from being slain only because his wife made payment without his knowledge. Since the man got a stroke and died when he heard what his wife had done, David was in a position to marry the widow and thereby attain influence among the Calebites to whom Nabal belonged. While Nabal lived at Maon his business was in Carmel. This Carmel's name still survives in *Kirmil,* a few miles to the north of Maon (see page 186). The place, primarily occupied by ruins of two forts of Roman and Crusader days, has long been exploited as a quarry for building materials by the people of nearby *Yaṭṭa,* which preserves the name of ancient Juttah (JOSH. 15:55). Iron Age sherds have also been found there. Above all, the enduring names bear unmistakable witness to the fact that the ancient places lay thereabouts, and that these are the scenes of the early history of David. The latter's success in winning the support of the Calebites eventually led to his kingship at Hebron (2 SAM. 5:1–3). His marriage to the widow was thus an important factor in his rise.

Another version of the betrayal of David by the Ziphites follows (1 SAM. 26, cf. 23:19). Gibeath-hachilah, or hill of Hachila, was evidently a hill on the rim of the tableland, east or southeast of Ziph. The British surveyors thought they had found a suitable equivalent for Gibeath-hachilah in a long ridge running out of the Ziph plateau, about five and a half miles from that place. The name of the suggested ridge, *Ḍahr el Kōla,* however, can hardly be connected with Hachila, and a long ridge is not a hill (Hebrew *gibeah*). An appropriate localization has yet to be found. The incident described as taking place here parallels the one that occurred near En-gedi (1 Sam. 24), in respect to David's magnanimity, his communication of it to Saul, and in Saul's seeming change of heart.

The final and historically most informative narrative about David's fugitive existence is that of his removal to Philistaea with his armed force of six hundred men. He gets Achish, king of Gath (see page 174), to assign him the outpost city of Ziklag. The latter was in old Simeonite territory (1 Chron. 4:30), in the same district with Beersheba. It probably lay between Beersheba and Gath. In the region north of Beersheba, there are no settlements of any consequence until one comes to *Tell el Khuweilfeh*. It seems probable that people living in towns up in the high country came down to the intervening area at sowing and reaping time, as is still the case to this day. *Tell el Khuweilfeh* thus seems to be a natural candidate for identification with Ziklag. It was probably crown property of Achish of Gath, and may have lain outside of the territory of that city-state. This would explain how the House of David could later claim it as crown property, since Achish bestowed it on David as a fief.

David now carried on a dangerous double-dealing role in his isolated situation. He used his troop of six hundred men in warlike raids and expeditions against the semi-nomadic groups dwelling to the south, who were actually under Philistine protection—the Geshurites, Gezrites and Amalekites (1 Sam. 27:8). Since David "went up," the groups in question lived on higher ground than Ziklag, but doubtless to the south. The Geshurites and Gezrites (R.S.V., Girzites) may be people from Geshur and the city of Gezer, who had migrated or been transplanted to this neighborhood. The fact that the Egyptians carried off populations has recently been made vivid by a newly-published stela of Amenophis II.

David followed a procedure of barbarous extermination, on the principle that "dead men tell no tales." At the same time he gave false accounting to Achish of Gath, pretending that he had made forays into the Negeb of Judah or of the Jerahmeelites or of the Kenites. Jerahmeel, we need only note in passing, was closely linked with the Kenites (1 Sam. 30:29). By killing off the allies of the Philistines, he did his own people a service and put himself in a position deserving their gratitude. At the same time he created the nucleus of a war-hardened private army, with a spirit quite different from that manifested at first (1 Sam. 23:3). As commander of six hundred veterans, he was thus in a position to capitalize on the chaotic situation that arose after Saul's death.

The Philistine War Begins

The Philistines now made a determined effort to subjugate the rising state of Israel. The information is very meager, however. We are not even told what city was dominant in Philistaea at this time, but merely learn that Achish of Gath was in the alliance and that David and his contingent were among his troops. In fact, David and his men were the guardsmen of Achish, in accordance with a system followed by many rulers to trust foreign mercenaries rather than their own people.

The text states:

"And the Philistines gathered themselves together, and came and pitched in Shunem: and Saul gathered all Israel together, and they pitched in Gilboa." (1 Sam. 28:4 a.v.)

"The Philistines assembled, and came and encamped at Shunem: and Saul gathered all Israel, and they encamped at Gilboa." (1 Sam. 28:4 r.s.v.)

The invasion route of the Philistines led them to the Plain of Jezreel. The fact that they chose to attack from the north, rather than to attempt an invasion through the valleys leading up into Judah or Benjamin, suggests that they enjoyed the support of the Canaanite cities of the plain and that the latter had a strong hand in the whole plan. The location of Shunem is well known; the name survives, slightly altered, in *Solem,* at the foot of the *Jebel Daḥi.* The city of Israelite times lay at a small but typical tell north of the present village. Below the tell there is a spring which supplied the ancient town with water, as it does the modern. The mound is surrounded by cactus growth and has been used for a cemetery in recent times, so that excavations are not feasible here. We know from the Tell el Amarna letters that Shunem had suffered a destruction in the late Bronze Age and that its lands were then being farmed by nearby Megiddo.

Saul's army is said to have encamped at Gilboa. This was probably only a village in those days. The name survives slightly altered in *Jelbōn,* which, however, lies some miles south of the area where the battle of 1 Samuel 29:1 f. must have occurred. The narrative of chapter 28 was not so much interested in the battle as in Saul's nocturnal trip to consult the witch of En-dor—one of the most dramatic stories to come down from ancient Israel. This town lay on the steep northern slope of the *Jebel Daḥi.* Its name, too, survives as *Endūr.* There is no indication of a true tell at this place, though there is a considerable depth of debris and some traces of an Iron Age settlement have been found. A recent suggestion would seek the En-dor of these days a half mile to the northeast at *Khirbet Ṣafṣafah* where there are Iron Age remains. A mile to the southwest of *Endūr* lie the ruins of an older Canaanite town which once must have ruled this neighborhood (*Tell el ' Ajjūl*).

En-dor was only three and a half miles northeast of Shunem, and hence very close to the Philistine camp as reported in this story. If Saul had started from Gilboa, En-dor would have been too distant to permit a return trip in a single night, if one allows for some protracted lingering for the seance. From Jezreel, the Israelite camp site as given in 1 Samuel 29:1, however, the trip is more feasible, requiring about three and a half hours each way. One must, therefore, suppose that 1 Samuel 28:4 is less exact as to the Israelite encampment.

David Pursues the Amalekites

The narrative of 1 Samuel 29 takes us back to the beginning of the Philistine campaign, and its initial statements are thus parallel to 1 Samuel 28:4. We learn at the outset how the enemy forces congregated at Aphek, and from this mustering place marched to Jezreel. Certainly the proper mustering place for the Philistines would be where their own contingents would converge. For this reason the Aphek in Sharon (Josh. 12:18), that lay at *Rās el 'Ain* and that was a gathering place for them at a previous occasion (1 Sam. 4:1), must be meant here. In this vicinity lay the northern border of Philistaea in the centuries that follow, and that makes it a particularly appropriate starting point. One can therefore disregard a number of more northerly localizations that have been suggested.

It was at this mobilization point, then, that the Philistine leaders objected to the presence of David and his contingent of six hundred men, and that Achish of Gath was compelled to dismiss his bodyguard.

Saul's Defeat

When the Philistines invaded the Plain of Jezreel, Saul's forces congregated at Jezreel. We may assume that the version of events from which 1 Samuel 28:4 was drawn was accurate in putting the Philistine camp at Shunem, opposite Jezreel, the name of which survives in slightly corrupted form as *Zer'īn.* If the whole Plain of *Merj ibn Amīr* is called Plain of Jezreel, this was hardly yet the case at the time with which we are dealing, for Jezreel certainly was too unimportant a place. A far more probable camping ground for the Israelites was at En-gannim (*Jenīn*), but the battle position was doubtless taken up at Jezreel. Nothing is said of the first phase of the fighting except that the Israelites were defeated. They retreated to Mount Gilboa. It was hereabouts that Saul preferred suicide to being slain by the Philistine archers.

One may suppose that Mount Gilboa of the narrative is the east-west ridge that separates the town of *Jelbōn* from the Plain of Esdraelon on the south. Up to this point the pursuit had been in open country, but from here southward was a forested region. Those who have passed through it report that there are virtually no traces of ancient settlements. In the woodlands the fleeing Israelites had prospects of escaping their pursuers. This ridge is the district upon which David invokes a curse in his elegy:

"Ye mountains of Gilboa, let there be no dew, neither let there be rain, upon you, nor fields of offerings: for there the shield of the mighty is vilely cast away, the shield of Saul, as though he had not been anointed with oil." (2 SAM. 1:21 A.V.)

"Ye mountains of Gilboa,
  let there be no dew or rain upon you,
  nor upsurging of the deep!
For there the shield of the mighty
  was defiled,
  the shield of Saul, not anointed
  with oil." (2 SAM. 1:21 R.S.V.)

The Philistine victory opened the way to the Jordan Valley. The inhabitants of nearby towns sought safety in flight. The city of Beth-shean, the first place the Philistines would have reached as they descended from the Plain of Jezreel to the bottom lands, was doubtless still in Canaanite hands and opened its gates without resisting. The name survives to this day in *Bēsān*, but *Tell el Ḥuṣn*, northwest of it on the south bank of the *Nahr Jālud*, marks the site of the ancient city. Before the excavations conducted here by the University of Pennsylvania Museum, 1921–33, the mound rose two hundred feet above the plain. The city which produced important finds from the Late Bronze Age, including two stelas of the Egyptian Pharaoh Seti I, seems to have been destroyed soon after Saul's time. On the northwest edge of the mound a gateway and buildings of the Iron Age were found, suggesting a partial rebuilding of the city by Solomon (1 KINGS 4:12). One may, therefore, surmise—though no historical report of it has survived—that the Israelites during David's reign avenged themselves on the Canaanites for having co-operated with the Philistines.

The bodies of Saul and his sons, found on the battlefield, were fastened to the walls of Beth-shean.

Burial of Saul and Jonathan

The sad news of the defeat of Israel at Mount Gilboa sped swiftly to every corner of the land, as fugitive soldiers returned to their villages. Within a day of the event, certainly the people of Jabesh in Gilead (see page 179) had heard what the Philistines had done with the bodies of Saul and his sons. All able-bodied young men of the city, which doubtless had furnished Saul with some of his most loyal officials, set out to perform the bold act of rescuing the corpses of the dead king and his sons from this dishonor. After a march of five hours or more, which no doubt was begun in the late afternoon, they came in the night to Beth-shean and carried out their sad task. They could have covered the nine and a half miles to the mouth of the wadi that led up to Jabesh before the light of the day broke over the Jordan Valley.

Saul and his sons were subjected to a purifying burning, and their bones were then interred "under the tamarisk tree in Jabesh." This tree, of course, was not inside the city, but somewhere nearby and was doubtless a local holy place.

CHAPTER XI

THE STORY OF DAVID

AFTER THE DEATH of Saul the path was open for David's rise. He saw at once that it was desirable for him to leave the remote Ziklag and go up into Judah. One might think that he would have gone to his native Bethlehem, but there were evidently weighty reasons for preferring Hebron. The Calebites, whose center this was, were among his strongest supporters. A movement was set on foot to make him king of Judah. It succeeded and he was anointed to that office by the representatives of the Judaean clans. With an eye to the future, David promulgated pan-Israelitic sentiments. He made the Judaeans feel that Saul was a national hero by requiring them to memorize his elegy on the passing of that king (2 SAM. 1:18); and he

sent envoys to Jabesh in Gilead, commending the leaders for their burial of Saul, and bidding for their support (2 SAM. 2:4-7).

Hebron and Mahanaim

The defeat at Gilboa did not yet mean the end of the Benjaminite kingdom. Saul had a young son named Eshbaal, whose name has been changed to Ishbosheth in the received Hebrew text. To counteract any possibility of Gilead's joining David's cause, Abner removed him to Mahanaim.

The realm ruled by Ishbosheth is described as follows:

"And [Abner] made him king over Gilead, and over the Ashurites, and over

Jezreel, and over Ephraim, and over Benjamin, and over all Israel." (2 SAM. 2:9 A.V.)

"And he [Abner] made him king over Gilead and the Ashurites and Jezreel and Ephraim and Benjamin and all Israel." (2 SAM. 2:9 R.S.V.)

The Transjordan territory of Gilead thus provided the real basis of the power still left to the House of Saul. The "Ashurites" are clearly an error; the Septuagint has "Geshurites" (see page 202). Mention of the city of Jezreel in connection with tribes or territories is peculiar. Perhaps it was crown property, and the only part of Issachar (to which it is reckoned in Joshua 19:18) that remained to the kingdom. Manasseh was apparently lost, too, and Asher was too remote to be held. Reading between the lines, one may assume that the independence of the Canaanite cities of the Plain of Esdraelon was re-established with Philistine help. Certainly nothing is said of any prolonged Philistine occupation.

War between the Kingdoms

Ishbosheth evidently made an attempt to re-establish the power of his house over the area of the Gibeonite league of Canaanite cities, but David did not propose to let that move succeed uncontested. His forces, led by Joab, met those of Abner at Gibeon, where they confronted each other on opposite sides of the city's pool or reservoir (which some scholars take to be identical with the "great waters," or "many waters" of Jeremiah 41:12, see page 317).

A century ago Edward Robinson sought to link this pool with an old reservoir lying below the fine spring on the east side of *ej Jīb*. It is about 120 by 100 feet in size and has a rock-hewn stairs in one corner. However, the antiquity of this installation is uncertain. In the recent excavations carried on at *ej Jīb* by Pritchard (see page 137), a very deep, round pool, held to have been made about 1200 B.C., and hence around the time of

the coming of the Israelites, was excavated; this pool has the very best claim to being the one meant in the narrative. It was cut out of the solid rock and has a circular staircase with a handrail carved out of the rock to make it easier for the water-carrying women of those days to get at the water supply when it receded in the dry season. The diameter of the pool is thirty-six feet, and it is deep enough to hold a three-story house.

The strange gladiatorial contest arranged by the two leaders by way of opening the fight would have taken place on the cultivated and terraced lands sloping off to the vale. The place ever after was known as Helkath-hazzurim. The name is thus supposedly derived from the incident. But almost invariably, such names are much older than the stories explanatory of them. Since it may mean "field of the stone knives" (cf. JOSH. 5:3), it could have gotten its name from a find of Neolithic tools or weapons. It is most improbable that such primitive weapons were used by soldiers of Eshbaal's and David's armies, living in the Iron Age. The correction of text sometimes advocated (changing *-hazzurim* to *-hazziddim,* "field of the sides") produces an improbable local name. This sort of suicidal fight is portrayed on a relief from *Tell Ḥalāf*.

In the battle that was opened by this tourney the forces of Ishbosheth were routed. Their flight will have gone in the direction of the Gibeah of Saul, but they apparently were not inclined to take refuge behind city walls where they could be hemmed in and starved out. Joab's fleet-footed brother Asahel was slain by Abner during the retreat—a particularly tragic and fateful occurrence. We must suppose that the place where he fell was marked in some way, because it was later customary among Benjaminites for those traveling this road to pause there and honor his memory (2 SAM. 2:23).

The course taken by the retreating Israelites is described as follows:

"And the sun went down when they were come to the hill of Ammah, that lieth before Giah by the way of the wilderness of Gibeon." (2 SAM. 2:24 A.V.)

"And as the sun was going down they came to the hill of Ammah, which lies before Giah on the way to the wilderness of Gibeon." (2 SAM. 2:24 R.S.V.)

In the vicinity of Gibeon, there was no "wilderness" that could be described as belonging to it. One must, therefore, hold that Gibeon here is an error for *Geba,* beyond which, indeed, lay the wilderness leading down to the Jordan country. Abner then must have taken the road past Ramah and Geba. The territory of the latter city lying between the *Wadi eṣ Ṣewēnīt* and the *Wadi Fārʿah* extended to the vicinity of *el Fauwār.* There is an important spring there, giving the place its name, for *el Fauwār* means "ebullition of waters." Since the Hebrew name "Giah" is probably synonymous in meaning, it may refer to the same place. This vicinity might, indeed, have been reached by sundown in a flight from *ej Jib.* One of the roads to Jericho crosses the valley above the spring and before descending into it passes two hills (*el Qrēn* and *Tell el Milḥ*). The latter, being closer to the spring and near the junction of two small valleys, may represent the "hill of Ammah" or Gibeath-ammah (said to mean the "hill of the dwarfs"), on which Abner made a stand. It was a suitable point for Joab to curb his desire for further pursuit, for the position was not easily stormed, and the tables might have been turned against him if his attack failed to carry it. A truce was now arranged between the two leaders and the fighting ended.

The descent of the weary warriors under Abner's command to the Jordan country and the crossing of the river in the night were followed by a forenoon march to Mahanaim (2 SAM. 2:29). Joab and his forces, too, returned home in the night. En route they

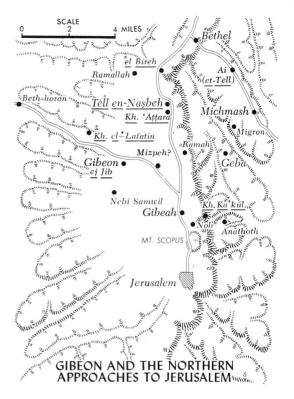

GIBEON AND THE NORTHERN APPROACHES TO JERUSALEM

buried the body of Asahel in the ancestral tomb at Bethlehem and reached Hebron by dawn (2 SAM. 2:32).

Abner's Death

The state of war between the two kingdoms lasted for some time, with David's kingdom growing ever stronger (2 SAM. 3:1 f.). Dissension between Abner and Ishbosheth arose and led the former to negotiate secretly with David. He offered to swing the northern tribes to David's side in the interest of national strength and peace. His price, of course, must have been the highest post in David's power to bestow—the post held by his kinsman Joab. Finally matters were advanced so far that Abner could travel to Hebron to seal the agreement. David had created an occasion for such a visit. He had demanded that his lawful wife, Saul's daughter Michal, be delivered to him. She was accordingly taken away from her husband Paltiel, son of Laish (i.e., a native of the town of Laish?) and conducted to Hebron by Abner. The bereft husband followed to

Bahurim (see page 204) where he was ordered to turn back.

The delicacy of the negotiations between David and Abner was greatly increased by the fact that Joab not only would have to be demoted or sacrificed, but that the slaying of Joab's brother in the battle at Gibeon had not been atoned for. David had carried on the dealing with Abner without knowledge of Joab and had sent the latter off on a raid so that he would be out of the way when Abner came. Unfortunately Joab returned when Abner had just left Hebron. After a furious interview with David, Joab sent messengers after Abner, without David's knowledge, recalling him to Hebron (2 SAM. 3:26 f.). They reached Abner at the cistern of Sirah (Bor-hassirah), a place hardly identifiable. Joab then murdered Abner in the gateway of Hebron.

The act of his chief aide caused David serious embarrassment, but he acted promptly to demonstrate to all the world that he disapproved of it. He commanded Joab and all his courtiers to mourn Abner publicly at the funeral, and he himself followed the bier as a mourner. He even composed an elegy about Abner's death (2 SAM. 3:33–34), and he refused to take food until sundown. Thus he convinced not only his own people but also the northern tribes that he had had nothing to do with this murder. He appealed for public understanding of his powerlessness against Joab and Abishai (2 SAM. 3:39). Joab would not have been under heavy public condemnation, since everyone understood and approved of the duty of blood-revenge.

With the great Abner, the architect of Israel's military successes in the growth and expansion of the first Hebrew Dynasty, removed from the scene, the temptation to do away with Ishbosheth was strong. Two army officers killed him in his sleep.

"The name of the one was Baanah, and the name of the other Rechab, the sons of Rimmon, a Beerothite, of the children of Benjamin: (for Beeroth also was reckoned to Benjamin.

And the Beerothites fled to Gittaim, and were sojourned there until this day.)" (2 SAM. 4:2–3 A.V.)

"The name of the one was Baanah, and the name of the other Rechab, sons of Rimmon a man of Benjamin from Beeroth (for Beeroth also is reckoned to Benjamin; the Beerothites fled to Gittaim, and have been sojourners there to this day)." (2 SAM. 4:2–3 R.S.V.)

The assassins of Ishbosheth travelled all night through the Ghor to bring their trophy, the head of the slain king, to David. Instead of rewarding them David had them executed and hung up their bodies by the pool of Hebron.

On Beeroth and Gittaim

Beeroth was an old Canaanite city, one of the four mentioned in Joshua 9:17 as controlled by Gibeon. Since Robinson, many scholars have favored placing Beeroth at *el Bîreh,* north of *Tell en Naṣbeh* (Mizpah); it has a fine spring which supplies both it and Ramallah with water. However, the absence here of visible remains of an old Canaanite city is disquieting. The remains of one could of course have been used up in the development of Ramallah.

The two army officers who murdered Ishbosheth are said to have been "sons of Rimmon." This is an unusual kind of personal name for Canaanites or Israelites, and one suspects that the original meaning was that they were from the town of Rimmon, which then was subject to Beeroth. We have already heard of the Rock of Rimmon (cf. JUDG. 20:45) and that modern *Rammūn* five miles northeast of *el Bîreh* occupies the site. Rimmon could well have been in the territory of Beeroth if that lay at *el Bîreh.*

The Beerothites are said to have fled to Gittaim. It seems probable that this flight took place in connection with the events just described, for the slaying of Ishbosheth by men of Canaanite stock and from a Canaanite community will have exposed that entire community to dire peril on the part of the enraged Benjaminites.

But where was Gittaim? No useful purpose would have been served by fleeing to any nearby town; the place meant must be quite remote, preferably outside of Benjaminite territory. Gittaim is mentioned again in Nehemiah 11:33, and if one connects it with the names that follow, a location in the coastal plain would be indicated. The name is only a longer form of Gath, and so it would not be surprising if certain Old Testament references to Gath really applied to Gittaim rather than to the more famous Gath of the Philistines that lay farther to the south. A site south of *Ramleh* has recently been suggested for it. The mound, *Tell Rās Abu Ḥamad*, is astonishingly large, covering twenty-five acres, but not very high, and was densely settled in the Early Iron Age. Its extraordinary size would be explained to some extent if an emigration of Canaanites from Israelite territory expanded the town.

David Becomes King of Israel and Acquires a Capital

The Israel tribes now had no leader of reputation to turn to, and the fact that David's queen was Michal, the daughter of Saul, will have weighed heavily in their readiness to make the Judaean ruler king over Israel. That they anointed him shows that this was a dual monarchy like that of Upper and Lower Egypt, or England and Scotland, or the former Austro-Hungarian Empire.

It was clearly impracticable for the king of Israel and Judah to govern from a point as far south as Hebron. But one can understand that David was reluctant to go to Saul's Gibeah. Here the adherents of the Benjaminite dynasty were too powerful. David's strength rested on his support by the Judaeans. As a king, furthermore, he wanted

property, and there was one attractive way of getting it—by taking some existing Canaanite city by force of arms. Jerusalem, though claimed for Benjamin in the tribal boundary system of the Book of Joshua, was so close to that boundary and so useless to Benjamin that its seizure could not raise strong objection. Besides, through his marriage to Saul's daughter he could exert strong influence in Benjamin. Apart from the dubious reports of Joshua 10:1 f. and Judges 1:5 f., we hear nothing of the city's setting up any resistance at the time of the conquest. From the point of view of a united Israel and Judah, it was an uncomfortable roadblock on the great north-south highway at the important point where the main artery from Moab and Ammon came in. So David determined to capture Jerusalem.

We have seen that David had a private armed force ever since his flight into the Negeb. The taking of Jerusalem was a coup by this unit. The leading objective on which David had his eye was the *meṣūdath Ṣīʿōn* or fortress of Zion.

The topography of Jerusalem requires some slight explanation at this point. (See Color Map XVII.) The city of the Middle Ages and of recent times lies on two hills, or more accurately on a plateau with a depression descending down in a north-south direction in the middle of it. The ridges thus formed on either side provided space for building and situations of strength. These ridges, furthermore, drop off with increasing height on their outer sides since the valleys east and west of them likewise taper off. The western ridge descends to the Hinnom Valley and the eastern one skirts the Kidron Valley. Misled by Josephus and the tradition of the early Church, men long believed Zion to have lain on the western ridge. But excavations carried on during the last century have shown that the old city of the Jebusites and of David was situated exclusively on the southern spur of the eastern ridge. It was not sprawled over both hills, like the city of

Josephus' day, whose economy was boosted by its being a mecca of pilgrimage, but was an ordinary Canaanite city of a few acres, supporting a small farming population. The Palestinian cities of the Late Bronze or Early Iron Age rarely had more than two thousand inhabitants. A hilltop location with a spring was the prime requisite. That condition existed only on the southeastern ridge. Actually, the Jerusalem that David conquered lay completely outside the walls of the present city—more precisely, south of the *Harām esh Sherīf*, the great sacred enclosure, that was the site of Herod's temple and in which the mosque of Omar now stands.

It seemed incredible to scholars, until quite recently, that this small and seemingly not very strong position could have been "the stronghold of Zion" that David renamed "the City of David." However, in Biblical times the southeastern hill was a good deal higher, relative to the valley-bottom, than it is today. The present hill has a drop on the east side of from ninety to one hundred and eighty feet as one descends from north to south; on the west side of from twenty to sixty feet. The level of the Kidron Valley has since antiquity risen from fifty-two to ninety-eight feet. The eastern declivity of the hill is composed of debris and rubble covering original steep rock terraces. On the western side one must dig from twelve to seventy-two feet down to reach the natural rock. If one allows for this accumulation of later ages, then the position was indeed very strong. Josephus even claims that there was a further elevation on the summit of the ridge which was shorn off in three years of labor at the time of Simon Maccabeus (142–134 B.C.). Since the level of the *Harām esh Sherīf* at present is sixty-four feet higher than the spur of the hill to the south, this would, if it were true, mean that the latter was even more impressive. While the foremost experts find Josephus' report unacceptable, the fact remains that the Jebusite city must in some way have had a defense line in

the north that was not subject to domination from the *Harām*. In shape Jerusalem was about three times as long as it was wide, and it may have covered an area of four to five acres. Population, accordingly, will have numbered 1230, at the rate of 250 per acre, with 300 fighting men. The excavations have shown that it had four gates, those on the north and south being guarded by towers, and the latter having a stair leading up to it.

We need not enter here into the question whether there was also at the time a second settlement on the western hill that perhaps was called Jerusalem, while the one on the eastern hill was called "fortress of Zion." The soundings thus far made on the western hill have not brought to light evidence of anything earlier than the Maccabean age. If the western hill is referred to as "the shoulder of the Jebusite" (JOSH. 15:8; 18:16 R.S.V.), this merely describes it as the most bulky height within the city's territory.

The water on which the city primarily depended was that of the Spring of the Steps or Spring of Our Lady Mary (see page 211), to which one went out by the eastern gate. A shaft through the rock gave the city access to its water supply in time of siege. It was rediscovered by the Warren excavations in 1867. An elbow-shaped tunnel staircase, so the Parker excavations of 1909–11 showed, led down through the rock on which the fortress was perched and gave access to shaft and spring. The city thus had an assured supply of drinking water and could not easily be reduced. The assumption that this shaft and tunnel were pre-Davidic in origin is supported by the existence of similar tunnels in Bronze Age cities like Gibeon and Ibleam.

The story of how David took Jerusalem is deplorably meager. It presupposes a siege, with the Jebusites taunting David, and the latter using this taunt in connection with his strategic dispositions (2 SAM. 5:6, 8).

Unhappily the text of what David said is not well preserved. The rendering of the

Revised Standard Version rests on the theory that the word *ṣinnōr* (which A.V. translates "gutter") means "water shaft," and that it refers to the shaft discovered by the Warren excavations. Through it, so it is held, David's men got up into the city. The theory is interesting, but faces objections. The word *ṣinnōr* would fit a sewer better than a water-shaft. But still other translations and inter-pretations of the important clause are possible, especially if emendations of text are resorted to; there is no way of deciding the issue at present. The text makes the im-pression of having suffered loss of words; something must have been done to the lame and the blind after the capture of the city. At any rate the story attempts to account for the fact that since then such unfortu-nates were forbidden to enter the house of the LORD (a Temple regulation otherwise unknown).

It would be difficult to exaggerate the im-portance of this conquest. The fact that David through his private army obtained the city, and took over intact a Canaanite city-state as his personal property, put him in a position to reward his henchmen and gave him a great degree of independence from both the Judaeans and the tribes of Israel. "King of Jerusalem" was no doubt one of his official titles ever after.

Brief as is the story of this action, equally brief is the account of what he did in organizing the city.

"So David dwelt in the fort, and called it the city of David. And David built round about from Millo and inward." (2 SAM. 5:9 A.V.)

"And David dwelt in the stronghold, and called it the city of David. And David built the city round about from the Millo inward." (2 SAM. 5:9 R.S.V.)

We must assume that Jerusalem was actu-ally rechristened "city of David," and that the ruler's purpose was to found it anew in

his name, just as Babylonian and Assyrian kings built cities in their own name. Kar Tukulti-Ninurta, "city of Tukulti-Ninurta," above the old Assyrian capital on the other side of the Tigris, built two hundred years before David, is an instance of a city of that kind. If he built the city from the Millo in-ward, that raises the possibility that the Millo —whatever that may have been—was a Jebu-site installation. However, other passages at-tribute the building of the Millo to Solomon (1 KINGS 9:24, 11:27), and it is quite possible that the text is merely mentioning a well-known place of the author's own day to make clear to the reader from what point on David began his rebuilding operations. We will defer discussing what is meant by the Millo until later (see page 220).

The building of a palace was of course a prime desideratum, for that of the Jebusite king was manifestly inadequate for the head of a kingdom extending from Dan to Beer-sheba. As ruler of a large state David now was involved in diplomacy and trade-relations. It is not surprising, therefore, that we hear that King Hiram of Tyre sent the necessary craftsmen and the required lumber (2 SAM. 5:11). This palace no doubt stood as long as Jerusalem was ruled by the Davidic Dynasty, but Solomon built one of greater size farther to the north (see page 218).

Two Victories Over the Philistines

In the present sequence of 2 Samuel two attempts of the Philistines to invade Judah are related. They are put after the capture of Jerusalem. For the first of these two events, the correctness of this placement must be doubted. If David had held Jerusalem at the time there would have been no need of his "going down to the stronghold", evidently meaning Adullam (see page 184). Such a move makes very excellent sense if the in-vasion occurred when he was still at Hebron, a site unsuited to defense.

"The Philistines also came and spread themselves in the valley of Rephaim. . . .

And David came to Baal-perazim, and David smote them there." (2 SAM. 5:18, 20 A.V.)

"Now the Philistines had come and spread out in the valley of Rephaim. . . . And David came to Baal-perazim, and David defeated them there." (2 SAM. 5:18, 20 R.S.V.)

The plain of Rephaim, noted for its grain (ISA. 17:5), lay west of Jerusalem (JOSH. 15:8, 18:16). It is obviously identical with the plain called *el Baq 'a.* Just why the name of the Rephaites, however, should be attached to this locality is not explained. In this narrative, as in the one which follows, David is portrayed as consulting the oracle of the LORD at every step (cf. also 2 SAM. 2:1; 1 SAM. 23:1 f.). Receiving a favorable augury he marched up to Baal-perazim, a point evidently held by the Philistines. Baal-perazim, referred to as Mount Perazim (ISA. 28:21), is taken by some scholars to be the ridge on which the monastery of *Mar Eliās,* three miles south of Jerusalem, now stands. One might think of the Philistines as encamped in the plain, with guards posted on the height to watch the road coming up from Bethlehem in the south. The storyteller would explain the name from the incident, and from David's words:

"The LORD hath broken forth upon mine enemies before me, as the breach of waters." (2 SAM. 5:20 A.V.)

"The LORD has broken through my enemies before me, like a bursting flood." (2 SAM. 5:20 R.S.V.)

In other words, David's attack was like the breaking of a dam—a comparison that would best suit a rush down a hill or valley. However, this name compounded with Baal will hardly have been coined by Judaeans. Local phenomena, such as particular breaks in a ridge would account much better for the name (cf. Perez-uzzah, page 199).

The other battle may well have taken place after David had established himself in Jerusalem.

"And the Philistines came up yet again, and spread themselves in the valley of Rephaim.

And when David enquired of the LORD, he said, Thou shalt not go up; but fetch a compass behind them, and come upon them over against the mulberry trees. . . . and smote the Philistines from Geba until thou come to Gazer." (2 SAM. 5:22–23, 25 A.V.)

"And the Philistines came up yet again, and spread out in the valley of Rephaim. And when David inquired of the LORD, he said, 'You shall not go up; go around to their rear, and come upon them opposite the balsam trees.' . . . and smote the Philistines from Geba to Gezer." (2 SAM. 5:22–23, 25 R.S.V.)

This battle can hardly have taken place in the plain of Rephaim, for there is a punning on the words "balsam trees" which indicates that the text originally read "valley of Bekaim." The mention of Geba (see page 180) is likewise inappropriate, since that town was remote from any point within reach in this connection. It is clearly a mistake for Gibeon, which, as we have seen, lay at *ej Jib* (see page 137). This is proven by an oracle of Isaiah:

"For the LORD shall rise up as in mount Perazim, he shall be wroth as in the valley of Gibeon." (Is. 28:21 A.V.)

"For the LORD will rise up as on Mount Perazim, he will be wroth as in the valley of Gibeon." (Is. 28:21 R.S.V.)

The second line has this second of David's Philistine victories in mind, just as the first line thinks of the attack at Baal-perazim. If the battle took place in a part of the valley of *ej Jib* then the pursuit to Gezer is completely understandable. Exactly where the "wood of balsam trees" may have stood in the valley of *ej Jīb* remains indeterminable.

David Brings the Ark to Zion

Once again we have occasion to observe David's remarkable insight. He had conquered a city, but it lacked any historic tie with Israel's past and with the LORD. It seems probable that an old Hurrian divinity, the goddess Khepa, was worshipped there since of old, for the king of Jerusalem in the Amarna Age was a servant of this goddess according to his name, Abdi-Khepa. David must have set up a holy place of some sort for the LORD, and there the ephod brought from Nob by Abiathar will have been installed. But with a sense of the value of the dramatic, David hit upon the idea of resurrecting the sacred object of the Ephraimite temple at Shiloh—the ark which had played such a role in the stories of the wilderness and of the conquest.

The poetic version of Psalm 132 suggests that David had to search to locate the ark. The story of chapter 6 does not refer to this matter of the search for the ark, but assumes that David knew where it was and went down with the whole army to Baale of Judah (*Baale-judah*, R.S.V.) to get it. The place where the ark was kept thus seems to have had a variety of names It was previously given as Kiriath-jearim, "city of the woods" (1 SAM. 7:1), which could be shortened to Jaar, "wood" (*fields of Jaar* R.S.V,). This was evidently the later name of the town, but the original one was Baalah (JOSH. 15:9). That name shows that it was previously the shrine of a Canaanite goddess. If it is called Baale-judah here, that is merely to distinguish it from several other Baalahs or Baalaths outside of Judah.

In connection with bringing the ark to Jerusalem two minor places are mentioned. One is a threshing floor called Perez-uzzah, allegedly so named because a man named Uzzah died there, for having touched the holy ark (2 SAM. 6:8). The name is probably much older than this event. Perez represents a topographic feature of some sort as was also the case with the plural of this word in Baal-perazim, and Uzzah may be indeed the name of an individual (cf. "Uzziah" as short for "Azariah"). There was a threshing floor at this place, and that indicates a location where the wind would strike. Presumably Perez-uzzah was somewhere on the road between Kiriath-jearim and Jerusalem. On the steep descent from *Qaṣtal* to *Qalōnīeh,* the oxen could well be imagined as slipping on the ledgy road of those days.

The unfortunate occurrence led David to defer bringing the ark to Jerusalem. Instead he "took it aside" to the house of Obed-edom the Gittite. This must have been a small town (cf. the "house of Micah," JUDG. 18:2) with a shrine dedicated to a pagan deity named Edom. The local magnate had the name "Obed [better, Ebed] -edom," "servant of the God Edom." There is some slight attestation for such a deity in Egyptian inscriptions. He is described as a Gittite or man from Gath—presumably the Philistine city. Since David had to "turn aside," the place was off the main road. East of *Qalōnīeh* there are localities that would be suitable, notably to the north of the road. Since the ark brought blessing to Obed-edom's house, David then is said to have made another expedition to bring it to Jerusalem (2 SAM. 6:12). It is quite possible, however, that the retarding elements in the narrative were introduced into the tradition later in connection with an annual ritual conducted with the ark (for which ritual Psalm 132 and Psalm 24 were composed), and that the bringing in of the sacred object progressed throughout in the triumphal manner that 2 Samuel 6:1-5 initiated.

Further Wars of David

The meager reporting of 2 Samuel 8 mentions further wars of David, without hint of the years of their occurrence or other desirable information.

A Philistine war is referred to in which David "took Metheg-ammah out of the hand of the Philistines" (2 SAM. 8:1). The name is a puzzling one and reminds one of the Gibeath-ammah of 2 Samuel 2:24; perhaps it has not been handed down correctly. Of the Moabite war of David we get only a brief record telling of the barbarous killing of the enemy, probably after the taking of their capital city (2 SAM. 8:2).

More is said of the war with a new element that now was rising to power to the north of Palestine—the Aramaeans (see page 171). They had permeated the existing Syrian kingdoms and gained ascendancy in some of them, much as the Israelites had done in Palestine. Zobah, sometimes called Aram-zobah (2 SAM. 10:6, 8 in the Hebrew) and Aram Damascus were states in which they had prevailed. The former at this time was the more powerful. While the information offered in 2 Samuel 8:3–8 is vague, we learn that a King Hadadezer of Zobah was David's contemporary, and that he was believed to have held sway over the Euphrates region adjacent to Syria. Since he had so much bronze, one must suspect that he also held much of the later territory of Chalcis in the Lebanon, where there were copper mines. If David went up into Syria and attacked Hadadezer, when he was engaged in regaining control of certain territories, he must have acted as an ally of some major power like Egypt or Assyria, perhaps in company with many other tributary kings. Allegedly David participated in two battles—one defeating the Aramaeans of Damascus in their attempt to join Hadadezer and the other in the defeat of Hadadezer himself. The city of Damascus then became tributary to David.

The story of the ambassador of King Thoi of Hamath, congratulating David on his victories over Hadadezer (2 SAM. 8:9 f.), gives us an interesting echo of those days. Hamath was doubtless still under a native dynasty, but was only with difficulty withstanding the rising Aramaean pressure. The city, whose name survives in Ḥamā on the Orontes River, was one of the most important places in Syria. The great tell of ancient Hamath is of imposing height and size. A Danish expedition under Harald Ingholt carried on several seasons of excavations there before World War II, but it will take many years of work to unlock all the secrets of Hamath. The so-called "Hamath stones," found on the tell by explorers early in the nineteenth century, provided the first examples of the so-called "Hittite hieroglyphic" script. The decipherment of this script has occupied many scholars, but it has now been made certain through the discovery of the bilingual Phoenician and Hittite hieroglyphic text of Karatepe in Cilicia.

A victory in the "valley of salt" is also referred to in this brief survey of David's early wars (2 SAM. 8:13). The Hebrew text

4.8 *Recently discovered stela with Hittite hieroglyphic inscription; storm god standing on sacred animal. Found at Jekke, near Aleppo. (Courtesy National Syrian Museum at Aleppo)*

gives the adversary as Aram (Syrians, A.V.), but this mistake has been rightly corrected to *Edom* by the Revised Standard Version. The valley of salt can only be sought in close proximity to the Dead Sea, perhaps near *Jebel Usdum*. The Edomite war, of which we hear more in 1 Kings 11:14 f., was a brutal war of extermination, and involved the annexation of that region by David.

The Ammonite War

Much fuller information is given about the Ammonite war and events in the life of David connected therewith (2 SAM. 10). The Ammonite capital Rabbath Ammon, or simply Rabbah, lay where *'Ammān,* capital of the Hashemite kingdom of Jordan, now stands. It is situated on the *Wadi 'Ammān,* as the upper course of the Jabbok is called, and on the main route coming from Gilead.

The Ammonite King Hanun insulted David's servants, sent to bring condolences to him at the death of his father. The provocation could only be answered by an attack on this formidable fortress. In expectation of it, Hanun acquired allies to aid him—the Aramaeans of Beth-rehob and those of Zobah, the king of Maacah, and the men of Tob (2 SAM. 10:6). Beth-rehob was doubtless the nearest of these kingdoms and for that reason it is put first. Perhaps its name survives in *Riḥāb,* north of *Jerash.* It is a very large site, but is covered with Byzantine-Arabic ruins; however, some Late Bronze and Early Iron sherds have been picked up at the northern end. The participation of this district in the war on the side of Ammon is quite understandable. Maacah, from which the Israelite city of Abel-beth-maacah gets its name, lay in the northern *Jaulān.*

Joab and "the mighty men" dispatched by David were forced to fight a two-front battle, since the Ammonites were drawn up before their city, while the Aramaean cohorts were posted by themselves in the open country. The Aramaeans were routed and the Ammonites took refuge in the fortress. But

Joab did not prosecute a siege at this time. He realized that he was not yet through with the Aramaeans. And, indeed, the powerful Hadadezer of Zobah sent an army under his chief Shobak to invade Israel. The army was defeated by David's forces at a place called Helam (2 SAM. 10:16). Unfortunately, there is no indication of where Helam lay, except that it was on the other side of the Jordan.

After peace was concluded with the Aramaeans, David could turn his attention to the siege of Rabbah. It was in connection with that siege that Joab was instructed to see to it that an officer called Uriah the Hittite was sacrificed in order that David could obtain his pretty wife, Bathsheba, for his harem (2 SAM. 11). The siege evidently took a long time, for engineering techniques were not as developed then as they were a century or two later, when the Assyrians showed how cities could be taken more speedily. We are still in the world of the "siege of Troy," made famous in Homer's *Iliad.* Rabbah's fate was sealed when Joab captured "the city of the waters." This was evidently a designation for the acropolis which must have controlled the brook. It is thus to be identified with the *Qal'a* of today, which lies on the north side of the *Wadi 'Ammān* and is isolated on the northeast and west by two valleys. The residential city lay west of the *Qal'a,* ripe for the plucking. Joab sent for David, who then supervised the final operations, and so was able to receive the credit of being the conqueror of Rabbah (cf. 1 CHRON. 20:2). The golden crown of Milcom, the god of the Ammonites, with its precious stone, David put upon his own head—in other words, he took the title of king of the Ammonites, in addition to king of Judah, king of Israel, and king of Jerusalem. The inhabitants became slave labor for David's building operations.

Absalom's Vengeance

The great king's family affairs naturally interested his people, and a good deal of reliable and colorful information has been preserved about them. These narratives all center about Absalom, the third of his sons. Amnon, a son by Ahinoam of Jezreel and David's first-born and heir-presumptive to the crown, defiled and mistreated Absalom's sister Tamar. Absalom determined to take vengeance on his half-brother, but he bided his time. Two years later, he issued an invitation to a sheep-shearing (2 SAM. 13:23).

Apparently the king's sons had estates of their own. Absalom's was at Baal-hazor. It is described as near "Ephraim." As the text stands, this must mean close to the Ephraimite boundary of Benjamin. Furthermore, the boundary between Benjamin and Ephraim passes north of a mountain range, the westernmost knoll of which is called el 'Aṣūr, and may well preserve the name Hazor. The mountain would be a suitable place for a Baal sanctuary. To this point the Genesis Apocryphon from Qumran, expanding on GEN. 13:3,14, has Abraham go. It calls it Ramath Hazor—avoiding the word Baal. At this highest point of central Palestine (3318 feet), he can see "from the River of Egypt to Lebanon and Shenir (see page 25) and from the great Sea to Hauran and all the land of Gebal (ej Jibāl, Color Map I, D-2) to Kadesh and all the Great Wilderness east of Hauran and Shenir to the Euphrates."

The murder of Amnon at that occasion leads to the flight of the other princes in fear of their lives. But rumor flew fast, bringing David the misinformation that Absalom had slain all the king's sons (2 SAM. 13:34).

"And the young man that kept the watch lifted up his eyes, and looked, and, behold, there came much people by the way of the hill side behind him." (2 SAM. 13:34 A.V.)

"And the young man who kept the watch lifted up his eyes, and looked, and behold, many people were coming from the Horonaim road by the side of the mountain." (2 SAM. 13:34 R.S.V.)

The dual form Horonaim is evidently used in this narrative for the two Beth-horons, upper and lower. The road meant, however, is the north-south highway, from which the Beth-horon road turned off to the west either a little to the north of Saul's Gibeah, as at present, or farther to the north at el Bireh. In view of the fact that much more traffic, notably from Transjordan, went to Beth-horon and the coastal plain than to Shechem and Jezreel, it was not unnatural for the first leg of the north-south highway to be included in the designation Horonaim road. That does not necessarily mean that the princes had gone toward Beth-horon.

The princes could only have been seen as they came to Mount Scopus. It is noteworthy that this point was visible from the tower of the north gate of the City of David.

If the "king's sons" fled to Jerusalem, Absalom fled in the opposite direction. From Baal-hazor, if situated at el 'Aṣūr, he was in a position to make a swift getaway across the Jordan. He went to the country of his mother's people. Her name was Maacah, and she was the daughter of Talmai, king of Geshur (2 SAM. 3:3). The land of the Geshur, which belonged to the sphere of Aram (2 SAM. 15:8), lay north of Gilead.

Absalom had powerful friends at David's court. Among them was Joab. By means of a stratagem, in which a woman of Tekoa co-operated, Joab implanted in David's mind the idea of recalling the absent son. It is the first time that Tekoa, a town of Judah, is mentioned in the Old Testament narrative. A more important personage than this nameless woman was to come from there—the prophet Amos (AMOS 1:1). The ancient name survives in Khirbet Teqū', south of Bethlehem.

Absalom's Rebellion

Absalom was born to be a king. He was blessed with those priceless gifts of a fine physical appearance and personal charm. His father left him idle instead of giving him an active role. Finally Absalom determined to assert himself. He organized a company of private soldiers. Allegedly, he even intercepted all those who brought law cases to Jerusalem for appeal to the king. Finally he applied to his father for permission to go to Hebron, ostensibly to fulfill a vow he had made while in Geshur. That suggests that Hebron was at this time the all-important sanctuary of the LORD for the men of Judah and especially for David's family.

Absalom had carefully laid his plans for a rebellion. In connection with the sacrificial ceremony at Hebron, he was anointed king and the trumpet was blown as a signal, announcing the event.

When the tidings came to Jerusalem, David immediately commanded flight. Since he would have been safe for a long time in his fortress, this reveals the depth of the disaffection existing. David's support rested on his bureaucracy, which fled with him, and on his armed force. We hear in this connection of the Cherethites and Pelethites who were under Benaiah's command (2 SAM. 8:18), and of the six hundred under Ittai the Gittite (i.e., from Gath). The Cherethites were a people of the Negeb (1 SAM. 30:14), and are mentioned along with the Philistines (EZEK. 25:16; ZEPH. 2:5). By origin they were Cretans. Pelethites, however, may be an artificially modified name to rhyme with Cherethites (Hebrew *kerēthi* and *pelēthi*). Who they were remains obscure. David had obviously emulated the example of the Egyptian Pharaohs and other potentates in surrounding himself with a solid core of mercenary soldiers of foreign origin. The six hundred men under Ittai of Gath were a personal following of that individual. That David and his family and courtiers all went on foot suggests a penitential act (cf. 2 SAM. 16:30).

At the last house—apparently outside the city walls—the king and his staff paused to review the force under their command. Careful note was taken, no doubt, of the absence of certain personages as well as of the presence of those who were willing to risk their fate in David's cause.

> "And all the country wept with a loud voice, and all the people passed over: the king also himself passed over [read *stood at*] the brook Kidron, and all the people passed over, toward the way of the wilderness." (2 SAM. 15:23 A.V.)

> *"And all the country wept aloud as all the people passed by, and the king crossed the brook Kidron, and all the people passed on toward the wilderness."* (2 SAM. 15:23 R.S.V.)

David stood near the Kidron while the throng went by, and thus was among the last to cross the brook. Their exit will have been by the eastern gate. The course taken was not via the road leading round to Bethany, but over the summit (the *Jebel et Ṭūr*).

Even in his sorrow and peril David showed that resourcefulness which marks the born leader. He sent back the ark and its priests, instructing the priests to send him intelligence through their sons. He saw a useful service that an aged counselor, who met him on the Mount of Olives, could do for him. This man was a member of an old Canaanite clan of Archites that had a territory between Bethel and Ataroth (JOSH. 16:2). He had evidently taken the short cut from Mount Scopus to intercept David on the summit. We learn in passing that a shrine existed on the summit where these roads met. Hushai was urged to pretend loyalty to Absalom in order to offset the counsel of Ahitophel.

Another meeting occurred after passing the summit. Here Ziba, the servant of Mephibosheth (Meribaal), came with supplies for David on his own initiative and apparently via a road from Anathoth. David noted the fact that Meribaal had not put in an appearance, and the crafty servant betrayed the fact that his master was speculating on a restoration of the monarchy of the House of Saul. Coming to Bahurim, David had a demonstration of the resentment of the Benjaminite family in the curses and stone-throwing of Shimei, which he bore with philosophic calm.

The exact localization of Bahurim is of some interest, since on it depends the determining of the route which the road of that day took in going to the Jericho area. It seems probable that the course of the later Roman road is essentially that of the more ancient one. Bahurim has been plausibly sought at *Rās et Tmīm,* a site where early Israelite sherds as well as Hellenistic and Roman are found. While *Rās et Tmīm* lies a certain distance from the road, it fits the situation here presupposed better than any other site recommended. Seeing the procession coming, Shimei might have left his village and proceeded eastward to the hill of *Sheikh 'Ambar.* The road passes along the foot of that hill, and for some distance Shimei could have traveled along the hillside above it keeping up the actions described.

The Situation at Jerusalem

Absalom victoriously entered Jerusalem "with all men of Israel." The counsel of Ahitophel was swift pursuit of David by a small force which he offered to select and lead. Obviously, then, Ahitophel was a military man of rank. Hushai opposed this plan for seemingly a very good reason: David's professional soldiers under his experienced leadership might ambush and defeat a small force; at the report of a reverse the revolution might collapse. Hushai advocated waiting for the arrival of further re-enforcements (cf. 2 SAM. 17:11), and proved a persuasive orator. Absalom and all the men of Israel were convinced by the picture he drew of the leonine fighter. Ahitophel, whose wisdom was proverbial, saw the handwriting on the wall. He went home to his native city Giloh (cf. 2 SAM. 15:12) and hanged himself.

Giloh is mentioned among eleven cities in the Judaean hill country (JOSH. 15:51). Its connection with *Khirbet Jāla,* a mile and a half west of *Beit Ummar,* receives some support from the fact that the town Holon mentioned before it in Joshua 15:51 may be linked with nearby *Khirbet 'Alīn.* However, some scholars seek both places farther south.

When the decisions had been taken, Hushai passed along the secret information and his counsel to the priests, and the priests sent word by a maid to their sons waiting, doubtless in the cover of darkness, at a pre-arranged rendezvous at the Fountain of Rogel. This fountain is to be identified with the so-called "Well of Job" (*Bīr Eyyūb*), originally perhaps "Well of Joab," since Job is not associated with this locality. Of course, the well that is there now is high above the level of the ancient spring, owing to the filling up of the valley (see page 211). The story of the messengers has been built up somewhat in the interest of suspense; furthermore, the unrealistic idea of repeated trips on their part has been injected into it. There was need and time for only one trip, and we may assume that it was made uneventfully. They reached the Jordan during the night, finding David encamped on the hither side of the river. The crossing may not have been an easy matter and David will have deferred it in the light of possible moves in other directions. Acting on Hushai's advice, however, he now forded the Jordan with the entire force of armed men and fugitives before the day broke.

Mahanaim

David and his retinue had reached Mahanaim before Absalom and his army crossed the Jordan (2 SAM. 17:24). We must thus assume that Absalom started his march on the forenoon of the next day with such forces as were available. Amasa, son of an Ishmaelite, was his commander instead of Ahitophel. They marched up into Gilead. Whether the term is used in the broader or narrower sense is a question that arises here, but can only be answered in the light of the subsequent developments. It is not at all clear that this march to Gilead had the purpose of immediately pursuing or striking at David. If Hushai's advice was being followed, a large mobilization was to take place, and the Gilead headquarters would presumably be the point where the forces would congregate.

David was supplied at Mahanaim from three loyal sources (2 Sam. 17:27 f.): 1) by his Ammonite tributary, son of the former king Nahash, residing no doubt at Rabbah; 2) by Machir of Lodebar 3) by Barzillai of Rogelim (see below on these places).

Informed by Hushai of Absalom's plans, David determined to attack rather than to await an attack. David's commanders persuaded him to stay at Mahanaim rather than risk his person in the fight—ostensibly for the national benefit but actually in order to have a free hand. Never did David show himself seemingly as small and yet as great as when he ordered them to see to it that no harm came to Absalom. His hopes for the future of his house rested on this son, who was of the stuff that kings are made of, and whose desire to reign, even at the cost of killing his father, David could fully understand and even condone. His aides were not able to rise to so large a view of things.

The factual information about this campaign is extremely meager.

"So the people went out into the field against Israel: and the battle was in the wood of Ephraim;

For the battle was there scattered over the face of all the country: and the wood devoured more people that day than the sword devoured." (2 Sam. 18:6, 8 a.v.)

"So the army went out into the field against Israel; and the battle was fought in the forest of Ephraim.... The battle spread over the face of all the country; and the forest devoured more people that day than the sword." (2 Sam. 18:6, 8 r.s.v.)

The location of this "Ephraim" is naturally a matter of interest. How far it was is not stated. The name of this place, like the one in 2 Samuel 13:23, is probably a miswriting for 'Aphrayin or Ephron. It is a type of name regularly replaced by Arabic et Taiyibeh. Now there is a place of that name in the region of the 'Ajlūn. It excellently fits the Gephrun (Ephron) of 1 Maccabees 5:46. There is thus good reason to suppose that it is also the place meant in the present connection. The 'Ajlūn still contains more forest than any other region in Palestine, and in antiquity, no doubt, was an extensive wilderness, in which men could get lost and starve to death as presupposed in the narrative. While there were some woods south of the Jabbok, there were none of an extent that would have proved such a menace as 2 Samuel 18:9 assumes. For Absalom to go to the 'Ajlūn was not unnatural. Here Israel's forces could congregate and he could expect aid from the kingdom of Geshur.

It was a long march from Mahanaim to "Ephraim," if Mahanaim lay south of the Jabbok, as some think it did. The fact that the story does not indicate a great distance to the battlefield, formerly led scholars to seek Mahanaim itself in the 'Ajlūn. There is a Khirbet Meḥnā along the route of the later Roman road from Pella to 'Ajlūn which was long believed to be the successor of Mahanaim, but its location is not a very strong or strategic one, nor is it in the area that other Old Testament indications point to. Khirbet Meḥnā is situated among thickets today and built on ruins, Arab or Byzantine, though the possibility that earlier ruins may lie beneath these is not excluded. It seems more probable, however, owing to considerations soon to be mentioned, that Joab and his fellow commanders had to march to the "forest of Ephraim" from a point south of the Jabbok.

The attack of David's men put the Israelites to flight. Absalom was allegedly slain while hanging by his hair in a tree, and Joab then sounded the signal to terminate the fighting. The rebel's burial was ignominious.

It seems likely that the burial place of Absalom would be known and long remembered, but there is no further clue or tradition as to its whereabouts. The "Tomb of Absalom" at Jerusalem is a work of the time of Christ.

The news of the victory and Absalom's death now had to be brought to David. Ahimaaz, one of the two priests' young sons, who had carried Hushai's message, was eager to go. Joab dissuaded him, sending a Cushite mercenary instead. (In the a.v. Cushi is used as though it were the man's name.) Ahimaaz thereupon insisted on going, too (2 SAM. 18:23). He took the way of the plain, i.e., the way that leads to the *kikkar,* or "circle," of the Jordan Valley (see page 65). He evidently continued through open and familiar districts and then went back up to the mountain country to Mahanaim. The Cushite runner, one must suppose, went by the army's back-track, keeping on the high ground through the forest.

If the starting point of this marathon was near *eṭ Ṭaiyibeh,* where was Mahanaim? Some scholars hold that *Tell el Hajjāj,* about the only important ancient site to the south of the Jabbok River, satisfies the requirements of the Jacob story best (see page 84). It also suits the story of Abner's march through the Jordan Valley (2 SAM. 2:29). It fits the indications for the boundary of Gad (JOSH. 13:26). Finally, it accords with the possibility of Ahimaaz and the Cushite reaching the place by different routes that converged north of the city. For Ahimaaz coming down the "plain" would have crossed the Jabbok near Succoth (*Tell Deir'allā*) and then taken the track to *Tell el Hajjāj.* The Cushite keeping on the ridge would have crossed the Jabbok at the tells of *edh Dhahab,* beyond which his course soon would have joined the one of Ahimaaz.

David's Return

Negotiations concerning the settlement of the rebellion now had to be carried on. The northern tribes first raised the question of recalling the king. Informed of this fact, David dealt through the priests Zadok and Abiathar with Absalom's general, Amasa, promising him the post held by Joab. Amasa persuaded the Judaeans to request David to return (2 SAM. 19:14).

When David came to the Jordan crossing near Gilgal, the Judaeans were on hand to receive him and with them were leading members of the House of Saul, who crossed the river to pay homage, and sought amnesty. David showed his usual wisdom in granting it, but in his mind their doom was sealed (cf. 1 KINGS 2:8). The aged Barzillai from Rogelim, whose aid to David had doubtless been a big factor in his victory, had come down to the Jordan crossing, a fact suggesting that Rogelim was not very far away. This place has usually been put in the north near *Irbid,* under the theory of a northern Mahanaim. One might perhaps think of the *es Salṭ* neighborhood.

David came to Gilgal attended by the Judaean reception contingent and half of the Israelite contingent (presumably the one thousand Benjaminites already mentioned). The rest of the Israelite contingent arrived after the river crossing had been effected and voiced their discontent that the Judaeans had taken the initiative out of their hands. This clearly reveals that David was king of Israel as well as of Judah, and that the two kingships were as separate as those of upper and lower Egypt. That the writer is primarily thinking of the quarrelsome Ephraimites (cf. JUDG. 8:1 f.) seems highly probable. The sharp rivalry between Judah and Israel, that was one of the misfortunes of Hebrew history, comes to the surface here.

David was not able to smooth over this quarrel. A man named Seba, son of Bichri (i.e., of the clan of Bichri, 2 Samuel 20:14 R.S.V.), preached secession. He is here called a Benjaminite but 2 Samuel 20:21 describes him as from Mount Ephraim. All the Israelites allegedly now forsook the king. One can hardly suppose, however, that the various members of the House of Saul, who had just received amnesty, risked their skins by joining in, and it seems probable that the Benjaminites were not committed.

The Judaeans now escorted David to Jerusalem. There is no mention of his reception there. Apparently the exercises had all been held at the Jordan. Besides, secession of the northern tribes must have put a damper on the occasion.

When David arrived at his capital he ordered Amasa to mobilize a Judaean militia force within three days and report to him. According to the version given in chapter 20, Amasa tarried unduly so that David feared treachery. Summoning Joab he charged him to take the mercenary troops and pursue Amasa.

"When they were at the great stone which is in Gibeon, Amasa went before them." (2 SAM. 20:8 A.V.)

"When they were at the great stone which is in Gibeon, Amasa came to meet them." (2 SAM. 20:8 R.S.V.)

We have seen that the Gibeonite question is now settled in favor of *ej Jīb* (see page 137). It has been suggested that one must infer from this particular story that the main highway to the north anciently went via *ej Jīb* rather than via the Gibeah of Saul. But no such assumption is necessary, if one supposes that Amasa had his headquarters at *ej Jīb* and that Joab and his men went there first for that reason. Their approach happened to coincide with the approach of Amasa himself, who may have been coming in from a different quarter. The story is not entirely clear, since a commander-in-chief like Amasa would certainly not have been unattended or traveling on foot. Such men as Joab and Abishai, too, would have been mounted.

The slaying of Amasa is in keeping with the character of Joab. The manner in which David held it against him (1 KINGS 2:5) suggests that the circumstances leading up to the event were rather different than is reported here. One suspects that Joab acted without instructions from David to rid himself of his rival. The "great stone" near Gibeon where the murder took place naturally arouses one's curiosity, for such objects are rather indestructible features of a locality. There is a large isolated stone block northeast of *ej Jīb,* hard by the roadside. It is about twelve feet long, four feet wide, and four feet high. The temptation is strong to regard it as the one referred to in the Biblical narrative.

A soldier was posted at the body of Amasa and was given the task of recruiting passing Benjaminites for militia in Joab's force. The latter with his regulars went northward in pursuit of Seba.

There was doubtless more to this campaign than the story recalls. In the end, Seba and his Bichrite clansmen took refuge in Abel-beth-maacah in the extreme north of the land. The site of this Abel is known; it lay on the east side of the westernmost Jordan source, the *Nahr Bareighīt,* on a hill overlooking the *Hūleh* marshlands that stretch away to the southeast. It is called *Tell Ābil*—another instance of the long continuance of an ancient name at one and the same site. This city is described as "a mother in Israel" (2 SAM. 20:19), i.e., a historic center of Israelitic life, and so its excavation is much to be desired. Looking over to this tell one can imagine Joab's force, augmented by the volunteers from various quarters, engaged in the siege operations, see the inhabitants throw the head of Seba over the wall, hear the trumpet blast calling off the battle, and see the irregular forces disbanding and the regulars marching back to Jerusalem.

David Exterminates the House of Saul

It was the usual thing in that ancient world for the founder of a new dynasty to exterminate a previous royal family, since that was the only way to safeguard himself and his descendants against revolutions. David, because of his friendship with Jonathan and as son-in-law of Saul, had not followed this custom, but his throne had become shaky through the recent events. The danger that members of the family of Saul might yet unseat his descendants was real. A cause was found to deliver up seven men of the House of Saul to execution by the Gibeonites, two of them sons of Saul by a concubine and five of them grandsons, children of Saul's daughter, Merab (2 SAM. 21:9).

The high place of Gibeon, where this was done, was considered the most important sanctuary of the LORD until the early days of Solomon (1 KINGS 3:4). According to 1 Chronicles 21:29 the tabernacle and altar of burnt offerings were there. This is very strange, in view of the fact that the city was admittedly inhabited by a Canaanite population. Evidently a highly esteemed sanctuary of the pagan sun-god had been turned into a sanctuary of the LORD. The mention that the execution took place at harvest time is of significance. It suggests that the act virtually amounted to human sacrifice.

It is of some interest just where this high place of Gibeon lay. Did it lie on a part of the hill that bore the ancient city, or south of it on the much higher hill now bearing the shrine in honor of Samuel (*Nebi Samwil*)? It seems rather probable that the hill of *ej Jib* itself is meant. This hill running north to south has two tops. The present village of *ej Jib* lies on the northern one, but the old acropolis lay on the southern one, for the spring on which the city depended was below this part of the hill on the east, and a tunnel was hewn through the rock to make the water accessible to the inhabitants in times of siege. There is thus reason to suppose that the sanctuary of the LORD, where the tragic sacrifice of human lives took place, and where the faithful Rizpah carried on her epic vigil that stirred the sympathy of all Israel, lay on the height occupied by the modern town.

David had to do something to counteract the effect of Rizpah's heroism. He went to Jabesh in Gilead and made the inhabitants give up the bodies of Saul and Jonathan (and of the other sons?) and buried them, along with the remains of the recently executed men, in Zela of Benjamin, where Saul's ancestors had their tomb. This place is mentioned as Zela-eleph ("ox-rib") in Joshua 18:28, but there is no clue as to its location except that it could be mentioned in the same breath with Gibeah and Jerusalem. Thus the resting place of Israel's first king remains as unknown as that of Moses, unless some future discovery brings it to light.

The Mighty Men of David

The towns referred to in the brief collection of incidents concerning feats of valor performed by David's men (2 SAM. 21:15 f.) include one of which we have previously heard nothing, but which played a role in the Philistine wars—Gob. In a parallel account that name is replaced with the more familiar one, Gezer (1 CHRON. 20:4 f.). This suggests that the later writer was puzzled by the name Gob. Perhaps it is a short form of Gibbethon (cf. 1 KINGS 15:27).

We cannot dwell here on the native places of the thirty mighty men of David of 2 Samuel 23:8–39. These "mighty men" represent a group of knights—a supporting aristocracy such as any monarchy requires. They must have had horses and chariots, though rather strangely the use of these is unmentioned in the stories of the early monarchy. They were an idle class, drawing their income from towns assigned to them.

A Census and Its Sequel

One of David's important acts—though only reported by a theologically oriented writer who had no appreciation of its political and economic necessity—was the taking of a census. A later version frankly regarded the idea of a census as an inspiration of the devil (1 CHRON. 21:1). Like the author of 2 Samuel 20:4 f., the narrator of Samuel 24 is friendly to Joab. The latter, he points out, vainly sought to dissuade David from the undertaking.

The army leaders are described as making a circuit of the boundaries in connection with this project.

> "And they passed over Jordan, and pitched in Aroer, on the right side of the city that lieth in the midst of the river of Gad, and toward Jazer:
>
> Then they came to Gilead, and to the land of Tahtimhodshi; and they came to Dan-jaan and about to Zidon." (2 SAM. 24:5 f. A.V.)

> "They crossed the Jordan, and began from Aroer, and from the city that is in the middle of the valley, toward Gad and on to Jazer, Then they came to Gilead, and to Kadesh in the land of the Hittites; and they came to Dan, and from Dan they went around to Sidon," (2 SAM. 24:5 f. R.S.V.)

The starting point is Aroer at the boundary of Moab at the Arnon (see page 120). The "city that lieth in the midst of the river of Gad," or better "in the middle of the valley, toward Gad," is a puzzling entity. Apparently a point in the middle of the Arnon Valley south of Aroer is meant (cf. DEUT. 3:16; JOSH. 12:2). Jazer has already been mentioned (see page 123). Gilead is used in a very broad manner to include the 'Ajlūn. The Authorized Version's rendering in 2 Samuel 24:6 needs adjustment in the light of modern textual criticism. With the Revised Standard Version one may hold that the northern terminus was "Kadesh in the land of the Hittites", i.e., the Syrian city Kadesh, which lay on the Orontes (at Tell Nebi Mind). That point seems rather remote, however, and it is quite possible that some town in northern Transjordan, from which the line could pass over the next mentioned point, Dan (see page 167), and then to

Sidon, was the one originally named here.

This narrative connects the story of the census with that of a pestilence, which the LORD allegedly inflicted on David as a punishment for his census. While the connection may be secondary, there is no reason to doubt that a pestilence did occur in David's time, and that it led to the founding of a new sanctuary of the LORD north of the capital. David, we are told, saw the angel of the LORD stretching forth his hand to destroy Jerusalem, much as Isaiah saw the Assyrian do (Is. 10:32). The angel obviously was approaching the north gate and had reached the area in front of it—the threshing floor of Araunah the Jebusite (Ornan in 1 CHRON. 21:15). At this juncture David offered a prayer of intercession. He then was instructed by the prophet Gad to build an altar on the threshing floor of Araunah. Going forth at once he negotiated the purchase of the land and of the pair of oxen engaged in threshing; he built an altar, and functioning as chief priest, sacrificed the two beasts so conveniently at hand. The altar, of course, stood on the exact spot where subsequently the altar of Solomon's Temple was erected.

This tradition lays considerable stress on the idea that David acquired by purchase the property on which the Temple was later reared. It thereby maintained that this sanctuary was a royal possession, not the property of the Hebrew people or of the tribe of Benjamin in particular. The Davidic kings, we must infer, advanced this claim, in effect making the Temple an annex of the palace. With the fall of the dynasty the people of Judah fell heir to it.

The sacred use of the area north of the city wall may have been older than this writer thinks. The name "threshing floor of Araunah," which lingered at the sacred rock, probably suggested the explanation the story gives. But holy places are usually holy since time immemorial, and one must suspect that to have been true of this one.

CHAPTER XII

SOLOMON IN ALL HIS GLORY

AFTER THE DEATH of Absalom it was more or less a foregone conclusion that Adonijah was next in line as David's successor, for he was second in order of birth. He enjoyed the favor of two of the most powerful leaders—Joab, head of the army, and Abiathar, chief priest. The trouble was that David did not want to name a successor while he was still able to exercise intelligent judgment.

Unfortunately, David lapsed into a senile condition, in which it was possible for those who happened to get his ear to influence him unduly. One of his wives, Bathsheba, the soldier's widow whom David had married, schemed to get the succession away from Adonijah and win it for her son, Jedidiah, who is better known to history by his throne name Solomon (Hebrew, *Shelō-*

mōh). She had the aid of the two younger, coming men, who had the ambition to replace Joab and Abiathar: Benaiah, a military man, who had all the "mighty men," or knights, under him, and Zadok, the priest. In addition she had on her side an individual belonging to a less "regular" class of religious personages—the prophet Nathan.

Adonijah's First Mistake

It is obvious that the kingdom was suffering under the lack of leadership. With a monarch unable to govern and unable to carry on the important function of supreme judge, things went from bad to worse. In this situation Adonijah felt that something ought to be done, but whatever was done had to be inaugurated with proper religious preparation. He made the mistake of arranging a sacrificial festival without informing David, and invited the men who were the real leaders of the state—Joab and Abiathar.

A sacrifice, of course, is held only at a holy place. The one selected must have served such a purpose since of old.

"And Adonijah slew sheep and oxen and fat cattle by the stone of Zoheleth, which is by En-rogel." (1 KINGS, 1:9 A.V.)

"*Adonijah sacrificed sheep, oxen, and fatlings by the Serpent's Stone, which is beside En-rogel.*" (1 KINGS, 1:9 R.S.V.)

The identity of the En-rogel, or "Fuller's Spring," can hardly be in doubt. The description of the boundary between Judah and Benjamin (JOSH. 15:7; 18:6) mentions it as being in the valley of the son of Hinnom. The latter was the valley south of the "southern shoulder of the Jebusite," i.e., the southern end of the western ridge.

There is today in this locality the so-called "Well of Job," where the suffering saint was supposedly healed, according to a belief first reported by an Arabic author in 985 A.D. Possibly Job got into this scene so remote from his proper habitat by confusion of his name with that of Joab. The Well of Job is no cistern, but a genuine well that taps ground water and is 125 feet deep. The inhabitants of *Silwān* greatly prefer it to the "Spring of the Steps" as a source of drinking water. Exploratory excavations carried on by Warren in 1867 showed that near the ancient well there is a subterranean cave, which was reached by a stairs from above. Since the ground level herabouts has been raised so much (see page 196), the Serpent Stone (stone of Zoheleth, A.V.), if it was not hacked to pieces in the time of Josiah's reformation (2 KINGS 23:4 f.), must lie buried in the depths. The name suggests that it was a stone with an encircling serpent sculptured on it. An object of this sort, though from a much later period, is still to be seen at the Nabataean city of Petra. Serpents were sacred to certain divinities, and the veneration of a Brazen Serpent at Jerusalem is attested to by 2 Kings 18:4. Nehemiah speaks of a "dragon well" (NEH. 2:13; Jackal's Well, R.S.V.), and since dragons were imagined as serpents it seems obvious that he means the well by the Serpent Stone.

The religious gathering thus convoked certainly could not remain unobserved, even if the preparations for it were kept secret. We find the prophet Nathan, one of those left out, hastening to Bathsheba with the news. Bathsheba, though certainly not queen, had influence with David and access to his quarters. She relayed the information. David determined to demonstrate that he was still the king and could do as he pleased. He summoned Zadok and Benaiah and told them to take the royal guards and to conduct Solomon down to Gihon. There Zadok [and Nathan?] should anoint him, and then the trumpet should be blown and the cry raised "Long live King Solomon!"

It is naturally a matter of great interest to identify the scene of this highly important event. The question is: Where was Gihon? We can gather from subsequent references that it was a spring on the east side of the City of David (2 CHRON. 32:30; 33:14). There is only one spring there now, called the Spring of the Steps, or Spring of Our Lady Mary, as the natives call it, or Fountain of the Virgin. A peculiar thing about it is its periodicity: it bubbles forth water twice a day in the rainy season. If that was characteristic of the spring in antiquity, it must have been regarded with awe, for such a mysterious phenomenon was interpreted supernaturally by ancient Orientals.

Riding the king's own mount and escorted by the foreign mercenaries, Solomon was thus conducted to Gihon and anointed there. The trumpet was blown and the loyal retainers in the City of David joined in the jubilation, as the new king returned to the palace and ascended the throne.

The procession to Gihon could not be observed from the En-rogel, but the noise of the celebrating could be heard. Abiathar's son, Jonathan, soon came with the clarifying news. One can imagine the consternation that fell upon the conspirators. Adonijah at once fled to the altar and seized its "horns" (as the curved projections at the corners were called), thus invoking asylum of the sanctuary. No doubt the altar in the tent of the LORD (1 KINGS 2:28) is meant, though it is uncertain where this tent stood in David's time and how Adonijah was able to get there without being intercepted. He refused to leave the place of safety thus embraced until he had Solomon's assurance that no harm would come to him. While David was alive, Adonijah was safe.

Passing of David

No detailed narrative has been preserved about the passing and burial of Israel's greatest king, founder of a dynasty that was to rule in Jerusalem for four hundred years. It was an event that certainly deserved recording. Only the fact of his death and his burial "in the city of David" is mentioned (1 KINGS 2:10). According to Nehemiah 3:15-16, the tombs of the Davidic kings (down to Ahaz, 2 KINGS 16:20) lay not far from the Pool of Shelah(Siloam), near the stairs of the City of David and below the "artificial pool" and the "house of the mighty men" (see page 208). The tomb of David was allegedly still pointed out in New Testament times (ACTS 2:29), but one cannot be sure that the geographical allusions of Nehemiah were understood at this period. Since Josephus and early Christian tradition sought Zion on the western hill, it is not impossible that David's tomb was (erroneously) pointed out in that quarter. From the time of the Crusades on, it was sought at the Cenacle (see page 414) and his supposed resting place is much revered by Mohammedans—the buildings over it being called "Prophet David" (en Nebi Dā'ūd).

The beliefs of the ancients, however, are only of minor interest since archaeology has shown that old Jerusalem lay on the southeastern hill. Some of those who excavated there sought with great zeal to locate the tombs of the Davidic kings. Unhappily, the southeastern hill was used as a stone quarry in Roman times, and it seems probable that little can have survived such destructive activity. However, two grottoes are unique among all the hundreds of tombs in and about Jerusalem. It seems possible that these are surviving examples of the tombs of the Davidic kings. There were, of course, a great many kings in the four hundred years of the dynasty's existence, and it is unwarranted to identify one of these tombs with that of David himself. That the ruler was buried "in the city of David" leaves the matter of the exact site completely open. It seems possible that like so many Assyrian kings he was buried in a crypt under his palace. It would have been robbed of any treasure it may have contained by callous descendants, and destroyed at the time of Nebuchadnezzar's conquest of Jerusalem.

Solomon Holds a Reckoning

No despot is ever safe while rivals live. To put them out of the way was standard procedure in the ancient Orient. Both Adonijah and Joab were slain. Joab was buried "in his own house in the wilderness"—doubtless a cave-tomb in the Wilderness of Judah. Whether the combing of that wilderness in the hunt for scrolls' caves will lead to the rediscovery of this tomb is a matter not without interest.

Another dangerous man still to be disposed of was the last survivor of the House of Saul, Shimei. Solomon skillfully set a trap for him and Shimei subsequently fell into it, when he traveled westward to Gath in Philistaea (see page 174) to recover runaway slaves. Solomon swiftly seized the opportunity and had Benaiah slay the individual who was the last hope of the Benjaminites.

SOLOMON'S PROVINCIAL SYSTEM

Consolidation of Affairs

The Hebrew state was now one of some consequence. In David's time there had apparently been little assertion of the ancient Egyptian rights over Palestine. The fact that the Pharaoh of Egypt—presumably the last ruler of the Twenty-first Dynasty, Psusennes II (c. 963 B.C.)—gave Solomon his daughter for a queen (1 KINGS 3:1) is indicative of Egypt's intentions to regain its influence in Palestinian affairs. This marriage must have taken place at the beginning of Solomon's reign (963–929 B.C.), for we are told that the princess had to be satisfied with the relatively plain accommodations of the City of David until a luxurious palace could be built.

A state act of great importance was Solomon's sacrifice. That Gibeon was the "great high place" is surprising, for Gibeon was a city with a Canaanite population. There may be some legal reason, not yet well understood, why this great ceremonial had to be held there. The pagan cult had long been abolished—it was a sanctuary of the LORD that witnessed this huge rite of a thousand burnt offerings. If one holds that the high place of Gibeon lay on the hilltop now occupied by ej Jîb (see page 208), then one will think of Solomon as spending the night there and dreaming that the LORD had appeared to him (1 KINGS 3:4 f.).

Solomon's Reorganization of the Kingdom

The small amount of realistic information preserved in the record of Solomon's reign shows that he had organizing ability. Of particular significance is the report of 1 Kings 4:7 f., about the "twelve officers over all Israel" set up by this ruler. Solomon modernized the state by dividing it into districts, which were placed under governors appointed by him. Unhappily, the list is not complete, for no mention is made of the foreign provinces or dependencies. "Israel" in this connection apparently does not include Judah (cf. 1 KINGS 4:20; 2 SAM. 5:5). The latter may have been under direct administration from Jerusalem. The names of the prefects must once have been listed on separate lines, and the right-hand edge of the leaf must have been damaged, for a number of the names are only half preserved. It is noteworthy that two royal sons-in-law held prefectures. The administrative divisions (see map on this page) show consideration for the older Hebrew tribal system in the areas where that was possible (I, VII–XII), but where the Canaanite city-states had an overriding importance the districts were based on their territories rather than on idealistic claims or aspirations of the tribes.

It may be noted that the list begins in the heart of the land, with the important Mount Ephraim. Some scholars think the term is employed broadly here to embrace all the territory between V and XI, being the mountain country east of the Sharon Plain. There can be little doubt that Shechem was the seat of the prefecture. Then follow the districts lying in a half-circle around Mount Ephraim, moving from southwest to north (II–V), and those lying to the east which were considered colonies of the Joseph tribes (VI–VII). Next comes the northern tier (VIII–X), and last the tier south of Mount Ephraim, Benjamin and the region east of it on the other side of the Jordan (XI–XII). In this list there are some troublesome spots. Thus in II, Makaz is not mentioned again in the Old Testament, but may be linked with a place mentioned in the Amarna Letters and in the list of Palestinian cities given by Pharaoh Thutmoses III (*c.* 1500 B.C.) (*Muḥ-ḥaṣi,* with a phonetic change). It is probably to be sought among the mounds in the vicinity of Gezer. Elon, according to a time-honored suggestion supported by a Septuagint reading, is probably Aijalon (page 138). Beth-hanan has been sought in *Beit 'Anān* on the Benjaminite border, east of Aijalon.

In III the mention of Socoh is of crucial importance. There are two places of that name in Judah. That there was actually such a town in western Manasseh is shown by the survival of that name in *Shuwēkeh,* situated where the valley coming down from Shechem enters the coastal plain. Here there is a high mound (*Rās Shu-wēkeh*), which fills the requirement of sufficient antiquity. This Socoh is already referred to in the Egyptian lists of Palestinian towns of the second millenium B.C. Its identification with the Socoh of III fits well with the indications for Hepher, referred to here as "land of Hepher" (cf. JOSH. 12:17). In the light of geographical considerations that we need not enter into, *Tell Ibshār,* lying in the coastal plain, has the best claim to being considered the center of the land of Hepher and therefore as the city of Hepher.

Arubboth does not occur again; its name should probably be corrected to Araboth, the form in which it appears in many Septuagint manuscripts. One of these adds the remark that Araboth belonged to Dor and was a district-capital of the coastal region. The northern limit of its territory probably was the spur of Mount Carmel that is called *el Khashm,* "the nose." The most important

site in this area, *Bāqa el Gharbīyeh,* which some have sought to link with Aphek, has a good claim to being regarded as Arubboth or Araboth. The adjacent district of Dor must have extended north from the *Khashm* to the Carmel promontory. The phrase Naphath-dor or "coast of Dor" describes it.

Another troublesome spot is found in the description of district V. This highly important area included some of the strongest and most historic Canaanite cities in the land: Taanach, Megiddo, and Beth-shean. The text is burdened at this point with descriptions of the extent of territory of the latter two cities (verse 12). We shall defer discussion of this passage until later (see page 219).

A further difficulty is the reference to Asher and Bealoth. Oddly, there is no mention of Zebulun and so the possibility exists that Bealoth is a corruption of that name.

In the case of District XII Gilead is an error for Gad. The use of "Gilead" in an expanded sense made possible the inclusion of Bashan, but that area belongs in District VI.

The Empire of Solomon

Later tradition claims that King Solomon held sway over all kingdoms from the Euphrates to the brook of Egypt (I KINGS 4:21), or, put differently, over all the region west of the Euphrates from Tiphsah to Gaza (I KINGS 4:24).

The mention of Tiphsah is of interest here (see Color Map XII). It is the only reference in the Old Testament to the place known to later geographers as Thapsacus. Because Alexander the Great crossed the Euphrates at that point, it attained a considerable celebrity with the Greeks. The Biblical reference is the oldest-known historical mention of it, except for a possible occurrence in an Assyrian inscription. The town probably lay on the left bank of the Euphrates near the point where the *Balīkh River* enters it from the north. Here an ancient mound, consisting of two summits rising nearly one hundred feet above the plain and one hundred and thirty-five

4.9 *The ruins of Palmyra. (Courtesy Institut Francais d'Archéologie, Beyrut, Liban)*

feet above the river, called *Tell el Thadayain* ("mound of the breasts") because of their shape and position, fulfills all the requirements for identification with Tiphsah, though only excavations can bring the final proof. Five hundred years after Solomon, Xenophon refers to Thapsacus as "a large, wealthy city." It had therefore become important in the Persian era. We can infer from its mention in 1 Kings 4:24 that in the time of that writer it was the main Euphrates crossing. This is the view of a later age. In Solomon's time, and in the Assyrian era generally, *Til Barṣip* and Carchemish were the great crossings. "From Tiphsah to Gaza" comprises the sphere of the whole caravan route from the Euphrates to the border of Egypt. Solomon is thus imagined as the man who could control this traffic and levy on it. No wonder that he waxed rich.

The sovereignty over Syria here claimed for Solomon need not be understood as involving actual administrative control. However, the ruler of a realm comprising all Palestine, with Edom and Moab annexed and the Philistines his vassals, was certainly able to dominate southern Syria in a period when Assyria or Egypt, immobilized by their own internal problems, failed to assert themselves in this sphere. If he controlled the southerly branch of the great trade route from the Euphrates, it does not seem unreasonable that he would try also to control the northerly branch. The one military exploit reported of him, though given only in a less trustworthy, later source, was apparently directed toward that goal.

> "And Solomon went to Hamath-zobah, and prevailed against it.
> And he built Tadmor in the wilderness, and all the store cities, which he built in Hamath." (2 CHRON. 8:3–4 A.V.)

> *"And Solomon went to Hamath-zobah, and took it. He built Tadmor in the wilderness and all the store-cities which he built in Hamath."* (2 CHRON. 8:3–4 R.S.V.)

Hamath of Zobah must be identical with the great Hamath (AMOS 6:2) on the Orontes River in Syria (see page 200 and Color Map III). It is presupposed here that this kingdom was under Zobah's dominion in Solomon's time. The reported building of "Tadmor in the wilderness" (desert) is interesting, for Tadmor was the predecessor of Palmyra that was to achieve great glory in Roman times. It is already mentioned by the

Assyrian king Tiglathpileser I (*c.* 1100 B.C.) as Tadmar. Its mention here is somewhat suspect, however, for in 1 Kings 9:18 the text must be corrected to Tamar (R.S.V.). There, as here, the further connection suggests towns and cities in Palestine rather than in Syria. But the Chronicles reading reflects the importance that Palmyra had attained in later times.

While Solomon was a man of peace he carried a big stick. This is illustrated by a large expansion of armaments. It is reported that he had forty thousand stalls (better "teams") of horses for his chariots and twelve thousand horsemen. This indicates that he went in heavily for the use of cavalry as well as of charioteers. No doubt the old Canaanite cities furnished most of the equipment available in the kingdom itself. In the 1928 excavations of the Oriental Institute of the University of Chicago at Megiddo, Guy found in stratum IV, which dates from Solomon's time, a large stable (with cobbled pavement in the center), partitions marked off by pillars, and stone cribs. No doubt a chariot detachment of the Hebrew monarch was stationed here.

Solomon and Hiram of Tyre

In 1 Kings 5:1 f., the spotlight falls on the Phoenician coastal city of Tyre, whose name (*Ṣōr*) meant "rock." It was, indeed, a city built on a rock, in fact, upon a rocky island in front of the Syrian coast. The Assyrian inscriptions speak of Tyre as lying "in the midst of the sea," and a scene on the Bronze Gates of Balawat shows the nobles of the city bringing tribute from their island to the Assyrian king Shalmaneser III (*c.* 850 B.C.) on the mainland. It seemed puzzling, formerly, that "Sidonians" was often used as a name for the Phoenicians not only in the Old Testament but also in Homer, and that even the kings of Tyre were called "kings of the Sidonians" in Assyrian inscriptions. The reason for this is that Tyre was destroyed in the thirteenth century B.C. and was resettled by people from Sidon—its traditional era beginning 1198-7 B.C. In fact, it was made the official seat of the Sidonian government, which it remained until the late eighth century B.C. Some Hellenistic writers, excerpts of whose works are preserved, tell that Hiram of Tyre built great harbor installations, and a temple for the deity Melkarth, "king of the city"; and that he conquered the people of Kition, capital city of Cyprus, thereby beginning the great Phoenician expansion and colonization that marked the next centuries. According to the list of the kings of Tyre, which Josephus has quoted from a Hellenistic writer Menander of Ephesus, he ruled thirty-four years. He was already at the helm of his state in David's time and was still active in Solomon's twenty-fourth year (1 KINGS 6:1; 9:10 f.). Hiram may be dated *c.* 969–936 B.C. or according to a different reckoning, 979–946 B.C.

4.10 *Tribute sent by the king of Tyre to the Assyrian king Shalmaneser III. (British Museum)*

King Solomon, desirous of building a first-class palace and temple, found it necessary to deal with the king of Tyre and to obtain building materials and skilled labor and architectural aid necessary to achieve his goal (1 KINGS 5:8 f.). He paid with farm products of which the Phoenicians were much in need. He also supplied the necessary labor battalions to carry on the lumbering operations. It is recorded that ten thousand men were kept at work in the Lebanon to fell and drag all this lumber to the sea. In addition, he had a very large force engaged in the mountain country adjacent to Jerusalem quarrying, hewing, and transporting the blocks of stone needed for the huge building project. Foreign architects and skilled labor drawn from various quarters doubtless aided in the task, for Jews and Israelites, as people but lately aspiring to civilization, naturally had no qualified personnel. Centuries later we find the Persian king Darius II also depending on imported skilled labor when building himself a palace (see page 333).

4.11 *The model of Shick shows the natural topography that was altered when Herod greatly enlarged the Temple area. Solomon's Temple can only have occupied the eminence. (Matson Photo Service)*

The Acropolis of Jerusalem

In many years of building activity there was thus created at Jerusalem an acropolis that included a Temple on its northern side. If we recall that the city was confined to the eastern ridge, this meant that one had to pass through the palace area to get to the Temple, or else to go around outside of the city walls to another entrance. In effect, therefore, the Temple was originally an appendage to the palace and a private sanctuary of the Davidic kings and their retainers. The public from the rural environment would hardly have been permitted to go through the palace area to get to the sanctuary. The gate for the public was probably on the east. It was only in the post-exilic city that things were radically altered, and then perhaps only after the old City of David was in foreign hands and a new residential city growing up on the western hill. At that time the Temple crowning the eastern ridge was left in possession of the name Zion, which at an earlier day had applied to the area of the City of David and its predecessor, the fortress of the Jebusites (1 KINGS, 8:1; 2 SAM. 5:7). The Hellenistic "Acra" founded on the site of the City of David in 168 B.C. had a new name of its own and to speak of it as "Zion" will have been repulsive to every patriotic heart.

Solomon's Temple was naturally built in accordance with an architectural style in vogue at the time. Nothing is said about temple courts, such as we hear of in Ezekiel's temple. The interest is focussed on "the house," a single building of three parts—a porch or vestibule, a main structure, and the "cella" at its rear. The description of 1 Kings provides interesting details about it. Ninth-century Assyrian temples furnish a particularly interesting comparison. They, too, were "long-house" buildings with vestibules, though these latter had greater breadth proportionally than is the case in Solomon's Temple. There, too, a cella at the rear of the house was a characteristic feature. However, the cella of the Assyrian temples was not set off as sharply as is the case with that of Solomon's Temple. Indeed, it seems that, like older Canaanite temples of the time of Amenophis III to Ramses II found at Beth-shean, the cella of Solomon's Temple was a sort of second-storey affair, up to which a staircase led (see 1 KINGS 8:8 and page 218).

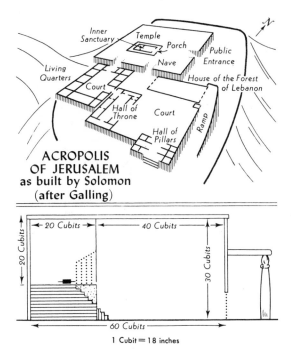

ACROPOLIS
OF JERUSALEM
as built by Solomon
(after Galling)

SOLOMON'S TEMPLE (after Galling)

The decorations of the sanctuary with wood carvings of open flowers, palm trees, and cherubim are all in approved Oriental style. The cella contained two statuesque gold-overlaid cherubim guarding the ark. These figures are primarily guardians of the throne of the deity, and Oriental kings, who liked to consider themselves as semi-divine, were fond of embellishing their own thrones with them (see fig. 4.6). There is thus some ground for the belief of various scholars that the ark was a "throne." Isaiah, standing in sight of altar and "house," has a vision of the LORD sitting on a throne, high and lifted up (corresponding to the raised platform of the cella), and his train filling the temple (i.e., the main part of the building, beyond the vestibule). Before the "house" was the altar of sacrifice. It is believed to have stood on the sacred rock which since about 70 A.D. has assumed a sort of mystical significance for the Jewish mind and which the Arabs called es Ṣaḵra. The mosque built by the Arab conqueror of Jerusalem, the Caliph Omar, now is reared over the site. Presumably this rock is where David erected the altar (2 SAM. 24:18).

A modern palace for the acropolis took much longer to build than the Temple— thirteen years. Unfortunately, it is not possible to get a very clear idea of the palace area from the description given in 1 Kings 7:1 f. The historical narratives furnish some additional helpful information, notably the account of the revolution against Athaliah (2 KINGS 11; 2 CHRON. 23; see page 289). Here we learn that there was a wall between the palace and the Temple and that at the time in question two gates permitted passage from the one to the other. The palace of Solomon lay in the southern part of the present quadrangle. Whatever vestiges of it may have existed in post-exilic times were destroyed when Herod greatly expanded the Temple area. Originally the latter will have been of very modest proportions.

On the left is a plan of the palace and Temple area as projected by a modern archaeologist. Its author has accepted the idea that the Forest of Lebanon House was a stable for Solomon's horses, and that a ramp, as in Sargon's palace at *Khorsabad,* led up to it. The Hall of Pillars is reconstructed after a distinctive type of building best known from the excavations at Sinjirli in northern Syria (the so-called *Bit Khilani*); the Hall of the Throne is given in accordance with a building of that nature at *Tell Ḥalāf* in Mesopotamia from a little before Solomon's time. West of the Hall of the Throne and encircling another court must have been the living quarters of the king and his harem, including the special palace built for his Egyptian queen (1 KINGS 7:8). However, no details at all are preserved about Solomon's buildings, and the drawing here is purely schematic, depicting the probable extent and a possible ground plan of the structures.

Metal Work and Foundry

By way of having an up-to-date establishment, Solomon obtained products of metal work for his temple. This was achieved under the direction of a Phoenician craftsman, whose mother had been a Hebrew of the tribe of Naphthali. His name, too, was Hiram (in Chronicles, Huram), like that of the Tyrian king. Hiram made the pillars on which rested the roof of the vestibule of the Temple, a noteworthy "molten sea," or font, and tripods of bronze. On page 153 is a specimen of Phoenician metal work centuries before Solomon—a golden bowl for a king of Ugarit (*Ras Shamra*). In the center of the bowl there is a frieze of alarmed gazelles, while around them whirls the mad chase. The king, with the reins of his team wrapped around his body, is drawing his bow at a wild bull, while cow and calf make good their escape and a frightened gazelle darts away. Such objects must have graced the table of Solomon, too.

Where the metal for the bronze work was obtained is not reported. We are told, however, where the casting was done, and this is a matter of interest to us in the present connection.

> "In the plain of Jordan did the king cast them, in the clay ground between Succoth and Zarthan." (1 KINGS 7:46 A.V.)

> *"In the plain of the Jordan the king cast them, in the clay ground between Succoth and Zarethan."* (1 KINGS 7:46 R.S.V.)

Succoth, as we have seen, is generally identified with the impressive *Tell Deir 'allā*, north of the Jabbok, at the point where that stream turns sharply southward toward the Jordan. If the foundries were between Succoth and Zarethan, then one would expect Zarethan to have been close to Succoth, for there were quite a few cities in this part of the Jordan Valley and it would be a confusing description if that were not the case. Elsewhere we hear that Adam was "to the side of Zarethan" (JOSH. 3:16), though unfortunately we are not told to which side. Since Adam is to be localized south of Succoth at *Tell ed Dāmieh*, near the ford of *ed Dāmieh* (see page 133), we at least have a fixed point for that item. Some perplexity is

caused, however, by the statement that district V of Solomon's realm included, beside Taanach and Megiddo,

> "All Beth-shean, which is by Zartanah beneath Jezreel, from Beth-shean to Abel-meholah, even unto the place that is beyond Jokneam." (1 KINGS 4:12 A.V.)

> *"All Beth-shean which is beside Zarethan below Jezreel, and from Beth-shean to Abel-meholah, as far as the other side of Jokmeam."* (1 KINGS 4:12 R.S.V.)

Originally Zarethan may have been described as beside Abel-meholah.

A recent suggestion would put Zarethan eleven miles north of Succoth at the magnificent site of *Tell es Sa'idīyeh* overlooking the southern side of the *Wadi Kufrinjeh*. But then a number of important places would have intervened between Succoth and Zarethan. The statement of 1 Kings 7:46 suggests that Zarethan is the next place of consequence north or south of Succoth. If one must look for a place to the north of *Tell Deir 'allā,* yet not too far from Adam, then the prominent *Tell el Mazār* is particularly attractive. Not far from it is the modern village of *Darar* that could conceivably continue the name of Zererah which is apparently an older or younger name for Zarethan (JUDG. 7:22). *Tell el Mazār* commands a view down to Succoth nearly two miles away, but also a good view to the north. The choice of a site for the foundries "between Succoth and Zarethan" was presumably governed by convenience to the transport of the ores. There were mines in the *Wadi Rājib,* and between *Tell Deir'allā* and *Tell el Mazār* was an appropriate point at which to process the metals brought down from the mountains.

A great festival of dedication was held at the time of the completion of Solomon's Temple, but the story about that event, while rich in religious reflection, is not very productive of realistic information. Delegations came "from the entrance to Hamath to the brook of Egypt" (1 KINGS 8:65)—a more extended way of describing the Hebrew territory than the older description "from Dan to Beersheba" (see JUDGES 20:1; I SAMUEL 3:20; 2 SAMUEL 17:11).

Debtor of the King of Tyre

The building of a luxurious acropolis was an expensive business. Solomon had to borrow money from Hiram of Tyre to carry through his undertakings. Apparently he sought to compensate Hiram by ceding or turning over to him a tract of land in Galilee containing twenty towns, at the head of which stood Cabul (I KINGS 9:11 f.). The latter was a border city of the tribe of Asher (JOSH. 19:27). This was hardly territory originally settled by Israelites, but more probably a Canaanite district that had been annexed by the tribe of Asher and that could easily be dispensed with to placate Hiram. Hiram, as we have heard, was engaged in considerable expansion of Tyrian power.

Cabul survives to this day in a village of the same name, *Kabūl,* situated at the western rim of the Galilean mountain country on a ridge sloping down to the plain with a valley on either side. The presence of debris of the Middle Bronze and Hellenistic periods shows that this is an ancient site. There can be little doubt but that excavations would produce Iron Age sherds as well. Cabul cannot very well have been the center for the towns of the plain below, for the latter would have been under the domination of one of the larger cities whose mounds are to be seen there; but it presumably dominated the towns of the forested hill country between the valley of *er-Rāmeh* in the north and the *el Baṭṭōf* Plain in the south. The submarginal nature of this district is reflected in the story of Hiram's disappointment.

Fortifications

In connection with Solomon's building operations we hear of the Millo (I KINGS 9:15, cf. 2 SAM. 5:9). We learn that he built the Millo after building a palace for his Egyptian wife (I KINGS 9:24). In connection with this is put a rebellion led by Jeroboam, who later became king of the northern tribes.

> "And this was the cause that he lifted up his hand against the king: Solomon built Millo, and repaired the breaches of the city of David his father." (I KINGS 11:27 A.V.)

> *"And this was the reason why he lifted up his hand against the king. Solomon built the Millo, and closed up the breach of the city of David his father."* (I KINGS 11:27 R.S.V.)

It is believed by some that the Millo was a raised area on which the buildings were put, for the word must mean something like "a fill," according to its etymology. However, it is also possible that it means a massive fortification structure. This interpretation is recommended by the fact that it is mentioned after the building of the palace. That Solomon closed up the breach of the City of David has raised many questions. When was the breach made? If one bears in mind that Solomon extended Jerusalem on the north, it seems obvious that he must have had the northern city wall dismantled, for it would have been most inconvenient for traffic between the city and the new palace to be funneled through a gate. He could thus have made a breach in the City of David. A new wall must then have been built around the new palace from the eastern and western points where the old wall had been cut, and this could be the closing of the breach of the City of David referred to.

The work on the Jerusalem fortifications was only a part of Solomon's undertakings of this nature. He also strengthened the defenses of the following cities:

1. Hazor in the extreme north, no doubt as outpost against the Aramaeans.

2. Megiddo in the center, bulwark against Phoenicia.

3. Gezer, at *Tell Jizr* in the Shephelah.

4. Beth-horon (lower), at the strategic

point of entry from Philistaea into the central hill country.

5. Baalath. Perhaps the Baalath of Judah is meant, since that controlled an important approach into Judah from the Philistaean coast; less probably the Simeonite Baalath (JOSH. 19:8). Baalath is better known as Kiriath-jearim (see page 199).

6. Tamar. This was essentially an outpost against the Edomites. A fort named Thamara still existed in the Negeb in Roman times and probably continued the old name. It is to be identified with *Qaṣr ej Jeheniyeh,* lying at the point where the road coming up from the *Ghōr* south of the Dead Sea, reaches the height of the pass. Solomon's Tamar no doubt lay below in the *Ghōr* itself, probably near *'Ain el 'Arūs.*

The mention of Gezer brings to the surface an item of considerable historical interest. A flashback is given (1 KINGS 9:16), according to which the Pharaoh of Egypt, who gave his daughter to Solomon as queen (see page 213), captured and destroyed Gezer and its population and gave it to his daughter as a dowry. Joshua is said to have defeated a king Horam of Gezer (JOSH. 10:33), but nevertheless it had remained independent (JUDG. 1:29). Evidently Egyptian rights of long standing would have been violated had David or Solomon sought to annex it.

Navigating the Red Sea

A concluding item in this chapter is of even greater interest.

"And king Solomon made a navy of ships in Ezion-geber, which is beside Eloth, on the shore of the Red sea, in the land of Edom.

And they came to Ophir, and fetched from thence gold." (1 KINGS, 9:26, 28 A.V.)

"King Solomon built a fleet of ships at Ezion-Geber, which is near Eloth on the shore of the Red Sea, in the land of Edom. . . . and they went to Ophir, and brought from there gold." (1 KINGS 9:26, 28 R.S.V.)

The Oriental rulers were at the same time merchant princes and so Solomon, too, sought to be a shipping and trading man. His province, Edom, subdued by David, touched the Gulf of Aqabah and therewith the Red Sea, beyond which lay untold sources of wealth. Eloth, or Elath, was situated at the head of that gulf, as we have already heard (see page 67). Ezion-geber, too, was mentioned as a station in the wilderness journey (NUM. 33:35 f.; DEUT. 2:8), but here we get our most specific reference to it.

The place was long sought many miles north of Aqabah at *Ghaḍiān,* which seems to preserve the name Ezion, but the theory sometimes entertained that the Gulf of Aqabah extended this far inland in antiquity has been disproved. The German explorer Frank rediscovered ancient Ezion-geber in *Tell el Kheleifeh,* situated some five hundred yards from the shore and halfway between the eastern and western ends of the head of the gulf. That Ezion-geber is described as "near Elath" shows that in the Biblical writer's day Elath was the better-known place. 1 Kings 22:48, being an earlier passage, mentions only Ezion-geber, while 2 Kings 14:22 and 16:6 mention only Elath, thus suggesting that Ezion-geber had ceased to be of consequence. Adjacent to the site on the south and west is a so-called *es sebkha* or salt marsh. The town thus could not have been built any farther to the west, since no fresh water is obtainable in that direction for several miles. The excavations carried on here by an American School expedition under Nelson Glueck, brought to light plants for smelting and refining copper and for manufacturing copper articles. The nearby copper mines of Sinai and of the *el 'Arabah* furnished the metal. The strong winds that blow here furnished an excellent draft for the operation of furnaces. The history of Ezion-geber ended in the sixth to the fifth century B.C. when Nabataeans rose to power and built up the town of Eloth (Elath or Aila) instead.

Solomon's harbor and its installations have been smothered with sand, for no doubt the city once lay directly on the shore of the gulf. If the king had ships built here he must have had the wood brought down from elsewhere. It is doubtful if any lumber suitable for that purpose was available except from the forests of Phoenicia. Solomon may have had the boats knocked down, carried overland, and then reassembled at the Gulf of Aqabah.

The State Visit of an Arabian Queen

Remembrance of the visit of an Arabian queen in Solomon's time greatly stirred the imagination of a later age. The writer who reports this was interested in Solomon's wisdom and hence says that she came to admire Solomon's wisdom and splendor. Such state visits, however, always have a political and economic background. Solomon's control of Edom put him athwart one of the great frankincense-trade routes of South Arabia, so it was quite essential for those whose existence depended on the frankincense traffic to have a commercial treaty with him. The story does not record the name of the Arabian queen.

We hear, however, of queens ruling in North Arabia under Tiglathpileser III (c. 735 B.C.). It is not impossible, therefore, that the queen who visited Solomon was really a North Arabian vassal or agent of the Sabaean rulers. However, proof may yet emerge that the Sheba of Solomon's day was governed by queens, and certainly a visit to Solomon by its ruler would be quite plausible for the economic reasons indicated above.

The Ophir Journeys

Whether the Ophir journeys hang together with these Sabaean trade relations is not clear. The initial mention of them in 1 Kings 9:26 f. suggests that they began before the visit of the Arabian queen. Renewed mention of them has been introduced by an editor into the story of that visit.

"And the navy also of Hiram, that brought gold from Ophir, brought in from Ophir great plenty of almug trees, and precious stones." (1 KINGS 10:11 A.V.)

"Moreover the fleet of Hiram, which brought gold from Ophir, brought from Ophir a very great amount of almug wood and precious stones." (1 KINGS 10:11 R.S.V.)

Here the Ophir fleet is strictly a Phoenician one belonging to Hiram; nor is it clear that it sailed from Ezion-geber. The reference to almug wood raises the question: What was it and where did it come from? The word has been vindicated as correctly reported by its occurrence in a tablet from *Rās Shamrā*, which gives a list of commodities. The usual rendering for almug is sandalwood, for which India was the only source of supply up to the eighteenth century A.D. But wood from India could hardly have been known in Syria in the fifteenth century B.C.

"For the king had at sea a navy of Tharshish with the navy of Hiram: once in three years came the navy of Tharshish, bringing gold, and silver, ivory, and apes, and peacocks." (1 KINGS 10:22 A.V.)

"For the king had a fleet of ships of Tarshish at sea with the fleet of Hiram. Once every three years the fleet of ships of Tarshish used to come bringing gold, silver, ivory, apes, and peacocks." (1 KINGS 10:22 R.S.V.)

Here are two separate fleets, each ruler having his own, and even composed of Tarshish-ships—the ocean liners going to Sardinia or Tartessus in Spain. Nothing is said here of Ophir, nevertheless Ophir must have been the goal of these voyages, in view of the products obtained. The author of this passage seems to have the idea that Solomon and Hiram sent Tarshish ships to the Red Sea, via a Nile-Red Sea canal, the existence of which at Solomon's time, however, is not yet established beyond doubt. If the translations "peacocks" were dependable, this would imply a journey as far as India. That, of course, would not be historically accurate, for it was not until Graeco-Roman times that journeys to India became possible. The word rendered "peacocks" is interpreted by some as "chickens" and by others as "baboons." On the seal of Jaazaniah from *Tell en Nasbeh* (*c.* 600 B.C.) there is a portrayal of a cock; however, that does not yet vindicate the existence of poultry in the Israel of Solomon's time.

Since ships were used, caravan traffic to Ophir must have been impossible. That makes it seem probable that Ophir lay on the other side of the Red Sea. Basically, the region meant must be the present Somaliland.

The Armaments Trade

The use of horses seems to have been very limited in David's time. They were evidently not raised to any extent in Palestine, and there was no money to buy them abroad. In a few short years this was all changed. It went hand in hand with the rising level of prosperity. Solomon not only acquired many horses for his army, but numerous chariots. Foreign import and export was more or less a royal monopoly for the simple reason that only the rulers were in a position to protect their commercial representatives and expedite their journeys. The private trader was handicapped at every point. The passage mentioning Solomon's dealing in horses is somewhat puzzling.

> "And Solomon had horses brought out of Egypt, and linen yarn: the king's merchants received the linen yarn at a price." (1 KINGS 10:28 A.V.)

> *"And Solomon's import of horses was from Egypt and Kue, and the king's traders received them from Kue at a price."* (1 KINGS 10:28 R.S.V.)

The reader will notice that in the Revised Standard Version a new geographical name "Kue" has replaced the "linen yarn" of the Authorized Version. Some ancient sources already suspected a geographical name in

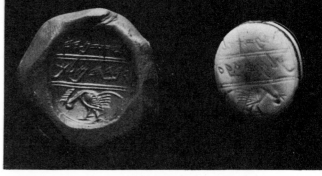

4.12 *Seal of Jaazaniah, found at* Tell en Nasbeh. (*Courtesy Palestine Institute of Pacific School of Religion*)

that word, and the Assyrian and North Semitic inscriptions have confirmed it. Kue (*Qwh*) was the name for a part of Cilicia. It was, as is so often the case, the name both of a city (not yet rediscovered) and a principality, and was adjacent to Mushki or Meshech (GEN. 10:2). There is, however, an inconsistency in the mention of both Egypt and Kue as points from which horses were imported. The kings of the Hittite succession states and of the Aramaean principalities did not need Solomon to import horses for them from Kue, to which they were much closer than he (1 KINGS 10:28–29). It seems likely and may have originally been so stated that Solomon was middleman in the sale of Cilician horses to Egypt and in Egyptian chariot sales to Syria. Since he was athwart the great trade route from Egypt to the Euphrates he was able to play a profitable middleman's role in this matter.

Seeds of Future Trouble

All the splendor of Solomon's period cannot efface certain disturbing facts that developed in the course of it. In the first place, he permitted a situation to arise that was bound to bring about serious religious disturbance. In the second place, there was a change of dynasty in Egypt, which also brought a change of policy (see page 213). That country now played a diplomatic game of aiding the external and internal enemies of the House of David. In the third place, there was the factor of Israelite separatism.

The rise of the religious crises is blamed

on Solomon's foreign wives. They wanted to worship their native deities. Chapels for them were built on the mountain east of Jerusalem (1 KINGS 11:7). We get more explicit information about this later, in the report of how these sanctuaries were destroyed by King Josiah.

> "And the high places that were before Jerusalem, which were on the right hand of the mount of corruption, which Solomon the king of Israel had builded . . . did the king defile." (2 KINGS 23:13 A.V.)

> *"And the king defiled the high places that were east of Jerusalem, to the south of the mount of corruption, which Solomon the king of Israel had built . . ."* (2 KINGS 23:13 R.S.V.)

Mount of corruption (or destruction) seems to be a figurative expression for the Mount of Olives. The name is a twisting of the appellation "Mount of anointing." The usual term for the latter "Mount of Olives" applied only to the part of the range directly opposite the Temple (the *eṭ Ṭūr* of today, see page 397). If Solomon's pagan chapels were south of it, that means that they stood on the eminence commonly called the Mount of Offence.

The foreign peril had two foci—Edom in the south and Aram in the north (1 KINGS 11:14 f.). With the Pharaoh's explicit permission, and no doubt active aid, Hadad, escaped scion of the royal family of Edom, returned to his own country and organized a successful revolution there.

The other rising peril was from the Aramaean chief, Rezon. His seizure of Damascus was a brilliant coup, quite analogous to Shamshi-Adad's seizure of the city of Asshur. Rezon's hatred of Israel is particularly stressed. The veil is slightly lifted for us, too, with respect to its cause in the statement that he fled "after the slaughter by David" (1 KINGS 11:24). In other words, David had brutally slaughtered the Aramaeans of Zobah after conquering them, just as he

had done to the Edomites.

The greatest danger to the Hebrew state lay in the underlying disunity. The northern tribes considered themselves to be Israel, the true people of the LORD, and resented the dominant role attained by Judah through its original support of David. The Israelites had conferred the rule of their land on David personally, not on Judah. They thought they had a right to withdraw it, as the rebellion of Seba shows (2 SAM. 20). That failed because of Joab's swift action, but the dissatisfaction smouldered, and it required only a strong leader to make it formidable.

Such a man of destiny appeared on the scene in Jeroboam, a high official of Solomon, who was in charge of all the labor conscription in the "tribe of Joseph" (i.e., in both Ephraim and Manasseh). He was an Ephraimite from Zeredah and was encouraged in his plotting against Solomon by the Ephraimite prophet Ahijah of Shiloh (1 KINGS 11:26 f.). The ambition to restore the House of Joseph to its position of leadership no doubt burned in the bosoms of these men, and dissatisfaction with the new absolutism imposed by Solomon will have added worthier motives. Jeroboam's plot was betrayed. He fled to Egypt where Shishak had now become Pharaoh (see page 270), and was held in reserve in that country for future eventualities.

The passing of Solomon is reported in the same meager manner as that of his father. We hear that he, too, was buried "in the city of David." That, as already suggested in his father's case, could mean in the palace, for the royal tombs that are attested as lying in the southern part of the City of David and close to its eastern wall (NEH. 3:16), could be those of subsequent rulers. Be that as it may, Solomon must be viewed as the founder of Hebrew civilization—borrowed civilization though it was. Since he cultivated architecture and the arts, he will also have cultivated letters, and the rise of a Hebrew literature will have begun in his time.

MAP I

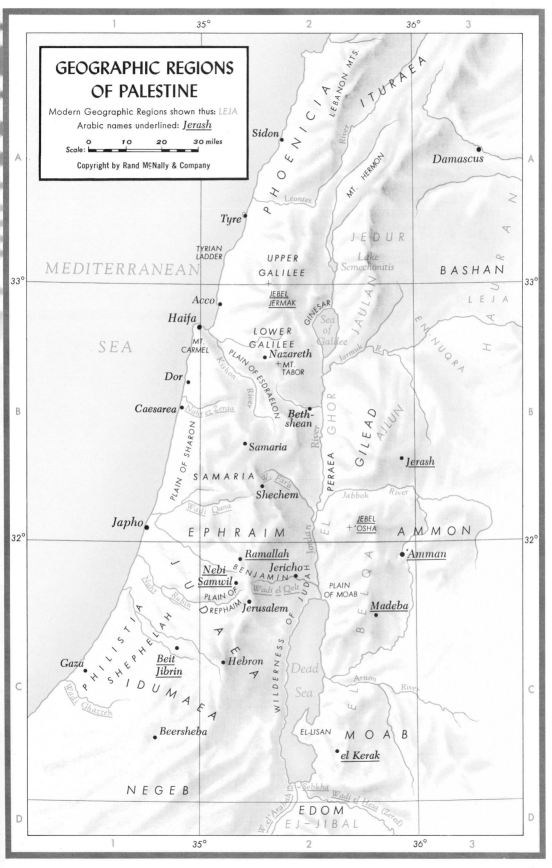

GEOGRAPHIC REGIONS OF PALESTINE

Modern Geographic Regions shown thus: LEJA
Arabic names underlined: *Jerash*

Scale: 0 10 20 30 miles

Copyright by Rand McNally & Company

MEDITERRANEAN

SEA

PHOENICIA

LEBANON MTS.

ITURAEA

Sidon

Damascus

River

MT. HERMON

Tyre

JEDUR

Lake
Semechonitis

BASHAN

TYRIAN
LADDER

UPPER
GALILEE

LEJA

33°

33°

Acco

JEBEL
JERMAK

GINESAR

JAULAN

EN NUQRA

HAURAN

Haifa

LOWER
GALILEE

Sea
of
Galilee

MT.
CARMEL

Nazareth

+MT.
TABOR

Jarmuk R.

Dor

Kishon

River

PLAIN OF ESDRAELON

Beth-
shean

GHOR

GILEAD

AJLUN

Caesarea

Nahr ez Zerqa

River

PERAEA

PLAIN OF SHARON

Samaria

Jerash

SAMARIA

W. Fara

EL

Jabbok

River

Shechem

Wadi Qana

Japho

EPHRAIM

JEBEL
+ OSHA

AMMON

32°

Jordan

32°

Ramallah

Jericho

BELQA

'Amman

Nebi
Samwil

BENJAMIN

Nahr

Rubin

PLAIN OF

Wadi el Qelt

PLAIN
OF MOAB

JUDAEA

REPHAIM

Jerusalem

Madeba

WILDERNESS

OF JUDAH

PHILISTIA

SHEPHELAH

Gaza

Beit
Jibrin

Hebron

Dead

Sea

IDUMAEA

Arnon

River

Wadi Ghazzeh

MOAB

Beersheba

EL-LISAN

el Kerak

NEGEB

es -Sebkha

Wadi el Hesa (Zered)

Wadi el Arabah

EDOM

EJ - JIBAL

225

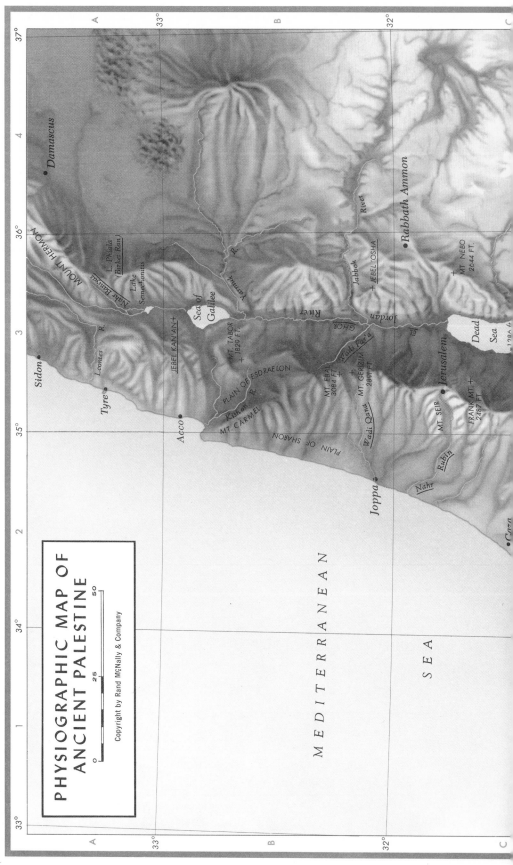

PHYSIOGRAPHIC MAP OF
ANCIENT PALESTINE

Copyright by Rand McNally & Company

0   25   50

MEDITERRANEAN

SEA

Damascus

MOUNT HERMON

L. Phiala
(Birket Ram)

Lake
Semechonitis

Nahr Banias

Leontes R.

Sidon

Tyre

Acco

JEBEL KAN'AN

Sea of
Galilee

MT. TABOR
1929 FT.

PLAIN OF ESDRAELON

Kishon R.

MT. CARMEL

PLAIN OF SHARON

Yarmuk

Jordan River

GHOR

Wadi Far'a

MT. EBAL
3084 FT.

MT. GERIZIM
2849 FT.

Wadi Qana

Nahr   Rubin

Joppa

Jabbok

River

JEBEL 'OSHA

Rabbath Ammon

MT. NEBO
2644 FT.

Jerusalem

MT. SEIR

FRANK MT.
2487 FT.

Dead
Sea

Gaza

226

MAP II

D

31°

30°

E

4

36°

•Ma'an

3

Brook of Zered (W. el Hesa)

Sebkha Araba

es-

Wadi el Arabah

JEBEL RAMM +
5397 FT.

B

35°

Ezion-
geber •

Gulf
of
Aqabah

N E G E

MOUNT
HALAK

Kadesh-
barnea

JEBEL KHARÛF +
3305 FT.

2

34°

JEBEL HELAL +
2026 FT.

JEBEL YELLEQ +
3566 FT.

1

31°

D

30°

E

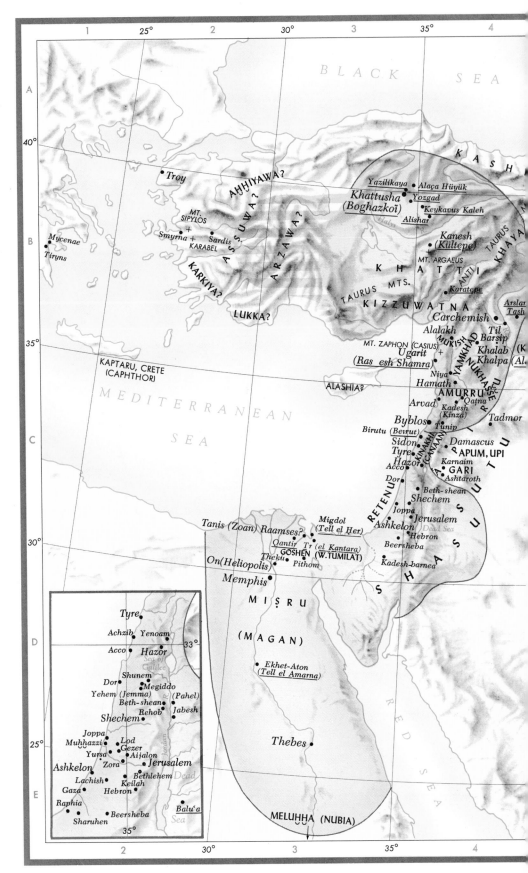

BLACK SEA

Troy

AHHIYAWA?

Yazilikaya   Alaça Hüyük
Khattusha   Yozgad
(Boghazköi)   Keykavus Kaleh
Alishar

MT.
SIPYLOS
Smyrna   Sardis
KARABEL

Kanesh
(Kültepe)

Mycenae
Tiryns

KARKIYA?

LUKKA?

ARZAWA?

MT. ARGAEUS

KHATTI

ANTI

KHAYA

TAURUS MTS.

KIZZUWATNA

Karatepe

Carchemish

Arslan
Tash

Alalakh   Til
Barsip

MUKISH

MT. ZAPHON (CASIUS)   Ugarit   Khalab
(Ras esh Shamra)   Khalpa

YAMKHAD

NUKHASSE

Al

KAPTARU, CRETE
(CAPHTHOR)

ALASHIA?

Niya
Hamath   AMURRU
Qatna
Arvad   Kadesh   Tadmor
(Kinza)
Byblos   Tunip
Birutu (Beirut)
Sidon   Damascus
Tyre   APUM, UPI
Hazor   Karnaim
Acco   GARI
Ashtaroth
Dor
Beth-shean
Shechem
Joppa   Jerusalem
Ashkelon   Dead Sea
Hebron
Beersheba

MEDITERRANEAN

SEA

RETENU

CANAAN

SHASU

Migdol
(Tell el Her)

Kadesh-barnea

Tanis (Zoan) Raamses?
Qantir   Tr (el Kantara)
GOSHEN (W. TUMILAT)
Theku   Pithom
On(Heliopolis)
Memphis

MISRU

(MAGAN)

Ekhet-Aton
(Tell el Amarna)

RED SEA

Thebes

MELUHHA (NUBIA)

Tyre
Achzib Yenoam
Acco   Hazor   33°
Sea of
Galilee
Shunem
Dor   Megiddo
Yehem (Jemma)   (Pahel)
Beth-shean
Rehob   Jabesh
Shechem
Joppa
Muhhazzi   Lod
Yursa   Gezer
Zora   Aijalon   Jerusalem
Ashkelon   Bethlehem   Dead
Lachish   Keilah
Gaza   Hebron   Sea
Raphia   Beersheba   Balu'a
Sharuhen   35°
25°

228

MAP III

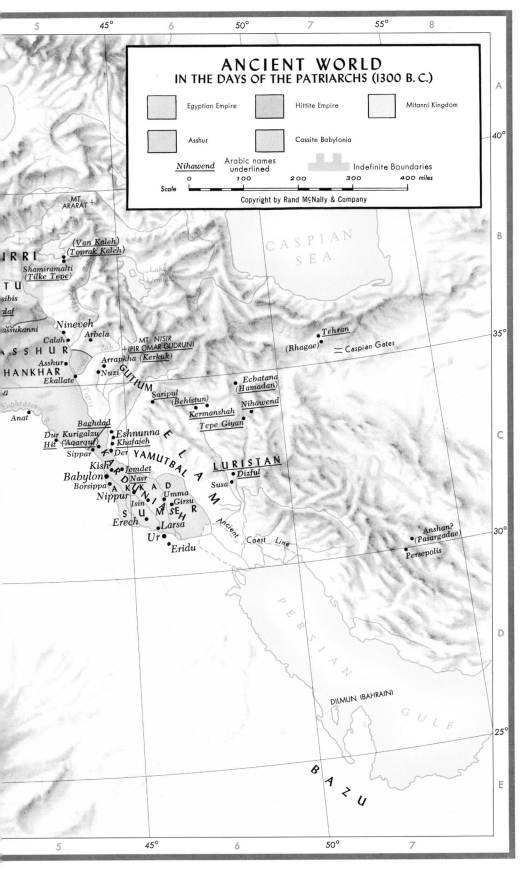

ANCIENT WORLD
IN THE DAYS OF THE PATRIARCHS (1300 B.C.)

Egyptian Empire   Hittite Empire   Mitanni Kingdom

Asshur   Cassite Babylonia

Nihawend   Arabic names underlined   Indefinite Boundaries

Scale   0   100   200   300   400 miles

Copyright by Rand McNally & Company

L. Van

IRRI

TU

sibis

slaf

assukanni

ASSHUR

HANKHAR

MT. ARARAT

(*Van Kaleh*) (*Toprak Kaleh*)

Shamiramalti (*Tilke Tepe*)

Lake Urmia

Nineveh

Calah

Arbela

Asshur

Nuzi

Ekallate

Arrapkha (*Kerkuk*)

MT. NISIR (PIR OMAR GUDRUN)

GUTIUM

Saripul (*Behistun*)

Tehran

(*Rhagae*)   — Caspian Gates

CASPIAN SEA

Ecbatana (*Hamadan*)

Kermanshah

Tepe Giyan

Nihawend

Anat

Euphrates

Baghdad

Hit   Dur Kurigalzu (*'Aqarquf*)

Sippar

Eshnunna

Khafajeh

Der

YAMUTBAL

LURISTAN

Dizful

ELAM

Kish

Babylon

Borsippa

Jemdet Nasr

AKKAD

Nippur

Isin

Umma

Girsu

SUMER

Erech

Larsa

Ur

Eridu

Susa

Ancient

Coast Line

Anshan? (*Pasargadae*)

Persepolis

PERSIAN

GULF

DILMUN (BAHRAIN)

BAZU

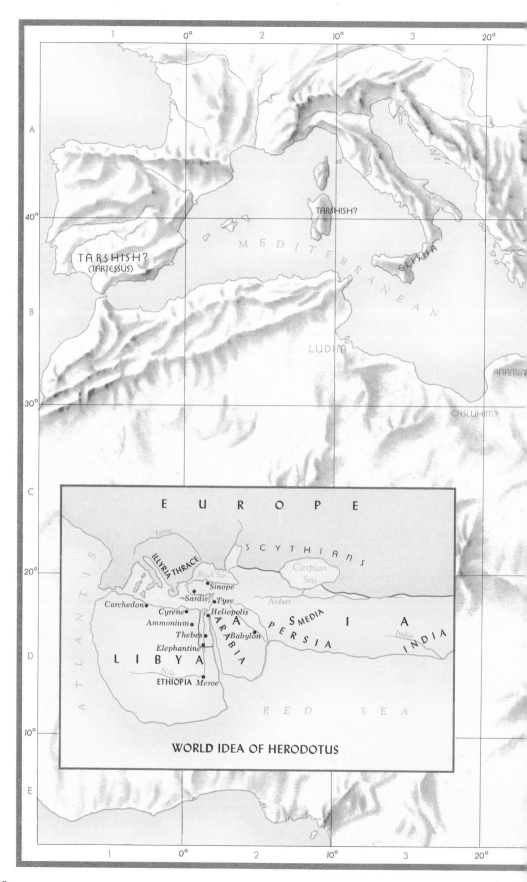

TARSHISH?

TARSHISH?
(TARTESSUS)

MEDITERRANEAN

ELISHA

LUDIM

ANAMIM

CASLUHIM?

EUROPE

Istros

ILLYRIA THRACE

SCYTHIANS

Black Sea

Caspian
Sea

ATLANTIS

Sinope

Carchedon

Sardis
Tyre

Araxes

Cyrene

Heliopolis

MEDIA

INDIA

Ammonium

ARABIA

PERSIA

India

Thebes

Babylon

Elephantine

LIBYA

Nile

ETHIOPIA Meroe

RED   SEA

WORLD IDEA OF HERODOTUS

MAP IV

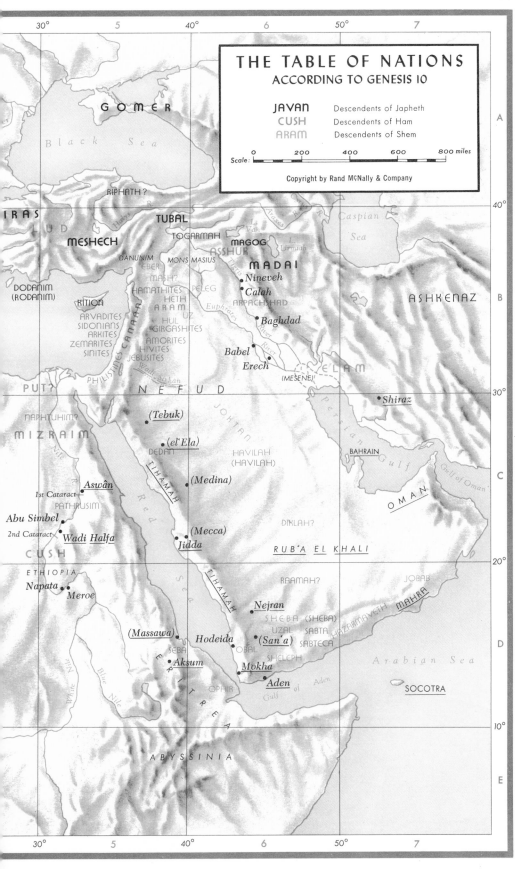

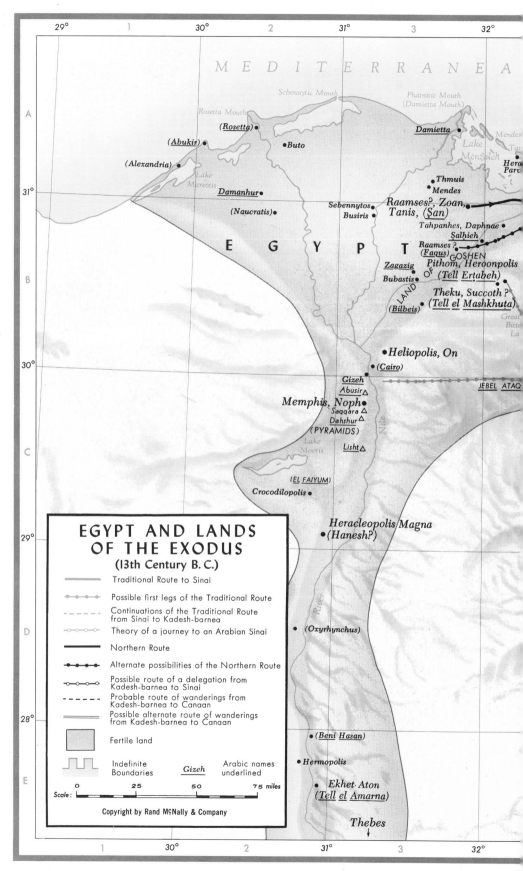

EGYPT AND LANDS
OF THE EXODUS
(13th Century B.C.)

———	Traditional Route to Sinai
—•—•—	Possible first legs of the Traditional Route
- - - - -	Continuations of the Traditional Route from Sinai to Kadesh-barnea
—○—○—	Theory of a journey to an Arabian Sinai
━━━	Northern Route
—●—●—	Alternate possibilities of the Northern Route
—○—○—	Possible route of a delegation from Kadesh-barnea to Sinai
- - - -	Probable route of wanderings from Kadesh-barnea to Canaan
═══	Possible alternate route of wanderings from Kadesh-barnea to Canaan

Fertile land

Indefinite Boundaries

Gizeh   Arabic names underlined

Scale: 0   25   50   75 miles

Copyright by Rand McNally & Company

MAP V

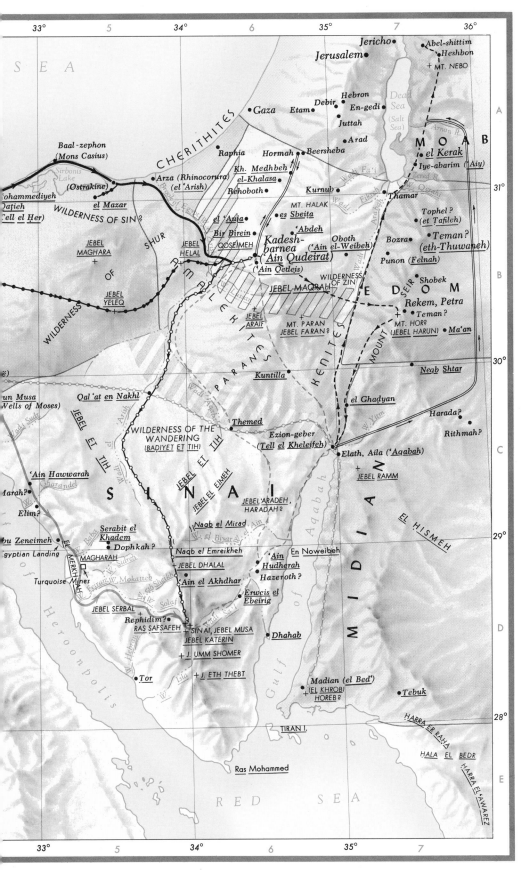

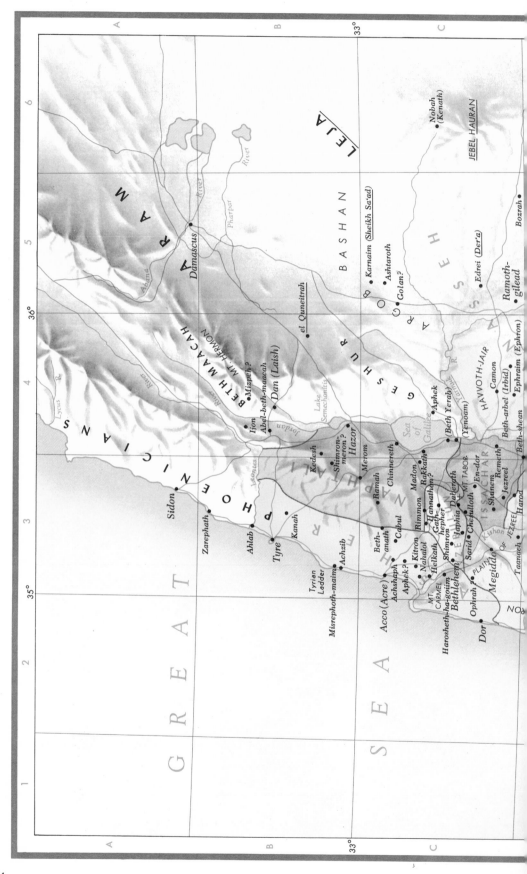

A
B
33°
C

A
B
33°
C

1   2   35°   3   36°   4   5   36°   6

GREAT

SEA

PHOENICIANS

Sidon

Zarephath

Ahlab

Tyre

Tyrian
Ladder

Kanah

Beth-
anath

Cabul

Misrephoth-maim

Achzib

Acco (Acre)

Achshaph

Aphek?

Helkath

Kitron

Nahalol

Rimmon

Hannathon?

Gath-
hepher

Shimron

Sarid

Japhia

Bethlehem

Harosheth-ha-goiim

MT.
CARMEL

Ophrah

Dor

KISHON

Megiddo

Taanach

Daberath

ZEBULUN

Chesulloth

En-dor

MT. TABOR

Shunem

Remeth

Jezreel

Shimron?
meron?

Kedesh

Ramah

Chinnereth

Madon

Rakkath

NAPHTALI

Merom

Hazor

ISSACHAR

PLAIN OF

Harod

JEZREEL

Kishon

Sea
of
Galilee

Lake
Semechonitis

Leontes

R. Leontes

Jordan

Dan (Laish)

Abel-beth-maacah

Ijon

Mizpeh?

MT. HERMON

BETH-MAACAH

A   R   A   M

Damascus

Abana River

Pharpar River

el Quneitrah

GESHUR

GESHUR

ARGOB

Golan?

Karnaim (Sheikh Sa'ad)

Ashtaroth

BASHAN

LEJA

Nobah
(Kenath)

JEBEL HAURAN

Edrei (Dera)

Bozrah

Ramoth-
gilead

MANASSEH

HAVVOTH-JAIR

Camon

Beth-arbel (Irbid)

Ephraim (Ephron)

Beth-shean

(Beth Yerah)

Yenoam)

Aphek

R. Yarmuk

R.

Lycus R.

234

MAP VI

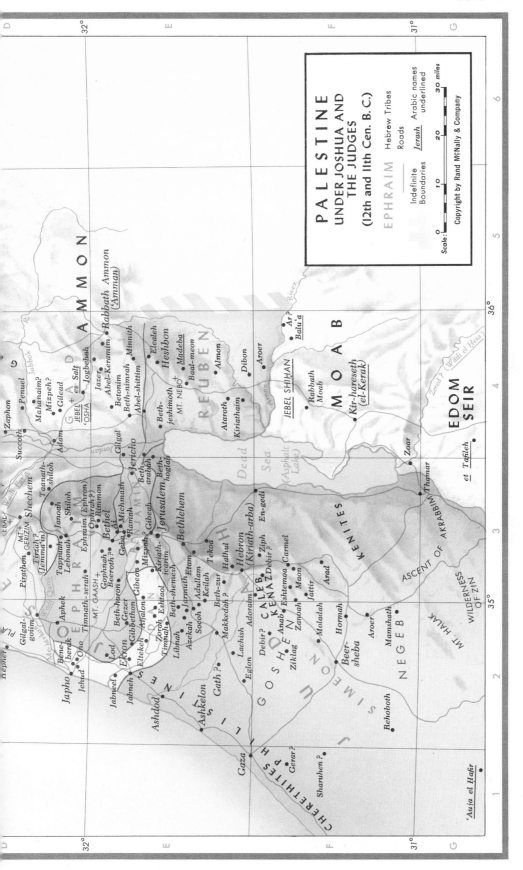

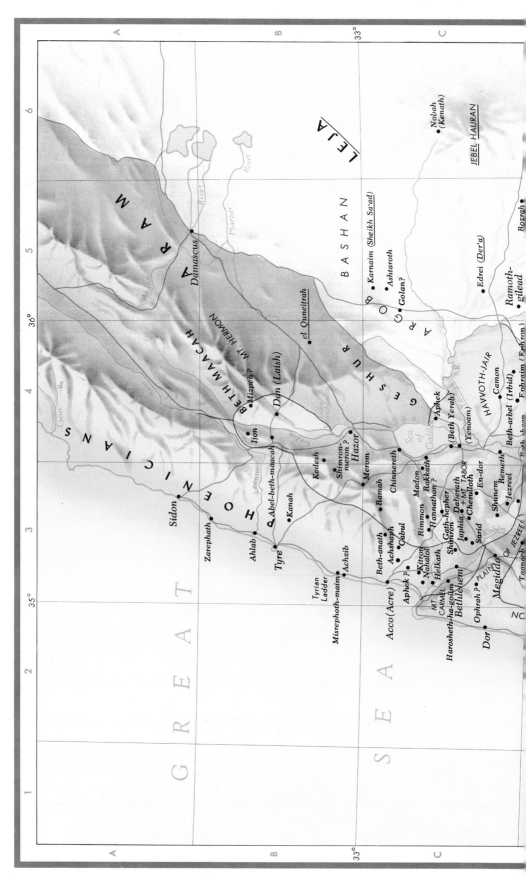

LEJA

JEBEL HAURAN

Nobah
(Kenath)

Bozrah

Edrei (Der'a)

Ramoth-
gilead

ARAM

Damascus

Pharpar River

BASHAN

Karnaim (Sheikh Sa'ad)
Ashtaroth
Golan?

ARGOB

Abana R.

el Quneitrah

GESHUR

HAVVOTH-JAIR

Camon

Beth-arbel (Irbid)

Ephraim (Ephron?)

MT. HERMON

BETH-MAACAH

Mizpeh?

Dan (Laish)

Ijon

Leontes

Abel-beth-maacah

Kedesh

Shimron-
meron?

Hazor

Jordan

Merom

Sea
of
Galilee

Aphek

Beth Yerah
(Yenoam)

Ramah

Chinnereth

Madon

Rakkath

Rimmon

Hannathon?

Remeth

Jezreel

PHOENICIANS

Sidon

Zarephath

Ahlab

Kanah

Tyre

Cabul

Beth-anath

Achshaph

Shunem

En-dor

Chesulloth

Japhia

MT. TABOR

Daberath

Sarid

Cath-hepher

Shimron

Helkath
Nahalol
Kitron

Aphek?

Acco (Acre)

Tyrian
Ladder

Misrephoth-maim

Achzib

MT.
CARMEL

Harosheth-ha-goiim

Bethlehem

Ophrah?

Dor

Megiddo

PLAIN
OF JEZREEL

Kishon

Taanach

GREAT   SEA

236

MAP VII

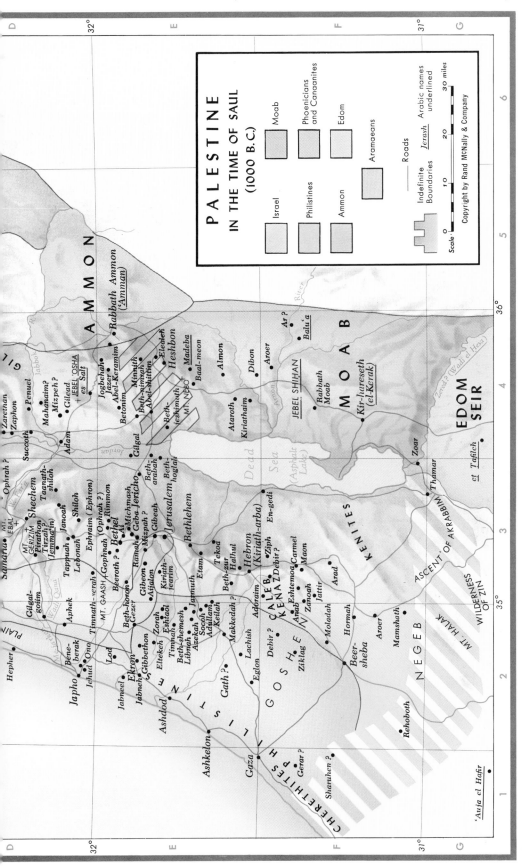

PALESTINE
IN THE TIME OF SAUL
(1000 B.C.)

Israel

Moab

Philistines

Phoenicians
and Canaanites

Ammon

Edom

Aramaeans

Roads

Indefinite
Boundaries

Jerash Arabic names
underlined

Scale

0   10   20   30 miles

Copyright by Rand McNally & Company

AMMON

Rabbah Ammon
(*Amman*)

GIL

Zarethan
Zaphon
Succoth
Penuel
Mahanaim?
Mizpeh?
Gilead
+ JEBEL OSHA
es Salt
Adam

Jabbok

Jogbehah
Jazer
Abel-Keramim
Betonim
Minnith
Beth-nimrah
Abel-shittim
Elealeh
Heshbon

Madeba

Baal-meon

Almon

River

Ar ?
Balu a

Dibon
Aroer

JEBEL SHIHAN

MOAB

Rabbath
Moab

Kir-hareseth
(*el-Kerak*)

Ataroth
Kiriathaim

Arnon

Zered (*Wadi el Hesa*)

EDOM
SEIR

et Tafileh

Zoar

Thamar

ASCENT OF AKRABBIM

WILDERNESS
OF ZIN

MT. HALAK

KENITES

Gilgal
Beth-
arabah
Beth-
hoglah

MT. NEBO
Beth-
jeshimoth

Samaria
MT.
EBAL +
MT. +
GERIZIM Shechem
Pirathon
(*Jemma'in*)
Tirzah?
Tappuah
Lebonah
Janoah
Shiloh
Ephraim (Ephron)

Wt Farah

Taanath-
shiloh
+ Ophrah ?

Ai
Michmash
Beth Jericho
Bethel Geba
Gibeah
Mizpah ?
Ramah
Gibeon
Ataloth
MT. GAASH (Gophnah (Ophrah ?)
Rimmon

Dead

Sea
(Asphalt
Lake)

En-gedi

Jerusalem

Bethlehem

Tekoa
Hathul
Beth-zur
Hebron
(Kiriath-arba)
Ziph
CALEB
KENAZ Debir ?
Eshtemoa Carmel
Maon

Arad

Anab
Zanoah
Jattir

Moladah
Hormah

Aroer

Mamshath

Beer-
sheba

NEGEB

Rehoboth

'Auja el Hafir

CHERETHITES PHILISTINES

Ashkelon

Gaza

Gerar ?

Sharuhen ?

Ashdod

Ekron
Jabneh Gibbethon
Eltekeh
Zorah Eshtaol
Timnah
Beth-shemesh
Libnah
Azekah
Socoh Adullam
Keilah
Makkedah ?
Adoraim

Gath ?

Lachish
Eglon

Debir ?

Ziklag

GOSHEN

Jamnia
Lod
Beth-horon
Gezer
Kiriath-
jearim
Jarmuth
Etam

Japho
Bene-
berak
Jehud Ono
Timnath-serah

Beeroth ?

PLAIN

Aphek

Hepher

Gilgal-
goiim

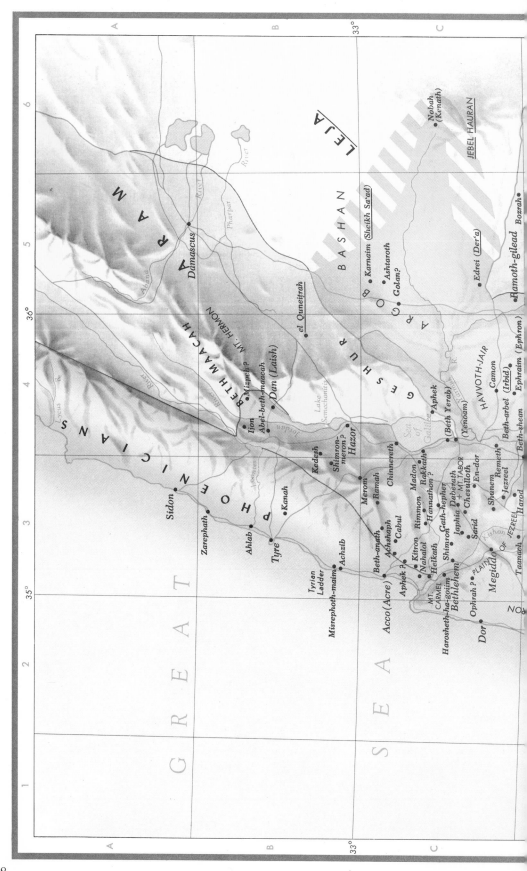

GREAT SEA

PHOENICIANS

Sidon
Zarephath
Ahlab
Tyre · Kanah
Tyrian Ladder
Achzib
Misrephoth-maim
Beth-anath
Achshaph
Acco (Acre)
Aphek?
Kitron
Nahalol
Helkath
Shimron
Bethlehem
Ophrah? · PLAIN
MT. CARMEL
Harosheth-ha-goiim
Dor
Megiddo
Taanach
NO

ARAM
Damascus
MT. HERMON
BETH-MAACAH
Ijon
Abel-beth-maacah
Mispeh?
Dan (Laish)
el Quneitrah
Kedesh
Shimron-meron?
Hazor
Merom
Ramah
Chinnereth
Madon
Rakkath
Hanathon?
Gath-hepher
Japhia
Dabareth
+ MT. TABOR
Chesulloth
Sarid
En-dor
Shunem
Kemeth
Jezreel
Harod
Kishon
PLAIN OF JEZREEL

LEJA
JEBEL HAURAN
Nobah (Kenath)
BASHAN
Karnaim (Sheikh Sa'ad)
Ashtaroth
Golan?
GESHUR
ARGOB
Aphek
(Beth Yerab)
(Yenoam)
Lake Semechonitis
Sea of Galilee
HAVVOTH-JAIR
Camon
Beth-arbel (Irbid)
Ephraim (Ephron)
Beth-shean
Edrei (Der'a)
Ramoth-gilead
Bozrah

Abana River
Pharpar River
Litani River
Leontes R.
Jordan
Yarmuk R.

238

MAP VIII

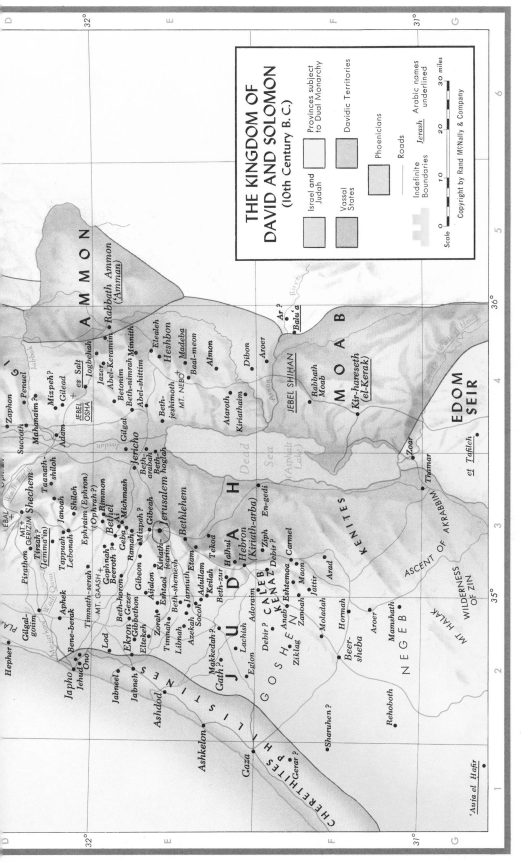

THE KINGDOM OF
DAVID AND SOLOMON
(10th Century B.C.)

Israel and Judah
Vassal States

Provinces subject to Dual Monarchy
Davidic Territories

Phoenicians

Roads

Indefinite Boundaries   Arabic names underlined

Jerash

Scale
0   10   20   30 miles

Copyright by Rand McNally & Company

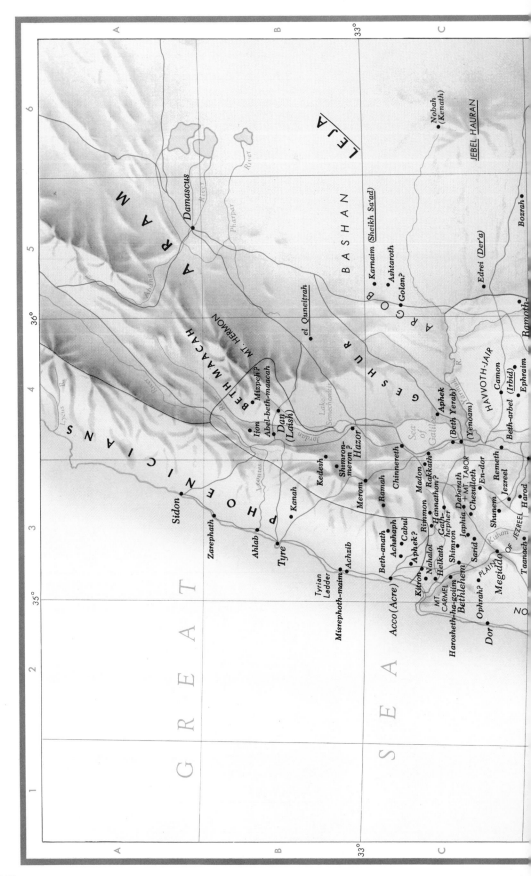

MAP IX

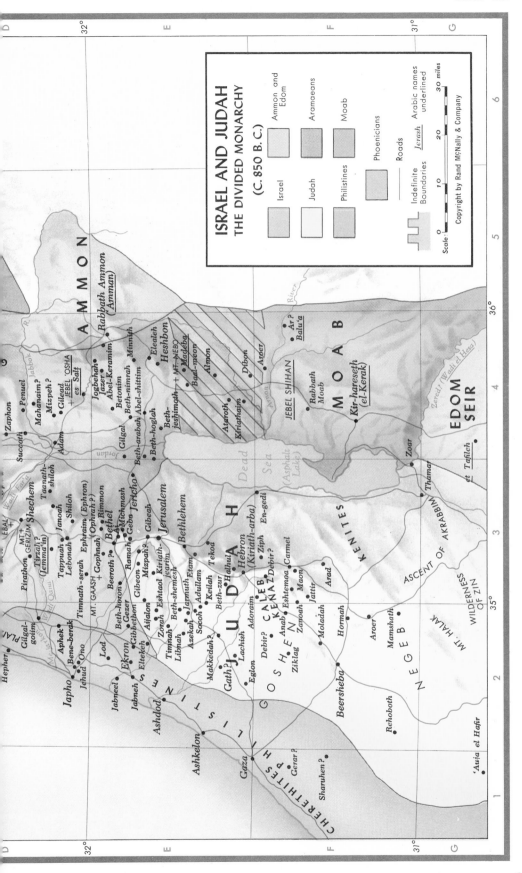

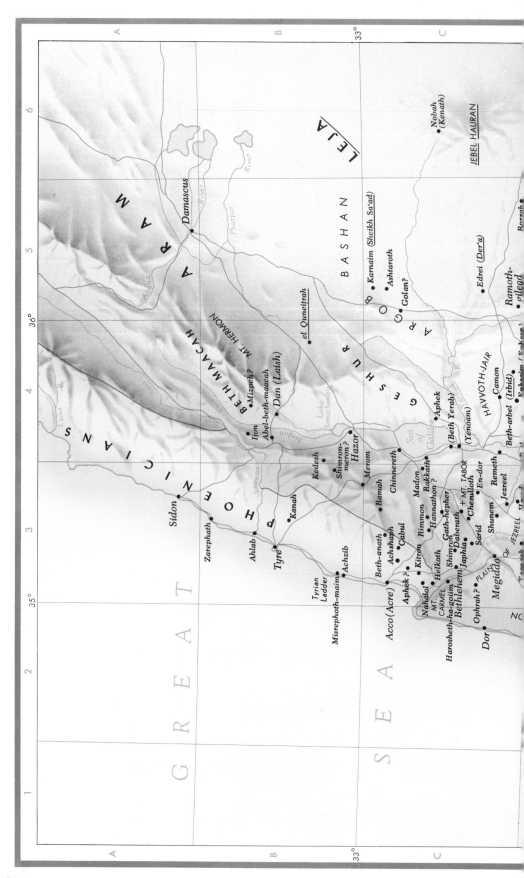

A
B
33°
C

6
5
36°
4
3
35°
2
1

33°

Damascus

ARAM

Pharpar River

River

MT. HERMON

BETH-MAACAH

LEJA

BASHAN

Nobah
(Kenath)

JEBEL HAURAN

Karnaim (Sheikh Sa'ad)
Ashtaroth
Golan?

ARGOB

GESHUR

Edrei (Der'a)

Ramoth-
gilead

Bozrah

el Quneitrah

Mizpeh?
Abel-beth-maacah
Dan (Laish)
Iion

Lake
Semechonitis

Jordan

Yarmuk R.

HAVVOTH-JAIR

Camon

Beth-arbel (Irbid)

Ephraim (Fahnac)?

Shimron-
meron?
Hazor
Merom

Kedesh

Aphek
(Beth Yerah)

Sea
of
Galilee

(Yenoam)

Ramah
Chinnereth
Madon
Rakkath
Hannathon?

+ MT. TABOR

En-dor
Remeth

Jezreel

Kanah

Jabneel

Beth-anath
Achshaph

Kitron
Helkath
Shimron
Japhia

Gath-hepher
Daberath
Chesulloth
Sarid

Shunem

Cabul

Rimmon

PHOENICIANS

Sidon

Zarephath

Ahlab

Tyre

Achzib

Misrephoth-maim

Tyrian
Ladder

Acco (Acre)

Aphek?

Nahalol
MT.
CARMEL
Harosheth-ha-goiim
Bethlehem

Ophrah?

Dor

Megiddo

PLAIN

OF JEZREEL

Kishon R.

NO

Taanach?

G R E A T

S E A

A
B
33°
C

242

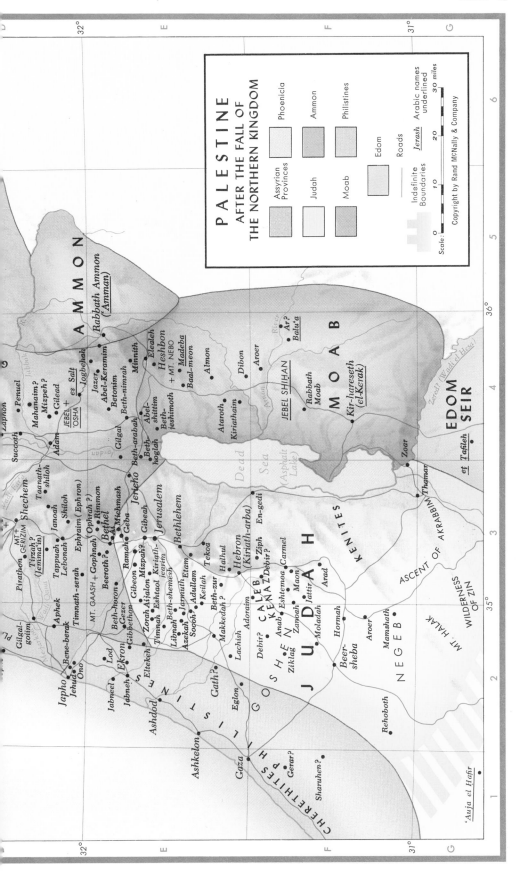

MAP X

PALESTINE
AFTER THE FALL OF
THE NORTHERN KINGDOM

Assyrian Provinces

Judah

Phoenicia

Ammon

Moab

Philistines

Edom

Roads

Indefinite Boundaries

Jerash Arabic names underlined

Copyright by Rand McNally & Company

Scale: 0   10   20   30 miles

AMMON

Rabbath Ammon ('Amman)

Penuel

Mahanaim?

Mizpeh?

Gilead

JEBEL 'OSHA

es Salt

Jogbehah

Jazer

Abel-Keramim?

Betonim

Beth-nimrah

Mimith

Elealeh

Heshbon

MT. NEBO

Madeba

Baal-meon

Almon

Dibon

Aroer

Ar? Balu'a

MOAB

JEBEL SHIHAN

Rabbath Moab

Kir-hareseth (el-Kerak)

Ataroth

Kiriathaim

Abel-shittim

Beth-jeshimoth

Succoth

Zaphon

Adam

Gilgal

Beth-arabah

Beth-hoglah

Jericho

Dead Sea (Asphalt Lake)

Zoar

et Tafileh

EDOM SEIR

Thamar

Shechem

MT. GERIZIM

Tirzah? (Jemma'in)

Pirathon

Taanath-shiloh

Janoah

Tappuah

Lebonah

Shiloh

Ephraim (Ephron?)

Ophrah?

Bethel

Rimmon

Michmash

Geba

Gibeah

Jerusalem

Bethlehem

Tekoa

Halhul

Hebron (Kiriath-arba)

En-gedi

KENITES

ASCENT OF AKRABBIM

WILDERNESS OF ZIN

MT. HALAK

Aphek

Timnath-serah

MT. GAASH

Gophnah?

Beeroth?

Ramah

Gibeon

Aijalon

Mizpah?

Kiriath-jearim

Ziklag

Timnah

Eshtaol

Beth-shemesh

Zorah

Libnah

Jarmuth

Etam

Azekah

Socoh

Adullam

Keilah

Makkedah?

Beth-zur

Adoraim

Lachish

Ziph

Debir?

Carmel

Maon

Ziph

Eshtemoa

Anab

Debir?

Jattir

Arad

Zanoah

Moladah

Hormah

Aroer

Mamshath

CALEB KENAZ

JUDAH

GOSHEN

NEGEB

Beer-sheba

Rehoboth

'Auja el Hafir

Gilgal-goiim

Bene-berak

Lod

Ono

Japho

Jehud

Jabneel

Jabneh

Ekron

Gibbethon

Eltekeh

Gath?

Eglon

Ashdod

Gaza

Ashkelon

Gerar?

Sharuhen?

PHILISTINES

CHERETHITES

PELISTIM

Jordan R.

Jabbok R.

Wadi Far

Wadi Qelt

Wadi el Hesa (Zered)

Arnon R.

243

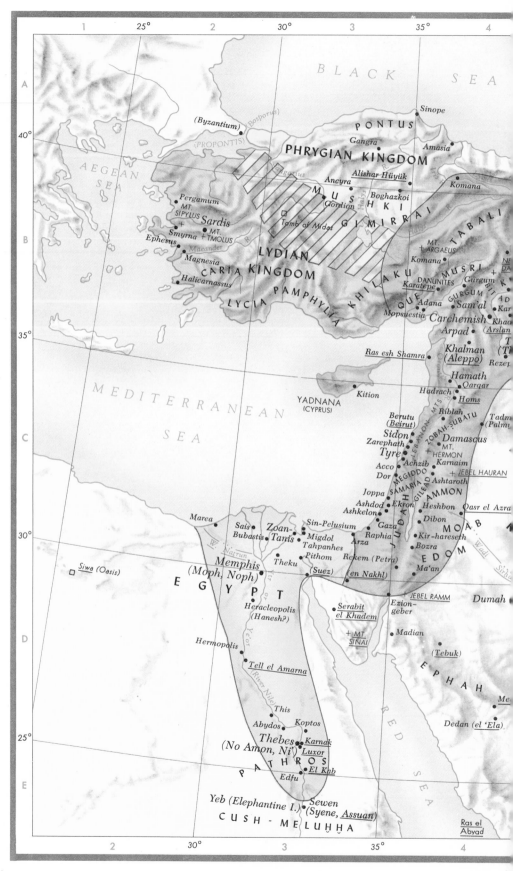

BLACK SEA

AEGEAN SEA

Sinope

PONTUS

(Byzantium) Bosporus

(PROPONTIS)

Gangra

Amasia

PHRYGIAN KINGDOM

Ancyra Alishar Hüyük

Komana

Sangarius M U S H K I

Pergamum
MT. SIPYLUS
Sardis
MT. + TMOLUS
Smyrna
Ephesus

Gordion Boghazkoi

Halys

Komana

G I M I R R A I

Tomb of Midas

MT. ARGAEUS

TABALI

Magnesia

LYDIAN KINGDOM

CARIA

MUSRI NE
DA

K H I L A K U

Karatepe DANUNITES Gurgum GURGUM

Halicarnassus

LYCIA PAMPHYLIA

QUE Adana Sam'al

AD
Kar

Mopsuestia Carchemish Khaa

Arpad (Arslan

T
(T

MEDITERRANEAN

Ras esh Shamra

Khalman
(Aleppo)

Rezef

Hamath Qarqar

Tadm
(Palm

SEA

Kition

YADNANA
(CYPRUS)

Hadrach Homs

Riblah

Berutu
(Beirut)
Sidon
Zarephath
Tyre
Acco
Dor

Damascus
MT. + HERMON
Karnaim

ZOBAH-ṢUBATU

LEBANON MTS.

Achzib
MEGIDDO
SAMARIA GILEAD Ashtaroth

Karaim
+ JEBEL HAURAN

Marea

Sais
Bubastis
Zoan-
Tanis

Sin-Pelusium

Joppa
Ashdod Ekron
Ashkelon

Heshbon Qasr el Azra
AMMON

Gaza
Raphia
Arza

JUDAH

Dibon
MOAB
Kir-hareseth

Migdol
Tahpanhes
Pithom

Memphis
(Moph, Noph)

Theku

(Suez)

Rekem (Petra)
(en Nakhl)

Bozra
Ma'an

EDOM

Wadi
Sirha

E G Y P T

W. Natrun

Heracleopolis
(Hanesh?)

Serabit
el Khadem

Ezion-
geber

+ JEBEL RAMM

Dumah

Hermopolis

Yeor (River Nile)

+ MT.
SINAI

Madian

RED

(Tebuk)

E P H A H

Tell el Amarna

This

Koptos

Abydos

Dedan (el 'Ela)

Me

Thebes
(No Amon, Ni')

Karnak
Luxor

PATHROS

El Kab

SEA

Edfu

Yeb (Elephantine I.) Sewen
(Syene, Assuan)

C U S H - M E L U Ḥ Ḥ A

Ras el
Abyad

Siwa (Oasis)

MAP XI

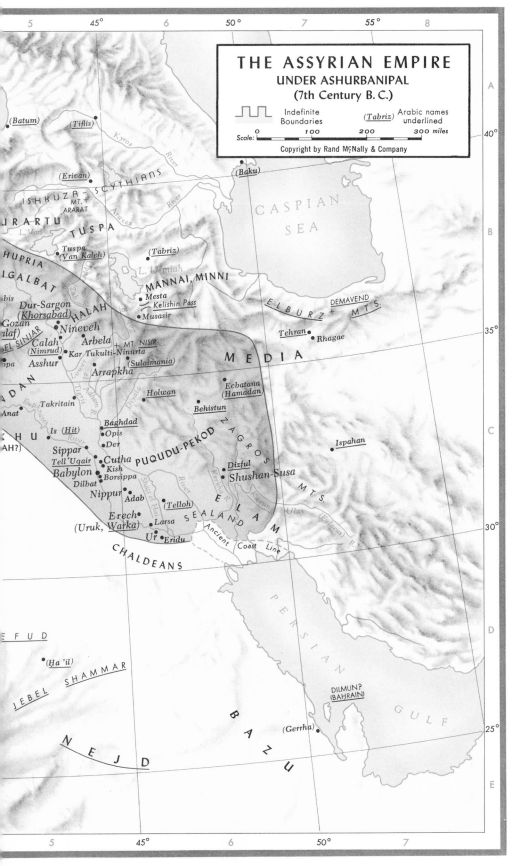

THE ASSYRIAN EMPIRE
UNDER ASHURBANIPAL
(7th Century B.C.)

Indefinite
Boundaries

(Tabriz) Arabic names
underlined

Scale: 0   100   200   300 miles

Copyright by Rand McNally & Company

(Batum)

(Tiflis)

Kyros

River

SCYTHIANS

(Erivan)

ISHKUZA
MT. + ARARAT

CASPIAN
SEA

(Baku)

River

Araxes

URARTU
L. Van

TUSPA

HUPRIA

Tuspa
(Van Kaleh)

(Tabriz)

DEMAVEND

ELBURZ + MTS.

IGALBAT
Zab

L. Urmiah

MANNAI, MINNI

Mesta
Kelishin Pass
Musair

bis

Dur-Sargon
(Khorsabad)

Gozan
alaf)

EL SINJAR

Nineveh

Arbela

HALAH

Tehran

Rhagae

Gozan

Kar Tukulti-Ninurta

Calah
(Nimrud)

MT. NISIR

MEDIA

pa

Asshur

Arrapkha

(Sulaimania)

Ecbatana
(Hamadan)

Holwan

Behistun

35°

40°

A

B

C

D

E

Takritain

Anat

Diyala

Is (Hit)

River

Baghdad
Opis

ZAGROS

Ispahan

SIppar
Tell 'Uqair

Cutha
Der

PUQUDU-PEKOD

Babylon
Dilbat

Kish
Borsippa

Shatt el Hai

Nippur

Adab

(Telloh)

Erech
(Uruk, Warka)

Larsa

Ur Eridu

CHALDEANS

EFUD

(Ha'il)

SHAMMAR

JEBEL

NEJD

Adhem R.

Lower Zab

Euphrates

AH?)

ADAN

KHU

Dizful

Shushan-Susa

Kerkha R.

Karun R.

Ulai

(Eulaeus) R.

ELAM

SEALAND

Ancient Coast Line

PERSIAN

BAZU

GULF

DILMUN?
(BAHRAIN)

(Gerrha)

30°

25°

MTS.

245

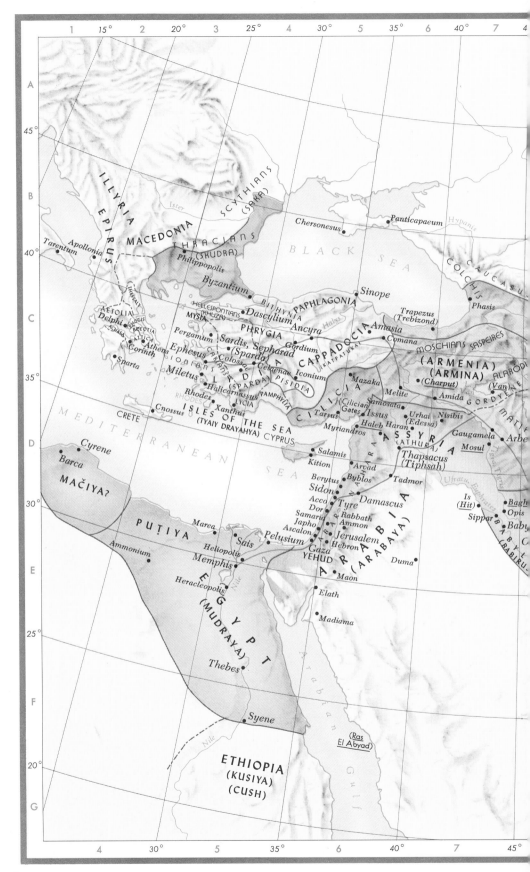

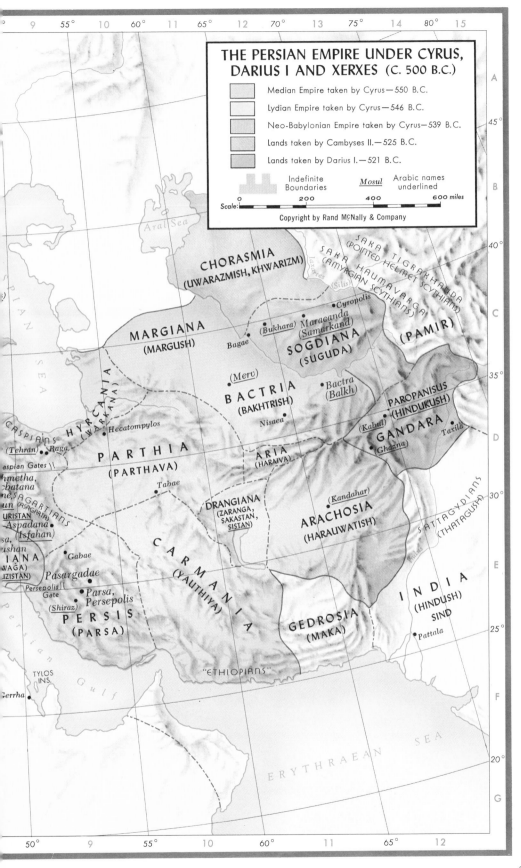

MAP XII

THE PERSIAN EMPIRE UNDER CYRUS, DARIUS I AND XERXES (C. 500 B.C.)

Median Empire taken by Cyrus—550 B.C.

Lydian Empire taken by Cyrus—546 B.C.

Neo-Babylonian Empire taken by Cyrus—539 B.C.

Lands taken by Cambyses II.—525 B.C.

Lands taken by Darius I.—521 B.C.

Indefinite Boundaries

Mosul Arabic names underlined

Scale: 0   200   400   600 miles

Copyright by Rand McNally & Company

Aral Sea

CHORASMIA
(UWARAZMISH, KHWARIZM)

SAKA TIGRAKHAUDA
(POINTED HELMET SCYTHIANS)

SAKA HAUMAVARGA
(AMYRGIAN SCYTHIANS)

(Silis)

Cyropolis

MARGIANA
(MARGUSH)

Bagae

(Bukhara) *Maracanda*
(Samarkand)

SOGDIANA
(SUGUDA)

(PAMIR)

(Merv)

BACTRIA
(BAKHTRISH)

Bactra
(Balkh)

PAROPANISUS
(HINDUKUSH)

Nisaea

GANDARA

(Kabul)

Taxila

HYRCANIA
(WARKANA)

Hecatompylos

ARIA
(HARAIVA)

(Ghazna)

CASPIANS

(Tehran) *Raga*

PARTHIA
(PARTHAVA)

Tabae

hmetha,
cbatana
ne,SAGARTIANS
un (ASAGARTA)
URISTAN
Aspadana
(Isfahan)

DRANGIANA
(ZARANGA,
SAKASTAN,
SISTAN)

(Kandahar)

ARACHOSIA
(HARAUWATISH)

SATTAGYDIANS
(THATAGUSH)

IANA
WAGA)
IZISTAN)

Gabae

Pasargadae

CARMANIA
(YAUTHIYA)

INDIA
(HINDUSH)
SIND

Persepolis
Gate

*Parsa,
Persepolis*

(Shiraz)

PERSIS
(PARSA)

GEDROSIA
(MAKA)

Pattala

TYLOS
INS.

"ETHIOPIANS"

Gerrha

Persian Gulf

ERYTHRAEAN SEA

247

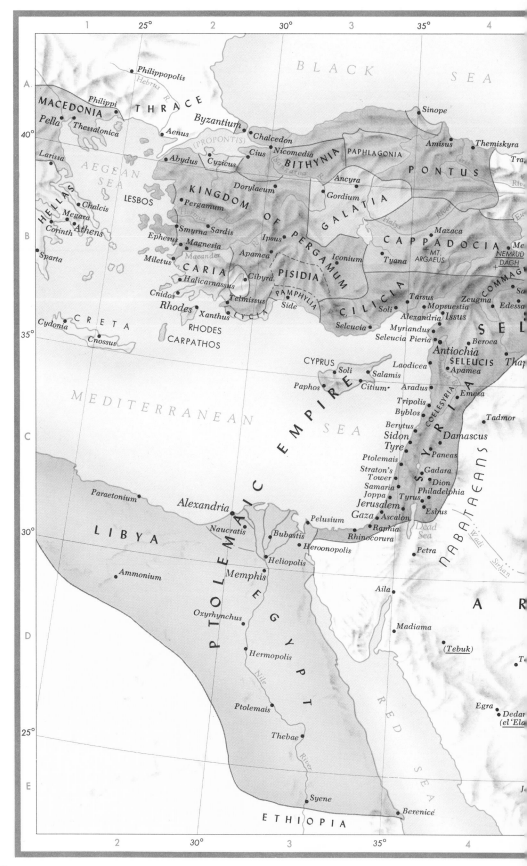

BLACK SEA

Philippopolis

MACEDONIA
Philippi
Pella
Thessalonica

THRACE
Hebrus R.

Aenus

Byzantium
Chalcedon

(PROPONTIS)

Cius
Nicomedia

BITHYNIA

PAPHLAGONIA

Sinope

Amisus
Themiskyra
Tra

PONTUS
River

LARISSA
Larissa

AEGEAN
SEA

LESBOS

Abydus
Cyzicus

Dorylaeum

Ancyra
Gordium

GALATIA

Mazaca

CAPPADOCIA

Me

HELLAS
Chalcis
Megara
Athens
Corinth

KINGDOM
Pergamum
Smyrna
Sardis
Ephesus
Magnesia

OF

Ipsus

PERGAMUM

Iconium

Tyana

MT.
ARGAEUS

NEMRUD
DAGH

COMMAG

Sparta

Miletus

CARIA
Maeander

Apamea

PISIDIA

CILICIA

Tarsus
Mopsuestia
Soli
Alexandria Issus

Zeugma
Edessa

Sa

Halicarnassus
Cnidos
Rhodes
Xanthus
Telmissus

Cibyra

PAMPHYLIA
Side

LYCIA

Seleucia

Myriandus
Seleucia Pieria

Beroea

SEL

Cydonia

CRETA

Cnossus

RHODES

CARPATHOS

CYPRUS

Soli
Paphos
Salamis
Citium

Laodicea

Aradus

Antiochia
SELEUCIS
Apamea

Tha

SEA

MEDITERRANEAN

EMPIRE

Tripolis
Byblos
Berytus
Sidon
Tyre

SYRIA

Emesa

Tadmor

Damascus

COELESYRIA

Paneas

Paraetonium

Alexandria

Naucratis

PTOLEMAIC

Pelusium

Bubastis
Heroonopolis

*Straton's
Tower*
Samaria
Joppa
Jerusalem
Gaza
Ascalon
Raphia
Rhinocorura

Ptolemais

Tyrus

Gadara
Dion
Philadelphia
Esbus

NABATAEANS

A

LIBYA

Ammonium

Memphis
Heliopolis

EGYPT

Oxyrhynchus

Hermopolis

Dead
Sea

Petra

Aila

Madiama

(Tebuk)

Wadi
Sirhan

R

T

RED

Ptolemais

Nile

Thebae

River

Egra
*Dedar
(el 'Ela*

SEA

Syene

Berenice

Je

ETHIOPIA

248

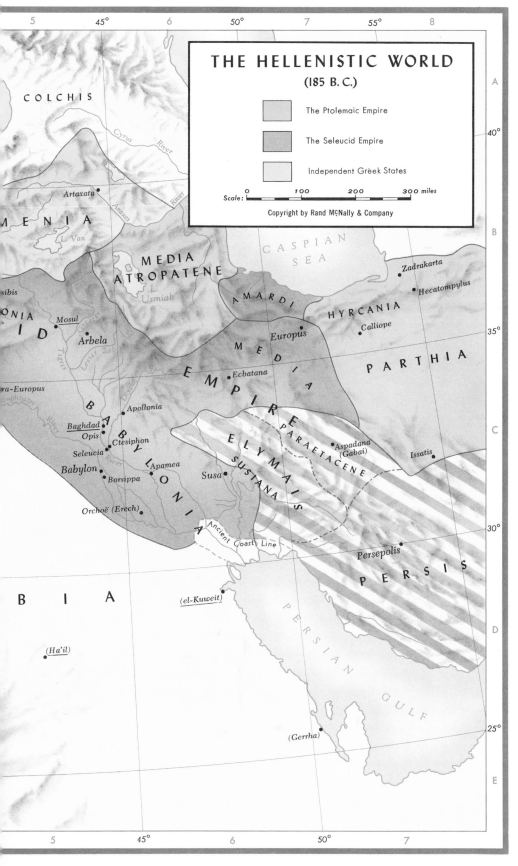

MAP XIII

THE HELLENISTIC WORLD
(185 B.C.)

The Ptolemaic Empire

The Seleucid Empire

Independent Grèek States

Scale: 0   100   200   300 miles

Copyright by Rand McNally & Company

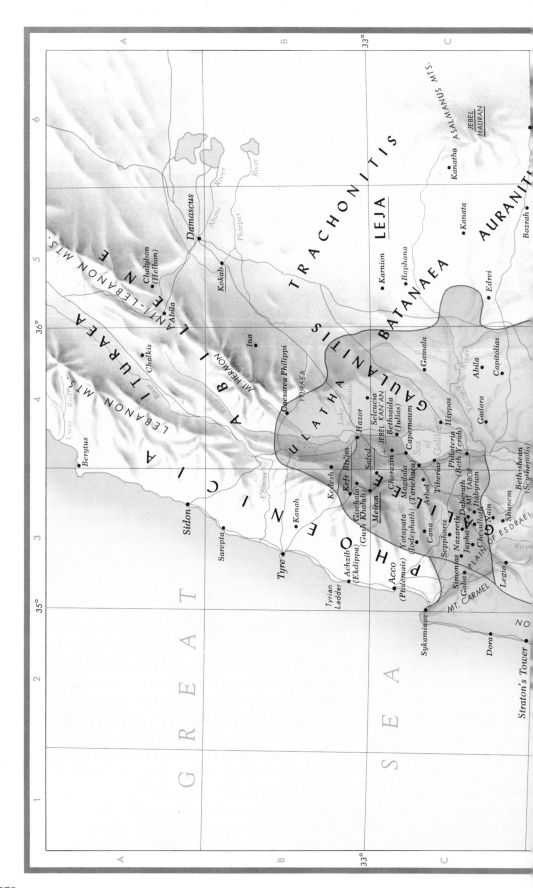

MAP XIV

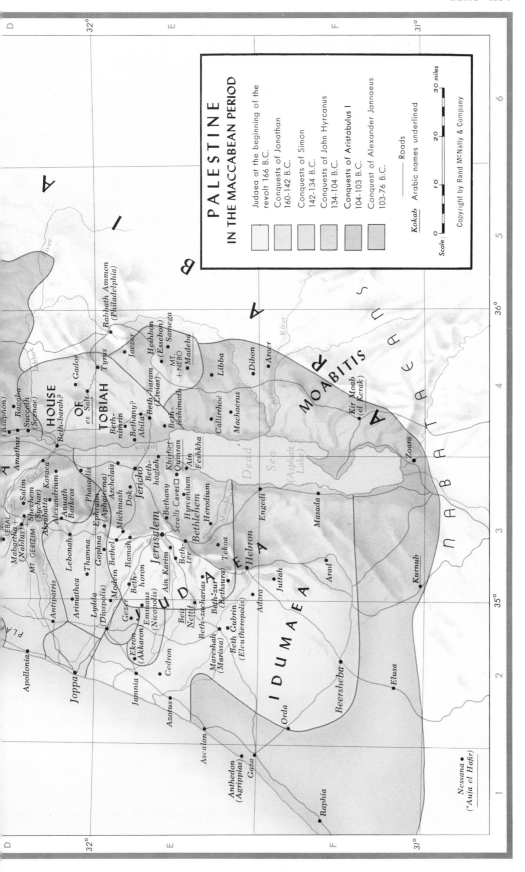

PALESTINE
IN THE MACCABEAN PERIOD

Judaea at the beginning of the
revolt 166 B.C.

Conquests of Jonathan
160-142 B.C.

Conquests of Simon
142-134 B.C.

Conquests of John Hyrcanus
134-104 B.C.

Conquests of Aristobulus I
104-103 B.C.

Conquest of Alexander Jannaeus
103-76 B.C.

——— Roads

Kokab Arabic names underlined

Scale: 0   10   20   30 miles

Copyright by Rand McNally & Company

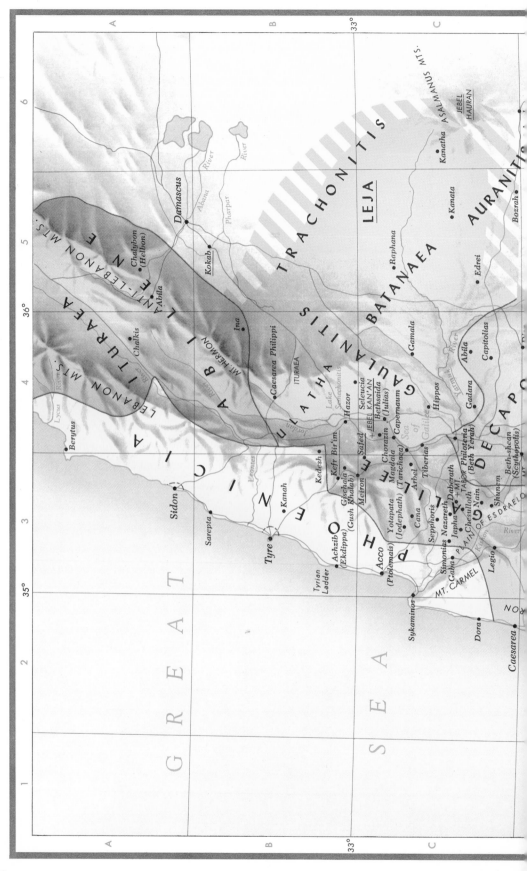

MAP XV

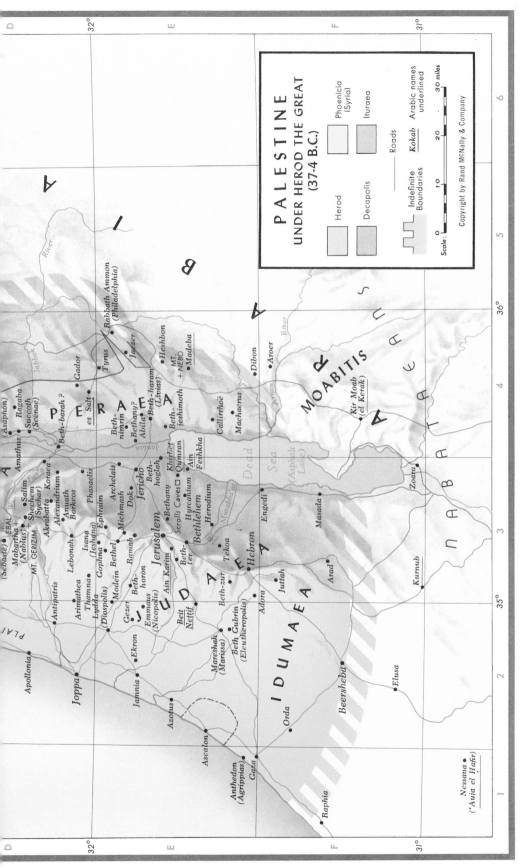

PALESTINE
UNDER HEROD THE GREAT
(37-4 B.C.)

Herod

Decapolis

Phoenicia
(Syria)

Ituraea

Roads

Kokab   Arabic names
underlined

Indefinite
Boundaries

Scale: 0   10   20   30 miles

Copyright by Rand McNally & Company

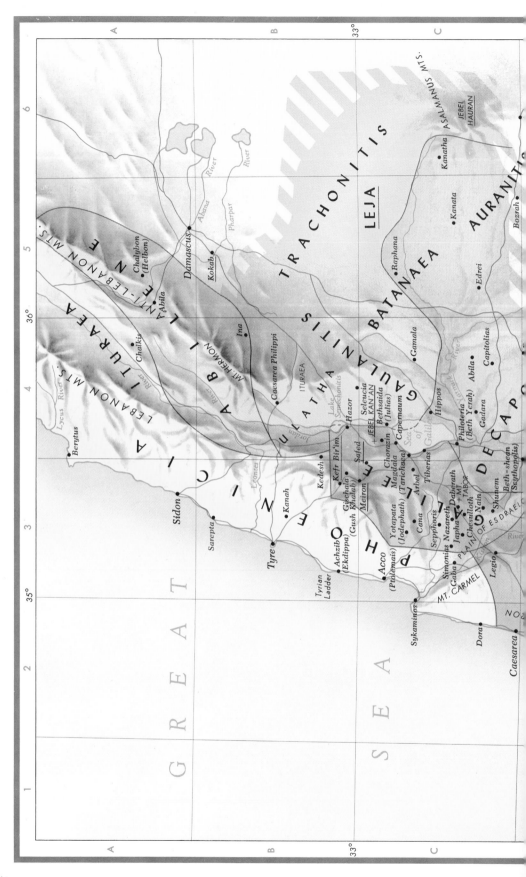

A

6

B

33°

C

ASALMANUS MTS.

JEBEL HAURAN

Kamatha

T R A C H O N I T I S

LEJA

AURANITIS

Kanata

Bozrah

Edrei

Chalybon
(Helbon)

Damascus

Kokab

Azana River

Pharpar River

BATANAEA

Abila

36°

ANTI-LEBANON MTS.

Raphana

ITURAEA

Chalkis

Ina

MT. HERMON

Caesarea Philippi

ITURAEA

S I L I N A I T I S

G A U L A N I T I S

Gamala

Capitolius

Abila

River

LEBANON MTS.

Lycus River

River

Berytus

Leontes

Lake
Semechonitis

Hazor

Seleucia

JEBEL KAN'AN

Bethsaida
(Julius)

KAN'AN

Capernaum

Sea of
Galilee

Hippos

Philoteria
(Beth Yerah)

Gadara

D E C A P O

Sidon

Sarepta

Kanah

Kedesh

Kefr Bir'im

Safed

Chorazin
Magdala

(Taricheae)

Arbel

Tiberias

Jordan

U L A T H A

Tyre

Achzib
(Ekdippa)

Gischala
(Gush Khalab)

Metron

Yotapata
(Iodephath)

Cana

Seppphoris

Simonias

Daberath

+ MT.
TABOR

Chesulloth

Nain

Shunem

Beth-shean
(Scythopolis)

G A L I L E E

Tyrian
Ladder

Acco
(Ptolemais)

Nazareth

Iapha

Gaba

PLAIN OF ES DRAELO

35°

MT. CARMEL

Legio

River

Sykaminos

Dora

Caesarea

G R E A T

S E A

RON

254

MAP XVI

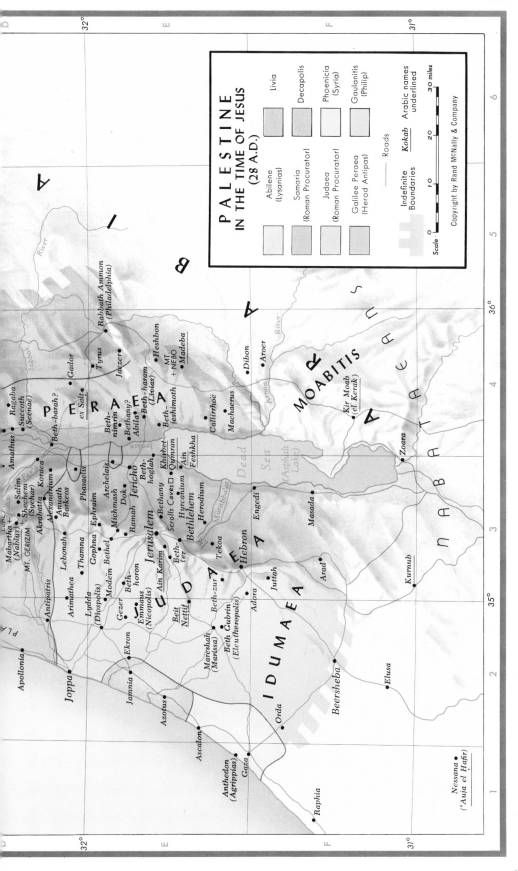

PALESTINE
IN THE TIME OF JESUS
(28 A.D.)

Abilene (Lysanias)	Livia
Samaria (Roman Procurator)	Decapolis
Judaea (Roman Procurator)	Phoenicia (Syria)
Galilee Peraea (Herod Antipas)	Gaulanitis (Philip)

Roads

Indefinite Boundaries

Kokab Arabic names underlined

Scale 0   10   20   30 miles

Copyright by Rand McNally & Company

MAP XVII

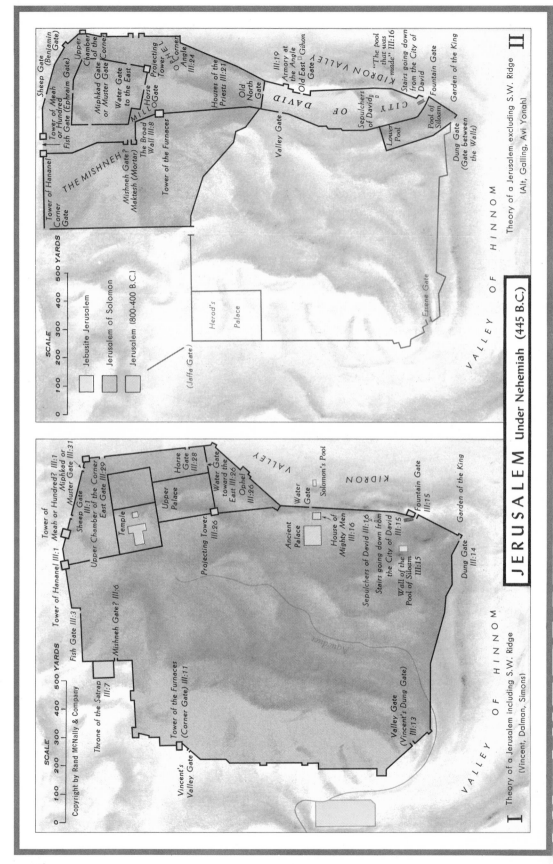

JERUSALEM Under Nehemiah (445 B.C.)

II Theory of a Jerusalem excluding S.W. Ridge (Alt, Galling, Avi Yonah)

I Theory of a Jerusalem including S.W. Ridge (Vincent, Dalman, Simons)

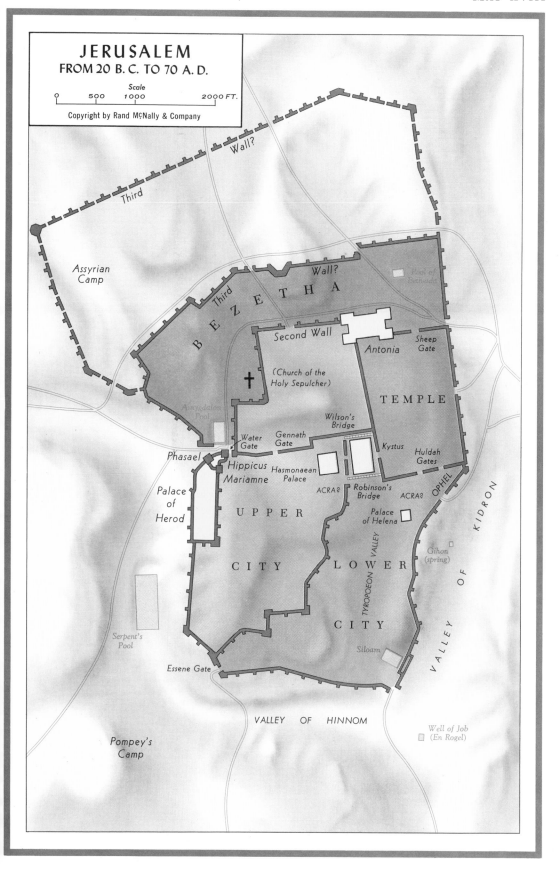

MAP XVIII

JERUSALEM
FROM 20 B.C. TO 70 A.D.

Scale

0   500   1000   2000 FT.

Copyright by Rand McNally & Company

Wall?

Third

Assyrian Camp

Third

B E Z E T H A

Wall?

Pool of Bethesda

Second Wall

Antonia

Sheep Gate

(Church of the Holy Sepulcher)

T E M P L E

Amygdalon Pool

Wilson's Bridge

Water Gate

Gennath Gate

Kystus

Huldah Gates

Phasael

Hippicus
Mariamne

Hasmonaean Palace

ACRA?

Robinson's Bridge

ACRA?

OPHEL

Palace of Herod

U P P E R

Palace of Helena

Gihon (spring)

C I T Y

L O W E R

VALLEY OF KIDRON

TYROPOEON VALLEY

C I T Y

Serpent's Pool

Siloam

Essene Gate

VALLEY OF HINNOM

Well of Job (En Rogel)

Pompey's Camp

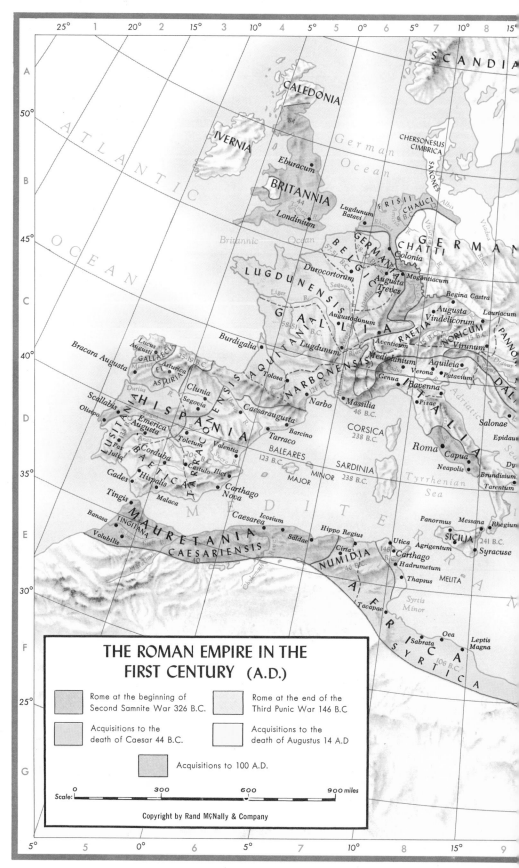

THE ROMAN EMPIRE IN THE FIRST CENTURY (A.D.)

MAP XIX

25° 11 30° 12 35° 13 40° 14 45° 15 50° 16 55° 17 60° 18 65°

A

50°

B

45°

C

40°

D

35°

E

30°

F

25°

G

10   25°   11   30°   12   35°   13   40°   14

R
M
A
T
I
A

ACIA

OESIA

DONIA

Niconolis

THRACIA

Danapris River

Hypanis River

Pyretus River

Tyras River

Ister River

ippopolis

Olbia

CHERSONESUS
TAURICA

Chersonesus

BOSPORAN
KINGDOM

Black   Sea

Byzantium

Nicomedia

BITHYNIA

Amastris

PAPHLA-
GONIA

Sinope

Amisus

PONTUS

CAUCASUS

COLCHIS

Trapezus

Caspian

Sea

Artaxata

ARMENIA

GORDYENE

ATROPATENE

Amida

ASSYRIA

Arbela

Opis

Artemita

Ctesiphon

Seleucia

Babylon

River

MESOPOTAMIA

Hatra

Carrhae Nisibis

Edessa

Circesium

Euphrates

Comana 64

Amasia

ARMENIA
MINOR

Ancyra

GALATIA

Melitene

CAPPADOCIA

Mazaca

Tyana

COMMAGENE

PHRYGIA

LYCAONIA

Dorylaeum

Sangarius

Pergamum

Sardis

Smyrna

Antiochia

Iconium

PISIDIA

PAMPHYLIA

Miletus

LYCIA

Selinus

CILICIA

Tarsus

64 B.C.

Antiochia

64 B.C.

Apamea

Laodicea

SYRIA

Palmyra

Aradus

Sidon

Tyrus

Damascus

Bostra

NABATAEANS

ASIA

Athenae

Ephesus

Corinthus

Sparta

Halicarnassus

Aegean

Sea

RHODUS
44

Cnossus

CRETA 67 B.C.

N   S   E   A

CYPRUS

Salamis

58 B.C.

PHOENICE

Caesarea

Joppe

Jerusalem

Gaza

Aelana

Madiama

Petra

ARABIA

Appollonia

rene

ICA

MARMARICA

Alexandria

Naucratis

Heliopolis

Memphis

Pelusium

Arsinoë

LIBYA

Ammonium

Heracleopolis

Hermopolis

Nile River

AEGYPTUS

30 B.C.

Coptos

Thebae

Arabian Gulf

Syene

Berenice

Nicopolis

Philippi

onice

ssa

Sparta

259

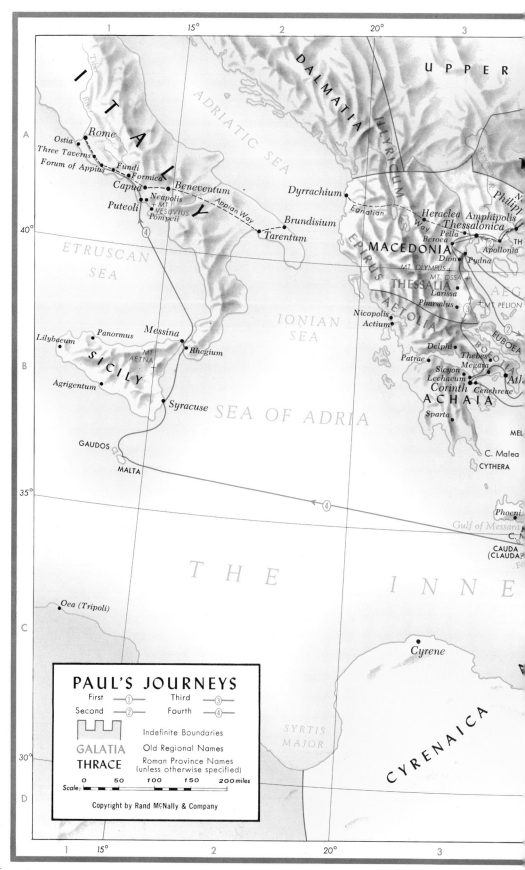

PAUL'S JOURNEYS

First ①   Third ③
Second ②   Fourth ④

⊔⊔⊔   Indefinite Boundaries

GALATIA   Old Regional Names

THRACE   Roman Province Names
(unless otherwise specified)

Scale: 0   50   100   150   200 miles

Copyright by Rand McNally & Company

MAP XX

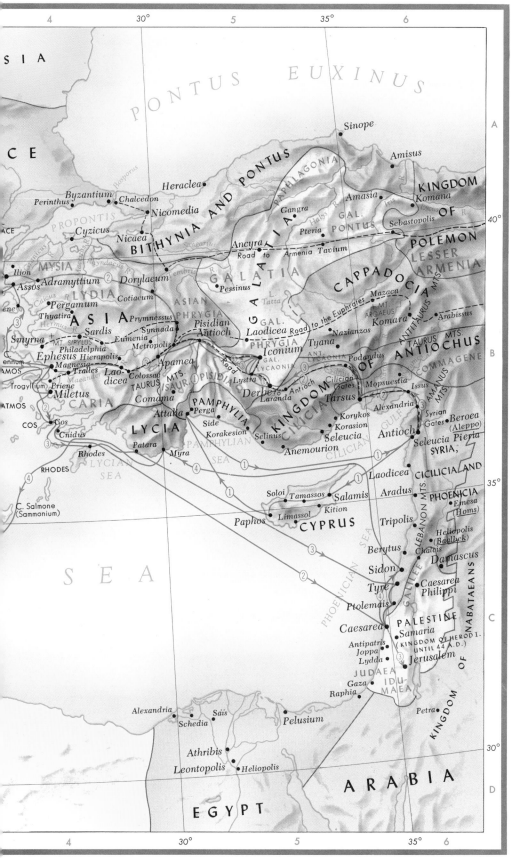

PONTUS EUXINUS

Sinope

Amisus

KINGDOM

Heraclea

Byzantium
Perinthus   Chalcedon
Nicomedia

PAPHLAGONIA

Amasia   Komana

OF

Gangra

BITHYNIA AND PONTUS

Cyzicus

Nicaea

PROPONTIS

Pteria   PONTUS

Sebastopolis

POLEMON

Ancyra
Road to Armenia   Tavium

LESSER

Ilion
Assos   Adramyttium   Dorylaeum

MYSIA

GALATIA

ARMENIA

Pessinus

CAPPADOCIA

Pergamum

LYDIA

ASIAN
PHRYGIA

Mazaca

Thyatira

ASIA   Prymnessus

Pisidian
Antioch

to the Euphrates
Komara   MT.
ARGAEUS   Arabissus

Smyrna
MT. SIPYLUS   Sardis   Synnada
Philadelphia   Eumenia

Laodicea Road   Nazianzos

Metropolis

PHRYGIA   Tyana

TAURUS MTS.

Ephesus Hierapolis
Magnesia

Iconium

ANTITAURUS MTS.

Tralles   Apamea
Laodicea
Colossae

GAL.
LYCAONIA

KINGDOM   OF   ANTIOCHUS

COMMAGENE

TAURUS MTS.
Priene   ISAURIA   PISIDIA

Comana

Lystra

Derbe   Antioch   Cilician
Gates   Mopsuestia   Issus

Miletus

CARIA

Attalia   Perga
Side

PAMPHYLIA

Laranda   Tarsus

AMANUS
MTS.

Cos

Cnidus

Korakesion
Selinus

Korykos
Korasion   Syrian
Gates   Beroea
(Aleppo)

Rhodes

Myra

PAMPHYLIAN
SEA

Seleucia
Anemourion

Antioch

RHODES

LYCIA

CILICIAN   Laodicea   Seleucia Pieria
SYRIA,

C. Salmone
(Sammonium)

Soloi   Tamassos   Salamis   Aradus

CICILICIA AND

Paphlos   Limassol   Kition

CYPRUS   Tripolis

PHOENICIA

Emesa
(Homs)

Heliopolis
(Baalbek)

Berytus   Chalcis

Sidon   Damascus

SEA

Tyre   Caesarea
Philippi

Ptolemais

Caesarea   PALESTINE

Antipatris   Samaria   (KINGDOM OF HEROD I.
UNTIL 44 A.D.)

Joppa
Lydda   Jerusalem

JUDAEA   IDU-
Gaza   MAEA

Raphia

KINGDOM OF NABATAEANS

Alexandria   Sais   Petra

Schedia   Pelusium

Athribis

Leontopolis   Heliopolis

ARABIA

EGYPT

261

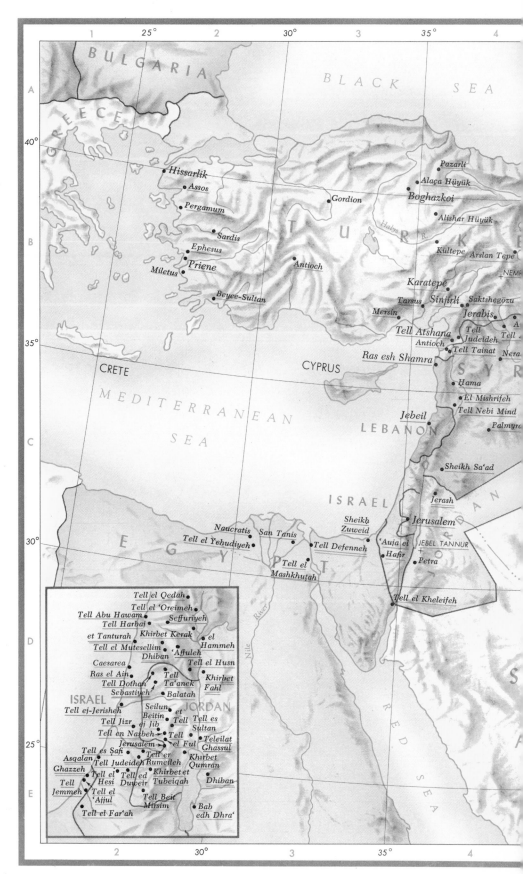

BULGARIA

GREECE

BLACK SEA

A

40°

Hissarlik
Assos
Pergamum
Sardis
Ephesus
Priene
Miletus
Beyce-Sultan

Gordion

Boghazkoi

TURKEY

Antioch

Pazarli
Alaça Hüyük

Alishar Hüyük

Halys

Kültepe
Arslan Tepe

NEMR

35°

CRETE

MEDITERRANEAN

SEA

Mersin
Tarsus

Karatepe
Sinjirli
Saktshegözu

Jerabis
Tell
Judeideh
Tell
Antioch
Tell Tainat
Nera

Tell Atshana

Ras esh Shamra

CYPRUS

SYR

Ḥama
El Mishrifeh
Tell Nebi Mind

Jebeil

LEBANON

Palmyra

C

Sheikh Sa'ad

Jerash

ISRAEL

Jerusalem

AN

30°

EGYPT

Naucratis
San Tanis
Tell el Yehudiyeh

Sheikh
Zuweid
Tell Defenneh

'Auja el
Hafir

JEBEL TANNUR

Petra

O

Tell el
Mashkhuṭah

Tell el Kheleifeh

Nile River

RED SEA

SA

D

Tell el Qedah
Tell el 'Oreimeh
Tell Abu Hawam
Seffuriyeh
Tell Harbaj
et Tanturah
Khirbet Kerak
el Hammeh
Tell el Mutesellim
Affuleh
Dhiban
Caesarea
Tell el Husn
Ras el Ain
Tell
Ta'anek
Khirbet Fahl
Tell Dothan
Sebastiyeh
Balatah
ISRAEL
Seilun
et
JORDAN
Tell ej-Jerisheh
Beitin
ej Jib
Tell es
Sultan
Tell Jizr
Tell en Nasbeh
Tell
el Ful
Teleilat
Ghassul
Tell es Safi
Jerusalem
Asqalan
Tell Judeideh
Tell er
Rumeileh
Khirbet
Qumran
Ghazzeh
Tell el
Hesi
Tell ed
Duweir
Khirbet et
Tubeiqah
Dhiban
Tell
Jemmeh
Tell el
'Ajjul
Tell Beit
Mirsim
Bab
edh Dhra'
Tell el Far'ah

E

25°

MAP XXI

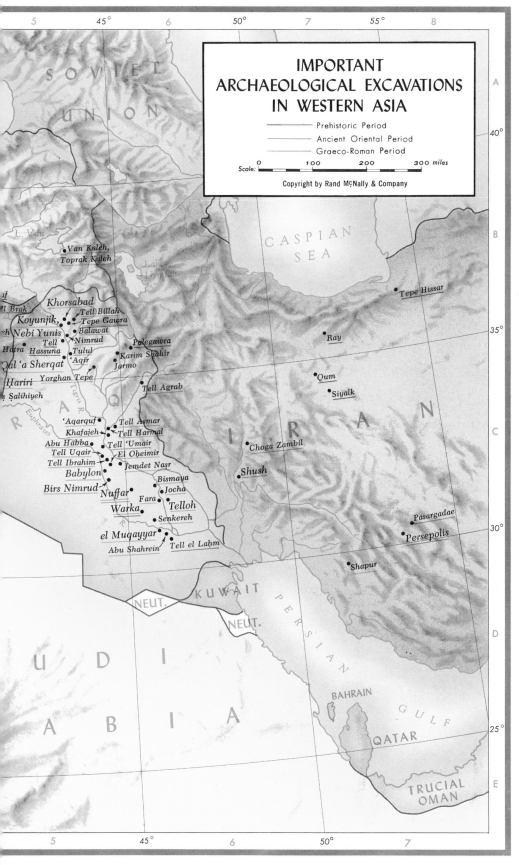

IMPORTANT ARCHAEOLOGICAL EXCAVATIONS IN WESTERN ASIA

——————— Prehistoric Period
——————— Ancient Oriental Period
——————— Graeco-Roman Period

Scale: 0   100   200   300 miles

Copyright by Rand McNally & Company

SOVIET UNION

L. Van

CASPIAN SEA

Van Kaleh,
Toprak Kaleh

Tepe Hissar

if
l Brak   Khorsabad
                     Tell Billah
Koyunjik,   Tepe Gawra
h Nebi Yunis   Balawat
Hatra Hassuna Nimrud Polegawra   Ray
Qal 'a Sherqat Tulul Karim Shahir
                'Aqir Jarmo
Hariri Yorghan Tepe   Qum
s Salihiyeh   Siyalk
                     Tell Agrab

R   I   R.
A   Q
                'Aqarquf   Tell Asmar   IRAN
                Khafajeh   Tell Harmal
           Abu Habba   Tell 'Umair   Choga Zambil
           Tell Uqair   El Oheimir
           Tell Ibrahim   Jemdet Nasr   Shush
                Babylon
                     Bismaya
Birs Nimrud   Jocha
        Nuffar   Fara
        Warka   Telloh   Pasargadae
                 Senkereh   Persepolis

        el Muqayyar
        Abu Shahrein   Tell el Lahm   Shapur

U   D   I
                         KUWAIT
                NEUT.
                     NEUT.   PERSIAN
A   GULF
B   I   A   BAHRAIN

                                 QATAR
                                 TRUCIAL
                                 OMAN

Euphrates

Tigris R.

MAP XXII

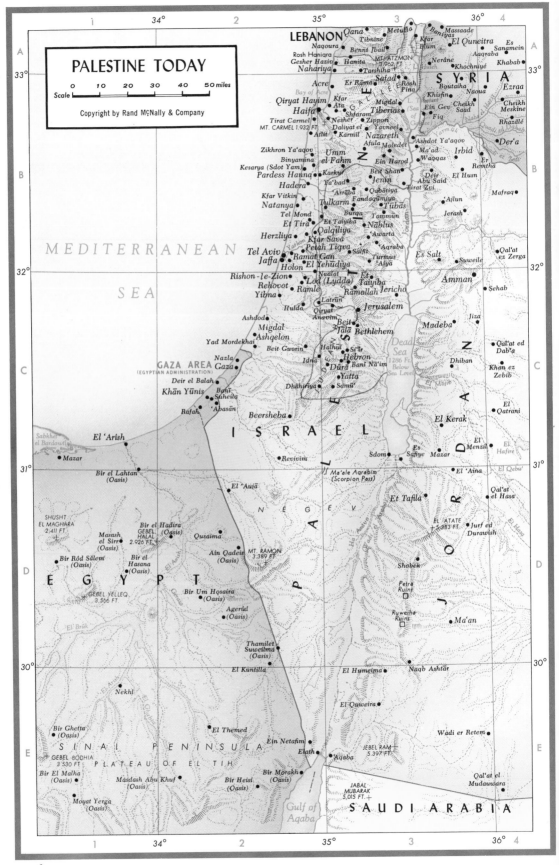

PALESTINE TODAY

Scale

0   10   20   30   40   50 miles

Copyright by Rand McNally & Company

THE DIVIDED KINGDOM

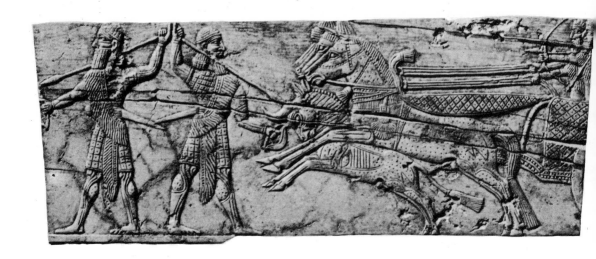

Top, *from Luristan north of Elam
came numerous objects with art of
this nature. They belong to a nomad
aristocracy—perhaps the "Scythians"
of Jeremiah's time* (c. 600 b.c.).
(*The Metropolitan Museum of Art*)
right, *engraved bronze bowl,* c.
700 b.c. (*Oriental Institute, The
University of Chicago*)

The DESIGN on the preceding page shows a winged figure and zodiacal signs from Assyrian reliefs, and a Hittite lion from Tell Halaf.

CHAPTER XIII

THE SECESSION AND
SUPREMACY OF ISRAEL

THE FLOWERING OF ISRAEL and Judah took place in the tenth century and was paralleled by a similar great development in Syria and in Phoenicia. The fact that the great powers on the Nile and Euphrates were unable at this time to wield any influence in these quarters created a favorable situation. The Aramaeans who had permeated Syria became so strong that they were able to throw off the Israelite yoke.

But the old city of Asshur on the Tigris, where Assyrian kings had reigned for over a thousand years, began to produce rulers who were able to master the Aramaean menace in Mesopotamia. With Tukulti-Ninurta II (*c.* 888 B.C.) we get more detailed information of events. Under Ashur-naṣir-pal II (*c.* 883–859 B.C.) the path of imperialism was again taken. This ruler warred with what has been called "calculated frightfulness." His armies went far into Syria, as well as into the northern regions, and therewith the problem of existence was posed for all the lesser states that co-existed in the Syro-Palestinian scene. Ashur-naṣir-pal moved the capital of his kingdom away from the historic Asshur and farther north to Calah. This city, then situated on the shore of the Tigris, was rediscovered by Sir Austen Henry Layard in 1845 at a place called *Nimrūd,* and here he procured reliefs from the king's palace portraying his campaigns. In recent years the excavations at *Nimrūd* have been resumed by the British School of ·Archaeology in Iraq under M. E. L. Mallowan.

The first contact of Israel with the power that was to be its undoing occurred under Shalmaneser III (858–824 B.C.).

As we have previously seen, Judah and Israel were a dual monarchy. It is not re-

5.1 *Sanctuary of Nabu (Nebo), a Babylonian deity that was very popular in Assyria. Paved forecourt and steps up to the platform on which the statue of the god once stood. (Released by permission of British Schools of Archaeology in Iraq)*

ported but seems probable that the Judaeans anointed Rehoboam (929–913 B.C.) king at Hebron. He had to go to Shechem to be crowned king of Israel (1 KINGS 12:1 f.). The Israelites, however, had summoned Jeroboam to come back from Egypt to be present at this occasion, and we may be sure that he came with a pocket full of Egyptian gold and promises; for it was clearly in Egypt's interest to encourage Israelite separatism. Before giving Rehoboam the crown the northern tribes made certain demands. They wanted a relaxation of the "yoke" of hard work and high taxes imposed by Solomon. This Rehoboam rejected under the influence of other young hotheads and in defiance of more sober counsels.

Israel Goes Its Own Way

The concessions refused, the Israelites now declined to crown Rehoboam their king, declaring their indifference to the House of David. When Rehoboam's taskmaster Adoram was ordered by him to start levying labor, he was put to death, and Rehoboam thereupon fled precipitately from Shechem to Jerusalem (1 KINGS 12:18).

The northern tribes now made Jeroboam their king (929–910 B.C.), thus destroying

the unified state that had attained such imposing strength and which under the right leadership could have become a great factor in Near Eastern history. When Rehoboam mobilized the Judaeans and Benjaminites in order to subdue the northern tribes (1 KINGS 12:21 f.), a prophet named Shemaiah is said to have interfered, and the action was abandoned.

Jeroboam's Cities

We are given a few brief items about Jeroboam, and one of them is a bit mystifying.

"Then Jeroboam built Shechem in mount Ephraim, and dwelt therein; and went out from thence, and built Penuel." (1 KINGS 12:25 A.V.)

"Then Jeroboam built Shechem in the hill country of Ephraim, and dwelt there; and he went out from there and built Penuel." (1 KINGS 12:25 R.S.V.)

That he carried on construction work of a new palace and fortifications at old Shechem seems to be implied. The excavations at the site of *Balāṭah* (see page 158) apparently struck no traces of his building activity, but it is hoped that the new McCormick and Drew Theological Seminary dig under George Ernest Wright will do so. The "going out" of Jeroboam to Penuel on the other side of the Jordan is usually taken to mean a change of capital, and then demands some historical explanation. The Egyptian invasion, of which something will be said shortly, is generally held to be the explanation. It seems more probable to us, however, that Jeroboam merely built himself another palace and stronger fortifications at Penuel, and that his "going forth" was in the nature of an expedition to supervise the construction work. The House of David had too many friends in Mahanaim to make that a particularly good choice. Penuel, not far from Mahanaim, served the same purpose. As we have seen, it probably lay at the eastern *Tell edh Dhahab* on the Jabbok River.

268

Since Jerusalem had become a national shrine through the Solomonic Temple and by virtue of possession of the ark exercised a continual attraction for Ephraimites and Manassites, Jeroboam established two royal sanctuaries for Israel, one in the south at Bethel and one in the north at Dan. He set up golden "calves" (a derogatory expression for bulls) at these temples—an act the prophetic narrators considered outright apostasy, and which, as many scholars believe, gave rise to the "Golden Calf" story of Exodus 32. The object was not intended as an idol, however, but as a symbol of the LORD. It seems probable that it is due to the influence of Hittite ideas emanating from Syria that Jeroboam was induced to adopt this symbol. The task of persuading the Canaanite population, which was, numerous in Israel, to accept the worship of the LORD was rendered easier by such means.

Jeroboam and Ahijah of Shiloh

The prophet Ahijah of Shiloh, who had originally been a supporter of Jeroboam, evidently withdrew his support as time went on. This is illustrated in the reception given by Ahijah to Jeroboam's queen, who went to Shiloh for an oracle concerning her sick son (1 KINGS 14:1 f.), a lad seemingly named after the prophet. The town of Shiloh had thus been rebuilt after its destruction at the hands of the Philistines. Ahijah predicted the boy's death as well as dreadful disasters for Israel because of the religious apostasy of Jeroboam. The woman returned to Tirzah and the child died as she reached her home, as Ahijah had foretold.

We have not heard of Tirzah before in the narratives. The storytellers have neglected to tell us that Jeroboam, after first residing at Shechem, had made Tirzah his residence. Since it remained the residence of his successors until Omri, Tirzah must be accounted a place of some importance in Hebrew history. Its situation must have been most attractive to the eye, for in the Song of

Solomon the beloved is said to be "beautiful as Tirzah." Where Tirzah lay is, alas, not yet established. Its identification with *Tell Fār'ah* northeast of Shechem (see page 154) is strongly urged by some authorities, largely because a crusader historian Brocardus (*c.* 1332 A.D.) was shown a place called Thersa, three hours' journey east of the city of Samaria—a description that would fit *Tell Fār'ah*. The excavations carried on there recently by the Dominican *École Biblique* of Jerusalem under De Vaux have lent some support to this view, for they show a decline of the site after the time of Omri. The Biblical evidence for the whereabouts of Tirzah seems to point to a more central location. The passage shedding the most light on this is 2 Kings 15:14 f. (see page 293)

On Rehoboam's Reign

The division of the kingdom must have hit Judah much harder than Israel. The latter will have experienced an upswing in prosperity, but the picture in Jerusalem must have been most discouraging—a mushroomed town that suddenly lacked income with an impotent ruler who was unable to keep former vassals in line. Since the Jordan Valley all the way down to the Dead Sea belonged to Israel, and since the regions from the Yarmuk River in the north to Moab in the south were Israelitic, it seems difficult to believe that the Ammonite crown still rested on Rehoboam's brow, even though his mother may have been of the old royal family of that country. That the Philistines remained subject is likewise most unlikely. Reassertion of Egyptian power in the coastal plain must have turned the flow of their tribute southward. Judah, however, held the Simeonite territory in the south, most of the Danite territory in the west, and much of Benjamin in the north. Benjamin was immediately adjacent and since David's time had been under the royal thumb. Still, the northern tribes were not disposed to recognize the loss of Benjamin, and much of the fighting that was done in the next century was due to a desire of Israel to regain control of it. We are given a hint to the effect that there was continuous warfare between Jeroboam and Rehoboam, but no details of it are provided (1 KINGS 14:30).

A whole group of fortresses was established by Rehoboam (2 CHRON. 11:5 f.). In this way four especially inviting avenues of invasion from the west and southwest were sealed off. The most northerly was that of the valley or plain of Aijalon, from which one ascended either via Beth-horon or via Kiriath-jearim in the direction of Jerusalem. Some six miles farther south was a second invasion route into Judaea. Here the *Wadi es Ṣarār* provided two tracks, one leading via Kiriath-jearim and merging with the southerly Aijalon route, and the other leading to Etam or Bethlehem. Since the valleys around Jerusalem are largely tributary to the *Wadi es Ṣarār*, Zorah, a fortress guarding this entrance, had a great importance. The third approach went up the *Wadi es Samṭ*. Routes coming from various quarters fed into it, and so three fortresses were required to guard it: Azekah, Socoh, and Adullam. The fourth avenue of approach, the *Wadi el Merj*, was guarded by Mareshah with the powerful outposts of Gath and Lachish. In the south the strategist who chose the fortresses contented himself with protecting positions on roads already in the Judaean mountain country. Three places are mentioned: 1) Adoraim—not referred to again until we hear of it as Adora in Hellenistic times (1 MACC. 13:20)—lay west of Hebron, where its name still survives in *Dūra,* and where there are abundant traces of remains of Graeco-Roman times; 2) Ziph, guarding roads to Hebron from the south; 3) Hebron itself—though not occupying a strong position. Three further places along the divide in the heart of Judah were also included— Beth-zur, Etam, and Bethlehem, all situated at important receiving points of routes from the west. Bethlehem at the same time served to guard tracks to the Dead Sea country, and therein was supplemented by Tekoa.

The surprising thing about this list is that it shows no defensive positions on the north against the kingdom of Israel. Some scholars believe that the Chronicler erred in making it a list of Rehoboam's fortresses and that it is rather to be understood as reflecting the time of King Josiah (639–609 B.C.). In any case, the list is based on possible peril from the west and leaves everything south of Hebron undefended. If it really reports the measures of Rehoboam, it must mean the Philistaeans or Egyptians were feared.

Shishak's Invasion

The invading Pharaoh was Shoshenk I, founder of the Twenty-second Dynasty. His name was given as Shushak in the Old Testament text, but was changed to Shishak by late editors. The narrative of 1 Kings 14:25 f. says nothing about his attempting a siege of Judaean fortresses. It does, however, give the impression that he came to Jerusalem. Rehoboam, we are told, bought him off with the palace treasures and even the golden shields of Solomon's bodyguard.

Fortunately we have a first-hand historical source available for this situation—the inscription of the Pharaoh himself on the south wall of the temple at Karnak. On it he lists the towns of Palestine that he visited in his campaign.

The Pharaoh, it seems, went up the coastal plain and crossed over to the Plain of Esdraelon. His objective, therefore, was the kingdom of Israel. Perhaps Jeroboam had to be reminded of tribute obligations. We hear of Shishak's visiting Taanach, Shunem, Beth-shean, Rehob (the one south of Beth-shean) and Mahanaim in Transjordan; perhaps on the way back he went via Gibeon, Beth-horon and Aijalon, which towns he mentions. Confirmation of his presence in the Plain of Esdraelon was provided by the fragment of an Egyptian stela discovered at Megiddo and bearing his name.

Jeroboam and Abijam

Jeroboam continued to reign over Israel after Rehoboam was succeeded in Judah by Abijam (913–911 B.C.). The record concerning his reign in 1 Kings 15 is meager. In the Book of Chronicles, however, (which gives his name as Abijah) more is reported about him (2 CHRON. 13). There is said to have been a battle between the forces of Jeroboam and Abijam. The sizes of the forces engaged have been greatly exaggerated, perhaps by some later hand. In the course of the fighting Abijam makes a speech to his opponents on Mount Zemaraim. Since Bethel, Jeshana, and Ephron were subsequently taken by Abijam, one must assume that at the beginning of the battle he and his forces were south of Bethel. Mount Zemaraim then must get its name from a town of Zemaraim which lay between Beth-arabah and Bethel (JOSH. 18:22). Beth-arabah was in the Jordan country near Jericho. The name may survive in 'Ain el Gharabeh. The Rās ez Zēmara between eṭ Ṭaiyibeh and Rammūn provides a name that could be reminiscent of Zemaraim.

Abijam's successor, Asa (911–871 B.C.), was still in his first years a contemporary of Jeroboam. Asa is especially lauded for having demoted his mother who apparently exercised regency owing to his youth (1 KINGS 15:9 f.). The reason given is that she set up a (wooden) symbol in honor of the goddess Asherah. Asa had it chopped down and burned in the Kidron Valley.

Asa and Baasha

When Baasha became king of Israel (909–886 B.C.), he blockaded traffic to and from Jerusalem by fortifying Ramah (1 KINGS 15:16 f.). Since the latter city lay in Benjamin, this meant seizure of valuable territory held by Judah. The northerly road was thus cut off, though apparently not the road that turned off to Beth-horon. The threat, however, was so serious that Asa used whatever treasure was left in the temple and palace to buy the aid of the Aramaean king, Benhadad

of Damascus. Asa knew that Benhadad had a covenant with Baasha, but he urged him to break it. The Aramaean heeded his plea and attacked Baasha. The cities whose territory he raided and devastated were Ijon, Dan, Abel-beth-maacah, and Chinnereth with all Naphthali.

Of these cities only Ijon has not been encountered previously. Its name survives in the district of Merj 'Ayyūn. On its northwest edge there is a steep mound called Tell Dibbīn, which rises over a hundred feet above the plain and dominates it and its waters. As Robinson first realized, this must be the site of ancient Ijon. The walls are still visible in places and have prevented spillage of the contents of the mound, so that no ancient sherds are to be found at its base. Its top, furthermore, is planted with gardens. That this is an important ancient city is obvious at a glance.

Baasha was now forced to take back his troops from Ramah and cease fortifying the city. Asa reoccupied it and removed the materials assembled by Baasha's labor force, utilizing them for fortifying Geba in Benjamin and Mizpah.

The site of Geba cannot be in doubt since the name survives to this day (see page 180). Correction of the name to Gibeah is not necessary, for Geba guarded an easterly road, while Mizpah guarded the main road—if its identification with Tell en Naṣbeh is accepted (see page 317). No particularly useful purpose would have been served by fortifying Nebi Samwīl, which ancient tradition identified with Mizpah, for that lay off the beaten track. Perhaps the city lying at Tell en Naṣbeh got the name Mizpah only in Asa's and Baasha's time, but was known previously by a different name (Ataroth?).

The excavations of F. W. Badé and the Pacific School of Religion at this important mound have shown that it was indeed powerfully fortified around this time. Very strangely, however, it had but a single gate,

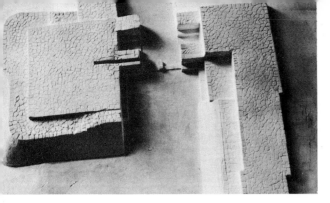

5.2 *Model of city gate of* Tell en Nasbeh. *Note stone benches in gateway alcoves. It was in such a spot that Abner was slain and that Boaz negotiated with the kinsman.* (*Courtesy Archaeological Institute, Pacific School of Religion*)

which faced toward Jerusalem rather than toward the north. The position of the city, furthermore, is not such that it commanded an extended view of the road to the north, such as one would expect of a border fortress built by Judah against peril from that quarter. That would indicate that it was really fortified by Baasha—perhaps before he captured Ramah. Ramah and Geba, lying in the same latitude, balance each other so excellently that one wonders why Asa did not merely rebuild the former as a fortress facing north instead of carting the materials away to Mizpah. The report may have become garbled in transmission—perhaps the materials were taken to Geba rather than to Mizpah.

The allusion to Asa as taking cities of Ephraim (2 CHRON. 17:2) refers to the Benjaminite cities held for a time by Baasha.

The account in Chronicles of the reign of Asa not only attributes to him the building of fortified cities (perhaps the same ones credited to Rehoboam previously), but claims knowledge of an invasion in his time by the Cushite or Ethiopian Zerah (2 CHRON. 14:9 f.). The Ethiopians did not come to power in Egypt until the next century, so this Cushite cannot be a Pharaoh. He may, however, have been an Egyptian governor of the colony at the "brook of Egypt" and Egyptian-held territory to the north of it as far as Gerar. We hear elsewhere, too, that

"children of Ham" (i.e., Cushites) lived adjacent to the tribe of Simeon in the south country (1 CHRON. 4:39 f.), and the Gedor there mentioned is to be read *Gerar*. Zerah carried his raid as far as Mareshah, where he was defeated by Asa and pursued to Gerar. The enormous figures given of the invading host must be drastically cut.

How the House of Omri Was Established

Prior events in Israel are a bit lost sight of in 1 KINGS 15:16 f. We hear later that before Baasha became king in that country Nadab, another son of Jeroboam, had reigned a brief two years (910–909 B.C.). The Issacharite, Baasha, had made a conspiracy against him and slew him while he and his army were besieging Gibbethon (1 KINGS 15:27).

Gibbethon saw more than one Israelite army at its gates. Twenty-six years later, after Baasha had been succeeded by his son, Ela, another siege of Gibbethon was in progress. Ela was at Tirzah, not with the army, when one of his military commanders, Zimri, assassinated him and destroyed his descendants. But Zimri had reckoned without Omri, the top commander of the forces in the field before Gibbethon. When Omri received the news of Ela's death he was declared king by the army and went up with "all Israel" to besiege Tirzah. Zimri perished in the flames of the palace built by Jeroboam.

The events are puzzling. Why should Israel be at war with the Philistines? What was Gibbethon that it should be such an important object that twice in a generation Israelite forces should be besieging it? Where did it lie? The place is mentioned only twice more in the Old Testament, as a Levitic city in the Samson country, and in a list of places on the western edge of the Judaean hill country (JOSH. 21:23; 19:44). In the latter connection, the names run in a northwesterly direction. The part of the series having relevance for the location of the city is: Timnah, Ekron, Elteke, Gibbethon, Baalah, and Jehud. Timnah, as we have seen, lay west of Beth-shemesh (see page 163). The last point, Jehud, lay in the plain of Ono (NEH. 6:2) east of Jaffa. The name has clung to a village of *el Yehūdīyeh*. The intervening places thus must lie in the area drained by the *Nahr Rubīn*. Eltekeh is seemingly an insignificant name in Old Testament history, but a great battle was fought there by the Assyrian king Sennacherib in 701 B.C., as we know from his inscriptions. *Khirbet el Muqennaʿ*, with which it has been identified, was much too important a site for Eltekeh.

Gibbethon is perhaps buried under *Tell el Melāt,* which stands isolated and visible from afar, three miles east of *ʿAqir*. It is the only tell in this area showing occupation since the late Bronze Age. While it is not the site of a great city, such as Ekron must have been, its position made it an outpost of Ekron or Gezer. It was a point about which the battle for the control of Philistaea could well have raged. Gibbethon is portrayed on one of the panels in Sargon's palace at Khorsabad, for he, too, besieged it; the name is *Gab-bu-tu-nu.*

Omri (885–874 B.C.) must have rebuilt the Tirzah palace, for he resided at that city for six years. Then, however, he built a new capital for himself on a noteworthy site that evidently was more suitable for city growth and roomy palaces—the hill of Samaria. Allegedly, he bought the property for the crown and so the place was his city while his dynasty lasted, much as Jerusalem was "the city of David." In the Assyrian inscriptions, Samaria is indeed sometimes called "House of Omri" (*Bīt Ḥumrī*). Why he named it Samaria (*Shōmerōn*) is hardly explained satisfactorily by the Biblical writer's reference to a supposed previous owner, Shemer. The name was doubtless coined by Omri to indicate the "guard" position of the city. Its situation above the present village of *Sebaṣṭīeh,* which merely clings to the east side of the hill, was favor-

able for fortification. The hill was roomy and was well isolated, except on the northeast, where it was connected by a saddle with the neighboring heights. It had a view over pleasant countryside, with the Mediterranean in the distance. An excellent site, indeed, for a city that later was able to tie down an Assyrian army to a three years' siege!

The general location of Samaria with respect to communications was also advantageous. It was situated above a valley tributary to the *Wadi esh Shaʿīr*—the route leading down from the heart of the Ephraimite country at Shechem to the coast, and to the north it had access to the highway to En-gannim (*Jenīn*), where roads fanned out to the cities of the Plain of Esdraelon, to Galilee and to Beth-shean in the Jordan Valley.

Excavations were first conducted in 1908–10 at Samaria by a Harvard University expedition under George A. Reisner, who had won fame for his work in Egypt and Nubia, and Clarence S. Fisher. Further campaigns were carried on with the aid of the Palestine Exploration Fund and the Hebrew University in 1931, with J. W. Crowfoot as director. Since Samaria was rebuilt by Herod the Great and named Sebaste, it is obvious that the Herodian city dominates the archaeological scene, and that it is a considerable undertaking to dig down to Israelite levels. Nevertheless, it also has been possible to get some idea of the fortifications and palaces of the kings of Israel.

Samaria in the days of its splendor must have presented an impressive picture in its verdant setting. Even a Judaean like Isaiah knew of its beauty for he spoke of it as the proud crown of the Ephraimites that is poised above a rich valley (Is. 28:1).

Omri must have been a great builder and organizer to create this capital city and to provide the Hebrew kingdom with an overweening power that soon made Judah its satellite; but he was also a great soldier. The inscription of the Moabite king Mesha tells us of his conquest of Moabite territory (2 KINGS 3:4 f.; see page 284). If we had narratives about Omri's achievements comparable to those which the Judaeans preserved about David, his name would be known to everyone.

Ahab of Israel

Omri was succeeded by his son Ahab (874–851 B.C.), who took for his queen Jezebel, a daughter of the Tyrian king Ethbaal. This led to the cultivation of the worship of Baal at Samaria—not, of course, as displacement of the God of Israel, but as a cult also recognized. The term Baal, however, is incomplete and requires further definition, for this deity is usually found in local manifestations. It seems probable that the Baal meant is the Tyrian Melqarth, a netherworld divinity. Around this same time even a king of Aram, of whom we will soon hear more, raised a stela to Melqarth. In both cases we evidently have a recognition of Tyre's tremendous rise in influence and wealth. The god who gave such success to the Phoenicians was naturally worthy of some attention. Ahab, furthermore, governed an area the economic and military strength of which resided in the old Canaanite cities. It is most unlikely that these ever completely abandoned their old gods, and it was necessary for a king who ruled a mixed population to make concessions to the latter element. Furthermore, Phoenician-held territory crowded Ahab's kingdom closely in the area of the Bay of Acre. Friendly relations with Tyre were most desirable and in antiquity this readily found expression in hospitality toward each other's cults.

The official recognition of a Canaanite cult in Israel's capital roused the indignation of the exponents of the Hebrew religion. The mighty Elijah, of whose activities some valuable narratives are introduced in 1 Kings 17 f., was a leader in this fight, though he was not to see it through to final victory.

It seems odd that in 1 Kings 16:34 we should get an item about the rebuilding of Jericho by "Hiel, the Bethelite." He was presumably the royal official in charge at Bethel, and the creation of a fortified city at the ancient site will have been ordered by his superiors. A fortress at this point meant a strong defensive position against any invasion of the upper Jordan Valley by Judah, and secured control of the fords to the Israelite cities in the east. The storyteller, however, is interested only in the fact that Hiel sacrificed two children—his oldest son and his youngest—in connection with the building of Jericho. This horrible lapse into heathenism caps the climax in the description of the religious apostasy in the northern kingdom. Child sacrifice was a Canaanite custom, as the Punic inscriptions and the excavations in Palestine have shown. A mighty religious question was thus posed: Shall the Canaanite religion be allowed to have equal status with the religion of the LORD? The strife this religious question engendered did much to destroy the power of Israel. It was the undoing of the House of Omri.

Elijah's Ministry

In the opening statement this prophet is described as "a Tishbite, of Tishbe in Gilead." It was long believed that modern *Lisdib* in a high location in the *'Ajlūn* represents this place. On an elevation some three hundred feet higher, with a sparse growth of scrubby oaks covering the slopes, lies *Mar Elias*. It is dedicated to the memory of the great man. However, Tishbe is a dubious place name. It has been suggested that "Tishbite" is a copyist's mistake for "Jabeshite."

Elijah is said to have foretold a drought to Ahab as punishment for the institution of Baal worship at Samaria. This drought seems to have been a widespread one and a matter of record on the part of Phoenician historians. Elijah himself was commanded by the LORD to go to the brook of Cherith "before the Jordan" which need only mean near to it. It is out of the question to identify this brook with the *Wadi el Qelt,* between Jerusalem and Jericho. It must be sought in the declivities of Gilead.

The drying-up of the wadi forced Elijah to depart. Since he was in danger of arrest he sought refuge in a foreign country. He went to Phoenicia to the city of Zarephath (Sarepta in LUKE 4:26). Zarephath's name survives to this day as *Sarafend* on the road going north from Tyre to Sidon. The spot where Elijah supposedly dwelt is still shown the credulous (the *Weli el Ḥiḍr*). The ancient city of the prophet's day, however, lay on the promontory *Rās Ṣarafend.* The Assyrian king Sennacherib two centuries later refers to *Ṣariptu* as one of the cities under the control of Sidon.

The narrative which began with a conflict between Ahab and Elijah requires another meeting between these two for its continuance. The ancient writer describes Ahab and Obadiah as engaging in a personal tour to find hay for their horses. The incident doubtless echoes the serious state of affairs that existed with respect to the supply of hay. The prophet confronted the king and demanded a clear-cut decision between Baal and the LORD. Israel could not serve two gods. He called for a trial of strength between them in an assembly to be convoked at Mount Carmel.

That name may not have been used for the whole range in this period, but only for a part of it. The promontory seems to have had its own name (see page 288). A Baal was worshipped there—in Roman times the Zeus of Heliopolis (*Baalbek*).

The reader with a strong sense of realism may wonder why it was necessary to go to Mount Carmel. Why not have the trial of strength at Samaria in the presence of Jezebel and her supporters? And how could "all Israel" be gathered in an out-of-the-way place like the mountain mentioned, at a time when the thirsty travelers could find no water to drink? Such considerations suggest that the story was originally concerned with a local religious contest and told how the religion of the LORD overcame the cult of the god worshipped at Mount Carmel. It was not, however, a first conquest, but a reconquest, for reference is made to the altar of the LORD that had previously stood there but had fallen down from neglect (1 KINGS 18:30). The writer used this local incident and gave it national significance.

There was more of a background to this than appears here. We may assume that the Israelites had incorporated the Carmel region in their expansion at the expense of Phoenicia (see page 148). But it is quite possible that the tribe of Asher, which claimed this area according to the theory of tribal allotments, had withdrawn from it, or that it had changed hands several times between Phoenicia and Israel. At any rate, the story of 1 Kings 18 mirrors the revival of the Hebrew worship and the ousting of the Baal worship in the Mount Carmel section. Whether the latter worship was fully identical with that introduced in Samaria by Ahab is problematic.

Where did the incidents so dramatically described in 1 Kings 18 take place? To answer that question requires some description of Mount Carmel. It is a mountain range which covers a great deal of ground. Roughly speaking, the Carmel area can be compared to a triangle, one of whose angles is the promontory extending into the sea south of Haifa, providing that place with shelter against the south wind, while one leg runs along the side of the Plain of Esdraelon for a distance of fourteen miles to the *Wadi el Milḥ* (salt valley). From here the line turns at right angles and goes out another fourteen miles toward the coast, including within its area the spur called "the nose" (*el Khashm*) which extends out into the maritime plain; turning at angles again we get the hypotenuse extending back to the promontory along the coastal plain for a distance of twenty miles. The mountain system rises gradually from the promontory to the southeast and is drained by numerous valleys tending toward the west. The comb of the range is toward the north and has a general height of sixteen to seventeen hundred feet, the true summit being the so-called Druze Summit of 1,810 feet. In spite of its modest height the sight of the mountain pleased the ancient Hebrews mightily. "Thine head upon thee is like Carmel" (Sol. 7:5) says the lover to his beloved, thinking of its forested slopes, and a Judaean prophet sees the top of Carmel withering when the Lord roars like a lion from Jerusalem (Amos 1:2).

The Carmelite monks in the sixteenth or seventeenth century, feeling the need of finding a spot suiting the Biblical requirements better, advanced the idea that the scene of the great contest must have been at a point on the range near to the Kishon stream (1 Kings 18:40). They selected the most easterly end of the Carmel comb that in consequence has come to be called *el Muḥraqa* ("place of the burnt sacrifice") by Arabs. Here the proximity of convenient roads would have made an assembly of Israelite delegations practicable and Elijah's race to Jezreel (1 Kings 18:46) would seem more reasonable. In general, these thoughts are well founded. However, the narrative of 1 Kings 18 requires a localization of the place of sacrifice at a point considerably lower than *el Muḥraqa* and closer to the city of Jokneam *(Tell Qēmūn)*, that stood by the Kishon stream. The nearby foothill of *Jelamet el Manṣūra,* which has been nominated for the honor, provides a more plausible location. The king could have reached this point and departed from it in his chariot (1 Kings 18:44) without having to climb the mountain itself. We see no reason for seeking any elevation point. Israel was to gather at (Hebrew "unto") Mount Carmel, not on it (1 Kings 18:19–20). The sanctuary of Jokneam itself may well be meant. A reluctance to mention it specifically could be due to subsequent revival of Canaanite heathenism at this place. The slay-

ing of four hundred priests of Baal at the Kishon, which the narrator attributes to Elijah, is in accord with the radical puritanism of this author; however, it is scarcely a realistic report in view of the time element involved in all that is said to have been done on that day before darkness fell.

The final scenes resuming the theme of the drought, with which the narrative began, possess a marvelous vividness. Elijah ascends the mountain, stopping short of the top and sending his servant up to the height to take an observation and return to him with a report. After repeated missions the servant states that a little cloud like a man's hand is rising out of the sea. Elijah then dispatches him to Ahab to announce the imminent arrival of rain.

The twenty-mile race of the prophet from Jokneam to the town of Jezreel ahead of Ahab's chariot and in the pouring rain provides a thrilling finis to the events. It was a marathon that indeed would have required the supernatural strength the story says was given Elijah.

The Journey to Horeb

Another immortal narrative about Elijah follows in chapter 19. Here the prophet is not the great victor in the religious struggle, but a defeated man (1 Kings 19:14) and a fugitive from the wrath of the queen. It is widely held that the transition from the one to the other is of editorial origin. The one story then must be completely independent of the other. Fearing the wrath of Queen Jezebel (whatever the original reason), Elijah flees to Beersheba. As we have seen, there was much religious pilgrimage from Israel to that ancient seat of reverence for Isaac (see page 80), and Judah must have tolerated this traffic, no doubt by arrangement with Israel. The prophet need not have gone through the heart of Judah but may have gone down through the Shephelah or low hill country. Leaving his servant at Beersheba, he goes a day's journey beyond this

5.3 *Beersheba.* (*Matson Photo Service*)

settlement into the desert. Here under a broom tree, or bush, he is refreshed with food and drink by an angel. There is clearly a relationship between this incident and those reported earlier from the same general locality (GEN. 16:7 f., 21:15 f.). We may accordingly hold that this is a further echo of the stories centering around Beerlahairoi, the very name of which suggested a "seeing" of a heavenly being, even though the place is not named.

Elijah is next commanded to go on a long journey. The food and drink given him by the LORD's messenger give him strength to travel continuously forty days and nights to Horeb, the mountain of God. The report of the journey gives no clear idea of where Horeb lay, and the round figure of forty days and nights of travel can hardly be stressed. It but poorly suits a journey to the Mount Sinai of Christian tradition which could be reached from Beersheba in less than ten days and on the basis of twenty-four-hour travel with supernatural aid, could be imagined as reached within three or four days. Possibly the narrator thought of Mount Horeb as lying far off in Arabia. Even the farthest point hitherto considered for the holy mount (see page 109) would at best have been a two weeks' regular trek from Beersheba. It seems probable that the storyteller's idea of the location of Horeb is hazy and that he has no knowledge of routes or distances.

The story speaks of a cave on the holy mountain into which Elijah went. It reminds one of the niches of the deity Dusares (*Dūshārā*) among the Nabataeans, the later inhabitants of the old Edomite country. There is a cave like this fashioned out of what was originally a natural cave. In it is a large stone pedestal, attached to the rear wall and probably considered the throne of the god. The entrance faces east, so that the morning sun strikes this throne.

Elijah's spending the night in the holy cave on the Mount of God must be viewed as an attempt to procure a message from the deity, as one did in a temple (cf. 1 SAM. 3:3; 21:9; 1 KINGS 3:5 f.; 9:1 f.). Nor was he disappointed. Summoned forth from the cave by the God of the Holy Mount, he was told to do three things: 1) to go to Damascus and anoint Hazael king of Aram; 2) to anoint Jehu king over Israel—while it is not said where he was to be found, we may infer from 2 Kings 9:1 that it was at Ramoth in Gilead, a place Elijah would be able to visit conveniently on his return from Damascus (see page 281); and 3) to anoint Elisha as prophet in his stead. The third item is climactic. When a new king was anointed the old one was king no longer; similarly, to anoint another prophet in one's stead is to abdicate. There can thus not be the slightest doubt but that this story intended to close the career of Elijah with three final acts, which (in the view of this particular narrator) brought about the victory of the LORD over Baal in the kingdom of Israel. To restate them in their significance, they were: 1) conjuring up the Aramaean peril in terrible reality (through Hazael); 2) bringing about a change in the dynasty of Israel; 3) appointing the prophet who would succeed in accomplishing what Elijah had vainly attempted, even though the remaining loyal worshippers of the LORD were only a small minority in the land (7,000).

This was the message of Horeb, given in a whisper in the night at the entrance of the cave after a fearful tempest, earthquake, and fire had prepared the way for the revelation.

The storyteller must have gone on to tell how Elijah fulfilled these commands, since it is unthinkable that they were not obeyed implicitly. Some statements, no matter how brief, about the trip from Horeb to Damascus, from Damascus back to Ramoth in Gilead, and from Ramoth to Abel-meholah must thus have followed.

The editors who created the Books of the Kings felt it necessary to omit the account of how Elijah had anointed Hazael and Jehu, because they wished to include other valuable narratives which attributed these things to Elisha or his agents (2 KINGS 8:1 f., 9:1 f.). Only the last of the three acts is reported—the anointing of Elisha. This may be derived from a different version of the incident, which describes it as a calling to personal service and discipleship, rather than as an abdication of Elijah and appointment of a full successor. In this way the narrative of 1 Kings 19 was robbed of some of the power that was inherent in it in its original form. Even with this abridgment it remains one of the greatest pieces of Israel's literature.

The Calling of Elisha

According to the version of this event preserved in 1 Kings 19:19 f., Elijah found a faithful servant, pupil, and later successor at Abel-meholah, where he happened on a man named Elisha plowing with twelve yoke of oxen, himself guiding the twelfth. We have already had occasion to speak of the location of Abel-meholah in connection with Judges 7:22 (see page 156). The present narrative presupposes that it lay in a good farming district. A man who had twelve yoke of oxen

to do his plowing was a big farmer and must have had a considerable tract of land. A poor man might plow with a single animal, an ox, an ass, or even a camel. The large-scale Arab farmer of more recent times hires men to work for him, not only in plowing but in harvesting and threshing, in return for their board and one-quarter of the crop. A traveler tells of an Arab landowner in those parts who had forty yoke of oxen doing his plowing and a boss for every ten yoke. Elisha in an individual operation on a smaller scale could supervise eleven yoke.

It would seem attractive to seek Abel-meholah at the *Tell el Meqbereh* discovered by Glueck (page 179), if one rejects it for Jabesh. It lies in rich bottom lands.

While Elisha was in the midst of plowing, Elijah threw his mantle over him, thereby, as it were, capturing him for his prophetic calling. The incident exercised a powerful influence nine hundred years later on the thought of Jesus of Nazareth (MARK 1:16 f.).

First Siege of Samaria

The rise of the Aramaean peril is vividly reflected in 1 Kings 20. The stories of this chapter make no reference to Elijah or Elisha, but only to nameless prophets, who act as self-appointed advisers to King Ahab. Written by adherents of the prophetic party, the stories naturally give only a one-sided portrayal of the happenings and play up the importance of these men.

Through Rezon, Damascus had become the seat of an important kingdom that took the place previously held by Zobah. As we have already heard, he had a hatred of Israel (1 KINGS 11:25). This anti-Israelitic tendency continued in Aram, and Benhadad I was only too ready to invade Galilee, when bribed to do so by Asa, king of Judah (1 KINGS 15:20). A full-scale invasion of the very heart of the Hebrew country by Benhadad now follows. In the first incident reported here (1 KINGS 20:1-25), Samaria was besieged by Benhadad and thirty-two vassal kings. A ater Benhadad led seventeen kings in an attack against a Syrian city, as we learn from the inscription of King Zakar of Hamath, found at *Tell el 'Afis* in the plain of Aleppo, probable site of ancient Hadrach. Ahab was ready to surrender, but when further humiliating terms were imposed, he and his councilors decided on further resistance. A sortie at the noon hour was made, led by the king himself and the "servants of the governors of the districts." These evidently represented professional soldiers that ordinarily were garrisoned in the districts, but had been concentrated for the defense of the capital. The site of the Aramaean encampment may have been around the present *Khirbet Basiʻeh,* at which point the *Wadi Shāʻir,* the city's main communication line to the south and west, would be cut off. In that case, the plain would be the scene of the attack which led to the discomfiture of the foe.

The Battle of Aphek

Ahab was warned that the Aramaeans would make another attempt to subdue him in the following year and could prepare himself for the eventuality (1 KINGS 20:22 f.). He had doubtless cleared the Ephraimite and Manassite area of the enemy after routing the foe before Samaria, but it may be assumed that the Aramaeans still held much of Galilee. In the new war the enemy proposed to give battle in more level country and took up its position at Aphek. The location of this Aphek is thus of some interest. The name is a common one, the word simply meaning the "bed of a brook." We have already heard of an Aphek near Acre (JUDG. 1:31), and of an Aphek in Sharon which was a mustering place for the Philistines (1 SAM. 29:1), but these lay far from the avenue of approach of the Aramaeans. One must thus seek the Aphek referred to here in a different quarter. A name derived from an ancient Aphek survives in *Afīq* or *Fīq* in the *Jaulān* in the plateau region east of the later Hellenistic city of Hippos. The word rendered "plain"

(mīshōr) in 1 Kings 20:23 seems particularly indicative of high tableland country. The location of this Aphek on the main road from Beth-shean to Damascus would seem to make it a suitable spot for the concentration of the Aramaean army. The Israelites in two divisions, which the storyteller neatly compares to two little flocks of goats, attacked and put the foe to flight. In the city of Aphek, where the collapse of a part of the city wall wrought additional havoc among the Aramaeans, Benhadad himself was captured. Ahab, instead of taking his life, spared him and negotiated a peace that regained for him the territory previously taken from Israel and, in addition, gave his traders rights in the bazaars of Damascus and hence a hand in the highly important and profitable trade that went through Damascus to the coast.

It may be that very Benhadad who set up the stela to the Tyrian god Melqarth which was discovered some years ago in the midst of Roman remains north of Aleppo, and which is now preserved in the museum of that Syrian city. Presumably, it was originally set up in the city of one of the tributary kings of the ruler of Damascus. It shows the god wearing the Syrian loincloth and carrying bow and battle axe. The inscription reads:

> The stela which did set up Bar Hadad [or Bir Hadad] son of . . . king of Aram to his Lord, to Melqarth, which [stela] he did vow [to erect] to him [if he answered his prayer] and he hearkened to his voice.

Naboth's Vineyard

A last story about Elijah and Ahab is found in 1 Kings 21. Chronologically, it probably preceded 1 Kings 17–18. It tells how Ahab acquired the vineyard of a man named Naboth. It adjoined Ahab's palace at Jezreel. We have already heard of this place as in the vicinity of Mount Gilboa (1 SAM. 28:4, 29:1, 11). This is the first mention of a royal palace here. It is not clear whether it was built by Omri or by Ahab. The town of Jezreel gave its name to the great plain that is called Esdraelon in Greek translation. It seems unlikely that the whole plain was called Jezreel in the older period. The term originally must have applied only to the neighborhood of the town of Jezreel itself, for prior to Omri or Ahab, Jezreel was certainly one of the least of the cities of the plain, and could scarcely have given its name to it. Seen from the valley coming up from Beth-shean, however, its location looms up far more impressively than when approaching it from the west.

The ancient name of Jezreel survives in slightly altered form in the village of *Zer 'in*. There is a low tell there, about three hundred yards long, the western half of which is occupied by the present village and the eastern part by a cemetery. Jezreel had no defensive location and was evidently just a country seat where the rulers found a refuge from the bustle of the city and the business of state. Unfortunately, the use of the mound as a burial site makes it an unfavorable place for excavations; it would be of great interest to uncover the palace of the Hebrew kings.

Where did the vineyard of Naboth lie? Generally speaking, rising ground that is not suitable for raising grain is utilized for vineyards. One might thus imagine it as having lain east of *Zer'in* on the way via *'Ain Jalūd* to Beth-shean. If so, then the palace of Ahab, being adjacent to the vineyard, must have lain at the eastern end of the mound. The conclusion of the narrative (1 KINGS 21:27-29) throws a kindly light on Ahab—so kindly that a later editor saw fit to bring up the idolatry charge in verses 25 to 26 by way of undercutting any sympathy for him.

Ahab's Last Battles

When the inscriptions of the Assyrian king Shalmaneser were first deciphered, an astonished world learned that Ahab of Israel had participated with other allies in a great battle fought at Qarqar (today *Khirbet Qarqūr*) on the Orontes River in Syria

against the invading Assyrian ruler in June of the year 853 B.C. The Assyrian dates being definite, this synchronism is of vital importance for the chronology of Israel. The biggest contingent was furnished by the king of Damascus, who therefore was at the head of the coalition. Shalmaneser calls him Adadidri, i.e., Hadadezer; however that is to be explained, he is surely identical with Benhadad. Israel and Hamath each supplied half as many soldiers as he.

The Old Testament chronological items, tallied with Assyrian reports, suggest that the battle of Qarqar took place near the end of Ahab's reign. Ahab was to meet his death, however, in a conflict with the king of Damascus. It seems improbable that he would have broken with Benhadad and gone to war against him in the same year, 853 B.C. A year or more must have intervened for diplomatic developments and recuperation from the defeat at Qarqar. It is of Ahab's final campaign, which we would put in 851 B.C., that a report is given in 1 Kings 22.

In Ahab's day the relations between Israel and Judah were amicable. They had been cemented by a marriage of the Judaean king Jehoshaphat (871-850 B.C.) who is described as visiting Ahab and participating in the campaign against Ramoth Gilead. The narrative of 1 Kings 22 regards Jehoshaphat as more religious than his Israelite colleague, for he urges seeking a word of the LORD with respect to the whole undertaking. No doubt the gate where they sat was the west gate, from which one has the best view over the countryside, and the benefit of the cooling breezes. Through the *Wadi Sha'ir*, which stretched out before them, one must imagine the kings starting off in their chariots for the journey to En-gannim, Beth-shean, and Gilead.

Why Ramoth in Gilead was such a bone of contention between Israel and Damascus can be understood only after one gets an idea of its location. It had been the government seat of one of Solomon's prefects (1 KINGS

4:13), and so must have been the dominant city of its district. Eusebius seems to have sought it at *es Salṭ,* but that is too far to the south. The site currently favored for the identification was found through the Archaeological Survey of the American Schools of Oriental Research, carried out by Nelson Glueck. About eleven miles southeast of Edrei *(Derʻa)* is a "three-knolled hill," which rises impressively above the fertile rolling plain and dominates the country round about. It was doubtless a powerful city, and its sherds show Iron Age as well as Bronze Age occupation. Its name is *Tell er Ramīth,* which corresponds excellently to the name Ramoth. Since the latter word is a plural meaning "heights" or "knolls," the three eminences characteristic of *Tell er Ramīth* would account excellently for the name. Here, too, is ideal ground for the maneuvering of the thousands of chariots that the Aramaean and Israelite kings threw into battle.

The story of the battle is unusually detailed and vivid. Ahab was struck by a stray arrow, and at sundown when the battle had ended he died, having literally bled to death.

Thus died one of Israel's greatest rulers, when greatness is measured by secular standards. From the standpoint of the representatives of the religion of the LORD, however, he was a hated apostate and the storyteller notes with satisfaction that predictions of doom uttered against him by Elijah (1 KINGS 21:19 f.) had come true.

Passing allusion is made in 1 Kings 22:39 to the "ivory house" built by Ahab, as well as to his city-improvement program. So far as we know, ivory was employed only in inlay work on furniture. The term "ivory house" was simply a popular designation coined by people who never saw the inside of a royal palace but had an idea it was built of ivory. Fine ivory carvings from the palaces of the Hebrew kings were found in the excavations carried on at Samaria by Crowfoot in 1932–33.

Ahaziah of Israel and Jehoshaphat of Judah

Ahab's son Ahaziah (851–850 B.C.) became his father's successor in this hour of crisis. We hear nothing of what Benhadad did after the retreat of the Hebrew forces from Ramoth Gilead. Did he take advantage of the situation and pierce more deeply into Israelite territory? Did Ahaziah have to accept a humiliating peace? Jehoshaphat of Judah, who had narrowly escaped death in the battle before Ramoth, acted more independently now.

The author of the Chronicles account of Jehoshaphat's reign credits him with strong militarization of his state, and with receiving tribute from the Arabs and unspecified Philistine cities or districts (2 CHRON. 17:11 f.). We learn, too, of an alleged invasion of Judah on the east by Moabites, Ammonites, and "some of the Meunites" (2 CHRON. 20:1 f. R.S.V.). In verse 10, "Mount Seir" is substituted for "the Meunites." The latter, therefore, are the people of a city of *Maon,* which is to be identified with the present *Maʻān* on the Hejaz railway to the east of Petra. The story is believed to be derived from a local report about a raid on the part of nomads from the other side of the *el ʻArabah* in the En-gedi neighborhood. It is, so to speak, the chronicler's substitute for the Edomite campaign of 2 Kings 3. The story seems to reflect the beginnings of Nabataean history of the late fourth century.

The picture we get of Jehoshaphat's relation to Edom in the more ancient narratives suggests that he had a strong hold on the country. It was governed by his deputy (1 KINGS 22:47), which would indicate that if Edom had been wholly or partially lost, it had been reconquered at least in part by Jehoshaphat. With the base at Ezion-geber once more in his possession, the king of Judah could aspire to resume the Red Sea commerce of Solomon's day. The weakened condition of Israel is reflected in Jehoshaphat's ability to refuse Ahaziah's bid for partnership in this profitable royal monopoly.

CHAPTER XIV

THE DOWNFALL OF ISRAEL

THE FASCINATING figure of Elijah comes to the fore again under Ahaziah (851 B.C.). The king sent messengers to Ekron to obtain an oracle from a god of healing, but the prophet, intercepting them, predicted the king's death (2 KINGS 2:1 f.). The sequel, relating how successive delegations were sent to arrest the prophet, thinks of him as sitting on the top of a hill, but does not tell us its location. It was obviously close to the road through the *Wadi Sha'ir,* which led to the coastal plain.

Last Story of Elijah

In 2 Kings 2 we hear of the passing of Elijah. The prophet, who was aware that his hour had come, tried to get rid of his servant; he urged him to stay at Gilgal, since the LORD had sent him on to Bethel. Elisha, however, insisted on going with him.

Since it is a three-thousand-foot climb from Gilgal to Bethel and the whole journey seemed useless, as they subsequently went back down to Jericho, some scholars have ex-

pressed doubt that the Gilgal near Jericho is the starting point meant. The words "so they *went down* to Bethel," furthermore, seem to demand a starting point north of the latter city. But the Hebrew verb "go down" is used in the opposite sense of "go up" (2 SAM. 5:17; JUDG. 11:37; 15:8), and that is probably the case here.

At Bethel Elijah sought to shake off his companion by saying that he was moved by the spirit to go down to Jericho. Arriving there, the prophet was moved to go to the Jordan, but again could not dismiss Elisha.

The road Elijah took from Jericho to the Jordan was probably the one passing Gilgal. He thus was heading for the region where Moses was mysteriously taken away. When he had accomplished the river crossing in a manner suggesting the miracle of Israel's crossing at the time of the conquest (2 KINGS 2:8), the moment of his translation came. Two-thirds of the spirit and power of Elijah now came over Elisha.

Elisha's Beginnings

Returning to Jericho, Elisha healed the spring of that city. This presumably refers to the 'Ain es Sulṭān, on the east side of the great mound of Tell es Sulṭān, or ancient Jericho. There had been nothing wrong with that water for three thousand years, for it was this spring that had attracted men to settle here in neolithic times and to continue here until the late Bronze Age. Apparently after Hiel had rebuilt Jericho (1 KINGS 16:34) there was trouble with it. The spring comes out beneath a wall, containing a small circular niche. A reservoir now receives this water, and the modern highway passes between it and the mound.

From Jericho, Elisha went back to Bethel where occurred the incident of the two voracious she-bears. There must still have been some forest in the district between Ai and Bethel at that time.

Elisha then went to Mount Carmel and from there to the city of Samaria (2 KINGS 2:25). His deeds or experiences at those places have evidently been deleted from the narrative; the incidents reported from Jericho and Bethel, however, give us an idea of the nature of what was told about him.

Israel and Moab

Ahaziah's reign in Israel was brief. He was succeeded by his brother Jehoram (850–842 B.C.). It is conceded that the latter did away with one great source of offense—the pillar of Baal which Ahab had made (2 KINGS 3:2). This Baal pillar may have been a bit more monumental than the stone set up by Jacob at Bethel (GEN. 35:14), and so was obviously a foreign symbol. The act shows that the ruler found it necessary to placate the rising influence of the followers of the LORD.

During the reign of Ahaziah the vassal kingdom of Moab had declared its independence (2 KINGS 3:4 f.). This meant the loss of a large annual tribute that was paid in livestock—indicating that the Moabites were still largely a pastoral people. When Jehoram became king he wanted to subdue the Moabite king Mesha once more, and to that end made an alliance with Jehoshaphat, king of Judah, obtaining the latter's help in the expedition.

The path chosen for the invasion was "by the way of the wilderness of Edom." It is apparent that Jehoram was reluctant to attack Moab from his own territory of Gilead in the north, perhaps because the Moabites had heavily fortified this boundary. An attack from the direction of Edom in the south, only possible with the permission and aid of Judah and his tributary, the king of Edom, must have seemed more promising. It was thus necessary to go from Jerusalem to the el 'Arabah south of the Dead Sea and ascend from there into the Edomite country. Such an enveloping movement to get to Moab from the southeastern side is indicated by the allusion to a "circuitous march" ("fetching a compass," A.V.), as well as by the length of time taken. Apparently the "way of the wilderness of Edom" means the way across the desolate el 'Arabah; the term is not otherwise found, and the "wilderness of Edom" is hardly to be equated with the "field of Edom" (GEN. 32:3; JUDG. 5:4), which means the Edomite plateau.

The allied army got into serious difficulties for lack of water in the course of this expedition. The king of Judah called for the advice of a prophet. Elisha was found present and predicted that the stream bed would be filled with water even though there was no wind or rain. As the story goes, water came from the direction of Edom on the following morning.

Such sudden coming of water down an entirely dry stream bed occasionally takes place in these regions, and is the result of a shower at some point higher up the wadi. That the Moabites allegedly saw the water opposite them red as blood and inferred that the allies had been fighting with each other is another item of local origin. It was evi-

5.4 *The old Moabite fortress Kir Hareseth stood here; the Crusader fortress' ruins now stand on the site (el Kerak). (Matson Photo Service)*

dently suggested by the sight of water flowing over the red sandstone which is typical of much of the Edomite country.

As predicted by Elisha, the campaign was a success. A typical "scorched earth" policy was followed. Finally the allies invested the Moabite capital Kir-hareseth, after ruining all the orchards round about it. The Revised Standard Version renders "the slingers . . . conquered it" (2 KINGS 3:25), but the statement seems too strong; the sequel shows that the city remained unconquered. In this instance the Hebrew word used must mean only "they assailed it."

Kir-hareseth (cf. Is. 16:7) is elsewhere called Kir-heres (Is. 16:11, JER. 48:31) or Kir-moab (Is. 15:1). It doubtless lay at the present *el Kerak,* situated on a crag east of the *Lisān,* the tongue of land that reaches out into the Dead Sea. The crusaders built a great fortress on this height, and in all probability much of the capital of King Mesha is buried beneath it. No certain traces of pre-Byzantine occupation were found, until in 1914 Albright located great masses of Late Bronze and Early Iron sherds on the steep southeastern slopes below the citadel. He also investigated a tunnel two hundred meters long, running from a fine spring at the *Wadi 'Ain es Sitt* toward the southern end of the citadel. It was probably dug by the ancient Moabites, but is a cul-de-sac, and so was not completed. One wonders if this engineering attempt was carried out by King Mesha after the siege by Jehoram and his allies had made him aware that his city was not safe without access to water.

The Moabite king did not remain on the defensive, but attempted a sortie, which however, was repulsed. He then resorted to an extreme measure to obtain the favor of his god Chemosh. He sacrificed his eldest son as a burnt offering on the wall of the fortress (2 KINGS 3:27). The sequel to this is stated rather cryptically: There came great wrath upon Israel. A calamity of some sort (spread of disease?) evidently befell the besiegers. The narrator has chosen to conceal the unpleasant truth. From the point of view of the Moabites, it was the wrath of their god Chemosh that visited the Israelites! They had to retreat to their own country.

In 1868 a stela (now in the Louvre) was discovered at *Dībān.* It bears an inscription of the very King Mesha mentioned here. The inscription is one of the most interesting and important Semitic texts ever found, for Mesha tells how he recaptured the northern portion of his country, which had been annexed by Omri, from the Israelites and how he exterminated the Israelite colonists ("men of Gad" as he calls them).

Elisha's Ministry

The next scenes of Elisha's ministry, insofar as they are reported in 2 Kings 4, are familiar. Shunem, Mount Carmel, and, in the Jordan Valley, Gilgal and Baal-shalisha (see page 177) require no further comment. There is no continuity discernible in his travels, however; these are all local reminiscences, gathered by a pious hand.

A major narrative and one of many-sided interests is that of 2 Kings 5, the healing of Naaman, "captain of the host of king of Syria" (Hebrew, king of Aram). It apparently presupposes that Elisha is living in or close to the city of Samaria, since he can act so promptly when Naaman arrives at court. The Aramaean, in coming from and returning to Damascus, had to ford the Jordan River, and so Elisha's advice that he should bathe in it seven times to be cured of his leprosy imposed no undue inconvenience.

The Jordan seems to him but a poor stream compared to the rivers Abana and Pharpar near Damascus, but on the advice of his servants he obeys and is rewarded. He went back again all the way from the Jordan to Samaria to render thanks to Elisha. Naaman's healing throws an interesting light on his character (cf. LUKE 17:18).

Another Elisha incident (2 KINGS 6:1 f.) implies that Elisha had numerous disciples, not just one, and that they suggested a removal from current cramped quarters in order to build themselves a dwelling more spacious in the Jordan River country. There trees could evidently be chopped down at will; each man was to provide a beam for the building (presumably only for its roof, for the sides would naturally be built up of stones). This suggests a sort of prophet-convent near the Jordan—the precursor of the monasteries that were to exist in later times. The incident is not definitely localized.

Several narratives about Elisha (2 KINGS 6:8 f.; 7:1 f.) report an Aramaean invasion with the prophet Elisha portrayed as close adviser of the king of Israel, who is not mentioned by name, and greatly feared by the Aramaeans. One incident highly stimulating to the imagination (2 KINGS 6:13 f.) is localized at Dothan (see page 91). Another (2 KINGS 6:24 f.) dwells at length and with some vividness on a new siege of Samaria itself by Benhadad I. On this occasion the LORD frightened the Aramaeans into headlong flight by causing them to hear "the sound of a great army," so that they thought "the king of Israel has hired against us the kings of the Hittites and the kings of Egypt to come upon us" (2 KINGS 7:6). By "kings of the Hittites" are meant the kings of the various Syrian city-states with primarily pre-Aramaean population, such as Hamath, Sam'al, Hadrach, and others. The allusion to "kings of Egypt" is significant; it suggests that this was written in the period of Egyptian history when that land was divided. Another Elisha story (2 KINGS 8:1–6), a

sequel to that of the Shunamite woman (2 KINGS 4:8–37), tells of a seven-year period of famine and the emigration of the woman and her family to Philistaea—an earlier counterpart of the emigration of the Bethlehemites Elimelech and Naomi to Moab in the Book of Ruth.

Of greater importance is a narrative taking Elisha to Damascus (2 KINGS 8:7 f.). It brings that city into very vivid focus, so something may be said here of this famous place. Several brooks, of which the largest is today called *Barada* (Cold River), come down from the Antilebanon range to water a plain south of it and convert it into a lovely garden district. The *Barada* is the river Abanah or Amana (cf. 2 KINGS 5:12), as the editors of the Hebrew text suggested reading. Amana was really the name of the Antilebanon range itself, as may be seen from the allusion to the "peak of Amana" (SONG OF SOL. 4:8) and then secondarily the name of the stream.

The identity of the Pharpar is less certain. It is commonly linked with the *Nahr el A'waj,* which the pilgrim route to Mecca crosses some six miles south of Damascus. All the brooks around Damascus end up in a marshy district some twenty miles to the east. Our knowledge of the Damascus district during the period 1850–1750 B.C. has recently been increased by the Egyptian Execration texts of the Brussels Museum, published by Posener, and the Mari documents. It was only through the Aramaean invasion and occupation of the region that Damascus became a great city. Since that time it has been continuously occupied, except perhaps for a short time after its destruction in 732 B.C., so there is scant possibility of excavating "the palaces of Benhadad" (AMOS 1:4).

The story of 1 Kings 8:7 f. assumes a certain international importance for prophets, as was also the case with the lost incident about Elijah's anointing Hazael (1 KINGS 19:15) which this one has replaced. The Elisha narrative says nothing about anointing

Hazael, however, but suggests that the prophet raised in Hazael's mind the thought of bringing about the death of Benhadad. It is important, too, for what it implies concerning the terrible blows Hazael later dealt Israel—events that have been only meagerly reported.

Two Kings of Judah: Jehoram and Ahaziah

The defeat of Jehoram of Israel and Jehoshaphat before Kir-hareseth in Moab must have had bad consequences for both. Jehoshaphat's son Jehoram, or Joram, king of Judah, not only lost the province of Edom, but in the campaign he undertook to subject the Edomites, he was surrounded and had to fight his way out of the hostile cordon in the darkness of night (2 KINGS 8:20 f.). This is said to have occurred at Zair, a place currently not identifiable. Another defection from the kingdom of Judah was the important city of Libnah (2 KINGS 8:22) on the Philistaean border. Some identify it with *Tell eṣ Ṣafi,* where Bliss and Macalister dug in 1879; others holding this to be Gath favor *Tell Bornāṭ.*

Jehoram of Judah was succeeded by his son, Ahaziah, whose mother, Athaliah, was either a sister or daughter of Ahab of Israel. We learn of his going with Jehoram of Israel to Ramoth in Gilead, which was in Israelite hands (cf. 2 KINGS 9:14–15), but was menaced by the troops of Hazael. Like his father Ahab, Jehoram of Israel was wounded, though not mortally, in an engagement near the city (2 KINGS 8:28 f.). Leaving the army, Jehoram returned to Jezreel to recuperate. Ahaziah, no doubt after returning to Jerusalem, subsequently "went down" to see him—the altitude of Jezreel being lower than that of Jerusalem.

Founding of the Jehu Dynasty

The story of 2 Kings 9:1 f. is one of the most vivid and best told of ancient accounts concerning a successful revolution. Taking advantage of the situation created by Jehoram's absence, the army chief Jehu, at Ramoth in Gilead, decided to follow the example of Omri and have himself made king by his officer-corps. A "son of the prophets" was easily found to anoint him. The narrative makes him an agent of the prophet Elisha. Whatever the origin of the rebellion, Jehu acts with lightning speed and a circumspectness coupled with craftiness. He makes sure that the exits of Ramoth are guarded so that no advance news can be carried, and then starts off for Jezreel.

The scene shifts to Jezreel where the watchman on the tower sees and reports to the king the approach of the troop that is coming up the valley from Beth-shean. Two horsemen sent out fail to return. The watchman recognizes in the hard driving of the horses on an uphill grade the manner characteristic of Jehu. Thereupon Jehoram and Ahaziah, totally unapprehensive, go forth in their own chariots to meet the leader, who, they must imagine, is the bearer of most important news. According to the story the encounter takes place on the old Naboth property. Too late Jehoram detects in the disrespectful approach of Jehu the signs of danger. He shouts, "Treachery, O Ahaziah!" and turns about to flee, but Jehu's arrow pierces his back so that he falls dead in his chariot. Time is taken to cast his body on Naboth's plot of ground, with a seemingly pious satisfaction at the fulfillment of the threat of 1 Kings 21:19, which Jehu claims to have heard in person (though without mention of Elijah).

It was a marvelous stroke of luck for Jehu that he also encountered the king of Judah in this exposed situation. It put into his hands a dazzling possibility of bringing about a reunited Israel and Judah, even though he was to be thwarted on that score. Ahaziah, seeing that Jehoram's body was being thrown out of his chariot, dashed off in the direction of Beth-haggan, or the "garden house," which, however, can hardly have been much more than a village. It probably is the En-gannim of Joshua 19:21 and the Ginaea (=Ginnayā) of Josephus; the name survives in modern *Jenīn*. Jehu commanded his charioteers to shoot the Judaean king, too.

Jehu meanwhile went on to Jezreel, where no resistance was encountered. When he entered the courtyard of the palace the queen mother Jezebel received him in a spirit worthy of a princess, taunting him as another Zimri (2 KINGS 9:31; cf. 1 KINGS 16:9 f.). Evidently she did not consider her husband's father Omri as on a par with that notorious assassin, but rather as the avenger of the lawful line of kings of the house of Jeroboam (1 KINGS 16:16 f.). At Jehu's command the chamberlains threw Jezebel out the window, where she was trampled under the hoofs of the spirited horses. It was even alleged that dogs devoured her and that there was little left for burial. Jehu then recalled the gruesome words attributed to Elijah in 1 Kings 21:23.

Jehu had won Jezreel, but the capital was not yet in his hands. To get possession of it by diplomacy was now his objective, for his own force was only a small one. Moreover, the army at Ramoth Gilead was distant and could not well be withdrawn. The leaders at Samaria showed astonishing lack of loyalty to the royal house, but we must suppose that the governing clique was largely of Canaanite extraction and indifferent as to who was the ruler. In response to an ambiguous request from Jehu, they sent out the heads of the seventy sons of Ahab in baskets. These Jehu had set up (no doubt in pyramidal form, after the manner illustrated on Assyrian monuments) at the gate of Jezreel. Hypocritically he disclaimed responsibility for this slaughter, but then turned about and suddenly held a series of executions at Jezreel, killing off all the people in any way connected with the house of Ahab or with the government, including priests; nor is it said in the case of the latter that they were priests of Baal. The narrator of 2 Kings 10 was not shocked at this, for to him anything connected with Ahab or Jezebel was under a divine curse. Others took a dim view of the matter. Long afterward we hear of an Israelite prophet naming his son Jezreel, as a living symbol of a word of the LORD concerning Jehu's crimes (HOS. 1:4).

After this holocaust of murder Jehu went on to Samaria, certain that its gates would swing open to receive him. On the way near "Beth-eked of the shepherds" he encountered forty-two Judaeans, who turned out to be Ahaziah's brothers, en route to Jezreel to visit "the children of the king and the children of the queen [-mother]" (2 KINGS 10:12 f.). Apparently no word had reached them of the happenings at Jezreel and Samaria. Jehu had all of them slain and their corpses cast into the cistern of Beth-eked. A possible though far from certain identification for that town is *Kufr Rā 'i,* which may preserve the last part of the name "Beth-eked of the shepherds," Hebrew, *rō-'īm.* This village and the neighboring one of *er Rameh* lie on prominent heights and both were inhabited in Israelite times.

In his further progression Jehu met Jonadab ben Rechab at some unmentioned point and hardly just by accident. This man belonged to a group of ascetics, about which we hear more in Jeremiah's time (JER. 35:1 f.). They were fanatically loyal to the old-fashioned simple life, and the old-time religion, and were apparently related to the Kenites (1 CHRON. 2:55). He and Jehu reached a working agreement.

There was apparently no resistance of any sort at Samaria. Jehu was able to murder without any difficulty all that were left of Ahab's kith and kin. The religious leaders cannot have been too openly involved in the revolution for the simple reason that it would have been impossible for Jehu to carry through the frightful deception of the Baal-worshiping aristocracy that then followed, had it been known or whispered that he was a sympathizer of the party of the LORD.

5.5 *Weathered figure of Shalmaneser III on left, inscription of Ramses II on right. At Nahr el Kelb. (Matson Photo Service)*

Pretending to arrange a festival in honor of Baal, Jehu summoned all the worshippers of that deity, though hardly those from afar, as the story would have it, since that would have involved too much of a time lag. He personally functioned in the role of officiating high priest of Baal. Then command was issued to the eighty guards posted outside to enter the temple and kill all the Baal worshippers. The number of those gathered in this royal temple must not be imagined as extremely large, for eighty men could not have overwhelmed a host, and the temple cannot be imagined as having occupied any great area of ground. A closed building is evidently presupposed in the style of the Assyrian "long-house" temples. One must assume that it was essentially the old Canaanite aristocracy that was thus liquidated— no doubt including the very men who had betrayed the city to Jehu. The story notes that the wooden Asherah and stone pillar, symbols of the Baal cult, were destroyed, that the temple was torn down, and that the very spot on which it stood was defiled by being turned into latrines. Just where this temple was located in the topography of Samaria has not been clarified by the excavations. However, there is some reason to

believe that it stood in the palace area, which, as the excavators have revealed, lay under the later temple that Herod built.

At about the time in which Jehu seized power in Israel, the Assyrian king Shalmaneser III (858-824 B.C.) was extending his control farther into Syria. It seems probable that there is a relationship between these events. Unlike Ahab, who had been allied with Benhadad in resisting the Assyrians, Jehu refrained from joining the present ruler of Damascus. Hazael had to face his attack alone and, according to Shalmaneser, made Mount *Saniru* (Senir, page 25) his fortress. Defeated, he fled to Damascus. The Assyrian ruler devastated the region around the city, but did not prosecute a siege. Instead, he penetrated as far as Mount *Baali-ra'si* where he set up his image. This is usually taken to be the promontory at the Dog River north of Beirut, where a weather-beaten sculpture is indeed found, but it seems very possible that Mount Carmel is meant. At that time Shalmaneser received the tribute not only of the Tyrians and Sidonians but of Jehu of Samaria whom he calls *Yaua* of *Bit Ḥumri,* or "House of Omri" (Israel). This tribute-presentation by Jehu is depicted on the so-called black obelisk from *Nimrūd* (Calah), one of the spectacular finds made by Layard in 1846 (see fig. 5.6). In 838 B.C. Shalmaneser again campaigned in Syria and took four of Hazael's fortress cities. For the remaining fourteen years of his reign he did not venture into Syria, and his son Shamshi-Adad V (823-810 B.C.) did not do so either. Under the four-year regency of Queen Semiramis (810-806 B.C.), there was likewise inaction in the Assyrian quarter. Hazael of Damascus was able to rebuild his power, and now turned once more against Israel.

The details of these wars between Israel and Damascus are unknown to us, but their result is given (2 KINGS 10:32–33, cf. 8:12). Hazael, we learn, conquered the whole country east of the Jordan, from Bashan in the north down to the Arnon. However, insofar as the region north of the Arnon is concerned, there is a discrepancy between this report and the inscription of Mesha, the king of Moab (see page 284). It seems probable that it was the Moabite king who conquered the Reubenites and Gadites from the Arnon northward, though his bailiwick will hardly have extended beyond the Jabbok. At that point, perhaps, the territory conquered by Hazael may have begun.

Judah Ruled by an Israelite Princess

An interesting account is included in 2 Kings 11 of what happened in Judah after the death of Ahaziah and the murder of the forty-two "sons of the king." Ahaziah's mother, who was either a daughter or sister of Ahab, had some of the mettle of worldly greatness in her and showed it by her actions. Her son being dead, she could no longer play an important role once a new king was chosen. With fierce resolve she killed off all the House of David, so that there was no eligible person available to be made king. In fact, she was not even going to spare her own grandchild, an infant son of Ahaziah by a wife from Beersheba (2 KINGS 12:1). A sister (half-sister?) of Ahaziah, however, saved the infant, and concealed him with his nurse in the Temple precincts for six years. No doubt Athaliah believed the child to be dead. The child's mother was certainly slain.

5.6 *Scene on famous black Obelisk from Calah, showing Jehu, king of Israel, prostrating himself before Shalmaneser III. (British Museum)*

Athaliah managed to hold her power as queen over Judah for six years (842–836 B.C.). Hers was apparently a tyranny supported chiefly by foreign mercenary troops.

In the seventh year, however, the priest Jehoiada organized a revolt against Athaliah. The boy Jehoash, now seven years old, was to be made king. The chiefs of the "Carites" (R.S.V.) and of the royal bodyguards had to be won over first. In this period the Carians, a people on the coast of Asia Minor, furnished mercenary soldiers for many rulers; we hear of their serving the Egyptian pharaohs as well. They had no doubt sworn to serve Ahaziah before serving Athaliah. When it was proved to them that a son of Ahaziah was alive, their loyalty to that king could readily lead them to espouse the cause of Jehoash against his grandmother, who had illegally seized the throne for herself. It must be recalled, too, that the high priest Jehoiada was married to a princess of the House of David (2 CHRON. 22:11), and that there was powerful opposition in Judah to Athaliah (2 KINGS 11:20).

The execution of the plot of the high priest involves the topography of the Temple and palace area of Jerusalem. It must be recalled that the Temple lay adjacent to and north of the palace district, with a wall between them that was pierced by two gateways which were exclusively for official use (see page 218). At this time the public had to enter the Temple area by a single gate in the northeast. One of the two palace gates to the Temple here is called the Gate of Sur (for which 2 Chronicles 23:5 substitutes "Gate of the Foundation"). Neither name can be regarded as reliably reported. The second gate is called "the gate behind the guards" (2 KINGS 11:6), or "gate of the guards" (2 Kings 11:19), and "the upper gate" (R.S.V.) in 2 Chronicles 23:2. Whatever its real name, it is clearly the one regularly used by the king and so most convenient to the royal quarters, for the "guards" (literally "runners") mentioned are the royal attendants.

289

The high priest chose a Sabbath for his revolution, when there would be a large crowd present in the Temple, and the hour when the detachment of troops guarding the gates between the Temple and palace was about to be relieved by another detachment. Instead of going off duty, it was prearranged that the first detachment was to join the second in forming a cordon around the entire "house" or Temple building. The boy Jehoash was led forth and anointed king, and received the acclaim of soldiery and no doubt of the astounded civilian crowd present. Athaliah, hearing the commotion and no doubt finding her immediate attendants uncooperative, hastened in person to the Temple; passing between the lines of posted soldiers toward the "house," she discerned the situation and cried, "Treason!" At the command of Jehoiada she was escorted back to the palace by the captain of the guards. The anger of the mob against the queen was diverted toward the destruction of her Baal temple, situated, no doubt, on the Mount of Offence (see page 224).

At the conclusion of the ceremonies the officers took the boy king through "the gate of the guards" into the palace, where he was put on the throne. His first act of state, inspired of course by Jehoiada, was to order the execution of his grandmother Athaliah.

Jehoash of Judah

Brought up in the Temple, the boy Jehoash (837-803 B.C.) was very much temple-minded. Credit is given him for inaugurating necessary repairs to the structure, though the high priest is given the credit for thinking up the idea of putting a collection box alongside of the pillar on the right side of the public entrance into the Temple (2 KINGS 12:9 f.). The idea persisted (MARK 12:41), though the place where the box stood was changed in later times. It was one of those inventions of a modest nature that had undreamed of possibilities. The incident reflects the general poverty of the time, and notably

of the House of David. The king was no longer able to pay for the maintenance of the Court-temple. By public participation in the cost of its maintenance, it gradually became more and more a people's rather than a dynasty's property. The fall of the dynasty, of course, made the people the sole heir to the title.

The political decline of both Israel and Judah and the ascendancy of Damascus is reflected in the fact that Hazael could besiege and capture the city of Gath. Even if the northerly Gath, or Gittaim (see page 195), is meant here rather than the Philistine Gath, it is still a venture far from Hazael's base and signifies a complete control over Israel. After conquering Gath he proposed to take Jerusalem. Jehoash bought him off with all the money and valuables he could scrape together out of Temple and palace and, of course, accepted vassaldom (2 KINGS 12:17–18). In this case piety and dutiful obeisance to priesthood certainly went unrewarded.

Jehoash was murdered by two of his "servants" (officials) who probably desired a more secular policy. The place of the slaying is noted. The text states:

"And his servants . . . slew Joash in the house of Millo, which goeth down to Silla." (2 KINGS 12:20 A.V.)

"His servants . . . slew Joash in the house of Millo, on the way that goes down to Silla." (2 KINGS 12:20 R.S.V.)

A locality named Silla is, however, unthinkable here and it is universally admitted that the text is unreliable at this point. All one can say is that the slaying took place at or near the Millo built by Solomon (1 KINGS 9:15, 24; 11:27; cf. 2 SAM. 5:9, and page 220), and hence south of the Temple. The slaying must have had a background of dissatisfaction with policy. What this background was can only be guessed, but it is worthy of note that about this time King Adad-nirari III (806-782 B.C.) of Assyria was well embarked on his reign, and bent on curbing the power of Damascus. The latter kingdom may have called for Jewish troops to help fight the Assyrians. Amaziah, the son of Jehoash, became his father's successor (803-775 B.C.).

Events in Israel

Jehu's son Jehoahaz (820-804 B.C.) evidently had to drink the cup of humiliation to the dregs (2 KINGS 13:3). A later reference speaks of cities taken from Israel by Hazael (2 KINGS 13:25). We learn that Israel's armament was reduced to fifty horsemen, ten chariots, and ten thousand infantrymen, "for the king of Syria had destroyed them and had made them like the dust by [*at,* R.S.V.] threshing" (2 KINGS 13:7). Terrible warfare, the details of which are entirely lost, had thus occurred. Who was the unspecified savior or deliverer given Israel by the LORD (2 KINGS 13:5) is not stated. Possibly Adadnirari III of Assyria is meant. The consequences might have been even worse but for his diverting Hazael's attention from Israel. Jehoash had angered the followers of the LORD by his religious liberalism.

Jehohaz, or Joash, (804-789 B.C.) reputedly carried on war with Judah and thus sought to re-establish his position there, but that was not the only region of his warring. The report of the passing of Elisha, which occurred in his time (2 KINGS 13:14-20), reflects knowledge of three victories of Jehoash over the Aramaeans, notably one in a battle fought at Aphek (cf. page 279). When Hazael was succeeded by a son named Benhadad, Jehoash was able even to regain the lost cities (2 KINGS 13:25). Inroads of Moabite raiders into territory west of the Jordan seem to be implied in the incident of 2 Kings 13:20-21, and suggests that Mesha's dynasty remained strong in southern Transjordan. One suspects that the Moabites were called in as allies by the Aramaeans.

Amaziah of Judah

Whatever encouragement Amaziah of Judah may have given the murderers of his father in order to get their support, he turned on them once he had the power in his hands and executed them (2 KINGS 14:5). He showed that he was of the stuff that kings are made of by seeking to subjugate Edom once more. It was no doubt the control of the great trade route that lured him. The report is very brief and incidental. It is said that he

". . . slew of Edom in the valley of salt ten thousand, and took Selah by war, and called the name of it Jok-theel unto this day." (2 KINGS 14:7 A.V.)

". . . *killed ten thousand Edomites in the Valley of Salt and took Sela by storm, and called it Jokthe-el, which is its name to this day.*" (2 KINGS 14:7 R.S.V.)

Even allowing for exaggeration in the casualties it must have been a great victory. The Valley of Salt may be the *es Sebkha,* south of the Dead Sea (see page 27), or the general vicinity of the *Jebel Usdum.* The Edomites would thus have sought to give battle near the point where the *el 'Arabah* begins. Amaziah pushed on and captured a city named Sela in Edom proper. The rock fortress of *Umm el Biyārah,* which is on an almost inaccessible mountain top in Petra, has recently been proposed for Sela, and abundant traces of Iron Age Edomite life exist nearby. If that identification were correct, the later Petra of the Nabataeans would conserve the original name, for Petra could be the Greek rendering of *sela',* "rock"; but the earlier name of Petra was Rekem, as Josephus states. Furthermore, a few miles northwest of ancient Bozrah *(Buṣeirah),* or five miles southwest of *eṭ Ṭafīleh,* there is today a village of *Sela',* near which also is a rock fortress, approachable only through a narrow gorge. It has a good claim to being considered the Sela of 2 Kings 14:7, for it is along a line which was more readily reached by the invaders after a victory at the head of the *'Arabah.* The present *Sela'* probably occupies the site of the old Edomite town. The name Joktheel did not endure.

A war between Judah and Israel now followed. Amaziah of Judah is blamed for it in the account preserved (2 KINGS 14:8 f.). However, the only battle mentioned took place on Judah's soil at Beth-shemesh; this suggests that Amaziah was on the defensive at one of the chief points of entry into his own country, and that the adversary took the offensive. Jehoash of Israel not only put the forces of the king of Judah to flight, but captured Amaziah, brought him to Jerusalem, and occupied the city. The victor is said to have broken down a four-hundred-cubit stretch of Jerusalem's fortifications "from the Ephraim Gate to the Corner Gate." The purpose of such an act was to destroy the city's defenses on its weakest side, i.e., in the north. We must infer from this that Jerusalem had grown in the course of time, and that a whole residential quarter had sprung up on the western hill. This meant that a wall encircling it had been constructed beginning at or near the northwest corner of the Temple-court wall. The Ephraim Gate presumably lay near the Temple-court on the west and led out to Ephraim. There was, however, considerable variation in the name of this gate (ZECH. 14:10 first gate; NEH. 3:6, 12:39 old gate?). The Corner Gate was probably the gate at the northwest corner, where the wall turned southward. Jehoash thus laid the city open and defenseless against attack from the north. He confiscated all the available treasure of Temple and palace and took hostages.

Discontent with this humiliating situation led to a plot against Amaziah on the part of the Jerusalemites. Amaziah had no hope of being able to crush the plot, and fled to Lachish in the Shephelah, where he was murdered. The people of Judah thereupon crowned his sixteen-year-old son Azariah (775–734 B.C.). This name could be shortened to Uzziah (cf. Is. 6:1). Early in his reign he extended his father's success in the Edomite quarter by recapturing and fortifying Elath

on the Gulf of Aqabah, thus regaining a place in the Arabian and African trade.

Israel's Brief Revival

Jehoash, by subjugating Judah, had won security in the south. By his victories over the Aramaeans he had liberated the lost cities (probably of Galilee and Transjordan). His son Jeroboam II (789–748 B.C.), whose name was evidently chosen with an eye to linking him with the founder of the Israelite kingdom, continued his work of reconstruction. He is said to have restored Israel's borders from the entrance of Hamath as far as the sea of the plain, i.e., the Dead Sea (2 KINGS 14:25). "Entrance of Hamath" should probably be read "Labo of Hamath," and means a city that lay north of Mt. Hermon. A final remark about Jeroboam alludes to his recovering for Israel (the portions of) Damascus and Hamath, which had belonged to Judah (2 KINGS 14:28). We will revert to this peculiar statement shortly.

A nationalistic prophet of that day is mentioned and praised for having given prediction of Jeroboam's success (2 KINGS 14:25)—a man named Jonah from Gath-hepher (2 Kings 14:25). This city lay in Galilee, north of the later Nazareth. The prominent and fairly extensive hill-site of *Khirbet ez-Zurra*, exhibiting Iron Age remains and situated west of the village of *el Meshhed,* doubtless represents the prophet's home town. The name *el Meshhed* applies originally to the supposed grave of the prophet, who is called *Nebi Yūnis* by Arabic-speaking people and has been commemorated there since Roman times.

Jonah was evidently a great figure, and an interesting though late story about him is told in the Biblical book dealing with a mission of his to Nineveh. He sailed from Japho (*Yāfa* or Jaffa), an ancient Canaanite port, to elude the LORD. "The gate of Jonah" on the Mediterranean coast west of Alexandrette is where the whale allegedly set the prophet ashore.

Amos and Hosea

A new kind of religious leader appeared on the scene in the Judaean Amos of Tekoa, who, we learn, appeared at Bethel with his message and was expelled by the high priest Amaziah of Israel (AMOS 7:12 f.). Perhaps his anger had been aroused by the invasion of Judah by Jehoash (2 KINGS 14:11 f.).

A little later a northern prophet named Hosea wrote down his oracles. There is no direct report of where he came from, but the highest point in southern Gilead is to this day called Hosea's Mountain (*Jebel Ōsha'*). The possibility that local tradition could have preserved his memory cannot be denied in view of the astounding persistence it exhibits in other instances. The designation of his wife as "daughter of Diblaim" may mean that she was from Beth-diblathaim in Moab (NUM. 33:46; JER. 48:22). Another indication of his Transjordanian origin is his allusion to "Shalman's" destruction of Beth-arbel (HOS. 10:14). This was a north-Gileadite city whose name survives to this day in *Irbid*. The great mound there is half again as large as that of Megiddo, and exhibits important Bronze Age remains, but sherds from Iron Ages I and II have also been found there. Shalman is Shalmaneser, but the city's real destroyer may have been Adad-nirari III. As is often the case in historical tradition, a better-known name has replaced one less familiar.

Menahem of Israel

The revived glory of Israel was shattered once more by internal revolution. Jeroboam's son and successor, Zechariah (748 B.C.), was assassinated by Shallum at Ibleam near the Plain of Esdraelon. The storyteller might have mentioned that this happened near the very spot where Zechariah's ancestor Jehu had murdered his king, and that therewith the sin of Jezreel was indeed being visited on the House of Jehu (HOSEA 1:4). Shallum's reign lasted only a month. Apparently one of his army commanders, Menahem from Tirzah, the old capital of Jeroboam I, rose up against him. The district of Tappuah (R.S.V., Tiphsah in A.V.), which refused to co-operate, was laid waste by him (2 KINGS 15:14–16). We have not encountered mention of the latter place in the narratives as yet. It lay in Manasseh, but its agricultural lands were primarily in Ephraim (JOSH. 17:8). In the boundary description of the passage just mentioned, we hear of the Manassite line as running from Michmethath, "which is east of Shechem," to En-tappuah, or "the spring of Tappuah" (JOSH. 17:7). For Michmethath *Khirbet Julējil* southeast of Shechem provides a plausible site. The Greek Bible translation in Joshua 17:7 preserved an additional name on the boundary, that of Jashib, or Jashub. Further references to the place occur in Jewish and Samaritan texts of the early Christian centuries. As the name clearly survives in the present *Yāsūf*, another fixed point of importance for the location of Tappuah has been found. In spite of this, its precise localization remains a matter of debate, though the prominent *Tell Sheikh Abū Zarad*, not far from *Yāsūf*, is a strong contender for the honor. Tirzah may have lain hereabouts, too. One is inclined to seek it north of Tappuah, since Menahem's action is best understood if the latter city blocked his way to Samaria. *Jemmā'īn* has been suggested as a likely location for Tirzah on all these grounds (but see page 269). After the demonstration of his ruthlessness at Tappuah, Samaria admitted Menahem—its Canaanite citizenry having no greater fondness for fighting him than they had had for resisting Jehu. Menahem was thus able to slay Shallum and make himself king of Israel (748–736 B.C.).

In Menahem's reign a greater usurper, Tiglathpileser III (745–727 B.C.), captured Assyria's throne and began to set up the great world empire of that nation. He is referred to in 2 Kings 15:19 as "Pul the king of Assyria," though his proper Assyrian name is used later in (2 KINGS 15:29). The identity of Pul with Tiglathpileser was revealed long ago by the cuneiform inscriptions, which showed that Pul (*Pulu*) was the name given him as king of Babylonia. At the approach of the mighty Assyrian, Menahem of Israel accepted vassaldom, paying one thousand talents of silver as tribute. To raise the money he levied a tax of fifty shekels on each man able to bear arms. Tiglathpileser in his own inscriptions mentions "Menahem [*Minaḥimi*] of the city of Samaria" (*Samerina*) among the western kings, whose tribute he received.

Menahem's son Pekahiah succeeded him but reigned only two years (736–735 B.C.); he was murdered in the citadel of the palace at Samaria by an aide named Pekah and a group of Transjordanians. Apparently there was dissatisfaction among the Israelites suffering under the Aramaean yoke.

Renewed Rise of Judah

Under Azariah (775–734 B.C.), Judah seems to have recovered from the disasters that had recently befallen her. The chronicler gives considerable additional information about Azariah's reign in 2 Chronicles 26, where he is called Uzziah. He fortified Jerusalem further by building towers at the Corner Gate, the Valley Gate, and the angle, points that receive mention by Nehemiah. Great success is claimed for him in warfare in Philistaea. The walls of Gath, Jabneh, and Ashdod are said to have been torn down by him and new towns built in Ashdod's territory (2 CHRON. 26:6 f.). Jabneh has not received mention hitherto in historical connections, but is the place called Jamnia in Hellenistic times, and lay on the Mediterranean coast south of the *Nahr Rubin.* Fighting with the Arabs that dwell in Gur-baal and with the Meunites is also mentioned (2 CHRON. 26:7). The rising importance of the Arabs is noteworthy, and the towers built by Azariah in the wilderness (2 CHRON. 26:10) were probably defenses against their inroads, and were predecessors of the Nabataean and Roman forts that have been discovered in the Negeb by modern explorers. Where Gur-baal lay, remains obscure—perhaps in the Gaza area. The Meunites were already referred to in connection with Jehoshaphat's reign (see page 281).

The annals of Tiglathpileser III mention an *Azriyau* of *Yaudi,* with whom the Assyrian concerned himself in a mountainous district of Syria, and the question arises whether he is not identical with Azariah of Judah. The date of the Assyrian campaign is controversial; it has usually been assigned to 738 B.C., but 743 B.C. is equally possible. Unhappily, the annals are very fragmentary at this point, and until a new copy of them or a corresponding text is found, we are left in the dark as to the actual role of this Azriyau. That *Yaudi* is the proper transcription of Judah into Assyrian is certain, and it is unwarranted to have recourse to the land of *Ya'di,* the territory of the kings of *Sam'al (Senjirli)* in northern Syria, as given in their Aramaic inscriptions. However, it is equally true that it is difficult to think of Azariah of Judah, or his son and co-regent Jotham, as taking a leading role in Syria. The Assyrian annals do not necessarily imply that Azariah was there or that there was any important fighting with him, for the initial statement refers to his paying tribute. Perhaps the peculiar item, to which reference was made in connection with Jeroboam II of Israel (2 KINGS 14:28), may have a bearing on the matter. Jeroboam allegedly had "recovered for Israel Damascus and Hamath which had belonged to Judah." Perhaps this is a reference to an enclave of territory in southern Syria that since the days of David or Solomon had belonged to the kings of Judah. After temporary confiscation by Jeroboam II, it could have passed back again into the control of the House of David. The Assyrian in coming to the district in question would naturally mention its owner, even if he were not there in person to defend it. Not only did he receive tribute from Azriyau; he was also the recipient of sums from numerous other kings, including Rezin of Damascus and Menahem of Samaria.

"The year that king Uzziah died" is given as the date in which Isaiah, worshipping in sight of "the house," saw his vision of the LORD (ISA. 6:1). In connection with Azariah's death, a plaque found at Jerusalem in 1931 is of interest (see page 170). It bears a Hebrew inscription that states:

Hither were brought the bones of Uzziah king of Judah—do not open.

The place where this plaque came from can no longer be ascertained, but one must suppose that the tomb of Uzziah was broken into, perhaps in connection with Herod's building operations, and that the remains had to be removed to a different resting place, which was marked by this inscription. The discovery of that tomb could be the historical fact behind the legend that Herod entered and robbed the tomb of David, as reported by Josephus.

Under Jotham (734–733 B.C.) the Ammonites were made tributary (2 CHRON. 27:5) and considerable building activity also took place, including the rebuilding of the wall of the Ophel (see page 307) and the construction of "the upper gate" of the Temple (2 KINGS 15:35; 2 CHRON. 27:3). It must be assumed that up to this time there was no exit from the northern part of the Temple quadrangle; some would identify this gate with the upper Benjamin Gate (JER. 20:2, R.S.V.). A seal bearing the name "Jotham" was discovered in the excavations at Ezion-geber in 1940; some believe it to have belonged to this ruler.

The Aramaean Peril

An officer named Pekah, who now became Israel's king (735–732 B.C.), presumably in revolution caused by Menahem's acceptance of Assyrian vassaldom, became a vassal of Rezin of Damascus instead and remained in that status for some years. He soon co-operated with Rezin in an attempt to bring Judah into the anti-Assyrian alliance. The preparations began at the end of the short reign of Jotham, according to 2 Kings 15:37, but the attack only developed under Ahaz (733–714 B.C.), as 2 Kings 16:5 f. relates. The occasion brought a man on the scene who is the most "classic" of all prophets—Isaiah, a citizen of Jerusalem, alert to all that was going on in court and palace. According to a partial version of the events (Is. 7:1–9), the plan of Rezin was to depose the Davidic king and make king there "the son of Tabel" (i.e., Rezin, the founder of the dynasty being Tabel, or better, Tabrimmon). Isaiah was divinely inspired to bring a message of reassurance to the young king Ahaz, who had been seen going forth to inspect the water supply of the city. The scene of their meeting is described as at "the end of the conduit of the upper pool in the highway of the fuller's field" (Is 7:3).

At this time there was as yet no sure access to a water supply, such as was later provided under Hezekiah. The "waters of Shiloah that go softly" (Is. 8:6) ran in an open conduit along the base of the eastern ridge (see page 300). But these waters, coming as they did from the Gihon spring, were not conveniently accessible to the inhabitants of the new quarter of the city that had grown up on the northern part of the western ridge. The new quarter must have developed its own water supply; the water works of this part of the city are meant. The conduit of the upper pool must be imagined as outside the north wall of the city, while the upper pool itself was within the city. There was naturally also a pool outside the city—a feeding reservoir, from which the water came via the conduit; but the king would have been wasting his time to inspect that reservoir, since in any siege it would be immediately in the hands of the enemy. He had to get as much water as possible into the pool inside the city before a siege began and to make sure that the point where the conduit entered was properly protected against enemy penetration. It has been suggested that the feeding reservoir lay in the depression northwest of the modern Damascus Gate, to which the term "land of the pool" (*Arḍ el Birḳeh*) clings to this day. The upper pool must have lain in the depression between the Temple quadrangle and the city's new quarter.

The feverish activity of preparing for defense of the city is well illustrated in Isaiah 22:8–11, which mentions the lower pool that no doubt gets its designation from the contrast to the upper pool. It must be sought at the lower end of the Tyropoeon Valley, and is probably the predecessor of the present *Birḳet el Ḥamrā*. The "old pool," which is mentioned in the same connection, is merely another term for this lower pool. The rendering of the word "ditch" (Hebrew *miqwāh*) as "reservoir" (r.s.v.) conveys the idea of a separate installation, but all that really is meant is the making of a deeper or stronger *basin* for the old or lower pool. Its location is described as "between the walls." It must have been close to "the gate between the two walls, by the king's garden" (2 KINGS 25:4)—in other words, at the point where a wall coming across the Tyropoeon Valley from the western hill joined the wall of the City of David (cf. page 316).

The words of 2 Kings 16:5 indicate that Jerusalem was actualy besieged by Rezin and his vassals, although unsuccessfully. However, the Aramaean king sent a force down to take Elath on the Gulf of Aqabah, and handed that city back to the Edomites, who retained it as long as a kingdom of Edom lasted. Perhaps it was in this desperate situation that Ahaz, like the Moabite king Mesha, sacrificed his son (2 KINGS 16:3). In his extremity he sent an appeal to Tiglathpileser III invoking his aid against Rezin and Pekah, and accepting Assyrian vassaldom (2 KINGS 16:7). It seems probable that Tiglathpileser at this juncture was already in Syria. He relates that he made a campaign into Philistaea (734 B.C.), presumably going down the coast, after skirting Tyre. Since he went as far as Gaza his purpose must have been to challenge Egypt and serve notice that he claimed Palestine.

Tiglathpileser's campaign to Philistaea must automatically have led the kings of Damascus and Israel to withdraw from Judah. Since they did not pay tribute, the Assyrian could regard them as enemies. In 733 B.C. and 732 B.C., Tiglathpileser finally delivered the deathblow to the Aramaean kingdom of Damascus. One must assume that Pekah, as Rezin's vassal, had to fight on his side, though the story of this warfare is not preserved in the Biblical narrative. However, we are told what the consequences were for Israel (2 KINGS 15:29–30). The Assyrian took the cities of Ijon, Abel-bethmaacah, Janoah, Kedesh in Naphthali, and Hazor. Janoah alone is new here; the name probably survives east of Tyre in *Yānūh*. By way of summary it is said that he annexed Gilead and Galilee, more especially the whole land of Naphthali, which was part of Galilee, and carried off the inhabitants. Isaiah 8:23 alludes to these great events.

Tiglathpileser's own account of how he regulated matters in the west is fragmentary here, but implies that he annexed everything except Samaria. The account refers to the capture of certain Israelite cities, but only three of the city names he listed are preserved. The first is *Ḥinatuna* (Hannathon in JOSH. 19:14) which probably lay at *Tell el Bedeiwiyeh,* a mound guarding the western exits of the *el Baṭṭōf* plain in Galilee and exhibiting remains of Middle Bronze and Iron I Ages. The others are *Aruma* and *Marum,* the former perhaps *Khirbet Rūmeh* in the plain mentioned, and the latter the Merom of Joshua 11:5. The annexed area became "the province of Megiddo," which city thus served as the provincial capital. Adjoining it on the west was the province of Dor. Karnaim in northern Gilead and perhaps the city of Gilead were also provincial seats. Israel, therefore, was reduced to the city of Samaria and the Ephraimite country south of it. In view of this calamity it is small wonder that Pekah was assassinated (2 KINGS 15:30). Tiglathpileser also mentions the event, calling the murderer *Ausi* (=Hoshea).

The brevity of the Old Testament narrative concerning this great history is such that these fearfully tragic events do not stand forth in all their significance. What disasters had followed on the overthrow of the house of Jehu! The latter groveling before Shalmaneser, as depicted on the black obelisk from Calah, had at least saved his people from invasion and his cities from ruin, and his descendants had achieved great success.

The fate of Damascus, its ruler and its people gets only brief mention in the Biblical narrative (2 KINGS 16:9). There was no Homer to sing of the epic siege. The Aramaean people, like the Israelites of Galilee, were deported. We are told that they were taken to Kir, a country that is referred to as the original home of the Aramaeans (AMOS 1:5) and that furnished Assyria with troops (Is. 22:6). Unfortunately the cuneiform inscriptions have not yet given us certain knowledge of a district of that name. Possibly the name refers to a mountain region on the northern frontier of Assyria.

Ahaz, we learn in 2 Kings 16:10, went to pay homage to the conqueror at Damascus; he was so impressed with a portable Assyrian altar that he saw there that he had one made like it at Jerusalem, and personally officiated before it on his return. This may signify that a new cult was prescribed by the Assyrian king. Another thing our story fails to relate is that Ahaz was sworn in at Damascus as an Assyrian vassal by a regular treaty, in which he had to call down on himself the most terrible curses and punishments in the event of breaking it. A treaty of this nature between Mati-ilu, king of Arpad in Syria, and his Assyrian overlord Ashurnirari V (753-746 B.C.) illustrates how an Oriental monarch bound his subject kings to himself.

Exit Israel

The new king Hoshea (732-721 B.C.), who supplanted Pekah, assumed a doubtful legacy. As we have seen, Tiglathpileser had left Israel only a rump state. Apparently the Assyrian was too busy with other matters to bring Hoshea to his knees when he rebelled. His son and successor, Shalmaneser V (726-722 B.C.), however, determined to subject Samaria completely. At his approach Hoshea, according to 2 Kings 17:3 f., gave in and paid tribute, continuing that for several years. However, after conspiring with "So, king of Egypt," Hoshea discontinued his tribute. Somehow Shalmaneser was able to seize and imprison him.

The people of the city of Samaria evidently were behind the resistance movement of Hoshea, and the Assyrian king now laid siege to the city. The three years' duration suggests that it was prosecuted only in a desultory manner, and that Shalmaneser V contented himself with starving the city out. No Assyrian inscription giving a detailed account of the event has yet been found. Shalmaneser V was apparently assassinated in Palestine or Syria, and a new king was elevated in Assyria in the person of Sargon II (722-705 B.C.). He takes credit in his inscriptions for the destruction of Samaria, which took place in 721 B.C.

Exile was the lot of the survivors. Sargon gave the number of those he deported from Samaria as 27,290. According to the Biblical account, he settled them in Halah on the Habor, the river of Gozan, and in the cities of the Medes. Halah lay northeast of Nineveh, which city at a slightly later day had a gate named the "gate of the land of Halah" (*Halaḥḥu*). Since there is reason to believe that the city lay between Nineveh and Sargon's new capital *(Khorsabad),* the large mound of *Tell 'Abassīyeh* has been nominated for it. Excavations there might give us traces of the ten lost tribes.

The Habor region, which is mentioned next, is that of the river which to this day bears the same name, *Khābūr,* and enters the Euphrates from the north. If this is the river described as "the river of Gozan," it has become more vivid through the rediscovery of the ancient city of Gozan. This city (*Guzana* in the cuneiform texts) is at *Tell Ḥalāf,* where interesting finds were made in excavations carried on by Baron M. von Oppenheim in 1911–13. It lay near *Rās el 'Ain* at the source of the *Khābūr* River. Whereabouts in the Gozan district the Israelites were settled is undisclosed; if any of them lived in the city itself the fact was not ascertained, but the excavations were focused on temple and palace areas, rather than on the quarters of the common people. Other Israelites were taken much farther to the northeast, to "the cities of the Medes." These people had only recently entered the world picture, and *Agbatana (Ecbatana),* today called Hamadan, was their capital. However, the reference to "cities of the Medes" remains vague. Cities under Assyrian control must be meant, and these will hardly have been very far to the north. As the Medes later inherited northern Mesopotamia, the phrase may refer to cities around the *Khābūr* sources.

An air of mystery thus hangs over the fate of the people carried off by Sargon II, and an even greater one over all those deported by Tiglathpileser III. The probability is that they lost their identity in the midst of mixed populations of deportees from widely diversified sections of the realm. In the rise and fall of kingdoms that took place in the centuries after their deportation, most of them may have perished.

Thus ingloriously ended Israel's history. Its spiritual heritage lived on in the memory of it preserved by men of Judah, who were more fortunate in being deported to Babylonia and in being liberated within a relatively short time.

Colonization of Israel's Cities

Sargon was not disposed to leave the cities of Israel desolate. One must assume in any case that the deportations carried on did not completely depopulate the country. Thousands will have fled when the war came and returned to their acres when the fighting was over. However, it was Assyrian policy to shuttle conquered rebel populations back and forth, and we learn in 2 Kings 17:24 f. that Sargon brought certain foreign groups to Israelite territory. Some were from Babylonia, for Sargon had had to subject that country anew. Deportees from the cities of Babylon and Cutha are specifically mentioned. Cutha lay ten miles northeast of Babylon at *Tell Ibrahīm,* where some British excavations were undertaken in 1880 by Rassam, in what was then a most desolate region. It is quite accurate if 2 Kings 17:30 speaks of the Cutheans as worshipping a god Nergal, the old Sumerian god of the nether world. The Hamath referred to is the city on the Orontes, though its deity, a goddess Ashima, is not yet very vivid to us. Perhaps these were people deported after the great uprising under *Yaubidi* of Hamath, which took place in the same year in which Samaria fell. Great uncertainty exists as to Ivvah and Sepharvaim, which also contributed to the foreign element. They occur again with other cities in 2 Kings 19:12–13 (Is. 37:12–13) and so we will defer speaking of them until later (see page 304). Sargon in his own inscriptions does not refer to any of these groups, but alludes to settling conquered Arabs, including such from Ephah (see page 73), in Samaria, a thing, however, which the Biblical writer does not mention.

CHAPTER XV

JUDAH'S VAIN STRUGGLE FOR SURVIVAL

THE ASSYRIAN RULER Sargon II, who had completed the conquest of Samaria, had a great deal of concern with the northern peoples. One of his adversaries was Mita of Mushki (Biblical Meshech), no doubt the man known to the Greeks as Midas of Phrygia. The kingdom of Urartu in Armenia was at this time facing invasion from the Cimmerians, and Sargon took advantage of this to conquer and destroy this northern neighbor. Assyria thereby lost the buffer state that shielded it from the hordes coming down out of inner Asia. In the south he had serious trouble with the ruler of *Bit Yakīn,* near the mouth of the Tigris, who seized Babylon and held it till Sargon could oust him in 709 B.C.

The situation in Syria and Palestine did not cause him too much trouble. In 720 B.C. he fought a coalition formed under the leadership of the king of Hamath. We learn that Hanun of Gaza, Sib'e of Muṣri, and the provinces of Arpad, Ṣimirra on the Phoenician coast, Damascus and Samaria were also involved. The northern group was defeated in battle at Qarqar (cf. the battle of 854 B.C., page 280), while Hanun of Gaza and Sib'e of Muṣri were defeated in a battle at Raphia. We have already spoken of Sib'e, who is probably identical with So or Sewe of 2 Kings 17:4. In the great new capital of Dur-Sargon *(Khorsabad),* which he built for himself, numerous reliefs were set up to commemorate his victories. One of them illustrates a scene from the battle of Raphia, in which the Ethiopian soldiers that fought under Sib'e are characteristically portrayed, while another scene shows a ruler, no doubt Hanun of Gaza, and his attendants as captives.

In 717 B.C. Sargon had to go against the old Hittite kingdom of Carchemish, which had been inveigled into rebellion by Midas of Phrygia. In 711 B.C. Sargon put down an uprising in Palestine led by Yamani of Ashdod. Allied with Yamani ("the Greek") were Philistaea, Judah, Edom, Moab, and Pir'u of Muṣri (a north Egyptian dynast?). Ashdod was taken and destroyed. An oracle of Isaiah is dated in the year when Sargon sent the Tartan (Assyrian *turtānu*), his military commander, to Ashdod (Is. 20:1).

The participation of Judah in the events of 720 B.C. and 714 B.C. has left no further echo in our sources. Apparently Sargon did not go out of his way to apply punitive measures to the inland regions.

Hezekiah of Judah

The son of Ahaz, Hezekiah (714–696 B.C.), gets much praise for his religious reforms. However, in other respects he did not prove to be very successful. That he sought to increase the country's defenses is apparent. In particular he strengthened Jerusalem itself by assuring its water supply (2 KINGS 20:20). Further information about the matter is given in 2 Chronicles 32:30. The Hebrew text of the Wisdom of Sirach mentions the fact that he hewed through rock with bronze (ECCLUS. 48:17). His concern was thus with the problem of getting water from the Gihon spring, which was situated on the eastern side of the City of David (see page 211) over to the west side of the hill.

Explorations along the foot of the ridge past the "Spring of the Steps" or "Well of Mary" have shown that several conduits to channel the waters of the spring in the desired direction were made at different times. The one running on the lowest level is that found by Shick in 1901 and examined in 1902 by Masterman, and is probably the oldest. A wall was built to block it. The one on the highest level ("the second aqueduct") was located by Shick in 1886 and was next

5.7. *Siege of Ekron (Amqarruna) by soldiers of Sargon II. (After Botta and Flandin)*

in age, probably dating from the time of Solomon. It is the one meant by Isaiah when he speaks of the waters of Shiloah (or Siloam) that go softly (Is. 8:6). It was primarily intended for the irrigation of the western slope of the Kidron Valley.

The conduit on the in-between level was cleaned out by the Parker syndicate exploring the area in 1911 and is the only one that corresponds fully to the description of the Chronicles passage cited above. This, then, must be the one constructed by Hezekiah according to 2 Kings 20:20. It had the purpose of leading water into the city by means of a tunnel bored through the hill itself to its western side. This necessitated a choking up of the eastern outlet, as 2 Chronicles 32:30 states. The tunnel that was cut through the ridge is much longer than necessary because it runs crookedly instead of in a straight line. Near the western exit of the tunnel a Hebrew inscription was discovered in 1880. The inscription was cut out of the rock by a vandal, but the broken pieces were confiscated and put in the museum at Constantinople. It commemorates the digging of the tunnel, and describes how the work was done by crews working from opposite sides of the hill. While Hezekiah's name is not mentioned in the inscription, there can be no reasonable doubt that this is the engineering achievement referred to in the Biblical passages mentioned.

There was naturally a receiving pool near the western exit of the tunnel to store the precious Gihon water. It is simply called "the pool" in 2 Kings 20:20 and in the Siloam inscription. Unfortunately, structures of Byzantine times were built where this pool must have lain, and obstruct the search for its remains. It is probable that the place where the spring issued from the tunnel was called "the lower Gihon," in contrast to "the upper Gihon" (as one should read in 2 Chron. 32:30). The receiving pool was certainly not called "pool of Siloam" at this time. As late as in Nehemiah's day the pool of that name lay on the eastern side of the hill, and was the one fed by Isaiah's "waters of Shiloah."

A further step of Hezekiah was a vigorous expansion of his power into Philistaea. He carried a raid up to the very gates of Gaza (2 KINGS 18:8). That city was loyal to Assyria, as it had reason to be, ever since Sargon had regulated matters there. That Hezekiah had some control over Ekron will appear shortly from the narratives to be cited.

Hezekiah was evidently very willing to make common cause with Babylonia and Egypt against the Assyrians. In Babylonia the Chaldean "Merodach-baladan" (Marduk-aplu-iddina II) had again issued forth from the safety of his lair in the marshes around the Persian Gulf and had seized the throne of Babylon. His ambassadors came to Jerusalem with alliance proposals, and were treated too trustingly by Hezekiah (Is. 39:1 f.). We hear, too, of an embassy of tall Cushites (Is. 18:1 f.), and of the sending of messengers of Judah to Egypt to make a covenant with Pharaoh (Is. 30:1 f., 31:1 f.). At the time of Isaiah's first oracle on the matter (Is. 30:4) a Pharaoh evidently controlled Zoan (Tanis) and Hanesh (i.e., Heracleopolis).

The days of grace for Judah were just about over. Sennacherib defeated Merodach-baladan in 703 B.C. and ended all hope of aid from Babylonia. In 701 B.C., the Assyrian finally came to Palestine via the cities of Phoenicia, whose submission he received.

The Assyrian Comes to Micah's Home

There was another prophet of woe in the Judaean country near the Philistine border—Micah, a man long remembered for an address he had given in Jerusalem (JER. 26:17-19). Prophecies preserved in a book bearing his name reflect the disastrous events of Sennacherib's invasion. The prophet's home was in Moresheth-gath (MICAH 1:1; cf. JER. 26:18). This place is to be differentiated from the similar-sounding Mareshah (Tell Sandaḥanneh), which Micah also mentions (MICAH 1:14-15). Moresheth-gath evidently was a town founded by the city of Gath at a time when it had expanded its power over the area in which the town lay—hence the name. The Mosaic map of Madeba puts it on the road leading northward from Eleutheropolis to Socoh. This fact and other information lend some basis to the belief that Tell ej Judeideh, a prominent mound on which some British excavations were conducted about 1900 and which shows habitation in Bronze Age, Iron II and Roman times, is the ancient site. In a particularly difficult passage in which he laments concerning the doom that is descending on his district, Micah gives a roll call of towns in his general environment, indulging in puns on their names. Except for Mareshah and Lachish, they are quite obscure or unknown.

The Assyrian Account of the War

The inscriptions of Sennacherib contain by all odds the most comprehensive account of the events of 701 B.C. The Assyrian states that he first marched down the coast to Ashkelon. It surrendered, but its territory, which at that time went as far north as to include Jaffa, was greatly reduced. He then proceeded against Ekron, for an army of the "kings" of Egypt, including chariot and cavalry detachments of the king of Ethiopia, was coming up from the south. Sennacherib does not mention any names, but the situation is quite clear. The Ethiopian ruler Shabaka had recently brought Egypt under his dominion, and therewith the various independent kings who at that time ruled parts of the Delta region had become his vassals. A battle was fought at Altaqū (Elteḵeh, cf.

Josh. 19:44), a few miles from the *Wadi eṣ Ṣarār,* and the Egyptian-Ethiopian army was put to flight. Thereupon Sennacherib went to Ekron, which surrendered. He executed all the ringleaders of the rebellion and decreed captivity for their supporters. Their king Padi, who was held captive in Jerusalem by Hezekiah, was to receive his throne back.

Having destroyed Hezekiah's allies, Sennacherib was now in a position to take up the cudgels against that ruler, who had not risked his forces as yet in the fight. The Assyrian speaks of reducing forty-six fortified cities of Judah. The Taylor Cylinder inscription does not specify the places, but the Old Testament narrative mentions his sieges of two major cities—Lachish and Libnah. The siege of Lachish must have been a particularly satisfying memory to Sennacherib, for he had it portrayed on the reliefs ornamenting the walls of the great palace which he built for himself at Nineveh, with an inscription reading:

> Sennacherib king of the world sat upon a throne, whereupon the captives of Lachish passed by.

Finally Sennacherib came to Jerusalem and besieged it. Left alone to face the Assyrian conqueror, Hezekiah gave up, accepting the humiliating terms imposed. He had to surrender his mercenary troops, all his treasures including thirty talents of gold and eight hundred of silver, his daughters, his harem and his musicians, and send them to Nineveh in charge of his ambassador. His territory, furthermore, was drastically reduced by Assyrian decree. Large numbers of men, women, and children were deported, though it is not quite certain whether the figure given in the cylinder inscription is correctly interpreted as 200,150, or is to be read as 20,150 or even 2,150. These people were taken to some totally unreported destination and pass into oblivion as did those deported from Samaria by Sargon. The terrible disaster is vividly reflected in an utterance of the prophet Isaiah (Is. 1:5–9)—cities burned, country desolate, foreigners in possession of it, and Zion left like a booth in a vineyard.

In the light of Sennacherib's report and Isaiah's words we must conclude that Sennacherib left the House of David nothing but a rump state, basically consisting of the old kingdom of Jebusite Jerusalem that was theirs by right of ancient conquest, with a strip of land in Benjamin and perhaps Bethlehem thrown in as home of the Davidic line. Judah as such was thus actually cut off from Davidic rule and its territory parceled out among the kings of Ashod, Ekron and Gaza and (a parallel inscription adds) Ashkelon.

Judaean Versions of the Events

The narrative of 2 Kings has two accounts of the catastrophe. The first (2 KINGS 18:13–16) is annalistic and comprehensive and evidently taken from dependable records. It states that in Hezekiah's fourteenth year Sennacherib came up against all the fenced cities of Judah and took them; that Hezekiah sent his message of complete surrender to Sennacherib at Lachish; and that the Assyrian imposed on him an indemnity of thirty talents of gold and three hundred talents of silver. No mention is made here of any siege of Jerusalem. And, indeed, Sennacherib himself speaks of no siege operations against the city, but speaks merely of blockading the roads and establishing some fortified points around it, evidently in preparation for a siege. The latter became unnecessary when the king surrendered.

Patriotic memory does not like to dwell long on national humiliation, and in retrospect something is always found that retrieves the situation or gives it an aspect of glory. A narrative of that nature elaborating on a dramatic incident in the war and giving the prophet Isaiah a patriotic role is appended in 2 Kings 18:17–19:37, as a supplement to the annalistic account. This account is really a combination of two versions; they have not, however, been interwoven, but merely joined together loosely by putting the conclusion of the first version (2 KINGS 19:36-37) at the end of the second version.

The first version is exceedingly vivid. The Assyrian military leaders have come from Lachish to demand Jerusalem's surrender, and are stationed at the very point where Isaiah had had his interview with Ahaz years before—at the conduit of the upper pool, on the highway of the fuller's field (2 KINGS 18:17; see page 295). Hezekiah's ministers go forth to deal with them. When the surrender demand was refused, it is said on Isaiah's advice, the Assyrians returned to Philistaea to report to Sennacherib, who in the meantime had gone on to Libnah. Here, so the story indicates, began the fulfillment of the oracle that Isaiah communicated to Hezekiah:

> "Behold, I will send a blast upon him, and he shall hear a rumour, and shall return to his own land; and I will cause him to fall by the sword in his own land."
> (2 KINGS 19:7 A.V.)

> *"Behold, I will put a spirit in him, so that he shall hear a rumor and return to his own land; and I will cause him to fall by the sword in his own land."* (2 KINGS 19:7 R.S.V.)

For at Libnah, Sennacherib is reported to have heard that Tirhakah, or Taharka, the third king of the Twenty-fifth Dynasty, had set out to do battle with him. That is the rumor that he was to receive. The story must originally have taken the exact course foreseen by the word of the LORD. The spirit put into Sennacherib, we may infer, moved him to quit Philistaea and go to the doom prepared for him in Assyria (as then described in 2 KINGS 19:36-37). The thought then must be that the Assyrian king retreated and left the field to Tirhakah, as though he were afraid to do battle with him.

There is noticeable here a telescoping of events, a circumstance suggesting that the narrative was written down after the passage

of considerable time, for we know that the campaign of Sennacherib occurred early in his reign in 701 B.C. and Tirhakah did not ascend the throne of the Pharaohs until 690 B.C. As we will see, a similar telescoping occurs in the matter of Sennacherib's death (2 KINGS 19:36-37).

The editor of these chapters had another narrative about Sennacherib's demand for surrender which likewise dealt with the role of Isaiah. The salient part of the second version appears in 2 Kings 19:9-35 and thus is inserted at the point where the previous account mentions Tirhakah's coming. This version again tells how messengers are sent to Hezekiah, and its parallelism to 2 Kings 18:17 f. is evidenced by the fact that the same sort of speeches as before are made by the Assyrian commander. This narrative ended in a manner far more satisfying to the pride of Judah than the other. Instead of just retreating on the strength of a rumor, Sennacherib suffered a fearful catastrophe in the outbreak of a pestilence.

A story about a disaster to Sennacherib's army during this period seems to have been current outside of Judah, too, for Herodotus heard it in Egypt two hundred and fifty years later. Field mice are said to have gnawed the quivers, bowstrings and leather shields of his soldiers during the night, so that the army, made defenseless, had to flee. Some scholars of great repute hold that there was a second campaign of Sennacherib, conforming more to the Biblical account and to the tale of Herodotus than the one he himself reports. The theory finds some support in the strange omission of the siege of Lachish and Libnah in the official inscription of the time.

The conclusion of the first version has been put at the end of the combined narratives. It saw the divine retribution befalling Sennacherib in his assassination by two of his sons in the temple of his god "Nisroch." The assassination of this ruler is confirmed by several Babylonian sources which, however, state that Sennacherib was slain by "his son." A god Nisroch is unknown and the name could be a mutilation of "Marduk" or of "Nimrod." The statue of the god Marduk was at this time in the temple of Nabu at Nineveh, for Sennacherib had destroyed Babylon. An inscription of his successor, King Esarhaddon, found at Nineveh in 1927–28, has shed fresh light on the happenings, but does not mention the names of the rebellious brothers. The Biblical narrative singles out two of them, Adrammelech and Sharezer. The rebels must have considered the success of their rebellion assured after the assassination of Sennacherib, because they began to fight for the crown among themselves. Esarhaddon hints at having been in hiding during the development of the rebellion. In the winter of 680 B.C., he marched against the rebels, who had concentrated their army north of Assyria. At the approach of his forces the rebellion collapsed. His brothers deserted their troops and "fled to an unknown land." The Biblical narrative asserts that they went to Ararat (*Urarṭu*). Esarhaddon victoriously entered Nineveh and held judgment over those who had been involved in the conspiracy.

The Lesson of the Fate of Kingdoms

In the speech of the Assyrian officer before Jerusalem's walls, some cities are listed which are said to have vainly relied on their gods and whose fate should be borne in mind by the Jews. We may briefly list and identify them as far as possible (see Color Map XI):

Gozan	Tel-assar	Sepharvaim
Haran	*Hamath*	Hena
Rezeph	Arpad	Ivvah (or Avvah)

The italicized ones have occurred already. Rezeph probably means the *Raṣappa* that lay west of Nineveh, between the Tigris and the Khabur, rather than the caravan town (*Ruṣāfeh*) west of the Euphrates, which attained significance only in later times when the Palmyra route attracted much travel. The only other well-known place not previously

mentioned is Arpad (cf. Is. 10:9, JER. 45:23) It was the goal of an Assyrian campaign by Adad-nirari III in 805 B.C. We have heard too, that King Mati-ilu, or Matiel, of Arpad made a treaty with the Assyrian king Ashurnirari V (753–746 B.C.). That treaty was most interestingly supplemented by an important Aramaic inscription found at a place called *Sujīn*, fifteen miles southeast of Aleppo; in it this same Matiel is party to a treaty with other Syrian rulers. That the king of Arpad in spite of all the curses invoked upon his head, broke the treaty with Assyria is seen from the fact that Tiglathpileser had to besiege the city for three years, taking it in 740 B.C. It lay at *Tell Erfād*, some twelve miles north of Aleppo.

More difficult is the allusion to Tel-assar said to be inhabited by people of Eden. The latter occurs in fuller form as Beth-eden in connection with God's judgment over Aram (AMOS 1:5; cf. EZEK. 27:3), and is evidently the district called *Bit Adini* in the Assyrian inscriptions. It was an Aramaean principality on the Euphrates in the ninth century B.C., but was fully subdued by Shalmaneser III who occupied its capital, *Til Barṣip (Tell Aḥmar)*, and renamed it "City of Shalmaneser *(Kar-Shalmaneser)*" after himself. Tiglathpileser III still used the name Bit Adini, but as a geographical rather than a political concept, and it likewise occurs in some Assyrian letters. Tel-assar is perhaps to be connected with *Tul-Ashurri*, to which Esarhaddon alludes when he says in one of his inscriptions, "I trampled on the people of Parnaki who dwell in *Tul-Ashurri*"—a statement formally much like "the people of Eden who were in Tel-assar." The connection suggests that the region is east of Tabali (see page 48) along the upper Euphrates.

The city of Sepharvaim has not yet been satisfactorily explained. The Dead Sea Isaiah Scroll here provides a variant spelling (*Spryym*) which lends attraction to a comparison of the name with the district of *Shupria* in the Upper Tigris country; others would connect Sepharvaim with the Shabarain, against which Shalmaneser V went soon after his accession (726 B.C.)—if that does not rather mean the Sibraim lying somewhere between Damascus and Hamath (EZEK. 47:16). The identification of Hena with the city of Anat on the Euphrates (still 'Ana) is unconvincing. Ivvah, or Avvah, has been very tentatively linked with the place called Imma in Roman times and today called 'Imm, three miles northeast of Ḥarim, which lies nineteen miles from Antioch in the direction of Aleppo. Since Hena and Ivvah occur together, they ought to lie in the same general area.

The list of cities and the manner in which it is introduced has some similarity with the question of the prophet Isaiah: "Is not Calno as Carchemish? is not Hamath as Arpad? is not Samaria as Damascus?" (Is. 10:9). This is a contemporary list, not one formulated in retrospect. The conquest of these six places is vividly in mind. Hamath and Arpad were already referred to. The name Calno has suffered a change-about of its middle consonants, probably because some Jewish text copyist did not know how to vocalize the letters in their original order, Knlw; the real name was Kunalua, as it is given in the Assyrian inscription. The Assyrian king Ashurnaṣirpal II came to this city on one of his campaigns, after leaving the Aprē (today 'Afrin) River, and before crossing the Orontes River. It is believed to be identical with a large tell a mile to the east of Ḥarim. The city was taken by Tiglathpileser III in connection with the campaign in which Azariah of Judah is mentioned (see page 294).

Carchemish, to which the prophet also refers, was one of the old Hittite principalities and lay on a promontory between the Euphrates and a small tributary stream, where the road coming from Aleppo crossed the river to go on to Haran and Nineveh. The mound of the old city is close to a village called Jerabis (often written Jerablus). When the Baghdad Railway was laid through here it cut into a corner of the ancient mound. Just before World War I, excavations were conducted there by Sir Leonard Woolley and T. E. Lawrence. Many great monuments of "Hittite" sculpture were found, some of them carved with "hieroglyphic Hittite" inscriptions and forming friezes that lined the base of the palace walls. Sargon made an end to the dynasty of Carchemish when he captured the city in 717 B.C. The oracle of Isaiah thus looks back on this event.

An Official of Hezekiah

Among the officials of Hezekiah who are said to have gone out to negotiate with the Assyrian general is mentioned Shebnah the scribe (2 KINGS 18:18). Either at an earlier date or later this man was "over the house," i.e., chief steward (a post held by Eliakim in 2 Kings 18:18). He angered the prophet Isaiah by having a fine new rock-cut tomb made for himself and brought on his head an oracle that has survived (Is. 22:14 f.). Perhaps this very tomb still exists at the village of Siloam, for sixty-five yards southwest of the so-called "tomb of Pharaoh's daughter" there is a tomb which had a panel with a Hebrew inscription to the right of the door over a windowlike opening. It was first noticed in 1870, cut out in 1879, and later taken to England. The writing was held illegible, but has recently been deciphered.

(1) This is [the sepulchre of   ]iah, who is over the house. There is no silver and no gold here,

(2) but only [his bones] and the bones of his handmaiden with him. Cursed be the man

(3) who will open this [sepulchre—]

5.8 *Inscription of Steward of the House. (After Avigad)*

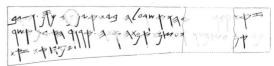

The name Shebnah is only a short form of Shebaniah and the latter could well have stood before the man's title. In any case, it is the tomb of a royal steward such as Shebnah was, and helps to make vivid this oracle.

The Era of Assyrian Vassaldom

Hezekiah was buried "in the ascent of the tombs of the sons of David" (2 CHRON. 32:33 R.S.V.). From now on we no longer hear of any burials in the royal necropolis itself. The reason for this may be that the available space had been filled. Hezekiah had to be buried on the slope of the hill, where nonreigning members of the Davidic family may hitherto have been entombed. As we will see, a further change was made in the case of the following kings.

Manasseh, the son of Hezekiah, had a very long reign (696–642 B.C.). The legacy of foreign oppression that his father had left him lay heavily on his amputated kingdom during a great part of his reign. He was ignominiously taken to Assyria at one time, for the Assyrian army commander

". . . took Manasseh among the thorns, and bound him with fetters, and carried him to Babylon." (2 CHRON. 33:11 A.V.)

". . . took Manasseh with hooks and bound him with fetters of bronze and brought him to Babylon." (2 CHRON. 33:11 R.S.V.)

"Babylon" is used broadly here to include Assyria (c.f. the Persian provincial title on page 331). If the king of Sidon is portrayed as held by a hook through his lips and the attached string being held in the hands of the Assyrian king Esarhaddon, this is clearly not just figurative, but represents a realistic instance of humiliating treatment (cf. also Is. 37:29). A prism of Esarhaddon written in 673–672 B.C. reveals the probable occasion of Manasseh's trip to Assyria: it was at the time when Esarhaddon had commandeered labor from the subject countries to rebuild the Front Palace.

I assembled the kings of the Hittites and of the other side of the river. Balu king of Tyre, Mannasseh king of Judah [*Menasi king of Yaudi*], Kaushgabri king of Edom, Musiri king of Moab, etc.

These and eighteen other vassals were required to direct their labor contingents in dragging the timber from the mountains and the colossi that had been hewn in the stone quarries and brought down on barges to the palace of his lordship at Nineveh. Hebrew tradition of a later age interpreted the absence of Manasseh in Assyria as an imprisonment.

Manasseh was forced to absent himself from his country on several other occasions. A tremendous event of his day was the conquest of Egypt by the Assyrian king Esarhaddon, and there can be little doubt but that Manasseh had to participate in it. Unfortunately no inscriptions of the Assyrian ruler giving us the details of that campaign have as yet been found. All we know is the brief mention in a chronicle kept by scribes at Babylon. It notes that a first attempt to invade Egypt took place in the seventh year; a second attempt in the tenth year resulted in the capture of Memphis. In the excavations carried out in 1954 at Nebi Yunis in Nineveh by the Iraq Ministry of Antiquities, fragments of three statues of Pharaohs, one of which bore the name of Taharka, were found in the entrance to what may be Esarhaddon's palace. En route for Egypt again in the twelfth year of his reign, Esarhaddon died. His son and successor, Ashurbanipal, however, continued the operations in Egypt in 667 B.C. and took Thebes, which the Old Testament calls "No-Amon." The impression made on the world by the fall of that city still rings through prophecy (NAH. 3:8).

Ashurbanipal's annals give many valuable details. He states that the twenty-two tributary kings and their forces had to aid in it, and among them specifically mentions Manasseh of Judah (*Minsie of Yaudi*). It seems quite certain, therefore, that he was also forced to do similar service under Esarhaddon, but of all this activity of Manasseh not the slightest echo has come down in the Book of Kings. An interesting instance of how exceedingly important facts have been forgotten or suppressed!

The excavations carried on at pre-exilic Judaean sites seem to provide evidence for an organization of territory in the southern area different from that which existed earlier or later. Numerous inscribed jar handles that have turned up, regularly name four different places, which must have been district centers for collection of taxes or tribute. Two of these places were in the Judaean mountain country, one being Socoh in the Shephelah and the other Mamshath on the southern border (called Mampsis in Roman times and identified with modern *Kurnub*).

The foreign domination evidently relaxed about the middle of Manasseh's reign, and the king took the opportunity to remilitarize his country. First of all he strengthened the defenses of Jerusalem. There can be little doubt but that these had been razed in some sector, though the rebuilding is not mentioned. We hear only that he built a high outer wall west of the Gihon spring and carried it round Ophel all the way to the Fish Gate (2 CHRON. 33:14). The Fish Gate, according to all the indications, was on the north side of the city. The wall thus ran up the Kidron Valley on its western slope. The "Ophel" in particular is mentioned as encircled by it. This word is sometimes used by modern writers for the entire southeastern hill of Jerusalem, but that is out of line with the ancient sources. Ophel must have been a locality in the immediate vicinity of the Temple, for the Temple slaves lived there (NEH. 3:26 f.; 11:21). Josephus, too, supports this when he refers to a sector as "Ophlas." This was encompassed by the "early wall" south of the southeast corner of Herod's Temple. This description points to Ophel as being the protruding bulge of the Temple hill. It probably was outside the original City of David. Jotham, we are told, had already given particular attention to the wall of the Ophel (2 CHRON. 27:3). A double-walled city meant an extra strong city. Thus on the sculptures of Sargon from Khorsabad, cities like Gaza and Raphia are shown as double-walled, while Gibbethon has only a single wall.

It is surprising to hear also of the existence of fortified cities of Judah under Manasseh (2 CHRON. 33:14). These had all been destroyed by Sennacherib. They must therefore have been rehabilitated by Manasseh. The remark indicates, too, that it was possible for this king to extend his control again over sections that Sennacherib had cut off from Hezekiah's kingdom and handed over to the Philistines. One must conclude that, seen from the secular angle, Manasseh was one of the ablest kings of the House of David. The Biblical authors, being concerned with the religious situation existing in his reign, have no kind word for him, while they give high praise to his father, who ran his country into untold calamity.

Manasseh's remilitarization spells a considerable relaxation of Assyrian rule which can hardly have taken place until the second half of the reign of Ashurbanipal. The Assyrian king probably made one concession after another owing to his absorption in the great struggles with Lydia, Babylonia, and Elam in the years 668–648 B.C. At this time, also, one of the numerous Assyrian appointee kings in Egypt, Psammetichus I (664–609 B.C.), made himself supreme over the rest, founding therewith the Twenty-sixth Dynasty of the Pharaohs.

Amon, who succeeded his father Manasseh, had only a brief reign (641–640 B.C.). He was assassinated in his palace, though the political reason for the act is not given (2 KINGS 21:23–24). Like his father he was buried in the "garden of Uzza." This garden is to be sought in the palace area (2 KINGS 21:18; 2 CHRON. 33:20).

King Josiah

There seems to have been a democratic movement in this time, for we hear that "the people of the land" took control of the situation. They slew all the conspirators and elevated to the kingship Amon's son Josiah, a boy only eight years old (2 KINGS 21:24). This young monarch (639–608 B.C.) was under the influence of priests and others loyal to the LORD, and so receives high praise on the part of the Biblical writers (2 KINGS 23:25).

This period gains especial vividness from the oracles of two prophets who lived in those days. The greater was Jeremiah, a native of Anathoth. The name of this town survives to this day as 'Anātā, north of Jerusalem. However, ancient Anathoth did not lie at the site of the present village, which is of very recent origin, but rather eight hundred and fifty yards southwest of it, on a summit (Rās el Kharrūbeh) that rises one hundred and fifty feet higher than the village. Here are to be found the remains of a settlement that endured from ancient Israelite times to the seventh century A.D. From this well-isolated height the eye can see far over the Jordan Valley to the east.

The other prophet, Zephaniah, was of princely extraction, a descendant of Hezekiah, but his prophesying shows a deep dissatisfaction with the royal princes (ZEPH. 1:8). In one of his oracles (ZEPH. 1:10–11) he alludes to points in the topography of Jerusalem. He mentions the Fish Gate, the Second Quarter, and the Mortar. The Fish Gate, as already noted, lay in the north of the city. The Second Quarter (Hebrew mishneh) is where the prophetess Huldah is said to have dwelt (2 KINGS 22:14). It evidently is a designation of the new suburb that had sprung up on the western hill. "The Mortar" (Hebrew maktēsh) was evidently the part of the city where the financial district lay, and the designation suggests that the terrain occupied by it originally had the shape of a basin. One must thus locate it at the very head of the Tyropoeon Valley (as it once was) and adjacent then to both Temple area and Second Quarter.

The prophet Jeremiah also has allusions to the topography of Jerusalem. We hear on one occasion (JER. 19:2) that he was to go forth to "the valley of the son of Hinnom, which is by the Potsherd Gate" (so the R.S.V. correcting the rendering "East Gate"). This gate is clearly identical with the one otherwise called the "Dung Gate," and the Valley of the Son of Hinnom, also called Valley of the Sons of Hinnom, or simply Valley of Hinnom (cf. JOSH. 15:8; 18:16), is the sweep of low ground that comes down past the western hill (Wadi er Rabābeh). In the same oracle we have repeated mention of the Tophet which evidently is a place in the Valley of Hinnom (2 KINGS 23:10), where in the time of Ahaz and Manasseh human sacrifice was carried on (sacrificing to "Moloch," JER. 19:4, 6). Jeremiah sees it as a fitting place for a future mass cemetery (JER. 19:11); it was thus identical with the widened end of the Valley of Hinnom, before it receives the Kidron ravine. Owing to the horrors of human burning that had been carried on here, Valley of Hinnom (Gehinnom) gave its name to the Gehenna of a later age (MATT. 5:22).

A veritable circuit of the city of Jerusalem is described in a later prophecy of Jeremiah (JER. 31:38–40). He starts from the Tower of Hananel and takes the line to the Corner Gate. These initial points cannot be in serious doubt; Hananel was in the north of the city and west of the Temple quadrangle, and the Corner Gate must lie to the west of it at the northwest corner of the city (cf. 2 KINGS 14:13; 2 CHRON. 25:23, 26:9). From the Corner Gate the line is described as going to (or along) the hill of Gareb and then making a turn to Goa. The only clear thing about this is that an angle was made before Goa was reached. The localization of these points depends on how one reconstructs the pre-exilic Jerusalem (see

Color Map XVII where, however, no attempt has been made to place either of these names). Jeremiah then mentions the whole Valley of Hinnom as far as the Kidron and ends up with the Horse Gate on the east of the city; that it lay close to the Temple appears from Nehemiah's wall description (NEH. 3:27 f.).

Jeremiah in some of his early prophecies is much burdened with the fear of a great peril impending from the north (JER. 1:14; chapters 3–6). The Assyrian records leave us in the dark for those years. Herodotus tells of a Scythian domination and an invasion of Palestine which allegedly was carried as far as Ashkelon, and Psammetichus stopping the invaders from entering Egypt by offering presents. It is only hearsay and may just be a refurbishing of the ancient events of the migration of peoples under Ramses III (see page 131). But western Asia was undoubtedly shaken when the Scythians came through the Caspian Gates and moved westward; kingdoms like that of Urartu were destroyed; peoples like the *Tabali* and *Mushki* (Tubal and Meshech) were driven out of their homes and forced to migrate northwestward; and new groups related to the Scythians came to the fore: Armenians, Medes, and Persians. Jeremiah's "foe from the north" is commonly believed to be the Scythians. The fear of an invasion from the north still rings through the words of Ezekiel (Ezekiel 38).

The time was ripe for Judah to wake up from a state of inertia and live again. In the sphere of religion there was a radical reformation. A law book (basically identical with that now contained in Deuteronomy 12–26) was brought forward by the priesthood of the Temple with the king cooperating, and a new covenant between God and the people was formed on the basis of it (2 KINGS 22:8 f.). Without mention of Deuteronomy 12:4–7, yet in accord with it, the narrative reports the abolition of all other Judaean sanctuaries—they are called "high places" in a derogatory manner—from Geba (see page 180), which thus formed the northern limit of Judaean territory at that moment, to Beersheba (2 KINGS 23:8).

Josiah must certainly have taken advantage of Assyria's difficulties to extend his power. One step in that direction was the occupation of Bethel, which had been reconstituted as an Israelite sanctuary by Assyrian authority (2 KINGS 17:27–28). The "high place" was destroyed and the tombs of priests and nobles broken open (2 KINGS 23:15 f.). As the fall of Assyria became more clearly indicated, Josiah went further. Significant is the remark about his activities in Samaria's old territory (2 KINGS 23:19 f.). This implies an invasion of the area by his forces. The priests of Israel's high places were slaughtered on the altars at which they had ministered.

According to a widely held view, certain materials preserved in the Book of Joshua (notably 15:21–62; 18:21–28; 19:2–6; 41–60) date from Josiah's time and show that under him the kingdom of Judah was organized into twelve districts. That headed by Jericho (JOSH. 18:21–24) includes Bethel and nearby "Ophra" (spelled Ephron in 2 CHRON. 13:19 and identical with the "Ephraim" of JOHN 11:54)—places that had previously belonged to the kingdom of Israel and hence to the Assyrian province that succeeded to its rights. Of particular interest likewise is the district headed by Ekron, which includes places like Lod (Lydda in the New Testament and today *Ludd*) and Japho (JOSH. 19:41–46).

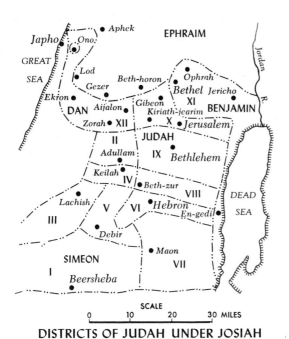

DISTRICTS OF JUDAH UNDER JOSIAH

And Great Was the Fall Thereof

Early in the reign of Sin-shar-ishkun (629–612 B.C.), an ominous event occurred in Babylonia. The country had been ruled by an appointee of Ashurbanipal named Kandalanu, after the Assyrian monarch had put down the secession of Shamash-shum-ukin in 648 B.C. Now, however, Nabopolassar, a Chaldean princeling from the marshes around the Persian Gulf, got control of Babylonia (626 B.C.).

In 1923 an important Babylonian text, the so-called "Chronicle of the Fall of Nineveh" was found in the British Museum's collections and published by C. J. Gadd in the same year. The chronicle, briefly recorded by a Babylonian scribe in the years 616–609 B.C., deals with the campaigns of Nabopolassar, king of Babylon, who is regularly given the title King of Akkad, and it gives us the first dependable account of the fall of Nineveh. The story begins with an invasion of Assyrian-held territory on the Euphrates and an indecisive battle between the Babylonians on the one hand and Egyptian and Assyrian troops on the other. In the following year

Nabopolassar sought to take the old Assyrian capital Asshur, but was driven off and himself besieged in Takritain (today *Tekrīt*). Here the Assyrians were repulsed and forced to retreat. In the fall of this year, however, the Medes came down from the north and took the city of Asshur. Nabopolassar, who had gone to join them in the attack, met with Kyaxares *(Umakishtar)* on the ruins of the city. Then each returned to his homeland. Nineveh was taken by the combined assault of Medes and Chaldeans in 612 B.C. and frightfully devastated. The text seems to imply that no quarter was given to the defenders—it was a case of complete extermination. The Assyrian king Sin-shar-ishkun (629–612 B.C.) must have perished.

The impression caused by the fall of Nineveh must have been tremendous. We get a glimpse from the prophecy of Nahum of the profound satisfaction with which the downtrodden peoples watched the happenings. He is called "the Elkoshite." His home thus must have been a place called Elkosh, but where that town lay is uncertain. There is an *el Qūsh* some fifty miles north of Mosul, and an Oriental tradition since the sixteenth century asserts it to be the prophet's home. Whether that be so or not, Nahum seems to show local knowledge of Nineveh in his words:

> "The gates of the rivers shall be opened, and the palace shall be dissolved." (NAHUM 2:6 A.V.)

> *"The river gates are opened, the palace is in dismay."* (NAHUM 2:6 R.S.V.)

For through Nineveh, indeed, flowed a river named the Choser. According to a Greek story of the fall of this city, it was the sudden rise of this river, causing a stretch of wall to collapse, which brought disaster to the defenders. The sketch-map on page 311 shows the plan of the ancient city walls, the location of its gates, and the course of the Choser. The excavations carried on at Nineveh thus far

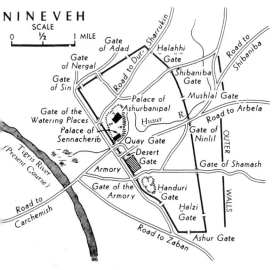

NINEVEH
SCALE
0   ½   1 MILE

do not as yet permit setting up a more detailed plan of the city. Nahum's final words (NAHUM 3:18–19) are a fitting requiem for this mighty capital of empire.

The end of Nineveh was not yet the end of Assyria. A leader who escaped from the city set up a government in Haran and took the throne name Ashur-uballit II. The chronicle of Nabopolassar, referred to before, mentions the *Umman-manda,* an old name for the northern peoples, as co-operating with Nabopolassar in 610 B.C. in the taking of Haran, where immense booty was obtained. Even that did not terminate matters, for Ashur-uballit was too smart to let himself be cooped up in the city. In the next year (609 B.C.) he even recaptured Haran with the aid of a large Egyptian army. The king of Babylon came up with his army and there was further campaigning in the regions north of Haran. The chronicle as originally published ends with Nabopolassar again starting out for a campaign in the following year (608 B.C.). It can be seen from this that the events connected with the death struggle of the Assyrian empire were far more complicated than the Greek accounts or the Old Testament allusions enabled anyone to guess.

Perhaps the most astonishing revelation given by the "Chronicle of the Fall of Nineveh" was that of the Egyptian role in these

events. It threw an entirely new light on the report of 2 Kings 23:29–30 about the end of King Josiah under Pharaoh Necho (609–593 B.C.). The Egyptian ruler did not go up "against the king of Assyria" but rather went up as his ally, and it was while he was en route to this objective that he killed Josiah at Megiddo, where the latter had gone "to meet him." The Revised Standard Version has changed the translation in 2 Kings 23:29 to read that Necho went up "to the king of Assyria," but we are of the opinion that the older version rendered the intent of the Hebrew quite accurately. It is rather a case of the Biblical writer misunderstanding the reports he was using. It is interesting to note that the Chronicles version does not repeat the statement but speaks of Necho's coming up "to fight against Carchemish by Euphrates" (2 CHRON. 35:20). That he seized Carchemish is indeed a fact, as we shall see.

The words of 2 Kings 23:29 do not necessarily imply that there was a "battle of Megiddo," though the Chronicles version does take this view of it (2 CHRON. 35:20 f.). Perhaps all Josiah wanted was to confer with Necho. The haste of the Egyptian to be on his way is stressed in the Chronicles version, and it would be in accord with the impatience of such a leader to have struck down a protesting Palestinian kinglet who bothered him at so important a time.

King Jehoahaz

The "people of the land," we learn in 2 Kings 23:30, now made Jehoahaz king in his father's stead. He was summoned to Necho's headquarters, which are said to have been at Riblah in Syria. As he left, Jeremiah mourned his going in a brief dirge (JER. 22:10). A prose supplement gives the departing king's original name as Shallum (JER. 22:11).

Riblah, mentioned here for the first time in the narratives, lay at the northern edge of the great valley (*el Biqā'*) between the Lebanon and the Anti-Lebanon mountain ranges. The city's name survives to this day at the village of *Rableh* on the west bank of the Orontes, where the river forms an elbow. The country south of here is barren for miles, since the river bed is cut too deeply to permit irrigation, but from *Rableh* on northward tillable soil begins. Not far beyond lay Kadesh, where Pharaoh Ramses II had fought his battle with the Hittites. Seen from *Rableh,* the eastern mountain range, cut through by a pass, sweeps around in an arc, while the Lebanon in the west sinks off to the north. At the modern town there are no ancient remains, but about nine hundred yards northeast of it, beside a small brook, there is a low, long-stretched tell with remains of ancient walls visible. Since sherds of late Bronze and Early Iron Ages are found there, this must be ancient Riblah; although no traces of Iron Age II sherds have been reported, they are probably there. There are no vestiges of remains of later eras. It was a strategic place, indeed, for Necho to pause. Here he could strike for the Euphrates either by Tadmor (Palmyra) or the more northerly route, and at the same time he was safe from surprise attack and had a line of retreat.

Jehoahaz was imprisoned at Riblah and later transferred to Egypt. Considering Palestine his dependency in accordance with ancient Egyptian claims, Necho appointed another son of Josiah named Eliakim, or Jehoiakim, ruler of Judah (2 KINGS 23:24).

Carchemish: One of History's Decisive Battles

The introduction to a great oracle of Jeremiah states that the utterance concerns the army of Pharaoh Necho "which was by the river Euphrates in Carchemish" and which Nebuchadnezzar defeated (JER. 46:2).

The "battle of Carchemish" has hitherto rested entirely on the Biblical evidence, though Greek sources, too, presuppose that there was a decisive struggle which terminated Egypt's pretensions to the control of Syria. The sources state that the Babylonian king Nabopolassar entrusted this campaign

5.10 *The newly-discovered Chronicle of Nebuchadnezzar which mentions and dates the first fall of Jerusalem.* (*British Museum*)

to his son Nebuchadnezzar; that during the victorious sweep of Nebuchadnezzar to clear the Egyptians out of Syria, Nabopolassar died; that Nebuchadnezzar, leaving his commanders to prosecute further activities, went by the shortest route through the desert to Babylon to receive the crown. What could thus be reconstructed has now been brilliantly confirmed by the publication in 1956 by J. D. Wiseman of a further Chronicle tablet, directly continuing that of "the Fall of Nineveh." The events of 608–607 B.C. have no relevance for us, but for 606 B.C. we hear of the Egyptian army taking a garrison city of the Babylonians south of Carchemish, annihilating its defenders, and of Nabopolassar's retreating from the place where he had subsequently pitched camp when the Egyptians crossed the river to attack him. In the following year (605 B.C.) the crown prince Nebuchadnezzar, who had already distinguished himself in the campaign of 607 B.C., marched against the Egyptian army which lay in Carchemish. The tablet states on the obverse side in Wiseman's rendering:

5. He accomplished their defeat and to non-existence [beat?] them. As for the rest of the Egyptian army

6. which had escaped from the defeat (so quickly that) no weapon had reached them, in the district of Hamath

7. the Babylonian troops overtook and defeated them so that not a single man escaped to his own country.

8. At that time Nebuchadnezzar conquered the whole of the Khatti-country.

What vividness this matter-of-fact chronicle lends to the oracle of Jeremiah! We now know that the Egyptian army lingered at Carchemish for several years, and have authentic word of the frightful disaster that befell it: "The nations have heard of thy shame, and thy cry hath filled the land" (JER. 46:12).

In Woolley's excavations at Carchemish a large private house was examined and produced finds bearing on these times. Bronze figures of Egyptian gods, a bronze ring with a cartouche of Psammetichus, and clay seals (once attached to papyrus rolls) bearing the name of Necho himself came to light, thus giving mute evidence of the presence of the Egyptians here. Finally there were some remains of the shield of a Greek soldier. It had a Gorgon's head in the middle and running animals, horses, dogs, deer, and rabbits, in circles around it. Necho thus had Ionian mercenaries as was indeed known from Greek sources.

The new Babylonian Chronicle text indicates that Nebuchadnezzar, after being enthroned at Babylon, returned to Syria and during the fall of the year "marched unopposed through Khatti-land." Early in the following year he took the heavy tribute of the Khatti territory to Babylon. The report makes exceedingly vivid the book of the Old Testament prophet Habakkuk, which reflects a vast astonishment at the speed with which Nebuchadnezzar took over the rule of the west (HAB. 1:5–11).

The official first year of Nebuchadnezzar began after he had "seized the hands of the god Marduk and his son [*Nabū* or Nebo]"

at the New Year's festival. According to the new Chronicle he mustered his army and went to Syria again in the late spring. This time all the kings of Khatti-land, and hence no doubt also the king of Judah, came before Nebuchadnezzar and he received their heavy tribute. There was only one who failed to pay, the king of Ashkelon. Nebuchadnezzar marched against that city in the fall and took it. He turned it into a ruin mound and carried off its king and its spoil.

An Aramaic letter found at *Saqqāra* in Egypt in 1942 by Egyptian excavators may have been written by this unfortunate king of Ashkelon, and if so it gives us his name. It is addressed to "lord of kings, Pharaoh" (or "lord of kingdoms," according to some translators), and the author calls himself "Adon, king of . . . " (name lost). He reports that the troops of the king of Babylon have advanced as far as Aphek, and begs for help. The Pharaoh addressed is probably Necho and the Aphek meant may be the important mustering place mentioned in the Old Testament (cf. 1 SAM. 4:1; 29:1). Egypt was still nursing its wounds from the battle of Carchemish and the Pharaoh seems to have left his vassal in the lurch.

The text of the new Babylonian Chronicle dealing with the events of Nebuchadnezzar's reign in the second and third years is not well preserved. In the second (603 B.C.), he was forced to attack some city of Syria, the name of which has been lost. In the third year (602 B.C.) he collected spoil in the same quarter. In the fourth year (601 B.C.) he marched through Khatti unopposed and undertook a campaign to Egypt in the fall. The Chronicle says:

> The king of Egypt heard [it] and mustered his army. In open battle they smote the breast of each other and inflicted great havoc on each other. The king of Akkad and his troops turned back and returned to Babylon.

The fifth year (600 B.C.) was devoted to assembling horses and chariots in great numbers. The sixth year (599 B.C.) was devoted to action against the Arabs (*Arabi*); companies were sent out from Khatti-land to scour the desert and plunder them. It was thus necessary to curb their inroads into Syria and to meet the same situation faced by Jehoiakim, who had suffered from raids from the Transjordan quarter (2 Kings 24:2).

Now that we know that Nebuchadnezzar had failed in his invasion of Egypt in 601 B.C., we can understand how it was possible that the Egyptian prestige recovered and that Necho could succeed in winning support in Palestine. If we learn in 2 Kings 24:1 that Jehoiakim, after serving the king of Babylon for three years, rebelled, we must interpret this as due to the machinations of the Egyptians. For how could he dare defy Nebuchadnezzar except in reliance on such an ally? In vain did the prophet Jeremiah warn against that decision. One of the most vivid chapters in the Old Testament, Jeremiah 36, tells how the prophet's aide, Baruch, read his dire predictions of disaster in the Temple, and how these were then read to King Jehoiakim in the secretary's chamber, which probably lay in the palace area close to the southeast corner of the Temple. The king contemptuously cut up and burned the scroll (JER. 36:22–23). Another warner, the prophet Uriah of Kiriath-jearim, made himself even more disliked and was extradited by Egypt to which he had fled, and slain (JER. 26:20–23). Jehoiakim's death prevented him from tasting the bitter fruits of his policy. This was the lot of his hapless son Jehoiachin.

King Jehoiachin

According to the Old Testament account Nebuchadnezzar's army came to Jerusalem three months after the passing of Jehoiakim (2 KINGS. 24:11 f.). Jehoiachin surrendered and "went forth" with his family and courtiers, in unconditional surrender. The event is said to have taken place in the eighth year of Nebuchadnezzar.

Here the new Chronicle of Nebuchadnezzar sheds new and welcome light. We quote it in Wiseman's rendering:

11 In the seventh year, the month of Kislev, the king of Akkad mustered his troops, marched to Khatti-land,

12 and encamped against [i.e., besieged] the city of Judah and on the second day of the month of Adar, he seized the city and captured the king.

13 He appointed there a king of his own choice [lit. heart], received its heavy tribute and sent [them] to Babylon.

The city of Judah (here for the first time written *Ya-a-ḫu-du*) is of course none other than Jerusalem. It is noteworthy, however, that the date of the capture of the city, as given in the Chronicle, is different than in 2 Kings 24:12. The Jewish editor calculated by a fall accession date, rather than by the Babylonian spring accession date. Since the capture of the city took place in Adar, the last month of the Babylonian year, the date of the capture was not in 598 B.C. but March 16, 597 B.C. This is indeed surprising information. If the Chronicle claims that Nebuchadnezzar seized the city and captured the king that raises the question as to which version of what happened is correct. The Chronicle being a priestly document does not necessarily represent official government reporting, but is rather a news-journal kept by priests of the temple.

Jehoiachin's uncle, Zedekiah, another son of Josiah by his wife Hamutal, was now made king by Nebuchadnezzar. However, it seems probable that he was regarded only as regent by the Judaeans, and that the captive Jehoiachin was considered their real king *de jure*. This is particularly evident from the fact that a dating by the *captivity* of Jehoiachin was in use, as reflected by 2 Kings 25:27 and the dates in Ezekiel. It was not possible to date by the *reign* of Jehoiachin, since that would have rendered any legal document so dated invalid.

Jehoiachin was taken to Babylon by Neb-uchadnezzar and no doubt was assigned a dwelling there. He apparently received income from crown properties in Judah. In 1928 there was found at *Tell Beit Mirsim* in a level of just this particular time, a jar-handle bearing the seal impression "Eliakim steward of Jaukin" (short for Jehoiachin). Subsequently, other handles with the same stamp were found there as well as at Beth-shemesh. Eliakim thus was probably the manager of the royal estates in Judah. While much of the income may have had to go to Zedekiah the title remained vested in Jehoia-chin. An even more surprising vestige of Jehoiachin's existence has come down in the Berlin Museum cuneiform texts from ancient Babylon published by E. F. Weidner in 1940. The tablets all relate to payment of rations in oil, barley, etc., to captives and others and are dated between 595–570 B.C. The fact that Jehoiachin received rations suggests he was free to move about. No doubt it was when his country revolted that he was put in prison (2 KINGS 25:27).

Prophet of the Exile

In the days when Jehoiachin was still free, a Jewish priest named Ezekiel had a visionary experience, whereby he was called to be a prophet of the LORD. The date of the vision is given in Ezekiel 1:2 as in the fifth year of the exile of King Jehoiachin (i.e., 593 B.C.). This marvelous experience took place "in the land of the Chaldeans by the River Chebar."

There is no clear indication as to where-abouts in Babylonia this stream was to be sought. In 1903, however, some Neo-Baby-lonian business tablets, written in the reign of Artaxerxes I and belonging to the business firm of the Murashu Sons in the Babylonian city of Nippur, were published. Here there appeared several references to a canal *Kabaru,* the exact equivalent of the Chebar! It seems certain that this "river" was a watercourse in the environs of this great Babylonian city.

The Nippur Map of the Jena Hilprecht collection published in 1956 by Samuel N. Kramer mentions canals, but the *Kabaru* is not among them and so must have lain outside the map limits. In Ezekiel 3:15 we learn that the settlement where the prophet lived was called Tell-abib. The settlement was probably a Babylonian *Til-abūbi*—a term used for any long-uninhabited mound.

Disaster Descends

Zedekiah, we are told, "rebelled against the king of Babylon" (2 KINGS 24:20). What led to this action is not explained. No doubt the Chronicler is right in assuming that Zedekiah had had to submit to an impreca-tory ceremony (2 CHRON. 36:13) of the kind we have already referred to in connection with Ahaz (see page 297). That Zedekiah was more a tool of others than a prime mover in the rebellion (cf. JER. 38:5) is shown by the fact that in the end his life was spared.

It is highly probable that the uprising of Judah against Nebuchadnezzar was inti-mately connected with other events of the times. Thus Tyre, too, seems to have rebelled. The uprisings of both were instigated and backed up by Egypt, where Pharaoh Hophra (JER. 44:30), or Apries, came to the throne succeeding Psamtik II early in 588 B.C. Ezek-iel has an oracle against Egypt (EZEK. 29:1 f.) probably uttered in January, 588 B.C. which was doubtless elicited by the military activities of Hophra.

The siege of Jerusalem began in January 588 B.C. and lasted until July of the following year. The accounts of 2 Kings 25:1–21 and Jeremiah 52:1–30 are focussed on the events at the city and are incomplete even as to these. It seems probable that while the pre-liminary operations were in progress other Chaldean forces were engaged in the task of subjugating the rest of the kingdom. This is revealed when reference is made to the reduction of the sole remaining Judaean fortresses, Lachish and Azekah (JER. 34:7).

The Lachish Ostraca

A new glimpse of the operations in that quarter was provided in 1935 by the excavations at *Tell ed Duweir*—ancient Lachish. In the guardroom of the eastern tower of the gate of the outer city wall eighteen inscribed sherds (so-called "ostraca") were found. They are all written in the old Hebrew script and date from the days just before Lachish was attacked. When the city was burned these ostraca were buried in the ruins. The ostraca are addressed "to my lord Yaosh," the style of those days equivalent to "Dear Mr. X." Yaosh was doubtless the commandant of the city and perhaps even of the district.

We can see from these short missives how a network of communication existed between the government at Jerusalem and the outlying garrisons and how messages were sent or received by the commanders.

Tragedy

The siege had begun in January. It ended the following year in the heat of summer, when the land was parched and the water supply at best was low. The food shortage alone, however, is mentioned (JER. 52:6). The wall was breached on the ninth day of the fourth month, and the Assyrian staff headed by Nergal-sharezer "came and sat in the middle gate" (JER. 39:3). No such gate is mentioned anywhere else, so that cannot have been its only name. If the breach was made on the north side of the city, as seems probable, since that side was the most favorable for siege operations, the middle gate would presumably be the "Ephraim Gate" (cf. 2 KINGS. 14:13; 2 CHRON. 25:23), lying between the northwest "Corner Gate" and the temple quadrangle. Others put it at the Fish Gate of the second wall, probably built by Hezekiah and Manasseh. That gate will have been situated where the depression dividing the western and eastern ridges, the Tyropoeon Valley, begins.

The narrative, after reporting the breach of the outer wall, states that Zedekiah and his men fled by night toward the Jordan Valley. They went out of the city by way of the gate between the walls, by the king's gardens (2 KINGS 25:4). It seems to us most probable that this was the Dung Gate. The two walls are then to be understood as follows: the first is the wall of the acropolis that lined the western rim of the eastern hill. The second is the long wall leading westward across the Tyropoeon Valley from the Dung Gate (called "Potsherd Gate" in JER. 19:2). A wall fitting the requirements and running to a junction with a younger wall *encircling* the western hill was discovered by Bliss and Dickie in their excavations of 1894–97. If that was the situation, the southern end of the Tyropoeon Valley could quite properly be described as "between the walls."

Issuing forth at the Dung Gate, the fleeing soldiers had to turn left around the base of the City of David to get to the Kidron Valley. They certainly had to break through the Chaldean line at this point. They then reached the "King's Garden," evidently a little "paradise" that the kings had created for themselves in imitation of the gardens the Assyrian monarchs. Hastening through this garden area, which was devastated by the besiegers, Zedekiah and his force poured down into the *Wadi en Nār*. Zedekiah was later caught by the Chaldeans.

Forsaken by king and defenders, the city was stormed and looted. The commanding general sent Zedekiah to Nebuchadnezzar at Riblah in Syria.

Here Zedekiah was judged. He got away with his life, but his little sons were slain before his eyes and he was then blinded and taken to Babylon in chains (2 KINGS 25:20).

Destruction of the City

The victorious Chaldean troops had to await orders as to the next step. Nebuzaradan brought the necessary instructions (2 KINGS

25:8). The Temple and palaces of Jerusalem and all large buildings were burned with fire, and the walls of the city were razed. The remnant of those trapped in the city and the deserters were taken to Babylon. Only vine dressers and farmers were allowed to remain in the land. The prophet Jeremiah, who was among the prisoners of war, was sought out and interviewed by Nebuzaradan, at the command of the king, and given his freedom (JER. 40:1–5).

Governor Gedaliah

Nebuchadnezzar appointed a native governor over those who were allowed to remain in Judah: Gedaliah, the grandson of a man who had occupied a high office under Josiah (2 KINGS 22:8). He must have been one of those who, like Jeremiah, had been opposed to the rebellion.

The provincial seat of government was at Mizpah. This presumably implies that Mizpah had not been burned to the ground. Jeremiah chose to cast his lot with those at Mizpah instead of accepting the invitation of King Nebuchadnezzar to go to Babylonia (JER. 40:6).

Various groups of soldiers from outlying areas now began to show up at Mizpah with their officers. Gedaliah reassured them with a solemn oath that they need not be afraid of Chaldean reprisals, and urged them to settle down to do their farming. Refugees who had fled to Moab, Ammon, Edom, and other lands, likewise started to come in.

Unfortunately, one of the demobilized army officers, a man named Ishmael, who was even of royal blood, had been incited by the Ammonite king Baalis to murder Gedaliah. Ishmael and his confederates, after carrying out their plot, seem to have established a reign of terror in Mizpah, though the meaning and purpose of all this is far from clear. They even slew seventy out of a group of eighty Israelites who were en route to the ruined Temple. The story seemingly implies the proximity of Mizpah to the highway coming down from Shechem and beyond. This excellently fits the situation of *Tell en Naṣbeh*.

The news of Gedaliah's death was, however, carried to Johanan and the other officers living in outlying places. They gathered swiftly and took up the pursuit of Ishmael, who had meanwhile departed from Mizpah with the population. They overtook him "by the great waters that are in Gibeon" (JER. 41:12). The emigrants all forsook Ishmael and placed themselves under the protection of Johanan and his fellow captains. Ishmael, however, escaped to the Ammonites with eight men.

The narrative is difficult to understand for we now know that Gibeon lay at *ej Jîb*. If Mizpah lay at *Tell en Naṣbeh,* Ishmael would be traveling in the wrong direction. We will confine ourselves to expressing the opinion that in Jeremiah 41:12 and 16 Gibeon is an error for Geba, as was the case in 2 Samuel 2:24. The "great [better, many] waters" would then be those of *el Fauwār*. The "great pool" of the Revised Standard Version rests on identification with the pool of 2 Samuel 2:13 (see page 192).

Prophet of the Fugitives

The murder of a governor appointed by Nebuchadnezzar and of some Chaldean soldiers was a serious business. Leaders like Johanan knew how such things were punished. Taking the liberated people under their wing they forsook the Mizpah neighborhood and fled southward past desolate Jerusalem to escape Chaldean vengeance.

Although Jeremiah prophesied that the people should stay in Palestine, the leaders had made up their minds to go to Egypt. Taking command of the situation, they led the group off to Egypt, compelling Jeremiah and his friend Baruch to go with them.

Thus, while a great migration of deportees was streaming toward the Euphrates, where the prophet Ezekiel and many leaders of Judah were awaiting them, this group, no doubt following many other bands of fugitives, took the track to the land of the Nile.

The Fate of the Mizpah Remnant

The objective reached in Egypt was Tahpanhes.

The location of Tahpanhes is known, for the later Hellenized form of the name, Daphne, survives to this day in *Tell Defenneh,* west of el Kantara. A prominent mound among the ruins was called by the natives "Palace of the daughter of the Jew." Some excavations were conducted there by Sir Flinders Petrie, which showed this "palace" to have been a strong fort. However, there must also have been a palace of the Pharaoh here, for Jeremiah performed a symbolic action at its entrance and predicted that Nebuchadnezzar would hold judgment on this spot. Ezekiel speaks of the pride of Tahpanhes (EZEK. 30:18), but like Jeremiah (JER. 43:9 f.) foresees the disaster for the city.

An utterance of Jeremiah concerning all the Jewish refugees in Egypt impressively concludes the ministry of the aged prophet to his people (JER. 44). The words are addressed to the Jews in Migdol, Tahpanhes, Noph and in the land of Pathros.

Migdol evidently is the Egyptian town nearest the continent of Asia in the northeast. The name is Canaanitic ("fortress"), and thus not the one which Egyptians themselves used. Whether the Migdol of the Exodus story (*Tell el Ḥēr*) is meant is not certain. At this time *Sin* (Pelusium) was the stronghold of Egypt (EZEK. 30:15 f.).

Noph is Memphis, the old Egyptian capital on the west bank of the Nile, south of Cairo. It is not surprising that there should have been a colony of Jewish exiles there. Pathros is viewed as the homeland of Egyptian sovereignty in Ezekiel 29:14—an echo, perhaps, of the Ethiopian domination. It appears as *Patures* in the inscriptions of the Assyrian conqueror Esarhaddon who called himself "king of the kings of *Muṣur, Patures* and Cush." It evidently specifies a district of southern Egypt. There were thus Jews who had gone up the Nile beyond Thebes.

The prophet uttered his solemn prediction that these refugees would all die by the sword, hunger and famine. He predicted, too, that Pharaoh Hophra, or Apries, (588–569 B.C.) would perish.

The story of the Mizpah exiles breaks off rather suddenly. Its continuation may have seemed irrelevant to the editors of the Book of Jeremiah and was left out. However, Josephus knew a longer version and on the basis of it gives a résumé of what happened. It seems that in 582 B.C. Nebuchadnezzar subjected the Ammonites and Moabites. He thereupon also invaded Egypt, so the report says. But there has been a telescoping of events, for that invasion did not take place until much later. Apparently the long siege of Tyre occupied him until about 570 B.C. (cf. EZEK. 29:18). That siege turned out more successful than Ezekiel anticipated.

As the prophet saw, time was ripe for a reckoning with Egypt. In 569 B.C. Pharaoh Hophra went to aid the Libyans against the Greeks, who had established themselves on the African coast at Cyrene. He was defeated and a rebellion broke out in his army, a part of which elevated Amasis as Pharaoh. In a battle fought between the opposing groups in 569 B.C., Amasis prevailed over Hophra. The latter was able to co-exist with his rival for some time but then was put to death. Thus were fulfilled the words of Jeremiah, who had said "he will fall into the hands of his enemies and into the hands of those who seek his life" (JER. 44:30).

However, Nebuchadnezzar availed himself of the prevailing rebellion and confusion to invade Egypt. It can hardly be doubted that he actually set up his court at the palace of Tahpanhes, as Jeremiah 43:8 f. predicted, and meted out death sentences there. When this narrative of Jeremiah 43 was written, furthermore, the terrible disasters that Jeremiah had predicted for the Jews of Egypt must have come true.

BABYLON TO JERUSALEM

The DESIGN on the preceding page shows a Persian king and procession of his spearmen from Persepolis relief, and writing on a silver tablet from foundation deposit at Persepolis.

LEFT, *head of a servant of Sargon.* (B. Meissner) MIDDLE LEFT, *"The handwriting on the wall" appeared in this language and must have looked something like this.* MIDDLE RIGHT, *Tiglathpileser III and his shield-bearer.* (B. Meissner) BOTTOM, *an Aramaic papyrus roll with seal and strings still in place.* (Brooklyn Museum)

CHAPTER XVI

IN THE LAND OF EXILE

THE LOT OF THE EXILES was bitter. A vivid remembrance of it lingers in the words of a psalmist: by the waters of Babylon they sat and wept; harps hanging on the willows; taunted by their captors; hearts filled with hatred for the Edomites, whose savage treatment of their land and its survivors had been reported to them (Ps. 137). All direct knowledge about the areas to which they were taken or about events that transpired has been completely lost. The only clues we have as to where some captives lived are a few places mentioned long afterward as the points of origin of some groups that returned from the captivity. Thus we hear of men from Tel-melah, Tel-harsha, Cherub, Addan and Immer, who were unable to prove their Israelite (Jewish) origin (EZRA 2:59), and of Casiphia where temple servants lived (EZRA 8:17). Speculations as to the whereabouts of these places is futile until the inscriptions provide us with better clues than is the case so far.

Ezekiel's Prophecy

In his contemplation of the future of the community restored in Palestine, Ezekiel foresaw new historical crises, but he believed that the people would be so godly and under such godly leadership that the LORD himself would put to nought all external foes. He anticipates a great invasion by Gog—a figure of the future that is evidently modeled on one of the past, namely King Gyges of Lydia (689–654 B.C.), whose name appears in the Assyrian inscriptions as *Gūg(u)*. That ruler evidently lingered in popular memory as a terrible scourge. For Ezekiel, Gog, or one of that name, is the future chief prince of Meshech and Tubal (*Mushki* and *Tabali*) in the regions west of the upper Euphrates (see page 48 and Color Map XI). Other peoples of Genesis 10 likewise appear in Gog's retinue. The LORD has already appointed a grave for Gog in the land of Israel "in the valley of the passengers [better, the travelers] on the east of the sea" (Hamon-gog). The rendering "east of the sea" is too explicit; the words need only mean *before* the sea" or near it. The sea referred to is probably the Lake of Galilee, and "the valley of travelers" must then be the "valley of the Violent Ones" (*Wadi Fejjās*) through which the "Way of the Hauranians" passes.

The restored community was to live in "the glory of all lands" (EZEK. 20:6, 15, i.e., the most glorious land) and thus had to have a suitable capital city with a temple and a supporting area. All this Ezekiel projected in his record of a vision granted him in the spring of 572 B.C. In that connection he speaks of a marvelous spring that would rise from the Temple (i.e., "the house") in the Messianic future. It was to be discernible at first as a mere trickle emerging from under the wall near the East Gate, but was soon to become rivulet, brook and river and turn the Dead Sea into living water, where fishermen could ply their trade from "En-gedi to En-eglaim" (EZEK. 47:10). En-gedi (see page 187) is evidently the southernmost of the two points named. En-eglaim is commonly believed to be the old name of *'Ain Feshkha*, situated close to *Wadi Qumrān*.

Ezekiel's blueprint also contained divinely fixed boundaries (EZEK. 47:15 f.). What he wants is a restoration of the united kingdom as it had existed in the days of David, except for the former possessions east of the Jordan. The northern limits given are important.

Daniel

In the Old Testament there is also preserved a book that tells of a Jew named Daniel (after an ancient wise man, EZEK. 14:14), who is said to have risen to prominence under the Chaldaeans and who continued to

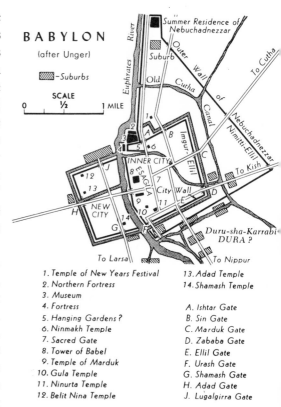

BABYLON
(after Unger)

▨ -Suburbs

SCALE
0   ½   1 MILE

1. Temple of New Years Festival	13. Adad Temple
2. Northern Fortress	14. Shamash Temple
3. Museum	
4. Fortress	A. Ishtar Gate
5. Hanging Gardens?	B. Sin Gate
6. Ninmakh Temple	C. Marduk Gate
7. Sacred Gate	D. Zababa Gate
8. Tower of Babel	E. Ellil Gate
9. Temple of Marduk	F. Urash Gate
10. Gula Temple	G. Shamash Gate
11. Ninurta Temple	H. Adad Gate
12. Belit Nina Temple	J. Lugalgirra Gate

enjoy high rank under the Persians. Nebuchadnezzar is described as recruiting young Jewish captives for his service (DAN. 1:3 f.), among whom Daniel proved outstanding.

In 1926 E. Unger published a roster of the high officials of Nebuchadnezzar as of around 570 B.C. It mentions the Nergalsharezer and Nebuzaradan of Jeremiah 39:13, but does not contain Daniel's name or that of any other Jew or Canaanite, except possibly that of the treasurer Ḥanunu.

The Image in the Plain of Dura

The interesting third chapter of Daniel tells of a golden image that Nebuchadnezzar set up "in the plain of Dura." The plain is of course named after a town that lay in it, for the word means "The Wall" and, as a name, is an abridgment (cf. Dur-Kurigalza, the city founded by a Cassite king, Kurigalzu). The abridged use is also illustrated by the Dura of Hellenistic times far up the Euphrates, where important finds were made by the Yale University Expedition. It seems attractive to connect this Dura of the Daniel narrative with a suburb of Babylon named *Duru sha-karrabi* (see map, page 322), which no doubt was popularly referred to as *Duru* and in Aramaic as Dura. One had to pass through this place when leaving the city via the Ellil Gate to go in the direction of Nippur. A location within easy reach of the capital is certainly required by the story.

Nebuchadnezzar's command that all should worship the image set up sounds very much like the introduction of a new chief god by royal fiat. It seems possible, however, that tradition here has credited Nebuchadnezzar with something that was really done by the last king of the Chaldean Dynasty, Nabonidus. A Babylonian text, which defames that ruler and seeks to justify the treason of the priesthood in betraying the country into the hands of a foreign conqueror, accuses Nabonidus of setting up a barbarous image.

The story of the three young men who were thrown into the fire because they would not worship the image (DAN. 3), brings to mind the great brick-kilns outside the city, where the bricks required for certain purposes in the vast building projects of Nebuchadnezzar were baked. Some of these great ovens were found in the excavations. Worth noting in this connection is a rather Solomonic judicial directive of the ruler Rim Sin (1750 B.C.), which appears in a recently published document of the Yale Babylonian Collection. He speaks thus concerning four men of Larsa: "Because they threw a young slave into an oven, throw ye a slave into a furnace." Clearly, that sort of thing was nothing new in Babylonia.

Is Not This Great Babylon?

Nebuchadnezzar, as just stated, was a mighty builder and many of his inscriptions commemorating his building-activities have come to light. Temples and temple-towers in various Babylonian cities were restored by him in great splendor. Above all, he lavished his attention on Babylon, its temples and palaces. The Biblical story of Daniel remembers this, when it describes him as boasting of his city's greatness, while walking on the roof of the royal palace (DAN. 4:50).

This Babylon of Nebuchadnezzar has been revealed at least partially by the great excavations carried on by Robert Koldewey in the decade before 1914.

A glance at the plan, page 322, will help us to visualize the Babylon of the times referred to in the Book of Daniel.

One distinctive contribution of Nebuchadnezzar was the *Ishtar Gate,* lying alongside the palace district, at the street intersection between the "south" and "main" palaces. Another was the laying out of the street that comes in from the direction of Akkad and leads past the "Gate of God" and the gates of the Marduk temple beyond it on the right.

The structure of the Ishtar gateway was covered with glazed bricks, exhibiting a row

6.1 *Dura-Europus where important finds were made from Hellenistic times. (Courtesy Institut Francais d'Archéologie, Beyrouth, Liban)*

of dragons and bulls in color, and the high and immensely thick walls of the palace, flanking the highway south of the gate, showed forth a parade of lions. An elaborate pavement seventy-five feet wide, named "May the foe not win the victory," went as far as "the Gate of God." Along this avenue came the great procession on the New Year's festival, when the gods conducted their king, Marduk, to his temple. It was a gala occasion and had great political importance, for at it the king "seized the hands of Marduk" and thereby was granted a renewal of his royal privileges for a year.

The palace of Nabopolassar, which had been damaged in its foundations by the Euphrates freshets, was replaced by Nebuchadnezzar with the entirely new southern palace that rose "like a forested height" and that was considerably enlarged on the eastern side. Nebuchadnezzar called it "the Palace at which Men Marvel." He made the city virtually impregnable. It is one of the ironies of history that a generation after his time it was to fall into foreign hands because of the dissatisfaction of its populace with its ruler.

Nebuchadnezzar's Dwelling
with the Beasts of the Field

One of the most intriguing of the Aramaic stories of the Book of Daniel is that relating how Nebuchadnezzar was driven from men till seven "times" (years) passed over him (DAN. 4:24 f.). The history of this king gives no inkling of any such prolonged absence from his throne, but that of his fourth successor, Nabonidus, does illustrate this very excellently, as we shall soon hear. Many scholars, therefore, believe that this incident, like the one about the image, has been transferred from the lesser to the greater figure.

Events under Nebuchadnezzar
and His Successors

The Chronicle text for the reign of Nebuchadnezzar does not extend beyond 594 B.C. He put down a rebellion in Babylonia in 595 B.C., and we have already heard that he invaded Egypt in the thirty-seventh year of his reign (568–567 B.C.) The period allotted to him comes to an end in 562 B.C.

Nebuchadnezzar was followed by Amel-Marduk (561–560 B.C.), whose name is given as Evil-merodach in the Bible. He is mentioned there because in the year that he began to reign, he mercifully freed King Jehoiachin from prison and dealt kindly with him (2 KINGS 25:27–30). If the date of this liberation is correctly given, it took place in April, 561 B.C. This was just before the first New Year's celebration of the new Babylonian ruler—a suitable time for acts of amnesty.

Evil-merodach's reign ended when it had hardly begun. He sought to curb the power of the priesthood, which therefore turned against him. Neriglissar thereupon seized the throne (558–555 B.C.). A new chronicle text tells of Neriglissar's campaign of 557 B.C. to Cilicia, where a rebellion had broken out. He even carried out the capture of a rocky island off the coast that was garrisoned with six thousand men—a most respectable military feat. He continued in the pious spirit of Nebuchadnezzar. His son and successor, Labashi-Marduk, however, was murdered after a few months. The man who replaced him was Nabonidus (555–539 B.C.).

Nabonidus and Belshazzar

Nabonidus came from Assyria. His father was a prince in that country, which now was under Median rule.

Nabonidus was particularly devoted to the moon-god Sin of Haran and to his temple E-khul-khul, of which his mother had been high priestess. This was displeasing to the priesthood of Marduk of Babylon. It seemed to them as though he were seeking to set up the moon-god Sin as chief god in place of Marduk.

The Last Years of Babylon

Due, perhaps, to this rift with the priesthood and the peril of assassination, Nabonidus absented himself from Babylon for seven years, not even returning for the New Year's festival for reinstatement in office. He built for himself a city and splendid palace at Tema in Amurru (the West-land). That this is the Arabian Tema of the Old Testament (cf. page 74) and identical with the oasis of *Teima* (Color Map XI, D-4), has now been made certain by stelas of Nabonidus found in the moon-temple of Haran in 1957. On these he speaks of his exile and mentions a campaign to *Yatribu*. This is without doubt the *Yathrib* to which a thousand years later Mohammed went on leaving Mecca; it is more commonly called Medinah. Teima has been rarely visited, owing to the hostility of the Arab population. Charles Huber, who in 1880 found an Aramaic inscription there of a priest of the gods of Tema, lost his life in securing it. The fathers Jaussen and Savignac state that the perimeter of the city walls, now in ruins, is about three kilometers.

That the story of DAN. 4 has been transferred secondarily from Nabonidus to Nebuchadnezzar has now been made clear by a Dead Sea Scroll fragment published in 1956 and called *The Prayer of Nabonidus*. It begins:

> The words of the prayer which Nabonidus (*Nbny*), king of Assyria and king of Babylon, the great king, spoke when he was smitten with a severe inflammation by the command of the Most High God in the city of Teiman (error for Tema): I was smitten for seven years and I was put far from men. But when I confessed my trespasses and sins he left me a seer. He was a Jew from the exiles of Babylonia. He gave his explanation and wrote that honor should be given and glory to the name of the Most High God.

The seer states that the king had prayed (in vain) to the gods of silver, gold, bronze, iron, wood, stone, and clay. The text breaks off at this point. No doubt it told how the king was healed when he praised the Most High (cf. DAN. 4:34 ff.).

The "King Belshazzar" of DAN. 5 was the crown prince. In Babylonian texts he is always called "son of the king."

Shadow of Things to Come

Revolutionary events on the world stage are bound to call into action the military powers of the age. We saw how at the time of the fall of Assyria, Egyptian armies intervened in far-off Syria and Mesopotamia (see page 311). It seems probable that Nabonidus' stay at Tema was not without relevance to what was going on in the outside world in his day, and that he occupied a position from which he could intervene in Mesopotamia, whether that was threatened by Egyptians or by a new rising power.

Lydia had since around 687 B.C. been the dominant state in western Asia Minor under the Mermnad Dynasty. While Gyges its great king had perished in trying to repel the Cimmerian invasion (*c.* 657 B.C.), his successors expanded their control eastward to the Halys River, and under Croesus (560–546 B.C.) subjected the whole coast of Asia Minor in the west.

Even more formidable was Media in the north. Media had received northern Mesopotamia as spoil, when Kyaxares and Nabopolassar divided the Assyrian realm between them, and from Ecbatana had expanded its power far eastward over the Iranian lands.

Both empires were about to fall, and we may be sure Nabonidus was watching the events very closely. He was not the only one who did so. The Jewish exiles, too, were watching the happenings with bated breath. A prophet, whose name is unknown, proclaimed that a new order was at hand and sent faith and hope tingling through the hearts of the captives. His prophecies were later appended to the Book of Isaiah (in chapters 40–55), and so scholars call him Deutero-Isaiah (or Second Isaiah). He exults over the coming fall of Babylon. If he speaks

6.2 *Tomb of Cyrus.* (*Courtesy Oriental Institute, University of Chicago*)

of a highway through the desert (Is. 40:3–4), the road Nabonidus built to Tema may have suggested the idea.

A Servant of the LORD and His Home

For Deutero-Isaiah a man named Cyrus was the Anointed of the LORD and the prospective bringer of redemption for those suffering in captivity (Is. 44:28; 45:1).

Cyrus was a subject king of the Median ruler Astyages. In the years 559–550 B.C., he built for himself a capital in the Iranian province of *Fars* at what the Greeks call Pasargadae (today *Meshhed i Murghab*). It lay in a plain of over five thousand feet elevation, northeast of the ranges separating it from the slightly lower plain in which Persepolis lay.

Part of the monumental gate of a palace still stands upright and shows the sculpture of a four-winged genius as the guardian of the gate. Above it there stood (until 1840) the inscription "I, Cyrus, the king, the Achaemenid," a general building inscription that had no specific connection with the relief, for the latter does not portray Cyrus as was long supposed, but rather a winged genius. Two hundred yards north of this gate is the Apadana or Audience Hall, marked by a single standing pillar forty feet high. On its account the ruins of the building that once stood here are called "the Palace of the Pillar."

West of the so-called "hill of the throne" (*Tul-i-Takht*) which constituted a fortress, an ancient highway leads off to Persepolis. Along this road, two-thirds of a mile south of the monumental gateway referred to above, lies the tomb of Cyrus, a small counterpart of the temple which was excavated

by Herzfeld in 1928. This is well known as one of the great places of the world.

Hammer Strokes of History

Cyrus had rebelled against his Median overlord in 553 B.C. and in 550 B.C. the Median army betrayed its king into his hands. He thus took over the Median capital Ecbatana and therewith the empire and its organization. He did not immediately turn his attention southward but rather to the west. He destroyed the Lydian Empire of Croesus by capturing Sardis in 546 B.C. This accomplished, he could move on Mesopotamia and Babylonia. Nabonidus had seized the Median property of Haran, where the rebuilding of the Temple of the Moon was a project dear to his heart. That may have led to the outbreak of hostilities.

For the year that saw the death of the king's mother (547 B.C.), whom some identify with the Nitocris of Greek legend, the Nabonidus Chronicle adds that in the spring Cyrus mobilized his troops and crossed the Tigris below Arbela. He occupied a city, the name of which is lost, and garrisoned it. It seems probable that all Mesopotamia was in

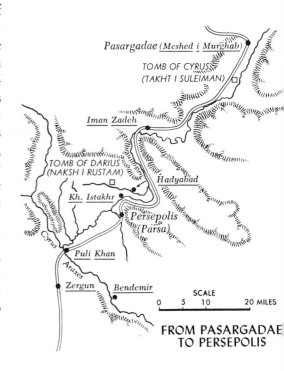

FROM PASARGADAE TO PERSEPOLIS

THE PALACE OF NEBUCHADNEZZAR

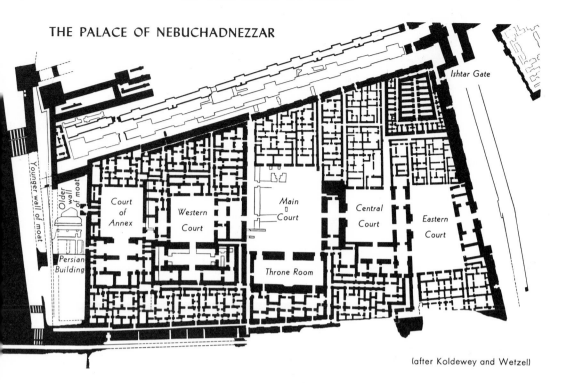

Ishtar Gate

Younger wall of moat

Old wall of moat

Court of Annex

Western Court

Main Court

Central Court

Eastern Court

Persian Building

Throne Room

(after Koldewey and Wetzel)

Cyrus' hands before he took the decisive step of invading Babylonia itself in 539 B.C.

Belshazzar's Feast

The fifth chapter of the Book of Daniel thinks of Belshazzar, who acted for so long as his father's representative, as the last king of the Chaldean Dynasty. The story of his feast conjures up the palaces of Babylon. The king may be imagined as celebrating his festivities in the southern or old palace, which was the one in which most affairs of state were conducted. The drawing gives a clear picture of the ground-plan of this palace, as revealed by the excavations. One entered it from the street leading to the Ishtar gate. On the south is the largest hall, the throne-room. It is fifty-six feet wide by one hundred and seventy-three feet long—a veritable ball-room suited for great public occasions. There was a large middle entrance and there were two side entrances, and the outer side was beautifully adorned with glazed bricks showing a pillar design on a blue background. In the rear wall opposite the middle entrance was a niche, once occupied no

doubt by the royal throne. Those waiting outside in front of the central door could thus see the king, much as one could see the image of the deity from the doorway of the Temple of Ninmakh. The walls of this throne-room were of white plaster. Here should be localized the great banquet of Daniel 5 and the mysterious Aramaic handwriting on the wall (see page 320).

It has often been noticed that the inscription that so alarmed Belshazzar, as given in Daniel 5:25, does not accord too well with the interpretation given in the verses that follow. From that commentary it would seem that it ought to read *"Mene, Tekel, Peres,"* whereas it was previously given as *"Mene, Mene, Tekel, Upharsin";* it is very probable that someone has improved on the original shorter reading, with an eye to a different application. The shorter reading of the commentary makes the whole thing very plain. At first sight a reader of the unvocalized words *mn', tql, prs* would think that they were the familiar nouns used every day in business dealings, "Mina, Shekel, half-mina." Daniel saw that they could be read as passive participles of the corresponding verbs and mean "numbered, weighed, divided." In the longer version of verse 25 this is not so clear. *"Upharsin"* can mean "and half-minas" or "and portions."

The Fall of Babylon

Neither the Biblical narrative of the fall of Babylon nor the accounts handed down in Greek sources, though justifiable in the light of subsequent minor uprisings, really give the full story of the initial downfall of the great Babylonian empire under the attack of Cyrus. Cyrus is not mentioned at all by Daniel. Instead Darius the Mede is made Babylon's conqueror. "Mede" was often used for "Persian" by those living at a distance, for the Persian realm could be regarded as a mere continuation of the Median. We find the author of the Hebrew chapters, which were appended to the older Aramaic ones, declaring that Darius was the son of Ahasuerus, by birth a Mede (DAN. 9:1). The latter assertion may only be an inference from the fact that Darius was called the Mede in Daniel 5:31. The writer was also confused as to the history of the Achaemenid kings, for Xerxes is the son of Darius and not vice versa. In claiming that Darius the Mede had conquered Babylon, the old Aramaic story is not entirely mistaken. Babylon rebelled against Persian rule after Cambyses' death and elevated Nebuchadnezzar III to the kingship. Darius, in all the campaigns he waged to get control of the empire, defeated this ruler in a series of battles, the decisive one taking place in December 522 B.C. That did not yet end matters, for Nebuchadnezzar IV continued the resistance, which was not overcome until a year later (November 521 B.C.). These events probably led the Jewish traditioners to link the fall of Babylon with Darius. But the story in Daniel has accurately retained remembrance of the overnight character of the collapse of Belshazzar's kingdom.

For the political and military situation leading up to Cyrus' taking of Babylon we must turn to the Babylonian sources, which for the present give the only light on the events. While there is a gap in the text of the Chronicle of Nabonidus after the eleventh year, we find the king back in Babylon in the seventeenth year (539 B.C.), where the text resumes. The New Year's festival was again completely celebrated in April. In October, Nabonidus met the forces of Cyrus in battle at Opis and was defeated. On the fourteenth of the month, Sippar was taken without battle, but Nabonidus, whose soldiers must have mutinied, managed to escape. The great Median wall running from the Euphrates to the Tigris west of Sippar was thus overrun by the Persians with the greatest of ease. On the sixteenth (October 14, 539 B.C.) Cyrus' general Gubaru (the Gobryas of the Greeks), governor of Gutium in the Zagros mountains, entered Babylon with his troops without battle. All this indicates that the land was honeycombed with treason. Nabonidus, again about to flee, was apparently caught in the city. The sacred areas were surrounded and guarded by the "shields of Gutium." On the third of the next month (October 29,) 539 B.C., Cyrus entered Babylon.

In his great cylinder inscription written in the Babylonian language, the Persian conqueror portrays himself as chosen by the god Marduk to make an end to the reign of terror that had prevailed under the evil Nabonidus. This clearly is a propaganda document composed by the Babylonian priests who had betrayed their national government to a foreign power. Nabonidus' share in the blame is, of course, great, since he originated the policies that aroused so much opposition.

It is a mystery how the vast historical transformation effected by Cyrus was possible, just as it is a mystery how the civilized eastern lands, more than a thousand years later, could fall to a handful of half-civilized Arabs. The Old Testament answer to the former problem was given by Deutero-Isaiah (Is. 45:1–3).

CHAPTER XVII

THE RECONSTRUCTION

At the beginning of the Book of Ezra there is quoted a proclamation or edict of Cyrus (Ezra 1:2–4), given in his first year as king of Babylon. That year began March 24, 538 B.C. The edict is said to have been doubly promulgated by criers as well as in writing. The God of heaven, Cyrus declared, had instructed him to build him a temple at Jerusalem in Judah. Permission was granted to the Jews who so desired to go up to Jerusalem and join in the task of this building. The trip of such emigrants was to be financed by the fellow Jews of their locality, who were also to give a free-will offering for the said temple.

Certain Judaean and Benjaminite heads of families, along with priests and Levites, thereupon are said to have felt the impulse to go. The leader was "Sheshbazzar." He had a Babylonian pagan name, *Shamash-ab-*

uṣur ("may the sun-god preserve the father"). Some scholars would identify him with Shenazzar, the fourth son of Jehoiakim (cf. 1 Chron. 3:17), but it seems improbable that a fourth son would have been chosen for an office that might develop into a revived kingship. Sheshbazzar may not have been a Jew at all, but rather a Babylonian administrator. A Persian official named Mithredat delivered to him the vessels of the Temple at Jerusalem, which had once been carried away by Nebuchadnezzar. Who Mithredat was, remains unexplained. We know from Babylonian sources that *Gubaru* (Gobryas), who played a role in connection with the fall of Babylon, was Cyrus' commissioner for the re-establishment of cults.

In a later connection we hear that there was not only an edict of Cyrus but also a "decree" or "memorandum" (Ezra 6:3 f.).

This is the term for a record of an official decree or decision. Such a decision naturally preceded any formulation of an edict for public announcement and was filed away with all other memoranda of royal decisions. In this memorandum it was recorded that Cyrus had in his first year commanded the rebuilding of the house of God at Jerusalem, prescribing its dimensions and the manner of its building, and directing that the costs be borne by the royal treasury. Also, he had ordered that the vessels which Nebuchadnezzar had taken from the Temple be given back to it.

Since the edict of Ezra 1:2-4 does not contain all the items mentioned in the memorandum, it seems probable that we do not have the original text of the edict, but merely a restatement of it. The text would in any case have been in the Aramaic language rather than in Hebrew.

It is strange that we hear nothing of how the Jews responded to Cyrus' edict. Instead, Ezra 2 offers a list of names of men and groups, giving the impression that these were the people who went back to Palestine with Sheshbazzar. Actually, however, this list, of which another copy is found in Nehemiah 7, was originally set up for a different purpose. As for the things commanded in the "memorandum," we hear only of the procurement of lumber needed to carry out the rebuilding of the Temple (EZRA 3:7). We learn in that passage that cedar logs were brought down from the Lebanon via the sea to Japho or *Jaffa*. The mention of Japho may be regarded as a rough approximation. It seems likely that the logs were brought into the mouth of the Yarkon River (Mejarkon, JOSH. 19:46) north of Japho to the town represented by *Tell Qasīle,* a site at which excavations were conducted in 1948-50 by B. Mazar and the Israel Exploration Society. The place was founded *c.* 1200 B.C.

According to Ezra 3, it is the community of 520 B.C. rather than of 538 B.C. that set up the Temple and altar—the things Sheshbazzar and his group were supposed to do. This is quite puzzling and the explanation can only be hypothetical. It is conceivable that Sheshbazzar's efforts to carry out Cyrus' order were thwarted by the same groups that later sought to prevent Nehemiah from executing his commission. What became of Sheshbazzar is unknown. His commission may have expired with the death of Cyrus or of Cambyses.

The Historical Background

Cyrus reigned until 529 B.C. but was succeeded by Cambyses (529-522 B.C.). The latter undertook a successful campaign to subjugate Egypt, which he put under a special satrap. He died from the consequences of an accidental wound—allegedly at an "Agbatana in Syria." If the reference of the Greek historian who states this were dependable that might mean Gibbethon in Palestine (see page 273), but the report may be partly false and Ecbatana in Media may be meant.

During Cambyses' absence a Magian impostor named Gaumata seized the throne, claiming to be Smerdis (*Bardiya*), a younger brother whom Cambyses had had secretly put out of the way. The Persian empire was shaken to its very foundation, for revolts broke out everywhere. In this dire situation a scion of another branch of the Achaemenid house, Darius I, assassinated Gaumata, in September, 522 B.C., and seized the throne.

Rarely has any king faced such a Herculean task as Darius. This ruler celebrated his triumph and gave a detailed account of the events in the relief and inscriptions carved into the face of a mountain, near the village of Behistun on the road from Baghdad to Hamadan. The inscription, in three languages—Persian, Elamite and Babylonian—is the longest and most important Achaemenid inscription known. The relief shows the king stepping on the prostrate Gaumata, behind whom are standing nine other bound rebels, the second of whom is the Babylonian

Nebuchadnezzar III, who was defeated in December, 522 B.C. The king with a motion of his hand wards off any suggestion of mercy for these captives. Overhead is the symbol of Ahuramazda, which is much like the symbol of the old chief god of Assyria.

The inscription also looks back on the rebellion of Nebuchadnezzar IV, who was defeated in November, 521 B.C., and on the expedition against the Scythians (summer of 519 B.C.). Not included, however, is the expedition in the winter of 519–18 B.C. against Egypt, where a rebellion had also broken out.

Zerubbabel

The curtain that shrouds Jewish events is briefly lifted in the second year of Darius, thanks to Ezra 4:24–5:2, and the Books of Haggai and Zechariah (chapters 1—8), which provide both the chronology and further insight. The community now had a governor named Zerubbabel ("seed of Babylon," and hence born there), a grandson of Jehoiachin—son of that ruler's first-born Shealtiel (1 CHRON. 3:17). He is referred to as "governor of Judah" (HAG. 1:1, etc.), or "the Tirshatha" (EZRA 2:63), a Persian title meaning "his excellency." The time of his appointment and the scope of his authority are in doubt. It seems likely, however, that he was appointed by Darius, who on seizing the throne must have filled all governorships with men sworn to him.

A scion of the House of David, the real heir-apparent to its vacant throne, Zerubbabel would seem to have been the logical man to manage the situation in Judah. Many Jews may have returned to Palestine with him, in expectancy of winning important posts in the event of a restoration of the monarchy. The rebellions in Babylon led by Nebuchadnezzar III and IV may have created a serious crisis for those who were supporters of the Persian empire. It is noteworthy that Deutero-Isaiah calls on the Jews to flee Babylonia (Is. 48:20), and that Zechariah too advises such a course (ZECH. 2:6 f.). The Persian crisis will have stirred the religiously oriented among the Jews to ask whether the great turning point of history had now arrived, of which the prophets had prophesied. Indeed, prophecy was not dead yet, but produced several men schooled in the old manner, who attempted to read the signs of the times and divine the will of the LORD. Thus on August 29, 520 B.C., a prophet named Haggai arose and called on Zerubbabel to take action in the matter of rebuilding the Temple (HAG. 1:2–4).

The movement thus initiated is successful. Work on the Temple is again begun. The foundation is laid December 18, 520 B.C. (HAG. 2:18). As the labor proceeded, so Ezra 5:1 f. relates, Tattenai, the governor of the province "Beyond the River" came (? or wrote), demanding to know by what authority the Jews were doing this building, and also to obtain the names of the men engaged in the building project.

The cuneiform inscriptions have confirmed the existence of this Tattenai, though for a later date, for a text from Babylon written June 5, 502 B.C., mentions a slave of *Ta-at-[-tan-ni]*, governor of "Beyond the River." The name itself has been previously vindicated by a text referring to "Tattannai, prefect of Susa." Possibly Tattenai has been confused with *Ushtanni,* who according to Babylonian texts was governor of "Babylon and beyond the River" and whose first recorded date is March 21, 520 B.C.

The "Golah" List

In this connection the list of Ezra 2 (-Nehemiah 7) may have a significance. The editor who put the list in its present position interpreted it as a list of returned captives, but it does not have the typical form of such a return document (cf. EZRA 8:1); it seems rather to be in the nature of an account of the communities supporting the Jewish Temple. It itemizes the number of men at the various outlying places. We see, therefore, that not just Jerusalem, but Judah itself (including Benjamin and some Ephraimite territory) was being re-established. The list, one may infer, was drawn up to satisfy the inquiries of the Persian governor of the whole Syro-Palestinian satrapy "Beyond the River" as to the groups under the command of the local governor who were willing to support the rebuilding of the Temple.

The Satrap Steps In

The letter of Tattenai to Darius (EZRA 5:6–17) reports the assertion of the Jews that Cyrus had permitted the rebuilding of their Temple, and suggests a verification of this with the aid of the archives at Babylon. A memorandum (see page 329) was thereupon found, not in Babylon but in Ecbatana (Aramaic, *Ahmetha*) in Media (EZRA 6:2). That this record was found there instead of at Babylon is a fact that seems beyond invention. It is quite reasonable, too, for with the fall of the Median empire in 550 B.C. and of Babylon in 539 B.C. Pasargadae can no longer have seen much of Cyrus. He will have spent the summer in Ecbatana and the winter in Babylon. It would thus be necessary to look up records of the acts of Cyrus in both places.

This reference to the Median capital is the only one found in the Old Testament. The apocryphal Book of Judith (1:1–4) gives a brief description of the fortifications of Ecbatana constructed by a legendary king Arphaxad, who ruled over the Medes. Herodotus tells a fanciful tale of the seven walls of Ecbatana. According to a more realistic report (by the Greek historian Polybius) the city had no wall at all, but its acropolis was astonishingly well fortified. Beneath it lay the palace area, four-fifths of a mile in circumference, which is less than that of Persepolis (one and a half miles).

Ecbatana lay on the site now covered by *Hamadan,* and native treasure-digging in the houses has brought to light numerous precious Achaemenid objects, such as gold and silver tablets with inscriptions of Darius, a golden goblet with an inscription of Xerxes and the gold tablet of Darius' great-grandfather Ariyaramna.

The roll found in Ecbatana (EZRA 6:3–5) vindicated the Jewish claims, and so Darius ordered that the Jews be permitted to continue their activity unmolested. Even more, he decreed that they were to receive subsidy from the taxes of the province "Beyond the River," and that sacrifices were to be brought there daily at government expense on behalf of the life of the king and his children (EZRA 6:6–12). All this sounds perfectly credible in the light of Darius' special interest in Egypt at this time, and the general desirability of creating more stable and prosperous conditions in the adjacent regions.

The project of rebuilding the Temple was evidently carried through and the work completed March 13, 515 B.C. (EZRA 6:15). It thus was in readiness for the (Babylonian) New Year's Festival of 515 B.C. that began a few weeks later. Zerubbabel, however, seems to have gotten into trouble with the Persians by nurturing hopes of a restoration of the Davidic throne.

An Incident from the Reign of Xerxes

Once the Persians had taken over the entire Chaldean realm and liberated the captive groups from the controls exercised by their captors, the Jews were able to move about freely like other people, and the path of progress was open to them. Many of them came to Susa which increasingly became the real administrative center of the Persian empire. In the course of time this Jewish community became wealthy and influential. In Hellenistic times it celebrated a festival called Purim at which was rehearsed the tale of Esther, allegedly queen of Ahasuerus or Xerxes (485–465 B.C.).

The name of Xerxes is carved indelibly into the history of the world through his effort to subjugate Greece. The invasion, by arousing Greek patriotism, had a vast stimulus on subsequent history. The foundation inscription of the harem built by Xerxes at Persepolis, discovered in 1931, revealed that he was not the first-born son, but that Darius himself chose him as successor and stepped down from the throne to make room for him.

The Glory That Was Susa

The tale of Esther puts Susa before the mind, and therewith one of earth's memorable cities. The name is written *Shushan* in Hebrew as well as in Assyrian, and these peoples no doubt thought that the name was derived from the word which in both languages means the lily. However, this is not the case, for Susa's name (really *Shushun*) is Elamitic and that tongue is totally unrelated to the Semitic family of languages.

The site of Susa was not lost sight of like that of Nineveh, for it still existed at the time of the Islamic conquest and only then fell into gradual decay. The name *Shush* continued to cling to the desolate mounds which lie fourteen miles south-southwest of *Dizful* by the *Shawūr* stream. It remained for Frenchmen under Dieulafoy, 1884–86, and De Morgan, 1908 f., to harvest the glory of Susa.

The most important Persian structure at *Shush* is the palace built by Darius I and rebuilt by Artaxerxes II. It was cleared in 1913. In 1929 there was published an elaborate inscription of Darius I commemorating and describing his building of this palace of Susa. It tells how workmen and materials from all over the realm were brought to this city for the great undertaking.

By the River Ulai

We have already noted the fact that part of the activities of the sage and prophet Daniel are given a background in the Persian era, and that Susa receives prominence in that connection. There we hear of the river Ulai (DAN. 8:2, 16), which is not referred to in the story of Esther. The same river name

6.3 *Ruins of Susa, ancient capital of Persia. "The Tomb of Daniel" can be seen by the banks of the* Shawur *(Saimarrah River). (United States Air Force Photo)*

appears in the Assyrian inscriptions. On the banks of this stream, near two towns which he mentions, Ashurbanipal's army fought a murderous battle with the army of King Teumman of Elam, and we learn that the corpses of the slain were cast into the Ulai. The Greeks reproduce the name as Eulaeus. Thus we read that Alexander the Great embarked at Susa and sailed down the Eulaeus to the Persian Gulf and along the gulf coast to the mouth of the Tigris. Now the Eulaeus is basically the *Karun* River, called Pasitigris in some Greek sources. How it was possible to sail down it from Susa to the gulf was long a perplexing question, since Susa is forty miles distant from the nearest point on the *Karun*. The mystery was solved in 1849 by Loftus, who heard from a native that formerly the *Kerkhah,* soon after its issuance from the mountains, divided into two parts, and that the eastern branch had flowed past *Shush* (about two miles to the east of it), and after absorbing the *Shawūr* at a point below a ford, had proceeded to a junction with the *Karun* at *Ahwaz*. In full accord with this tradition Loftus found the bed of the eastern and extinct branch of the *Kerkhah* on the road from *Dizful* to *Shush*. It was not less than nine hundred feet wide and had a depth varying from twelve to twenty feet. It could thus be considered an

6.4 *Palace of Darius at Persepolis (Courtesy Oriental Institute, University of Chicago)*

6.5 *Silver votive bowl of a King of Kedar (see page 337). (Courtesy Brooklyn Museum)*

upper reach of the Ulai or *Karun,* or again be called the *Kerkhah* or Choaspes—a circumstance accounting for the confusion in the reports of the classical authors as to the river on which Susa lay. It is the extinct side-channel of the *Kerkhah* that is meant when it is reported that Alexander sailed down the Eulaeus. It cannot be the *Shawūr* (which gets its name from the Sassanian king Shapur), though it skirts the mounds of *Shush* on the west, for according to Loftus that is "only a narrow stream, at certain seasons expended in cultivation before it forms a junction with the *Dizful* River."

If the Mohammedans show a tomb of Daniel beside the *Shawūr* it was evidently because they thought that this was the Ulai.

Persepolis

From Susa a road led up through mountain gorges to the high plateau in which Persepolis lies. It is unfortunate that we get no clear mention in the Bible of that city which Darius I made the capital of the Persian kings during the long hot season of the year. Its name was *Parsā,* and the name was extended to the region of which the city was the center; it is the region or people that is meant when the Bible refers to Paras. From Persepolis communications to Susa and Babylon were more swift and convenient than from Pasargadae—hence the abandonment of the latter place as a residence. The ruins of Persepolis are among the most noteworthy in the entire East. The building of a royal residence there was undertaken by Darius between 518 and 515 B.C.— at the very time when the Temple at Jeru-

salem was being rebuilt. The great terrace and the Audience Hall, as well as the main gateway and part of the city walls, which rested on a foundation of stone masonry sixty feet high, were undertaken by him. Xerxes finished what Darius had begun, and started construction of the Hall of a Hundred Columns, built a small palace of his own (see fig. 6.4 on this page), and also the Harem for which Darius had laid the foundation. Artaxerxes I completed the Hall of the Hundred Columns.

Excavations were begun at Persepolis in 1931 by Ernst Herzfeld and the Oriental Institute, and later continued by E. F. Schmidt. Particular attention was given from the outset to the area of the stairways leading up to the great terrace, of 1500 by 1000 feet dimension, on which stood the Audience Hall. Under twenty-six feet of rubbish and masonry were found a series of wall sculptures which, put together, would make a panel of reliefs five to six feet high and a thousand feet long. Originally all these sculptured figures were colored, and one well-protected relief of the Persian emperor showed him wearing garments hemmed with scarlet and purple. The theme of the whole series is to show the emperor receiving representatives of the twenty-one provinces of the empire with their gifts, no doubt at the occasion of the New Year's festival.

That Persepolis was "home" to the Achaemenids after Cyrus is underlined by the fact that they were buried there. In the hillside in the rear of the fortress are the tombs of Artaxerxes II and Artaxerxes III and the unfinished one of Darius III, whom

Alexander the Great drove out of his realm. Nearby, on the other side of the stream called the Pulwar, at *Naḳshi-i-Rustem* in the wall of a cliff, are the tombs of Darius I, Xerxes, Artaxerxes I and Darius II. Several of these tombs bear inscriptions and sculptures over their entrances.

Decisive Developments

Xerxes was followed by Artaxerxes I (465–425 B.C.). No inscription of Artaxerxes I was known—for not even his tomb at Persepolis bears one—until 1934 when one was published that had been found on a vessel that may once have been used by a colleague of Nehemiah to bring food to the king's table. It bore an old Persian inscription around half of its rim giving the king's name, his titles, and his lineage.

According to Ezra 4:7–23, fresh building operations were undertaken at Jerusalem under this ruler. It seems probable that the incident narrated took place at the beginning of his reign. Judah's neighbors, notably those of the adjacent province of Samaria, immediately lodged a complaint with Artaxerxes. A certain Rehum, who must be imagined as the governor of Samaria, and Shimshai the scribe (his executive secretary), protested on behalf of the aristocracy of their province. This is described as composed of Persians, men of Erech, Babylonians, men of Susa (that is, Elamites), and the rest of the nations whom Osnappar (Ashurbanipal) had deported and settled in the cities of Samaria and in other sections of the satrapy "Beyond the river." (Ezra 4:10). Nothing is said here of the people of the various cities originally brought to Samaria by Sargon II

(2 Kings 17:24). Evidently, then, there were subsequent deportations, including one under Esarhaddon (Ezra 4:2), and the descendants of these later arrivals now were more prominent than those of the earlier ones. In the letter sent by Rehum, which was written in Aramaic but was read to the king by a Persian translator, the ruler was informed that the Jews were building fortifications and he was warned of the consequences that this might have. If he would look up the history of the Jewish kingdom he would find that Jerusalem was always a source of peril. When Artaxerxes found that substantiated by the records, he gave the Samarians permission to order cessation of the building activity. There is no indication who the Jewish leaders of that day were.

The Coming of Ezra

A tremendously significant event for the whole future of the Jewish people to this day was the coming to Jerusalem of Ezra "scribe of the law of the god of heaven" in the seventh year of Artaxerxes (Ezra 7:6, 12). Unfortunately, it is not clear which of the two rulers of that name is meant. That Nehemiah came under Artaxerxes I is indubitable, in view of the state in which he found Jerusalem, but it is a moot question whether Ezra's coming can have preceded his. The

6.6 Elamites with bows, long daggers, and lioness with cubs; Armenians with stallion and vase. (Courtesy Oriental Institute, the University of Chicago)

editor of the great historical work to which the Books of Ezra and Nehemiah once belonged may have thought that Ezra came under Artaxerxes I, since the two kings are not distinguished in any way in the original records. That fact was brought home very vividly to the present writer when he prepared for publication the Brooklyn Museum collection of Aramaic papyri, ten of which were dated under "King Artaxerxes." He, too, assumed at first that this meant Artaxerxes I. The family history as well as the double chronology of these documents (Babylonian and Egyptian dates) soon established the fact that several of them were from the reign of Artaxerxes II. It is thus very possible that the Chronicler, when he read a date "King Artaxerxes" in the memoirs of Ezra and in the memoirs of Nehemiah, assumed that in both instances Artaxerxes I was meant. It seems probable, however, that Ezra came later than Nehemiah. If he came under Artaxerxes II he would have come in 398 B.C. instead of in 458 B.C. Whatever the truth of the matter may be, we will first deal with Nehemiah.

Nehemiah Goes to Jerusalem

The action taken by Artaxerxes I of stopping the building activity at Jerusalem (EZRA 4:17 f.) was reversed later in his reign through the diplomacy of Nehemiah, a cupbearer at his court, whose aid the Jews sought.

The next incident (NEH. 2:1 f.) is put in the spring of 445 B.C.—a fact necessitating the correction of the preceding date. Nehemiah deftly places his request before the monarch: to be allowed to rebuild the city of his forefathers! The king is willing to grant him a short leave of absence. Provided with letters to the governors of the (subdivisions of the) province "Beyond the River" and with a military escort, Nehemiah departs, apparently in the spring of that same year—perhaps after the monarch went north to Persepolis. Nothing is said about the itinerary or the duration of the trip. Nehemiah

notes that his arrival was very displeasing to two men about whom we shall hear more later—Sanballat the Horonite and Tobiah the Ammonite.

Tour of the Walls

After three days Nehemiah rode forth on a secret nocturnal tour of inspection (NEH. 2:12 f.). His exit was via the Valley Gate, and he traveled counter-clockwise. The residential quarter from which he issued must thus have lain inside the old walls above the Valley Gate. The crucial question therefore is: where did the Valley Gate lie? Color Map XVII shows two different theories of the matter which are widely held at present. The whole matter hinges on the larger question whether the southwestern hill was included in the pre-exilic city. This can only be decided by the spade of the excavator. The only "valley" near Jerusalem is the "Valley of Hinnom," or of the "son of Hinnom," and hence some scholars believe the Valley Gate must have lain adjacent to it. However, the gate could well be named after a farther objective.

Rebuilding the Walls

The restoration text of the third chapter of Nehemiah is by all odds the most important document for the topography of old Jerusalem. It describes how various sectors of the wall were rebuilt by teams working under their own leaders, and suggests that Nehemiah skillfully used the factor of rivalry as an incentive to expedite the work. Only one group, the men from the town of Tekoa, is criticized for not showing sufficient energy (NEH. 3:5). In listing the forty-one teams that went to work and the sectors in which they labored, Nehemiah gives due honor and distinction to the high priest of the day, Eliashib, whom he names first of all.

The Supporting Jewish Community

Those who labored on the building project were not all from Jerusalem. We learn from the third chapter of Nehemiah that work teams came from certain outlying places, and therewith we get an idea of the extent of the province of Judah at this time. The account of the celebration adds several more places (NEH. 12:28 f.). According to these indications Judah in the south included the territory up to the line Tekoa–Beth-zur–Keilah; on the west the territory extended from Keilah to Zanoah—a place we have not encountered in the narratives, but which lay near Samson's home town of Zorah at *Khirbet Zanū',* which still preserves the ancient name. Beth-haccerem (Beth-hacherem, R.S.V.), probably lay south of the Holy City at an Iron Age tell near *Ramat Raḥel* (see pages 68, 340). The Jerusalem district included places south, north, and east of the city. On the south, Bethlehem and Netopha belonged to it. The latter is sought two and a half miles southeast of Bethlehem at an ancient site occupying the spur of a ridge (*Khirbet bedd Falūḥ*). Joined to Bethlehem and Netopha on the north were Anathoth and Beth-asmaveth (*Ḥezmeh*), and in the east a "house of Gilgal," or Beth-gilgal, which some identify with the Gilgal of Joshua 15:7. Farther to the north lay the district of Mizpah, in which Gibeon was included. Jericho, too, was the center of a district, and "the plain" is also referred to, though only the portion of it west of the Jordan and adjacent to Jericho on the north and south can be meant.

Jealous Neighbors

The swift progress made could not escape the attention of those who feared Jerusalem's resurgence.

The most important and meddlesome neighbors were the inhabitants of Samaria. Their representative at the time was San-ballat (Babylonian, *Sin-uballiṭ*) who, as Josephus states and as an Aramaic papyrus has confirmed, was governor of that province. He is referred to sometimes as the "Horon-ite," a designation that is usually taken to mean that he was from Beth-horon, but the vocalization is uncertain; for all that he might be a Harranite (cf. his Sin-compounded name) or a Hauranite.

On the east were the Ammonites, and here Tobiah, "the Ammonite servant" (NEH. 2:10, 19; 3:35), is especially singled out for mention. He was evidently of Israelite or Jewish origin as his name shows, and had close connections with the aristocracy at Jerusalem (NEH. 6:17 f.; 13:4 f.). His descendants, the "Tobiads," were to play a powerful role in the following centuries in Jewish affairs. They had a fortress named Tyrus at *'Arāq el Emīr,* where the name Tobiah is inscribed in the rock. Excavations were made there by the American Schools in 1960–61.

The mention here of the Ashdodites is puzzling, since it seems peculiar that the inhabitants of one relatively unimportant Philistaean city should be singled out in such a manner. That is again the case in Nehemiah 13:23 f., where one must wonder how Jews should come to have wives from Ashdod. "Ashdodites," however, is used as a designation for the inhabitants of Philistaea as a whole, and this is due to the fact that it was the provincial capital ever since Sargon II of Assyria annexed the region (711 B.C.).

The fourth in the group of the surrounding enemies are the Arabs. This is surprising, since one thinks of them as living east of the Ammonites. However, so remote a localization would not have made them a factor in the immediate situation (cf. NEH. 4:7). They must, therefore, be the southern neighbors of Judah. Sometimes Nehemiah mentions Geshem or Gashmu as an enemy, instead of the Arabs. It is evident that this man was the ruler of the Arab group. The name has lately taken on new meaning through some inscriptions, notably that on a silver vessel which is now in the Brooklyn Museum, said to be from *Tell el Mashkhūta* in Egypt (see fig. 6.5 on page 334). It bears the name of Qainu, son of Gashmu, king of Kedar, and was dedicated to the goddess *Han'ilat.* The

Geshem of this inscription may have been Nehemiah's foe.

Nehemiah Sees It Through

Within fifty-two days (in the year 444 B.C.?), the breaches in the walls were repaired, and the city was once more rendered defensible. Haste was imperative, lest his enemies get Artaxerxes to countermand his previous order. No one could count very long on the favor of an Oriental ruler.

The enemies now sought to lure Nehemiah to a conference in the plain of Ono (NEH. 6:2), the broad *Wadi Muṣrāra,* in which the village of *Kufr 'Āna* preserves the ancient name. It was apparently royal domain, and formed a sort of neutral zone between Ashdod and Samaria. Nehemiah believed that their purpose was to assassinate him and did not go. He also saw through the scheme of a traitor who wanted to bring about his undoing (NEH. 6:10–13).

Having successfully achieved the rebuilding of the walls, Nehemiah held a celebration (NEH. 12:27–43). Two processions started off on top of the walls, heading in opposite directions. We must assume that the starting point was the Valley Gate, which is the one important point that is not mentioned (see Color Map XVII).

Later Trip of Nehemiah

Nehemiah left Palestine in 433 B.C. to return to King Artaxerxes. There is thus a surprisingly long hiatus between his arrival in 445 B.C. and this departure. He returned again, however, at a subsequent date and presumably held the post of governor all the time.

Nehemiah seems to have persuaded the leaders of the community to sign an agreement of policy which is preserved in Nehemiah 10. The item about the annual religious contribution of one-third of a shekel (NEH. 10:32) is of interest in the light of an Aramaic papyrus from Elephantine giving a list of contributors to the maintenance of a

temple of the LORD in that Egyptian town.

With this visit Nehemiah disappears from the scene. The reign of Artaxerxes I lasted until the spring of 423 B.C. and we may assume that his cup-bearer continued in favor and kept an eye on Jerusalem's affairs until that date.

Light on Judah under Darius II

An Aramaic papyrus found by Rubensohn in the Berlin Museum excavations on the island of Elephantine in 1907 has cast a flood of light on the situation in Judah as of its date, November 25, 407 B.C. We learn from it that Bagoas (Bagohi), to whom the letter was addressed, was the Persian governor of Judah (*Yehūd,* as also on the coins of this period) and that the high priest was a man named Johanan. We hear that Sanballat was governor of Samaria, and we find that one of his sons, Delaiah, issued the reply to the letter. The papyrus also mentions the Persian satrap of Egypt, Arsham or Arsames.

The Bagoas letter makes it reasonable to believe that Nehemiah came to Jerusalem under Artaxerxes I, since the high priest Johanan of the papyrus of 407 B.C. probably is the grandson of the Eliashib who was the high priest in Nehemiah's time. A list of the high priests to the time of "Darius the Persian" reads as follows: Eliashib, Joiada, Johanan and Jaddua (NEH. 12:22). Since the list obviously extends beyond the reign of Darius II (405 B.C.), it seems probable that "Darius the Persian" means the last of the Achaemenids, Darius III (335–331 B.C.). Josephus makes a Jaddua the high priest at the coming of Alexander the Great in 331 B.C. If that is correct and if there was only one high priest named Jaddua, several names must have dropped out between Johanan and Jaddua in Nehemiah 12:22. In any case, the Johanan "son" of Eliashib of the Ezra memoirs (NEH. 13:28) is the high priest Johanan of the Bagoas letter (see page 339). The identification of the two makes the coming of Ezra after the time of the Bagoas letter, and therefore under Artaxerxes II, increasingly probable. This is confirmed by the whole situation. According to the letter, there is close co-operation between Samaria and Jerusalem, and intermarriage between the leading families. It is hard to understand how this could have occurred after the coming of Ezra. Indeed, it would necessitate supposing that Ezra's work was quickly undone.

The Journey of Ezra

In Ezra 7 f. we get some excerpts from the memoirs of the priest Ezra, "the scribe of the law of the god of heaven." This title is not a Jewish formulation, but conferred by the Persians. "Scribe" could be a term of some dignity. Ezra's role is only understood if he held a government post as secretary for Jewish religious affairs. He apparently had a predecessor (or successor, depending on the dating preferred) who influenced Darius II to issue the royal order, of which a copy was found among the Aramaic papyri from Elephantine, directing the Jews of that colony to celebrate the Feast of Unleavened Bread in 419 B.C.

According to the narrative about his mission Ezra traveled to Jerusalem from Babylon in the seventh year of Artaxerxes. If this is Artaxerxes II, then his trip took place in 398 B.C. Particularly important was the juridical aspect of the trip. Just as Darius I had found it necessary to have a special legislation promulgated in Egypt that would command the loyalty of the people and of its leaders, so Artaxerxes here sends Ezra to introduce a legislation and organize a judiciary that will act on the basis of it. There must have been some special cause or occasion for this action, but it is not related.

Many Jews decided to go to Palestine with Ezra. He assembled his party, fifteen hundred strong, "by the river that flows to Ahavah" (EZRA 8:15), later simply "River Ahavah" (EZRA 8:21). It must have been named after a district or town and it seems

likely that it was a canal or side arm of the Euphrates or Tigris. It cannot very well have been the *Diyāla,* since that was called the *Ṭurnat.* Until Babylonian texts provide us with a comparable name we are totally in the dark as to Ezra's starting point; nor is it of much help if we hear of his sending messengers to the evidently nearby town of Casiphia to recruit some descendants of former Temple servants who had settled there (EZRA 8:17), for we cannot locate that place at present either. A fast was held at the River Ahavah, before starting on the journey, for Ezra intended to proceed without military escort, relying only on God's help.

There is not a word about the course followed on this journey. The trip took five months—an extraordinarily long time. If they left the Ahavah in the middle of April, it was late in September before they arrived.

At Jerusalem Ezra was induced to take strong action in the matter of mixed marriages. An important item mentioned in that connection is that he spent the night fasting in the chamber of "Johanan the son of Eliashib" (EZRA 10:6). As already suggested (see page 338) that individual must be identical with the Johanan who appears as high priest in the Elephantine papyrus and with the unnamed son of Joiada, son of Eliashib, whom Nehemiah had driven out of Jerusalem because he was a son-in-law of Sanballat (NEH. 13:28). We must infer that he was high priest, but was currently *in absentia.* If there is any truth in what Josephus tells about him, viz., that he slew his brother in the Temple and that Bagoas (Bagoses) imposed penalties on the Jewish community for seven years on account of this murder, his absence would be quite understandable. The fact that Johanan is called the "son of Eliashib" in Ezra 10:6 rather than "son of Joiada, son of Eliashib," as Nehemiah 13:28 would lead one to expect, has caused some difficulty; but the Aramaic papyri published by this author in 1953 suggest that it was quite in order for a man to omit the name of his father and use that of his grandfather instead. Thus, an individual at Elephantine whose full name was "Anani son of Haggai son of Meshullam" is called "Anani son of Meshullam" on a papyrus endorsement. Josephus can hardly be right as to Johanan's having committed the crime at the time when he first became high priest, for the Elephantine Jews in their letter to Bagoas refer to having written to the high priest Johanan as well. The event must have occurred somewhat later.

The Publication of the Law

The supreme act of Ezra at Jerusalem was the presentation of a set of laws to the Judaean community, and the latter's acceptance of them (NEH. 8). A great assembly was convoked in the square before the Water Gate, and Ezra, standing on a wooden platform constructed for the purpose, read the law to the people, with the gate behind him and the square before him.

This Water Gate, as we have already had reason to note, was on the east side of the City of David (NEH. 3:26; 12:37). It was the gate that led out to the Gihon spring. The open space (or "square") in front of the gate must have been sufficiently large for a good-sized public gathering.

The choice of the place is significant. The law was not read in the Temple, but in the area of the old city of the kings of Judah. The function of Ezra is political; he is an appointee of the Persian ruler, and he wants an act of endorsement from the community, which is to take upon itself a set of laws by which it is willing to be governed.

Persian Judea

New light on the obscure Persian period comes from the excavations conducted at *Ramat Raḥel* (see page 68), between Jerusalem and Bethlehem, by Y. Aharoni and a Hebrew expedition in 1959. Jar-handle stamps were found giving not only the name of the Persian province of Judah

(*Yehūd*), but also the name of an individual and his title: *Yehud. Yehoazar the governor.* Another stamp has: (belonging) *to Ahio the governor (phw')*. The only governor since Nehemiah known hitherto was Bagoas. In the light of these stamps, the one found at Jericho reading *Yehud. Urio* may give the name of another governor (or local prefect?), and a coin from Beth-zur reading *"Hezekiah. Yehud"* could mean the high priest Ezekias mentioned by Josephus (*Against Apion*, I, 22) and prove that he served also as governor. If what Josephus relates of Bagoses' (i.e., Bagoas') reign of terror (*Antiquities*, XI, 7) is true, one can see why Jews would again have been appointed to the office. As the coin mentioned above shows, coinage was first minted in Judea in this period.

Jews in Egypt

The proximity of Egypt to Palestine had made that country a natural haven for Jewish fugitives since of old. We have seen that the Jeremiah narratives predicted the destruction of the Egyptian Jews of that day and that there is every reason to believe that this had come about (see page 318). New groups of Jews may have gone down late in the Chaldean era. The Egyptian Pharaohs always needed mercenary troops, and, while most of them were drawn from other quarters, there were among them some western Semites, including Jews. This has been made particularly vivid by the Elephantine papyri, of which mention was made above. The Jewish colony on that island in the Nile was a part of a military colony guarding Egypt's southern border. The fact that it had a temple for its own god proves that sovereign power had aided in its establishment, for its existence was obnoxious to the priesthood of the god Khnum. The island of Elephantine, of which the Egyptian name was Yeb, is not mentioned in the Old Testament, but Sewen (Assuan) on the mainland is referred to. The northernmost and southernmost points of Egypt are mentioned in Ezekiel 29:10, cf. Ezekiel 30:6. It is possible that Deutero-Isaiah already knew of the Jewish colony when, in hailing the returning Jewish exiles, he singled out those from the land of Sinim (Is. 49:12; Dead Sea Scroll: Siniyites), which, according to the context, lay far away either to the south or to the east. These Jews had been settled in a colony of Aramaeans and had become Aramaic speaking. The Aramaeans must have been brought there in the days of Pharaoh Hophra (588–570 B.C.), presumably to replace a garrison at Elephantine that had mutinied, as is known from the inscription found at that place of an Egyptian official named Nesuḥor.

We have said something above about an Aramaic papyrus-letter from Elephantine. The astonishing revelation that there was a Jewish colony at or near Assuan was first brought to the attention by a collection of Aramaic papyri obtained there and published in 1906 by two Oxford scholars, Sayce and Cowley. The Berlin Museum expedition was able to locate the spot where these had been found by native diggers and recovered an even greater number of documents, among which the letter referred to on page 338 was of outstanding importance. We have already mentioned what it reveals about the situation in Judah, but may say something here of what it tells us of the Jewish colony. Its temple of the Lord was destroyed at the instigation of the priests of Khnum, the ram-headed Egyptian god of Elephantine in 410 B.C. The Jews had fasted and mourned for three years and the letter to Bagoas, which is only one of a number sent out to influential persons, asked aid to have the temple restored. Arsham or Arsames, the satrap of Egypt, was absent at the time, for another related document speaks of his having "gone to the king." The appeal of the Jews found a hearing, for Sanballat's son Delaiah, to whom the matter was evidently referred, gave an order in the matter. The transcript of it entitled "memorandum" is preserved. The Jewish messenger was to convey to Arsham, who therefore must have been back in Egypt, Delaiah's recommendation that the temple be rebuilt and that (non-bloody) sacrifices should be permitted there.

Concerning this Arsham, some Aramaic Leather Documents bought in Egypt by the Egyptologist Borchardt, 1932, and published by G. R. Driver in 1954, have provided additional interesting information. Arsham is likewise mentioned in cuneiform documents, for he owned estates in Babylonia.

It had been questioned whether the Elephantine temple was rebuilt, since it was believed that Persian rule ended very soon, with the accession of Artaxerxes II (404–359 B.C.). However, the oldest collection of papyri from Elephantine—those acquired by the American Egyptologist Charles Edwin Wilbour in 1893, but only published in 1953, by the present writer—showed that the temple was functioning as late as 402 B.C. and that the Persian king Artaxerxes II was still sovereign in Egypt at that time. The rebellion of Egypt must thus have taken place in the spring of 401 B.C., at the very time when Cyrus the Younger led an army against his brother King Artaxerxes II from Asia Minor to Babylonia. Ten thousand Greek mercenaries took part in this adventure, which ended disastrously in the battle at Cunaxa (an as yet unidentified place). The Greek writer Xenophon who took part in the expedition has given a vivid account of it.

The Jews of Egypt were apparently left undisturbed under the Egyptian ruler Amyrtaeus, for an Elephantine papyrus dated in his reign (June 19, 400 B.C.) has survived. One of the papyri in the Brooklyn Museum is a letter written October 1, 399 B.C. In it the writer informs a personage in Elephantine of the death or capture of Amyrtaeus and the accession of Nepherites I, founder of the Twenty-ninth Dynasty. This was an ominous event, for the dynasty came from Mendes, where the ram-god was supreme. It seems certain that Nepherites heeded the desire of

341

the Elephantine priests of that deity and directed the abolition of the Jewish temple. The colony was bereft of its livelihood, and its members were no doubt removed elsewhere.

Artaxerxes III

Darius II was succeeded by Artaxerxes III. We have no direct reports about how the Jewish community fared under this ruler, but the Old Testament probably contains some materials from his time. An important event of his reign was the sacking in 348 B.C. of the Phoenician city of Sidon, which the Persians had preferred to Tyre. One of the kings of fourth-century Sidon had been Eshmunazzar, whose basalt sarcophagus, bearing a lengthy Phoenician inscription, was found in 1855 southeast of the present city of Ṣaidā. The dirge over Sidon now found in Isaiah 23:1–14 and wrongly labeled "the burden of Tyre" is believed by many to have been composed at this time. .

Another important act of Artaxerxes III was the renewed subjugation of Egypt, first attempted by him in 350 B.C. and successfully achieved in the onslaught launched in November, 343 B.C. Nektanebos II, the last of the Pharaohs of old Egypt, retreated to Memphis and then, deserted by his Greek mercenaries, fled up the Nile to Nubia. It seems likely that "the burden of Egypt" which is found in Isaiah 19:1–15 mirrors one of the campaigns of Artaxerxes III.

Geographical Elements in Some Late Prophetic Writings

We may turn briefly to the prophecy of Joel which was elicited by a terrible locust plague.

There are also some elements of geographical interest in the Book of Joel, though the sections in which they occur may be supplements to the basic prophecy. Among them is the prediction of a convocation of all nations for judgment in the Valley of Jehoshaphat (JOEL 3:2, 12), also referred to as the

Valley of Decision (JOEL 3:14). Christian tradition since the fourth century A.D. identified the place with the Kidron Valley. However, the Old Testament writers never call the Kidron a valley, but rather consider it a ravine (naḥal). It seems probable that the vale of Jehoshaphat was named for King Jehoshaphat and that it is identical with the Valley of Shaveh (GEN. 14:17), as well as with the king's dale, where Absalom erected a pillar or funeral monument and where he expected to be buried (2 SAM. 18:18). According to Josephus, that monument stood at a point about four hundred yards to the north of Jerusalem. The name "king's dale," or Valley of the King, suggests that it was royal property. The stone quarries existing in this area will have been of particular importance to the royal builders. Certainly only a large area of ground such as that which exists north of the city, not a constricted valley like the Kedron, could be conceived of as the setting for such an assemblage as the prophecy has in mind. The assumption that all peoples could be gathered there suggests that the prophet had a very limited idea of the size of the human race of his day.

Another geographical allusion is found in the closing verses of the book. Like Ezekiel, this writer thinks of a fountain coming forth from the temple of the future. He describes it as watering the valley of Shittim (JOEL 3:18). This might better be translated "valley of accacia trees," for it is unthinkable that the Shittim on the other side of the Jordan (JOSH. 2:1) should be meant. He is evidently thinking of the *Wadi en Nār,* the continuation of the Kidron Valley. Perhaps there was a grove of accacias near its entrance in those times.

Some late prophecy in the Book of Zechariah also speaks of places. The whole land of Judah from Geba to Rimmon shall be turned into a plain, but Jerusalem will remain elevated (ZECH. 14:9 f.). Benjaminite Geba is evidently the northern boundary point, while Rimmon is said to be south of Jerusalem. It may be En-rimmon (JOSH. 19:7) in the Judaean mountain country. It is believed to have lain about eleven miles northeast of Beersheba (at *Khirbet Umm er Ramāmīm*). Jerusalem's confines are described as extending "from the Benjamin Gate to the place of the First Gate, to the Corner Gate and from the Tower of Hananel to the King's wine presses." The Benjamin Gate and the Corner Gate are the most easterly and westerly points on the north side of the city. The allusion to the First Gate or Gate of the First (*former gate,* R.S.V.), is obscure, but probably has reference to the Ephraim Gate lying between the two others mentioned. The northern and southern limits of the city are indicated by the Tower of Hananel and the King's wine presses. Some scholars believe the text originally read "the King's sepulchres" instead of wine presses, but in any case a point at the foot of the southeastern ridge must be meant. It is noteworthy that no need is felt to indicate a point on the southwestern ridge.

Late prophecy is much concerned with the Edomites, who took advantage of the fall of Jerusalem to invade southern Judah and the Negeb. In this way it came about, when Edom proper was overrun by the Arabs and became the seat of the Nabataean kingdom, that the names Edom and Seir came to be applied to the regions west of the *'Arabah*. If in the closing verses of Obadiah's prophecy the "mount of Esau" is an important objective of Hebrew reconquest, this means the Negeb. Other goals are mentioned, such as Zarephath in Phoenicia, and returned exiles from Sepharad (Sardis in Lydia) are given a prominent role.

Geography in the Wisdom Literature

The ascendancy of the Arabs in this period is also reflected in the Wisdom Literature. Appended to the Book of Proverbs going under the name of Solomon, we find some alleged sayings of Arab wise men—of Agur of Massa and Lemuel, king of Massa (PROV. 30:1; 31:1). We have heard of Massa as one of the sons of Ishmael (GEN. 25:13 f., cf. page 74).

A work showing considerable interest in north Arabia and its frontiers is the Book of Job. Tradition since early Christian days put his home in the Hauran region. That excellently suits the idea that he had cattle and carried on plowing, for the Hauran is a rich agricultural district. His name may well hang together with that of a King Ayab, of whom we hear in the *Tell el Amarna* Letters. The northern localization of the scene of the book fits in with the fact that Job suffers raiding at the hands of the Chaldeans (cf. 2 KINGS 24:2). Mention of the Sabaeans is indicative of the fact that at the time when this was written these people were dominating the trade route from Arabia to Syria. The friends of Job augment the Arab background, though only the home of the first can be identified with any assurance. For his city, Teman, must have lain in northern Edom (EZEK. 25:13). An Iron Age site near Petra (*eṭ Ṭawīlān*) has been suggested for it. This far-flung Arab world representation suits the universalistic outlook of this greatest poetic production of the ancient Semitic peoples. Priestcraft, ceremonialism, religious fanaticism, nationalism and racialism are lost sight of, and we move in a world where a man faces the facts of life and the religious questions in full freedom, yet under God.

TABLE OF BIBLE HISTORY

CHRONOLOGY	HEBREW	WESTERN ASIA	EGYPT	WESTERN WORLD
1400 B.C.		Amarna Age. Egypt in nominal control of Palestine and Syria. c. 1370 Hittites defeat Mitanni and seize Syria. Assyria independent of Mitanni. 1363–1328 Ashur-uballit I. End of Mitannian Kingdom. 1348 Hittite prince sent to wed widow of Tutankhamen; slain on way. 1345–1315 Murshilish II. Seti I campaign to Palestine. 1315–1290 Muwattalish, Hittite king.	1377–1358 Amenophis IV Akhnaton. 1358–1349 Tutankhamen. 1349–1345 Hui. 1345–1200 XIX Dynasty. 1345–1318 Haremhab. 1318–1317 Ramses I. 1317–1301 Seti I. 1301–1234 Ramses II.	1400 Mycenaean Civilization at height.
1300 B.C.	c. 1300 (1700?) Abraham. c. 1230 Exodus of a Hebrew group? c. 1220 "Israel" group defeated by Merneptah (on Palestine borders?)	1296 Battle of Kadesh under Ramses II. 1257–1221 Tukulti-Ninurta I of Assyria.	1234–1220 Merneptah reigns; pacifies Palestine; Israel mentioned 1220–1200 Seti II.	
1200 B.C.	c. 1200–1100 Palestine conquered by Hebrews. Tribal confederacy formed.	c. 1197 Sea-peoples migrate on Asiatic coasts, try to invade Egypt. Philistines settle. 1160 End of Cassite Dynasty at Babylon. 1112–1074 Tiglathpileser I of Assyria. Aramaean migration in Mesopotamia.	1200–1085 XX Dynasty. 1200–1197 Sethnakht. 1197–1165 Ramses III wards off great invasion of sea-peoples. 1165–1085 Ramses IV-XI.	1200 Beginning of Greek colonization of Aegean coast of Asia Minor.
1100 B.C.	Battle of Taanach. Midianite invasion. c. 1010 Philistine invasion of Central Palestine.	1010–970 Ashur-rabi II of Assyria.	1085–950 XXI Dynasty; Thebes and Tanis, Smendes and Herihor.	
1000 B.C.	c. 1000–985 Saul. c. 985–963 David. c. 963–929 Solomon. c. 959 Temple completed. c. 929 Secession of northern tribes. **ISRAEL** c. 929–910 Jeroboam. c. 910–909 Nadab. c. 909–886 Baasha. **JUDAH** c. 929–913 Rehoboam. c. 913–911 Abijah. c. 911–871 Asa.	969–965 Ashur-resh-ishi II. 964–933 Tiglathpileser II. 932–910 Ashur-dan II. 909–889 Adadnirari II.	950–730 XXII Dynasty (Libyan). 950–929 Shishak (Sheshonk I). 929–893 Osorkon I.	
900 B.C.	**ISRAEL** c. 886–885 Ela. c. 885 Zimri. c. 885–881 Tibni. c. 885–874 Omri. c. 874–851 Ahab. c. 851–850 Ahaziah. c. 850–842 Joram. c. 842–820 Jehu. 842 Jehu submits to Shalmaneser III. c. 820–804 Jehoa- **JUDAH** c. 871–850 Jehoshaphat. c. 850–843 Joram. c. 843 Ahaziah. c. 842–836 Athaliah. c. 836–803 Jehoash or Joash. c. 803–775 Amaziah.	888–884 Tukulti-Ninurta II. 883–859 Ashur-nasir-pal II. 858–824 Shalmaneser III. 823–810 Shamshi-Adad V. 809–782 Adad-nirari III.	870–847 Osorkon II. 815–730 Synchronous XXIII Dynasty, King Petubastis and others.	

					750–550 Second Greek colonization.
	755–740 Ashur-nirari V. 745–727 Tiglathpileser III. 726–722 Shalmaneser V. 721–705 Sargon II. 704–681 Sennacherib. 703 Merodach-baladan II of Babylon.	*c.* 734–733 Jotham. 733–714 Ahaz. *c.* 714–696 Hezekiah. 701 Hezekiah surrenders to Sennacherib.		720–715 XXIV Dynasty: Bocchoris. 715–663 XXV (Nubian) Dynasty. 712–700 Shabaka.	
700 B.C.	... Shallum. *c.* 748–736 Menahem. 738 Menahem pays tribute to Tiglathpileser III. *c.* 736–735 Pekahiah. *c.* 735–732 Pekah. 733 Tiglathpileser III appoints Hoshea. *c.* 732–721 Hoshea. 721 Samaria falls.	**JUDAH** *c.* 696–642 Manasseh. *c.* 641–640 Amon. *c.* 639–609 Josiah. *c.* 609 Joahaz. 608–598 Jehoiakim.	687 Lydia rises to power in Asia Minor. 680–669 Esarhaddon. 668–648 Shamash-shum-ukin of Babylon. 668–626 Ashurbanipal. 657 Gyges of Lydia dies fighting Cimmerians. 639 End of Elamite kingdom. 625–621 Ashur-etil-ilani. 625–585 Cyaxares of Media. 625–605 Nabopolassar founds Chaldean Dynasty at Babylon. 620–612 Sin-shar-ishkun. 611–606 Ashur-uballit II. End of Assyrian Empire. 605 Battle of Carchemish. Egyptian army crushed. Others defeated at Hamath. 604–562 Nebuchadnezzar II. 604 Nebuchadnezzar interrupts campaign. Visits Babylon to succeed father. Returns to Syria. Sacks Ashkelon in Kislev. 601 Nebuchadnezzar tries to invade Egypt. Checkmated in bloody battle.	700–688 Shabataka. 688–663 Tirhaka (Taharka). 670 Egypt conquered by Esarhaddon of Assyria. 667 Ashurbanipal destroys Thebes. 663–525 XXVI Dynasty (Saites). 663–609 Psamtik I. 650 Founding of Naucratis in Egypt. 609–593 Necho.	*c.* 650 Second Messenian War. 650–580 Corinth powerful in Greece. 650–550 Lydians subdue Greek Asian cities. *c.* 621 The "Draconic" laws.
600 B.C.		598 (Dec.) Siege of Jerusalem. 598–597 Jehoiachin. 597 Jerusalem surrenders to Nebuchadnezzar 2 Adar (March 16). *c.* 597–587 Zedekiah. Fall of Jerusalem (July 30, 587). 561 Jehoiachin freed. 538 Cyrus' edict restoring Temple vessels. 520 Temple building begun; Haggai and Zechariah. 515 Temple completed.	599 Operations in Syria and against Arabs. 561–560 Evil-Merodach (Amel-Marduk). 559 Cyrus, Astyages' vassal, begins reign. 559–556 Nergal-shar-usur. 556 Labashi-Marduk. 555–538 Nabonidus. 550 Cyrus takes over Median realm. 546 Cyrus annexes Croesus' Lydian realm. 539 Cyrus takes Babylon. 529 Cyrus II king of all Western Asia. 529–522 Cambyses: conquest of Egypt. 525 At death rebellion of Gaumata (Pseudo-Smerdis). 521–486 Darius I.	593–588 Psamtik II. 588–568 Hophra (Apries). 568–525 Amasis. 525 Psamtik III. Cambyses conquers Egypt.	594 Solon lawgiver at Athens. 561–528 Pisistratos dictator at Athens.

Table of Bible History, continued

CHRONOLOGY	HEBREW	WESTERN ASIA	EGYPT	WESTERN WORLD
500 B.C.	495 Oldest papyrus on Elephantine Island attests Jewish colony and temple. 458 Ezra's coming? (See 398). 445 Nehemiah comes to Judaea. 428 A corrected date for Ezra? 410 Elephantine Jewish temple destroyed. 407 Elephantine Jews' letter to Bagoas.	486-465 Xerxes. 465-424 Artaxerxes I. 424-405 Darius II. 405-359 Artaxerxes II. 401 Revolt of Cyrus. March of 10,000 Greeks.	463 Inaros and Amyrtaeus revolt in Delta. 404 Amyrtaeus (II) rules in Delta. 401 Amyrtaeus sole king of XXVIII Dynasty, rules all Egypt. Persian rule ended.	493-492 Themistocles, Archon. Naval program. Fortification of Piraeus, harbor. Miltiades comes to Athens. 490 Darius punishes Greeks. Athenian victory at Marathon. 489 Miltiades dies; Themistocles rules. 480 Persian war of Xerxes. Greeks defeated at Thermopylae; Athens burned. Persian navy defeated at Salamis. 479 Athens again scourged. Battle of Plataea, Pausanias expels Persians. 478-477 Kimon drives Persians from Thrace. 431-404 Peloponnesian War. Breaks power of Athens, weakens all Greece.
400 B.C.	399 End of Elephantine colony. 398 Coming of Ezra to Jerusalem? Founding of Samaritan sect? 348 Rebellion in Syria and Palestine against Artaxerxes III. Jewish groups deported to Hyrcania? 332 Jews come under Macedonian control. 320 Ptolemy I attacks Jerusalem; carries off many captives. 314 Antigonus conquers Palestine. 312 Battle of Gaza gives Ptolemy renewed control.	359-338 Artaxerxes III. 338-336 Interregnum. Arses. 336-330 Darius III. 333 Battle of Issus won by Alexander the Great. 332 Siege of Tyre. Invasion of Egypt. 331 Battle of Arbela. 330 Alexander burns Persepolis. Ends war of revenge. Dismisses Greek troops. 330-327 Alexander's campaign into Central Asia. 327-325 Alexander's march to India. 324 Marriage festival of Susa. 323 Alexander dies at Babylon. 312 Battle of Gaza; Ptolemy and Seleucus defeat Demetrius. Seleucid era begins. 301 Battle of Ipsus. 301-280 Seleucus I Nicator.	398-393 Nepherites XXIX Dynasty from Mendes in Delta. 358-341 Nektanebos II last of Dynasty XXX from Sebennytos. 343 Artaxerxes III begins Egyptian conquest. 332 Alexander the Great conquers Egypt. 323-306 Ptolemy, satrap of Egypt. 301-31 Ptolemaic Dynasty. 301-285 Ptolemy I Lagi.	386 Peace of Antalcidas. Greek cities of Asia Minor recaptured by Persians. 338 Philip defeats Greeks at Chaeronea, establishing Macedonian rule. 338-337 Philip elected Greek Commander of War of revenge against Persia. 336 Philip begins Persian War; murdered. 336-323 Alexander the Great. 335 Alexander destroys rebellious Thebes. 334-331 Conquests of Asia Minor, Syria, Palestine and Egypt. 323-322 Lamian War. Greeks fail to win freedom from Macedonia.
300 B.C.	218 Palestine occupied by Antiochus III. 217 Ptolemy IV retakes Palestine at Raphia. 202 Palestine retaken by Antiochus III.	280-261 Antiochus I Soter. 261-246 Antiochus II Theos. 261-260 War between Ptolemy II and Antiochus II. 246-226 Seleucus II Callinicus. 226-224 Seleucus III Keraunos. 224-187 Antiochus III the Great.	285-246 Ptolemy II Philadelphus. 246-221 Ptolemy III Euergetes. 221-205 Ptolemy IV Philopator. 205-181 Ptolemy V Epiphanes.	264-241 First Punic War. Romans take Sicily. 238 Sardinia and Corsica taken from Carthaginians. 218-201 Second Punic War. 218 Hannibal crosses the Alps. 216 Battle of Cannae. Hannibal wins, but not strong enough to attack Rome. 209 Scipio takes Carthago Nova in Spain. 202 Scipio invades Africa. Hannibal defeated. Carthage forced to give up Spain and its navy.
200 B.C.	200 Palestine lost to Scopas, Ptolemy's general. 198 Palestine definitely becomes Seleucid. Scopas beaten at Paneas and Sidon. 190 Simon the Maccabee is high priest. c. 176 Heliodorus seeks to rob Temple for Seleucus IV.	187-175 Seleucus IV Philopator. 175-164 Antiochus IV Epiphanes. 174 Antiochus IV visits Jerusalem. 169 First Egyptian campaign of Antiochus. 168 Second Egyptian campaign of Antiochus. 167-166 Appeal of the Samaritans.	181-146 Ptolemy VI Philometor. 164-162 Jewish temple founded at Leontopolis in Egypt by Onias IV, son of high priest Onias III.	197 Philip V of Macedonia defeated by Romans under Flaminius at Cynoscephalae. 196 Flaminius declares Greeks liberated. 178-168 Perseus, last king of Macedonia. 168 Battle of Pydna; Romans destroy Macedonian kingdom.

	Judaea	Syria / Near East	Rome & West
	172 Jason replaced by Menelaos. 170 Onias III assassinated. 169 Antiochus plunders the Temple. 168 Revolt in Jerusalem. Punitive raid of Apollonius. Theocracy abolished. Greek *Polis* founded in City of David (*Acra*). 167 Temple polluted. Maccabeans revolt. 166-165 Death of Mattathias of Modiin. Book of Daniel. 165 Gorgias proceeds against Maccabees. Campaign of Lysias. 164 Persecution ceases. Temple rededicated (*Hanukkah Festival*). 163 At death of Antiochus IV Judas besieges Acra. Campaign of Antiochus V. 162 Peace made; Temple returned to Jews. Menelaos executed. Alcimus high priest. Demetrius overthrows Antiochus V. 161 Jews rebellious; Judas' victory over Nicanor. Judas' treaty with Rome? 160 Campaign of Bacchides. Judas slain. 160-142 Jonathan. 159 Alcimus dies; no successor appointed. c. 157 Jonathan makes peace with Seleucids. 152 Alexander Balas appoints Jonathan high priest.	163-162 Antiochus V Eupator. 162-150 Demetrius I Soter, son of Seleucus IV.	149-146 Third Punic War. Carthage razed. 148 Macedonian uprising. Macedonia, Epirus and Thessaly made Roman province. 146 War between Sparta and Achaeans. Roman general Mummius destroys Corinth. Greece tributary. 133 The Gracchi begin movement to help the poor.
150 B.C.	143 Trypho, commander of Antiochus VI, seizes and executes Jonathan. Simon Maccabeus sides with Demetrius II. 142-134 Simon. 142 Demetrius II gives autonomy to Jews. 141 Simon captures the Acra. 140 Simon appointed Ethnarch. 139-138 Antiochus VII grants Jews privileges. 134 Simon assassinated; son of John Hyrcanus becomes high priest. Antiochus VII takes Jerusalem, but he confirms autonomy. 134-104 John Hyrcanus. 104-103 Aristobulus. 103-76 Alexander I Jannaeus.	151-145 Alexander Balas, usurper. 146-138 Demetrius II Nicator. 140 Parthian campaign of Demetrius II. Falls into captivity. 138-129 Antiochus VII Sidetes. 133 Attalus of Pergamum wills realm to Rome. It becomes province of Asia. 128-125 Demetrius II Nicator. 128-122 Alexander Zabinas. 125 Seleucus V. 125-113 Antiochus VIII Grypos. 113-95 Antiochus IX Kyzikenos. 111-96 Antiochus VIII.	96 Apion, son of Ptolemy VIII, bequeathes Cyrenaica to Rome. 42-31 Antony ruler of East. 37 Antony weds Cleopatra. 32-31 Octavian wars on Cleopatra, deposes Antony. Egypt made a province.
100 B.C.	76-67 Salome Alexandra. 67-63 Aristobulus II younger son prevails over Hyrcanus II elder son. 63 Romans take Jerusalem Temple. Judaea Roman dependency; Hyrcanus made high priest. Origin of the Decapolis. 63-40 Hyrcanus II. Antipater governor of Judaea. 47 Hyrcanus hereditary high priest and ethnarch of the Jews.	93 Tigranes of Armenia takes Cappadocia. 89-88 Mithridates of Pontus conquers Bithynia, Phrygia and Mysia. Athens allies itself with Mithridates. 88-85 First Mithridatic War. Sulla. 85 Mithridates forced back into Pontus. 83 Tigranes conquers Seleucid realm. 83-81 Second Mithridatic War. 69 Tigranes defeated at Tigranocerta by Lucullus. Disaster in Parthian campaign.	92 Contact between Rome and Parthians. 87-86 Sulla besieges Athens. Fortifications razed, Piraeus burned. 63 Conspiracy of Catiline. 58-51 Caesar's Gallic Wars. 55-54 Caesar's expedition to Britain. 44 Caesar slain. Antony rules Rome. Opposed by Octavian and Consuls. 43 Triumvirate of Antony, Octavian, and Lepidus.

347

Table of Bible History, continued

CHRONOLOGY	HEBREW	WESTERN ASIA	EGYPT	WESTERN WORLD
100 B.C.	46 Antipater's sons Phasael and Herod commanders of Judaea and Galilee. 44 At death of Caesar, Antipater and Herod support Cassius. 43 Antipater assassinated. 41 Phasael and Herod tetrarchs. 40 Parthian invasion; Hasmonaean Antigonus made king, Rome offers kingship to Herod, if he can win it. 38 Herod defeats Antigonus' commander at Isana. 37 Herod captures Jerusalem. Antigonus executed at Antioch. 20 Herod receives from Augustus the Hauran and Batanaea; also Ituraean Tetrarchy of Zenodorus. 20-19 Begins rebuilding of Temple. 10 Temple completed. 7 Alexander and Aristobulus executed. 6-4 Varus, legate of Syria. 4 Herod's son Antipater executed. Herod dies. Uprising suppressed by Varus. 4-6 A.D. Archelaus Ethnarch of Judaea, Idumaea and Samaria. 4-34 A.D. Philip Tetrarch of Batanaea, Trachonitis, Auranitis and "Ituraea." 4-37 A.D. Lysanias Tetrarch of Abilene in Syria. 4-39 A.D. Herod Antipas Tetrarch of Galilee and Peraea.	68-64 Antiochus XIII, last Seleucid king. 54-53 Crassus, legate of Syria. Invades Mesopotamia, is defeated by Parthians at Haran (Carrhae). 52 Pompey sole Consul. 49 Break between Caesar and Pompey. Caesar gets control of Italy and Spain. Pompey goes to Greece. 48 Battle of Pharsalus. Pompey defeated by Caesar; flees to Egypt and is slain. 48-47 Alexandrian War. Caesar intervenes in Egypt. 47 End of Kingdom of Pontus through Caesar's defeat of Pharnaces. 39 Antony defeated in Parthian venture.		42 Battle of Philippi. Death of Brutus and Cassius. 36 Lepidus retires. Octavian ruler of West. 33 Break between Antony and Octavian. 31 Battle of Actium. 30 Death of Antony and Cleopatra. Octavian rules Roman realm. 27 Octavian becomes Augustus Caesar.

(Table continued from left)

CHRONOLOGY	HEBREW	HEBREW	ROME
1 A.D.	6 Second term of Quirinius. Census of Palestine. Uprising of Judas of Gamala, "the Galilaean." c. 29 John the Baptist executed. c. 30 Death of Jesus. 34 Tetrarchy of Philip abolished. c. 35 Paul's conversion. 37 Herod Agrippa I given tetrarchy of Philip and that of Abilene. 38-39 Anti-Jewish rioting in Alexandria. 40 Agrippa gets Tetrarchy of Antipas. 41-44 Herod Agrippa I made king and rules realm of Herod the Great by favor of Claudius. 41-48 Herod of Chalcis, husband of Berenice. 44 Dispersal of the Apostles. James the Just at helm of Jerusalem Church. 44-48 Procuratorial government for Judaea under Cuspius Fadus and Tiberius Alexander.	49 Claudius expells Jews from Rome. 50 Herod Agrippa II gets kingdom of Chalcis. 52-60 Antonius Felix procurator. 53 Agrippa II gives up Chalcis but receives old tetrarchies of Philip and Lysanias. 57 Paul goes to Jerusalem. 58-60 Paul prisoner in Caesarea. 60-62 Porcius Festus procurator. 64 Persecution of Nero. 64-66 Gessius Florus procurator. 66 Cestius Gallus gives up siege of Jerusalem. 66-73 Jewish War. 67 Vespasian subjects Galilee and Samaria. 68 Peraea and Idumaea pacified. 70 Titus begins siege of Jerusalem. City falls in September. 73 Fall of Masada. Jewish uprisings in Alexandria and Cyrene.	14 Death of Augustus. 14-37 Tiberius. 37-41 Caius Caligula. 41-54 Claudius. 54-68 Nero. 68-69 Galba. Otho. Vitellius. 69-79 Vespasian. 79-81 Titus. 81-96 Domitian. 96-98 Nerva. 98-117 Trajan (co-regent in 97).
100 A.D.		100 Death of Agrippa II. His kingdom made part of Syrian province. 106 Nabataean kingdom becomes province of Arabia. 116-117 Jewish uprisings in Alexandria, Cyrene, Cyprus, Mesopotamia, Palestine. 132-135 Uprising of Barcochba. Beth-Ter last resistance. Aelia Capitolina found-	117-138 Hadrian.

THE TIME OF JESUS

The DESIGN on the preceding page shows a Roman triumphal arch, Roman soldier, and a coin of Augustus.

LEFT, *head from colossal statue (about eight feet high) of Antiochus I of Commagene found at Nemrud Dagh. (Courtesy Theresa Goell)* MIDDLE, *sketch of synagogue façade at Capernaum. (After Sukenik)* BOTTOM, *synagogue of Beth Shearim. (Courtesy Archaeological Department, Hebrew University)*

CHAPTER XVIII

THE WORLD INTO WHICH JESUS WAS BORN

"But when the fulness of the time was come, God sent forth his Son." (GAL. 4:4)

It was in this way that the greatest of Christianity's early teachers, Paul of Tarsus, viewed the coming of Jesus Christ. Paul held that a historical process had been completed and the juncture was at hand for something new and different: for a leadership of the spirit that would carry the world to new and undreamed-of possibilities. That leadership was provided by Jesus of Nazareth.

Was the judgment that a historical process had been completed right?

Everywhere the vigor of nations was gone. With incredible good fortune the Romans with their legionaries recruited from con-quered peoples had successively wrecked the Carthaginian, Seleucid and Ptolemaic Empires. With no future left for them, the Greek states and heroic Macedonia sank into helpless dependence. That inevitably affected all aspects of culture as well. The great history of Greek thought had run its course. Greek religion had lost its vitality, and the religion of the conquering state could not replace it in the hearts of men. Eastern cults were imported by faddists and gained adherents because of the attraction exercised by mystification and odd or intriguing rituals. There was life in only one place: in mighty Rome itself. Thither was brought the spoil of nations, there the conquered kings and chieftains marched in the triumphs of the victorious generals. A poet-prophet of the

Latins, Virgil, could eloquently hail the very times in which Jesus was born as a Messianic Age, such as was predicted in eastern books utilizing Hebrew prophecy.

But this was merely Latin pride and patriotism; the heart of humanity was not in it. A heathen Rome, though it could prepare the way for the Gospel by treading down the whole world, could not provide the spirit of life to animate that world. And for Rome itself this very age was the end of creativeness. What follows is only decadence, a succession of tyrannies, an epic of human selfishness and bestiality.

Yes, Paul was right in his judgment. The world was waiting, though it knew it not, for the messenger of glad tidings, for a peace different from the *pax Romana*.

The Caesars Appear on the Scene

The story of Rome's rise is as remarkable as the rise of the United States or of the Russian Empire. A glance at Color Map XIX makes plain how from the city of Rome there evolved the greatest empire the earth had yet known.

In the period of 264–133 B.C. the Roman Republic had paved the way for the assumption of a powerful position in the world. In the period of 133–31 B.C., the Roman Republic was rent with internal dissension and civil war, but at the same time made further progress in the conflict with external enemies. Beginning with Sulla, who first used the army against the state's own citizens, the path to dictatorship was opened.

Julius Caesar, who had trained his legions to the highest state of military efficiency in the Gallic wars, was thus enabled to defy the senate and seize power. His murder in 44 B.C. by representatives of the senatorial party once more posed the question whether a return to republican government was possible. Octavian, the adopted son of Julius Caesar, was at first on the republican side, and opposed Mark Antony, who was seeking to succeed to the position and power of Caesar. But

Octavian soon reached an agreement with Antony and the two, with a third man named Lepidus, formed a so-called triumvirate or "three man rule." The senatorial party led by Brutus and Cassius, Caesar's slayers, lost out in the defeat of their army (42 B.C.).

But the triumvirate could be no lasting arrangement. With Mark Antony operating in the east and lingering in Egypt at the court of Cleopatra, Octavian took measures to increase his power in the west, first by ridding himself of Lepidus and then by putting down all of Antony's partisans. Antony himself was finally defeated by him in the naval battle of Actium (31 B.C.) and, forsaken by all of his supporters, committed suicide in Egypt.

Octavian, having attained full power and being recognized as first citizen (*princeps*), now put aside legally the institution of the triumvirate. He first relinquished the command which had been entrusted to him by the senate in 32 B.C., whereupon that body then gave him full military power (as *imperator*), the decision over war and peace, and the title of "Augustus" (27 B.C.), which was commonly used as though it were his name (LUKE 2:1). He rejected the title of king and in addition to the title Augustus bore only the family name of "Caesar."

The reign of Augustus from 31 B.C. to 14 A.D. was a period of peace. The old national barriers had fallen; it was possible to travel about in one world, and with a degree of safety previously unknown, for Roman soldiery curbed local conflict and punished banditry and piracy. The peoples flourished in a material way at least under the aegis of a stern but fairly just government.

It was providential that Christianity's beginnings should have occurred under Roman rule. At no previous period could this religion have spread so rapidly from city to city and country to country. In that respect, too, it was the "fulness of the time."

The boyhood of Jesus fell during the time of the reign of Augustus, and his young manhood, ministry, and death on the cross came under Tiberius (14–37 A.D.). The great years of the beginning of the Church were those under Caligula (37–41 A.D.) and Claudius (41–54 A.D.). It was under Nero (54–68 A.D.) that the Church was to go through the fire of trial and witness the passing of its greatest leaders.

The Provinces of the Roman Empire

The "world" of Roman days (see Color Map XIX) was still essentially composed of all that circle of regions contiguous to the Mediterranean. Like two crescents these regions lay about that sea. The lower crescent began with Cilicia and Syria. It took in Palestine, the Nabataean realm from the Bostra area to the Arabian coast south of Madiama, Egypt (Aegyptus) as far as Syene on the Nile, Libya, Africa (a term originally restricted to the region between Cyrene and Carthage [Carthago]), and finally Mauretania in the extreme west. The upper crescent began with Hispania, Gallia and with the lower Rhine (Rhenus), and followed the Danube (Danuvius) to the Black Sea; skirting the shores of that sea it took in all of Asia Minor to the northwest corner of Syria in the south, and in the north as far as the upper reaches of the Euphrates, behind which lay the Armenian kingdom. The latter gravitated toward the Parthian realm, which had control of ancient Mesopotamia and the Babylon area, Media and Persia and the regions east as far as the Indoscythian states (see Color Map XII). These easterly areas, which once had been a vast source of wealth to the Achaemenids and the Seleucids, Rome was content to leave under Parthian rule. The Arsacids, as the Parthian royal house was called, no longer menaced the control of the west. Indeed, the Roman leaders realized that a strong Parthia was the best safeguard to security in the eastern world by barring off the invasion of peoples from beyond the Oxus River. To police all these regions was unattractive.

The provinces (Greek "eparchies") of the Roman Empire were divided into those under the administration of the senate, and those under the administration of the emperor. Those which involved any hazard for the security of the frontiers were under the emperor. When the situation with respect to peril changed, the status of the provinces changed from senatorial to imperial or vice versa. The size of the provinces, too, was not established once and for all, but was subject to adjustment. Syria was one of the most important provinces and exposed to danger of invasion from Armenia, Parthia and Arabia. It was, therefore, under imperial administration. A few subject kingdoms were allowed to exist, such as the one of Herod and of Antiochus of Commagene, but these rulers occupied their posts only as long as it pleased Rome.

The Political Situation in Palestine

Looking at the Palestinian scene in particular, we note that it had changed considerably in a century of Roman rule. The Greek cities that had been victims of Jewish vengeance or had languished in weakness were all re-established and strengthened by Roman favor. Herod, king over all Palestine and adjacent regions, by the grace of Augustus Caesar, promoted the welfare of his territories irrespective of Jewish national interests, and was a mighty builder. New Hellenistic-type cities like Caesarea with its harbor and Sebaste (Samaria) were monuments to his cultural efforts. He also did much building in Jerusalem, and brought water to the growing city by means of an aqueduct all the way from the so-called Pools of Solomon southwest of Bethlehem. But above all he rebuilt the second Temple on a grand scale. Perhaps to avoid the sort of contest over the throne that had destroyed the Hasmonaean House, Herod in his final testament divided his realm among three sons, the brothers Archelaus and Herod Antipas, and their half-brother Philip. This

353

testament, however, could stand only if approved by Augustus. It was contested by Archelaus, who in an earlier testament had been named successor, but in the end it was confirmed.

Archelaus received Judaea, Samaria and Idumaea, but for the present only with the official title of ethnarch. Of course the common people will have called him "king," and so does Matthew 2:22. Antipas received Galilee and Peraea as a "tetrarchy" and with the title "tetrarch," while Philip got the tetrarchy of Batanaea (Bashan), Trachonitis (the *Leja*), Auranitis (the *Hauran*) and the district of Paneas, which was cut off from the Ituraean kingdom of southern Syria to which it had previously belonged. Another tetrarchy was made up of a further portion of Ituraea called Abilene—the district around the city of Abila, west of Damascus—and this was given to Lysanias, a descendant of the Ituraean royal house.

Archelaus, who had the chance to continue with much of his father's power and influence, quickly lost out. After his accession (4 B.C.) the Jews became extremely unruly. Archelaus governed with brutality. He furthermore incensed public sentiment by putting aside his wife Mariamne and entering into a second marriage with Glaphyra, widow of his step-brother Alexander. Since this woman had had children by Alexander, the marriage was contrary to Jewish custom. Judaean and Samaritan delegations went to Rome with their complaints. Augustus summoned Archelaus and after giving him a hearing banished him to Gaul in 6 A.D. His territory was now taken over by the Romans and administered by a procurator residing at Caesarea.

The Jews under the Procurators

The procurator was an especial type of imperial governor and was so named because procurement or financial management was his prime concern. The Gospel writers do not use his proper title, but simply call him

governor (LUKE 3:1; ACTS 23:24), and the same designation is given the legate of Syria (LUKE 2:2). Procurators were appointed where conditions were particularly difficult. They were as independent as the legates, though the nearest legate could override them. This procuratorial government became a major source of trouble and unrest in Judaea, and led finally to the great disaster of the Jewish war. The Roman business men who were given the procurator jobs were totally at a loss in dealing with an Oriental people bound by so many ceremonial laws, and capable of such fanaticism in matters of their religion. The procurators were apt to make one mistake after another.

The taking over of Judaea and Samaria into direct imperial government necessitated a census. This took place under the first procurator, Coponius (6–9 A.D.). Luke, who connects the birth of Jesus with the event, does not mention the procurator's name because the order was issued by the legate of Syria, P. Sulpicius Quirinius, who had assumed that office for the second time in the same year, 6 A.D. Luke has universalized this census. He may have thought that it coincided with an enrollment that was conducted in the provinces every year to register all those liable for the poll tax. If the great Pharisaic teacher Gamaliel in addressing the council says that Judas the Galilaean rebelled at the time of the census (ACTS 5:37), that agrees with Josephus; but the main rebellion took place during the unrest immediately after the death of Herod in 4 B.C. and was quelled by C. Quintilius Varus, who was legate of Syria at the time—the same man who was later to meet an inglorious end in the forests of Germany. Sepphoris in Galilee, the center of Judas' activities, was destroyed at this time, and its inhabitants were sold into slavery.

These events, which may have taken place in Jesus' childhood, must have left a deep impression on the minds of the people of nearby Nazareth. They will have helped to

7.1 *Herod's fortress, Masada, was on this crag above the Dead Sea.* (*Courtesy Department of Archaeology, Hebrew University and Louis M. Rabinowitz*)

convince Jesus that political Messianism was not the road to salvation for God's people.

In the main the situation established by Augustus Caesar continued in the years to come. Judaea and Samaria had been under procurators since 6 A.D. In the years of Jesus' ministry the incumbent was Pontius Pilate (26–36 A.D.). Complaints lodged against him by the Jews finally brought about his removal from office in the last years of Tiberius (14–37 A.D.). The procuratorship of Marullus from 37 to 41 A.D., under Caligula (37–41 A.D.), was marked by a serious crisis, owing to the emperor's demand that he be accorded divine worship. The statue of the emperor was to be set up in the Temple of Jerusalem for that purpose, and the governor of Syria, Petronius, was ordered to smash all resistance. But Herod Agrippa, a grandson of the old king and son of Aristobulus (put to death by Herod in 7 B.C.) was in Rome and succeeded in getting the order withdrawn. Caligula

died in 41 A.D. and was succeeded by Claudius (41–54 A.D.).

A brief interim of change in the status of Judaea now followed. It was due to the fact that Herod Agrippa had played an active role in supporting Claudius' aspirations to become emperor. Out of gratitude toward him, Claudius appointed him king of Judaea and Samaria. He thus was given much of the power held by his grandfather, Herod the Great. Like him he was a Jew to the Jews and a Greek to the Greeks. Herod Agrippa presumed unduly on the royal favor, however, when he began to build the so-called "third wall of Jerusalem" to embrace the suburban district that had grown up north of the second wall (see Color Map XVIII). The legate of Syria soon stopped the undertaking.

At Agrippa's death in 44 A.D. no successor was appointed. Judaea and Samaria again came under procurators and stayed under them until the Jewish War in 66 A.D.

CHAPTER XIX

THE GOSPEL STORY

THE GOSPELS WERE NOT intended to be biographies of Jesus of Nazareth, although one modern book about him, written by a noted historian, regularly speaks of them as "Lives." For these writers the theme was the origin of the Christian message, for which and by which the Church lived. And when early in the second century "the Gospel According to the Four" was set up, as the initial stage in the creation of an authoritative New Testament, the thought was that none of these four by itself sufficed to give a complete account, but that each made a valuable contribution to the picture. Nor was the Church troubled by seeming divergences in the parallel narratives. The thing that mattered most was the spirit that breathed from these pages. Like the different stops of an organ the four blended into a beautiful harmony.

We of today are wont to ask questions that did not occur to the authors of the Gospels. We are, for example, keenly aware of the importance of environment. We would like to identify the scenes in which Jesus of Nazareth moved about, and are eager to go with him from place to place. We would like to have the times in which he lived re-created in a realistic manner. To these ends we must analyze the old narratives and try to bring to bear on them such illumination as may be obtained from outside literary sources, from early Christian tradition, and from archaeological research. But the road back is not easy. This is especially true with respect to the daily life of the ordinary people. Not even an "assemblage" of tools and wares, such as archaeologists have set up for periods millennia earlier has been attempted. The first authentic illustration of Jewish life in those times has come from the excavations at the Qumran settlement near the Dead Sea (page 369), the home of the community to which we owe the preservation of the Dead Sea Scrolls. But this ascetic group hardly lived a normal Jewish existence. Perhaps some site in Galilee will yet produce for us a record of typical Jewish village life of the time of Jesus.

But while archaeological exploration can yet reveal a great deal, we must realize that there are limitations to the prospects. Remains of the time of Christ are "recent," archaeologically speaking, and hence lie near the surface, except where covered by later strata. Surface remains of the village variety, however, had small chance to survive through the ages. In the places most appealing to Christian interest, any vestiges of the first century lie under later massive structures, difficult or impossible to remove, or under modern towns. We must resign ourselves to the fact that there is no way to re-create the Bethlehem or the Nazareth of Jesus, as Mr. Rockefeller has re-created Colonial Williamsburg in Virginia.

In the following pages, we will consider the geography of the life of Christ in the sequence suggested by the narratives. Since the Gospels, especially the first three, parallel each other to a great extent, it would be unprofitable to follow the account of each separately. The indicated course is to take the oldest one, that of Mark, as a basis and consider the variations or extra materials of the other Gospels at the points where they become relevant.

Mark begins with the ministry of John the Baptist and links with that the beginning of Jesus' prophetic ministry (MARK 1:14). He feels no need to enlighten the reader on Jesus' birth. That was not as yet a matter of great concern. Matthew and Luke, however, do feel the need of telling about Jesus' birth,

7.2 'Ain Kārim, *the supposed home of John the Baptist.* (*Matson Photo Service*)

and the latter includes also one episode of his boyhood. Therein both, and Luke especially, make a slight concession to the side of a rising "biographical" interest on the part of people of Greek extraction and training. For about this same time a man named Plutarch was writing about the lives of famous men, and teaching the world what a fascinating subject that can be. Since Luke goes into more detail than Matthew with respect to the birth of Jesus, his infancy narrative has become dominant in the mind of Christendom, and Matthew's contributions are merely used to fill out the picture.

The Home of John the Baptist

For Luke, as for Mark, the Gospel story begins with John the Baptist, except that Luke (unlike Matthew) feels the need to tell us also of John's parentage and birth. It is rather strange that Luke does not tell us where John was born. If he knew it he may have omitted the fact intentionally in order to discourage further interest in a man who still had his own following apart from the Christian Church (ACTS 18:25; 19:3). An early but unverifiable tradition asserts that John's birthplace was 'Ain Kārim (mentioned as *Karem* in the Greek translation of Joshua 15:59 but missing in the Hebrew). It is a village situated in a lovely, secluded valley three and a half miles west of Jerusalem. And, indeed, the account of Mary's journey into the "hill country . . . to a city of Judah" (LUKE 1:39) clearly means a place west of Jerusalem. John's father, Zacharias, was a priest of the Abijah order, which is eighth among those listed in 1 Chronicles 24:7 f. We must not think of priesthood as a full time job. There were so many priests that each one only got a chance to serve for a week twice a year. They owed their right purely to their descent. It was thus quite possible for priests to live far from the Temple and merely travel there when their period of service was scheduled. Indeed, one could raise the question whether Luke's belief that the priest Zacharias dwelt in Judaea within easy reach of the Temple was not just an inference on the Evangelist's part. An important Jewish poem of the ninth century A.D., written by a man named Kalir and containing ancient information (second to third century) about the homes of the priestly clans, reveals that the Abijah order lived at that time in Kephar Uzziel in Galilee. This town lay at *Umm el 'Amad* in the plain of Beth Netophah (*Baṭṭōf*) north of Nazareth. The ruins of a synagogue still exist there (fig. 7.3),

7.3 *Ruins of the synagogue of Kephar Uzziel in Galilee, a town where the priests of the Abijah order of Luke resided. (Courtesy Archaeological Department, Hebrew University and Louis M. Rabinowitz)*

probably on the site of an earlier one of the time of Christ. He will surely have visited this synagogue. Mary's going to see Elizabeth at this nearby town would certainly have been more feasible than a trip to Judah (LUKE 1:39).

The Early Life of Jesus

A harmonized version of Matthew 2:23 and Luke 2:4 lives in the Christian mind, with the second, that of Luke, dominant. But no matter whether Joseph came from Nazareth originally or went there secondarily, it was the city where Jesus grew up, and with which he was so firmly associated that he became "Jesus of Nazareth" to his contemporaries (if the customary interpretation of Greek *Nazarenos* is correct).

Nazareth

The allusions in the Gospels to Nazareth are the oldest known references to this town. It is not among the places mentioned in Joshua 19:10 f., nor is it referred to by Josephus, who gives the names of forty-five Galilaean towns, nor by the Talmud which names sixty-three. The sole reference to it in Jewish literature is in the elegy of Kalir, referred to above, according to which a town named *Nṣrt* (so written in the unvocalized Hebrew) was the home of the priestly order of Happizzez (A. V. Aphses, 1 CHRON. 24:15) in the second or third century A.D. Eusebius says of Nazareth that it lies in Galilee fifteen Roman miles from Legio in the direction of Mount Tabor.

Legio (*el Lejjūn*) lay, near the tell of Megiddo, in the Plain of Esdraelon, and was the district center in the Church Father's day. To go to Nazareth from the coastal plain one will have gone to Legio and then on to Mount Tabor, to avoid crossing the plain and the Kishon stream, for that more direct course was not feasible for a good part of the year.

The early Christian pilgrims doubtless sought Nazareth at the place where it is still shown today, *en Nāṣira,* which preserves the old name in Arabic adaptation. But the New Testament form of the name, Nazareth, is not quite the original Hebrew form either, but a modified pronunciation given it in its passage into Greek. The original name must have been *Nāṣerāth,* corresponding in formation to that of Daberath, a nearby town (JOSH. 19:12).

The Nazareth of Joseph's time was clearly not of great consequence (JOHN 1:46). It was not, so far as we know, a very ancient place, for no tell indicates the existence of a Bronze Age or even Iron Age settlement in that vicinity. If one wonders why no city of importance had arisen in this otherwise favorable neighborhood, the answer must be that this territory belonged to a strong town a mile and a half to the west, the Japhia (better Japha) of the tribe of Zebulun (JOSH. 19:12), a place already mentioned in the Palestine list of Thutmosis III (1500 B.C.), and still bearing the name of *Yāfa* today (fig. 7.4). According to Josephus this was the strongest fortress of lower Galilee in his time. Another town of consequence, the Chesulloth of the tribe of Issachar (JOSH. 19:18), lay a mile and three-quarters southeast of Nazareth (at *Iksāl*). Under those circumstances one can see why Nazareth never grew to be strong. Its name probably means "guardplace"—a fitting name for an outpost of Japhia. It was doubtless just a small village, where people tilled the hillsides or made a living from trades.

By no stretch of the imagination can Nazareth be said to have lain on an important artery of traffic. The great route from Damascus to the sea nowadays goes to Beirut in Syria, but that was not the case in antiquity. The best route to the sea from Damascus crossed the Jordan a little below the Lake of Galilee and went via Sepphoris out to Ptolemais, as Acco was called in Jesus' time. It may be that since Herod had built up Caesarea much travel went to the latter place, rather than to Ptolemais. But such caravans would have gone via Scythopolis (Beth-shean), Samaria, and Dothan. Only travel bound from the south to Sepphoris would have had occasion to pass through Nazareth.

Nazareth has a pleasant location in a basin or amphitheater on the south side of the *Jebel es Sīkh.* Since the rock in this area is limestone into which cisterns can easily be cut, the storage of rain water is readily possible. That has been a big factor in the town's existence. There is, indeed, in present-day

7.4 *Japhia, on the northern edge of the Plain of Esdraelon. An important town and fortress stood here and held sway over the region of Nazareth. (Courtesy Archaeological Department, Hebrew University and Louis M. Rabinowitz)*

7.5 *Nazareth.* (*Keren Hayesod, Jerusalem*)

Nazareth one good spring, which emerges from the ground about 150 feet north of the Church of St. Gabriel. The waters of the spring are conducted under the church and led into the so-called "'Well of Mary," where the women gather to obtain their drinking water.

Edward Robinson in 1838 found such a crowd waiting around it to fill their jars and such strife as to who should come first that he never could get near it. Pious imagination pictures the mother of Jesus as frequenting this place with her waterjar.

The most suitable site for an old Hebrew settlement, such as Nazareth undoubtedly was, is the hill above the "new fountain" (*'Ain Jedîde*), so called because for a time it ran dry and then started up again. This fountain is more likely to have been the one to which Mary went. There is a monastery on the hill now, but it cannot be learned whether any ancient remains were exposed when its foundations were laid. If Nazareth did not lie on that hill, then it may have lain below it, on the site where the Nazareth of early Christian travelers must admittedly be sought. The oldest buildings of the present-day city all lie in this vicinity. Some Jewish tombs of the second century have been found at Nazareth, and there is an ossuary with a brief inscription in the museum of the Franciscans. But what the Nazareth of today has to offer is all of much later vintage. Moslem fanaticism carried on a veritable obliteration here in the Middle Ages, and the Franciscan efforts to get a foothold and revive defunct tradition deserve admiration, for it is a story full of sacrifice and suffering.

He who would commemorate Jesus in the spirit, however, would much prefer to find a spot not "consecrated" by the hand of man. As far back as 1838 Edward Robinson, who regarded all "holy places" with skepticism, sought escape from those forced on him at

7.6 Ṣafed, *the "city set upon a hill."* (*Matson Photo Service*)

7.7 *View from the north toward Mount Tabor.* (*Keren Hayesod, Jerusalem*)

Nazareth by going alone to the Mohammedan *Weli* of *Nebi Ismaīl* on the height west of the town. Here he remained for some hours, lost in the contemplation of the wide prospect. In the north he could see Sepphoris, with the plain of *el Baṭṭōf* beyond it, while to the northeast lay the higher mountains of the *Jaulān,* overtowered by Mount Hermon with its snowy crown. The sight of *Ṣāfed* on its height beyond the *el Baṭṭōf* Plain, Robinson thought, must have been in Jesus' mind, when he spoke of the city set upon a hill that cannot be hid (MATT. 5:14). But even more impressive in many ways was the view to the south and southwest over Esdraelon and over the Mediterranean Sea.

This was the environment that, in conjunction with heredity and special influences from on high, formed the character of Jesus.

"O Little Town of Bethlehem"

The nativity narratives of Luke and Matthew have raised Bethlehem to celebrity in the eyes of mankind. Luke tells us nothing of the long, hard journey, but immediately takes us to the point of arrival and the birth of Mary's child. As Bethlehem lay on the important artery leading south to Hebron and the Negeb, the overcrowding of facilities is reasonable, even without the special situation created by the census. What constituted an "inn" to Luke is not clear, for even the Greek and Roman sources give us no satisfactory account of this institution. One thinks of the *Meḍāfeh* of the modern Arab village, which merely provides a shelter for strangers.

Very early tradition held that a cave on the east of the city was the place of the nativity. Indeed, it seems likely that Justin Martyr (*c.* 150 A.D.), a native of Palestine, already was thinking of the traditional site still revered to this day as Christ's birthplace, when he said that Joseph had to be contented with a cave because he found no lodgings *in the town.* It is reported by various writers of antiquity that the cave of the nativity was desecrated in Hadrian's time (137 A.D.) by a cult of Adonis, and that it lay in a sacred grove. Jerome compares its recovery for Christianity with that of the recovery of the Ark of the Covenant for Jerusalem by David. It was Constantine to whom this recovery had been due, for he caused the place to be purged of the last vestiges of heathenism (*c.* 326 A.D.), and had a beautiful church built over what Eusebius calls "the mystic grotto."

While the present Church of the Nativity at Bethlehem may have undergone rebuilding, notably in the sixth century under the emperor Justinian, the nave of Constantine's structure is still there. That makes it one of the most ancient churches of Christendom. Stairways lead down from the choir on the north and south sides to a grotto thirty-three feet long by thirteen feet wide, clearly the cave as the Christians of the fourth century knew it. The floor level is somewhat lower on the south side of the grotto and there is a niche in the rock on the right, which can be construed as a manger.

361

7.8 *The shepherds' fields with Bethlehem in the background.* (*Matson Photo Service*)

There can be no disputing the venerable antiquity of this crypt. There is even a possibility that it is the place that was regarded as that of the nativity in the days before Hadrian. The defilement of a Christian holy place at Bethlehem would be quite in line with what allegedly happened to Golgotha and Christ's tomb under Hadrian (see page 408).

But the thing that is doubtful is whether the Church of the apostolic age sought to ascertain and thought of honoring the birthplace of Jesus. If the identity was established after 100 A.D., Christian title to the place is not as good as it might be. The proximity of the grotto to "the field of the shepherds" could have suggested that it was the appropriate spot. There is also the possibility that the ancient sanctuary of Bethlehem lay here, and that age-old veneration was just renewed with Christian reinterpretation.

Whether the tradition about the sacred grotto of Bethlehem is reliable or not, its hoary antiquity has hallowed it. One cannot forget all the Christian devotion that has been poured out here through the ages. What remains the same as it was when Jesus was born is the topography. West of the Church of the Nativity was doubtless the old city's eastern gate. As one goes down the narrow east-west street south of the church, one gets to a point where there is a noble prospect. In the distant background lies the rugged wilderness of Judah and behind it the strip of the Dead Sea. On the horizon looms the high tableland of the Transjordan country,

with the fortress of old Moab (today *et Kerak*) in the south a shining point on its high crag. Truly, Bethlehem was a city worthy of being the birthplace of Jesus, though it was not predestined to be the scene of his preaching or of his death.

The field where the shepherds experienced the vision of angels was sought by the early Church in the nearer foreground of the scene just described. Here, east of Bethlehem, is indeed the natural quarter in which to look for it.

In the springtime, with grass abundant, the shepherds would not yet have strayed far from the town, though of course keeping outside of its arable lands. They would be within an easy walk of the cave.

But there was also a scriptural reason for locating the field there; for near the tomb of Rachel is put "a tower of Eder," (A.V. Edar, GEN. 35:21), or better a place named Migdal-eder, with the meaning "tower of the flock." Tradition identified Migdal-eder with the nearby village of *Beit Sāḥūr,* a name derived from that of Ashhur, "father" of Tekoa (1 CHRON. 2:24). The prediction that the kingdom of the daughter of Jerusalem was to come to the "tower of the flock" (MIC. 4:8) was understood as referring to the angelic announcement of the birth of the Messiah to the shepherds of this Migdal-eder.

The Magi

Matthew's Christmas story, however, has also contributed vastly to the composite ver-

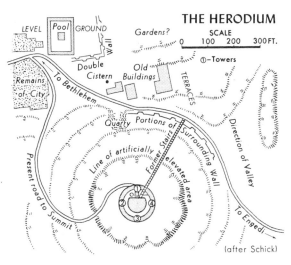

(after Schick)

sion of the events of which we hear each Yuletide. There are first of all the glamorous figures of the Wise Men from the East. Whence they came is not made very clear. If the Greek word "east" is a translation of the Hebrew word *qedem*, then they would have been from among the "sons of the East," i.e., the Arabians. Old Testament prophecy, it was thought in the early Church, had predicted the coming of men from that quarter (Is. 60:6). The astrological interest of the Wise Men, on the other hand, pointed toward Chaldea, where Orchoë (Erech) was still a noted center for that sort of learning. On the other hand, the term Magi suggested a home in Iran. Their coming to Jerusalem and Bethlehem in any case must have been by the north-south highway. If they were warned in a dream not to return to Jerusalem, but "departed to their own country by another way," one may imagine them as going eastward, past the Theodosius monastery (*Dēr Dōsi*) toward the Jordan ford above the head of the Dead Sea, thus bypassing not only Jerusalem but Jericho as well.

Herod and the Herodium

But Matthew also brought evil King Herod, whom Luke does not mention, into the Christmas picture. Herod was unforgotten and unforgettable in Bethlehem, for southeast of this city he had one of his castles built, the "Herodium." Perhaps we may digress here to speak of it, for it looms large on the horizon of Jesus' birthplace. It was rediscovered by Edward Robinson, who was able to identify it with the so-called Frank Mountain or *Jebel el Fūreidīs*, where, so fifteenth-century tradition claimed, the Crusaders had held out for forty years after the fall of the Kingdom of Jerusalem. Herod's choice of that place for a castle was due to his fondness for the locality as such, for here he had won an important victory over the supporters of the last Maccabean king. Josephus relates that the place was a hill that was

raised artificially to a further height by the hand of man till it was the shape of a woman's breast. It was encompassed with circular towers and had a staircase of 200 steps of polished stone leading up to it. Within were luxurious apartments. Around the base of the hill there were other fine buildings. He notes especially that water had to be conducted here from a great way off (from *Arṭās*) at vast expense. The plain round about was full of large houses, such as are found in cities— no doubt the villas of relatives and courtiers. Indeed Herod liked it so well here that he chose this hilltop for a final resting place.

7.9 *The Frank Mountain. (Matson Photo Service)*

7.10 *Statues of gods Ahuramazda, Mithras, Vereth-ragna, Commagene, and Antiochus on* Nemrūd Dagh. (*Courtesy T. Goell and F. K. Doerner*)

One can hardly be in doubt where he got the idea: it was from King Antiochus of Commagene, who had himself buried on the *Nemrūd Dagh* in the Taurus, and had gravel piled over his tomb to a depth of hundreds of feet, thus elevating the summit of the entire mountain. Herod had gone to Samosata to pay his respects to Mark Antony, at the time when the Roman general was besieging Antiochus in that capital (38 B.C.). No doubt he met Antiochus when the latter surrendered, and later heard about the magnificent and original memorial which that ruler had created for himself. The Herodium was Herod's bid for a similarly unique mausoleum. Whether the crypt is still there amid the ruins, perhaps deep down in the hill, can only be determined by archaeological investigation. Perhaps his sarcophagus will yet be found undisturbed, as it is hoped that of Antiochus of Commagene will be recovered by the *Nemrūd Dagh* expedition of Theresa Goell and F. K. Doerner.

In the war of 70 A.D. Jewish rebels held out in the Herodium for some time, and when the Romans captured the castle they destroyed it. It was at that time that the summit took on the crater-like appearance so characteristic of it.

The death of the "Holy Innocents," which Matthew attributes to Herod's command, puts into vivid light what depravity the old rogue was held capable of. On the other hand the allusion to Rachel "weeping for her children" proves that Rachel's tomb must have been shown in the Evangelist's time where its more recent counterpart now stands. For only the proximity of the ancestral mother's supposed resting-place explains her particular concern for the children of Bethlehem.

"Out of Egypt Have I Called My Son"

The flight of the Holy Family to Egypt is another contribution of Matthew to the Christmas story as it lives among us. Nothing is said about the route they took. The traveler of those times in going from Bethlehem to Egypt would probably have gone via Beth-zur or Hebron to the coastal plain and then down the regular highway to Pelusium. The sojourn in Egypt has left no further echo.

At *Maṭarīyeh,* close to the ruins of Heliopolis, a so-called "tree of Mary" was shown as early as the fifth century, while a mediaeval traveler speaks of a "well of Mary"; both no doubt are fancies of the imagination.

The return from Egypt is connected with the accession of Archelaus in 4 B.C. (MATT. 2:22). If Joseph desired to avoid Judaea in going to Galilee, he might have kept up the coastal highway through Sharon and then have taken the road to Legio and Scythopolis, turning off it near Mount Tabor to strike for Nazareth.

Going to Jerusalem

What impressions of life can compare with those received in one's childhood? Think of what it means for a small-town boy to visit Washington, D.C., and all the patriotic shrines of its environment! It meant even more for a boy from little Nazareth in Galilee to go to Jerusalem, because not only patriotism was involved, but religion above all. The patriotic side cannot be overlooked, however, for the Galilean Jews were ardent patriots.

Galilee owed its Judaization to the imperialism of the Maccabees, and Jerusalem was their city. King Herod was in debt for what hold he had on the Jewish people to the fact that his wife, Mariamne, was a princess of the Maccabean house. His slaughter of all those of that blood, including his own sons by her, had done more than anything else to arouse hatred for him.

But Jerusalem was above all the seat of a religious empire. Prophecies such as had never been spoken of any city on earth gave it an aureole of glory. Millions of Jews and proselytes in that Roman world were praying daily with faces turned toward Jerusalem. Pilgrims came thither from all the earth. Going up to Jerusalem was thus a marvelous experience for the boy Jesus.

The Passover journey of the Galileans would have consumed three days by the shortest route, for it was sixty-two miles as the crow flies from the southern boundary of Galilee to Jerusalem. While there are several different roads that could be taken, the shortest and most attractive one for residents of Nazareth and its environs led through the Samaritan country. They would have gone via Mount Tabor to Ginnaia (*Jenīn*) and then to Samaria and Shechem. This route had the further advantages of easier traveling and more comfortable temperatures than the route via the Jordan Valley, which, however, might well be preferred in the wintertime.

The first night's stop might have been at *Ṣānūr* north of the city of Samaria and the second at ancient Lebonah (*el Lubbān*) on the northern border of Judaea. If Joseph and Mary later traveled a day's journey in the homeward direction, hoping to find the lost boy among the other pilgrims, this same valley of Lebonah, where there was a good caravanserai near a spring, would probably have been the locality where they sought him in vain and had to turn back. Crusader tradition, it is true, found the place at *el Bīreh* and built a church of St. Mary there; but that is only half a day's journey from Jeru-

7.11 El Lubban, *probable overnight stopping place of caravans from Galilee to Jerusalem.* (*Matson Photo Service*)

salem. A full day's journey brings one to Lebonah as the indicated stopping place.

Boys of Jesus' age just were beginning to attend the synagogue service and so were not yet familiar with all the Bible stories. A father taking his son to Jerusalem for the first time would naturally point out to him the places that had played a role in their people's history, wherever ancient names were still alive, and would tell him something about those happenings. What great events had taken place at Jezreel, Samaria, Shechem, Bethel!

What anticipation must have gripped the boy Jesus when he asked, "How far is it yet?" to learn that they were almost there. At last at the place called *Ṣāfīn*, "the watchers" (Greek: Mount Scopus), Jerusalem burst into view, one and a half miles distant. Here the pilgrims paused, their breath taken away by the sight! And the boy Jesus must have looked wide-eyed on the city of his dreams. The City of David! Think what that would mean to a lad whose father was a descendant of the king who had made this city important in the eyes of the world! On the spot where the pilgrims stood, surveying with rapture the glorious scene, had halted many a general and potentate in ages

365

7.12 *Jerusalem from the west.* (*Courtesy Bavarian State Archives*)

past. One could see in the mind's eye the Rabshakeh of Sennacherib and his officers, coming to demand the surrender of the city; the generals of Nebuchadnezzar examining the defenses with the eyes of eagles to divine where they might be breached. Here according to ancient story the High Priest Yaddua had received mighty Alexander the Great, when he was en route to Egypt. In the depths of a future yet unborn, others were waiting for their turn to step forth upon this stage: Roman emperors, Saracen generals, Crusader kings.

"A City That Is Compact Together"

As Jesus saw it from the north, Jerusalem presented a face of thirty-foot walls with many towers rising as high again above them.

The eastern part of the city, with the Temple, projected out beyond the western area, though the exact course of the north wall in the western section is still a matter of debate. This projecting part of the north wall was straddled on its right hand corner by a great citadel which Herod had named the Antonia, in honor of Mark Antony (page 402). On its towers now stood helmeted Roman soldiers, keeping an eye on the Temple courts immediately to the south. The ground to the north of the Antonia inclined upwards, so that from where Jesus stood one could also see part of the Temple courts and discern "The House" on the west side. A valley sloped off past the Temple on the east, and one could see that the Temple quadrangle stood on what quickly became a precipitous height. There was also a "draw" or valley leading down in the middle of the city, dividing it into two parts. The main residential part lay on the higher western hill and was called the Upper City, and from here a bridge led across the city-valley to the temple. Near the gate through which the pilgrims were going to enter the city one could see the palace of the Hasmonaean kings, whose dynasty had ended with the coming of the Romans.

The northwestern corner of the Upper City was marked by the palace of King Herod, which now was at the full disposal of the Roman procurators. Three prominent towers were visible on its northern side, and were known as Phasael, Mariamne and Hippicus; they were named after Herod's brother, wife, and a friend. One of them was destined to survive for long ages, being part of the present Tower of David (probably Phasael).

The two hills sloped off to the south, so that even the high towers of the southern wall of its defenses were not visible from the north.

As they approached the Gennath or "Garden" gate the eyes of the boy Jesus will have seen the city's place of execution, known as Golgotha.

Passing through the impressive gateway and the courtyard between its flanking towers they found themselves in the city, where the first task will have been to seek lodgings and prepare themselves for a visit to the Temple, according to the elaborate requirements laid down by the Pharisaic teachers.

What an experience it must have been for the boy to enter those sacred courts, which Herod's building activity had rendered so beautiful. We may imagine him walking about in the halls or colonnades on the sides of the Court of the Women, which lay on a level lower than that of the inner sanctuary (see page 400). In this area pious visitors such as Anna (LUKE 2:36 f.) could linger. It is here where Jesus is later said to have taught (JOHN 8:20), and it presumably was here also where the boy Jesus approached some Teachers of the Law—who were laymen, not priests—with his eager questions. The sudden love the boy developed for the Temple, which made him forget parents, friends and the passing of time, is revealed by his reply to his worried mother's reproaches. Thus early did the boy reveal the bent of mind and the singleness of purpose that were characteristic of the adult. All this came out of "going down to Jerusalem" at an impressionable age and of seeing with the idealistic eyes of youth.

The Baptism and Ministry

The story of the Gospel is the account of how Jesus brought the heaven-born "good tidings" of God's love and mercy to men. But the work of Jesus was preceded by the brief ministry of John the Baptist. The latter's preaching of an impending world-crisis and his baptismal rite, whereby he effected a cleansing and hallowing of men's lives, were

7.13 *Airview of the Qumran excavation. (Palestine Archaeological Museum)*

7.14 *Storage bins in the Qumran settlement. (Palestine Archaeological Museum)*

viewed as an indispensable part of the Gospel story. Jesus himself had put John above all the prophets (MATT. 11:9).

In the Wilderness

According to the Gospel of Mark (1:4), John the Baptist appeared in the wilderness. That immediately suggests the "wilderness of Judah," by which term was meant the area of rugged gorges and bad lands on the east side of Judah, where the land slopes off to the Jordan Valley (see page 31). Matthew, too, drew this conclusion, as his wording shows.

Some have wondered how a man preaching in that wilderness could get an audience. Baptism, too, could not have been performed in many places in that parched land. However, it seems likely that the verbiage of the Evangelists is governed by prophecy. Since the voice was to cry in the wilderness (Is. 40:3), John is described as preaching in the wilderness. The fact that he baptized in the Jordan, however, shows that that area is meant. Josephus, too, speaks of the country

east of Jericho and down to the Dead Sea as desert and barren.

Was John at Qumran?

But the Gospel of Luke seems to have distinctive information when it says that John was in the wilderness until the time came for him to take up his ministry to Israel (LUKE 1:80). This suggests that he was attracted to some such monastic community as that of the Essenes, whose monastery at *Khirbet Qumrān* above the Dead Sea has recently been discovered and excavated, and part of whose library has been found in caves in the nearby cliffs, where it was stored when their settlement was threatened with destruction. Indeed, until another community center is found, this one has the odds in its favor of being the one in which John had tarried. For if he was about the same age as Jesus (as Luke presupposes) then John must have been in the wilderness quite a long while. Individual hermit life only became popular later in Christian history. It is very probable, therefore, that John joined a monastic group.

staircase, and was possibly used for ritual immersion. A large room was evidently an assembly room. In one of the inner rooms was found an object which, when assembled, turned out to be a long table. It had fallen from an upper story room. With it were ink-pots, suggesting that this was a scribes' writing table.

Luke continues his distinctive remarks about John when he states that after the word of God came to John in the wilderness, he went into all the country about the Jordan, delivering his message (3:3). The term used in the Old Testament, *kikkar hayyar-dēn,* "the circuit of the Jordan," was evidently in the mind of the one who formulated the words. To some extent this is supported by the Fourth Gospel, when it describes John as baptizing in several places that would seem to be at opposite ends of the Jordan Valley region (see page 390 f.).

7.15 *Main assembly room at the Qumran settlement. (Palestine Archaeological Museum)*

The Scene of Christ's Baptism

The place of Christ's baptism seems to be in the southern sphere of John's roving (if rove he did). We have heard that the thought of Jesus' likewise having been a member of the Qumran community has been put forth quite seriously.

If so, he separated from it on receiving a divine call and turned from legalism to become a prophetic figure. Only his baptism still reserves a slight link with a possible Essene past.

Before the discovery of the Dead Sea Scrolls, our knowledge of the Essenes rested on what a few ancient writers reported about them—notably Josephus (*Jewish War,* II, 8). There are some things in his story which may be discounted. Thus, if he says that they have no certain city, but that many of them dwell in every city, one must suppose that he is describing the situation existing after 68 A.D. when their center was destroyed.

The Qumran excavations have given us an idea of how the Essenes lived. They had a self-contained center with potters' workshops, flour mills, ovens, storage bins, and twelve cisterns, to which an aqueduct brought down water in the rainy season. The main building was 121 feet square, with a strong tower at the northwest corner. To the south and west of this building were the work-shops and cisterns. One cistern has a

7.16 *One of the tables on which many of the Dead Sea Scrolls probably were written. (Palestine Archaeological Museum)*

7.17 *View of the Jordan near the place of baptism.*
(*Elsie D. Kraeling*)

Jesus' coming to John at the Jordan near Jericho, it must be admitted, becomes natural and vivid when one thinks of it in terms of a departure from the Qumran settlement. However, the oldest tradition no longer remembers or does not choose to mention any such connection in speaking of his baptism

7.18 *Reproduction of a piece of the Madeba Map.*

(MARK 1:9). But the popular impression that Jesus worked as a carpenter in Nazareth until this time is hardly correct. It is virtually a necessity to assume that he spent years with some ascetic group for the simple reason that celibacy was utterly unknown in a Jewish village. A young man's family arranged a marriage for him at an early age. If Jesus was thirty years old when he began his ministry he was probably gone from Nazareth for a decade. The fact that he is called "teacher," furthermore suggests that he had had an education. It was certainly not in the schools of the Pharisaic teachers, against whom he is in opposition and whose legalism is foreign to his taste. It was the sort of learning cultivated at Qumran, whether that be the exact community in which he dwelt or some other one.

The Fourth Gospel alone names the place of the baptism (JOHN 1:28). The locality meant is not too certain, if one leaves aside what early tradition claimed to know about it. The best ancient manuscripts have "Bethany." While one can assume the existence of a Bethany beyond Jordan, it cannot be proven and is otherwise unknown. Origen, the great Church Father and first textual critic of the New Testament, held that the reading of some ancient manuscripts, *Bethabara,* was to be preferred. But his only reason was that the Biblical Bethany lay elsewhere. The reading *Bethabara* could well point to a different locality entirely, reflecting the fact that John had sometimes preached and baptized there as well. If it is not a miswriting for Betharabah (JOSH. 15:6), which we know lay near the Jordan fords, then it must be connected with Beth-barah (JUDG. 7:24), a shortened form of Beth-abarah, "ford-town," a place considerably to the north of the traditional scene of John's activity.

The Madeba map and the early pilgrims put the scene of John's activity just north of the *Hajleh* ford on the west side of the river. Here the spot where Jesus had been baptized was marked with a cross set in the Jordan, while at the edge of the stream stood a

7.19 *The traditional Mount of the Temptation,* Mons Quarantana (Jebel Qaranṭal). (*Keren Hayesod*)

church (on piles), and farther back was a monastery of St. John the Baptist (fig. 7.18). But while tradition may not be far out of the way it can hardly be absolutely accurate. For the Fourth Gospel asserts that John baptized on the other side of the Jordan. That he must have been active in Peraea, the region beyond the Jordan, is proven by the fact that Herod Antipas, the tetrarch who ruled Peraea along with Galilee, had him arrested and later executed. We know that this ruler would have had no authority on the west bank of the Jordan.

Scene of the Temptation

In its present connection in the Synoptic Gospels, the temptation follows the baptism. This suggested that if Jesus went into the "wilderness" he would have sought out that area which lay close to the Jordan Valley on the west. Crusader tradition identified the place of the temptation with the prominent mountain top northwest of Jericho and called it *Mons Quarantana* (a name surviving as *Jebel Qaranṭal*). In Maccabean days, this height was crowned by the fortress of Dok, which guarded a path leading up toward Bethel; its name still survives in the spring called *'Ain Dūq,* at the foot of the mountain. Simon the Maccabee was murdered in this fortress (1 MACC. 16:15), and John Hyrcanus vainly besieged it for a long while. We do not know whether it still existed in Jesus' time. A church has been built in recent years on this mount and the remains of a monastic establishment of 340 A.D. were uncovered in connection therewith. For here of yore stood the "Laura [or monk's cell] of Duka," founded by a man named Chariton, whose name survives farther south in the *Wadi Khrēṭūn*. With its view over the Jordan Valley this is, indeed, a suitable spot

371

to commemorate the temptation, but since scripture does not localize that event all identifications are purely speculative.

From the Jordan to Galilee
(According to John)

John's Gospel not only omits the temptation but it places the calling of an original five disciples in the Jordan Valley scene. From there Jesus, it would seem, started for Galilee, reaching Cana "on the third day" (JOHN 2:1). But that statement should not be pressed; it could be based on the general supposition that it was a three-day trip from Jerusalem to the border of Galilee. Actually the place to be identified with Cana could not be reached in normal travel from the *Hajleh* ford before the fourth day. If the party took the road running on the west side of the Jordan Valley they would have passed Koraea (*Qarāwā*) and Scythopolis (*Bēsān*), at or near which places the nights would be spent. That would have meant a daily march of twenty-two miles. Another day's trip would have brought them to Nazareth.

The designation "Cana in Galilee" in John is clearly the customary designation of the place meant, and like "Bethlehem in Judah" differentiated the town from another place of the same name elsewhere. There was a Cana (or Kanah, Hebrew *Qānāh*) in the area near Tyre (JOSH. 19:28); the designation "Cana in Galilee" was needed to prevent confusion.

Ecclesiastical tradition identifies Cana with a town called *Kufr Kenna,* an hour and a half from Nazareth in the direction of Tiberias. This was very convenient for pilgrims traveling from Nazareth to the Lake of Galilee, and saved them the exertion as well as the perils of a side-trip to the pocket in which the real Cana lies. The name *Kufr Kenna,* however, goes back to a Kephar Kanna.

The Cana of the marriage feast probably is farther to the north, on the north side of the *el Baṭṭôf* plain at a place locally known as *Khirbet Qānā.* It has a far better claim than *Kufr Kenna* to be considered the home of Nathanael (JOHN 21:2) and of a Simon (MATT. 10:4) and as the place where miracle and faith began (JOHN 2:11). Its spelling corresponds to that of the Tyrian Kanah mentioned above. Josephus speaks of staying

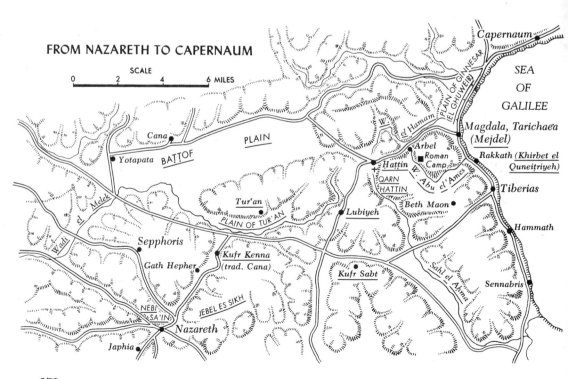

FROM NAZARETH TO CAPERNAUM

7.20 *The Lake of Galilee from* Horns of Ḥaṭṭīn. (*Matson Photo Service*)

for a while at "Cana, a village of Galilee," and this site excellently suits his narrative. It was not very far from Yotapata (Jode-phath), the chief fortress of the Jews in northern Galilee, where Josephus was taken prisoner by the Romans and ingloriously ended his military career. The Cana of his day doubtless lay on the summit of the hill, where there are cisterns and other ancient vestiges. According to recent reports there may be remains there of the third century A.D., but some sherds and coins from the time of Christ have also been found. This out-of-the-way place merits archaeological in-vestigation and Christian interest.

The Transfer to Capernaum

According to John's Gospel, Jesus went down from Nazareth to Capernaum with his five disciples and his family, but stayed there only a short time (JOHN 2:12). The Gospel of Mark, on the other hand, describes Jesus as going alone and finding his first disciples at Capernaum, making the town his head-quarters between trips.

In journeying from Nazareth to Caper-naum one would first cross the *Nebi Sä'in* ridge and pass the non-Biblical Gubabta (*el Meshhed*), somewhat to the south of which lay ancient Gath-hepher (2 KINGS 14:25 and page 292). Then came Kephar Kanna, al-ready referred to above. Soon one reached a route that led from Acco to Tiberias. But a person bound for the district north of Ti-berias would follow that road only a short distance and then go left to *Lubīyeh*, beyond which he could take either the road via the *Wadi el 'Amēs,* which reaches the lake shore halfway between Tiberias and Magdala, or the one via Arbel and the *Wadi Ḥamām,* or Valley of Doves, which led directly to Mag-dala. If Jesus took the latter route it would have led him past a mountain of peculiar shape, which the natives have named the *Horns of Ḥaṭṭīn.* On its top in the remote past had lain a city of the Canaanites (page 139) and on its south side, in a cave, was found the skull of the "Galilaean man." The plain near these horns was to become one of the most famous battlefields of history, for

7.21 *Synagogue of Beth Arbel. Jesus must have passed through here on his way to Capernaum from Nazareth. (Courtesy Archaeological Department, Hebrew University)*

here the Crusaders were to suffer their decisive defeat at the hands of Saladin (1187 A.D.). The village of *Ḥaṭṭīn* gets its name from a town that the Jewish sources call *Kephar Khaṭṭīā*.

The plain hereabouts was noted for its excellent wheat. In Jesus' time it must have been controlled by the town of Arbel (*Irbid*),

7.22 *Caves in the Valley of the Doves. (Courtesy American Geographical Society)*

which lay near the entrance to the *Wadi el Ḥamām*, the gorge leading down to the Lake of Galilee. Josephus held an important conference at Arbel with the representatives of Galilee. At Arbel one still can see the ruins of a synagogue of the third century A.D., perhaps on the site of an earlier structure that Jesus must have visited in the course of his Galilean ministry (fig. 7.21).

The road now enters the *Wadi el Ḥamām* and goes in serpentine manner through this gorge. A short distance below Arbel on the south side there are caves high up in the wall of the precipice. An event of some importance had taken place here several generations before Jesus' time, and there can be little doubt that he often had heard of the story. Brave men (Josephus calls them "brigands" to please his Roman readers) who were opposed to Roman rule and the kingship of Herod, doubtless adherents of the last Maccabean king, Antigonus, had taken refuge in these caves and from this safe retreat fought against Herod's authority. A military expedition had to be undertaken to destroy them. Soldiers were lowered down from the tops of the crags to smoke out these caves, but the heroic defenders preferred death to capture. An investigation of these caves by a modern archaeological expedition might find many things of interest here, but that would require special equipment not ordinarily available to archaeologists. Farther down the wadi, near its emergence into the plain, were other caves in the same south wall of the precipice. These were converted into a four-storied fortress in Islamic times.

Coming out into the plain one reached the town of Magdala, possibly the home of the "Magdalene," the Mary from Magdala (MARK 15:40). The tenacity of the survival of names is illustrated by the fact that *Mejdel* is still the name of the place. In the Talmud it is called "The Tower of the Dyers" (*Magdal Ṣabbā'āya*). Josephus calls it by the Greek name Tarichaea. The city lay directly on the shore of the lake. Josephus claims to

7.23 *View over the Plain of Gennesaret looking toward Capernaum.*
(*Matson Photo Service*)

have built (rebuilt?) the walls protecting it on the landward side. He attributes a fishing fleet of 230 boats to the town and a population of 40,000; these figures have to be taken with a grain of salt. The road coming up from Tiberias passed through the narrow plain between the city walls and the mountain.

From Arbel Jesus had descended over 1000 feet, for the Lake of Galilee lies 682 feet below sea level. He need not have entered Magdala itself unless he chose to do so. Going northward he must have traversed the little plain that today is called *el Ghuwēr* and that in his time was called Ginnesar (so the Talmud, while Josephus transcribes "the Gennesar"). The Lake of Galilee, too, was called the Lake of Ginnesar, and there was a small town north of Magdala bearing the same name; it is called Gennesaret in Mark 6:53 and Matthew 14:34, and the lake gets the same name in the Gospels. But this form of the name is hardly accurate. In the Aramaic translation of Numbers 34:11, Lake of Chinnereth is rendered Lake of Ginnesar. Since Josephus says "the Gennesar" the definite form *Ginnesārā* will have been the current one of New Testament times.

Jesus, in going up the lake, will soon have come to the neighborhood of *Khirbet Minyeh*. This was long believed to be the site of Capernaum, but the excavations carried on there in 1931 and the following years have disproven that. The structure has turned out to be an Islamic building, and the name, instead of possibly being connected with the *Mīnīm* (a Jewish term for "Christians"), is to be derived from Arabic *Munyat* (*Hishām*), or "dwelling" of the Caliph Hisham (723–742 A.D.).

Ahead of Jesus lay a height barring the road, and necessitating a detour to the west. This height, *Tell el 'Oreimeh,* once bore the city of Chinnereth (page 139). It lay desolate in Jesus' time. North of this height the road forks, though whether that was the case in antiquity is not so certain. The left-hand fork ascends and veers away from the lake, making for the Jordan crossing at the "Bridge of the Daughters of Jacob." The Crusaders used this as a leg in the route to Damascus and called the entire road the *Via Maris,* or "Way of the Sea" (MATT. 4:15). It is possible that Matthew is thinking of the road from *Beth Yeraḥ* to Capernaum with his "way of the sea," though that was hardly

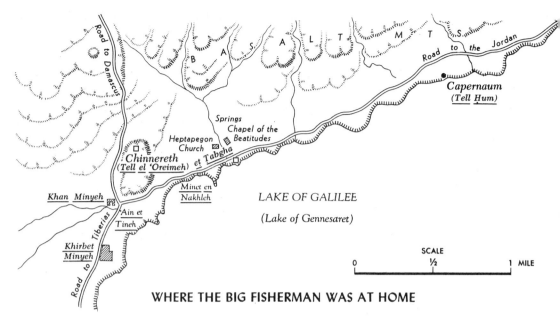

WHERE THE BIG FISHERMAN WAS AT HOME

the meaning of the prophet whose words are quoted in a free manner (Is. 9:1).

The road Jesus took, in any case, will have veered off to the left and crossed the *et Tabghah* area, now owned by a German Catholic Society. The name is an attempt to say in Arabic the Greek name Heptapegon, "the seven spring-place." A considerable riddle is posed by Josephus, who speaks of having been injured near Julias (Bethsaida) and then being brought to a place where there is a most fertile fountain, which the people of the country call *Kepharnokos*. It is generally believed that this is only a corruption of the name Capernaum (due to some text copyist). Many have concluded from this account of Josephus that Capernaum lay at *et Tabghah*, for there is no such remarkable spring at the site most scholars now accept as Capernaum. Was Capernaum, perhaps, destroyed in the days of the early Church, so that the name clung only to the spring at *et Tabghah* in Josephus' time? At any rate there are no remains of a town of the time of Christ at *et Tabghah*.

Josephus notes the peculiar fish-fauna of the "spring of Capernaum" but he fails to state a fact very characteristic of the place to-day, namely that the water of these springs flowing into the lake and loaded with vegetable matter attracts a great many fish to this point, so that, indeed, it is one of the best fishing areas of the lake as such. Fishermen make it their headquarters for the early months of the year. That was doubtless the case also in antiquity. And so this is quite probably the locality where Jesus happened on the fishermen and fishing boats, as described in Mark 1:16 f.

The fishermen were engaged in throwing the cast-net, then wading into the water to tread the net down and enmesh the fish it had covered and then hauling out the catch. The skill and persistence with which they operated convinced Jesus of their fitness for a different task and led him to address them with the words "Come ye after me and I will make you to become fishers of men."

It seems odd that the Christians of the early centuries did not particularly commemorate the calling of the disciples here, but instead located other things in this vicinity. The map shown above indicates where a basilica stood, supposedly on the site of the Multiplication of the Loaves and the Fishes, as well as the Chapel of the Beatitudes and the rock on which the risen Lord was believed to have laid the fishes when he appeared to the disciples by the lakeside (JOHN 21:9). Some beautiful fourth century A.D. mosaics were found by Mader in excavating that Heptapegon church, and it is touching indeed to sense here the faith and the devotion of Christian people of times so remote. But so far as the Miracle of the Loaves and Fishes is concerned, its localization here can hardly be reconciled with the narratives of the Gospels (see page 386).

Jesus then goes on with his four disciples to their town of Capernaum. There being no town at *et Tabghah,* this must be sought at *Tell Ḥūm.* It was a matter of a twenty-five minute walk. The hills soon approached the shore so that the road had to leave the lakeside and cross the spur of a ridge. Beyond in the narrow plain, which is only 350 yards wide, must have lain the village. There is no tell here in the true sense of the word. The designation is a European seventeenth-century reproduction of Arabic *Talḥūm,* which in turn reproduced sixteenth-century Jewish *Tanḥūm.*

The belief that the name Capernaum meant "town of Nahum" was challenged

7.24 *Mosaic floor of old Christian church at* eṭ Ṭabghah. (*Matson Photo Service*)

until very recently, but an Aramaic inscription found by Sukenik in his excavation of the synagogue at Hamath Gader (*el Ḥammeh*) near the mouth of the Yarmuk River has confirmed the spelling. It invokes remembrance for persons who donated memorials and among them is a Dositheus of Capernaum (*Kephar Nahum*). However it

7.25 *The synagogue of Hamath Gader.* (*Courtesy Archaeological Department, Hebrew University and Louis M. Rabinowitz*)

7.26 *The synagogue at Capernaum, partially restored. (Courtesy American Geographical Society)*

is unlikely that this Nahum is the Biblical prophet. The Church Fathers never avail themselves of that thought, but interpret the name as "town of consolation."

The ruins of Capernaum cover a strip of land a mile long. Unfortunately, no excavations have been conducted there yet except on the site of a single edifice. This building, which was first identified by Robinson as a synagogue, was explored by H. Kohl and C. Watzinger in 1905–6. There would probably be nothing left of it had not the Franciscans bought the property in 1894 from the Bedouin owners to stop the pilfering of stones for building purposes. In 1926 these fathers, under P. Orfali, began the restoration of parts of the building out of the jumble of fallen materials.

Is this the synagogue visited by Jesus on the evening of his arrival at Capernaum with the four fishermen? One may be quite sure that it stands on the very site of the synagogue to which Jesus went. But it is certainly not the same building, for it was constructed in the third century A.D., at which time there was a great revival of Jewish life in Palestine, especially in Galilee. It was built of white limestone, brought from elsewhere, for the volcanic rock of the area is black basalt, and it is from the latter that the synagogue of Jesus' day must have been constructed. The synagogue surviving there is a basilica-type building. A staircase led up to its four-columned front, with its large central portal and two smaller flanking doorways. There were nine columns on either side of the building and there were five in the rear. Like many of our churches the synagogue had galleries for the women, to which access was had by two stairways that ran up on either side of a small annex in the rear of the northwest corner. On the east side of the building was a courtyard.

This synagogue, too, will have had its "Seat of Moses," to which Jesus referred when he said,

"The scribes and the Pharisees sit in Moses' seat." (MATT. 23:2)

This was evidently a stone chair with a back rest for the use of some esteemed Teacher of the Law who might drop in at a synagogue service in his travels. The custom no doubt was in imitation of the Hellenistic-Roman one of providing some high-backed chairs for dignitaries at the theaters. Such Seats of Moses have been found in other synagogues. The nearby synagogue of Chorazin had one of solid basalt; it was provided with a back rest and decorated arm-rests (fig. 7.27). It bears an Aramaic inscription which reads, "Remembered be for good Judan, son of Ishmael, who made this portico and its staircase. As his reward may he have a share with the righteous!" In Jesus' day the Seat of Moses in the Capernaum synagogue may have borne the name of that gentile centurion who built the synagogue for the people there (LUKE 7:5). A like blessing may well have been invoked on him in a similar inscription.

The ruins of this third-century synagogue show rich ornamentation, for it would appear that the Jews of that era sought to share in the general culture of the time and were even willing to permit decorative use of flora and fauna, mythological creatures, astrological symbols, and geometrical designs. But we must imagine that in Jesus' day a stricter observance of the law prevailed in such matters.

From the synagogue Jesus went with the disciples to the house of Peter and Andrew,

7.27 *Seat of Moses with inscription in ruins of the third-century synagogue of Chorazin. (Courtesy Archaeological Department, Hebrew University and Louis M. Rabinowitz)*

where he healed the former's mother-in-law and other sick people that were brought to him there.

Galilean Wanderings

The following morning Jesus left Peter's house when it was still dark and went to a "solitary" (literally, "desert") place and prayed. Since Capernaum lay in a narrow, fully cultivated plain, this place must be imagined as on the rising hillside northwest of the town. If the spot Jesus sought was merely one where he would be alone, the cultivated hillside would have sufficed; but if Mark's word "desert" is taken literally, he must have gone beyond this cultivated zone

to the district strewn with blocks of basalt and with traces of habitation by Neolithic man.

Hereabouts, then, those who went in search of him found him. Jesus expressed the wish to travel about to preach his message in other towns, which presumably implies that he did not go back to Capernaum that morning. It stands to reason that the next place to which they went was nearby Chorazin (*Kerāze*). While the evangelists do not mention any visit to the place, the woe pronounced over Chorazin (MATT. 11:21) makes it certain that Jesus often went there. Like the synagogue of Capernaum, that of Chorazin probably stands on the site of the one at which Jesus preached, but the building itself was a third-century A.D. structure, made of the dismal basalt rock found in this area.

Jesus thereupon went "into the synagogues of all Galilee" (MARK 1:39). Many other third- through sixth-century synagogues besides those of Arbel, Capernaum and Chorazin are known and have been partially or wholly explored. Great finds in particular were made at Beth Shearim, where there is not only a synagogue but where there are tombs of important Jewish teachers. But no synagogue of the time of Christ has as yet been uncovered.

However far Jesus may have roved, he returned to Capernaum. After healing the

7.28 *Capernaum from the Sea of Galilee. (Matson Photo Service)*

paralytic in the house of Peter he went down to the lake shore and there spoke to a crowd. On going farther (perhaps up the lake toward the boundary of the tetrarchy of Herod Antipas) he passed the booth of the tax collector Levi, or Matthew, who became his disciple. After further unlocalized incidents Jesus "withdrew himself with his disciples to the sea of Galilee." But people from all over the country—not just Galileans, but Phoenicians, Judaeans, Idumaeans, and Transjordanians—followed him. He found it necessary to have a boat kept at his disposal to escape the pressure of the crowd (MARK 3:9). It seems likely that the place presupposed was where he had first encountered Peter and the others, namely at et Ṭabghah. It was at this time that he appointed The Twelve as his official family (MARK 3:13).

Into this situation the parallel version of the First Gospel puts the "Sermon on the Mount" (MATT. 5:1 f.). One may thus imagine the Sermon on the Mount and the appointment of The Twelve as having taken place on the hillside above et Ṭabghah. This

7.29 *View of Nain and Mount Tabor.* (*Matson Photo Service*)

was also the belief of the early pilgrims. A twelfth-century monk speaks of a "cave" in a mountain near Heptapegon, where Jesus uttered the beatitudes. Above the present road the remains of a chapel have actually been found (see sketch map, page 376). Luke, however, imagines the sermon as delivered on the plain below, after the appointment of the disciples had taken place on the mountain (6:17 f.). A large audience could be more suitably assembled there.

A Special Journey in Luke's Narrative

At this point Luke departs somewhat from the Gospel of Mark. After the healing of a servant of the centurion in Luke 7:1–10 (cf. MATT. 8:5 f.), Jesus goes on the following day to Nain (LUKE 7:11–18). According to Eusebius, it lay south of Mount Tabor, near Endor. And here, indeed, a *Nēn* still continues the name as found in the Gospel story. The old Hebrew name must have been *Na'īm,* but Nain evidently sounded better to Greek ears.

If Jesus really made a special trip to Nain from Capernaum he might have gone to Magdala and taken the road up through the *Wadi el 'Amēs* to *Lubīyeh.* Continuing southward on the east side of Mount Tabor he would have come to Endor and there taken the branch road to Nain, a village at the foot of the *Jebel ed Daḥi* on a low spur of the mountain and on the divide between waters flowing toward the Jordan Valley and the Mediterranean. The spring of the town lies on the west, where the road goes out toward Nazareth. In the construction of a new house in this part of the village some years ago, foundations of older buildings were allegedly uncovered by the natives, and both Israelite and Roman sherds are said to have been found there. In any case the ancient Nain will have lain convenient to the spring.

Nain had an eastern and a western "gate," or point of entry. Before the eastern gate, which Jesus may have approached if he came from Capernaum, there are rock tombs

7.30 *Aerial view of the Lake of Galilee.* (*Courtesy Institut Francais d'Archéologie, Beyrouth, Liban*)

which still remind the passerby of the objective of the funeral procession that stirred Jesus' sympathy. Luke's statement that the incident of the raising of the dead youth spread through the whole of Judaea is surprising, since Nain was in Galilee. He is evidently using Judaea in a broad sense here.

Lakeside Scenes

After appointing The Twelve, Jesus returned to Capernaum (MARK 3:19), and there must have occurred the incidents related in Mark 3:20–35. This is succeeded by renewed teaching of the crowd on the shore of the lake, from the boat held in readiness for Jesus and presumably in the same setting as before, at *eṭ Ṭabghah*. After the dismissal of the crowd, Jesus suggests crossing to the eastern side of the lake (MARK 4:35 f.). Other boats accompanied them. On the way occurred one of those sudden gales characteristic of the Jordan Valley (see page 37) and which can quickly produce six-foot waves on this sheet of water.

It seems very probable that some of these trips on the lake had a material as well as a spiritual purpose. Unless one is willing to imagine the disciples as mendicants, they must have done something to provide food and minimum earnings, and the natural thing for them was to go fishing when circumstances required it.

K. E. Wilken, a German traveler who visited the Arab fishermen of *el Mejdel* on the Lake of Galilee and was permitted to join them in one of their excursions, has drawn an interesting picture of their activities. These will have been the same in the time of Jesus as they were until recent Israeli occupation. The fishermen slept until evening in their mud huts and went down to the shore shortly before sundown. Night descends very suddenly in this deep valley. After the fishermen had prayed facing toward Mecca, they embarked and pushed out into the lake. The rowing was done as silently as possible and not a word was spoken; every ear was listening for the sound of a possible whirlwind starting to develop in the gorges descending from the mountains. This could bring on just such a situation as is reported in Mark 4:37. They crossed over to the eastern shore of the lake, where swarms of fish are to be found at night. This seems to be due to the fact that there, in the deepest water, which attains a depth of 705 feet, some twenty mineral springs boil up during the night. Here the fish like to congregate for this period. Two boats operated together dragging a weighted net between them.

7.31 *Ruins of the forum at* Jerash (*ancient Gerasa*). (*Ewing Galloway*)

Every now and then the fish were taken out of the drag-net with the aid of small nets. After the danger of surprise storms was over, the fishermen conversed freely. Around 2:00 A.M. they returned homeward. They reached the western shore around dawn, washed and dried their nets, and then had breakfast in the manner described in John 21:9, roasting fish on hot stones by the shore. The swarms of fish change their station at the end of the night, and go over to *eṭ Ṭabghah,* where the springs become active after daybreak and send their waters into the lake, or to the Jordan inlet. If any fishing is to be done by day, the cast-net method already described (see page 376) is employed.

The species of fish caught are no doubt the same as in the days of the disciples. The chief food-fish are two carp varieties; Jewish people have a predilection for carp to this day. A catfish variety which is notably found at the mouth of the Jordan is held undesirable as its taste is very bitter. It is immediately thrown away, like the bad fish in the parable (Matt. 13:48). There is also a sardine-like fish which is caught in great numbers near the shore; perhaps these are the "small fishes" of John 6:9.

In the lake crossing related in Mark 4:35 f., the objective reached is variously designated as the country of the Gadarenes, or Gerasenes, or Gergesenes (Mark 5:1; Matt. 8:28; Luke 8:26).

In the best ancient manuscripts Mark and Luke have Gerasenes and Matthew has Gadarenes. The Gergesenes, no matter how they may have gotten into the text-tradition, must hang together with the Girgashites of the Old Testament; a place name Gergesa seems improbable. The other two names are derived from famous cities of the Decapolis, Gadara and Gerasa.

The Decapolis, which is mentioned in this narrative (Mark 5:20), merits a moment's consideration. In the vast building activity of the early Seleucid rulers, the east had been dotted with cities that were rebuilt or newly built in the Greek manner. Transjordan, too, was the scene of such great development. Its cities were seriously menaced in their prosperity and independence by the rise of the Maccabean-Jewish state. But when Pompey regulated the affairs of Syria in 63 A.D., he decided that these cities of Transjordan still had vitality and could be made the main props of Roman rule. He reduced the Jewish dominion in Transjordan to Peraea, a narrow strip east of the river from south of Pella to the Arnon, and gave back to the Greek cities their old position. They began a new era with this liberation by Pompey, and dated their coins accordingly. The use of the term Decapolis to comprise them appears first in Pliny (23–79 A.D.), in the Gospels (Mark 5:20; Matt. 4:25), and in Josephus. The most vivid impression of the culture and life of these cities in Roman times is given by Gerasa (today *Jerash*), which has been quite thoroughly explored and described by a Yale University expedition (fig. 7.31). It is true that the remains one sees are much later than the time of Christ. But the earlier buildings will have been similar, if less grand. At Gadara (*Mukēs*), south of the *Yarmuk* River and overlooking the Lake of Galilee from the southeast, there are also important remains; but this city still awaits the explorer who will resurrect it.

It seems unlikely that the land on the east of the Lake of Galilee was called "land of the Gerasenes," for that city lay too far to the east. It could have been called "land of the Gadarenes" more readily, though the actual owner of the territory will rather have been Hippos, or Susitha as it was called by Aramaic-speaking people. It was enthroned near *Fīq* on the bold height of *Qala 'at el Ḥuṣn*, where the ruins of Roman times still mark the existence of an important place. Hippos had an important function in guarding the road to Damascus. Its water was brought all the way from the headwaters of the *Wadi es Samak* fifteen miles to the south. Like Gadara it has not yet been explored.

Just where Jesus landed and where the healing of the man possessed of a demon took place has been the subject of much speculation. The story of how the swine ran down the slope (MARK 5:11 f.) is commonly localized in the vicinity of *Kurse*, where there is a steep bank such as is presupposed, but where, unfortunately, there are no tombs such as are also required.

After the return from the trip to the eastern shore, a multitude gathered and Jesus again taught them by the lakeside (MARK 5:21 f.). The healing of the daughter of Jairus, which follows, is not expressly localized, but the "ruler of the synagogue," Jairus, presumably lived at Capernaum.

Journey to Nazareth

We then find Jesus going to "his own country" (MARK 6:1; MATT. 13:53), which Luke identifies more precisely as Nazareth (4:16 f.). The route mentioned above in connection with his first coming to Capernaum may have been that of this trip as well. At the synagogue, where Jesus arises to read Scripture, he is given the book of the prophet Isaiah. This incident has received fresh vividness for us through the discovery of the Dead Sea Scrolls. The Bible was not "the Book" in his time, but rather "the Books," or a sacred library. A scroll of a single major book, written on leather in parallel columns, so that one kept unrolling the strip on the left, while rolling it up on the right, was bulky enough for handling. Isaiah was evidently the favorite prophet, and it was above all that last portion of the book, which begins at chapter 40, that was much beloved for its imperishable words of faith, comfort and courage. The Isaiah Scroll of Mar Athanasius has provided us with exactly the sort of "book" that will have been handed to Jesus, and its script is no doubt virtually identical with that upon which his eyes rested on that day. Figure 7.32 shows how the very passage he read must have looked.

7.32 *A column from the Dead Sea Isaiah Scroll (Is. 59:17—61:4). The script on which Jesus' eyes rested looked like this, and the place he found (Luke 4:17) is at the break in the fourth line from the bottom. (Courtesy American School of Oriental Research)*

The address given by Jesus aroused sharp opposition, even resulting in physical violence. We are told that the people of Nazareth put Jesus out of the city, and led him to the brow of the hill on which it was built. It was here that they wanted to throw him down headlong (LUKE 4:28). This passage invites local comment in the light of the topography of Nazareth. As already set forth (see page 360), it is extremely difficult to get any certainty as to the exact location of the town of Jesus' day, which naturally was much smaller than the present one. To find the "brow of the hill," from which the Jews sought to cast Jesus, tradition has picked a bluff a mile and a half south of the city, overlooking the Plain of Esdraelon. It was believed that Jesus had leaped across the gorge to the hill opposite, and hence the height is known as *Jebel el Qafza*, "Mount of the Leap."

But the requirements of Luke's narrative make it imperative to seek the "brow of the hill" immediately at the synagogue from which Jesus was expelled. High points were usually chosen for synagogues if such were available. If the building had been situated above the so-called "New Fountain," where there is a drop-off of some twenty-five feet, the situation could be realistic enough. Grave injury would be expected from a fall from that height, and the next step would have been stoning the injured person to death.

Where did tradition seek the location of the synagogue? There was still a synagogue at Nazareth in the days of the pilgrim Antoninus (570 A.D.). Like most excavated Galilean synagogues it was probably built in the second to third centuries, but presumably on the site of the older one that had been destroyed by the Romans in 70 A.D. It is unlikely that the building shown today as "School of the Messiah" marks the site meant by the ancient traveler. A better case can be made out for the synagogue's having lain at the *Maqām el Arba 'īn,* "the place of the

7.33 *View over Tiberias. (Courtesy American Geographical Society)*

Forty," where once stood a Church of the Forty (Armenian) Martyrs, who were much celebrated in the East. But that tradition is reasonable only if one seeks the Nazareth of Jesus' time in the north, near the church of St. Gabriel. Exploratory excavations alone can determine the town-history of Nazareth, and until this is done speculation is futile.

We must infer that Jesus returned to the lakeside area after his rejection at Nazareth. This is clearly the scene of his preaching in villages and of the sending forth of The Twelve (MARK 6:6 f.), as is made evident by the sequel (MARK 6:31–33).

Tiberias and Machaerus

At this point, however, the story of Jesus' ministry is interrupted by an account of the fate of John the Baptist (MARK 6:17–29). John had been imprisoned, says the Evangelist, for criticising "King Herod." The Herod meant is Herod Antipas, tetrarch of Galilee and other areas. The fact that he had taken his brother's wife had met with widespread disapproval. However, the brother whose wife he took, according to Josephus, was not the Tetrarch Philip, mentioned in the story used by the Gospel, but rather one who was also named Herod, and who had in fact been designated in the first testament of Herod the Great as his father's successor. It was when visiting Rome, where this Herod was living, that Antipas persuaded the ambitious daughter of the Maccabees to cast in her lot with him.

The capital of Antipas had been at Sepphoris, but about 26 A.D. he decided to build himself a new one on the shores of the Lake of Galilee. He named it Tiberias in honor of the emperor Tiberius. It was thus a brand new city in the time of Jesus (c. 28–30 A.D.). To populate it, persons had been drafted from various quarters, for law-abiding Jews did not want to live there, owing to its having been built on the site of a cemetery. It was given city government, such as the cities of the Decapolis had. The location was an attractive one—not far from the warm springs of Hamath (not the same as those of Hamath Gader, see page 377), or from Sennabris (today Ṣinn en Nabra). Tiberias was also convenient to *Beth Yeraḥ* at the outlet of the lake, from where the important pass leading up into the high country of the *Jaulān* was readily reached. On the south side of modern Tiberias there are still the ruins of fortifications, but not those of Antipas' day. His palace may lie in the hill called "Castle of the King's Daughter" (*Qaṣr bint el melek*), which bears the tomb of Rabbi Meir. Tiberias was an important center of Jewish learning in the third and fourth centuries A.D., but still had its heathen temple.

It was here at Tiberias, the Gospel author seems to think, that John's death took place. Mark says that a banquet was held in honor of Herod's birthday to which all the leading men of Galilee were invited. At this occasion the daughter of Herod's wife, a girl named Salome, was given permission to ask a favor of the "king," and instigated by her mother requested the head of John the Baptist. The story implies that John was in prison in Tiberias, and that the executioner could straightway deliver the head on a platter. We may note in passing that this Salome, who has so well served the purposes of modern writers and composers, became the wife of the Tetrarch Philip and later married Herod of Chalcis; and it is her portrait which graces some of the latter's coins. While Mark mentions the reverent burial of John by his disciples in a tomb, he does not tell where this tomb was situated.

Josephus, who was very fully informed on all matters pertaining to the House of Herod, puts the imprisonment and death of the Baptist at the fortress of Machaerus. This was east of the Dead Sea in the extreme south of the district of Peraea, which, as we have

7.34 *View of the southern end of the Lake of Galilee. Here lay the city of* Beth Yeraḥ (Philoteria *in Greek times*). (Courtesy Archaeological Department, Hebrew University and Louis M. Rabinowitz)

heard, was also part of the domains ruled by the tetrarch. It would have been a very inconvenient place to which to bring the Galileans for a birthday party. Indeed, it is so out of the way that it has not been much visited even by modern scholars, and has never had any thorough exploration by an organized expedition. Not even a topographic plan of it worthy of reproduction has ever been published. The place was discovered a century and a half ago by the German traveler Seetzen. It is called *el Mekawer,* thus continuing the old name to this day. According to Pliny it was the strongest fortress of Palestine, with the exception only of Jerusalem. The hill of *el Meshneqeh,* opposite *el Mekawer,* was evidently part of the fortress, and according to Glueck large waterworks are still visible there. Founded originally by Alexander Jannaeus (103–76 B.C.), Machaerus was destroyed by Pompey's general Gabinius (63 B.C.), but was rebuilt by Herod the Great. Not far north of there is the *Wadi Zerqā Ma'īn,* with the warm springs of Calirrhoë, famous in Roman times.

The stones of Machaerus tell of the wife whom Antipas was going to put aside, when he plotted to marry his sister-in-law, Herodias. His wife asked for permission to make a trip to Machaerus, and he, believing her to be ignorant of his plans, readily granted the request. From there she made good her escape to her father, the King of the Nabataeans. While this left Antipas free to wed Herodias, he henceforth had a deadly enemy. But the great walls of Machaerus speak even more eloquently of John the Baptist, if this was where he was incarcerated.

Scene of the Miracle of the Loaves

After the return of the disciples from their missionary journey (a "field-work" trip in preparation for their later occupation), Jesus suggested a "retreat" for them, and so they crossed the lake to go to a lonely place (MARK 6:31–32).

Their ship was observed from the shore and a multitude preceded them. Jesus, therefore, taught the people until the disciples called his attention to the lateness of the hour and the need of dismissing them that they might go into the village to buy food. But instead he provided a repast miraculously. He then sent his disciples off in the boat to Bethsaida, and after he had taken leave of the crowd went into the hills to pray. Later he rejoined the disciples near Bethsaida, and crossed the lake with them to "Gennesareth," (MARK 6:53), here evidently a village on the western shore (see page 375).

The events described are not very definitely localized. Tradition, as we have read (page 377), sought the place of the feeding of the multitude on the hillside above *eṭ Ṭabghah.* But we must recall again our earlier remark that there was a tendency on the part of the ancients to locate holy places where it was convenient for the pilgrims to reach them. In John 6:1–24, furthermore, the feeding of the five thousand, which is clearly another version of this same event, is put on the eastern shore of the lake. And if the feeding of the four thousand in Mark 8:1 f. were a parallel to Mark 6:35 f., as some scholars hold, then it would be significant that this event, too, seems to be localized on the eastern shore. But other considerations, besides those of a critical nature, buttress the thought that Mark 6:3 f. took place on the Decapolis side of the lake. 1) The suggestion to go by boat to a place where privacy could be had involved crossing the lake, for by staying on the hither shore they could not hope to escape the multitude. But one could not foresee that the people would go around the lake. 2) There would have been no need of a miracle if the people who had preceded Jesus to the objective were just from the towns and hamlets between Tiberias and Capernaum; they could all have gone to their homes. 3) A crossing of the lake is implied in the storm scene on the return trip—not just some trip hugging the western shore. 4) The landing at "Gennesaret" or Ginnesar implies a crossing.

Attempts have been made to find the exact locality on that eastern shore where the feeding of the multitude could have taken place. A "grassy" spot large enough to accommodate a multitude and a nearby hill where Jesus went to pray are presupposed. Jesus' command to the disciples to cross over to Bethsaida would be most understandable if given at a point southeast of that city, while John's reference to boats coming over from Tiberias would point toward a more southerly locality. For John's version of the incident, a particularly suitable setting has been suggested in a lonely neighborhood between *Wadi es Samak* and *Wadi en Neqēb,* where the high tableland approaches the lake; here *Mōqa Edlo* would provide a suitable hill to which Jesus might have gone to pray.

The Journey to Phoenician Territory

Jesus, after further activity in the general vicinity of Capernaum (MARK 6:56 and 7:17, where the "house" referred to must be Peter's), departed to go to the district of Tyre (MARK 7:24). We have already seen that northern Galilee gravitates very much toward that famous old Phoenician city, and it would be natural for one who was traveling about in Galilee to cross over the line into Tyrian territory. The latter at that time extended well into Galilee and even included Kedesh. The example of Elijah's sojourn in Phoenicia (1 KINGS 17:9 f.) could have suggested a similar course on Jesus' part. For just as Elijah had fled before Ahab, so Jesus had good cause not to linger near the capital of Herod Antipas, since the latter had just ordered the execution of John the Baptist. Jesus would have reached Tyrian territory in a day's journey from Capernaum by going to *Ṣāfed* (an ancient Zephath, in Josephus called "Seph") and to the plain of *Mērōn,* thence on to Gischala (*ej Jish*), the most important city of Upper Galilee and *Kefr Bir 'im.* It is uncertain whether he went on

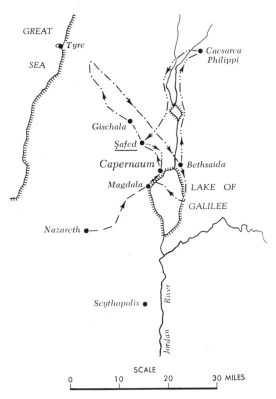

JOURNEYS OF JESUS
(According to Mark)

to the Tyrian Kanah and the vicinity of Tyre itself.

Somewhere in the rural border districts with partly Jewish, partly gentile population, Jesus healed the daughter of the Syro-Phoenician woman. Mark's report that he "returned" from the region of Tyre and went through Sidon to the Sea of Galilee via the region of the Decapolis is not as clear geographically as one might wish. Matthew's account escapes this difficulty by stating at the outset (15:21) "he withdrew to the district of Tyre and Sidon" (i.e., to Phoenician territory, generally speaking). If Jesus had gone as far north as Sidon, he could have gone from there to the Decapolis, via Caesarea Philippi. But such a visit to that neighborhood seems unlikely in view of the journey made to it soon afterward (MARK 8:27). If it was his purpose to avoid the Tiberias-Capernaum area for the present,

7.35 *The mouth of the Jordan. (Matson Photo Service)*

Jesus might have gone from the Tyrian district to Bethsaida and then to the adjacent Decapolis territory.

It is not said where Jesus went in the Decapolis, but the connection implies that he stayed near the Lake of Galilee. A healing and another feeding—that of the four thousand—are reported from there (MARK 8:1–10). Next came an eastward crossing of the lake. The landing-place Dalmanutha is uncertain, however, for the parallel account in Matthew 15:39 has "Magadan" in place of it, and Eusebius asserts that this is the right reading. A recently discovered third-century Biblical papyrus also has that reading instead of Dalmanutha in Mark 8:10. The important Palestinian Syriac Gospel, a text which reflects native Palestinian tradition, has *Magdal* (Magdala), and that is probably the name originally intended in the Greek. By a series of miswritings by copyists of manuscripts to whom these names were foreign and meaningless, it became Dalmanutha.

In the Tetrarchy of Philip

After a discussion with the Pharisees, Jesus re-entered the boat and crossed over again to the eastern shore (MARK 8:13). We next find him at Bethsaida where he performs a healing (MARK 8:22 f.).

It is odd that Bethsaida is twice called a "village" in this connection. This seemingly agrees very poorly with Josephus' report about Bethsaida, for he says that it had been raised to city status by the Tetrarch Philip

and named "Julias" after the daughter of the emperor Augustus. But perhaps a fishing village of Bethsaida had continued to exist all along directly on the shore in the shadow of the city of Julias, which may have lain farther back from the lake. According to Josephus, Julias lay near the entrance of the Jordan into the lake, and Pliny puts it on the eastern bank of the river.

The logical place to look for Julias is thus at *et Tell,* a mound about 800 by 400 feet in extent, that rises to the height of 100 feet nearly a mile inland in the fruitful alluvial plain. Several archaeologists who have visited the place were unable to find any evidence of its having been inhabited in Hellenistic-Roman times, but there have been reports that the Bedouin found pillars and hewn stones on the eastern part of the southwestern declivity. K. E. Wilken, who heard this from the Bedouin's own lips, speaks of finding some Hellenistic-Roman, as well as Iron Age sherds on the northern inclines. A strong spring emerges at the southwestern end of the mound and flows into a pool, and thence into the Jordan. The tell is now surrounded on three sides by swamps, and so the locality is malarial. No doubt proper drainage existed in the days of the Tetrarch Philip, who resided at Julias in winter and must have liked the place a great deal, for he was buried there in 34 A.D. Perhaps the spade will yet bring his tomb to light.

It seems probable that Bethsaida, which Mark calls a village (MARK 8:23, 26), remained distinct from Julias, and was on the shore of the lake. And, indeed, about fifty yards from the present shore, on the east side of the Jordan mouth there is a site 656 by 918 feet which is called *Khirbet el 'Araj.* The traveler already mentioned had an unusual opportunity to examine the stratification there when the wall of a cistern, that workmen were constructing for his host, collapsed. There was an upper layer of about twenty inches composed of alluvial sand; below that was a layer of about six inches with sherds of the Roman period down to about 250 A.D. He mentions the typical red-colored ones and painted jar-handles. Another layer of alluvial sand of twelve to fourteen inches lay above the next lower stratum of twelve inches. This last layer he confidently assigns to the time of Christ, for from it he was able to extract four lamps and eleven small coins showing three ears of grain on one side; these, he asserts, were minted in the time of Pilate (26–36 A.D.). He notes that the stratum in question was destroyed by fire, and finds therein a remarkable vindication of Jesus' woe over Bethsaida (MATT. 11:21). In any case the situation observed here warrants further investigation, when the times and the opportunity are favorable. It would be of great interest to have the very streets of Bethsaida through which Jesus walked brought to light again.

Caesarea Philippi

If we may suppose that it was from the Bethsaida area that Jesus started on his journey to Caesarea Philippi, we may imagine him as following the good road that must have connected the tetrarch's winter residence of Julias with his summer residence. This road ran above the Jordan on the east, but forked near the so-called "Bridge of Jacob's Daughters." The course to the left continued up the river valley while that to the right merged for a while with the Damascus road coming from across the Jordan, but soon turned off from it again and headed northward into the highlands, going via *Sqēq* and descending past *Za'ōra* to Caesarea Philippi. On the way (i.e., on the high plateau before one descends to the city) may have occurred the conversation in which Peter uttered his belief that Jesus was the Messiah (MARK 8:27 f.).

It is not clear whether Jesus and the disciples entered Caesarea Philippi itself, for Mark speaks only of "the towns" belonging to it. They doubtless avoided the Paneion grotto, from which a branch of the Jordan

emerged and where the heathen cult of Pan was carried on. The older name of this Caesarea, Paneas, has outlived both the name that Philip gave it and the later name "Neronias" which Agrippa II gave it, for it still clings to the village of *Baniās*. The mediaeval walls and towers on the height above the village may stand on the site of the acropolis of ancient Caesarea. The amphitheater, where 2500 captive Jewish soldiers had to kill each other as a spectacle for Titus, Agrippa II and Bernice, seems to have disappeared. The Mohammedan shrine of *Sheikh Khudr* (St. George) may occupy the site of the temple Herod the Great had built here in honor of Augustus.

The Scene of the Transfiguration

The transfiguration incident occurs next after the departure from Caesarea Philippi. In view of the loose-knit connection it seems doubtful whether the "six days afterward" of Mark 9:2 should be stressed as implying six days of travel.

Tradition sought a setting for the Transfiguration and found it in Mount Tabor, which rises from the Plain of Esdraelon on the northeast. It was a conveniently accessible spot for those who visited Nazareth and the

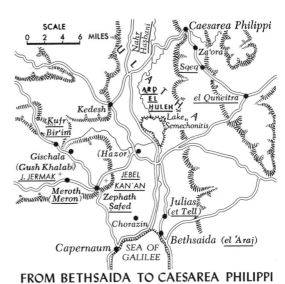

FROM BETHSAIDA TO CAESAREA PHILIPPI

389

sacred sites on the Lake of Galilee, and there was something ethereal about this dome-shaped mountain which made it seem a most appropriate setting for so mysterious an event. An old apocryphal gospel, "The Gospel according to the Hebrews," localized either the Transfiguration or an appearance of the risen Christ here, and 2 Peter 1:18 may already have the same site in mind. Fourth century tradition firmly assumed it to be the place. In the sixth century there were three churches (in commemoration of the three booths or tabernacles of Mark 9:5) on the eastern end of the summit, from which one looked forth over part of the Lake of Galilee to Mount Hermon. But historically Mount Tabor seems to be an unlikely localization, for there was a fortress on this mountain top in antiquity, which Josephus provided with a new wall in 66 A.D. The cult of a heathen god, Baal Tabor, too, was carried on here, and the place would probably have been considered "unclean" by law-abiding Jews like Jesus and his disciples. The fact that Jesus soon after rejoining the main group of disciples "enters the house" (MARK 9:28), his Capernaum headquarters, suggests that the high mountain meant was in that locality. This could be the *Jebel Kan'ān* north of Capernaum or even the *Jebel Jermak* near *Mērōn,* the highest elevation in Galilee, from which a marvelous prospect is to be had not only over Upper Galilee to the Lebanon Mountains and Mount Hermon, but especially also over the *Jaulān* with its extinct volcanoes and even to the Hauran. In the south the view goes beyond Mount Tabor to Mount Gerizim, and in the southwest to Mount Carmel and the blue Mediterranean.

A renewed wandering "through Galilee" (MARK 9:30) is followed by another return "to the house" in Capernaum (MARK 9:33).

Special Journeyings of Luke's Central Section

At the point where the crucial journey of Jesus to Jerusalem begins (MARK 10:1 f.), the Third Gospel's parallel account introduces a special travel narrative of its own (LUKE 9:51 f.) and does not rejoin the main current of Mark's story again until Luke 18:31 f. The geographical progression, however, is quite uncertain, and it would seem that Luke was governed by considerations other than creating a reasonable itinerary when he arranged his materials. It seems unnecessary, therefore, for us to dwell on most of what he reports.

As though a new beginning were being made to the start from Galilee, Luke relates how Jesus, when on the way to Jerusalem, passed along between Samaria and Galilee, and came to a village where he healed ten lepers (LUKE 17:11 f.). The literal rendering of the text brings to light the geographical difficulty it poses. Passing *between* Samaria and Galilee might seem to be impossible unless one took the boundary line. But following that would lead away from the objective, Jerusalem. Actually, however, Luke's statement may be quite accurate. It probably refers to passing through the Plain of Esdraelon, which was more or less debatable ground since cities of Galilee lay on the northern side of it and cities of Samaria along its southern rim. Mediaeval tradition put the incident of the lepers at *Jenīn* (Ginnaia), which, however, is quite definitely on the Samaritan side and hence does not quite suit the requirements of Luke's words.

Journeys of Jesus in the Gospel of John

The Gospel of John has some distinctive journeyings of Jesus to report. From the Jordan valley, where he gathered his first disciples, he goes to Cana in Galilee (JOHN 2:1), moves to Capernaum with his family for a short time (JOHN 2:12), and then embarks on a Passover journey to Jerusalem (JOHN 2:13–21). A short trip follows after the Nicodemus incident, in which Jesus went into the land of Judaea and remained there, baptizing with his disciples. John was also baptizing close by at Aenon near Salim. Jesus already was in Judaea by virtue of

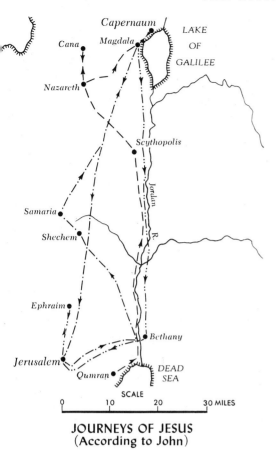

JOURNEYS OF JESUS
(According to John)

though it was actually a good distance away. Josephus mentions an *Aïn* as the base from which Simon Maccabeus carried raids into the north against Akrabeta and south into Idumaea. It is possible that the Evangelist has the same place in mind. If Jesus baptized in Judaea he would have been farther to the south, for the northern boundary of that region was near Koraea.

At the Well of Jacob

Jesus is described as returning again from Judaea to Galilee via Samaria (JOHN 4:1 f.). The narrative suggests that he had come up from Jericho and was taking the road that went through the vale of Shechem and on via Sebaste to Ginnaia. The reference to the city called Sychar is puzzling. The name is sometimes linked with a place today called *'Askar,* a mile northeast of the traditional Well of Jacob. But that seems improbable. It is more likely that Sychar is a corrupt writing of Sychem (Shechem). The *'Askar* theory rested on the belief that Shechem lay at *Nāblus.* Since we now know that Shechem lay at *Balaṭah,* there is no need of it. The latter site is closer to Jacob's Well and was inhabited until about 67 A.D., as Sellin's excavations have shown. It was destroyed in 67 A.D. by Vespasian.

The "Well of Jacob", of which John 3:6 makes the first mention, lies at a point where the roads from Jerusalem and Jericho converge and where those going to *Nāblus* and *Jenīn* separate. It was known to an early pilgrim in 333 A.D., and by 400 A.D. there was a church over it. The well has a diameter of over six feet and a depth at present of 75 feet; since there is considerable debris in the bottom it may have been deeper originally. It is stoned up in the upper portion, but pierces rock lower down, and strikes groundwater that pours in from several directions. The mouth narrows like the top of a bottle, and a heavy stone with a round hole, through which a bucket can be lowered by a rope, covers it. A Greek Catholic chapel now

being at Jerusalem, so the statement that he now came into Judaea sounds surprising, and invites critical explanation, over which, however, we need not linger. He evidently went into the Jordan Valley, for his ministry is now brought into close parallelism with that of John the Baptist. The latter does not seem to have been in the same locality as in John 1:28, but farther to the north. Jesus himself, it would seem, sought the Jericho neighborhood, since a start from there makes his subsequent visit to Sychar (JOHN 4:5) reasonable.

Where shall one seek John's Salim, near which there was an Aenon (spring place)? The early Church sought it near Scythopolis (Beth-shean), though the Salim near Shechem also had its adherents. Under the latter theory Aenon would be in the well-watered *Vadi Fār'ah,* and Salim would only be mentioned as the nearest Samaritan town,

391

7.36 Jacob's Well at Shechem, as it was before a chapel was built over it. (Matson Photo Service)

owns and shelters the site. There can scarcely be any doubt but that this is the place John's Gospel had in mind, and where Lord Christ spoke to the Samaritan woman.

Jesus stayed two days at Sychar, winning believers among the Samaritans, and since it was the rainy season, as the allusion to four months before the harvest shows (January), he certainly must have received hospitality there. After leaving Sychar he continued on to Galilee (JOHN 4:45 f.).

Bethesda

Another festival journey to Jerusalem leads to the mention of a locality in the Holy City itself—the Pool of Bethesda. It lay by the Sheep Gate (Greek *probatikē*), and the five porticoes erected there were a favorite gathering place for invalids (JOHN 5:2 f.). It seems a disturbance of the water was interpreted popularly as due to the touch of an angel, and it was believed that the first one who stepped into it after that phenomenon occurred would be healed. This particular information has evidently been supplied from some non-canonical gospel, for it is not found in the best manuscripts of the New Testament and hence is relegated to the margin in the R.S.V. At this pool, then, Jesus healed a man who had never been able to get into the water first, though waiting many years for the opportunity.

The name Bethesda has engraved itself deeply into the hearts of Christian people everywhere. The old Syriac translation gives it as *Beth-ḥisdā*, "House of Mercy" (i.e. of God), and this is probably what the Greek transcription Bethesda attempts to reproduce. That does not necessarily mean that Bethesda was the true name of the place, but could indicate that that is what Christians living at Jerusalem in the early centuries had come to call it, in commemoration of the healing of the sufferer by Jesus. The oldest manuscripts of the New Testament have the name Beth-zatha, which therefore is used by the R.S.V. This is no doubt identical with *Bezatha*, the name of the city-district that had grown up north of the second wall. This name too presents problems, on which, however, we cannot dwell here. It was scarcely an appropriate name for a pool, and in view of the traditions quoted below it seems probable that the sentence in John 5:2 should be rendered "There is in Jerusalem by the sheep *pool a place* called Bethesda."

Of greater interest and consequence is the fact that the site of the Pool of Bethesda can be identified with a high degree of probability. The names of G. Schick, L. H. Vincent, and N. van der Vliet are closely linked with this painstaking work. We can only give the resultant picture. Two pools have indeed been found on the property of St. Anne which fit the description given by Eusebius and Cyril, and the remains of pillars confirm the existence of porticoes thereabouts. The sketch on page 393 shows the shape of these pools. In addition to four porticoes surrounding both of them there will have been the portico between them, in which Jesus may have healed the unfortunate sufferer. It seems almost certain then, that a place playing a role in the story of Jesus, as related by John, has actually been identified. True, the intermittent "troubling" of the waters in the pool has led some

392

scholars to identify Bethesda with Siloam (of which that is very typical), but since the Evangelist shortly afterwards refers to the pool of Siloam (JOHN 9:6–7) he clearly differentiates them.

Further Journeyings

We next find Jesus "at the sea of Galilee, which is the sea of Tiberias" (JOHN 6:1), and carrying on a brief Galilean ministry, beginning with the incident of the feeding of the multitude opposite Tiberias, already considered (page 386). We soon find him going to Jerusalem again for the Feast of the Tabernacles, which was celebrated in the fall of the year. He made several appearances in the Temple, and was nearly stoned on one occasion (JOHN 8:59). Somewhere in the city he healed a man who was born blind, by bidding him to go wash himself in the Pool of Siloam. The text adds parenthetically "which is by interpretation, Sent" (JOHN 9:6–7). This interpretative remark evidently suggested itself because Jesus "sent" the man

to Siloam; it seemed to the Evangelist prophetic that the pool should have had this name. The incident may have taken place in the southwestern part of the city, for then this pool, which, we have said, lay in the Tyropoeon Valley in the shadow of the old City of David, definitely would be the nearest one.

Jesus stayed in Jerusalem for the Feast of the Dedication, called Hanukkah (JOHN 11:22 f.). This was not a festival commanded in the Old Testament law, but a new and popular one that had come up in commemoration of the purification and re-dedication of the Temple after its defilement by the Seleucid Antiochus Epiphanes. The Evangelist notes that it was the winter season. The only local point referred to is the hall of Solomon in the Temple, in which Jesus walked about.

Bethany

After escaping from the hands of the Jews (presumably as he had done in Nazareth, according to Luke 4:30) Jesus went to the other side of the Jordan, where John had baptized him (JOHN 10:40). Here he gained followers among those who had admired John. In that neighborhood he was informed of the illness of Lazarus of Bethany (JOHN 11:3), and soon afterward received the report of his friend's death. He delayed going to Bethany, however, timing his arrival for the third day after receiving this message.

The Bethany here referred to obviously lay close to Jerusalem, and is the one mentioned in the Passion narratives (MARK 11:1; 10:46; 14:3). It is described by John as "fifteen furlongs" (literally 15 stadia, or a half hour's walk) from Jerusalem (JOHN 11:18). The name is written *Beth 'Anyā* in the Syriac version, which may be correct and could be a shortened form of Beth Ananiah. An Ananiah is mentioned right after Anathoth and Nob (NEH. 11:32) and may be the same place. The ancient settlement lay on a rocky

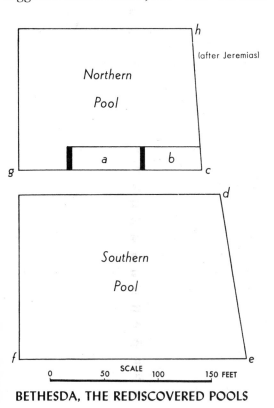

BETHESDA, THE REDISCOVERED POOLS

7.37 *The traditional tomb of Lazarus.* (*Matson Photo Service*)

height some three hundred yards west of *el 'Azarīyeh,* where cisterns, burial caves and hypogea (underground tombs), some Canaanite, others late Jewish, have been found.

The supposed tomb of Lazarus below the present village has been regarded as the scene of the raising of the dead man since about 300 A.D. A church was even built there before 380 A.D. The sepulchre is described as a "rock chamber with recessed vaults on three sides." This scarcely fits the description of John's narrative, which calls for "a cave with a stone lying upon it." However, the antiquity of the identification renders this a venerable place.

Since Martha went forth to meet Jesus, when she heard that he was coming, the point where she would have encountered him was also the subject of pious speculation at an early date. The exact spot was shown to the pilgrim Etheria (380 A.D.), 500 paces west of the tomb of Lazarus in the direction of the Mount of Olives. In the sixth century it, too, was marked by a church. However, this identification is predicated on the belief that Jesus came from Jericho via the round-about way of the northerly Roman road (see page 398). It has been suggested that if he came via the direct, southerly route a more suitable point for the meeting of Jesus and Martha would be where the road comes up from the *Wadi es Sikkeh,* near the Greek monastery *ej Jeneineh.*

Ephraim

Jesus did not return to the Jordan after the raising of Lazarus, according to John, but went into seclusion to avoid premature seizure by the Jews. He sought out a town called Ephraim; and there he stayed with the disciples. Ephraim is a tribal or regional name in the Old Testament, except in 2 Samuel 13:23, where, however, the Jewish editors call it a misspelling of Ephron. Josephus, too, mentions an Ephraim near Bethel that was taken by Vespasian in the Jewish war. It seems likely that both mean the same place and that it is identical with the Aphairema of 1 Maccabees 11:34, the capital of a district bordering on Samaria. The real Hebrew name was doubtless Ephron or Ephrain (so 2 CHRON. 13:19), and the place is best sought at *eṭ Ṭaiyibeh,* four miles northeast of the town of Bethel. It is a very secluded neighborhood south of *el 'Aṣūr* (page 202) and close to the wilderness (the barren gorges leading down to the Jordan Valley). Jesus may well be imagined as sojourning there with adherents, or with relatives of disciples, for the inclement rainy season would certainly have been unfavorable for any outdoor camping.

At this point the special journeyings of John's Gospel end, and we again may follow the track laid out by the oldest Gospel.

The Last Journey to Jerusalem

From Capernaum, whither he had come after his travels through the high country of Galilee, Jesus took the first step in the final, fateful journey to the Holy City.

According to Mark 10:1 f. he went to the region of Judaea beyond the Jordan. One may think of him, perhaps, as going down the lake and to Scythopolis without the detour up into the mountains. If the "region of Judaea" is to be taken literally he would have had to go at least to Koraea. That he went to "beyond the Jordan" implies a crossing over into Peraea, perhaps at *ed-Dāmieh*. It would involve a recrossing of the river at the fords east of Jericho. While nothing is said of this, the arrival at Jericho is mentioned (MARK 10:16).

The Jericho of the days of Jesus did not lie at modern *Erīḥa,* but rather a mile to the northwest of it, where the *Wadi el Qelt* opens into the plain. This was established by the German expedition under Sellin (page 134). According to Josephus, Herod had a palace here and had even provided the city with an amphitheater and a hippodrome. Since the road from Jerusalem came down through the *Wadi el Qelt,* the latter was guarded by two fortresses on the peaks at its exit. The southern peak commands a view both of the Jericho plain and part of the western approach to the city, and the remains on it suggest that it once bore the fortress of Kypros, mentioned by Josephus. The northern peak commands another part of the western approach to the city, and opens up a large prospect over the whole country of the Jordan to the Dead Sea. No pre-Byzantine remains seem to be preserved there, however.

On issuing from the *Wadi el Qelt,* one immediately entered Herodian Jericho, which lay spread out on the northern bank and may have extended for a mile and a quarter northward. Lower down the wadi, which carries a good stream of water in the wintertime, were two additional forts or towers. The two tells *Abu 'Alayiq* covered them until recent excavations. The southern tower lies farther out in the plain than its opposite number, being about a half mile from the mountains. Warren dug there in 1868 and Sellin in 1909 and 1911, but it remained for a joint expedition of the American Schools and the Pittsburgh-Xenia Theological Seminary under James L. Kelso to make real progress. The core of the southern tell, we now know, was a Hellenistic fortress, erected on

7.38 *Excavation of Herodian Palace by American School of Oriental Research. (Elsie D. Kraeling)*

the flat plain where it slopes off to the wadi. The excavator suggests that it was originally built by Bacchides (1 MACC. 9:50) in 160 B.C. Josephus speaks of two towers which Pompey captured near Jericho in 63 B.C., naming them Threx and Taurus. The excavated one may well be one or the other of these.

Unlike the older Canaanite and Hebrew town the Roman town of Jericho had streets and public places where shade trees could flourish. In a sycamore tree—a type of tree growing only in the Jordan Valley and on the coast—Zaccheus, the publican, sat in the branches to get a good view of Jesus (LUKE 19:2–10). A piece of ancient wood found in the excavations and used for bonding the wall of the tower, was identified as sycamore at the Yale School of Forestry.

As he left the city Jesus was importuned by the blind beggar Bartimaeus who sat by the roadside (MARK 10:46). The road up to Jerusalem skirted the south bank of the *Wadi el Qelt* and went up the "Ascent of Adummim" (today, *Ṭal 'at ed Damm*) to the "Inn of the Good Samaritan." Here one had a first view of the Mount of Olives. The road then descended into a plain and, after crossing another valley (*Wadi es Sidr*), divided.

Which fork did Jesus take? That would have depended on his objective. If his goal

7.39 *View over Bethphage and Bethany from the Mount of Olives with the wilderness of Judaea and the Dead Sea in the background.* (*Matson Photo Service*)

was the north gate of Jerusalem he would have taken the right-hand road, which is the one the Romans at a later date built into a regular paved road and marked with milestones, and which crosses north of the Mount of Olives. If he had a preliminary objective in Bethany he would, presuming that Bethany lay at *el 'Azarīyeh,* have taken the left-hand road which led through the *Wadi es Sikkeh* and up a steep gorge to the promontory east of the Mount of Olives.

The statement of the Evangelists as to Jesus' objective is not as clear as one might wish (MARK 11:1; LUKE 19:29; MATT. 21:1). The mention of two places in Mark and Luke, who reverses their order, seems artificial. There is reason to believe that one of them is secondary. The great Church Father Origen held that Bethany alone was originally mentioned. The two names in Mark and Luke may represent a combination-reading of two separate text-traditions, one exclusively mentioning Bethphage (as Matthew has it) and the other only Bethany.

The Mount of Olives

What is the Mount of Olives? Where were Bethany and Bethphage? These, of course, are the essential questions that one must ask if one would attempt to trace the route of Jesus' journey. "Mount of Olives" (literally,

THE MOUNT OF OLIVES

SCALE

0 2 4 6 Tenths of Miles

"of olive trees") was hardly the name of the whole eastern range that, with its series of four eminences, can be seen from Jerusalem. We have had occasion to note that Palestinians look at the terrain less broadly than we do, and that what we would consider a single river valley or mountain range has different names in its different sectors. Today the name *eṭ Ṭūr*, "the Mount" (*sc.* "of Olives"), applies exclusively to the third or southwestern height which is opposite the Temple and to the slope stretching down from it to the Kidron Valley. The two more northerly heights and the fourth more southeasterly height of the range are not part of "the Mount," but have their own names. There is every reason to believe that this continues ancient Hebrew usage. The second northerly height is the highest, though only exceeding *eṭ Ṭūr* by twenty-one feet, a difference hardly detected by the eye.

When the Mount of Olives was named, the whole hillside was doubtless covered with orchards. In Acts 1:12 and various other sources it is called the "olive grove" (Latin: *olivetum*) or Olivet, so that it must still have

been an orchard area. According to Josephus the Mount (i.e., the summit meant) lay five stadia east of Jerusalem or a Sabbath's journey (cf. Acts 1:12), about a ten minutes' walk. We must remember that the "lower city" of that day lay to the south of the Temple quadrangle, so that only the hill directly opposite the City of David can be referred to with the term "the Mount," and this accords fully with the use of *eṭ Ṭūr*.

We have already discussed the location of Bethany in the light of John's Gospel (page 393). There is no clue to it except that of early Christian tradition which sought it at *el ʿAzarīyeh*. It is on the southeast side of the range. The eminence above it on the northwest is not included in *eṭ Ṭūr*, but has a special name, *Rās esh Shiyāḥ*. Precisely speaking, therefore, Bethany did not lie either on or at the Mount of Olives, though in going from it to Jerusalem one would, after crossing the ravine west of the *Rās esh Shiyāḥ,* pass around the south and west sides of the Mount of Olives.

It is different, however, with Bethphage, if ancient tradition located it correctly. For its site was shown north of the *Rās esh Shiyāḥ*

7.40 *An aerial view of the Mount of Olives Range. (Bavarian State Archives)*

and here one is really on the rear side of *eṭ Ṭūr,* and hence "at" the Mount of Olives (MATT. 21:1). While Bethany is not referred to in Talmudic sources, Bethphage occurs a number of times. It is always mentioned as the easternmost point in Jerusalem's territory. It was indeed the appropriate place from which to start the ride into Jerusalem, and so Matthew's version that an ass was secured there is plausible. The name Bethphage (*Bethpage* R.S.V.), we may note in passing, is usually explained as "town of unripe figs," but the rendering is by no means certain.

While some of the early pilgrims imagined Jesus as having gone over the northern (late Roman) road and then turned off it in a southerly direction to get to Bethphage, this would seem much less natural than his taking the southern road to Bethany and then proceeding northward to Bethphage and crossing the heights of *eṭ Ṭūr.*

On the way down from the summit the Holy City must have lain before Jesus' eyes, notably the Temple courts which were in plain view.

It is in this area between Bethphage and the present Church of the Ascension that one must imagine the popular demonstration to have taken place (MARK 11:8 f.). The branches that people laid in Jesus' path were doubtless broken from the olive trees.

At some point in the descent from the Mount of Olives Jesus wept over the city and spoke prophetic words concerning its future, according to Luke 19:41 f.

Entering Jerusalem

In descending to the city Jesus had a choice of paths. The direct one was rather steep for riding, and so can hardly have been the one used at this occasion, though the early Church in its Palm Sunday processions followed this route. The other ran more circuitously and comfortably, crossing the Kidron Valley by a bridge or causeway. The ancient situation, however, has been interfered with here by the construction of the Church of the Tomb of the Virgin, and so it is no longer possible to say just how the road ran in Jesus' time.

It seems unlikely that Jesus entered the eastern gate of the Temple, even though Matthew 21:12 f., describing his visit to the sanctuary, might lend itself to such an interpretation, and though that was the accepted view at the time of the Crusades. But one did not ride into the Temple, and to use the sanctuary as a passage was regarded as a profanation of it. But there seems to have been a city gate through which he might have entered on the east side of the city's northeast corner. Some steps which once led up to it can still be seen above today's road. There thus may have been a street or passage between the city wall and the Temple court. Such a passage would be most desirable in any case for the movement of soldiers in defending the city walls.

In the city of Christian times, in which the Temple area lay desolate, this gate was called the Gate of Benjamin, continuing the name of a gate of earlier days. The sixth-century Christians, at any rate, believed that Jesus had entered the city here. On Palm Sunday a festive procession was held, which began on the Mount of Olives and passed through this gate, halting briefly at the nearby "Sheep Pool" (page 392) and then passed on to the Church of the Holy Sepulchre. There was a north gate which that narrow street passed; Josephus alludes to it, and the Mishnah calls it *Tadi Gate,* but it was probably only for use of the priests, as it led into the Temple area. Possibly in Jesus' time, one coming from the east of the city would have had to go around the walls past the Antonia to the Gennath Gate (so-named by Josephus), which is the Ephraim Gate of much earlier days (cf. NEH. 8:16). The Fourth Gospel's localization of the demonstration (JOHN 12:12 f.) would fit well with this course, for it thinks of it as taking place directly in front of the north side of the city. Hearing that Jesus is coming, the crowd of visitors in

Jerusalem goes forth to meet him, taking *palm* branches. Since palms do not grow in the vicinity of Jerusalem, these branches must be imagined as having been brought up from Jericho for festive purposes.

Jesus Visits the Temple

After entering the city Jesus paid a visit to the Temple, in the course of which "he looked round about upon all things" (MARK 11:11). We, too, may appropriately do that at this point. It was, indeed, worth seeing—this temple that Herod had rebuilt in such magnificence. The disciples later marveled over it in viewing it from the Mount of Olives (MARK 13:1). Herod had vastly increased the area, and built a huge substructure on the sloping ground in the east to provide the foundation that has withstood the wear and tear of the ages. The mighty Herodian masonry, of which some drafted stones are to be seen at the Wailing Wall (fig. 7.41), still speak of this great builder.

If Jesus was in the northern part of the upper city he will have crossed a bridge over the Tyropoeon Valley that begins to form here and will have entered through the Coponius Gate. Wilson's Arch is a remnant of a somewhat later bridge in the same neighborhood, and the so-called Gate of the Chain (*Bab el Silsile*) is the near equivalent of the Coponius Gate. After passing through this gate Jesus found himself in the great court encircling the whole sanctuary and known as "the Mount of the House." While the area belonged to the Temple, it was not holy ground, and non-Jews, as well as Jews who had broken Hebrew law by being defiled by contact with corpses, had access here. Standing in the shade of the roofed colonnades or porticoes that ran around the quadrangle, Jesus will have seen the walls of the sacred enclosure containing the "House"— the Temple proper. One stood in the rear of it here, and to get into the sacred precincts it was necessary to get to the other side of the quadrangle. Jesus will have gone to the

7.41 *Herodian masonry in the Wailing Wall.* (*Ewing Galloway*)

right, and turning the corner will have proceeded first through the southern portico known as "the Royal Portico" into which two gateways, known as the Huldah Gates, entered, admitting visitors from the southwestern part of the city. Turning the corner once more Jesus will have passed into the portico on the east side known as "Porch of Solomon" (ACTS 3:11). Abuses such as those mentioned in Matthew 21:12–17 may have gone on either in the Royal Portico or in that of Solomon in Jesus' time, when the Sadducees were still strong, but will have had the disapproval of the Pharisees. As he proceeded Jesus will have seen at the left the entrance to the inner courts. But we may imagine him as first continuing through Solomon's Portico and going past the Susa Gate, on which the acropolis of Susa was pictured in relief; it was, no doubt, a gift of the Elamite Jews, but was only used in connection with the red heifer ceremony (NUM. 19:1–10). Rounding the northeast corner Jesus would have come to the Tadi Gate, reserved for the use of priests (page 398), and then would have seen bulging out into the Temple quadrangle the great fortress called Antonia by Herod, in honor of Mark Antony. Here Roman soldiery was now in

THE SECOND TEMPLE ACCORDING TO JEWISH TRADITION
(after G. Dalman)

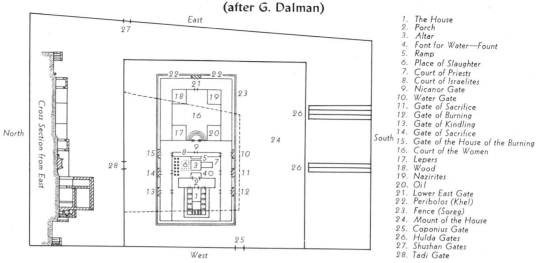

1. The House
2. Porch
3. Altar
4. Font for Water—Fount
5. Ramp
6. Place of Slaughter
7. Court of Priests
8. Court of Israelites
9. Nicanor Gate
10. Water Gate
11. Gate of Sacrifice
12. Gate of Burning
13. Gate of Kindling
14. Gate of Sacrifice
15. Gate of the House of the Burning
16. Court of the Women
17. Lepers
18. Wood
19. Nazirites
20. Oil
21. Lower East Gate
22. Peribolos (Khel)
23. Fence (Soreg)
24. Mount of the House
25. Coponius Gate
26. Hulda Gates
27. Shushan Gates
28. Tadi Gate

power, holding the city in check just as the Ptolemaic and Seleucid kings had once done from the Acra in the south.

We may think of Jesus as retracing his steps and passing again through Solomon's Porch to the point where one turned to go to the sacred precincts. Approaching the latter one saw a wall and before it a low balustrade which Jews called the *soreg* ("hedge"). The space between the *soreg* and the wall was the *peribolos*. Here stone tablets, one of which has been preserved, proclaimed to the gentiles in the Greek language:

Let no gentile enter within the hedge
and the *peribolos* around the sanctuary.
Whoever is caught shall have himself to
blame for his consequent death.

Stepping over the balustrade Jesus would have had to ascend twelve steps and pass through a gateway with gold-overlayed doors.

Jesus now entered the Court of the Women, so named because it marked the limit beyond which women were not allowed to go. This court, too, had a roofed portico around it, and in the corners there were four high-walled unroofed chambers, one for wood-storage and inspection (for no wormy wood could be used for the altar-fire), one for storage of oil and wine, one for the checking of those claiming to be cured of leprosy (MATT. 8:4), and one for those seeking purification from failure to carry through Nazirite vows (cf. ACTS 21:24–26).

Beyond the Court of the Women on another raised terrace and walled off by a high wall was the holy area of the actual sanctuary. One ascended a stair of fifteen steps and stood before the Gate of Nicanor, probably the one called "the Beautiful" (ACTS 3:2 f.). Its doors were artistically wrought in Corinthian bronze. To these steps Mary might have gone (LUKE 2:22 f.), but not beyond, for it was here a priest declared women cleansed after childbirth.

Jesus, of course, could pass through the Nicanor Gate. He now found himself within the "hangings" (Hebrew *ḳelāʾīm*)—the reserved area—and had a first full view of the altar and House. Only a narrow strip of space on the east side of the court was available to a layman such as he, and it was known as the Court of the Israelites. West of it, perhaps raised or in some way partitioned off, was the Court of the Priests. Three steps led up to the vicinity of the altar and on these the Levitic minstrels made music during the seasons of the daily offerings. The altar was a great cube made of unhewn stones, and had a ramp leading up to it, for steps were prohibited (Ex. 20:26).

Around the whole court area were chambers for various purposes, including the "Hewn-stone Chamber" where the Council is said to have met (page 405). An open space lay between the Altar and the House. No layman had any business there, and the Zechariah who was slain in this area (MATT. 23:35) must have been a priest. His being killed at this holy spot was regarded as a horrible thing—a desecration of God's House.

The House had a high vestibule with pillars. On the steps leading up to it the priests, before (not after) the morning and evening sacrifices, stood and gave the benediction (NUM. 6:25) that they alone were privileged to utter. Around the House itself were chambers for various purposes. Behind the vestibule the visitor saw the great curtain, for the doors stood open except during the night, when no one was admitted to the Temple.

It already being late when he had completed his Temple tour, Jesus went out to Bethany to spend the night (MARK 11:11). Mark may have thought of him as enjoying the hospitality of Simon the Leper (MARK 14:3). In view of the congestion in the city caused by the multitude of pilgrims coming to the Passover, many people must have been forced to seek accommodations in the outlying villages. On the return to the city the following morning, the fig-tree incident of Mark 11:12–14 occurred. Jesus may have expected to find fig buds (Arabic 'ajr), which are still eaten today by those who are hungry enough not to mind their bitter taste. April was hardly yet the time for fajj (Hebrew paggim), the unripe, juiceless figs, which do not reach the stage when they are given that designation until seven weeks after the leaves appear. Mark's sequel to this incident (11:19 f.) is made unnecessary in Matthew's version (21:18 f.) and Luke and John have omitted the whole episode.

Scene of the Last Supper

From John's account one would infer that Jesus, after leaving Bethany for Jerusalem, stayed in the city itself. His arrival on the fifth or sixth day in advance of the Passover implies his desire to follow Jewish custom in respect to purification requirements (JOHN 11:55). Furthermore, John has cancelled the account of the Passover meal, for in his view the death of Jesus preceded the Passover (JOHN 19:31).

According to Mark, Luke and Matthew, Jesus sent his disciples into the city from Bethany or Bethphage to find a place where they could hold the Passover. It was obligatory to eat the meal in Jerusalem and even to spend the night of the meal there, though the rabbis probably relaxed the latter requirement by extending "Jerusalem" to include the villages in its area.

The question of the location of the "large upper room, furnished and ready" (provided with the essential mattresses or cushions for a party of at least ten persons) was, of course, bound to arouse later Christian interest. While it is not stated in the New Testament that this upper room is identical with the upper room where the first Christian gatherings were later held (ACTS 1:13, etc.), it is only natural that such an identification was bound to be made.

The preparations for the Passover supper required that someone take a lamb to the Temple, kill and skin it there and return with the meat, carried in the hide, to the house where the meal was to be held and where it had to be cooked. The Evangelists do not dwell on these very essential matters which doubtless consumed a considerable time. It is difficult, even with all that may be gleaned from Jewish sources, to get any clear picture as to how all the practical things involved in the situation were handled. Josephus asserts that 256,500 Passover sacrifices were counted on one occasion of this nature. The amount of time that would be consumed and the congestion that would result, both in the Temple courts and in the entrances, if only one-tenth of that number of persons sacrificed in the inner court be-

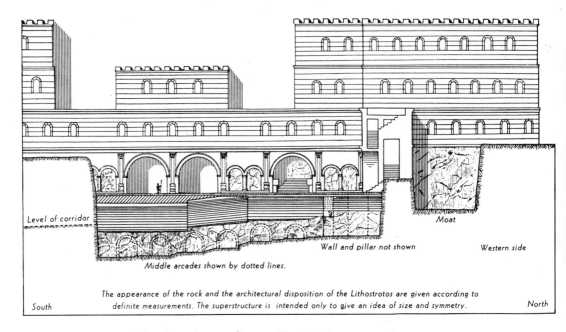

Level of corridor

Middle arcades shown by dotted lines.

Wall and pillar not shown

Moat

Western side

South

North

The appearance of the rock and the architectural disposition of the Lithostrotos are given according to definite measurements. The superstructure is intended only to give an idea of size and symmetry.

The Antonia according to Père L. H. Vincent. A sectional diagram on the axis of the western basin and figurative restoration of the fortress above ground.

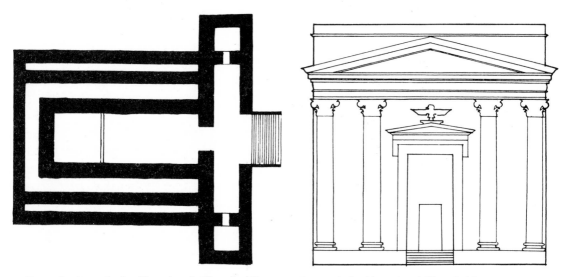

Ground plan of the Temple of Herod. (Reconstruction of Watzinger)

Front of the Temple of Herod. (Reconstruction of Watzinger)

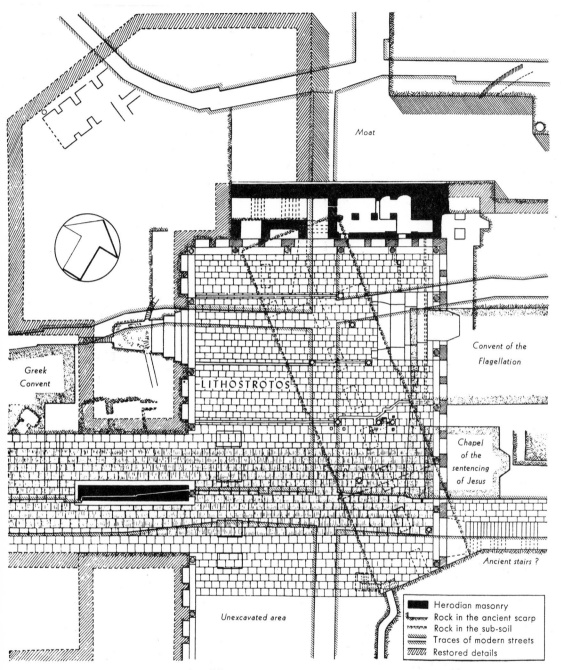

Moat

Greek
Convent

LITHOSTROTOS

Convent of the
Flagellation

Chapel
of the
sentencing
of Jesus

Ancient stairs ?

Unexcavated area

	Herodian masonry
	Rock in the ancient scarp
	Rock in the sub-soil
	Traces of modern streets
	Restored details

The Lithostrotos according to modern exploration. (After Vincent) tween 2:30 in the afternoon and sundown, would still have been terrific.

Gethsemane

After the singing of the hymn, the second part of the Hallel (Ps. 113-118), which followed the recital of the Passover Haggada and the drinking of the third cup of wine, Jesus went out with his disciples to the Mount of Olives to a place called Gethsemane (MARK 14:26, 32).

Matthew, too, gives the name (MATT. 26:36) but Luke and John do not mention it. The name Gethsemane, familiar and beloved as it is to Christian ears today, was thus not considered important by these two Gospel writers. One must reluctantly admit, furthermore, that its meaning is dubious. The usual assumption that it means "press of oils" faces serious philological objections, and even the very spelling of the name is uncertain. The Church Father Jerome, who had studied Hebrew, gives it as *Gesamani* and connects it with the "fat valleys" (Hebrew, *ge'ē shemānīm*) of Isaiah 28:1.

Quite distinctive and of interest for the localization of the place of Jesus' praying is the version of the Fourth Gospel. According to John there was a garden across the Kidron Valley which Jesus entered with his disciples (JOHN 18:1).

This report should not be combined with that of Mark, who knows of no "garden," but only of a "place." It seems likely that when John's words were written down the locality of Christ's "agony" had been converted into a garden. There was no garden, but only the orchard hillside, in Jesus' time.

Tradition presents no less than four candidates for identification with Gethsemane— all situated above the present road from Jerusalem to Bethany. That of the "Latins" (as the Roman Catholics are called in the Orient) with a wall around it and containing very old olive trees; that of the Russians; that of the Armenians; and that of the Greek Orthodox Church. The visitor can thus have his choice. The Latin Gethsemane naturally attracts Occidentals most.

There is nothing in the Scriptures to indicate how far up the Mount of Olives the place Gethsemane is to be sought. One can therefore only say: somewhere on the other side of the Kidron on the hillside. If we are willing to listen to tradition at all in this matter, our choice can only be the oldest tradition of which there is record. In the fifth century and up to the time of the Crusades, Gethsemane was held to lie on the ground now occupied by the Church of the Tomb of the Virgin. The place of Jesus' prayer, however, was held to lie a stone's throw up the hill (LUKE 22:41).

The Scenes of the Proceedings

After his betrayal and arrest on the Mount of Olives Jesus was conducted to the palace of the high priest (MARK 14:53). "Caiaphas," the name supplied by the other Evangelists, was only a surname, the meaning of which is uncertain. The man's real name was Joseph, and he held the high priestly office 18-35 A.D. The conclusion sometimes drawn from John's remark, "who was high priest that year" (18:13), that the priestly office changed hands annually, is erroneous.

Early in the fourth century Christians claimed to have knowledge as to where Caiaphas' palace had stood; its ruins were pointed out in the upper city. This accords well with the fact that the high priest Ananias of Acts 23:2 lived in that district, according to Josephus. In the sixth century a Church of St. Peter stood on the supposed site. The Bordeaux Pilgrim (333 A.D.) was shown the ruins of Caiaphas' house outside the south wall of the city of Aelia, and the Madeba mosaic puts it south of Sion Church (see page 414).

Oriental houses incline very much to the use of a central court, from which entrance then is had to rooms or halls round about it. It is in such a court that Peter must be imagined as denying that he knew Jesus and where he heard the cock crow. That cock will have been very close at hand, for such a bird was kept by travelers and, we may suppose, privileged residents of cities, like high priests, as a sort of "clock." Thus the mediaeval traveler Felix Fabri relates that his caravan took a large white cock along from Gaza on the trip through the desert that "standing on the coop he might during the desert journey indicate to us the hours of the night." The cock's crow has definite regularity, but hourly performance is hardly implied. Two crowings are presupposed in the narrative (MARK 14:30, 72).

The place where Peter was supposed to have stood when he heard the cock crow was naturally marked by a church in the early centuries. The present Armenian Church of Caiaphas, 160 feet north of the Cenacle, may be on or near the site of that Byzantine structure since the remains of a mosaic floor are preserved outside of it.

According to Mark, a meeting of the Council, or Sanhedrin, was held at the high-priest's house during that night and another in the morning, presumably at the regular place of meeting, which Josephus calls by the Greek name *Boulé*. The Mishnah tract *Sanhedrin,* which gives much information about that twenty-member council, speaks of its meeting in the Temple in the "Hewn-stone Chamber." That could reflect a situation that arose during the Jewish war. The *Boulé* of Josephus was no doubt an independent building. It lay below the Temple, near the bridge leading over to the eastern hill. Oddly enough the Mohammedan court of *el Meḥkameh* of today stands just about in the same locality. It was in the council house that the decisive vote was cast on the morning after the arrest. The decision was to ask the Roman governor Pontius Pilate for the execution of Jesus.

Jesus was next led to that official, who held open-air court in front of the "Praetorium" (MARK 15:16). One must not, however, look for a definite building of that name. In the Roman view a Praetorium existed wherever a praetor held court.

There is conflict of opinion as to where Pilate would have sat in judgment. The Roman governor did not reside at Jerusalem, but rather at Caesarea on the coast of the sea, and normally a prisoner would have been sent down there (as was later done with Paul); his accusers, too, would have had to go there (cf. ACTS 23:33, 24:1). But Pilate was in Jerusalem at this time because of the Passover, when the influx of so many Jews into the Holy City created a situation that bore watching. Where would he have stayed? In the palace of Herod or in the Antonia citadel? That is the question.

Josephus tells of a later occasion when the seat, on which Gessius Florus sat in judgement, was set up before the entrance of Herod's palace. In other words that place served as the Praetorium. It thus seems natural to suppose that this was also the scene of the trial of Jesus, though the word the R.S.V. translates "palace" instead of A.V. "hall" (MARK 15:16) does not, as one might think, clinch the matter.

John's version suggests that all the questioning of Jesus by Pilate took place indoors, and that Pilate had to go outside to consult with the accusers, who were unwilling to defile themselves by entering the domicile of a heathen (JOHN 18:28). Pilate, then, occupied the judgment seat only when he rendered the verdict at a place called the "Pavement [Greek, *lithostrotos*], but in the Hebrew, Gabbatha" (JOHN 19:13). The word Gabbatha is Aramaic (*gabbetā,* "elevation"), and is the term evidently in ɪse to describe the *Bema,* or platform, that was a familiar installation of every Hellenistic city. Herod naturally had such a one in front of his palace for his judicial functions.

The earliest ecclesiastical tradition sought the "Praetorium" in the vicinity of the Jewish council house or of the Hasmonaean palace. The steps that supposedly led up to it were brought to Rome (allegedly in 326

A.D.) and set up in 845 A.D. as the *scala sancta*. The place where they were obtained must thus have had ascending ground before it. In the Middle Ages the Franciscans sought the Praetorium at the Antonia castle up to which a stairway actually led. This theory has received support recently through the excavations of Vincent at the Convent of Our Lady of Zion, which showed that the *Ecce Homo* arch (dating from the time of Hadrian) stands on a pavement of Herod's time in a part of Antonia's central court, which was fifty yards square. The large stone blocks used for this pavement would excellently fit the word "lithostrotos" used by John. But a similar pavement may have existed in front of Herod's palace. The discovery can scarcely overbalance the weight of the incident from Josephus mentioned above. The Antonia was a crowded place, as seat of the Roman garrison, and Pilate would have desired more luxurious quarters than it was able to furnish, if such were at his command.

Since the location of Herod's old palace is known (page 367) the general vicinity of its entrance can be fixed. In terms of present-day Jerusalem, the place may have lain south of the eastern side of the present "Pool of Hezekiah."

The Roman soldiery then took Jesus into the "Praetorium" and there bound, mocked and scourged him (MARK 15:16 f.), an incident which Luke does not relate. Presumably the guard house or guard rooms of the palace would have been the scene of the scourging of Jesus by the Romans.

All Evangelists except Luke immediately pass over to the crucifixion. That writer provides a retarding element with the account of how Jesus was sent by Pilate to Herod Antipas, who was present in Jerusalem for the Passover celebration (LUKE 23:6–12). The tetrarch may have occupied the old palace of the Hasmonaeans, to which his father Herod had gained title by virtue of his marriage to Mariamne. It lay on the east side of the hill of the upper city, according to Josephus. Luke substitutes a mocking of Jesus by Herod's soldiers for the one Mark attributes to the Romans (LUKE 23:11). This would seem to involve a protracted interruption of the proceedings at the Praetorium and their resumption and conclusion later.

The Roman soldiery then led Jesus forth to crucify him (MARK 15:21). They compelled an individual who was approaching the city gates, a man from Cyrene in North Africa, to carry "the cross." The popular representations of Jesus bearing the cross are inaccurate, since the prisoner of the Romans only bore the *patibulum* or cross-piece. A place of execution did not have to be found—it was well established and the upright post already stood there.

The Church of the early centuries did not dwell on the matter of the *Via Dolorosa* and so there is no ancient tradition with respect to it. The stations of the cross only became a matter of Christian interest since the thirteenth century under the influence of the Franciscans. It was assumed at that time that the Praetorium was the Antonia and that the exit of Jesus from the city took place via the Damascus Gate. But if the Praetorium was the palace of Herod then it seems likely that the procession would have taken a different course than that of the traditional *Via Dolorosa*.

Golgotha

The place of execution bears the name of Golgotha in Greek transcription, and Mark interprets it as "place of the skull." The Aramaic word for "the skull" is *gulgultā* and so if Mark's rendering is correct and not, as some hold, a popular etymology, there has been a loss of one letter in the transcription of it into Greek. The familiar name "Calvary" comes to us from the Latin Bible translation, which renders "place of the skull" as *locus calvariae*.

The question of the location of Golgotha has agitated Christian minds a great deal.

It stands to reason that the place was outside the city wall and most probably north of the city near a thoroughfare. The question is complicated by the fact that we do not know to what extent the land west of the Antonia was built up in Jesus' time, or how the "second wall" embracing the *Bezatha* area (cf. page 392) ran. The "authenticity" of the traditional holy places depends on this and only future excavations can clarify things. If the situation was like that on Color Map XVIII, the traditional localization of Golgotha and the Holy Sepulchre would not be proven correct, but could be maintained.

The Christians of the Apostolic Age can hardly have thought of Golgotha with any particular veneration. Numberless other men, mostly criminals, had doubtless been crucified on the same spot before and after Jesus, and those who vividly remembered that fact could not yet have regarded it as hallowed ground. Considerations of this sort may still have influenced Constantine's advisers, for nothing is said of Golgotha and the site of the Holy Cross at this time. Eusebius in the *Onomastikon* merely says that Golgotha is shown in Aelia (Jerusalem) toward the north of "Mount Sion" (the city's western ridge). Golgotha became of interest three hundred years later. The supposed discovery of the Holy Cross at that time played a great role in the matter.

The kleig lights of interest and attention in Constantine's day were focused on the *tomb* of Christ. That the two places were believed to be fairly close to each other, however, may be seen from the brief account of the Pilgrim of Bordeaux (333 A.D.). To understand his words one needs to know that the boundaries of Aelia Capitolina, the city established by Hadrian, did not coincide with the walls of Jerusalem of 70 A.D. In the north they extended out beyond the old city's area, while in the south they left much of it lying outside the new walls. Thus the sites of Golgotha and the tomb of Christ were now located *within* the city, as this pilgrim saw it.

There is no warrant in the Gospels for thinking of Golgotha as a "hill." Mark merely calls it a "place," and the other Evangelists followed suit. It is purely a fancy of western readers to assume that the place was a cranial-shaped eminence. The site could have been called "the skull" for other reasons: because a single skull lay there, or was elevated on a pole there, at the time when the name was first coined.

Those who discount the tradition about the location of Golgotha and seek it farther away have other sites to choose from. Some, who have been impressed with the idea that it must be a hill, have sought it in the hill of *ez Zāhira,* north of the Damascus Gate. This is "Gordon's Calvary," named after the British general Charles G. Gordon, who, however, was not the first to advocate this site. Stone-quarrying carried on there at some time has given it a skull-like appearance. But the early Church did not seek the place of the crucifixion at this point, and its tradition deserves careful consideration, for the exact spot was certainly known to the Christians before 70 A.D., and it is probable that those who returned to the area some years later would still have been able to identify it.

The Holy Sepulchre

The story of the burial of Jesus centers about a Jew praised highly by Mark for his piety and even termed a secret disciple of Jesus by John—one Joseph of Arimathea. His birthplace is identified by Eusebius, on what ground we do not know, with a *Remphthis,* about nine miles north of Diospolis (Lydda), and that form of the name survives today in *Rentīs,* a village in the Shephelah, lying on a hillside below the probable ancient town-site. We have already heard of it in connection with the home of Samuel (see page 177).

What is the Biblical evidence for the location of the tomb of Jesus? The oldest Evangelist, Mark, tells us that Joseph of

407

Arimathea obtained permission from Pilate to take the body of Jesus from the cross; that he purchased linen in which to wrap the body according to the custom of the time; and that he (apparently unaided) took the body from the cross and laid it in a tomb that had been broken out of the rock and rolled a stone before the entrance.

One must infer that the tomb was rather close by the place of crucifixion. Two women observed what Joseph did—the same two, who, with a third companion, went to the tomb the day after the Sabbath and found it empty (MARK 15:42–16:1). Luke substantially follows Mark, merely emphasizing the fact that it was a *new* tomb in which no body had ever been put. Matthew tries to clarify the ownership: it was Joseph's own tomb which he had hewn into the rock. John, who differs in his details, offers some more explicit information concerning the location of the tomb (JOHN 19:41–42). According to him, it lay in a garden near the place of crucifixion. Owing to the imminence of the Jewish Day of Preparation, Joseph put the body in the tomb, but it was only a temporary haven. Joseph used it because it was close at hand and without having any title to it. But John's words confirm what those of Mark imply, that the tomb was close by Golgotha. Indeed, one may suspect that here, as elsewhere, John reflects a nascent curiosity of Christendom about the exact places where events of singular importance for its history had taken place, and that he is reporting local knowledge of the Palestinian Church of the period between the fall of Jerusalem and the persecution of Trajan. His words also make it very probable that devoted Christian sentiment had by that time created a garden spot here.

An important change in the state of affairs that existed when the Gospel of John was written took place around 137 A.D., for at this time the Roman emperor Hadrian founded a new city named Aelia Capitolina amid the ruins of the city of Jerusalem. He did not simply rebuild the place within the course of its one-time walls. The city was to be a heathen city, to repel the Jews with its uncleanness. Its patron divinity was the goddess Aphrodite, and a temple in her honor formed the center of it. It was built, we are told, on the very site of the Holy Sepulchre. Coins of Aelia from Hadrian's time and that of the emperors who followed show a temple with a goddess in its arched entrance. Christians regarded the choice of the site of the Aphrodite temple as a deliberate attempt to destroy and defile the Holy Sepulchre. When the mighty wheel of events in its turning finally brought a Christian emperor to the helm, it became possible for them to recapture this and other holy places, such as the grotto in Bethlehem.

There is every likelihood, then, that the present Holy Sepulchre is the spot that was pointed out to Constantine's officials as the tomb of Christ. Whether that identification itself was in error cannot be determined. But in the light of present knowledge it seems likely that Golgotha and the Sepulchre were, indeed, in that neighborhood. Beyond that everything rests on the integrity of the ancient churchmen who advised Constantine.

Scenes of the Easter Visions

In the Gospel of Mark the women who come to the tomb of Christ on Easter morning are told by the angel to inform the disciples that Jesus was risen and would appear to his disciples in Galilee (MARK 16:7). It was there that the visions of Peter and of The Twelve (1 COR. 15:5) must have taken place. Matthew's account adheres to Mark's pattern in predicting a Galilean appearance to the disciples, but it relates an appearance to the women after they have left the tomb (MATT. 28:7 f.). This Evangelist does not mention the vision of Peter, however, and implies a rendezvous of the eleven with the risen Christ on a mountain to which Jesus had directed them (MATT.

28:16). This meeting was at the same time the final parting (Luke's "Ascension"), but with assurance of Christ's continued invisible presence, and the assignment of a great task to the disciples.

There is no clue as to the location of Matthew's mountain, but it seems likely that it is the same one mentioned in connection with the Transfiguration. That a certain height in Galilee was held in particular reverence by Galilean Christians as the scene of these two incidents is also supported by the epistolary allusion to "the holy mountain" (2 PETER 1:18 and see page 390).

In Luke's narrative the initial appearances of the risen Christ are localized in Judaea. He omits the message sent by the angel to Peter and the others. The basic appearance to Peter is only mentioned in passing (LUKE 24:34), for to relate it was troublesome, since that appearance had taken place in Galilee, probably at the lakeside (cf. JOHN 21:4 f. and page 410). In Luke the spotlight falls on two disciples who were not even members of the original Twelve, and one of whom was named Cleopas. Luke has developed in a most beautiful manner how, on the way to Emmaus, they met a stranger with whom they conversed about the sad events, and who in the end turned out to be the risen Lord himself.

Where was Emmaus? Eusebius says "it is now Nicopolis of Palestine, a noteworthy city." It received that new name in the third century. It still occurs under the older name in Josephus, according to whom *Ammaous* (as he spells it) lay south of *Tamna* (Old Testament Timnah). The place was the scene of a battle in the wars of the Maccabees (1 MACC. 3:40 f.) in 166–165 B.C. Its very name has survived to this day in *'Amwās*.

But many people find an obstacle to accepting *'Amwās* as the town meant in the Easter narrative because Emmaus is described as a village sixty stadia (seven miles), or a walk of nearly two hours, from Jerusalem (LUKE 24:13). Nicopolis is twenty miles from Jeru-salem—a five-hour march, from which a return on the same evening (LUKE 24:33) and in the darkness of night would be quite arduous. For this reason many favor other identifications. But *'Amwās* has the best claim to being considered the true Emmaus, in spite of the difficulties this causes for the interpretation of Luke's narrative, for at that place alone is the name historically established. Emmaus is a Greek reproduction of a Semitic place name, *Hammā,* which means "warm well." *'Amwās* has two wells of lukewarm water that could account for the name. Furthermore, Eusebius and Jerome both sought Emmaus at *'Amwās,* and the *Codex Sinaiticus* reads 160 stadia (seventeen miles) instead of sixty (seven miles) in Luke 24:13 in an obvious desire to bring Luke's text into conformity with geography. This fits the actual distance on the particular road which the disciples must have taken. One must imagine them as leaving the city by the north gate and going past Golgotha and the site of the tomb, and following the north-south road to the point where one turned off it to the left and went down to Beth Horon and thence to Emmaus. It was the road most commonly used in going on farther to Lydda and Joppa, for there was not as much uphill and down dale as on the straighter road to Jaffa through the Wadi *'Ali* used by the highway of our day.

John's account of the Easter events follows Luke's example in placing the setting of the decisive happenings at Jerusalem. There is no mention of the disciples having left the holy city after the holidays. Mary Magdalene is accorded a preliminary vision in the garden in which the tomb lies (JOHN 20:14 f.). The vision to the disciples occurs in their gathering behind closed doors "where the disciples were assembled" (JOHN 20:19 f.) and is repeated a week later at the same place for the special benefit of Thomas (JOHN 20:19–29). The localization is thus extremely indefinite (as was also the case with the scene of the final repast and the

7.42 *Ruins of the chapel of the "Table of the Lord"* (mensa Domini). (*Matson Photo Service*)

washing of the feet—John 13:1 f.). But no doubt the gathering place of the disciples is the same as the one presupposed in Acts 1:13. Since John omits any account of the Ascension, the appearance before the doubting Thomas is the last one in the original Gospel (chapters 1–20) and is the occasion of the final parting.

In Galilee and on the Way to Olivet

A supplementary chapter (chapter 21) has, however, been affixed to the original Gospel, which tells of an appearance of Jesus before Peter and six other disciples at the "Sea of Tiberias." The story of this chapter, many scholars believe, is an echo of the lost account of the appearance of Christ to Peter (1 COR. 15:5; LUKE 24:34) which according to Mark must have taken place in Galilee.

Thus, at the conclusion of the "Gospel according to the Four," we are taken back to the early scenes of Jesus' ministry. We must imagine the disciples as in Capernaum and as starting for their fishing trip to the eastern shore of the lake at sundown (see page 381), but as failing to find the swarms of fish. The "spring holes" are not always easy to locate, notably on dark nights. If their boat was at *eṭ Ṭabghah* their return will likewise

have been to that point. Tradition of the early Church imagined it thus, for at this place was shown the rock called "the table of the Lord" (*mensa Domini*) on which lay the fish when the disciples came ashore and were invited to a repast by the risen Christ (fig. 7.42). The spot lies about 575 feet from the Church of the Multiplication of the Loaves, close to the shore. Here there is a rock platform thirty-two feet wide and forty-five feet long from which a stairs of six steps leads down to the water's edge. It evidently marks the supposed site of the boat landing. The stairs is already mentioned by Etheria (390 A.D.). Pious sentiment may well join in Christian fellowship with the ancients in indulging the thought that it was hereabouts that one of the most beautiful and memorable incidents in the story of the disciples of Jesus took place.

In the concluding paragraph of Luke's Gospel, Jesus leads the disciples out to Bethany. If the Ascension had followed on the return of the Emmaus-disciples, it would necessarily have taken place during the night or toward morning, in view of the length of the journey back from Emmaus. But the connection between incidents is often loose-knit. Luke is seeking to bring the Gospel to a conclusion, and so one should not insist on a literal sequence of events. If the point of departure was "the house" and hence from the southern part of the western city, they would have gone forth from a southern gate such as that of the Essenes and turned eastward to the junction of the road with one that comes down the Kidron Valley from the north and heads for Bethany. Since Luke deals with the Ascension again and in more detail in the second volume of his historical work (which was cut off from the Gospel when the latter was made the third book in the collection called *The Gospel according to the Four*), we will revert in the next chapter to the matter of the scene presupposed for the parting. The Ascension is not only an ending, but a new beginning.

THE GROWTH OF CHRISTIANITY

The Acropolis seen between pillars of Theseion. (J. Lane Miller)

The DESIGN on the preceding page shows a section of a basilica, plan of another basili
fish and anchor from earliest catacomb paintings.

CHAPTER XX

THE EARLY CHURCH OF PALESTINE

DURING THE EARLY years of the Christian movement, innumerable things happened of which we have no detailed record. A strong Jewish-Christian Church with world-wide missionary effort among the Jewish Dispersion was established. The events transpired against the backdrop of increasing Roman-Jewish tension, with the final explosion of the Jewish war and the destruction of Jerusalem by the Romans in 70 A.D. After the collapse we find Jewish Christianity reduced to sorry remnants. On the one hand it was now outlawed by the Jews, and on the other hand it was looked upon as backward or even heretical by the Gentile Church, which had taken over the Jewish Christian elements in the Dispersion and which now regarded itself as representing Christianity.

In this situation Luke, writing of the progress of the Gospel to the West, gave in his Book of Acts some account of the early Jerusalem Church, which, however, when the sermons are discounted, will be seen to be exceedingly meager in factual detail. This is but the afterglow of a great history, painted with nostalgia by a loving hand.

Olivet Once More

Luke begins his story of the Christian Church at Jerusalem. The Ascension of Christ and his parting directives are not only a great conclusion to the account of his work, but form a magnificent introit to the history of the Church, much as Moses' blessing and disappearance on Mount Nebo serve both to round out his existence in glory and to provide a noble prelude for Israel's triumphal march into the Holy Land.

In Luke's Gospel we are told that Jesus led the disciples out to Bethany and there parted from them (LUKE 24:50). The village itself (page 393), of course, will hardly have been pictured as the scene of an event so private. "To Bethany" thus means "toward Bethany" and does not intend to be very specific as to the spot.

In the account of Acts the leading forth is not repeated; the Ascension is described and in the end we hear that the Eleven returned to Jerusalem from Olivet (ACTS 1:12).

We have already had occasion to note that the term "Mount of Olives" was probably restricted to that portion of the range called *eṭ Ṭūr* (page 397). One would think that the eminence south of it would have been more convenient to the road leading out to Bethany (LUKE 24:50). However, the early Church did not localize the Ascension there; instead, it put the "certain place" of the Lord's Prayer (LUKE 11:1) at that spot, and today there is a Church of the *Pater Noster* there. The church marking the supposed site of the Ascension and founded by Constantine's mother Helena, was erected farther to the north on top of the true Mount of Olives (*eṭ Ṭūr*). The indicated distance of a Sabbath day's journey from Jerusalem would fit, for that was set at 2000 cubits (about five stadia), or a little over half a Roman mile.

Luke's transfer of the final vision of the risen Lord from a mountain in Galilee, where Matthew 28:16 put it, no doubt in conformity with Mark's original conclusion, to the Mount of Olives, illustrates how indifferent he was to the historical localization of the events, and that he was writing for people who cared little about obscure Palestinian scenes, but were interested in Jerusalem and its neighborhood.

The Upper Room

At Jerusalem a new life began for the disciples, in a house which is often referred to but never clearly localized.

Here in the "upper room" they devoted themselves to prayer together "with the women, and Mary the mother of Jesus, and with his brethren." The election of a man to take Judas' post (ACTS 1:15–21) evidently was held in this same upper room. Nor is there any indication that Pentecost found the disciples in a different locality. For we hear that "they were all with one accord in one place," and there is reference to "the house in which they were sitting" (ACTS 2:1–2). It is no doubt the one where Jesus celebrated the Passover according to the Synoptic Gospels (MARK 14:15).

There is every probability that the third-century Christians sought to continue the tradition of the Apostolic Age with respect to the upper room. They identified it with a house in the western part of the city, outside of the walls of the new Roman city of Aelia, and later tradition calls it "the Cenacle" (Latin *coenaculum*). Adjoining the cenacle was the *Sion Church* (first mentioned by the pilgrim Aetheria, *c.* 370 A.D.), later also called the *Church of the Apostles*. If that church, indeed, was the successor of the earliest meeting house in Jerusalem, it well deserves the title of "the Mother of Churches" (*mater ecclesiarum*).

In and Around the Temple

The early congregation was still a Jewish "sect," a dedicated holy group. Luke speaks of their "continuing daily with one accord in the Temple" (ACTS 2:46). Such daily attendance at the Temple sacrifices was possible only for those who did not labor in an occupation. The first Christians may have maintained themselves by the proceeds of the sale of private property (ACTS 4:34–35) so long as these lasted.

An incident is reported in connection with Peter's and John's going up to the Temple at the hour of evening prayer (ACTS 3:1 f.). They were importuned by a lame beggar at "that gate of the temple which is called

Beautiful." This is doubtless the Nicanor Gate of Jewish tradition (page 400). Josephus speaks of it as the "brazen gate which looked toward the sunrise," and localizes a popular assembly there at a certain occasion. In the Acts story, however, the healing of the beggar brings about a gathering in "the porch that is called Solomon's," on the east side of the outer court (page 399). We find the Apostles there again at a later occasion, holding a Christian gathering (Acts 5:12–13), and the same place is probably meant in Acts 5:21 f. Their healing and teaching in the Temple at that occasion brought on interference by the Temple police. The gathering in Solomon's Portico was interrupted, and the Apostles were put in detention for the night. Just where they would have been kept is not clear. Perhaps in a special cell in the Temple (Jer. 20:2). They were arraigned on the following morning before the council, doubtless in the same building where Jesus had confronted this body (see page 405). They were subsequently arrested once more, when their healing activity received prominence, and were put into "the common prison" which, of course, was outside the Temple. An angel is said to have delivered them, instructing them to go again to the Temple with their message (Acts 5:20).

When the fact of their escape was reported and their presence in the Temple ascertained early in the morning, the Temple police brought them respectfully before the council. Their responses to interrogation "cut to the heart" or enraged this judicial body which "took counsel to slay them." On the advice of the famous Pharisaic teacher Gamaliel the disciples were released, though only after being beaten.

The Stoning of Stephen

According to Luke's narrative, Hellenists or Greek-speaking Jews played a role at first in the old Jerusalem Church. Such Jews were an important object of Christian missionary interest after the fall of Jerusalem in 70 A.D., and so Luke has lovingly dwelt on the figure of one of their kind, a man named Stephen, giving him the distinction of being the first Christian martyr. In this connection we hear of the synagogue of the Libertines (freedmen), Cyrenians, Alexandrians and those from Cilicia and Asia (Acts 6:9).

The old rendering "Libertines" is misleading in view of the meaning commonly attached to that word. The Jews originally gathered into this congregation for the purpose of hearing the Scriptures read in the Greek language were all men who had been set free from slavery. One can only speculate how they had gotten into that state. The name stuck to the synagogue, even though its membership at this time may no longer have been composed of such people.

What concerns us here is the possibility that the site of this synagogue may have been located. In the excavations carried on by the Frenchman Raymond Weill in the area of the old City of David in 1913–14, a bathing establishment of Roman times was found, and in a cistern there was deposited a limestone plaque thirty inches long and sixteen inches wide with a Greek inscription reading as follows:

1 Theodotos (son of, or of the family of) Vettenos, priest and
2 Archisynagogos, son of an Archisynagogos,
3 grandson of an Archisynagogos,
4 built the synagogue for the reading
5 of the law and for the teaching of the commandments. Also
6 the hostel and the chambers and
7 the water-installations for those
8 having need of them from abroad; which (synagogue)
9 his ancestors had founded,
10 and the Presbyters and Simonides.

There was a Roman family called the *gens Vettena,* of which this Theodotos may have been a freedman. But his ancestors had already built a synagogue on the same spot, and had like himself held the title of "ruler of the synagogue" (Greek *Archisynagogos*), i.e., the man who was elected or appointed to conduct or manage the service of the synagogue so that things were done decently and in order (cf. LUKE 13:14), and to tend to its property concerns. Scholars are agreed that this inscription, like the warning tablet in the Temple (page 400), belongs to about the time of Christ. The possibility exists, therefore, that it is from the very synagogue whose members disputed with Stephen and stirred up the authorities and the mob against him. Since Stephen was a Hellenist he will have attended this synagogue before joining that of the new Christian group, and no doubt it was Paul's spiritual home as well.

Stephen is haled before the council by his accusers. Their meeting place will again have been the regular one in the council house west of the Temple. The sequel, however, completely loses sight of the scene, or fails to mention a change in it. A shift is made from the council chamber to the street, where mob violence can take place. The crowd cast Stephen out of the city and stoned him and "devout men" (Greek-speaking proselytes) buried him (ACTS 7:58; 8:2).

Luke evidently had no interest in the precise place where the stoning of Stephen had occurred. Since the Sanhedrin's meeting place lay in the north near Wilson's Arch, an exit from a northern gate naturally suggests itself. That Stephen had to be taken out of the city prior to stoning followed from a rule deduced by the Pharisaic teachers (cf. DEUT. 17:5). It was further required by the rabbis that before an individual was stoned he must be cast down from a height of at least eleven feet. In recent time the *Zāhira* hill (Gordon's Calvary) has been thought by Jews to be Jerusalem's ancient "place of stoning" (Hebrew *bēth hasseqīlāh*). But there is no evidence that there was any definite place set apart for this purpose, or that this particular hill had a precipice in antiquity as it now has, for its present shape is due to quarrying that was carried on there

later (see page 407). A Church of St. Stephen was built in 460 A.D. on the site of the eastern one of two churches that once stood in what is now the Convent of the Dominicans. But if one assumes a release of Stephen by the council (which did not have the authority to put him to death), and places the mob action at a slightly later occasion, the stoning of Stephen might just as well have taken place south of the city near the synagogue of the "Libertines." "The Gate of Stephen" was the name given in the sixteenth century to the eastern gate, north of the Temple area (see page 398). At this time it was believed that he was led out there.

The Travels of Philip

A persecution now scattered church members, with the exception of the Apostles, throughout Judaea and Samaria (ACTS 8:1). Perhaps Luke's statement should be limited to a dispersal of the Greek-speaking members, since Stephen and the man who next receives particular prominence, the deacon Philip, whose origin is left unmentioned, belonged to that group. The expulsion of such alien residents was certainly much easier than that of people rooted in the native community. Philip is said to have gone down "to a city of Samaria," where he made converts. Just what city of Samaria is meant is not directly stated. It hardly seems likely that it was ancient Shechem, the seat of orthodox Samaritanism. Sebaste, nobly rebuilt by Herod as a Hellenistic city, is probably meant. The vagueness of the author of Acts on this may be due to his reluctance to put the Apostles in this scene, where worship of the late emperor Augustus was the order of the day. Herod had greatly increased the area of the city so that it was now two and a half Roman miles in circumference, and had settled here many colonists, notably retired soldiers.

In the excavations carried on at Samaria by the Harvard University expedition under George A. Reisner and Clarence S. Fisher

8.1 *Staircase leading up to the temple at Samaria. (Courtesy American Geographical Society)*

(1908–10) and continued under J. W. Crowfoot (1931–35), a good deal was learned about Hellenistic-Roman Samaria, as well as about the Samaria of earlier times (see page 273). The great city wall is the work of Herod. The western gate, with its two round towers, is particularly well preserved. Within the city there was a great deal of rebuilding around 200 A.D., so that much of the Herodian city may have been altered. But the two streets bisecting the city in an east-west direction will have been those Herod laid out, even if the colonnades are not his. The foundations of the great temple to Augustus exist, however. It was built on a terrace to which a staircase of twenty-four steps led up, and was elevated high above all other buildings of the city. Sebaste naturally had all the appurtenances of a Hellenistic city, such as market place, theater, hippodrome, etc.

Among Philip's converts was a man who had previously practiced magic in the city, and whose name was Simon. Many echoes have come down in early Christian writings about this Simon Magus. His birthplace was Gitta, which lay at a place still called *Jett;* the town of Roman days probably was situated at the foot of the high hill, from which an earlier Canaanite city looked forth over the coastal plain toward Caesarea.

Whatever the place where Philip was laboring, the Apostles Peter and John went down to it in person "and prayed for them that they might receive the Holy Spirit." In connection therewith they find it necessary to reprimand the brazen Simon Magus

(Acts 8:14–23). Missionary work "in many villages of the Samaritans" attends the return to Jerusalem. Philip must be imagined as participating in it (Acts 8:25).

A second journey of Philip took him in the opposite direction.

"And the angel of the Lord spake unto Philip, saying, Arise, and go toward the south unto the way that goeth down from Jerusalem unto Gaza, which is desert." (Acts 8:26 A.V.)

"But an angel of the Lord said to Philip, 'Rise and go toward the south to the road that goes down from Jerusalem to Gaza.' This is a desert road." (Acts 8:26 R.S.V.)

In our opinion the A.V. rendering is better here. In the underlying Semitic, we believe, the reference was to Gaza as desolate. Strabo in enumerating the coastal towns says:

Then after Ascalon follows the harbor of the Gazaeans; and above it lies in a distance of seven stadia [a little less than a Roman mile], the city itself, once famous, but destroyed by Alexander and since then desolate [the same word as "desert" in Acts].

But Strabo was mistaken in thinking of Gaza as destroyed by Alexander the Great. Its actual destroyer had been another of that name—the Jew Alexander Jannaeus, who

8.2 *Ruins of senate hall at Samaria. (Courtesy American Geographical Society)*

therewith fulfilled the prediction "Baldness has come upon Gaza" (JER. 47:5). He not only wrecked this Hellenistic city, but all others in the southern coastal region. It was Pompey who thrust the Jews back from this area in 63 B.C. and gave these wasted cities independent status, and it was his general Gabinius who re-established them in 59 B.C. "New Gaza," which the ancient geographers distinguish from "old" or *desert* Gaza, thus was built up before the time of Christ at a point south of old Gaza, but equidistant from the harbor, which had a separate existence and, indeed, its own name. It was evidently more important for the city to be on the caravan road than on the coast. If the angel bids Philip take the road to "desert" Gaza, one may suppose that the terminology here echoed arose before new Gaza was established, and merely continues a long existing phrase. Besides, "desert" Gaza was a landmark of conquest that stood vividly before the patriotic Jewish mind, and reference to it arose on the lip or flowed from the pen most naturally and readily.

The road that Philip would have taken from Jerusalem to Gaza was already a subject of curiosity in antiquity. The words directing him to go south seemed to suggest a course down to Beth-zur, where one would turn off from the Hebron road to go toward the plain. Here tradition, as illustrated by the Madeba map, sought the place of the baptism of the Ethiopian eunuch. A later theory held that Philip went via Beth-ter and *Beit Jibrīn* and sought the place of baptism at a spring near the former place.

But if one understands "go toward the south" as indicating only the general sphere to which Philip is now to turn his attention, after having previously done missionary work in the north, the route taken by him and by the driver of the Ethiopian's cart might have been the regular one from Jerusalem via Emmaus. And since Philip, after baptizing the eunuch, turns up at Azotus (ACTS 8:40), the point of the baptism ought

to have been near there. South of Azotus, however, water for immersion is difficult to find, for the road passes through dreary wastes. The best suggestion so far made is that the place of the baptism is to be sought about two miles north of Azotus, which lay on the coast, near the mound of old Philistine Ashdod. Here the highway reaches the source of the *Nahr Sukrēr,* at present the only water on this sector of the caravan road to Gaza. The report of Philip's going to the city of Azotus reflects the existence there of a Christian congregation founded by him.

The conclusion of the narrative then brings him rather quickly to his final objective: "passing on he preached the gospel to all towns till he came to Caesarea" (ACTS 8:40). He certainly would not have bypassed such places as Lydda and Joppa. But the author of Acts wanted to stress the ministry of Peter at these towns, and for that reason does not mention them in this connection. While he gives Peter a great role at Caesarea, he also reports Philip's going there (ACTS 8:40); indeed, this was really Philip's bailiwick and we still find him living there many years later when Paul came to Caesarea on his final journey to Jerusalem (ACTS 21:8).

The story of Paul's beginnings (ACTS 9:1 f.) dates back to the period before the scattering of the "Hellenists," for like them he was a Greek-speaking Jew, a native of Cilicia. In connection with their dispersal also occurred the immensely important event of the founding of a Christian church at Antioch (ACTS 11:19-20 f.; see page 429).

A Chapter in the Travels of Peter

The Book of Acts has given Peter an important role in the coastal area of Palestine. In the course of his travels, which seem to have been concerned chiefly with visiting the Christian congregations already established, he comes to Lydda where he performs a healing that greatly impresses the Christians not only of Lydda but of the Sharon district north of it.

Lydda, called Lod in the Old Testament, was ceded to Jonathan the Maccabee by the Seleucids in 145 B.C. Pompey took away the Jewish rights in this city but Caesar restored them. Josephus once calls it "a village which was not less than a city in largeness." It was the capital of a Judaean district. Its ancient name still survives as *Ludd,* and there is here an impressive ruined church of the Crusaders, dedicated to St. George, who allegedly was born as well as buried here. But no trace of the town of Peter's day, nor of the ancient Lod that had a history reaching back into Canaanite times, has been found as yet—these remains doubtless lie under the present settlement. Then as now the region round about was a garden district.

Lydda lay on the road from Jerusalem to Joppa, so it is not surprising that we hear of Peter going to the latter place also. It was called Japho in the Old Testament, *Yapu* in the Assyrian inscriptions, and the name still lives as *Yāfa* (Jaffa); but in the ancient times the Hebrews never had possession of the place. It was a Canaanite town, and in the Persian era we find the Phoenicians in control of it. The Maccabees, however, succeeded in getting hold of it; in fact Simon Maccabeus drove out the native inhabitants and fortified it. Caesar confirmed Jewish possession of it. With the rest of Judaea it passed from control by the Herodians to that by Roman procurators. But the house of Tabitha, where Peter miraculously restored the charitable widow to life, or that of Simon the Tanner, situated "by the seaside," where Peter lived and had his strange vision and at which he subsequently received the emissaries that Cornelius sent him, all lie buried with the rest of ancient Joppa beneath the more recent habitations. As the natural harbor town for Judaea, Joppa had played a considerable role in earlier days, though after Caesarea was built and provided with a harbor by Herod, its importance must have been greatly reduced. When Caesarea itself declined and perished, which was not until the

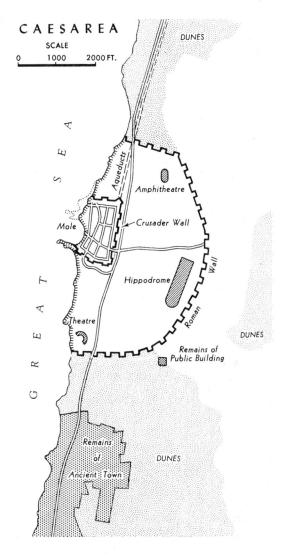

thirteenth century A.D., Jaffa enjoyed a revival.

But the story of Peter also takes the reader to Caesarea. Since it was the Roman seat of government for Judaea, there naturally was an important contingent of Roman troops stationed there. Caesarea had a large element of Jews, who presumably lived in their own district, though they had equal rights with the pagans and shared in the city's government. In the main, however, it was a Hellenistic city, which Herod had built on the site of the earlier town of "Straton's Tower." He had named it Caesarea in honor of Caesar Augustus and had dedicated it in 12 B.C. The temple to the divine Caesar stood on an

8.3 *Pavement of synagogue at Caesarea on the site of one that may have been visited by Cornelius. (Courtesy Archaeological Department, Hebrew University and Louis M. Rabinowitz)*

eminence facing the harbor's mouth and was noted for its beauty and its grand proportions. It was visible to sailors from a great distance and perhaps lies buried on the hill south of the city limits, where the outlines of a large building are to be seen.

A semi-circular wall surrounded Roman Caesarea, though the town later expanded out beyond it toward the south. Caesarea was laid out according to plan and divided into about three hundred blocks. Herod also had constructed great harbor installations, with quarters for the sailors of ships docking there. Colossal figures of Roma and of Augustus flanked the harbor entrance. The city not only had a theater, from whose seats the spectators looked westward over the harbor and the sea, but an amphitheater and a hippodrome as well. It is a great place, and while some of it is overlaid with a Crusaders' city and some has been eaten away by the sea, much of it lies buried under the sand dunes. Excavations have been carried on there by the Department of Antiquities of the Government of Israel, but it will take a long while to dig it out.

A soldier like Cornelius lived, no doubt, in the heathen part of the city, and so the scruples of a law-abiding Palestinian Jew like Peter, who could readily be "defiled" by entering a heathen's house, become understandable. The conversion of Cornelius is, according to the author of Acts, the first

conversion of a Roman, and it is eminently appropriate that such a conversion should be localized at the point where the ships sailed to and from Rome. The incident foreshadows Peter's particular concern with Rome and its soldiers, at whose hands he probably perished beside the Tiber. Figure 8.3 shows the pavement of a Jewish synagogue found here—perhaps a successor of the very one to which Cornelius and Peter may have gone, and where Philip and his daughters may have attended until it became necessary for Christians to have their own gathering place.

Peter no doubt went back to Jerusalem by the regular road past Beth-horon. There must have been much travel between the two points in those days, official as well as commercial.

The Dispersal of the Apostles

The arrest of important leaders by "King Herod" was a more decisive event in the history of the Primitive Church than the author of Acts makes evident.

How was it possible for King Herod to make such arrests? This is not explained in Acts, but can be answered on the basis of other sources. There had been a change in the governmental situation in Judaea and Samaria, in 41 A.D. Instead of being ruled by a Roman procurator they were now, for a brief season, ruled again by a king of the House of Herod, Herod Agrippa I. His father was Aristobulus, a son of Herod the Great and Mariamne, a man who thus had the blood of the Maccabees in his veins as well. Under Caligula he had already been made king of the northern "tetrarchies" previously ruled by Philip, Herod Antipas, and Lysanias. Caligula's successor, Claudius, decided that it was best to let Agrippa also govern Judaea and Samaria. And so there was once more a sovereign in the palace at Jerusalem, a man with a knowledge of the Jews and of their customs, and with a great family tradition behind him. This Agrippa

I, then, who was virtually entrusted with the realm of his grandfather, is the "King Herod" of Acts 12:1. His was an almost incredible rise to power, just what Herodias had dreamed of for her husband Antipas, with whom she went into exile. But ironically it was her brother who, thanks to his contacts with the men of destiny in Rome, fell heir to the role of the last king of the Jews. It was toward the end of Agrippa's short reign that he "laid violent hands upon some who belonged to the church." James, the son of Zebedee, was executed—for what reason is not reported; he must have aroused the royal ire to an especial degree. Perhaps, like John the Baptist, he had criticized the king's private morals, which were not above reproach. The killing of an important Christian leader was favorably received by the Jews, and so Agrippa also arrested Peter at the time of the Passover festival, intending to try him publicly after the festival was over. The charge that could be brought against Peter is not specified. He was evidently considered an important prisoner if it required four squads of soldiers to guard him. But Peter escaped from prison by night and went "to the house of Mary the mother of John, whose surname was Mark; where many were gathered together praying" (Acts 12:12). After sending a message to James and to the brethren, he "went into another place" (Acts 12:17).

The house of Mary has often been regarded as identical with the house of the upper chamber where Jesus held the last supper and where the disciples gathered after the Ascension. The earliest tradition vacillates, sometimes considering the Cenacle also the house of James and sometimes that of the Apostle John, where he lived with the mother of Jesus. The narrative of Acts gives no clear support to either view.

The message sent by Peter to James clearly involved the final passing of all responsibility for the Jerusalem Church to the latter. The James meant, as we know from the writings of Paul and the early church historians, was not one of the twelve disciples of Jesus, but one referred to as "the brother of the Lord," later also called "James the Just." It seems doubtful whether any of the original Twelve were left at Jerusalem or that Peter himself ever went back there again. A surprising thing about Luke's narrative is that he has omitted making clear who James was and has given no inkling of the tremendously important role he played in the Jerusalem Church. We would be totally in the dark about him if it were not for the letters of Paul. No less strange is Luke's silence about most of the original Twelve.

The early church historian, Eusebius, believed that the dispersal of the Twelve into all the world took place only after the death of James, "the brother of the Lord." But this may well rest on a misunderstanding—the dispersal will have taken place after the death of James, the son of Zebedee. Luke reports only Peter's departure, and does not say where he went. Since Agrippa I ruled all Palestine, Peter had to travel far to get out of his clutches. We may assume that the houses of Christians formed a sort of "underground railway," which aided his escape. There is every reason to believe that he went to Antioch, where we find him in Galatians 2:11 f.

Luke gives no inkling as to what happened to any of the other apostles. He is writing of the progress of the gospel to the west—from Jerusalem over the land bridge to Greece and Rome—and he will not be diverted to speak of its progress into other regions, such as the Parthian East or Arabia and Africa. He has given hint of its expansion into such areas in the story of the Ethiopian eunuch and in the words of the crowd at Pentecost. When Luke wrote, there were doubtless Christian communities in Egypt, in Arabia and Crete, and in all the Parthian lands and in the Asia Minor provinces which he enumerates (Acts 2:9 f.).

After the escape of Peter, Herod Agrippa went to Caesarea (cf. Acts 12:19–23). Here

8.4 *The square at the foot of Masada is one of the camps of the Roman besiegers of the fortress in the Jewish War of 70* A.D. (*Courtesy Archaeological Department, Hebrew University and Louis M. Rabinowitz*)

he is believed to have participated in the celebration of a quadrennial festival in honor of Caesar, which would have taken place in 44 A.D. His brief reign ended with his death in that year and his privileges were not granted to a successor. He had aroused Roman suspicion by building a new wall for the defense of Jerusalem and other acts of an independent nature. Procuratorial government was again established over Judaea, but a brother of the late king, called Agrippa II, who had been made ruler of the kingdom of Chalcis in the Lebanon area, was given the right of supervising peculiarly Jewish affairs and appointing the high priests.

The history of the Palestinian Church is not pursued further in the Book of Acts. The little we hear of it comes up in connection with the church of Antioch or of the story of Paul. Luke brings the mother Church back into the center notably with the so-called Council of the Apostles (ACTS 15), but many believe that the incident is reported there for other than chronological considerations. Historically, the dispersal of the Apostles must have taken place with the death of James and the departure of Peter prior to the death of Herod Agrippa I in 44 A.D. After that the Primitive Church must

have stood entirely under the leadership of James, the brother of Jesus. James' martyrdom, which took place soon after the end of Paul's imprisonment at Caesarea, is not related in the Book of Acts, but is recorded by outside sources, including Josephus (if this report is not a Christian addition).

The consequences of the Jewish War of 70 A.D. must have been disastrous for Jewish Christianity, for its members were regarded as Jews and hence suffered all the consequences of that fearful chastisement meted out by the Romans—execution, enslavement, and burning of towns and villages. "The churches of Judaea which were in Christ," stood importantly before Paul's mind at the time when he referred to them (GAL. 1:22). These congregations must have been wiped out. Refugees from them settled in certain communities in Transjordan, particularly at Pella across the river from Scythopolis. It is noteworthy that the author of the Book of Acts does not mention the former Judaean churches (other than that of Jerusalem) or the churches of Galilee, but gives information about those in Samaria and the cities of the coastal plain. That is because these areas were not involved in the terrible war that had raged in Galilee and Judaea.

CHAPTER XXI

FROM ANTIOCH TO ROME

CHRISTIANITY, once it began to radiate out from Palestine, first sought to obtain a foothold in Syria. Its beginnings in Phoenicia, Cyprus and Antioch are expressly connected (ACTS 11:19) with the flight of refugees from the persecution that arose over Stephen. Philip's ministry at Caesarea, an important harbor in the coastal trade with the northern cities, provided a ready point for the transition of the gospel to these areas, with Antioch, the Syrian capital and metropolis, as the crowning objective. Converts were at first sought only among Jews and proselytes. But some men of Cyprus and Cyrene also undertook to convert gentiles, and found great success. This indication of divine blessing on such work could not be ignored. And Providence had in readiness for Antioch a mighty man of valor in the person of Saul of Tarsus in Cilicia, who later took the name Paul.

Cilicia was the region lying in southeastern Asia Minor, across the Gulf of Issos from Antioch's seaport, Seleucia. The heart of the country was a fertile plain in which was situated the city of Tarsus which Paul proudly says was "no mean city" (ACTS 21:39). It lay on the river Cydnus about ten miles from the coast. Some distance south of the city the river formed a lake in ancient times, and here was a good harbor to which ships could ascend, and light craft could even go up to Tarsus itself. Lying at the starting point of the great trade route across the Taurus mountains into Asia Minor, Tarsus was naturally a highly important place. It had been a free self-governing Hellenistic city since 170 B.C. It had received favorable treatment from Julius Caesar; Mark Antony had received Cleopatra here at a magnificent occasion in 38 B.C. and had bestowed this city with others of the Syrian coast on this daughter of the Ptolemies. Augustus had increased the privileges of Tarsus when he united Cilicia with Syria into one province. It was third among the centers of Greek learning, being rivaled only by Athens and Alexandria. A Stoic philosopher named Nestor was the most influential man of Tarsus in Paul's day, and the latter can hardly have been entirely ignorant of his teachings.

It would lead us too far afield to give an account of the long and checkered history of Tarsus, as a result of which that city sank into such a wretched state that hardly a trace remains of its ancient Hellenistic-Roman splendor. The so-called Tomb of Sardanapalus (Ashurbanipal) is about all that is discernible of antiquity on the surface, and that is actually but the substructure of a terrace on which rose a Graeco-Roman temple. However, one may be sure that in the highest part of the city one stands above the ancient acropolis, and the imagination can fondly picture the sight of the shining marble buildings that crowned it.

Why Paul should have become a persecutor of Christians remains a mystery. Judaism tolerated quite a few sects; beliefs did not matter too much, so long as one fulfilled the law, and tradition claims that the Jerusalem Christians were law-abiding.

Paul was present at the stoning of Stephen, though he is not said to have cast any stones himself (Acts 7:58). While Paul directly admits having persecuted the Christians (1 Cor. 15:9; Gal. 1:13), he does not say in what way he did so. It seems likely that he incited other mob actions like the one to which Stephen had fallen victim, but the report of Acts that he entered houses and dragged men and women off to prison (Acts 8:3) may be based on the sort of thing done to Christians in the author's own time by

Roman authorities. And the same thing may be true of the statement that Paul went to Damascus to bring Christians from there bound to Jerusalem (Acts 9:1-2). If Paul had expressed himself on the purpose of his going to Damascus we suspect that he would have worded it differently.

The Road to Damascus

On the road to Damascus, so Acts 9:3 relates, occurred the event that convinced Paul of the reality of Christ's resurrection. One can only speculate as to the route Paul would have chosen. He could have taken the road up from Scythopolis or the way of the Hauranians (page 322), or the one passing the outlet of the Lake of Galilee. But one would like still more to think of him as going up through Tiberias and on by the Via Maris of the Crusaders to the Bridge of the Daughters of Jacob. Passing through the country where Jesus had lived and labored might have made Paul particularly receptive for the experience that befell him. He might have had his vision near that very mount on which the Disciples had their rendezvous with the risen Lord (Matt. 28:16). Luke's account, however, suggests that the vision took place in the proximity of Damascus itself. Tradition of the Middle Ages held that it happened at *Kokab,* on the *Jebel el Aswad,* which was about twelve miles from the city.

The Damascus of Paul's day is now buried beyond hope of recovery beneath the present city. Paul is said to have lodged in the house of a certain Judas "on the street called Straight." This is but the familiar *via recta* that was characteristic of the Hellenistic-Roman cities of Syria, and can still be seen in the ruins of Bostra, where the ancient town-plan has not been destroyed. Several centuries later than Paul's time it was the fashion to line such streets with roofed colonnades. Damascus still has one tolerably straight and partly roofed street, which runs through the city from the western to the eastern gate and which is called in Arabic *el darb el mustaqīm,* "the straight way," in obvious continuation of the ancient designation *via recta.* It seems highly probable that it follows the general course of the street of Paul's day. Until recently the Jewish quarter of the city still lay on this "straight way" in the southeastern part of the city.

One would expect that a church of Paul's conversion would have been a feature of the early Christian Damascus. But the pilgrim Arculf, who passed through here in the seventh century, shortly after the Arabs had seized the city, reports that a large church in honor of John the Baptist existed there, and says nothing of places commemorating events of the life of St. Paul. The local Christians seem to have had no knowledge of them. The mighty pressure of Moslem life in the days when the city was the capital of the Omayyad Caliphate not only robbed Christians of the three-naved Basilica, which had been built in the fourth century on the site of the Roman temple and which then was converted into the great Omayyad mosque, but tended to destroy whatever Christian tradition may have existed there earlier.

It was doubtless very significant for the expansion of Christianity into central Syria and the Euphrates-Tigris regions, as well as into Arabia, that it gained a foothold at Damascus early in the Apostolic Age. There is only one Damascus! The highroads of the commerce of the east had their hub here. Situated in an oasis on the edge of the desert, it was the favorite mart of the caravans that bore the products of the East to the West and of the West to the East. It was not by nature a fortress like Jerusalem. But though conquered again and again it always rose to new prosperity and greatness, for it was indispensable. The beauty of its surroundings gave it a semblance of paradise to the ancients.

In and Out of Damascus

According to the author of Acts, the converted Paul began at once to preach Christ among the Jews of Damascus, and so enraged them that they sought to kill him, watching at the gates for him day and night. Paul's disciples, however, lowered him over the city wall in a basket, thus enabling him to escape the plot (Acts 9:22–25). Allegedly, he then went to Jerusalem.

But when Luke wrote, the details of Paul's early career were already obscured. Paul's letters reveal things not known to that author. Speaking of the situation immediately after his vision of the risen Christ Paul says that he did not go up to Jerusalem but went to Arabia and then returned again to Damascus (Gal. 1:16–17).

It is obvious that Paul's escape from Damascus must have taken place at the end of the second visit, since he would not have been able to go back there if it had occurred at the end of the first visit. Assuming that Paul's vision of the risen Christ took place on the road to Damascus—his own words do not permit any inference as to this—the departure to "Arabia" could have been in the nature of a return to the very place where he had had the vision.

The word "Arabia" is misleading to the modern mind. In Paul's day one was in Arabia as soon as one got out of the bailiwick of Damascus. Paul could have gone back again to Damascus rather soon. Indeed, a part of the three year interval between the vision and the trip to Jerusalem to consult Peter (Gal. 1:18) may well have been spent in missionary activity at that city (Acts 26:20). That work was then terminated by his flight (Acts 9:22 f.).

Luke attributes this departure of Paul from Damascus to the discovery of a Jewish plot to assassinate him. But Paul's own words suggest that there were other unreported factors in the situation: he faced arrest or seizure (2 Cor. 11:32–33).

His adversary was the representative of the King of the Nabataeans, Aretas IV (9 B.C.–40 A.D.), the very man whose daughter had been married to Herod Antipas (page

386). But when the translations render the title of that representative as "governor" they are assuming that Aretas reigned over Damascus. One must regard that as extremely unlikely. The Romans would scarcely have permitted Aretas to hold a place so important. Damascus is counted among the cities of the Decapolis, and was thus a free city under the general aegis of the Province of Syria. The word rendered "governor" is really the Greek title "ethnarch," and merely means the ruler of an ethnic group in a city. Thus the Jews of Alexandria were under an ethnarch, whose job it was to manage and judge this foreign group of people; he was responsible to the civic authorities, but no doubt was recommended for the post by the Jews themselves, and perhaps even endorsed by leaders at Jerusalem. The Nabataeans may have been a similarly numerous element in Damascus, owing to the great Arabian caravan traffic, and this group will have been put under an ethnarch who would supervise their affairs.

What could have led the Nabataean ethnarch to seek Paul's arrest? Did he act in concert with the Jews? Had Paul caused unrest among the Nabataeans by his missionary zeal, or had he violated a pagan sanctuary in some way? Apparently through his residence in "Arabia" Paul was counted as under the jurisdiction of the Nabataean ethnarch. If the latter guarded the city against Paul this need only mean that his watchers were posted at certain strategic points to seize him. The "garrison" of the Authorized Version is properly omitted by the Revised Standard Version.

As for Paul's account of the manner of his escape, tradition of recent origin has combined his statement with the version of Acts 9:25 that he was let down "over the wall," and has imagined him as let down out of a window of a house built against the wall. The tourist is even shown a building fitting that supposition close by the gate called *Bāb Kīsān* in the southeastern part of the city.

But this is unlikely, for the ancient city walls were wide and unencumbered so that the defenders could rush from one point to another to meet attacks, and no house would have been built over them. What Paul must mean is that he was let down through an opening in a tower of the city wall.

Jerusalem and Tarsus

According to Acts 9:26 f. Paul returned to Jerusalem after his escape, but was regarded with suspicion by the Christians. It required the intervention of Barnabas to open the way for him. He spoke in public and engaged in deals with the Hellenistic Jews. According to Acts 26:20–21 he preached "at Damascus, at Jerusalem, and throughout the coasts (*the country* R.S.V.) of Judaea." As in Damascus he aroused such hatred that a murder plot was hatched against him there, too. When the brethren got wind of it they took him to Caesarea and shipped him off to Tarsus (ACTS 9:30–31).

Paul's own account in the first chapter of Galatians suggests that Luke has simplified the events. He implies that his visit to Jerusalem was a secret matter, and this has all the earmarks of plausibility in view of the fact that he had escaped from Damascus and might be extradited to the king of the Nabataeans. If he spent fifteen days with Peter and saw only one other "apostle," James the brother of the Lord, it is difficult to see how he could have done any preaching or disputing in Judaea. Indeed, he declares that he was not known by sight to the churches of Christ in Judaea (GAL. 1:22). But if in the Acts version Paul is sent back to Tarsus this accords fairly well with his own statement of what he did after his visit to Peter, namely, that he afterwards went into the regions of Syria and Cilicia. (GAL. 1:21).

How long Paul lingered in Tarsus we do not know. Nor is it clear whether he attempted to spread the new faith in this place. According to the Acts narrative he was induced by Barnabas, who had been sent up from Jerusalem to Antioch to see about the mission that had been started there among the Greeks, to leave Tarsus and share in the work in the Syrian capital (ACTS 11:22 f.).

Antioch the Beautiful

If Paul and Barnabas left Tarsus to go to Antioch we may imagine them as embarking in a merchantship in the "Rhegma" (the bay) and sailing down the Cydnus River to its mouth and then going on to Seleucia Pieria. Behind them loomed the great Taurus mountains, barring off the interior of Asia Minor. Before them on the Syrian coast they saw the Amanus Range ending in the Anti-Casius, and south of that the great Mons Casius, sacred to the god Zeus Kasios (page 106). Between these ranges lay their objective, the Orontes River Valley, in which Antioch was situated. A day's sail brought them to Seleucia Pieria, five miles up the Orontes and the port serving the Syrian capital. Seleucia was in those days a noble city lying in the shadow of Mount Rhosus (*Jebel Mūsa*). It was considered an impregnable fortress. Two great moles extending out into the sea are all that remain of the harbor installations. Excavations carried on in Seleucia in 1937–39 by the Princeton University expedition brought to light a Christian "Martyrion" or memorial church of the fifth century A.D. that was almost totally destroyed in the earthquake of 526 A.D.; however no light has been shed on the Seleucia of Paul's day. Through the Antioch Gate and up the north side of the river the road led out in the direction of the capital. As one stands before the ruins of that gate one must think of how often Paul must have passed through here, not only on his arrival with Barnabas, but in the course of his later goings and comings.

After five or six hours of walking the travelers ascended the last hill and from it saw Antioch before them in a great and fertile valley. It was a thrilling sight, even to men like Paul and Barnabas, who were accustomed to Hellenistic cities. What town

in all that eastern world could equal it? "Antioch, the Beautiful," "The Queen of the East," or "Antioch the Great" were some of the superlatives heaped upon it. In size, only Alexandria and Seleucia on the Tigris could be compared with it among the cities of the Orient. Founded by Seleucus I in the year 300 B.C. on a site indicated by the oracle of the god Zeus Kasios and named after the king's father Antiochus, it had for 250 years been the capital of an empire, and in the period of the latter's prosperity its rulers had striven to provide it with great monuments of architecture. When Pompey administered the final *coup de grâce* to the Seleucid House in 64 B.C., a new chapter in Antioch's history had begun. He bestowed great favors on the city and repaired recent earthquake damage. Caesar coming from Egypt in 47 B.C. entered the city amid vast acclaim and granted it freedom in all its internal affairs. He presented the city with a great Basilica, the Caesarium, in the apse of which was set up a bronze statue of Roma. Tradition attributed many other buildings to him. The gratitude of the Antiochenes toward him was displayed by the fact that from then on they counted their years from the date of the battle of Pharsalus. Here at Antioch Mark Antony had celebrated great festivities in honor of Cleopatra and had even put the city under her sway in recognition of ancient Ptolemaic claims. To Antioch came Augustus after his victory over Antony, and conferred the governorship of Syria on his son-in-law, Agrippa. The latter immortalized himself here with construction of a public bath, the Agrippianon, and a whole block of houses constituting a sort of Roman district became known as the quarter of the Agrippites. Herod of Judaea, no doubt to please Agrippa (after whom his grandson Herod Agrippa was named), built a marble-paved road to Daphne, a sort of Versailles, about two and a half miles from the city. The emperor Tiberius built several temples at Antioch, including one of Jupiter Capi-

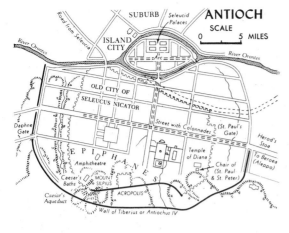

tolinus; he rebuilt some public buildings that were destroyed in a great fire in 23 A.D. and provided a broad marble-paved street, four miles long, bisecting the southern part of the city from east to west. When a terrific earthquake visited Antioch in 37 A.D., soon after Caligula had become emperor, Roman relief funds were made available and a Roman delegation was sent to see to the repair of the damage; some of these men even put their hands into their own pockets to lend aid.

Paul and Barnabas will have crossed the bridge over the Orontes River to the island, where lay the quarter called the New City, built by Antiochus III, "the Great" (242–187 B.C.). Here stood the palace of the Seleucid kings, at the time of Paul the residence of the governor of Syria. Then they will have crossed over the left arm of the Orontes to the main city by another bridge, and entered it from the north. The oldest portion of the town was in the west, where the gate led out to Daphne, a suburb so important that Antioch was called "the one by Daphne." The "old city" formed a separate compartment within the town, for it was barred off by a wall. This wall followed the north-south street that ran straight ahead through the city to the intersecting east-west main street, which it then pursued in the westerly direction. It was thus separated

from the district of Epiphania, which lay beyond it to the south, and extended up the slopes of Mount Silpius. Epiphania was built by and named after Antiochus IV Epiphanes. The mighty outer city walls girdling it could be seen ascending the mountainside to embrace the acropolis. Near the wall between the Old City and Epiphania, but within the latter, lay the agora. It had witnessed the spectacle of the crucifixion of Antigonus, the last Jewish king of the house of the Maccabees—an execution that Herod the Great had requested and that Mark Antony, then tarrying at Antioch, had ordered. As a friend of Greek civilization, Herod had given the town a colonnade to beautify the easterly portion of its main street.

There was an important Jewish element in Antioch. It had equal rights with the Greeks and its privileges were engraved on bronze tablets. Its loathing of polytheism and consequent separatism naturally made it disliked, and the role the Maccabees had played in destroying the Greek cities of Palestine provided a further cause for anti-Semitism on the part of the Antiochenes. Probably during the time when Paul was there an unfortunate episode occurred. It is not mentioned by Josephus, but by a later writer, who has preserved a great deal of information about the history of Antioch. It took place two years after the earthquake of 37 A.D. A fight had arisen in the circus between two partisan groups and in some way it had come to involve the Jews. Many of them were killed and their synagogues burned. Then a Jewish priest, Phineas of Tiberias in Galilee, allegedly assembled an expeditionary force, which invaded and terrorized the city. Caligula sent Roman soldiery in pursuit of them, and many of the Jews involved were executed. The head of Phineas was set up on a pole on the other (western?) side of the Orontes. Several Roman officials, too, were removed and punished for not having prevented the tumult and not having resisted the Jewish invasion. The incident helps to explain why there was less hindrance to Christianity here from the Jewish side than was the case elsewhere.

The Church at Antioch

There were Jewish Christians in Antioch when Paul and Barnabas came there. But there were also the gentile converts, for whose sake Paul had been called. The ministry that Paul now began in this city was evidently bent on creating a Christian fellowship in which believers of Jewish and gentile origin lived in full concord with one another. Jewish dietary laws and prescriptions about clean and unclean will have seemed of small importance to a group living in the great Hellenistic Roman world.

8.5 *City wall of Antioch on Mount Silpius, encircling Epiphaneia. (Matson Photo Service)*

The existing concord was temporarily disturbed, however, at the time of Peter's visit (Galatians 2:11 f., see further page 435). It is not impossible that the Jewish Christians formed a separate organization at this time and that Peter ministered to them—thus giving rise to the theory later accepted that he was the first bishop of Antioch. But the gentile group was the more important and adhered to Paul. The emphasis placed on the person of Jesus Christ by Paul, as manifested in all his later Epistles, was doubtless present from the beginning in his preaching, and if we are told that in Antioch the disciples were for the first time called "Christians" by outsiders (Acts 11:26), this excellently reflects the "'Christological'" character of the new religion as promulgated by Paul. What the visit of a "prophet" from Jerusalem named Agabus signified (Acts 11:27–28) is not clear; only his prediction of a coming world disaster is mentioned.

According to Acts 11:29–30, Paul made a journey to Jerusalem with Barnabas to bring relief to the congregation in connection with a world-wide famine that occurred in the time of Claudius and which was held to be the fulfillment of what Agabus had foretold. We know something about this famine from other sources. It did not hit all countries at once, but passed from east to west. Rome did not have it until the winter of 50–51 A.D.; Greece was struck in the year before, 49 A.D. According to Josephus there was a serious famine in Palestine at the time of the Procurator Tiberius Alexander. This crisis must have taken place in the winter of 48–49 A.D., prior to the Greek famine of 49 A.D. The attempts, for example by Eusebius, to date the famine at Jerusalem earlier than the Greek famine run contrary to the best ancient authorities, and are based on the fact that Luke relates it before the death of Herod Agrippa (44 A.D.). An illustrious convert to Judaism, Queen Helena of Adiabene in Mesopotamia, who had a palace at Jerusalem's eastern hill and the remains of whose tomb still exist north of the city, made large purchases of grain in Alexandria and of figs in Cyprus to bring aid to the inhabitants. It seems likely that Paul and Barnabas, too, will have supervised the transport of similar victuals, contributed by the congregation at Antioch for the brethren at Jerusalem.

The second journey of Paul to Jerusalem thus took place in 48–49 A.D., at which time, as we already have seen, James the brother of the Lord was head of the Church. The coming of Peter to Antioch, of which Paul tells in Galatians 2:11 f., thus lay in the past. It seems necessary to assume, therefore, that Paul tarried at Antioch longer than the one year mentioned in Acts 11:26 or else that the famine occurred after the first missionary journey.

From Seleucid Antioch there went forth in the pre-Christian centuries mighty kings and captains with their mercenary troops and elephant brigades to fight for the preservation of the empire of Alexander of Macedon, to which they considered themselves the true heirs. From Roman Antioch, in the course of the forties and fifties of the first century A.D., there went forth again and again a man named Paul, wielder of the sword of the spirit, who was destined to be the bearer of the Christian evangel to the western world. His were the more abiding victories. On each return from a great journey he held fellowship with the Christians at Antioch, and told them of the field white with the harvest. Would that we knew where in that great area of ruins around *Antakīyeh* stood the church of Paul's day out of which sprang the great Antiochene church of the following centuries: the church of the bishop and martyr Ignatius, of the polemical writer Theophilus, of the biblical scholars Lucian and Theodore, of the great orator Chrysostom. Paul had a great part in laying that church's foundations, and the very stones of Antioch proclaim that the work was well done. It was to endure until the Sassanian ruler Chosroes Anushirwan, whose immortal monument the *Tak-i-Kesra* still broods over the Babylonian plain at Ctesiphon, destroyed the city in 538 A.D. and deported the surviving population to Media.

Paul's First Missionary Journey

The first missionary journey reported in Acts, chapters 13-14, took Paul and his co-worker Barnabas to Cyprus, of which island the latter was a native. They must have started at the opening of the sailing season (around March 5), since they were able to get across to Salamis, which lies on the east coast of the island opposite Syria. Very soon after that date starts the period of westerly winds, which blow through the summer. These winds forced sailing ships to take a roundabout course; they first had to travel along the Cilician coast and then make for the north coast of Cyprus with the aid of land breezes and ocean currents.

Cyprus

Salamis was the largest city of the island in those days and lay at the edge of a fruitful plain extending westward between two parallel mountain ranges. It was about three miles from modern Famagusta and had an excellent harbor, which now is sanded up. The aqueduct, still preserved, could have taken care of the needs of over 100,000 people. There was an immense limestone forum there, and on a platform at its southern end was a temple dedicated to the Olympian Zeus.

Cyprus had been under Roman rule since 58 B.C. and was a senatorial province. Among its governors was the great Cicero, whose year of benevolent administration contrasted markedly with those of his predecessors, under whom the people had been harshly exploited. At the great Christian council of Nicaea of 325 A.D., three bishops from Cyprus were in attendance, a fact showing that Christianity had made great progress on the island. Legend claims that Barnabas suffered martyrdom at Salamis, and a church devoted to his memory existed there.

While Paul and his companion were bent on converting gentiles, they could not bypass the synagogues of their own Jewish people. And so we find them visiting these. The Jews on Cyprus were very numerous. This is quite surprising and helps lend credibility to the theory of Rosen that this people had largely absorbed the Phoenicians in the Hellenistic era. For it is a real question how the Phoenicians could have disappeared and how the Jews could have become as numerous as they were in the first century A.D. But Judaean Jews must have come over to Cyprus, too, in some numbers, at the time when Augustus granted King Herod the exploitation of the Cyprian copper mines ("copper" gets its very name from Cyprus). The time was to come when terrible tragedy was to befall these Cyprian Jews, in consequence of a great rebellion on their part (115–116 A.D.). They were exterminated, and no Jew was allowed to set foot on the island—even one who landed there by reason of shipwreck was executed. Contemporary history shows that the people of this island are still capable of extremism. Whether Paul and Barnabas had much success with the Jews of Cyprus is not recorded.

Luke tells us of the missionaries journeying through the island to Paphos (Acts 13:16). There is no definite information on their route, but they may have gone through Tamassos and Soloi. With Paphos is meant the administrative capital of the Roman province, New Paphos, the ruins of which lie about a mile from the modern town of *Ktima*. The more ancient city of that name, with its famed Aphrodite sanctuary, had stood at a point ten miles away. The ruins of Roman Paphos still reveal a theater, amphitheater, and parts of the city wall.

At Paphos, Barnabas and Paul were invited by the Roman proconsul, Sergius Paulus, to tell him of their message. A Jewish "magician" named Elymas strove to "turn away the proconsul from the faith," but to no avail. Sergius Paulus evidently became a convert. It is noteworthy that the author of Acts, who has persistently used the name "Saul" for the man from Tarsus, from this point on (Acts 13:13) calls him Paul. This indicates that Paul took the name of the Roman proconsul for his own name. It signalized one of his great early achievements to win for the faith a man of such high position and rank. It is worthy of remembrance, then, that Paul is Paul to us rather than Saul, because of this distinguished Roman, whom he sought to honor in this fashion.

Since the missionaries left Paphos by ship (Acts 13:13) we can visualize them embarking at the moles of the ancient harbor, which are preserved to this day, and setting sail to Pamphylia on the Asia Minor coast. The journey to Cyprus had doubtless been undertaken on the suggestion of Barnabas. The determination to enter the heart of Asia Minor was surely on the initiative of Paul, for as a native of Tarsus he was naturally greatly interested in the territory adjoining his homeland. How often in boyhood he must have looked with longing eyes toward those mysterious Taurus Mountains, and dreamed of visiting all the great cities that lay beyond them in that vast upland country.

It was an important move, this first foray into a world that was to become one of the main centers of Christian thought and life in the centuries to come. The narrator notes that John (Mark) here quit the party to return to Jerusalem (Acts 13:13). And no wonder, the thought of climbing those Asia Minor mountains to get into the interior could make even a stout heart quail.

Asia Minor Ahead

We must glance for a moment at this great land we call Asia Minor. It is held by the Turkey of today. But for a thousand years after Alexander's conquest it was part of the Greek world. The various non-Greek peoples of far more ancient times such as Lydians, Carians, Celts, Armenians, Hittites and others had been more or less absorbed into the great Hellenistic civilization. The decline of this whole region was brought about in the twelfth century A.D., when the nomads from inner Asia moved in and interrupted communications between the cities. This led to a disintegration of civilized life.

Asia Minor is the land bridge from Europe to all the easterly regions that were the home of earliest empire and culture. There is a high central plateau, forming a sort of basin surrounded by a rim of mountains. This leaves the coastal regions at the foot of the mountains in a peripheral position. They could only with difficulty dominate the central plateau and were more apt to be dominated by it. The movements of history in this great theater have always been from east to west or west to east, and since there are only a few good points of entry into the plateau region, history followed certain well-beaten paths. On the east the southern entrances deserve particular attention. The great mountain wall, here called the Taurus, has been described by no less an authority than Sir William Ramsay as a great dividing line between two worlds. East of the Taurus you are in the Eastern world, west of it you are in the Western world. Hence the passes through the Taurus, notably the one through the Cilician Gates (cf. page 436), are of immense importance. Cilicia, and notably the section around Tarsus, thus already belongs to the East, and Tarsus more than any other city was the meeting place of East and West.

If one looks at the western part of Asia Minor one sees there, too, certain gates through which travel must pass. A double zone of mountains runs vertically across central Phrygia and this forces travel to take either a northerly or southerly route. He who started overland from Ephesus passed around these mountains on the south. He who came from Smyrna or northern Lydia went via the north. Here a lofty ridge coming down from Mount Ida near ancient Troy approaches close to the mountains just mentioned, so that a narrow glen divides them. This glen is the northern passage-way to the Asia Minor plateau. Emerging from it the east-bound traveler found himself in the broad plain of the Kaystros River.

Asia Minor, over which the great House of the Seleucids had held loose sway, but in which it had permitted many vassal kingdoms to exist, was Roman when Paul and Barnabas went there. The Romans had not had to fight for this part of their empire; it just fell into their lap by bequests made by rulers of dying dynasties. Attalos III of Pergamum had opened this series of generous bequests; Nikomedes of Bithynia had followed suit. Cyprus had come in along with Cyrene in Africa by virtue of the testament of its last ruler. The necessity of suppressing piracy had led the Romans to the seizure of Cilicia, and this region became unified with Syria administratively through Pompey. Since the time of Augustus new territories, thus far only tributary to Rome, became Roman-owned: in 25 B.C. the kingdom of Galatia; in 7 B.C. a kingdom centering at Gangra in Paphlagonia; in 17 A.D. the kingdom of Cappadocia; in 43 A.D. the federation of Lycian cities; two principalities, one on the border of Cilicia and one in northeastern Asia Minor. The kingdoms of Antiochus and of Polemon were still left to be swallowed up a little later.

The Romans did not redistrict Asia Minor, but took over the earlier political units pretty much as they were. In the division of provinces between Augustus and the Senate a considerable part of the country was conceded to the latter's management, namely, 1) "Asia" 2) Bithynia and Pontus. The term "Asia," used as a provincial name, included Mysia, Lydia, Caria and a great part of Phrygia, with the western coastal cities and the islands off the coast. The nucleus was the old Hellenistic kingdom of the Pergamenes, whose rulers the Romans had called "kings of Asia" in the second century B.C. and whose territory they called "the province of Asia" after they took it over. While Pergamum was the capital at first, Ephesus became the real administrative center under Augustus. Its governor, selected from among the ex-consuls, bore the title of Proconsul. In eastern and southern Asia Minor, where military dangers existed, the provinces were imperial. Under Augustus a new province of Galatia was formed in Asia Minor. It consisted of the Galatian kingdom, which had been greatly enlarged by Mark Antony (in 36 B.C.). The province retained this expanded form, except that Pamphylia was kept out of it and received an imperial governor of its own, who under Claudius was also awarded control of Lycia. Cappadocia had become an imperial province under Tiberius. Cilicia already had been put under Syria by Augustus. The consolidated Roman situation now prevailing must have made the Asia Minor lands particularly inviting to Paul.

8.6 *Remaining arches of ancient aqueduct of Pisidian Antioch. (Courtesy American Bible Society and T. Goell and F. K. Doerner)*

Penetrating Pamphylia and Galatia

The Christian invasion, led by the humble travelers Paul and Barnabas, made a landing on the shores of Pamphylia, that narrow region ringing the "Pamphylian Sea" with Lycia on the west and Cilicia on the east, and then went north into the mountains.

The first objective of Paul and Barnabas was Perga in Pamphylia (ACTS 13:13), which lay on the Kestros River seven or eight miles above its mouth. Possibly the point of debarkation was Attalia where we later find the travelers embarking for home. Perga was an important city with a great temple of Artemis. But it was a center of the old native element and apparently not fertile soil for the Gospel, which could expect a better reception where the ground had been prepared by Jewish proselytism. Nothing is said in any case of the missionaries preaching there at their first visit, though they did so on the return journey. Instead they went on up for 100 miles through the mountain country of Pisidia into Lycaonia to the city of Antioch (ACTS 13:14), often called "Pisidian" Antioch because under Diocletian a new province called Pisidia was created here with Antioch

as its capital. In Paul's time these regions, as already mentioned, were all in one province often called for short "Galatia." It is rather surprising that the old name Antioch is used, for Augustus had made the place a colony with Roman laws and given it the name Caesarea. Latin and not Greek was thus the official language there. But it was doubtless a Greek-speaking audience that Paul addressed on the two Sabbaths on which he spoke in the synagogue. His success in impressing the proselytes aroused jealousy on the part of the Jews, who saw their own converts slipping out of their control, and led to an open break. Paul announced that salvation was for the gentiles, without proselytism. But with the aid of prominent proselyte women and leading men of the city, the Jews stirred up mob action against the missionaries and they were driven out of Antioch, though not without leaving disciples behind who were full of enthusiasm.

Then they journeyed some eighty miles in an easterly direction on the "royal road" from Antioch to Lystra, but diverged from it to go first to Iconium (ACTS 13:52). An old Christian document of the second century tells how Paul was induced by a certain Onesiphorus to do so. Iconium—existing today with its name shortened to *Konia*—has a situation much like that of Damascus; it is

433

8.7 *The Plain of Lystra as seen from the Mound.* (*Courtesy American Bible Society and T. Goell and F. K. Doerner*)

a garden spot in an arid region, with the river that creates the oasis petering out in the plain to the east. At Iconium things took much the same course as at Antioch. In the end the missionaries, hearing that they were to be stoned, fled to Lystra and Derbe, cities of Lycaonia, and their neighbourhood. This sounds as though Iconium did not lie in Lycaonia. Actually it did, in Paul's day, but apparently the people regarded themselves as Phrygians. It is interesting to note that Xenophon, too, early in the fourth century B.C., describes Iconium as last of the Phrygian cities, beyond which he entered Lycaonia.

Lystra was some eighteen miles from Iconium in a vale, about a mile in breadth, which is watered by a stream that flows east between the hills, only to lose itself in the plain beyond. The fortified town lay on a rise north of the stream. Its site was not definitely identified until 1885, when an inscription in honor of Augustus was found there by the Wolfe Expedition to Asia Minor.

Paul's healing of a cripple awakened the superstitious belief that he and Barnabas were the gods Mercurius and Jupiter (*Hermes and Zeus,* ACTS 14:12 R.S.V.). That Barnabas was equated with the greater divinity does not, as one might think, indicate

that he was displaying greater activity than Paul, but rather quite the opposite; for to the ancient mind the more active individual is the lesser of two. Of course one may also concede the possibility that Barnabas had a more distinguished appearance. The priest of Zeus even wanted to bring sacrifice in honor of these gods. The god Zeus is here described with the Greek technical term *propoleos,* the one whose temple is in front of the city. The gates to which the sacrifice was to be brought were probably those of the temple precinct. The missionaries, hearing of these preparations, went forth from the city to interfere. However, the change of public sentiment that followed was comparable to that which Jesus experienced soon after his entry into Jerusalem; Jews from Antioch and Iconium came and incited the people. They stoned Paul and dragged his body outside the city, thinking him dead. But when his converts gathered about him he rose up and entered the city with them. The following day he and Barnabas went on eastward to Derbe (ACTS 14:20).

Derbe, too, was in the Roman province of Galatia, for it had been annexed to the kingdom of Galatia by the last king. It was now the eastern frontier city of this province and was honored with the title Claudio-Derbe by the emperor Claudius. It was soon after it had received this distinction that Paul came there. The site of Derbe was established in 1956, when an inscription mentioning the Claudio-Derbenes was found at *Kerti-Hüyük* in what is now a marshy district thirteen miles from present *Karaman* and north-northeast of ancient Laranda. No particular incident is reported from Derbe, but numerous converts were made, one of whom, Gaius, later appears among Paul's companions (ACTS 20:4).

At Derbe the missionaries had reached a boundary of importance: that of the kingdom of Commagene, whose king, Antiochus, though a Roman vassal, was nominally independent. This was hardly a fertile field for

Christian mission just then, for kings were protectors of certain cults and by virtue of their powers could act drastically. Commagene was devoted to the cult of Mithras. Figure 8.8 from Nemrud Dagh shows this god receiving the earlier Antiochus, of whose mountain tomb we have already spoken (see page 364). So Paul and Barnabas decided to retrace their steps.

On their return journey the missionaries revisited their congregations, preached their message at Perga and went down to Attalia, which lay to the west of Perga and on the sea. This city had been founded by Attalus II of Pergamum in the second century B.C. as a seaport to serve the southern part of his kingdom. Its name survives, slightly changed, as *Adalia*. Nothing is said of any preaching here, and so conditions must have been unfavorable for such activities. A ship may have been about to sail. The missionaries, weary from their long marches, struggles and hardships, will have been eager to seize the opportunity to return home to Syria.

Back at Antioch

It can be imagined how glad the gentile portion of the congregation at Antioch was to hear the report of its missionaries concerning their successes in the Roman provinces of Cyprus and Galatia. But now there arose trouble in the Jewish portion of the congregation. It was being persuaded by emissaries from the Jerusalem Church, in which numerous converts from Pharisaism were playing an important role (ACTS 15:5), that gentiles ought not to be admitted to the church without first becoming Jews (ACTS 15:1). According to the account of Acts, Paul and Barnabas went down personally to Jerusalem to thresh out the matter. Paul's own account of the events, given in his Epistle to the Galatians, suggests that Luke was guided by other considerations than those of chronology in assigning this trip and the so-called Council of the Apostles to this particular time. What took place now was the conflict with Peter, described in Galatians 2:11–12. Luke says not a word about it. But at the time it was a serious matter and the Judaistic faction that had gotten control of the Church at Jerusalem, under the aegis of James the brother of the Lord, sent out its emissaries and made serious trouble for Paul in the very congregations he had founded. It is to this state of affairs that we owe the existence of Paul's Epistle to the Galatians, the *magna carta* of Christian liberty. The "Galatians" are simply the people of "Pisidian" Antioch, Iconium, Lystra and Derbe, who belonged to the congregations established in his first missionary journey. Paul's repeated mention of Barnabas in this epistle is quite apropos in view of the fact that the members of these churches knew him personally and no doubt esteemed him highly. The so-called "North Galatian" hypothesis, according to which the real Galatians or Celts that formed the core of the Galatian

8.8 *Mithras Relief from Nemrud Dagh showing god on right and king on left. (Courtesy F. K. Doerner)*

kingdom of old are the addressees of this Epistle, seems improbable. There is no record of Paul's having done any work among them at the time of the first journey, and since they were not yet absorbed into the Hellenistic world, but spoke Celtic, he would have had scant prospects of making himself understood by them.

The Second Missionary Journey

Paul was not content to stay long in Antioch. He had a great desire to revisit the churches he and Barnabas had founded. Unfortunately Barnabas insisted on taking John Mark along, and this led to a termination of their joint activity. The modern reader of Acts is apt to feel that Paul was too harsh in this attitude toward Mark, but there were doubtless other factors involved besides the one Luke mentions. Without lingering over these we will merely note that the incident reveals Paul's emancipation from the patronage of Barnabas. There could be no doubt that the successes both in Cyprus and Galatia had been due chiefly to Paul. The man of Tarsus was conscious of the invisible forces working with him and through him; the eagle has found his wings and is going to use them as he wills. Like Abraham and Lot the two men chose separate areas. Barnabas went off to Cyprus with Mark, leaving the Galatian congregations to Paul, who took with him a man named Silas.

From Antioch to the Aegean Sea

This time Paul did not go by boat to Pamphylia but rather traveled on foot, for we are told they "went through Syria and Cilicia, strengthening the churches." This shows that the church at Antioch must have sent out other missionaries besides Paul and Barnabas. We hear nothing of the long and arduous journey that took them past the lake and plain of Antioch and through the forests of the Amanus. They reached the so-called "Syrian Gates" at the narrow pass near the present *Beilān,* about twenty-eight miles from Antioch. From here they descended the slopes of Mount Rhosus into the plain of Issos in Cilicia. Not far from that famous battlefield, where Alexander had won his first victory over Darius, lay a city called Alexandria (now *Alexandrette*) with the best harbor on the whole coast. Further stations en route will have been Mopsuestia (already mentioned in the *Karatepe* inscription of the ninth century B.C. and centuries after Paul the home of some great Christian theologians), Adana, and Tarsus. But we hear nothing of what transpired in these places.

From Tarsus the travelers went across Cilicia to the Taurus. At some time in the remote past a wagon road had been cut through a gorge whose rock walls rise to a height of 500 to 600 feet on the west bank of a small stream. These rock walls were the Cilician Gates and one followed this road upwards across a bare mountain summit and then down by another small stream to the vale of Podandus on what is now the *Tschakut Su* River, 2800 feet above the sea. Continuing up that watercourse one reached a point where the gorge is so narrow that the road must detour and cross a ridge for four or five miles, coming back to the river in the vale of *Loulon* or *Halaba,* near the northern end of the great passageway. This road perhaps had been made in the second millennium B.C.

The Cilician Gates were a great funnel, through which in ages past had moved the armies of the empire builders, the migrating tribes and the caravans of the merchants. Sargon of Akkad, Hittite kings, Assyrian kings, Alexander and the Diadochi, Seleucids, and Roman generals had all passed through here, going east or west, as the tides of history ebbed and flowed. And now a great captain of a new religion, with a lone adjutant toiled westward over this track.

Those who know the Taurus say that no one could suppose Paul to have crossed it before the middle of May; June first is more probable. If he took the route to Derbe via Laranda and marched daily, except on the Sabbath, he would have reached Derbe eight days after passing the Cilician Gates. Two days more would have taken him to Lystra, where he must have spent some weeks, since he performed an operation there on Timothy (ACTS 16:3), from which the latter had to recover before joining in the trip on which Paul proposed to take him. It was another day's march from Lystra to Iconium, and four days thence to "Pisidian" Antioch. In all these places Paul must have lingered a few days to strengthen and give fresh inspiration to the young churches.

Where did Paul go after leaving "Pisidian" Antioch?

"Now when they had gone throughout Phrygia and the region of Galatia, and were forbidden of the Holy Ghost to preach the word in Asia,

After they were come to Mysia, they assayed to go into Bithynia: but the Spirit suffered them not." (ACTS 16:6–7 A.V.)

"And they went through the region of Phrygia and Galatia, having been forbidden by the Holy Spirit to speak the word in Asia. And when they had come opposite Mysia, they attempted to go into Bithynia, but the Spirit of Jesus did not allow them." (ACTS 16:6–7 R.S.V.)

The exponents of the so-called "North Galatian hypotheses" assume that Paul journeyed into the heart of the old Galatian kingdom. That would have meant going north toward the Black Sea, or *Pontus Euxinus,* and would have taken more time than was at Paul's disposal. However, there is a very slight difference in the Greek manuscripts in verse 6, and the best reading makes it possible to render not only as the R.S.V. does "the region of Phrygia and Galatia," but "the Phrygian and Galatian region"—in other words, the single region west of "Pisidian" Antioch which could be described as Galatian from the point of view of the Roman provincial name, but which sometimes also was called "Phrygian" by those thinking in terms of the older nationality of the people. It was here in *Phrygia Galatica* that Paul and his companions were forbidden by the Holy Spirit to speak the word in "Asia," at whose boundary they now stood. This did not forbid them to *pass through* "Asia," however, and

8.9 *The Vale of Podandus. (Courtesy American Bible Society and T. Goell and F. K. Doerner)*

8.10 *Ilion, or Troy. Here Achilles and Hector fought. (Ewing Galloway)*

we must imagine them as crossing a portion of that province.

They may therefore have gone from "Pisidian" Antioch via Cotiaeum to Adramyttium, where the question whether to go into Mysia will have arisen, and then to Troas. From Pisidian Antioch to Troas was a journey of seventeen days. The shipping season had not yet come to an end when Paul reached Troas. Even without any "North Galatian" detour, which was certainly entitled to more precise description if it had occurred, the time from June 1 would barely have sufficed to bring him to Troas before the sailing of the last boat.

The name Troas reminds one of Troy, but was really the name of the whole district in which ancient Troy or Ilion was situated. Ilion itself (*Hissarlik*) lay farther to the north near the entrance to the Dardanelles. The Romans had a particular fondness for this whole area because it was the legendary home of their people. The real name of the city Paul visited was Alexandria, lying ten miles south of the Dardanelles, and it was called Alexandria of Troas to differentiate it from other Alexandrias. When it became a Roman "colony" under Augustus its official name was *Colonia Alexandria Augusta Troas*. But it is easy to see why the last word

would win favor and be used by ordinary folk as the name of the place. The city had an excellent harbor, ringed by heights, and was the great port of traffic between Asia and Macedonia. There was an "old city" with an acropolis surrounded by a wall, and a "new city" that had grown up outside of it and also was walled in. There are still remains there today of temples, a theater, circus and baths. The chief sanctuary, that of Apollo Smintheus, was quite far away to the south (twelve miles). For ages the ruins of Troas have been used as a stone quarry. Large parts of the area are covered by thickets. The town standing there now amid the remnants of ancient civilization is called *Eski-Stamboul*.

It seems doubtful whether Paul attempted to do any mission work here at this time, though on a later visit he found that "a door was opened" at Troas (2 COR. 2:12). One can imagine Paul looking down upon this harbor and its ships and pondering what he should do. The Spirit had prevented him from going north into Bithynia and Mysia or west into "Asia." Whither was he to turn? To the right lay the Hellespont; Byzantium may have lured him. Directly ahead lay large Greek islands. Then in the night came the dream of a summons from the other side of the sea (ACTS 16:9). Europe called him. And so he and his companions took passage for Macedonia.

On to Macedonia

The voyage is succinctly described in the first person plural, and so the author of Acts is able to avail himself of an account given by one of Paul's companions. The points mentioned are Samothrace and Neapolis (ACTS 16:11).

They passed Imbros before coming to Samothrace, and finally the island of Thasos before getting to Neapolis. Nor is it clear to the reader of this diary entry until he looks at a map that Neapolis was the end of the boat trip, and that from here Paul had to go on foot in order to get to Philippi.

438

Neapolis (now Kavalla) lay on a hillside above the Strymonian Gulf. A temple of Diana crowned the height and was visible far out at sea. To the rear was the great Pangaeus mountain range. While the harbor was not very good, it was the terminus of the Egnatian Way, a great road constructed by the Romans leading from here to Philippi and westward to the Adriatic port of Dyrrachium (today Durazzo). This great throughway to the Italian Sea naturally attracted much traffic.

It was a walk of eight miles, about three hours, to Philippi. The Pangaeus Range had to be crossed through a narrow pass. From here they had a marvelous view. To the south lay the Aegean Sea with its isles and to the north they saw below a lovely plain, the plain of Drama, surrounded by mountains and watered by a stream, the Zygactes. On a hill dominating the plain lay Philippi. It was founded by Philip of Macedon, who in 338 B.C. succeeded in uniting the Greek states under his control. They declared him leader of a Pan-Hellenic expedition of revenge against the Persians. It was left to his son Alexander to carry out this great task. Inestimable effects flowed from that conquest. Indeed, one may assert that if Alexander had not gone to the East, Paul would never have come to the West. For through the decree of providence Alexander created the one world of Hellenistic speech that made the spread of the Gospel possible. But Macedonia's great days were over. The Greek states, ever fighting among themselves and hating the war-like Macedonians, who alone could have saved them from their fate, had been gobbled up by Rome. On the battlefield of Pydna another Paul, the Roman general Aemilius Paulus, had overcome the last Macedonian king (168 B.C.) and annexed his country. Near Philippi had occurred the battle in which Brutus and Cassius were slain (42 B.C.) and out of which arose Octavian's claim to the Roman crown.

Augustus had honored Philippi by making it a Roman colony, as Acts 16:11 properly notes, so Latin was the official tongue now and many Romans lived there.

A French expedition carried on archaeological exploration at Philippi from 1914–38, but most of its discoveries concern the history of the city long after Paul's time. Where the Egnatian Way entered the city there were found the ruins of a gate, which may well mark the very point where Paul entered the city and where he went forth to find his co-religionists.

The travel-account speaks of the missionaries going outside the city to a place by the riverside, "where prayer was wont to be made" (Acts 16:13).

The word translated "where prayer was wont to be made" is synonymous with "synagogue." These were often built outside the city and near water—sea, lake, or river, as the case might be—for it was obligatory to wash one's hands before prayer, and hence before entering the synagogue, and it was extremely convenient to have water close at hand. In this case the building suspected of being a synagogue stood by the banks of the Zygactes River. The Egnatian Way came close to the stream at a point about a mile from the gate mentioned above, and some have held that this must be where the synagogue stood. Excavation may yet find some traces of it. Here the missionaries made the acquaintance of Lydia, a woman from Thyatira, a seller of purple goods. She is described as one "which worshipped God" (Acts 16:14, i.e., a Jewish proselyte). The presence there of this Greek woman illustrates the success that Judaism had in winning proselytes among her sex. Lydia now became the first Christian convert in Philippi and was baptized with her entire household.

Paul's healing a slave girl who had "a spirit of divination" proved less fortunate. Her owners apparently were Romans and were making money out of her soothsaying. If Paul hitherto had faced trouble caused only by Jewish instigators, he here found Roman adversaries who dragged him and Silas to the market place, before the court. The market place and platform on which orators appeared or judges sat has been discovered by archaeologists, though as rebuilt in the second century. The charge of being Jews and creating a disturbance and of teaching customs "which are not lawful for us to receive, neither to observe, being Romans," was brought against the missionaries. The last point had grave implications, for Roman law forbade the promulgation of a new religion. Christianity could escape this ban only through claiming to be a form of Judaism, which was a recognized existing religion.

The "justice" meted out here was evidently of a kind that gave the defendants no hearing. They were beaten with rods and put into the prison, which was close to the market place, with feet placed in stocks, a mode of punishment still popular in Colonial America.

An earthquake in the night, however, terrified the jailer and led to his conversion by Paul. When the order to release the prisoners came, Paul revealed his Roman citizenship and refused to accept a mere dismissal. The magistrates, afraid of what might happen to them if the case were reported to higher authority, apologized but requested the missionaries to leave town. After a farewell visit to Lydia, they departed escorted by some of the brethren.

Paul's later letter to the Philippians, the most beautiful of his letters, reflects the noble Christianity of the members of this church, who shone like stars in a dark world (Phil. 2:15).

The Egnatian Way turned sharply southwest from Philippi. Following it the missionaries passed through Amphipolis, capital of the first district of Macedonia. Its name probably means "the all around visible city," for it lay on a terraced hill protected on three sides by the winding Strymon River and was conspicuous from land and sea. A brief dig carried on here at one point in 1920 brought to light an early Christian basilica, but otherwise there is little known as yet of the ancient town. But there is a monument there called "the lion of Amphipolis,'" commemorating a victory of the fourth century B.C.; on this Paul's eyes surely rested. Apparently there was no synagogue at Amphipolis or at the next point mentioned, Apollonia, thirty miles farther, for nothing is said of any attempt to make converts at these places.

After thirty-eight miles of walking across the peninsula called Chalcidice, Paul and Silas came to Thessalonica, more recently called *Saloniki* but now officially named "Thessaloniki." The Egnatian Way went right through the city, and there are still remains of arches that mark the site of the eastern and western gates. It was the capital of one of the four Macedonian districts, and was really the administrative center for the whole province and the residence of the proconsul. Having sided with Octavian it received especial favors and "autonomy" as well. Hence we hear in Acts 17:5 of "the people," i.e., the assembly or the *demos*. But Thessalonica of Paul's day is gone beyond hope of recovery, for the remains of antiquity are buried beneath the flourishing modern city. The fourth-century arch of Galerius spans the Egnatian Way at one point, and is the city's most venerable monument.

Paul and Silas found no such hospitality here as at Philippi. In a letter that Paul later wrote to the Thessalonians, he mentions how he and his companion worked night and day that they might not become a burden to anybody (1 Thess 2:9). The Philippians, hearing of his hardships, twice sent Paul help (Phil. 4:16). The Book of Acts says nothing about all that, but merely reports how they went to the local synagogue, preached their message and gained converts, among whom were a great many of the "devout Greeks" (i.e., proselytes) and not a few leading women. A band incited by the Jews and composed of market-place idlers sought to lay hands on the missionaries, but failing to find them took their host, Jason, and some of the other converts before the city authorities (*politarchs,* officers elected by the *demos*) on the charge of harboring anti-Roman revolutionists. They were released on giving bail, but immediately sent Paul and his companions out of the city by night, considering it hazardous for them to remain.

Paul and Silas now continued on to Beroea (ACTS 17:10), which lay some forty miles away in the district of Emathius. They must have turned off to the left from the Egnatian Way, which led in a northeasterly direction to Pella, for Beroea lay to the south. It was a town of considerable importance and today is called Veroia. There, too, was a Jewish synagogue. These Jews are described as "more noble" than those in Thessalonica, willing to hear and consider what was presented to them. Converts were made, including "honorable" Greek women, i.e., women of high station, as well as some men (ACTS 17:12). However, the Thessalonica Jews soon came down there to stir up trouble, and so Paul was immediately sent off toward the sea, a distance of twenty-five miles, no doubt to Pydna, the Macedonian Waterloo. While we are not told that Paul took a ship from there to Athens it seems to be implied. If he went by land he would have gone via Dion, Heracleion, Larissa, Pharsalus, Lamia, Orchomenos, and Thebes. But one would expect some mention of a place between Beroea and Athens in such a long journey. We may, therefore, assume that Paul sailed down the Aegean coast from Pydna. In the west loomed Mount Olympus, rising to a height of 9793 feet. No doubt many aboard the vessel still revered the gods who supposedly dwelt on its lordly summit.

Athens

From Piraeus it was five miles to the city. Paul would have walked by the new road called the Hamaxitos, which kept north of

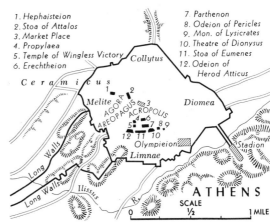

the earlier road, for the latter was encumbered with ruins of the "long walls" built by Themistocles. Along the road were altars to unknown gods, as mentioned also by Paul's contemporary, Philostratus. As the apostle approached the city he passed on the left the *Keramikos* or ancient cemetery, where lay many of the great men of Athens. At last he stood before the Piraean gate on the west side of the city. Did he think in his heart: What of Jerusalem? For Athens had a glamour second to none of the western world's cities because of its poets, its thinkers, its artists, and more anciently its lawgivers and soldiers. But it had fallen from its once proud pedestal. It was like Vienna of today—a city with a great past, but with a sorry present. Rob a people of its power and wealth, and its culture must inevitably decline. This was what Rome had done to the Greeks, and all the benefactions of its Caesars could not halt the downward trend. The age of the Greek "doer" was at an end; it was an age of the Greek talker. Athen's populace is neatly characterized by the author of Acts, when he says they spent their time in nothing except telling or hearing something new (ACTS 17:21). It was a decadent society, living in a tomb of ancient greatness, with the foreign tourist trade providing much of its support.

Passing through the gate Paul entered a street leading eastward to the market place

441

(*agora*). This was an open rectangle, bordered by many fine public buildings. Recent excavations in the agora area have identified on its west side the ruins of the Stoa, or portico, of Zeus, the Boulouterion, in which the council of the five hundred met, the Odeion, or music hall, where contests in music and oratory were held, and a number of temples. On the south side of the agora, two great stoas or porticoes running parallel have been found. On the eastern side lay the Stoa of Attalos. Only the north side is unexplored, owing to the railroad line; here probably lay the *Stoa Poikile,* or Painted Stoa, where Zeno the "Stoic" had lectured.

If Paul proceeded eastward he would have come to the new market place that Julius Caesar and Augustus had provided, because by the first century B.C. the old market place had become much congested with monuments. It was an open square with shops and arcades around it. Passing around the north and east slopes of the Acropolis one might follow the "Street of Tripods," where those who won success in sponsoring a dramatic contest were commemorated by bronze tripods set on pedestals. One of these pedestals, that of Lysicrates (335 B.C.), is still standing, though its tripod is no longer on it. Paul doubtless saw this monument. Circling the Acropolis on the east he would have come to the theater of Dionysus, where the great Greek plays had first been produced.

From the agora Paul might have taken a street leading around the east side of the hill called the Areopagus to the main entrance of the Acropolis, which lay on a higher and larger summit. Here stood the ornamental gateway called the Propylaia, flanked by the little temple of the Wingless Victory. Passing on, one ascended to the great Parthenon, of which Emerson sings

Earth proudly wears the Parthenon
As the best gem upon her zone.

Beyond it on the northern side of the hilltop was the graceful Erechtheion with its "Porch

8.11 *The Parthenon seen through two pillars of the Propylaea. (J. Lane Miller)*

of the Maidens." But Paul will hardly have visited these buildings.

According to the story of the Acts, Paul on arriving at Athens sent home the men who had conducted him from Beroea, with orders to Silas and Timothy to come to him at once (ACTS 17:15). However, his own remarks (1 THESS. 3:1 f.) suggest that one or both had come to Athens with him, and that Paul then sent Timothy back to Thessalonica.

The great missionary argued with Jews and proselytes in the synagogue on the Sabbaths, and also spoke daily in the market place to those who would listen. He is described as provoked because of the many idols he saw at Athens, a typically Jewish reaction, since it was a cardinal commandment "Make thee no graven images." An "Apollo Belvedere" or a "Venus de Milo," so different from the barbarous divine statues of the Orientals, were only idols to him.

Invited by Epicurean and Stoic philosophers to set forth his teaching, Paul is said to have addressed them, standing in the middle of the Areopagus, or Mars' Hill. The Areopagus was a small rocky hill, on the summit of which the court held session; whoever spoke there was vindicating himself before the judges. There was a stone on which the accused stood and another from which the prosecutor spoke. It was not a forum for philosophizing addresses. It is possible, perhaps, to imagine Paul as speaking on the *slope* of the Areopagus. But we have had occasion to observe before that Luke does not always have full and accurate reports to rely on; actually Paul may have been charged with a crime, as he would have been at Philippi and Thessalonica had he not quickly left those places. It thus seems possible that Luke has fused several occasions into one—a court appearance and an address to the philosophers. The latter would probably have been delivered in the agora area, or in the "Painted Stoa," which gave the "Stoic" philosophy its name. The address attributed to Paul in Acts 17:22 f. was quite suitable for such an occasion. But if he was charged with an offense against Roman law and haled before the court on the Areopagus he must have spoken in a very different vein to meet the issue.

Paul's missionary success at Athens was slight. True, Luke credits him with a number of converts including two prominent ones, Dionysius the Areopagite (a member of the high court that sat on the Areopagus) and a woman named Damaris. But in 1 Corinthians 16:15, Paul calls Stephanas of Corinth "the first convert of Achaia" (to which province Athens belonged), and so these people cannot yet have publicly declared their allegiance to the new religion, or have been baptized when Paul left Athens. Paul's departure seems to have been free from compelling necessity.

Corinth

The author of Acts says nothing of the cities Eleusis and Megara through which Paul must have passed, if he went on foot to

8.12 *A view of the Lechaeum Road in Corinth. (J. Lane Miller)*

Corinth. The road from Athens after skirting a bay in the Gulf of Aegina on the left crossed the line of the present Corinth Canal. That artery was not built until 1881–93; it had been projected by Nero but was, of course, opposed by all those who made money out of hauling smaller vessels and freight across the isthmus, and by the politicians who could levy tolls on this commerce. Corinth was called "the Rich" by a poet because of its trade, says Strabo. With two harbors, one (Lechaeum) facing toward Italy and the other (Cenchreae) facing toward Asia it was a great crossroads, for navigation around the Cape of Malea at the southeastern tip of the Peloponnesus was so hazardous that the merchants preferred the route via Corinth. Out of such ability to levy tolls on trade the city had grown wealthy.

In the vicinity of the present canal lay the temple of the Isthmian Poseidon, surrounded by a grove of fir trees. Here the celebrated Isthmian Games were held in alternate years. Paul was to hear a great deal about

443

8.13 *The archaic Temple of Apollo at Corinth.* (*J. Lane Miller*)

them, and had them in mind when he later wrote to the Christians of this city and compared the Christian's course to that of the runners competing for a prize (1 Cor. 9:24).

As Paul approached the city he will have seen a long line of jumbled rocks, the ruins of the ancient city walls, which the Romans had razed. For the Corinth which he was entering was no longer the old city of classic days. That city, which gave the world the famous Corinthian pillar, had been laid low by the Roman general Lucius Mummius in 146 B.C. Unfortunately the account that the historian Polybius gave of this event is lost; only a fragment of it is preserved by Strabo, in which he speaks of how wantonly the Roman soldiery dealt with masterpieces of Corinthian art. We do not know, therefore, how extensive the devastation was. But the destruction of Corinth was one of two deeds out of which Rome rose to wealth— the other being the destruction of Carthage.

Corinth had been newly founded by Julius Caesar as a Roman colony with the title *Colonia Laus Julia Corinthiensis* and with Latin as the official language. There must have been a vast difference in the population, for the Roman element consisted largely of freedmen, no doubt Greek-speaking, even when they bore Latin names. The city was now the capital of Achaia. That, of course, brought much Roman officialdom into the

town. Being under Senatorial administration this Roman province was under a proconsul, who usually held office for only one year. The new incumbent, whose term began in April, had to be on hand by July.

The visitor who comes to this scene of ancient Greek culture today is struck first by the sight of seven Doric columns on a small eminence in the old city area. They belong to the temple of Apollo, and have stood there since the sixth century B.C. Paul must have passed this temple many times during his long stay at Corinth. But the second landmark to strike the visitor's eyes is the gray mass of the rocky hill farther to the south, called Acrocorinth, the city's acropolis. Here the remains of antiquity are overlaid with later structures. But once a beautiful little temple of Aphrodite, visible far out at sea, was among the buildings on its summit. In the great field of ruins of the city itself archaeologists have been at work since 1858, and since 1896 the American School of Classical Studies has carried the task forward. It is thanks to their labors that one can get some idea of how matters lay in Paul's time.

If Paul entered by the road coming from the harbor town east of Corinth it led him directly to the market place, or agora. On the right he would have passed the fountain house of Peirene, the chief reservoir in the great water system of the city, north of which lay an Apollo sanctuary. Keeping right he would have passed the Propylaea, a monumental gateway, through which one ascended by stairs to the road that led out to the westerly harbor of Lechaeum. Along that street the excavators found indications that there was a *macellum,* or meat market, there, perhaps the one Paul referred to when he suggested raising no questions of conscience in eating what was bought in the market (1 Cor. 10:25).

If Paul walked farther along the north side of the agora he would have passed a line of shops. These were simply rooms opening out on the streets, or on courtyards. At the northwest corner of the agora there was an exit whence one took the street leading to the city of Sicyon. If Paul explored that for a distance he would have seen on the right the temple of Apollo already mentioned. To the left lay the reservoir called the Fountain of Glauke. Then came the small theater called Odeion, built in the first century B.C. for those still interested in plays and music. Beyond that he would have come to the large theater. Here were held in those days the gladiatorial games and fights of gladiators with wild beasts. The high wall around the orchestra was adorned with paintings.

Returning to the agora Paul would have seen that on its west side were more shops. Looking toward the south he would have observed that the southern half of the market place was about eight feet higher than the northern half on which he was standing, while beyond there lay the south stoa or portico. In the middle of the agora, projecting out from the upper level into the lower, was a platform or *bema,* used as a speaker's rostrum, or even as a judicial seat. In the southwest corner of the agora a street issued in the direction of Acrocorinth, the acropolis on the hill, with its shining temple of Aphrodite. It was served by a thousand slave girls, who had been donated to the temple as prostitutes.

There were Jews in Corinth and Paul will have had no trouble in locating the synagogue. A stone bearing the Greek inscription "[Sy]nagogue of the Hebre[ws]" was found by modern excavators at the foot of the Propylaea, suggesting that a synagogue stood there in Christian times. However, in Paul's time the synagogue must have been situated elsewhere, though it is not impossible that it bore a similar inscription. The use of the word "Hebrews" rather than "Jews" is interesting, for Paul, too, employs it (2 COR. 11:22, PHIL. 3:5). Paul went to the synagogue, of course, and took advantage of the privilege to address the congregation (ACTS 18:4). Here it was, no doubt, that he met

Priscilla, whose name suggests that she may have been a Roman, with her Jewish husband Aquila, a native of Pontus. They had been forced to leave Rome because of the edict of Claudius banning all Jews from the city (probably in 50 A.D.). Through this couple Paul found work in the textile business that he had learned in his youth. Perhaps Aquila had a shop on the north or west side of the agora, where he would have had his "tentmakers" at work.

When Silas and Timothy arrived (ACTS 18:5) Paul took a more aggressive line, and this soon brought on a break with the Jews. He declared that he would henceforth at Corinth concern himself only with the gentiles; of course, that meant first of all the proselytes. The ruler of the synagogue, Crispus, whose Latin name suggests that he may have been a convert to Judaism, was baptized with his household. A special divine revelation encouraged Paul to speak out even more fearlessly than he yet had done (ACTS 18:9 f.). And so we must imagine him as appearing in public and attracting attention. In all he spent eighteen months in this city. The noble letters that he later wrote to the congregation at Corinth bring home vividly to the reader the moral and religious problems faced by the people, and the skill of the great missionary in dealing with them.

In the summer of 51 A.D., a new annual proconsul, Gallio, came to Corinth, a brother of the Stoic thinker, Seneca. A Delphic inscription, really a letter of the emperor Claudius, has helped to make the above date of this proconsul's term likely, because it refers to him, and was written late in 51 or in the first half of 52 A.D. The Jews haled Paul before the new governor's tribunal with the charge "this man is persuading men to worship God contrary to the law." It was a new manner of worship, or in other words a new religion; and the propagation of a new religion was forbidden by Roman law. There is reason to believe that the hearing was held in the agora and that the proconsul heard the case, seated on the platform (*bema*), with the defendant and his accusers on the lower level before him. Excavations have revealed that a church was erected later over this spot, and that fact would indicate that the place had had a significance for the beginnings of Christianity in Corinth. Of course, it is also possible that the hearing took place in the Basilica northwest of the Propylaea, or in the Julian Basilica, which was situated behind the south stoa. That building, in which the excavators found some fine statues of members of the family of Augustus, was certainly of importance for the Roman administration.

The proconsul Gallio dismissed the charge of the Jews, holding that this was a dispute among the Jews and no concern of a Roman court concerned only with Roman law. There followed a riot, in which the Archisynagogos or "ruler of the synagogue," Sosthenes (successor to the converted Crispus?), was beaten, apparently by the crowd of bystanders, in an outburst of "anti-Semitism," such as at that time was manifesting itself in other cities of the empire. Gallio, Luke points out, paid no attention to this, thereby showing his dislike of the Jews. Paul could thus continue his work. It was during his stay at Corinth that he wrote his two letters to the Thessalonians.

But Paul now decided that his mission at Corinth was accomplished. The couple Priscilla and Aquila, too, determined to leave with him. They must have taken the road leading to the eastern harbor town of Cenchreae. Taking passage thence they sailed for Ephesus. Aquila and Priscilla apparently intended to stay there for a time, but Paul, though invited to stay for a longer period, departed, with a promise to return later. We will therefore say more of this great city in connection with his second arrival.

From Ephesus Paul sailed to Caesarea in Palestine (Acts 18:22). The report that he went and "saluted the church" means that he made a very quick visit to the church at Jerusalem. If he "went down" from Jerusalem to Antioch this expression shows that the writer is more conscious of altitude than of latitude, for Antioch is only a few hundred feet above sea level. The reader cannot help being struck with the meagerness of the account of Acts in this whole connection. Much will have happened, but the author can give only a few bare facts. So great an event as Paul's homecoming from this missionary journey deserved fuller reporting.

The Third Missionary Journey

A fresh missionary journey is begun in Acts 18:23, though the fact is not emphasized by the author. Paul is said to have gone from place to place in "Galatia and Phrygia." This means the territory of the Roman province of Galatia (see page 437). We are not told whether Paul trudged over the Taurus once more or went by ship to Attalia. His concern was with re-visiting those churches previously founded.

Ephesus
At "Pisidian" Antioch, Paul once more stood at the point at which he had been deterred from entering the province of Asia (Acts 16:6). But this time there was no such hindrance. "Paul passed through the upper country," i.e., the inland high plateau region of Phrygia through which the highroad led via Apameia, Colossae, Laodicea and Magnesia to Ephesus. The last stage of the journey involved a descent from the plateau to sea level. Paul was determined to make good his promise to the Ephesians of returning to them if God willed (Acts 18:21).

In western Asia Minor there are four prominent river valleys, and the entrance to each one was guarded in those times by an important city. In the north is the Caicus Valley to which Pergamum, situated on its north side, held the key. South of that is the Hermus, near the mouth of which lay Smyrna. Next in order comes the Cayster and then the Maeander (from which we get our verb "to meander"). At the latter's mouth lay Miletus, at the former's, Ephesus. One might think that Miletus and Smyrna would have been more important than Ephesus, for their rivers were larger, but Ephesus actually held a central position and by virtue of certain mountain passes had access to both the Hermus and Maeander valleys. Here at Ephesus, and not at Sardis as in Persian and Lydian days, was the beginning of the great trade-route to the Hellenistic East. Not only did ocean commerce adjust itself to that fact, but politics, too, took note of it. For Ephesus was the capital of "Asia," the former kingdom of the Pergamenes, though the proconsul of this senatorial province still resided officially in Pergamum. Ephesus was thus a strategic place for the planting of Christianity.

Since Paul came to the city from the east he must have entered it by the Magnesian Gate. On the right he will have seen the hill today called *Ayasoluk*, a Turkish corruption of the Greek *Hagios Theologos*, "The Holy Divine" (i.e., St. John), in whose honor a church was built there in later centuries. At the foot of this hill there lay in Paul's time the temple of Artemis. When rediscovered in 1877 by J. T. Wood after years of search, this deeply buried temple was found to have stood on a platform 418 by 239 feet. A flight of ten steps led up to the platform, and three further steps to the pavement of the peristyle. The temple itself was 163 by 342 feet and had over a hundred columns supporting its roof. These had a diameter of six feet, and thirty-six of them had sculptured drums with life-size figures at their bases, donated by old King Croesus of Lydia in the sixth century B.C. The foundations of the altar were twenty feet square. Behind it was the cella, or Holy

8.14 *Agora of Ephesus. (Courtesy F. K. Doerner)*

of Holies, having a width of seventy feet and containing the statue of the goddess Artemis. Another valued sacred object of Paul's day seems to have been a sacred stone— a meteorite that was doubtless regarded as *omphalos* or "navel of the earth." The temple, brilliantly finished in colors, was considered one of the seven wonders of the world. Pausanias the Greek geographer called it the largest building in existence. Paul will hardly have looked on it with aesthetic feelings, however, and his Jewish repugnance for idolatry will not have permitted him to go near it.

While old Greek Ephesus had lain in close proximity to the temple, the city newly built by Lysimachus, one of the Diadochi, or successors of Alexander the Great, clustered about double-topped Mount Pion across the vale to the west. Entering by the Magnesian Gate, Paul would soon have seen the Odeion, where music festivals were held. Then he would have come to the agora, or market place, as important in the life of any ancient city as the business district is in a modern one. Northeast of the agora was a great open-air theater, with rows of seats rising in a vast semicircle up the slope of Mount Pion.

It is estimated that it could seat 24,500 people. Standing on the summit above, one can look down upon its well-preserved ruins.

Before the theater was a small square, and opposite that was a great double-arched gate. Here one passed into a great marble-paved street about thirty-six feet wide and called the Arkadiane, which ran northwest for about 1735 feet to the harbor. It was lined on either side with a roofed colonnade, behind which were storerooms and shops. At the terminus of the Arkadiane there was the Harbor Gate. Ephesus had a narrow inner harbor, which one reached by sailing up into the broad mouth of the Cayster River. The water was rather shallow and silted up easily; no doubt occasional dredging was necessary to keep the harbor open.

Today there is no harbor there and no vessel could approach the sandy beach that now, due to centuries of alluvial deposit, lies four miles distant from the city. Standing at the Harbor Gate and looking over all the masts of the sailing ships to the northwest, Paul would have seen the Hill of Astyages, which dropped off to the left into a saddle leading over to Mount Koressos. On that Hill of Astyages, which, with its height of 450 feet, virtually dominates Ephesus, there is a fort traditionally called "the Prison of Paul." It is a structure of much later times, but the designation is curious; we will revert to it again later.

Since the previous visit of Paul a small group of people interested in Christianity had formed. Apparently they were disciples of the Alexandrian Apollos, whose coming to Ephesus and later departure for Corinth are particularly noted by the author of Acts (18:24 f.). He makes it clear that Apollos was really a disciple of John the Baptist, but belonged to a group that had also made room for Jesus in its beliefs—perhaps much as Islam later made room for Jesus beside Mohammed. Aquila and Priscilla, who must have departed before Paul's coming, had been able to lead Apollos over into Chris-

tianity more definitely. But the group of twelve that Paul found were baptized only with John's baptism, a fact showing that they were Apollos' converts. Nevertheless, they all felt themselves pretty much "Christian," and Apollos had been given letters of recommendation to the church at Corinth, where he attained such esteem that Paul later had to take note of it in his letter (1 Cor. 1:12). The twelve now received Christian baptism, probably at the hand of one of Paul's aides.

Paul again followed his regular custom of speaking in the synagogue. After three months, however, this led to a rupture with the Jews, and Paul left the synagogue with his followers. They held daily meetings from now on "in the hall of Tyrannus." Presumably this was the lecture room (*schola*) of a Greek teacher of philosophy, deceased or absent, which was rented for the purpose. Since Paul worked for his living (Acts 20:34, 1 Cor. 4:12), we must imagine him as starting his trade several hours before daybreak and continuing to the fifth hour (an hour before noon), which was the customary closing time of the work-day. He then could apply himself to his teaching in the afternoon, instead of to relaxation. One manuscript of Acts adds quite appropriately that he taught from the fifth to the tenth hour.

Ephesus was noted as a center of magical practice, and "Ephesian writings" was a familiar term in the Graeco-Roman world for magical texts. Many such texts have been found in the sands of Egypt. Paul had an experience with Jewish exorcists, the seven sons of Sceva, which mightily increased his reputation and led to a great public burning of magical books, allegedly worth fifty thousand pieces of silver (Acts 19:13-19).

The two years of Paul's daily teaching perhaps were the most important of his whole career. For here at this metropolitan center, he reached so many people that he could say that all Asia had heard the word of the Lord (Acts 19:10). People who came from the inland cities, whether on public or private business, had an opportunity to go and hear this teacher of a strange new message which was akin to the well-known Hellenistic Judaism, but freed of the distasteful aspects that made acceptance so humiliating. Out of this grew the establishment of numerous new congregations at inland places like Colossae and Laodicea, to which Paul wrote letters (that to the Laodiceans mentioned in Colossians 4:16 having been lost). Paul's helpers played a role in this work, for we find him joining Timothy with himself when he later wrote to the Colossians.

It was during this ministry in Ephesus that Paul wrote his two letters to the Corinthians. These epistles give us some idea of further travel plans entertained by Paul. He at first intended to go from Ephesus to Corinth, to Macedonia, back to Corinth and then to Jerusalem (2 COR. 1:16). He gave up that idea and sent the Corinthians a letter instead, in which he expressed the intention to remain in Ephesus till Pentecost (1 COR. 16:8) and then go through Macedonia to Corinth (1 COR. 16:5). He sent Timothy and Erastus to Macedonia in advance as substitutes (1 COR. 4:17–19).

According to Luke's narrative, Paul's teaching affected the prosperity of the local craftsmen making votive objects for sale to visitors who desired to make a donation to Artemis. While the humbler folk used terracotta objects, the more prosperous donated silver or gold objects. Demetrius the silversmith aroused his fellow tradesmen in the matter and a public demonstration took place, the crowd following to the theater crying, "Great is Artemis of the Ephesians!" and dragging with them two of Paul's companions whom they had apprehended. Paul is said to have been restrained from going among the crowd by messages of the "Asiarchs." There really was only one Asiarch at a time. He was the official who was guardian of the rites of the imperial Roman cult, and held office for only one year; his predecessors, as ex-Asiarchs, may, however, have continued to use the title so that one could speak of them in the plural, as Acts does here. It is interesting to find these pagans siding with Paul over against the dominant Artemis cult. The crowd was quieted by an address of the foremost local official (translated "town-clerk"), who not only reproved Demetrius and his partisans, but warned against incurring Roman wrath by rioting, and demanded the release of the two captives. He suggested orderly legal procedures. The affair quieted down, but Paul now left Ephesus by ship.

In connection with Paul's stay at Ephesus one is struck by the fact that the author of Acts tells us nothing that would explain Paul's words when he speaks of being pressed to the point of despair and of having fought with beasts (2 COR. 1: 8–9; 1 COR. 15:32). It is difficult, to say the least, to take Paul's fighting with beasts as figurative and as referring to the mob scene described by Acts. And the despair of which he speaks is likewise not explained by that account. Fearful things happened at Ephesus, and Paul was sent into the arena: that is the inescapable conclusion, if words mean anything. So the curious local tradition about "Paul's Prison" on the Hill of Astyages may not be entirely unfounded.

A Visit to Macedonia and Greece

The story of Paul's travels is again continued in summary form in Acts 20:1 f. He went first to Macedonia, where the congregations formerly founded were revisited, and then to Hellas (Achaia). Here he must, of course, have gone to Corinth. And it must have been during his stay at that city that he wrote his great letter to the Romans, in anticipation of visiting a congregation that had sprung up at Rome, some of whose leading members—headed by Prisca (Priscilla) and Aquila—were Paul's converts and were currently residing there. The personal greetings he sends these people (ROM. 16:3–16) show

449

what a large number of friends he had at the capital. And his remarks are like rockets in the night, revealing in a flash important happenings of which the author of Acts makes no mention: Priscilla and Aquila had "risked their necks" for Paul's life; Paul's kinsmen Junias and Andronicus, "men of note among the apostles" and converted before he himself had been, had once been in prison with him. Allusion is made to the hitherto unmentioned church of Cenchreae, near Corinth, and to Phoebe, a deaconess there, who had been of so much help to him and others. Since he so warmly recommends her to the Roman congregation, it is probable that she carried to Rome this document of incomparable importance for the history of the church in ages to come.

From Greece Paul intended to go to Jerusalem for the Passover (ACTS 20:3). His purpose was to have his gentile missions show their fellowship with the Christians of Jerusalem by bringing them a collection (ROM. 15:25). Since navigation opened on March 5, after cessation of the winter storms, and it was a month's voyage, he could hardly have reached his destination in time in years when the Passover fell early. In 57 A.D. the Passover fell on April 7.

A murder plot of the Jews, of which Paul got wind, caused him to change his plans. Perhaps the plot was to be executed at Cenchreae or on whatever vessel he might take from there. There would have been many Jews aboard ship on the same errand of celebrating the festival at the Holy City. Paul decided to postpone his departure and go to Jerusalem for Pentecost instead. Hence he returned to Macedonia and proposed to leave from there for Troas. Some members of his party took an earlier boat, but he and others, including the diarist who speaks in the first person plural in Acts 20:6 f., spent Passover and the Feast of the Unleavened Bread at Philippi, and then sailed from Philippi (or rather its harbor, Neapolis) to Troas, a five day journey. There they were reunited with their companions and spent seven days, on the last of which, a Sunday, the incident with the youth Eutychus took place. (ACTS 20:7–12).

From Troas to Assos

Rather strangely, Paul separated from his companions to go a day's march by land to Assos, instead of embarking with the others (ACTS 20:13). Since they were to take him aboard at that harbor he could not have lingered en route for any missionary purpose. Perhaps Paul desired to be alone to commune with his Creator; for crucial months lay ahead of him, as he well knew. His name had become anethema to the Jews. The murder plot he had just escaped lifts the curtain a bit on the situation, and the subsequent happenings in Jerusalem fully reveal it. What, one wonders, was the reason for such enmity?

For nearly two centuries the Jews had with great success made converts for their religion in the Hellenistic world. And now this one great Christian missionary was attracting proselytes to Christianity in increasing numbers, partly by relaxing ritual laws the Jews believed important. Christian teaching, furthermore, as formulated by the Apostle was particularly offensive to them: ". . . Christ crucified, unto the Jews a stumblingblock" (1 COR. 1:23). Hatred of Paul was becoming world-wide among them. Why Paul under these circumstances risked going to Jerusalem remains hard to understand. The author of Acts reveals only later, through Paul's own mouth, that everywhere, in the churches he visited in these months, attempts were made to dissuade him from going (ACTS 20:23). But he seems to have known with the certainty of intuition that the road to Jerusalem was the road to further missionary conquest, through the aid of Him "who moves in a mysterious way his wonders to perform."

The road from Troas to Assos led south and was parallel to the coast, although several miles inland. Whether he went down to the cape and then east along the coast of the Gulf of Adramyttium, or cut off that corner by following a river valley to a point north of Assos is hard to say. The vessel on which Paul's companions traveled had to go around the Cape of Sminthium and through the channel between the peninsula and the island of Lesbos to get to Assos.

Coming from the north across the river valley, Paul had to ascend half a mile to high ground and then found himself at the gates of Assos, famed as the home of the Stoic philosopher, Cleanthes, and noted for the excellent wheat that was exported from there. No Greek city of Europe or Asia had a more imposing or beautiful location. It rose terrace-like up a conical hill, a half mile from the sea. A magnificent view presented itself here. One could look across to Lesbos and the small islands east of it, as well as to the coast on the opposite side of the gulf. The ruins, only partly occupied by the present village of *Behram* and explored by the American Archaeological Institute in the eighties and nineties, speak impressively of a venerable past. The city walls which encircled Assos for more than two miles and which were originally sixty-five feet high date mostly from the fourth century B.C.

Where Paul must have entered the city, he would have been close to the acropolis on which stood an ancient Doric temple of the goddess Athena. Below it lay the agora and on its northern side was a wide stoa or portico. Still lower down was a theater, whose ancient spectators sat looking out over the sea. The city also had a gymnasium, a Bouleuterion and public baths. East of the present harbor is an ancient mole leading into the gulf. It was probably here that Paul found the vessel from Troas. His companions will have rejoiced over his safe arrival.

Around the Coast of Asia Minor

Ships doubtless anchored for the night in these parts, for the wind dies away in the late afternoon. But a northerly breeze sets in very early in the morning, suggesting a start at or before daybreak. The next morning, therefore, Paul's ship set sail and, leaving the Gulf of Adramyttium, turned into the channel of Mytilene, stopping for the night at the important city of that name of the mountainous island of Lesbos (ACTS 20:14). Mytilene originally lay on a separate small island, but a causeway forming two excellent harbors now connected it with Lesbos. Back in the fifth century B.C. the city had played a role in history. The Romans destroyed it in 84 B.C., but Pompey gave it its freedom in 63 B.C.

From here Paul's ship might readily have gone into the Gulf of the Hermus River to Smyrna, but instead it passed through the channel between the island of Chios and the peninsula jutting out from the mainland. Here it must have anchored for the night, probably near Cape Argennum. Leaving Ephesus to the east, they then went through a narrow channel to get to the island of Samos, where they must have touched Trogyllium, though the mention of that port is omitted in the best manuscripts and hence in the Revised Standard Version. Heading southeast Paul's ship next made for Miletus at the mouth of the Maeander River.

Miletus was a celebrated city, second only to Ephesus, among the cities of "Asia." Founded by Ionians in the eleventh century B.C., it was destroyed by Alexander the Great in 334 B.C., but was soon rebuilt. The excavations carried on here by the Berlin Museum 1900–06 have clarified the topography of the town. Much of what was found belongs to an age either long before or long after Paul. But the great temple of Apollo Delphinios must have struck Paul's eyes from afar. He was evidently able to arrange for a stop of a few days at this port, for the representatives of the church at Ephesus were summoned. The messenger may have taken a sailboat to Priene, and thence gone on foot to Ephesus. The Ephesians would hardly have reached Miletus until the third day of Paul's stay. His parting words to this group (ACTS 20:18-35) give a stirring revelation of the picture of him that lived in the minds of his followers. The elders of Ephesus went down with Paul to the harbor and saw him off in the saddest of all partings.

The ship now took a "straight course" to the island of Cos at the entrance to the Ceramian Gulf (ACTS 21:1). Perhaps it stopped at the city of Cos, at the eastern end of the island. This fertile island was noted for silk production, ointments, wine and wheat, and was the scene of luxurious country life. It was also noted for its medical school, for this was the home of Hippocrates, whose name is alive to this day because every medical doctor graduated in the western world must still swear the oath to which Hippocrates pledged his students. Fittingly, the chief god of Cos was Aesculapius, the god of healing.

Cos was always closely linked to Rhodes. To this island, forty-three miles long and twenty miles wide, Paul's vessel continued on the following day, passing the peninsula of the Chersonnesus on the left and a series of islands on the right. The city of Rhodes, founded in 408 B.C., lay on the northern tip of this island. At the harbor entrance once had stood the famous Colossus of Rhodes, one of the Seven Wonders of the World. It was a statue of the sun god, 105 feet in height, erected in commemoration of successful resistance to a siege of 280 B.C. Strabo, the Greek geographer, calls Rhodes the most splendid city known to him with respect to harbors, streets, walls and other equipment. He notes its excellent government and the social-mindedness shown in care for the poor and unemployed. Rhodes had once been mistress of Caria and Lycia on the mainland opposite, but had been too powerful to suit Rome. Like its colossus, which was toppled over by an earthquake in 224 B.C., broken off at the knees, so the city's might, too, was

broken. In the time of Paul it enjoyed Roman favor, however, and was a free city, continuing to play an important role in trade.

From Rhodes the vessel sailed to Patara. This was a city of the Lycian coast, near the mouth of the Xanthus River and chief port for a group of inland cities farther up that valley. It was an important point in the coastal trade, though the more easterly city of Myra (mention of which is added in some Greek manuscripts at the end of Acts 21:1 and which we will meet later in Acts 27:5) outstripped it. At Patara Paul found a ship bound for Phoenicia and transferred to that.

To Syria and Palestine

Approaching Cyprus and keeping south of that island, the ship headed for Tyre, for which its cargo was destined. Paul had doubtless seen this city before in the course of his early travels between Cilicia or Syria and Palestine. Once upon a time it had been an island city; it had been joined by a mole to the mainland by Alexander the Great, and this mole by constant accretion of ocean sands has now become a veritable isthmus. Here thirty thousand women, children, and slaves were taken and sold into slavery by Alexander; nearly one-third as many men were killed in the defense of the city or executed. The woe of an Ezekiel over Tyre (EZEK. 27-28) was thus completely fulfilled, though later than the prophet expected. But the city was rehabilitated by the Seleucids and became quite splendid again. After a checkered political history it was annexed by Rome in 65 B.C., receiving the status of a free city. Paul and his companions had time to go ashore and contact the local congregation (ACTS 21:4). We learn by this allusion that Christianity was already established there.

From Tyre the voyage continued down the Palestinian coast the short distance to Ptolemais (ACTS 21:7), successor to the Acco of Old Testament times. It was an important place, indeed, though in modern times it has yielded its position to Haifa, across the bay. Here at Ptolemais, too, there were Christians with whom Paul and his companions could profitably spend the day.

The following morning their vessel went on to Caesarea, the capital of the Roman province embracing Judaea and adjacent areas (see page 420). Therewith the long sea voyage, that may have begun about April 15 (if this was the year 57 A.D.), finally terminated about May 14, two weeks before the Pentecost festival that Paul wanted to spend at Jerusalem.

At Caesarea Paul stayed at the home of "Philip the evangelist" (ACTS 21:8). Here he again had to listen to the voice of ominous prophecy and tearful pleading not to go to Jerusalem. But it was useless to try to dissuade him. He was under a compelling necessity imposed on him by a higher power. When the little group finally started on foot for the Holy City they took two days for the journey, spending the first night with an early disciple named Mnason, a Cyprian. What town this man lived in has been left unmentioned; perhaps it was Antipatris. From there they must have gone on to Jerusalem via the Beth-horon Road.

Jerusalem and Caesarea

The diarist who was also present at Paul's meetings with the Jerusalem Christians tells us of Paul's reception by James and the Elders (ACTS 21:17 f.). Paul was more or less on trial before them, but this was not so apparent to a Greek. The fact that Paul brought a goodly charitable contribution from gentile Christians (a circumstance not mentioned here, but alluded to in Acts 24:17 in Paul's speaking to Felix) will have helped to soften the attitude toward him. But the demand was made of Paul at this occasion that he show his respect for the Mosaic law by doing something in the nature of "good works." This, the leaders, held, was essential to please the "many thousands" of Jewish Christians who were zealous for

the law. They suggested he help four indigent brethren to pay their Nazirite vows. Paul, who had dealt too sternly with Peter at Antioch for "dissembling" (GAL. 2:13 f.), was thus forced to do some dissembling himself, and participate in ceremonies which he considered of no value. He may have justified this before his own conscience with thoughts like those he advances in 1 Corinthians 8:9 f. He had to go to the Temple with the Nazirites and state that he was bringing the offering for them and desired purification for himself. We have already made mention of the particular chamber in a corner of the Court of the Women which was reserved for Nazirites (page 400). Since Paul came from the land of the gentiles, his own purification could not be achieved just by an immersion at sundown of the same day, but involved the procedures connected with the more serious degree of uncleanness (such as that after contact with a corpse). Then he had to be sprinkled twice by a priest on the third and seventh days with water of purification. It was probably after this second sprinkling that he was recognized and that the riot broke out over his presence in the Temple.

The mob action in the Temple precincts was observed by the Roman watchman on the Antonia citadel and brought immediate interference. Paul was delivered from his assailants by the soldiers. We must imagine him as standing on the stairs of the Antonia leading up from the Temple's outer court when he addressed the crowd in Hebrew (Aramaic) speech (ACTS 21:40).

It is not necessary to go into detailed comment on the following events: Paul's claim to Roman citizenship came in good stead. Secret information was brought by his nephew of a plot to assassinate him, causing the Roman officer in charge to transfer Paul by night and on horseback to Caesarea. His case was heard there by the Roman procurator Felix, who to please the Jews kept Paul in prison for two long years. The

453

newly-appointed procurator, Festus, handled his case, and consulted King Agrippa II, who in 53 A.D. had received dominion over the former tetrarchies of Philip and Lysanias and had a supervisory role over the Temple and high priesthood at Jerusalem. Paul's request to have his case judged in Rome was finally granted.

The Journey to Rome

One cannot view the remains of the old Roman harbor installations at Caesarea, and notably those of the mole that ran out into the sea, without visualizing the scene of parting that took place when Paul finally sailed in a ship of Adramyttium that was bound for Syrian and Asia Minor ports (ACTS 27:1 f.). We may imagine Christians of the city, including Philip and his family, watching the embarkation. Aristarchus of Thessalonica in Macedonia went with him. Unless another of those mentioned in Acts 20:4 was also a companion but out of modesty fails to mention himself, we would have to conclude that this Aristarchus is the diarist whose journal has been used by Luke, for the narrative again is in the first person plural.

Sidon to Myra

The ship must have left late, for it was the next day when it put in at Sidon, which lay on the coast twenty-three miles north of Tyre (see page 452). Old Sidon had been laid in ashes in 351 B.C. when it revolted against the Persian monarch, Artaxerxes III, 40,000 people perishing in its flames. Under the Seleucids of the third century a new Hellenistic Sidon had come into being. It was in Paul's day a free city with its own magistrates and municipal government, and was noted not only for its artists but for its scholars, notably its astronomers and mathematicians. There were already Christians in Sidon. The Roman centurion, Julius, to whose charge Paul and other prisoners were committed, allowed him to visit them while the ship was in port (ACTS 27:3).

Leaving Sidon the following day they had to sail under Cyprus, i.e., keep around to the east and north of it on account of the winds. Skirting Cilicia and Pamphylia, they came to Myra in Lycia (the so-called "western" text of the Greek Book of Acts adds "after 15 days"). This was a most important place for ocean commerce, especially for direct voyages from Alexandria to Asia Minor, which had been made possible in Roman times by the larger vessels and the progress in the science of navigation. The grain ships bound for Rome could not go directly to their objective, Italy, but took advantage of the prevailing westerly winds to get over to Myra, and then of the local coast winds to travel westward. A Christian pilgrim of a later era held Myra to be the gate to the eastern Mediterranean in the same sense that Constantinople was the gate to the Aegean. The city of Myra lay two and a half miles inland from the coast; the harbor town was really named Andriake, but it was customary to refer to it, too, as Myra. Here, at the terminus of long ocean voyages across the open sea, the sailors were wont to pay their vows to the deity, probably the god Poseidon (in Christian times replaced by St. Nicholas, one-time bishop of Myra). Here the centurion in charge of Paul found a ship from Alexandria that was bound for Italy, to which he transferred his party. It was probably a grain-carrying vessel, for grain was one of the main export products of Egypt and much needed in Rome. A westerly breeze was fine for a direct run from Alexandria to Myra, but if the wind shifted slightly to the north such a ship was deflected to the Syrian coast and had to follow the course taken by Paul's Adramyttium vessel. The second-century author Lucian in his dialogue *The Ship* gives an interesting account of a voyage made under such circumstances.

Myra to Crete

Creeping along the coast the Alexandrian vessel finally came opposite the Carian city of Cnidus, situated on a peninsula on the southwest coast of Asia Minor. The diarist speaks of sailing slowly for many days (ACTS 27:7). Cnidus was only 130 geographical miles from Myra and the run could have been made in a day with favorable wind. Obviously, then, the ship had to face contrary winds. At Cnidus the Aegean Sea comes down, and here the advantage of being able to stay in smooth water under the lee of the shore came to an end. They might have put in at Cnidus and waited for better weather, but the lateness of the season made continuance of the voyage urgent. The only course now was to try and round Cape Salmone on the eastern end of Crete and go up the sheltered shore of that long island. This they were able to accomplish and get under the lee of Crete (ACTS 27:8). With a west wind it was not possible to round Salmone, as Lord Nelson and his fleet found out in 1798, and the success of Paul's vessel in doing this proves that the wind must have been northwest.

They kept along the Cretan Coast with difficulty until they reached the Fair Havens (Greek, *kaloi limines*) near the city of Lasea. This was a small bay, east of Cape Matala, and the nearest sheltered spot available. It still bears the same name in modernized form (*Limeonas Kalous*). The coast then turned off northward and afforded no protection against a northwest or north wind.

The journey from Myra to Fair Havens must have taken about twenty-five days. The author of Acts notes that the "fast" was now past (ACTS 27:9), i.e., the Day of Atonement, which in the year 59 A.D. fell on October 5.

It was now getting late for ocean travel; from September 14 to November 11 was considered a dangerous period, while from November 11 to March 5 sailing was suspended. Paul was more experienced in ocean travel than the account of his ministry in Acts would lead one to believe. We learn from 2 Corinthians 11:25 that he had three times suffered shipwreck, and once even had spent a night and a day adrift on the ocean. He thus felt free to offer some advice and warned against going farther. But the centurion, who seems to have had the deciding voice, gave heed to the captain and the ship's owner, who was also on board, and who wanted to take the gamble of proceeding farther. Fair Havens was not too attractive for wintering, and they hoped to find a more suitable berth at Phoenix, a harbor looking northeast and southeast (ACTS 27:12). In such a matter, where everyone's life was at stake, the majority seems to have ruled, and Paul was outvoted. The harbor of Phoenix, or Phenice (modern Lutro), was forty geographical miles farther up the Cretan coast. It was better protected and in every way more attractive, and there was reasonable hope of being able to make it in a few hours under favorable circumstances. But if the best manuscripts, as rendered by the Revised Standard Version, state that Phoenix looked northeast and southeast, this is erroneous; the harbor looks southwest and northwest.

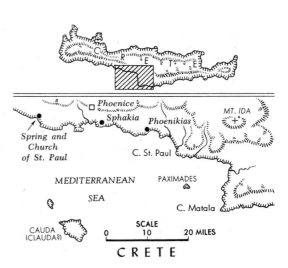

CRETE

455

THE WIND EUROCLYDON
(Euro-aquilo)

The arrival of a southerly breeze provided a good opportunity to depart, and so they set sail. Ahead of them Cape Matala projected six miles out to the south and it was difficult to clear it. But they succeeded and then went up the Gulf of Messara.

Danger at Sea

The risk, however, soon became apparent. The south wind can shift very suddenly, particularly in a mountain country; and the mountains of Crete, dominated by Mount Ida of legendary fame, arose to a height of seven thousand feet. Suddenly they were struck by a wind, called the "Euroclydon," or the "Levanter" (Greek *Eurakulon*), roaring down from those mountains. The ship, with a single large sail which could not be slackened quickly, was in great peril. They drifted with starboard toward the wind until they got into calmer water under the shelter of an island named Cauda or Clauda (Gozzo), some twenty-three miles to the south. Here they were able to take refuge. The waterlogged lifeboat, which they had been towing, was got aboard—a hard job, in which the diarist seems to have helped. The ship was then undergirded with ropes to reinforce her, lest she break apart from the strain caused by shifting cargo. This could be done by lowering a cable under the hull in U-shaped manner, drawing it along both sides to the center and fastening it there.

If they left the protection of Cauda the wind would blow them directly toward the African coast. Here the text speaks of fearing the quicksands, or Syrtes (ACTS 27:17). The Syrtes were two areas on the coast of Africa—the westerly one being the Syrtis Minor and the easterly one the Syrtis Major; both were greatly feared by ancient navigators. Precautions were taken to reduce the hazards by "straking sail," or "lowering of the gear." This meant getting flat on the deck every bit of fairweather sailing equipment such as spars, rigging, sails, etc. But this precaution was not enough to keep Paul's ship from being blown southward. A ship in this situation had either to scud or heave to. The former was out of the question, since that would have taken them to the Syrtis. They had to heave to with some storm-sail set. This was necessary to keep the ship from pitching and rolling, and to keep her on the starboard tack in order to hold a course west by north.

The storm did not let up. The next day they began to lighten ship and kept this up until cargo and even ship's furniture were thrown out, the passengers helping. Under cloudy skies no bearings could be taken astronomically to determine their location. The ship's inmates had had no food, since cooking was impossible under such conditions, and were in a weakened and dejected condition. In this situation Paul counseled courage, predicting on the basis of a vision that he had in the night, that all would be saved, but the vessel would be lost.

Events came to a crisis on the fourteenth night of this incessant storm. They were drifting across the Sea of the Adria (ACTS 27:27). The term Adriatic is used nowadays for the waters east of the Italian peninsula, but Ptolemy distinguishes between the Gulf of Adria and the Sea of Adria, the former being the waters east of Italy, and the latter extending southward from the Italian boot. Of Sicily, too, he says it is bounded on the east by the Adria, while Crete is bounded by it on the west and the Peloponnesus on the west and south. It was thus the name of the middle basin of the Mediterranean.

For some reason the sailors suspected that land was near. Perhaps the roar of the breakers was heard. They took soundings and got twenty fathoms and later fifteen fathoms. They put four anchors overboard from the stern, and fearing that these might not hold, anxiously awaited the break of day. This ancient mode of anchoring had the advantage that when the anchors were out the ship was under full command. Paul now became aware that the crew was planning to abandon the ship in the lifeboat under cover of the darkness, and warned the centurion of the dire consequences. The officer took action and had the boat cast adrift. Paul then urged all to eat and strengthen themselves for the impending crisis.

Malta

When day broke they saw the land before them, but did not recognize it. This is not surprising, for even if the sailors knew Malta, they were not at a familiar harbor. They saw that there was a bay with a beach, and they planned if possible to bring the ship ashore on it. So they threw out the anchors, at the same time loosening the ropes with which the rudders were tied up out of the water when not in use. The ship, therefore, was immediately under steering control. Hoisting the foresail to the wind, they made for the shore. But before attaining this objective the vessel hit a shoal; the bow stuck fast, and the stern was pounded to pieces by the surf (ACTS 27:39–41).

There seems to be little doubt as to the general locality in which these events took place. It is obvious from the subsequent narrative that the shipwreck occurred on the north side of the island of Malta. Since the Middle Ages a bay there has been called "St. Paul's bay." It lies eight miles from Valetta and nearly five miles from the ancient capital

Melite (Cittá Vecchia), which is in the heart of the island. The description of the Book of Acts excellently fits the situation. A ship riding a gale from the indicated point of the compass would have been driven past Koura Head, which bounds the bay known as St. Paul's on the east. This point of land is 476.6 nautical miles from Cauda, and thus fits a drift of the length of time mentioned and the speed of drift estimated.

Tradition has localized the shipwreck on the eastern side of the bay and here was built a church of St. Paul ad Mare; that church was rebuilt in 1610, at which time the Tower of St. Paul was also erected nearby. But the natural drift of a vessel driven as described would have been to the west side of St. Paul's bay, which is rocky, but has two creeks, one of which has a beach. The other creek, however, may also have had a beach in former times, and here may best be sought the spot where the ship was run toward shore, because it fits the description of "a place where two seas met." While the Revised Standard Version renders "shoal" the meaning is really "a place between two seas." The same term is applied by Strabo to the Bosporus, and so in the opinion of James Smith it would also fit the channel that exists here between the mainland and the rocky ridge of which Selmun Island

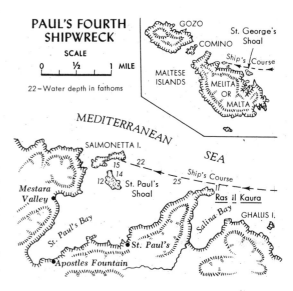

PAUL'S FOURTH SHIPWRECK

SCALE

0   ½   1 MILE

22 – Water depth in fathoms

GOZO

COMINO

St. George's Shoal

Ship's Course

MALTESE ISLANDS

MELITA OR MALTA

MEDITERRANEAN

SEA

SALMONETTA I.

15   22

14

12   St. Paul's Shoal

25

Ship's Course

Mestara Valley

Ras il Kaura

Salina Bay

GHALLIS I.

St. Paul's Bay

St. Paul's

Apostles Fountain

(crowned since 1845 by a statue of Paul) is the visible part. The ship must have plowed into the mud where three fathoms are indicated on the Admiral Smyth chart.

The vessel now began to crack up. The centurion out of respect for Paul forbade the customary killing of the prisoners. He ordered all to swim ashore or drift ashore on planks. One wonders that the diarist says nothing of how Paul and his companions personally fared in this situation. On getting out of the water they learned, from inhabitants of the island who had observed their shipwreck, that they were on Malta (Greek, *Melite*), the largest of the Maltese islands, about seventeen miles long and eight miles wide.

Malta was Roman in 218 B.C. and was part of the province of Sicily, which island is only sixty miles distant. The Romans did not treat them as enemies but at once gave them "municipal" privileges. The Publius mentioned in the narrative as "chief man of the island" and owner of lands in the neighborhood was probably the Roman official in charge. The province of Sicily was under a *propraetor,* and Publius may have been his *legate.* One would expect the official to have resided at the capital (Città Vecchia). And indeed tradition, which would make him the first bishop of Malta, seeks his residence where the cathedral of that town now stands; but he may have had a country estate near the seashore. A prominent villa, found near the church of St. Paul ad Mare, but covered up again for protection, is a candidate for identification with the country house of Publius, if one favors the traditional landing place.

Paul and his company stayed three months in Malta. It seems probable that he did not remain inactive here, even though he was under arrest. Whether a Christian group was created through his efforts is, however, unknown. The language barrier may have made it difficult for him to preach the gospel in Malta. There are believed to be traces of Christian influence in second-century art on the island, but the first reference to a churchman from Malta dates from the fifth century.

To Sicily and Italy

The shipwrecked company was not the only one to winter at Malta. There was another Alexandrian vessel which spent the long months there. With this ship the centurion and his party sailed for Sicily, perhaps even before the start of the normal navigation period on March 5. A favorable wind may have tempted them to risk the short run. Their objective, Syracuse, was the principal city and capital of the eastern half of that island; for each half stood under a *quaestor,* and the whole under a *praetor.* Once upon a time Syracuse had been one of the most prosperous and important of Greek colonies, but it sank into poverty and decay under Roman rule in the second century B.C., and had been recovering but slowly since the time of Augustus.

At Syracuse Paul's vessel stayed three days. The wind must meanwhile have become unfavorable, necessitating a wait for a change. When it came they ran on to Rhegium on the Italian coast, probably by tacking back and forth. This city lay hard by the narrowest part of the Strait of Messina. Here were the famous Scylla and Charibdis, the former a rock around the cape north of Rhegium and the latter a whirlpool near Messina. Ships often had to lie at Rhegium for some time to await a favorable wind and avoid dangerous currents. The twin brother gods, Castor and Pollux, were much invoked at this port and appear on its coins. No doubt Paul's Alexandrian ship had them on its prow (ACTS 28:11) as a bid of the shipowner for their favor in the frequent run through these straits.

Advantage was taken of a fortunate south wind to make the passage and reach Puteoli (now Pozzuoli). They had to sail past Pompeii, with great Vesuvius in the background, and Neapolis (Naples) to reach this great

8.15 *Puteoli, landing place of St. Paul in Italy.* (*J. Lane Miller*)

harbor. This was the regular landing place for cargoes destined for Rome. The ruins of the ancient mole, where Paul first stepped on the shores of Italy, are still to be seen there. Otherwise there is not much left of the city of his day, except for the amphitheater, in which Nero once played an actor's role, and the Serapeum.

There were Christians at Puteoli and Paul was permitted by the centurion to spend a week with them. Julius may have had to await instructions from his superiors before proceeding farther. Finally on the eighth day he started for the city with his prisoners.

Along the Appian Way

The journey through the Campagna in the early spring gave Paul a glimpse of Italy. North of Capua, where a great old amphitheater still speaks of Roman days, the road merged with the Appian Way, which ran from Rome to Brundisium on the Adriatic. Marvelous views over the sea were had at some points. Perhaps halt was made for the night at Formiae, a favorite stopping place. The following day they would have gone on and, passing the country estate of the great Cicero as well as his tomb, they would soon have entered a rugged hill country. Emerging from it they would have reached a plain in which the town of Fundi lay. A promontory loomed up forbiddingly ahead of them, but the Roman engineers had carved away

enough of it to permit the road to pass through by the seaside. It was a historic spot, this pass of Lantulae, for here a Roman general had once barred the way against Hannibal. Beyond this pass they came to the town of Terracina on its shining, rocky height overlooking the sea. Here they probably spent the second night.

From this point on the Appian Way left the sea. Two days of marching through the vast Pontine marshes followed. A canal, built by Augustus, now ran beside the highway and permitted hauling of freight and passengers in barges towed by mules. The first lap of the journey through the marshes ended with an overnight stop at the Forum of Appius at the forty-third milestone from Rome. It was an important way station where travelers changed horses and here, too, the canal ended. The Roman poet Horace once satirized what went on at this hangout of boatmen, innkeepers and travelers. But Paul had a pleasant surprise here. His coming had been reported to his friends in Rome and a number of them had hastened forth to meet him. And here at this caravanserai they came together.

The next day at noon the travelers reached the end of the Pontine marshes at a place called Three Taverns, ten miles nearer to Rome. The flimsy buildings have naturally disappeared, so that the exact place where they stood can hardly be identified, but they were in the vicinity of the present Cisterna. Here the second group of Paul's reception committee met him, and once more there was rejoicing over the reunion with former converts, made in Asia Minor, Macedonia, and Greece, who were now living in Rome.

From here on the scene changed. The road led up into the Albanian Mountains. At Aricia, on the shores of the Albanian Lake, the last night's stop was probably made. Here a great Roman viaduct, over which Paul must have passed, still greets the eye. The next morning the party began the last lap of the journey. On the height before

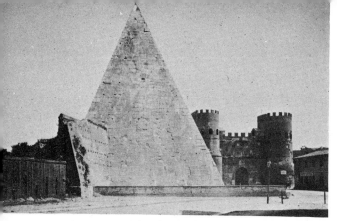

8.16 *Left, Pyramid of Cestius who died in 12 B.C. and right, the Ostian Gate. (Ewing Galloway)*

coming to what is now Albana, they beheld the wide plain of the Campagna lying open before them, and Paul's friends will have pointed out to him where Rome lay in the haze of the distance.

From now on the Appian Way went straight through the plain. On the right and on the left funeral monuments made their appearance. Here lay men of illustrious name, who had raised an Italian town to a martial glory exceeding that ever attained by any other. Along this road many of them had traveled on returning from the wars, to be welcomed with a triumphal celebration on reaching the city. But the prisoner who approached Rome that day, with a retinue of friends and a few soldiers as guards, was destined to carve his name more deeply into the hearts of the men of a coming world-age than any Roman general was able to do.

Rome

Rome at last! The Porta Capena, over which an aqueduct ran, lay open before the travelers. After many weary months Paul entered the world capital. A man who thought in terms of world-wide Christianity, he had made this his greatest objective. For here all threads of the far-flung empire converged; here opportunity would present itself to spread the gospel to a thousand places through those whom, God willing, he would encounter and instruct. As they approached the *Circus Maximus,* the Ostian Way came

in from the left. Out there, though he did not know it, Paul was to find his final resting place.

The merging roads now ran northeasterly. To the left lay the Palatine Hill, on which stood the palaces of the emperors. That of Augustus with the temple of Jupiter, that of Tiberius, and that of Caligula were doubtless pointed out to Paul. They soon crossed the street leading westward to the Forum, around which clustered many of the most important buildings of the city. If they kept along the street, called *Vicus Patricius,* they had on the left the Viminal Hill and on the right the Mons Cispius. One may think of them going straight ahead to the *Castra Praetoriana,* where the centurion Julius would have had to report with his prisoners, and where the charges were examined and the necessary preliminaries attended to. According to another view, however, the centurion Julius was not of the praetorian guard, but of a different class and would first have taken Paul to the Caelian Hill on the right opposite the Palatine Hill, for here the commander of the class in question, the *Princeps Peregrinorum,* is believed to have had his camp. Paul's case would have come before the praetorian council composed of

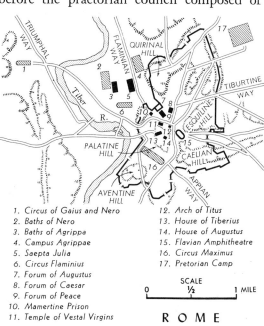

1. Circus of Gaius and Nero
2. Baths of Nero
3. Baths of Agrippa
4. Campus Agrippae
5. Saepta Julia
6. Circus Flaminius
7. Forum of Augustus
8. Forum of Caesar
9. Forum of Peace
10. Mamertine Prison
11. Temple of Vestal Virgins
12. Arch of Titus
13. House of Tiberius
14. House of Augustus
15. Flavian Amphitheatre
16. Circus Maximus
17. Pretorian Camp

SCALE

0   ½   1 MILE

ROME

the *Praefecti in Praetorio* and their aides, and so he would have been brought to the *Castra Praetoriana* later. This must be the praetorium referred to in Philippians 1:13 in the Greek (the A.V. renders "palace," the R.S.V. "praetorian guard").

The legal case against Paul was not of a serious nature, and so he was allowed much liberty while awaiting trial. He was merely provided with a single guard and allowed to seek his own lodging. On the third day he summoned the local leaders of the Jews, who disclaimed having received any letters about him from Jerusalem and were willing to hear his message. The meeting broke up, as so often, with some in favor of the new gospel and others against it. Therewith Paul considered himself to have done his duty by the Jews of Rome and declared, as he had done at Corinth (ACTS 18:6), that he would confine himself henceforth to the gentiles.

For two years, while he waited for his case to come up, his lodging was the scene of religious instruction. It was the great opportunity of his life and he hoped to carry his witness before Caesar himself. One may surmise that his purpose was to win for Christianity the benefit of being a religion recognized by the state. Since 54 A.D. the sovereign was young Nero. There can be no doubt that Paul's case came before him, for the message that he received in Acts 27:24 definitely presupposes this. If only light charges stood against him, as Acts 26:31 declares, we must infer that he was set free. In the letter he wrote to the Philippians during his captivity he was confident of being vindicated (PHIL. 1:25; 2:23–24). He succeeded in making converts among the slaves of Nero (PHIL. 4:22). The martyrdom of Paul must have come about, therefore, in a second captivity and on graver charges.

A Possible Journey to Spain

When Paul was in Ephesus he wrote to the Corinthians that he was looking forward to preaching the gospel in lands beyond theirs (2 COR. 16:16). Later, he wrote the Romans from Corinth and said that he would visit them when he went to Spain (ROM. 15:24). Here the magnificent scope of Paul's missionary idea stands forth—from the Cilician Gates to the Pillars of Hercules, that was his course! Rome was only a brief stop on the last part of the way. In him lived a spirit akin to that of the mighty empire builders like Alexander, but infinitely more noble.

Paul uses the name Hispania for Spain. That name had only recently gotten into Greek use, though the Romans had employed it since the second century B.C. Strabo, the Greek geographer, born about 30 B.C., still speaks of Spain as Iberia—the land of the Iberus River (now the *Ebro*), that enters the Mediterranean near Tortosa. Spain was long in Carthaginian hands, and in fact provided the base from which Hannibal was able to invade Italy in his grandiose crossing of the Alps in the second Punic War (218–205 B.C.). The Romans, however, invaded and occupied southern Spain, terminating the Carthaginian hold on the country. Pompey, Caesar, and Augustus in succession later completed the conquest of the rest of the Iberian peninsula.

Three rivers run through southern Spain, in a southwesterly direction and parallel to each other, to enter the Atlantic. The most westerly was called the Tagus, the central one the Anas and the easterly one the Baetis. Near the mouth of the latter river once lay Tartessus, held by many to be the Tarshish of Old Testament times (page 222); but in Paul's day it no longer existed. Farther up the river, however, lay Hispalis (Seville) and Corduba (Cordoba). If one spoke of Hispania, one thought first of all the country round about Hispalis, for the former name

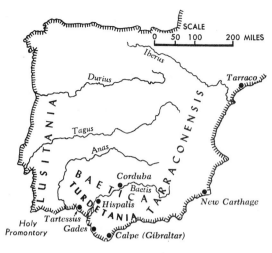

FINAL SCENE OF PAUL'S MINISTRY ?

is derived from the latter (with a slight phonetic change of *l* to *n*). Good-sized freighters could ascend the river as far as Hispalis. This Baetis River country, or Turdetania, had a glamour in Paul's time. It was blessed with a goodly climate and had a teeming population—Strabo speaks of two hundred cities! Hispalis and Corduba were Roman colonies, and that meant that there were numerous Greek-speaking people there, for Rome had enslaved the Greeks by the hundreds of thousands. It is in this area that one must look for the lost footprints of Paul. This was near enough to the Pillars of Hercules.

Since of old that term had marked the farthest point west, the "ends of the earth." Like many another name that made sense when it was first used "Pillars of Hercules" was mystifying to later ages, and Strabo gives various theories that were put forward to explain it. Some held it applied to the Rock of Calpe (Gibraltar) and the opposite Mauretanian mountain Abylax; others identified it with two islands in the straits area; still others held it had originally referred to two stelas, inscribed with ancient writing, which Hercules set up at Gades, to mark this as the farthest point reached by him in his expedition to the setting sun. For Gades, or Gadeira (Cadiz), lying in the Atlantic mouth of the straits, was an old Phoenician

colony, and still had a population chiefly of Semitic origin. In this area with its mild climate and gentle west winds Homer had sought the "Isles of the Blessed."

A scientific geographer, of course, knew that Gades was not at the end of the world. Strabo asserts that the "Holy Promontory" (Cape St. Vincent) on the west coast of Spain "is the westernmost point, not only of Europe, but of the entire inhabited world." But such advanced knowledge is not to be expected of the average person. The old traditional view that Gades was the ultimate settlement of the West will have prevailed in Paul's mind as in everyman's. One would like to think of him visiting Gades. But as at Malta, Paul would probably have been unable to understand the Phoenician dialect spoken or to make himself understood.

The view that Paul actually undertook a Spanish journey is strongly supported by the words of Clement of Rome (*c.* 95 A.D.), who may have known him personally and who certainly had rich information about him.

> Through jealousy and strife Paul showed the way to the prize of endurance; seven times he was in bonds, he was exiled, he was stoned, he taught righteousness to all the world, and when he had reached the limits of the west he gave his testimony before the rulers, and thus passed from the world and was taken up into the Holy Place—the greatest example of endurance.

Clement would certainly not have regarded his own city of Rome as the "limits of the west." The phrase quoted above from Strabo and the remarks on the Pillars of Hercules show where those limits lay.

In addition, second-century sources, notably the *Canon Muratori,* speak specifically of Paul's going to Spain. But whatever traces may have existed of Paul's work in Spain, they were wiped out through all the vicissitudes of history affecting that land when Rome declined.

462

An interesting question is raised by Clement's mention of an exile of Paul. This could only have been an exile by Roman decree, and lends strong support to the view that banishment was the outcome of his trial at Rome. Since Augustus there were two kinds of exile—deportation and relegation. Deportation meant exile for life under military surveillance and with loss of citizenship and property. The deported person was usually sent to an island: Gyarus (Guira, one of the Cyclades in the Aegean Sea), Sardinia and an oasis in the Libyan desert were considered the worst places one could be banished to; Crete, Cyprus and Rhodes were not considered too bad. Sometimes a whole group could be deported; thus Tiberius sent 4000 freedmen to Sardinia for adhering to Jewish and Egyptian "superstition." Relegation was a milder form of exile. The person affected was merely banished from a specified district, either to a prescribed place or with permission to choose a place; and the term might be for life or for a period. It seems quite clear that Paul's exile must have been a relegation, banishing him for a time from Judaea or Rome. It is very probable that he would have chosen to go to Spain.

Crete and Nicopolis

Did Paul make still other journeys after leaving Spain? The answer is intimately bound up with problems critical and historical posed by the so-called "Pastoral Epistles": 1 and 2 Timothy and Titus. The Second Epistle to Timothy presupposes another captivity of Paul, and the postscript found in some younger manuscripts and quoted in the Authorized Version (but omitted in the Revised Standard Version) says that "it was written from Rome, when Paul was brought before Nero the second time." These Epistles mention journeys that do not fit well with those reported in Acts, and so are assigned by many to this time after the Spanish journey. We need not here go into the chronological aspect of this matter, but can confine ourselves to the supplementary geographical items provided by these Epistles. The Epistle to Titus refers to a sojourn of Paul in Crete; he left Titus there to tend to affairs of church organization, but this helper is to follow him to Nicopolos and spend the winter with him there (Tit. 1:5; 3:12). These two points thus enter into the field of vision for the geography of the life of Paul.

Crete was a large place and promised contact with North Africa, for the island, which is 156 miles long and 30 miles wide, was joined to the latter region in a single Senatorial province "Cyrenaica and Crete." It was a fertile island and hence thickly populated. Here once had flourished the great Minoan civilization, of which the palaces of Cnossus, excavated by the modern archaeologist, have provided a vivid record. According to the Iliad, Crete had a hundred cities, of which seven, headed by Cnossus and walled Gortyna, are named. Gortyna lost its walls somewhere in history, however, for it was not thus protected in Strabo's time. But it had for a while been more important than Cnossus, for it is among the places directed by a Roman consul to take a friendly attitude toward the Maccabean state (1 Macc. 15:23) and to extradite fugitives from Judaea to Simon Maccabeus (141 b.c.). In Strabo's day the chief cities were Cnossus, Gortyna, and Cydonia. Only the last named lay on the coast, more specifically on the western end of the island. It might have been the natural point of entry for Paul returning from Spain. But there is no further information about this Cretan ministry.

An interesting question is raised by the mention of Nicopolis, whither Titus is to go from Crete. A postscript to the Epistle of Titus that is included in the Authorized Ver-

8.17 *Ruins of Phaestus, one of the great cities of Crete's early days. (Ewing Galloway)*

sion claims that the letter was written "from Nicopolis in Macedonia." This is manifestly inaccurate, since Paul speaks only of planning to go there, but it gives an idea as to where Nicopolis was sought by tradition. The only Nicopolis of that period passably fitting that description was the one in Aetolia, which was west of Macedonia, so that someone thinking of it from a vantage-point like Mount Athos might inexactly place it in Macedonia. This must be the city meant.

Paul might even have gone there at an earlier occasion than after his first captivity, for in writing to the Romans he says that he has preached the Gospel "from Jerusalem and round about unto Illyricum" (ROM. 15:19). He does not say that he preached in Illyricum, but implies that he had gotten to a point close to it, which can only mean Aetolia. That was another journey the author of Acts failed to mention.

If he came to Nicopolis in Aetolia, Paul found himself among Greek-speaking people in a beautiful new city. For Nicopolis was the fruit of an emperor's whim. In September, 31 B.C., Octavian had encamped for a night at what then was a bare spot on the cape on the north side of the Gulf of Ambracia (Arta). On the opposite cape to the south lay Actium, with its temple of Apollo. There his adversary Mark Antony had found more comfortable quarters. The next day the decisive battle between the fleets of these rival commanders was fought. A sudden storm put Antony's sailors at a disadvantage. The

Battle of Actium, as it is known to history, ended in victory for Octavian, the master of Italy, who now achieved the rule of the Adriatic and Greece. While Antony escaped to the Near East and still had the possibility of making a comeback from there, events proved that Actium was the turning point.

Augustus (Octavian) certainly regarded it in that light. He decided to found a city on the cape where he had camped, and named it Nicopolis, "City of Victory." It was not built or organized in the Roman manner, but in the fashion of the Hellenistic cities, and was to be a center of a revival of Greek life. He joined together a number of existing towns in adjacent localities (in a so-called *synoikismos*), transferring the population to this new center. He gave it freedom and autonomy, and a fifth of the votes in the Federation of the Greek States. A new temple of Apollo was built by Augustus at Actium after the model of the one at Olympia, and a quadrennial festival instituted, whose games ranked with the four Greek games—the Olympian, Pythian, Isthmian, and Nemean. One can see, therefore, that Nicopolis was important for a time, and that the thought of going there could have had great attraction for Paul. At the same time it was a place where the cult of emperor-worship must have been prominently carried on. It is quite conceivable that Paul may have gotten into trouble there on that score, and have been taken to Rome for a second trial.

The Christian leaders, when confronted with the demand to worship the Caesars or die, answered in the spirit which the Book of Daniel had instilled into Jewish hearts (DAN. 3:17–18). We must suppose that both Paul and Peter perished in consequence of the policy put forward by Nero, of subjecting those accused of being Christians to this test, of requiring them to sacrifice to Divus Julius, Divus Augustus, Divus Tiberius, and Divus Claudius. Paul was doubtless put to death with the sword, the customary mode of execution for a Roman citizen.

CHAPTER XXII

GEOGRAPHY OF THE REVELATION

THERE ARE NO RECORDS in the New Testament describing the progress of Christianity in the last third of the first century. But the Book of Revelation gives us a glimpse of the Asia Minor scene a few years before the century closed. For that book was written during or right after the persecution that came upon the churches of this area at the end of the reign of the Roman emperor Domitian (81–96 A.D.).

Patmos

The author has incorporated in the Revelation a vision describing Christ as writing letters to the angelic patrons of seven Asia Minor churches. He even quotes their text verbatim. They are not private letters, but rather public—each congregation can know what was said to the others as well as to itself. In introducing his story of this vision, the author of The Revelation states,

> "I, John, . . . was in the isle that is called Patmos, for the word of God, and for the testimony of Jesus Christ." (REV. 1:9 A.V.)

> "I, John, . . . was on the island called Patmos on account of the word of God and the testimony of Jesus." (REV. 1:9 R.S.V.)

The early Church Fathers assert that John was banished under Domitian, and his own words suggest it was for preaching and for confessing Christ.

We have already seen that there were two types of exile, deportation and relegation.

This would seem to be an instance of deportation to an island. It does not seem to have been the intention of the governor of Asia at this time to condemn Christians to death. A single martyr is all that we hear of in the Revelation (2:13); otherwise only arrests are in prospect (2:10). But deportation to an island, for those of the lower social level, was essentially life imprisonment at hard labor. The individual wore chains, was poorly fed and clothed, slept on the bare ground and worked under the lash of a military overseer. If one is unwilling to believe that anything but a death penalty could have been decreed under Roman law by the governor, then one may suppose that John took refuge on Patmos secretly to escape the persecution.

Patmos is an island lying off the coast of Asia Minor. In recent times its natives have been noted for their skill in seamanship. Strabo, who mentions it as one of the Sporadic group of Aegean Islands, has no comment on its natives such as he offers on the inhabitants of nearby Leros, who, he tells us, were of ill repute. Patmos is ten miles long and six miles wide in the north, and contains three groups of volcanic hills, of which the highest, St. Elias, rises to a height of 800 feet. The shore line is jagged, with many cliffs and precipices. Palm trees abounded here once, and in the Middle Ages it was even called Palmosa, "the one rich in palms," but it is now quite bare. On the eastern side the island is nearly pierced in the middle by the deep Bay of Scala. As one follows the road from this landing place to the modern town, which lies a mile and a half uphill to the south, one passes a grotto, which is supposedly the one where John had his visions. But since the island was deserted during the Dark Ages owing to the pirates infesting this area, there is little likelihood of any continuity of tradition. Above the modern town, on the top of the hill, is the Monastery of St. John, which looks for all the world like a mediaeval fortress. To the monks is due the

new beginning of life here on the island; the monastery was founded in 1088 by grant of the Byzantine emperor, Alexius Comnenus.

But the ancient town of John's day did not lie under the monastery. It was situated on the narrow isthmus between the Bay of Scala and the Bay of Merika on the west. Here there are still ruins of the citadel, and here it must have been where John went forth and returned with the chain gang and the hard taskmaster. The book looks back upon the experience, however, and so it seems probable that he was freed from this captivity under the new emperor, Nerva (96–98 A.D.), as Eusebius claims.

But it was on Patmos that his mind was occupied with the vast perspective of time and eternity, with the kingdom of God and that of the beast. But at the same time John also was concerned with the congregations of the mainland close at hand. The sheaf of letters addressed to them show him using both the shepherd's rod and staff. He accords high praise to Ephesus, Smyrna and Philadelphia; praise qualified by warning to Pergamum and Thyatira; and sharp criticism or warning to Sardis and Laodicea. These cities, in the order in which they come up in the text, lie in a rough circle that swings north from Ephesus and returns to it. It seems natural that John should start with this city, the most important of all of them in that day. But since we have sufficiently dealt with Ephesus in connection with Paul's ministry there, we may turn forthwith to the second.

Smyrna

This city lay across the peninsula at the next great bay north of Ephesus. It is praised by Strabo as the fairest city of "Ionia" (an old term embracing a league of twelve cities, supposedly founded by Ionian Greeks). A hill named Matusia, lying close to the sea on the western side of the city, was included in its area, while in the south Mount Pagos, rising 400 feet, provided a site for its acropolis. The residential part of the city then stretched from the slopes of Pagos toward the bay. It had a nearly-closed inner harbor, which, however, having been completely sanded up, now lies under the bazaars of present-day Smyrna (Izmir). The rectangular division of the city's quarters (arranged according to the so-called Hippodamian system), the well-paved streets, and the great colonnades were a striking sight. A street called "The Golden" was particularly noteworthy; it reminds one of the street of the eternal city (REV. 21:21).

The topography of old Smyrna can be reconstructed only tentatively, for there are but slight remains of its ancient temples and public buildings. The modern city covers the site, and in all such cases the ancient towns were gradually dismantled as convenient sources of building materials. The temple of Aphrodite Stratonikis, where the documents were kept and which had the right of asylum, is believed to have lain near the present Rothschild Hospital, while the Metröon, or temple of the Mother of the Gods of Mount Sipylos, was situated toward the east. Elsewhere in the town was a temple in honor of the emperor Tiberius and his mother Julia Augusta; a number of cities had contended for the privilege of having the temple, but Smyrna had won out, partly because of its importance and partly because of its pro-Roman record in earlier days. And of course, there were a number of other temples in and around Smyrna.

The agora or market place has been found and excavated. The stadium lay on the western slope of Mount Pagos and its location can still be traced despite the modern structures covering part of it. Here occurred the martyrdom of Polycarp in 155 A.D., one of the most important of early Christian martyrdoms, since this bishop of Smyrna was a great figure in the Church. The theater, which could seat 20,000 people, lay on the northern slope of Mount Pagos. Hard by was the Stratoniceum named after the wife of the Seleucid ruler, Antiochus II. It was a colonnade offering protection against rain and the heat of the sun. The walled acropolis overlooking the city gave it the effect of wearing a crown, as already observed by some ancient writers and as seen by John as well, when he holds out to Smyrna the promise of a very different crown—"the crown of life."

Smyrna had a glamour in the eyes of the Greek world as the alleged birthplace of Homer. It even had a hall or temple dedicated to the poet and containing his portrait, the Homerium. But the Smyrna in which Homer may have lived did not stand on the site of Roman Smyrna. It had lain several miles away at the northeast end of the bay, by the banks of the Meles stream (probably the present Chalka Punar). The old city was destroyed in the period of the Lydian domination. Alexander the Great planned to rebuild Smyrna, but did not live to carry out his purpose; his successors, notably Lysimachos, executed the plan, choosing the new site at the foot of Mount Pagos in place of the steep and lofty crag.

Roman Smyrna had three gates—one leading out to the northwest to the coast, one leading eastward to the city of Magnesia at the Sipylos Mount, and one leading south toward Ephesus. It was an important place for the economic life of Asia Minor.

The letter quoted by John reflects the fact that there were Jews at Smyrna and that they were particularly hostile to Christianity. The poverty of the Christian group is recognized, but stands in contrast to its wealth in the spiritual things. A brief persecution impends, but the crown of life will be the prize for its fidelity. Jewish hatred continued long here, for when Polycarp was martyred the Jews even violated the Sabbath to carry wood to the stadium for a pyre to burn the bishop.

Pergamum

The third church addressed by John is that of Pergamum (a latinized form of Greek Pergamos or Pergamon). This city lay to the north of Smyrna, on the road from the

8.18 *Pergamum, the Gymnasium Terrace.* (*Courtesy F. K. Doerner*)

latter port to Adramyttium (ACTS 27:2). It guarded the next river valley, that of the Caicus, and the region in which it lay belonged to Mysia. Pergamum was not on the sea, but rather fifteen miles from it, between two branch streams of the Caicus called the Selinus and the Cetius. But ships could ascend the Caicus so that the location was not too inconvenient. Pergamum had attained sudden importance in the third century B.C., when its governor seized the treasure which Lysimachos, one of the successors of Alexander, had stored there. With Attalus I (241 B.C.) it had become a kingdom, after that individual had won fame as defender of Greek civilization against the inroads of the barbarous Celts or Galatians. Co-operating with the Romans in their struggle against Hannibal, Attalus I was awarded the Seleucid dominions west of the Taurus. But Rome did not trust him too far and hence did not allow him to absorb the Galatian kingdom; its separate existence was recognized and supported. In 133 B.C. Attalus III bequeathed the Pergamene kingdom to Rome. Early in the first century A.D. the Romans established a "province of Asia," substantially identical with the kingdom of Pergamum and with that city as the provincial capital. In John's time Pergamum still held this position and was the residence of the Proconsul.

Roman Pergamum was a splendid city. When Pliny calls it "the most distinguished city of Asia" he is probably thinking of it in the light of its historical importance in the Hellenistic period. More recently the provincial council had built here the official Temple of Roma and Augustus for its meeting place. When the letter of John to the city's angel refers to the throne of Satan being at Pergamum, he is evidently thinking of the place as the seat of the Roman governor; the Persian satraps of old were sometimes described as occupying thrones, and an Oriental writer could well view a Roman governor in the same light. As the center of the province of Asia, Pergamum was also the place where the state religion was most thoroughly promoted. That state religion, as we have seen, involved the worship of the emperors. The specific mention in the Pergamum letter of the martyrdom of a Christian named Antipas (REV. 2:13) is especially noteworthy; he may have been the first to suffer martyrdom in Asia under the Roman policy established by Nero. Here, if anywhere, an example had to be made.

Pergamum lay on a tongue of land that drops off southward from the thousand-foot level to the valley of the Caicus. On the side toward the Cetius River there is a steep declivity, while on the side toward the Selinus there are gentle slopes with fertile farm lands. On the height, of course, stood the acropolis, and on the slope below it the older part of the city. Excavations carried on at Pergamum by the Berlin Museum since 1878 have revealed much of the glory of the city and notably of the acropolis. On the most prominent spot and visible from afar stood the temple of Athena, the patron goddess of the city. Its priestesses were highly respected, and memorial inscriptions to some of them stress the fact that they had conducted their office in a manner worthy of the goddess and of their native land. North and east of this temple were colonnades; behind the easterly one lay the palace of the old kings, while behind the northern one was the famous library, rivaling the one at Alexandria in Egypt. Parchment was raised to high prominence in bookmaking at this city, and so the city name lives on forever in our word "parchment" (Latin *pergamentum*).

On a terrace below this topmost area, and south of the Athena temple, stood a gigantic altar of Zeus, which was one of the Seven Wonders of the World because of its marvelous sculptures portraying Zeus' battle against the primeval giants. Excavated by a Berlin Museum expedition this was until recently one of the treasures of that institution, in which it was built up anew. On the next lower level below the altar lay a colonnade-surrounded area with the temple of Dionysus in the west and the agora in the east. The old city wall was reached at the Dionysus temple, and there was a gate here through which one entered into the southern end of the theater-terrace. If one turned and followed that terrace, one came to the theater, which lay directly below the Athena temple.

In Roman times the god Asklepios had gained the chief popular favor at Pergamum and is sometimes referred to as "the Pergamene god." His temple was devoted to the cure of diseases, and many sufferers from all over came there to get help, medical and magical, from doctor and priest. The biographer of the wonder-worker Apollonius of Tyana calls Pergamum "the holiest place of Asia," for it was an ancient Lourdes or St. Anne de Beaupré.

The newer parts of the city naturally had further installations of various kinds, notably those for the kind of amusements favored in Roman times—a more modern theater, a stadium and an amphitheater. In the stadium, probably, the martyr Antipas met his fate. John's letter praises the congregation for its loyalty at this time, and chides it only for tolerating the teaching of the "Nicolaitanes" (cf. REV. 1:6 R.S.V., Nicolaitans), the followers of a certain Nicolaos, whom the early Church Fathers would identify with the Nicolas mentioned in Acts 6:5. The same group was also operative at Ephesus.

Thyatira

The fourth city honored with a letter from St. John is Thyatira, which lay on the road from Pergamum to Sardis, on a branch of the Hermus River called the Lycus. The city has a particular interest as the home of a woman who played such an important role in Paul's ministry—Lydia the seller of purple goods, who aided him at Philippi (ACTS 16:14). Since she was a proselyte, there must have been Jews in Thyatira. Seleucus I, who founded the city, settled many Jews in "Asia," and allegedly gave them citizenship rights in the cities he founded. Thyatira was usually considered a Lydian city, and the woman "Lydia" from Thyatira represents an interesting example of a person named after a region. In those days Thyatira was becoming a manufacturing town. More trade guilds from this place are known from the Greek inscriptions than from any other city of "Asia." We hear of linenworkers, woolworkers, tailors, leatherworkers, tanners, dyers, potters, bakers, bronzeworkers, and slave dealers. It is unlikely that Lydia was in Philippi in Macedonia on purely private business; she must have represented a guild and have been an agent in Greece for Thyatiran textiles for women's wear. The color particularly associated with cloth or dresses from Thyatira was a bright red ("purple" is a word used for several colors in the ancient sources). This dye was derived from the madder-root found in this region.

Thyatira's transition to a commercial city was partly due to the change in the political situation brought by Roman domination and partly to its location. It had originally been established as a military outpost, either for or against Pergamum, depending on who held it. It occupied a key position, guarding the approach to the Caicus Valley from the Hermus Valley or vice versa. This strategic

469

point had not, however, been endowed by nature with a commanding site suitable for a great fortress. Primarily a garrison town, it naturally was as well fortified as its location permitted; but it was its fate to be taken and retaken in the wars of the Hellenistic era. But when the *pax Romana* descended on this region and warfare ceased, there was no longer any need for a military post here. Then the fact that the city stood on the trade route leading north to Troas led to the commercial and industrial development already mentioned.

As a Hellenistic-Roman city, Thyatira had all the equipment for civic, religious and amusement purposes. But archaeologically we can know only little about this town, for the modern *Ak-Hissar* occupies the site, and so the remains of antiquity are covered up or obliterated.

The particular patron of Thyatira was a heroic figure of uncertain origin named Tyrimnos, who is portrayed as riding forth on his charger with a battle-ax over his shoulder. This hero was merged with Apollo and subesequently appears on coins as a standing rather than a mounted figure, but still carrying the ax. He was a "propolis" god, having his temple outside the city walls. The goddess most prominently worshipped was Artemis; curiously the highpriest of the "Pythian-Tyrimnaean-Apollo" and the highpriestess of the "Boreitene Artemis" (as these deities were officially called) were husband and wife.

The importance of guilds was great in a place like Thyatira. It was impossible to thrive in business without being a member of one, but at the same time this membership confronted Christians with grave problems of conscience, owing to established heathen customs connected with the life of these societies. Thyatira is rebuked in the letter for tolerating a prophetess, who is called Jezebel, one who leads the people of God astray. It seems likely that she was of the same mind as the *Nicolaitanes* of Ephe-

sus and Pergamum (REV. 2:6, 15). Her position must have been one endorsing guild membership and telling Christian people to be unconcerned about regulations laid down by the Apostles in Acts 15:23–29. Apart from this situation, however, the congregation receives high praise.

Sardis

Following the northward road one comes next to Sardis. It was a name out of a dead past, for Sardis had once been the capital of a kingdom that ruled most of Asia Minor. Its best known ruler was the fabulously wealthy king Croesus, who fell from the pinnacle of power almost overnight in 546 B.C., when he lost his kingdom to half-nomadic tribesmen from the Persis, led by a man of destiny named Cyrus. Here subsequently resided the Persian satraps, and here was the terminus of the imperial Persian road from Susa, over which the hosts of a Xerxes traveled en route to the invasion of Greece. Sardis surrendered to Alexander the Great; later it was the residence of the Seleucid governors of Asia Minor. Liberated by the Romans from the Seleucids in the battle of Magnesia in 190 B.C., it was given to the Pergamene kingdom and became Roman with the latter in 133 B.C. In the first century A.D. it was still the metropolis of a group of Hermus-Valley cities. In 17 A.D. it suffered a terrific earthquake. The emperor Tiberius not only remitted its taxes for five years but contributed ten million sesterces toward rebuilding the stricken city. Its long history ended in 1402 A.D. with its destruction by Tamerlane, the great Asiatic conqueror who invaded Asia Minor, after taking Baghdad and Damascus.

The Sardis of old Oriental days lay in what seemed an impregnable position on a spur of Mount Tmolus. Past it on the west flowed the Pactolus stream, on its way to join the Hermus River a few miles to the north. There was not much room on the hilltop, and so only the acropolis could perch there, while the residential town lay at its feet. It is an arduous climb up this hill, whose summit is 800 feet above the plain, and there was only a single avenue of access by a steep and winding path from the south. The fortress on the hill was thus a place of refuge in peril, rather than a place where people lived. The city's fall to Cyrus seems to have been effected after the manner of Jebusite Jerusalem's fall to David: skillful climbers scaled the crag undetected at a point believed so secure as to require no guarding.

8.19 *Artemis Temple at Sardis. (Courtesy Ahmet Donmez)*

In Roman times, of course, the defensive position of Sardis no longer had any meaning. The city of Hellenistic days had lain at the foot of the acropolis on the west, but the Roman city occupied a terrace on the north. The chief temple was that of Artemis, the goddess identified with the native Cybele. It lay west of the acropolis near the banks of the Pactolus and had an area of 327 feet by 163 feet. It was not destroyed by the hand of man, but rather by earthquakes and decay. On the sacred way leading to the temple still crouch the flanking lions. The day was to come when the goddess Artemis was ousted and the temple turned into a place of Christian worship. The excavations carried on here by an American expedition reveal how the sign of the cross was engraved in the temple in many places, indicating the new use to which it was put.

The letter of Christ to the angel of Sardis conveys a solemn warning to its congregation, which, though having the reputation of being a living one, is declared spiritually dead, notwithstanding that there are a few in it who are worthy. The warning apparently was of some avail. For soon, in the second century, Sardis was to have a great spiritual leader in the person of Bishop Melito, one of the great lights in early Church history.

Philadelphia

If, instead of continuing north from Sardis toward Adramyttium, one turned east on the road that leads to the Euphrates crossing, one came to Philadelphia. This city was founded by and named after Attalus II of Pergamum (159–138 B.C.), who was called Philadelphus, "brother-loving," because of his loyalty toward his predecessor Eumenes II. The city lay in the valley of the Cogamis River, a tributary of the Hermus. Its site may have been chosen with an eye to its excellent defensive position, for it was situated on a broad hill which slopes up toward Mount Tmolus, though it was not destined to have need of this strength in Hellenistic-Roman times. But tragic days were to come in the fourteenth century, when it played a heroic role as a free Christian city in a land overwhelmed by Turkish armies, and when it twice resisted grim sieges, till in the end it was done to death by a combination of Turk and Byzantine soldiers.

Philadelphia was founded as a Hellenistic city to spread the gospel of Hellenism in the heart of a barbarous land, and it fulfilled that mission with great success. The letter to the angel of the church of Philadelphia says to this city, "I have set before thee an open door," assigning to it a new role in a different mission. Its gateway-role is apparent from its location, for from Philadelphia the road ascends to Phrygia and the great central plateau of Asia Minor that forms the main land-mass of that region. The railroad engineers of modern times still considered this the natural point of entry into the interior and laid their tracks here.

Like Sardis, Philadelphia suffered fearfully

in the earthquake of 17 A.D. Strabo, who wrote a few years later, states that the seismic shocks continued for some time and kept the population in terror, so that people lived in huts in the countryside. Since it shared in the bounty of Tiberius, which was conveyed by his adopted son and heir, Germanicus, it assumed the name of Neo-Caesarea for a while. Archaeologically its history is very much a blank. The modern town of Ala Sheher lies on the site. Most of the information about ancient Philadelphia rests on literary references, the coins of the city and a few inscriptions.

The church of Philadelphia was still young and apparently in no great danger of persecution. There were Jews in the city, but though they are harshly judged as a "synagogue of Satan," that criticism seems to rest more on their disloyalty to Jewish principles than on their hostility to Christianity.

Laodicea

If one left the west-east Hermus Valley route at Philadelphia and struck southward by a crossroad leading to the Maeander Valley, one passed Hierapolis of Phrygia (Col. 4:13) and then after six miles came to Laodicea. Here the road met the main west-east trade route of those days, coming up from Ephesus.

Laodicea was situated on a spur of the hills adjoining the valley of the Lycus (a branch of the Maeander) on the south, and a smaller stream, the Asopos, passed by on the west. South of it rose Mount Salbakos and farther to the east Mount Kadmos, summits over 8000 feet high. The city was founded by the Seleucid ruler Antiochus II (261–246 B.C.) and named after his queen Laodice. It was essentially a garrison city for the purpose of strengthening the Seleucid hold in this region. Among those settled here in the course of time were numerous Jews, though the city of Apamea farther to the west, beyond Colossae (see page 449), had five times as many. Laodicea had grown greatly since the Roman

annexation and was highly prosperous. When it was hard hit by an earthquake in 60 A.D., it did not ask help from the emperor, but proudly repaired its damage out of its own pocket. The boast of prosperity and complete self-sufficiency that the letter to the Laodicean church attributes to it (REV. 3:17) echoes the spirit of the city itself in that earlier crisis. Laodicea was a center of banking and exchange. A great source of wealth lay in the glossy black wool produced by a highly developed breed of sheep (now extinct) raised in this region in those times, and in the manufacture of garments from this superfine wool. Perhaps John's counsel to buy from Christ "gold tried in the fire that thou mayest be rich" and "white raiment that thou mayest be clothed" is suggested by way of contrast to its position in exchange and in the textile trade. Near Laodicea, furthermore, was a great medical school, and a drug called "Phrygian powder" was developed there for treatment of eye-diseases. John's recommendation to Laodiceans to obtain "salve to anoint your eyes that you may see" seems to hint of knowledge of Laodicea's place in the pharmacological trade.

While we hold it certain that Paul passed this way he evidently did not do any missionary work at Laodicea (Col. 2:7), though his assistant, Epaphras, may have (Col. 1:7). But Paul wrote the Laodiceans a letter (Col. 4:16). A postscript appended to the First Epistle to Timothy (omitted in the R.S.V.) claims that this letter was written from Laodicea, metropolis of Phrygia, and thus would seem to imply a later personal visit of Paul to this church. But this postscript is of too late origin to have much weight. The city, however, was the leading bishopric of Phrygia in the early Christian centuries. An Epistle to the Laodiceans, allegedly written by Paul, has come down in Latin, but represents a late attempt to supply the lost letter to this congregation.

Hellenistic-Roman Laodicea is a ruined site today. No thorough exploration of it has as yet been attempted, nor are the remains very impressive. This is due to the fact that its surface remains have been carried off since the eleventh century to build the city of Denizli, which lies six miles away at the foot of Mount Salbakos.

Armageddon

The visions that follow in the Revelation are partly concerned with the celestial scene and partly with the terrestrial. One of the latter, at least, must arouse some curiosity from the geographical angle—that of 16:12-16. The visionary sees the sixth of seven angels pour his bowl on the great River Euphrates. The waters are dried up in consequence, "that the way of the kings of the east might be prepared" (REV. 16:12). The coming of these kings from the east (rather than from the north, as in older prophecy) was suggested by the Parthian menace. For the pouring out of the bowl on the river, presumably the point of the great Euphrates crossing into Syria is the one the seer has in mind. Unclean spirits are then sent out—but rather surprisingly not just to the kings from the east, but to the kings of the whole world, to assemble them for battle on the great day of the Lord Almighty.

> "And he gathered them together into a place called in the Hebrew tongue Armageddon." (REV. 16:16)

The matter is not pursued further in this connection, but is resumed in Revelation 19:19, where "Faithful and True" on his white charger leads the celestial cavalry against the kings of the earth and the demoniac triad that convoked them.

Armageddon is the mobilization point, not necessarily the battlefield. One could suppose, therefore, that it was imagined as lying north of the Euphrates, which the mobilized army of the eastern kings is to cross dry-shod. That may have been the original meaning of the material used by

John (for he is heavily dependent on previous apocalyptic prophecy), but he has broadened the scope of the earlier prediction: Not only the eastern kings, of whom Ezekiel spoke (chapters 38-39), but those of *all the earth* are to assemble. He may thus be transferring the mustering place to a point south of the Euphrates, in Syria or even Palestine. But the matter remains vague. Here the name Armageddon takes on great importance as possibly providing a localization. A widespread interpretation holds that this Hebrew phrase means "the mountain [*har*] of Megiddo," the old Canaanite city which lay at the edge of the Plain of Esdraelon. General Allenby, because of a victory won nearby over the Turks in 1918, has become Allenby of Armageddon. Since the *tell* of old Megiddo can hardly be termed a mountain or provide a place for congregating more than a regiment, it is held that Mount Carmel is referred to in this veiled manner, for its slopes come down this far. But there is no reason in apocalyptic tradition to look for decisive events in this vicinity. Nor is it likely that in John's time or even in that of Jesus there was any knowledge of the name Megiddo, except as it occurred in Biblical history. The place was long since desolate and forgotten. Other towns near it held the limelight. The spelling Armageddon in our translations, furthermore, does not accurately reproduce the Greek original, which has *Armagedon*. In the Septuagint translation the name Megiddo is spelled Mageddo. The single *d* and the final *n* in (Ar-) magedon are unfavorable to a comparison with it. Greek transcriptions of Hebrew or Aramaic words sometimes cause great difficulty, because one cannot always be sure as to the identity of one or more of the underlying Semitic consonants, and it is possible that the *g* is used here for an entirely different letter which the Greek alphabet does not have. It would be tedious to consider here the various solutions of this name that need to be weighed by the philologist.

Only new texts like the Dead Sea Scrolls can bring clarification. We will merely hazard the thought here that Magedon is more apt to be an appellative than a true geographical name. In view of the deep influence which Ezekiel's Gog prophecy (EZEK. 38) had on apocalypticists, one is inclined to seek the solution of the name in the sphere of ideas expressed or called forth by it.

It may be of interest to note that a Qumran scroll fragment, published by P. Milik in 1956 and giving the Aramaic original of a page from the Testament of the Twelve Patriarchs (a work of the second to third century B.C.), shows that some apocalypticists localized events of great importance in the vicinity of Mount Hermon. The city of Abel-maim (2 CHRON. 16:4), otherwise called Abel-beth-maacah, is mentioned in that connection.

Jerusalem the Golden

Jerusalem had obtained an incomparable place in the affections of the Jewish people. It seemed impossible to them, and to Jewish Christians that the culminating events in the history of the Kingdom of God should not take place there. The Holy City and the Holy Land round about it—were not these fixed realities of Old Testament prophecy? Even the fall of Jerusalem in 70 A.D. could not destroy this hope. And the visionary of Patmos sees a new Jerusalem coming down from heaven in place of the one that was destroyed. Certain prophecies of the Old Testament had even predicted a readjustment of topography—the raising up of Zion above the hills (MIC. 4:1) and the emergence of a genuine river that would create verdure in the barren wilderness and sweeten the Dead Sea (EZEK. 47)—and John presupposes and adapts all that too. With this apocalyptic picture of the future the great history of salvation is seen as reaching its finale.

The mind of the Jewish-born visionary, we note, is still bound to the land from which Jewish hearts could not be separated. Whether in Babylonian exile or in Roman exile the vow remained the same,

"If I forget thee, O Jerusalem, let my right hand forget her cunning [wither R.S.V.]." (Ps. 137:5)

This mental bondage to a land and place was not entirely shaken off by Christianity. It remained a potent factor in its life, and under Constantine led to the construction of churches at the supposed Holy sites in Palestine, and to the mighty history of the Crusades, with their immeasurable consequences for civilization. But it was a limitation that could not be adhered to permanently. Fortunately, there was operative also in Christianity, like an undertow, a different line of thought, that sublime indifference to any localized sanctity which is proclaimed by Jesus in the Fourth Gospel, as he sat by the Well of Jacob and spoke to the woman of Samaria:

"Believe me, the hour cometh, when ye shall neither in this mountain, nor yet at Jerusalem, worship the Father.

God is a Spirit: and they that worship him must worship him in spirit and in truth." (JOHN 4:21, 24)

INDEX

This geographical index includes the place names which appear on the maps and in the text. To make it easier for the reader, two kinds of type are used to distinguish map references from text references. All place names which are map references appear in roman type. Each map name has an index reference key, always a letter and figure combination, and the plate numbers of the maps in roman numerals. The place names which are text references appear in italic type; a dagger (†) after the page number of a text reference means that a photograph of the place also appears on that page.

A

Abana, riv.......A5 VI, VII, VIII, IX, X; B5 XIV, XV, XVI
Abarim, mts., 124
Abdeh...................B6 V
Abel-beth-maacah......B4 VI, VII, VIII, IX, X
Abel-beth-maacah, 207
Abel-Keramin....E4 VI, VII, VIII, IX, X
Abel-Keramin, 161
Abel-meholah...D4 VI, VII, VIII, IX, X
Abel-meholah, 278
Abel-mizraim, 94
Abel-shittim...A7 V; E4 VI, VII, VIII, IX, X
Abel-shittim, 124, 132, 134
Abila......E4 XIV, XV, XVI
Abila, 354
Abila (in Abilene)...A5 XIV, XV, XVI
Abila (in Batanaea)...C4 XIV, XV, XVI
Abilene...A5 XIV; B4 XV, XVI
Abu Habba..........C5 XXI
Abu Hawam, Tell....D2 XXI
Abukir..............A2 V
Abu Shahrein.......C6 XXI
Abu Simbel..........C5 IV
Abu Simbel, 98
Abusir, pyramid.........C3 V
Abu Zeneimeh.........C5 V
Abu Zeneimeh, 104
Abydos......D3 XI; A2 XIII
Abyssinia.............E5 IV
Accad, 47
Acco..................B3 II
Acco (Acre)...B2 I; E2 III; C3 VI, VII, VIII, IX, X, XI; D5 XII
Acco ('Akka, Acre), 33, 148
Acco (Ptolemais)...C3 XIV, XV, XVI
Achaia...C3 XII; D10 XIX; B3 XX
Achor, valley of, 136
Achshaph...C3 VI, VII, VIII, IX, X
Achshaph, 139
Achzib (Ekdippa)...D2 III; B3 VI, VII, VIII, IX, X, XIV, XV, XVI; C4 XI
Achzib, 149
Acra................XVIII
Acre: see Acco
Actium.....D10 XIX; B3 XX
Actium, 352, 464
Adab................C6 XI
Adam...D4 VI, VII, VIII, IX, X
Adam, 133, 134†
Adana...............B4 XI
Addan, 321
Aden, gulf.........D6 IV
Admah, 71
Adora...F3 XIV; F2 XV, XVI
Adoraim...E2 VI, VII, VIII, IX, X
Adoraim, 270
Adramyttium.........B4 XX
Adria, sea...........B2 XX
Adria, sea 456
Adriatic, sea...C9 XIX; A2 XX
Adullam...E2 VI, VII, VIII, IX, X
Adullam, 90, 184–85, 270
Aegean, sea....B1 XI; B2 XIII; D10 XIX; B3 XX
Aegyptus..........F12 XIX
Aelana..........F13 XIX
Aelia Capitolina, 408
Aenon......D3 XIV, XV, XVI

Aenus...............A2 XIII
Aenus, riv..........B8 XIX
Aetna, mtn..........B1 XX
Aetolia...........C3 XII; B3 XX
Affuleh............D2 XXI
Africa.............E8 XIX
Agabah, gulf.......E2 II
Agora, 442, 443
Agrab, Tell.........C6 XXI
Agrigentum..D8 XIX; B1 XX
Ahavah, riv., 339
Ahhiyawa...........B2 III
Ahlab...B3 VI, VII, VIII, IX, X
Ahlab, 148, 149
Ahmar, Tell........B4 XXI
Ahmetha Ecbatana....D8 XII
Ai...E3 VI, VII, VIII, IX, X
Ai, 64, 135, 136
Aijalon...D2 III; E3 VI, VII, VIII, IX, X
Aijalon, 270
Aila..............D3 XIII
Ain...D6 V; E3 XV, XVI
Ain el Akhdhar.......D6 V
Ain es Sultan, 283
Ain Feshkha...E3 XIV, XV, XVI
Ain Hawwarah........C4 V
Ain Hudherah, 114, 115
Ain Karim...E3 XIV, XV, XVI
Ain Karim (Karem), 357
Ain Qedeis.........B6 V
Ain Qedeis, 117, 118
Ain Qudeirat........B6 V
Ajjul, Tell el.......E2 XXI
Ajlun...............B2 I
Ajlun, 205
Akkad..............C5 III
Akrabatta...D3 XIV, XV, XVI
Akrabbim, Ascent of...D3 VI, VII, VIII, IX, X
Aksum.............D3 IV
Alaca Huyuk......A4 III, XXI
Alalakh...........B4 III
Alalakh, 96
Alarodians..........C7 XII
Alashia, isl........C3 III
Albis, riv.........A8 XIX
Aleppo.........B4 III, XI
Aleppo, 304
Alexandria (in Seleucis)...B4 XIII; B6 XX
Alexandria (Alexandrette), 436
Alexandria (in Egypt)...A1 V; C3 XIII; E11 XIX; C4 XX
Alexandria of Troas, 438
Alexandrium...D3 XIV, XV, XVI
Alishar............B4 III
Alishar Huyuk...A3 XI; B4 XXI
Allon-bacuth, 87, 88
Almon-diblathaim, 124
Altaqu, 301, 302*
Alush, 112
Amalekites..........B6 V
Amanus, mtn........B6 XX
Amardi.............B6 XIII
Amarna, Tell el...D3 III, XI; E2 V
Amarna, Tell el, 97
Amasia......A4 XI; B6 XII; C13 XIX; A6 XX
Amastris.........C12 XIX
Amathus...D4 XIV, XV, XVI
Amida...C7 XII; B5 XIII; D14 XIX
Amisia, riv.......A7 XIX
Amisos...A4 XIII; C13 XIX; A6 XX
Amman...C2 I; C3 II; E4 VI, VII, VIII, IX, X
Amman: see Rabbath Ammon

Ammon...B3 I; D5 VI, VII, VIII, IX, X; C4 XI; D6 XII
Ammonium...D1 IV; E4 XII; D2 XIII; F11 XIX
Amorites............B5 IV
Amphipolis.........A3 XX
Amphipolis, 440
Amurru.............C4 III
Amygdalon, pool......XVIII
Anab...F2 VI, VII, VIII, IX, X
Anamin.............B4 IV
Anas, riv..........D4 XIX
Anat...............C5 III, XI
Anat, 305
Anathoth, 308
Ancyra...A3 XI, XIII; B5 XII; D12 XIX; A5 XX
Anemourion..........B5 XX
Anshan (Pasargadae)...C7 XII
Anthedon (Agrippias)...E1 XIV, XV, XVI
Anti-Lebanon, mts...A5 XIV, XV, XVI
Antioch (in Pisidia)...B5 XX; B3 XXI
Antioch (in Syria)...B6 XX; B4 XXI
Antioch (in Syria), 418, 423, 427–30, 446
Antiochia (in Phrygia)...D12 XIX
Antiochia (in Syria)...B4 XIII; D13 XIX
Antiochus, Kingdom of...B5–B6 XX
Antipatris...D2 XIV, XVI; XV; C5 XX
Antitaurus, mts..B4 III; B6 XX
Antonia...........XVIII
Antonia, 367, 453
Anuath (Borkeos)..D3 XIV, XV, XVI
Apamea (in Asia Minor)...B3 XIII; B5 XX
Apamea (in Babylonia)...C6 XIII
Apamea (in Seleucis)...B4 XIII; D13 XIX
Aphek (in Ephraim)...D2 VI, VII, VIII, IX, X
Aphek (in Geshur)...C4 VI, VII, VIII, IX, X
Aphek, 149, 173, 279, 313
Aphik: see Aphek
Apiru..............C4 III
Apollonia...B2 XII; C6 XIII; D2 XIV, XV, XVI; E10 XIX; A3 XX
Appian Way.........A2 XX
Appian Way, 459, 460
Apum...............C4 III
Aqabah, 109, 114
Aqabah, gulf..........D6 V
Aqabah, Gulf of......E2 II
Aqabah, gulf, 221
Aqabah, riv.........C6 V
Aqarquf...........C5 XXI
Aqir..............B5 XXI
Aquileia..........B8 XIX
Aquitania.........B6 XIX
Ar...F4 VI, VII, VIII, IX, X
Arabah, riv.........B7 V
Arabia (Arabaya)...D2 IV; D6 XII, XX; D4 XIII; F4, 5 XIV; E5 XV, XVI; F14 XIX
Arabian, gulf...F6 XII; F13 XIX
Arabian Sea........D7 IV
Arabisus..........B7 XX
Arachosiash (Harauwatish)...D12 XII
Arad..A7 V; F3 VI, VII, VIII, IX, X, XIV, XV, XVI
Arad, 147

Aradeh (Haradah), mtn.....C6 V
Aradus...C4 XIII; E13 XIX; B6 XX
Araif, mtn...........B6 V
Aral Sea..........B10 XII
Aram...B5 IV; A5 VI, VII, VIII, IX, X
Aram, 224, 274, 278
Aramnaharaim, 82
Arar, riv..........B6 XIX
Ararat, mtn........B5 III, XI
Ararat, mtn, 45
Arar Nahara.........D6 XII
Araxes, riv...D2 IV; B6 IV, XI, XIII; C8 XII; D15 XIX
Arbel.......C3 XIV, XV, XVI
Arbel (Irbid), 374
Arbela...B5 III, XI, XIII; C7 XII; D14 XIX
Archelais...E3 XIV, XV, XVI
Areopagus, 442, 443
Argaeus, mtn....B4 III, XI, XIII; B6 XX
Argennum, cape.....B4 XX
Argob...C5 VI, VII, VIII, IX, X
Aria (Haraiva).......D11 XII
Aricia, 459
Arimathea...D3 XIV; D2 XV, XVI
Arkites..............B5 IV
Armageddon, 473
Armenia (Armina)...C7 XII; B5 XIII; D14 XIX
Armenia Minor.......D13 XIX
Arnon, riv...C2 I; C3 II; A7 V; F4 VI, VII, VIII, IX, X, XIV, XV, XVI
Arnon, riv, 29, 120, 121, 288, 289
Aroer (in Judah)...F2 VI, VII, VIII, IX, X, XIV, XV, XVI
Aroer (in Moab)...F4 VI, VII, VIII, IX, X, XIV, XV, XVI
Aroer (in Moab), 161, 209
Arpachshad..........B6 IV
Arpad (Arslan Tash)...B4 XI
Arpad, 304
Arrapkha (Kerkuk)...B5 III, XI
Arsinoe.......C4 V; E12 XIX
Arsinoe, 102
Arslan Tash......B4 III, XXI
Arslan Tepe........B4 XXI
Artaxata..B5 XIII; D15 XIX
Artemita..........E15 XIX
Artemis Temple, 471
Arubboth...D2 VI, VII, VIII, IX, X
Arubboth (Araboth), 214
Aruma, 296
Arumah, 159
Arvad...........C4 III; D6 XII
Arvadites...........B5 IV
Arza (Rhinocorura) (el Arish)...A5 V; C3 XI
Arza, 103
Arzawa.............B3 III
Asalmanus, mtn...C6 XIV, XV, XVI
Ascalon...D5 XII; C3 XIII; E2 XIV, XV
Ashdod, 173, 337
Ashdod...E2 VI, VII, VIII, IX, X; C3 XI
Ashkelon...C3 III, XI; E2 VI, VII, VIII, IX, X, XVI
Ashkelon ('Asqalan, Ascalon), 164, 301
Ashkenaz...........B7 IV
Ashtaroth...C4 III; C5 VI, VII, VIII, XI, X
Ashtaroth, 67
Asia...D2 IV; D11 XIX; B4 XX

Asia, prov., 432
Asia Minor, 325, 431–34
Asian Phrygia........B5 XX
Asmar, Tell.........C6 XXI
Aspadana (Isfahan) (Gabai)...
    D9 XII; C7 XIII
Asqalan.............E2 XXI
Asshur.....B5 III, XI; B6 IV
Asshur, 56, 267
Assos.........B4 XX; B2 XXI
Assos, 450, 451
Assuwa..............B2 XI
Assyria.....C6 XII; D14 XIX
Assyrian Camp.......XVIII
Asturia.............C4 XIX
Asturica...........C4 XIX
Astyages, Hill of, 448
Aswan...............C5 IV
Ataqa, mtn..........C4 V
Ataroth...E4, VI, VII, VIII,
    IX, X
Athens (Athenae)...C3 XII;
    B1 XIII; D10 XIX; B3 XX
Athens, 441, 442
Athribis.............C5 XX
Athura.............C6 XII
Atlantic, ocean.......A2 XIX
Atlantis.............D1 IV
Atropatene..........B6 XIII;
    D15 XIX
Atshana, Tell........B4 XXI
Attalia.............B5 XX
Attalia (Adalia), 435
Attica..............C3 XII
Augusta.............B8 XIX
Augusta Treves.....B7 XIX
Augustodunum......B6 XIX
Auja el Hafir...G1 VI, VII,
    VIII, IX, X; C3 XXI
Avaris, 92, 99
Aventicum..........B7 XIX
Ayun Musa (Wells of Moses)
    ....C4 V
Azekah...E2 VI, VII, VIII,
    IX, X
Azekah, 138, 139†, 183, 270,
    315
Azotus....E2 XIV, XV, XVI
Azotus, 173, 418

B

Baalath: see Kiriath-jearim
Baale of Judah, 199
Baalirasi, mtn., 288
Baal-Meon.......E4 VI, VII,
    VIII, IX, X
Baal-perazim, 198
Baal-shalisha, 177, 284
Baal-zephon (Mons Casius)....
    A5 V
Baal Zephon, 105, 106, 107
Baba, riv............D5 V
Bab ed Dhra.........E2 XXI
Bab ed Dhra, 72
Babel..............B6 IV
Babel, 47, 53, 54
Babylon.........C5 III, XI,
    XIII, XXI; D2 IV; D7 XII;
    E14 XIX
Babylon: on ancient world map,
    43; origin of, 54; raided by
    Hittites, 96; used to include
    Assyria, 306; under Nebu-
    chadnezzar and successors,
    323–25; fall of, 327–28;
    archives at, 332
Babylonia (Babirush).........
    D7 XII; C6 XIII
Babylonia, 42†, 43–45, 53, 55, 66
Bactra (Balkh) ....C12 XII
Bactria (Bakhtrish)...C11 XII
Baetica............D4 XIX
Baetis, riv, 461, 462
Bagae.............C11 XII
Baghdad...C5 III, XI, XIII;
    B6 IV; D7 XII
Baghouz.............B5 XI
Bagistane...........D8 XII
Bahrain......C7 IV; D7 XXI
Bahurim, 204
Baku..............A6 XI
Balah, lake...........B4 V
Balatah.............D2 XXI
Balawat.............B5 XXI
Baleares............C6 XIX
Balua...E2 III; F4 VI, VII,
    VIII, IX, X
Bamoth, 125, 126
Banasa.............E4 XIX
Barca......D3 XII; E10 XIX
Barcino............C6 XIX
Bashan...A3 I; B5 VI, VII,
    VIII, IX, X

Bashan, 28, 288
Batanaea Auranitis...C5 XIV,
    XV, XVI
Batum..............A5 XI
Bazu.........E7 III; D6 XI
Beerlahairoi, 69–70, 72, 78, 80,
    277
Beeroth...E3 VI, VII, VIII,
    IX, X
Beeroth, 137, 194
Beersheba...C1 I; C2 II; C3,
    E2 III; A6 V; F2 VI, VII,
    VIII, IX, X, XIV, XV, XVI
Beersheba: southernmost town of
    Palestine, 31; probably visited
    by Abraham, 64; origin of
    name, 75; associations with
    Isaac and Jacob, 80–82, 93;
    flight of Elijah, 276
Behistun..........C6 III, XI
Behistun, 330
Beirut.............C4 III, XI
Beitin.............D2 XXI
Beit Jibrin............C1 I
Beit Mirsim, Tell.....E2 XXI
Beit Nettif...E2 XIV, XV,
    XVI
Belgica.............A6 XIX
Beneberak...D2 VI, VII, VIII,
    IX, X
Beneventum.........A2 XX
Beni Hasan..........E2 V
Benjamin........C2 I; E3 VI
Bered, 69, 70
Berenice (in Cyrenaica).......
    E9 XIX
Berenice (in Egypt)...E4 XIII;
    G13 XIX
Beroea (Aleppo)....B4 XIII;
    B6 XX
Beroea (in Macedonia).......
    A3 XX
Beroea (in Macedonia), 441
Berutu (Beirut).......C4 XI
Berytus...D5 XII; C4 XIII;
    A4 XIV, XV, XVI; C6 XX
Bethanath...C3 VI, VII, VIII,
    IX, X
Bethanath, 151
Bethany...E3 XIV, XV, XVI
Bethany?..E4 XIV, XV, XVI
Bethany, 393, 396, 397, 410, 414
Betharabah, 271
Betharabah...E4 VI, VII, VIII
    IX, X
Beth-arbel (Irbid)...C4 VI,
    VII, VIII, IX, X
Beth-aven, 182
Beth-barah........D4 XIV,
    XV, XVI
Beth-barah, 156, 370
Beth-car, 176
Beth-eden, 304
Beth-eked, 287
Bethel...E3 VI, VII, VIII, IX,
    X, XIV, XV, XVI
Bethel: Abraham in vicinity of,
    63–64; visited by Jacob, 82,
    87, 91; taken by Joseph, 147–
    48; taken by Abijam, 271;
    under Jericho, 309
Bethesda, Pool of.......XVIII
Bethesda, Pool of, 392
Beth Gubrin (Eleutheropolis)...
    E2 XIV, XV, XVI
Beth-haccerem (Beth-hacherem),
    68, 337
Beth-haggan, 286, 287
Beth-hanan, 214
Beth-haram(Livias)...E4 XIV,
    XV, XVI
Bethhoglab...E3 VI, VII,
    VIII, IX, X, XIV, XV, XVI
Beth-horon..E3 VI, VII, VIII,
    IX, X, XIV, XV, XVI
Beth-horon, 137–38, 182, 202,
    221
Bethjeshimoth...E4 VI, VII,
    VIII, IX, X, XIV, XV, XVI
Bethjeshimoth, 124, 125
Bethlehem...E2 III; E3, C3
    VI, VII, VIII, IX, X, XIV,
    XV, XVI
Bethlehem, 15, 168, 270, 361–63,
    408
Beth-millo, 158
Beth-nimrin...E4 VI, VII,
    VIII, IX, X, XIV, XV, XVI
Beth-peor, 125, 126, 128
Bethphage (Bethpage), 397, 398
Beth-rehob...D5 VI, VII,
    VIII, IX, X
Beth-rehob, 201

Bethsaida (Julias)...C4 XIV,
    XV, XVI
Bethsaida, 386, 388, 389
Beth-shean (Scythopolis)..B2
    I; E2 III; C4 III, VI, VII,
    VIII, IX, X, XIV, XV, XVI
Beth-shean, 219
Beth-shemesh...E2 VI, VII,
    VIII, IX, X
Beth-shemesh, 163, 174–75, 292
Beth-shittah, 155
Bethter....E3 XIV, XV, XVI
Beth-yerah...C4 VI, VII,
    VIII, IX, X, XIV, XV, XVI
Beth-zacharias.......E3 XIV
Beth-zur (Bethsura)...E3 VI,
    VII, VIII, IX, X, XIV, XV,
    XVI
Beth-zur, 270
Betonim...E4, VI, VII, VIII,
    IX, X
Beulah, 38
Beyce-Sultan........B2 XXI
"Beyond the River," 331–32
Bezek...D3 VI, VII, VIII, IX,
    X
Bezek, 146, 179
Bezetha.............XVIII
Bilbeis.............B3 V
Billah, Tell.........B5 XXI
Biphath.............A5 IV
Bir Birein...........B6 V
Birs Nimrud.........C5 XXI
Birutu (Beirut).......C4 III
Bismaya............C6 XXI
Bitadini............B4 XI
Bithynia...B5 XII; A3 XIII;
    C12 XIX; A5 XX
Bit Yakin, 43
Black Sea............A3
    III, XXI, XI, XIII; A5
    IV; B5 XII; C12 XIX
Blue Nile.............D5 IV
Bochim, 150
Boeotia......C3 XII; B3 XX
Boghazkoi......B3 III, XI;
    A3 XXI
Borsippa..........C5 III, XI;
    C6 XIII
Bosporan, kingdom..C12 XIX
Bosporus, strait......A2 XI;
    A4 XX
Bostra.............E13 XIX
Bostra, 424
Bozra............B7 V; C4 XI
Bozrah...C5 VI, VII, VIII,
    IX, X, XVI, XV, XVI
Bracara Augusta.....C3 XIX
Brak, Tell.........B5 XXI
Britannia...........A5 XIX
Britannic, ocean......B5 XIX
Brook of Egypt (el Arish riv.)...
    B6 V
Brundisium..C9 XIX; A2 XX
Bubastis...B3 V; C3 XI, XIII
Bubastis, 102
Buboea.............B3 XX
Bukhara............C11 XII
Bulgaria............A1 XXI
Burdigalia...........C5 XIX
Burg, 64
Busiris.............B3 V
Buto...............A2 V
Byblos...C4 III, XIII; D6 XII
Byblos, 145
Byzantium...A2 XI, XIII;
    B4 XII; C11 XIX; A4 XX

C

Cabul...C3 VI, VII, VIII, IX,
    X
Cabul, 220
Caesaraugusta.......C6 XIX
Caesarea....B1 I; C2 XV, XVI;
    E13 XIX; C5 XX; D2 XXI
Caesarea, 418–23, 453, 454
Caesarea (in Mauretania).......
    D6 XIX
Caesarea-Philippi (Ituraea)....
    B4 XIV, XV, XVI
Caesarea-Philippi, 389
Caesariensis.........E5 XIX
Caicus, riv..........B4 XX
Cairo..............B3 V
Calah (Nimrud)...B5 III, XI;
    B6 IV
Caleb Kenaz...F3 VI, VII,
    VIII, IX, X
Calliope...........B7 XIII
Callirrhoe..E4 XIV, XV, XVI
Callirrhoe, 52
Calno, 305

Camon...C4 VI, VII, VIII,
    IX, X
Camon, 160
Cana.......C3 XIV, XV, XVI
Cana (Kufr Kenna), 372
Canaan..........C4 III; B5 IV
Canaan, 24, 63, 65
Capernaum.....C4 XIV, XV,
    XVI
Capernaum, 375–79, 383, 387,
    390, 410
Caphtorim.........B4 IV
Capitolias..C4 XIV, XV, XVI
Cappadocia (Katpatuka)......
    C5 XII; B4 XIII; D13 XIX;
    B6 XX
Cappadocia, 432–33
Capua......C8 XIX; A1 XX
Capua, 459
Carchedon..........D1 IV
Carchemish........B4 III, XI
Carchemish, 96, 300, 305, 311–
    13
Caria....B2 XI, XIII; B4 XX
Carians............C4 XII
Carmania (Yauthiya).E10 XII
Carmel...F3 VI, VII, VIII,
    IX, X
Carmel, 183, 187
Carmel, mtn...B1 I; B3 II;
    C3 VI, VII, VIII, IX, X,
    XIV, XV, XVI
Carmel, mtn, 30, 33, 38, 275
Carpathos, isl........B2 XIII
Carrhae...B4 XIII; D13 XIX
Carthage...........D8 XIX
Carthago Nova......D5 XIX
Casiphia, 321, 339
Casluhim............C3 IV
Caspian Gates..B7 III;C9 XII
Caspian Sea...B7 III, IV, XI,
    XIII; C2 IV; B9 XII; C16
    XIX; B7 XXI
Castra Praetoriana, 460, 461
Castulo............D5 XIX
Cataracts (of the Nile) ..C5 IV
Caucasus, mts.......B7 XII;
    C14 XIX
Cauda (Clauda), isl. ....C3 XX
Cauda (Clauda), isl., 456, 457
Cedron............E2 XIV
Celaenae...........C5 XII
Cenacle, 414, 421
Cenchreae..........B3 XX
Chagar-Bazar.......B5 XXI
Chalcedon..A2 XIII; A4 XX
Chalcis...B1 XIII; A4 XIV,
    XV, XVI; C6 XX
Chaldeans..........C6 XI
Chalybon (Helbon)..A5 XIV,
    XV, XVI
Charput...........C6 XII
Chatti.............A7 XIX
Chauci.............A7 XIX
Chebar, riv., 315
Chephirah, 137
Cherethites....A6 V; F1 VI,
    VII, VIII, IX, X
Chersonesus.........B5 XII;
    C12 XIX
Chersonesus Taurica...B5 XII
Cherub, 321
Chesulloth...C3 VI, XIV, XV,
    XVI
Chesulloth, 359
Chinneroth......C3 VI, VII,
    VIII, IX, X
Chinneroth, 139
Chios, isl...........B4 XX
Choga Zambil........C6 XXI
Chorasmia (Uwarazmish
    Khwarizm).......B11 XII
Chorazin...C4 XIV, XV, XVI
Chorazin (Keraze), 379
Choser, riv., 310
Chylemath, riv.......D6 XIX
Cibyra.............B2 XIII
Cicilicia...........B6 XX
Cilicia...C5 XII; B3 XIII;
    D12 XIX; B5 XX
Cilicia, 324, 418, 423, 432
Cilician Gates........C6 XII;
    B5 XX
Cilician Gates, 432, 436
Cilician, gulf........B6 XX
Cimmerians..........A4 XI
Circesium.........D14 XIX
Cirta..............D7 XIX
Citium............C3 XIII
City of David, 196–97, 220, 224,
    415
City of Moab, 125
Cius..............A2 XIII
Clunia.............C5 XIX

Cnidus......B2 XIII; B4 XX
Cnidus, 455
Cnossus...C4 XII; B2 XIII; D11 XIX; B4 XX
Cnossus, 463
Coelesyria............C4 XIII
Colchis..B7 XII; A5 XIII; C14 XIX
Colonia..............A7 XIX
Colossae......C4 XII; B4 XX
Colossae, 449
Comana..B6 XII; C13 XIX; B4 XX
Commagene........B4 XIII; D13 XIX; B6 XX
Commagene, 434–35
Coptos.............F12 XIX
Corduba, 461, 462
Corinth (Corinthus)...C3 XII; B1 XIII; D10 XIX; B3 XX
Corinth, 443–45, 449
Corinth Canal, 443
Corner Gate, 292
Corsica, isl.........C7 XIX
Cos, isl.............B4 XX
Cos, isl., 452
Cotiaeum.............B4 XX
Crete (Creta), isl...C3 XII; B1 XIII; E10 XIX; B3 XX; C2 XXI
Crete, 455, 463
Crocodilopolis..........C2 V
Ctesiphon..C5 XIII; E15 XIX
Ctesiphon, 430
Cunaxa, 341
Cush............C5 IV; F5 XII
Cush, 42
Cush-Meluhha........E3 XI
Cutha.................C5 XI
Cutha, 298
Cydnus, riv.........B5 XX
Cydonia.............B1 XIII
Cydonia, 463
Cyprus...C5 XII, XX; B3 XIII, XXI; D12 XIX
Cyprus, 430–32
Cyrenaica...E10 XIX; C3 XX
Cyrene...D1 IV; D3 XII; E10 XIX; C3 XX
Cyrene, 318, 423, 432
Cyropolis.........C12 XII
Cyrus, riv...B6 IV; B8 XII; A6 XIII
Cythera, isl........B3 XX
Cyzicus.....A2 XIII; A4 XX

D

Daberath...C3 VI, VII, VIII, IX, X, XIV, XV, XVI
Dacia..............B10 XIX
Dahshur, pyramid....C3 V
Dalmanutha, 388
Dalmatia...C9 XIX; A2 XX
Damanhur...........A2 V
Damascus...A3 I; A4 II; C4 III, XI, XIII; A5 VI, VII, VIII, IX, X, XIV, XV, XVI; D6 XII; E13 XIX; C6 XX
Damascus: tributary to David, 200; importance under Aramaeans; 278–79; description of city, 285; ascendancy in 9th century B.C., 290; recovered by Israel, 294; taken by Assyrians, 296–97; in Paul's time, 424–26
Damascus Gate, 296
Damietta.............A3 V
Dan (Laisch)....E2 VI; B4 VI, VII, VIII, IX, X
Dan, 167
Danapris, riv.......A12 XIX
Danube, riv........A4 IV
Danunim............B5 IV
Danunites...........B4 XI
Danustris..........B11 XIX
Danuvius, riv.......B9 XIX
Daphne, 427–28
Dascylium..........B4 XII
Dead Sea (Asphalt Lake)...C2 I; C3 II; E2 III; A7 V; F3 VI, VII, VIII, IX, X, XIV, XV, XVI
Dead Sea, 27, 36
Debir...A7 V; F2 VI, VII, VIII, IX, X
Debir, 146, 147
Decapolis...........C4 XV, XVI
Decapolis, 382, 385, 386, 388
Dedan (el 'Ela)...C5 IV; D4 XI, XIII

Defenneh, Tell......C3 XXI
Deir el-Azhar: see Kiriath-jearim
Delos, isl............B4 XX
Delphi......C3 XII; B3 XX
Demavend............B7 XI
Der................C5 III, XI
Dera, 123
Derbe, 434
Derbent............B8 XII
Derber.............B5 XX
Dhahab.............D6 V
Dhalal, mtn........D5 V
Dhiban.......D2, E2 XXI
Dibon...E4 VI, VII, VIII, IX, X, XIV, XV, XVI; C4 XI
Dibon, 123, 124
Diklah.............C6 IV
Dilbat.............C5 XI
Dilmun (Bahrain)...D7 III,XI
Dion...C4 XIII; D4 XIV, XV, XVI; A3 XX
Diospolis...E2 XIV, XV, XVI
Diyala, riv......C6 XI, XIII
Dizahab, 116
Dizful......C6 III, XI
Dodamim (Rodamin)...B4 IV
Dok......E3 XIV, XV, XVI
Dophkak............D5 V
Dophkak, 111, 112
Dor....B1 I; E2 III; C3 III, XI; C2 VI, VII, VIII, IX, X; D5 XII
Dor, 132, 139, 214
Dora.....C2 XIV, XV, XVI
Dorylaeum..........B3 XIII; D12 XIX; B4 XX
Dotha, Tell, 91, 92
Dothan...D3 VI, VII, VIII, IX, X, XIV, XV, XVI
Dothan, Tell..........D2 XXI
Dothan, 91, 92, 285
Drangiana (Zaranga)..D11 XII
Dravus, riv.........B9 XIX
Driton, riv........C10 XIX
Duma......D6 XII; C4 XIII
Dumah (ej-Jauf)......D4 XI
Dura, 322–23
Dura-Europus.......C5 XIII
Durius, riv.......C4 XIX
Dur Kurigalzu (Aqarquf)....C5 XI
Durocortorura.......B6 XIX
Dur-Sargon (Khorsabad)....B5 XI
Duweir, Tell ed......E2 XXI
Duweir, Tell ed: see Lachish
Dyrrachium..C9 XIX; A2 XX

E

Easr el Azraq.........C4 XI
Ebal, mtn...B3 II; D3 VI, VII, VIII, IX, X, XIV, XV, XVI
Ebal, mtn., 158
Ebenezer, 173, 176
Eber...............B5 IV
Eburacum...........A5 XIX
Ecbatana (Hamadan)..C6 III, XI, XIII
Ecbatana, 325–26, 330, 332
Eden, 42, 43
Edessa...B4 XIII; D13 XIX
Edfu..............E3 XI
Edom...D2 I; B7 V; C4 XI
Edom: location of, 29; sprung from Esau, 81; agricultural civilization in, 89; name applied to Negeb, 116–17; avoided by Israelites under Moses, 119–20; in Solomon's time, 221, 224; tributary to Judah, 281, 283, 286, 291
Edom Seir...G4 VI, VII, VIII, IX, X
Edrei (Der'a)...C5 VI, VII, VIII, IX, X, XIV, XV, XVI
Eglon...E2 VI, VII, VIII, IX, X
Eglon, 137
Egnatian Way........A3 XX
Egnatian Way, 439, 440, 441
Egra..............D4 XIII
Egypt, Brook of......C3 III
Egypt (Mudraya) . . B2 V; D3 XI, XIII; E5 XII; D5 XX; C2 XXI
Egypt, 223, 306, 318, 340–42
Egyptian Landing......D4 V
Eikreh, riv.........B7 V
ej Jib.............D2 XXI
ej Jib, 207–08; see Gibeon
Ej-Jibal.............D2 I

Ekallate.............B5 III
Ekhet Aton (Tell el Amarna)...D3 III; E2 V
Ekron (Akkran)...E2 VI, VII, VIII, IX, X, XIV, XV, XVI; C4 XI
Ekron, 174, 300†, 301, 302, 310
Elah, valley of, 183
el Ain, riv............C6 V
Elam...C6 III, XI; B6 IV
Elam, 66, 67, 144
el 'Arabah, Mines of, 67
el 'Arabah, riv...D2 I; D3 II
El Arish, riv...C3 III; C5 V
Elath.......C7 V; E6 XII
Elath, 221, 292, 296
el 'Auja............B6 V
El-Belqa...........C2 I
El-bethel, 87
el Biyar, riv..........C6 V
Elburz, mts..........B7 XI
Elealeh...E4 VI, VII, VIII, IX, X
el Ejmeh, mtn.........C6 V
el' Ela...............C5 IV
Elephantine..........D1 IV
Elephantine, 338–42
Eleutheropolis......E2 XIV, XV, XVI
El Faiyum............C2 V
el Ghadyan..........C7 V
El Ghor..............C3 II
el Hamam, riv, 374
El Hammeh........D2 XXI
el Hesa (Zered).......D2 I
El Hismeh...........C7 V
Elim.................C4 V
Elim, 107, 109, 111
Elisha..............B3 IV
El Kab..............D3 XI
el Kantara..........C3 III
el Kantara, 102, 103, 106
El Kerak...C2 I; A7 V; F4 VI, VII, VIII, IX, X, XIV, XV, XVI
el-Khalasa...........A6 V
el Khalil, 77
El Khrob (Horeb?), mtn..D6 V
Elkosh, 310
Ellasar, 66
el-Kuweit...........D6 XIII
El-Lisan............C2 I
el Mazar............B5 V
el Mejdel, 381
El Merkh Ah.........D5 V
El Mishrifeh........C4 XXI
El Mojib, riv.........C3 II
el Mugayyar........C6 XXI
el-Oelt, riv..........C2 I
El Oheimir..........C6 XXI
Elon, 214
Eloth: see Elath
El-paran, 67, 75
El Peraea Ghor........B2 I
el Qafza ("Mount of the Leap"), 384
el Qelt, riv., 395
el Quneitrah...B4 VI, VII, VIII, IX, X
Eltekeh...E2 VI, VII, VIII, IX, X
Eltekeh, 273
Elusa......F2 XIV, XV, XVI
Elymais............C6 XIII
Emerica Augusta....D4 XIX
Emesa (Homs)......C4 XIII; C6 XX
Emmaus (Nicopolis)...E2 XIV, XV, XVI
Emmaus, 409, 410
Enaim, 90, 91
En-dor...C3 VI, VII, VIII, IX, X
En-eglaim, 322
En-gannim......D3 VI, VII, VIII, IX, X
En-gedi...A7 V; F3 VI, VII, VIII, IX, X, XIV, XV, XVI
En-gedi, 186–87, 322
en Nakhl...........C3 XI
En Noweibeh........D6 V
En-Nuqra...........B3 I
En-rimmon, 343
En-rogel, 211
En-mishpat, 67, 68
Ephah...............D4 XI
Ephah, 298
Ephesus...B2 XI, XIII, XXI; C4 XII; D11 XIX; B4 XX
Ephesus, 432, 446–48, 466
Ephraim (Ephron) (Aphairema)...B2 I; E3 VI, VII, VIII, IX, X, XIV, XV, XVI; C4 IV

Ephraim (Ephron), 202, 205, 213 272, 394
Ephraim Gate, 292
Ephrath, 88
Ephron: see Ephraim
Epidaurum..........C9 XIX
Epiphania, 428
Epirus...B2 XII; D10 XIX; A2 XX
Erech (Uruk, Warka)...C5 III; B6 IV; C6 XI
Erech, 47, 54
Eritrea.............D6 IV
er Raha, 112
Erweis el Ebeirig.......D6 V
Eridu..............C6 III, XI
Erivan.............A5 XI
Erythraean, sea......F11 XII
Erzerum............A5 XI
Esau, mtn., 343
Esdraelon, plain of...B2 I; B3 II; C3 XIV, XV, XVI
Esdraelon, plain of, 30, 358, 361, 384, 390
Eshnunna...........C5 III
esh Sheikh, riv........D5 V
Eshtaol...E3 VI, VII, VIII, IX, X
Eshtaol, 163
Eshtemoa...F2 VI, VII, VIII, IX, X
Eshus..............C4 XIII
es Salihiyeh........C5 XXI
es Salt...D4 VI, VII, VIII, IX, X, XIV, XV, XVI
es Sbeita...........B6 V
es-Sebkha...C2 I; D3 II
Essene Gates..........XVIII
Etam....A6 V; E3 VI, VII, VIII, IX, X
Etam, 164, 270
Ethiopia (Kusiya-Cush)...D5 IV; F5 XII; E3 XIII
Ethiopians..........E10 XIX
Eth Thebt, mtn........D6 V
Etruscan, sea........B1 XX
et Tabghah, 380, 381, 382, 386
et Tafileh...G4 VI, VII, VIII, IX, X
et Tanturah.........D2 XXI
et Tell............D2 XXI
et Tih, mtn..........C6 V
Eumenia............B4 XX
Euphrates, riv...C5 III, XI, XIII; B6 IV; B4 XI; D7 XII; B5 XIII; E14 XIX; C5 XXI
Euphrates, riv., 43, 55, 62, 68
Euphrates, Road to the...B5 XX
Europe.............C2 IV
Europus............B7 XIII
Euxinus (Black Sea)...A5 XX
Ezion-geber (Tell el Kheleifeh)...E2 II; C6 V; D4 XI
Ezion-geber, 110, 221–22

F

Fadak...............D5 XI
Fahi,' Khirbet........D2 XXI
Fair Havens.........B3 XX
Fair Havens, 455
Fai, riv............A7 V
Fara...............D2 XXI
Far 'a, riv...B2 I; B3 II; D3 VI, VII, VIII, IX, X, XIV, XV, XVI
Far'ah, Tell el.......E2 XXI
Faran (Mount Paran), mtn...B6 V
Feiran, riv..........D5 V
Fejj el Aseiker, riv., 120
Fekheriyeh, Tell......B5 XXI
Fish Gate, 308
Formica............A1 XX
Forum of Appius......A1 XX
Forum of Appius, 459
Frank, mtn.........C3 II
Frisii..............A7 XIX
Ful, Tell el.........D2 XXI
Fundi..............A1 XX

G

Gaash, mtn . . . E3 VI, VII, VIII, IX, X
Gaba......C3 XIV, XV, XVI
Gabae.............D9 XII
Gabbatha (judgment seat), 405
Gad................D4 VI
Gadara...C4 XIII, XIV, XV, XVI

479

Gadara, 382
Gades..............D4 XIX
Gades, 462
Gador.....D4 XIV, XV, XVI
Galatia...B3 XIII; D12 XIX;
    B5 XX
Galatia, 432–37
Galilee...B2 I; C3 XIV, XV,
    XVI; C6 XX
Galilee, 29, 373, 408, 409, 410
Galilee, Sea of . . . A2, B2 I;
    B3 II; C4 VI, VII, VIII, IX,
    X, XIV, XV, XVI
Galilee, Sea of, 26, 37, 322,
    373†, 381, 383
Galilee, Lower..........B2 I
Galilee, Upper..........A2 I
Gallaecia............C4 XIX
Gallia................B6 XIX
Galatian Lycaonia.....B5 XX
Galatian Phrygia......B5 XX
Galatian Pontus.......A6 XX
Gamala....C4 XIV, XV, XVI
Gandara...............D13 XII
Gangra.........A3 XI; A5 XX
Gangra, 432
Gari...................C4 III
Gath...E2 VI, VII, VIII, IX,
    X
Gath, 174, 184, 188, 270, 290
Gathhepher . . . C3 VI, VII,
    VIII, IX, X
Gathhepher, 292
Gaudos, isl..........B1 XX
Gaugamela.............C7 XII
Gaulanitis..C4 XIV, XV, XVI
Gaza...C1 I; C2 II; E2 III;
    A6 V; E1 VI, VII, VIII, IX,
    X, XIV, XV, XVI; D5 XII;
    C3 XIII
Gaza, 32, 52, 165, 301, 417–18
Geba...E3 VI, VII, VIII, IX,
    X
Geba, 180–82, 271, 309, 317
Gedrosia (Maka).....E11 XII
Gennesaret, plain of, 375, 386,
    387
Gennath Gate........XVIII
Genua................C7 XIX
Gerab, 166
Geraia................D4 XIV
Gerar...F1 VI, VII, VIII, IX,
    X
Gerar, 52, 72, 80, 272
Gerasa...........D4 XV, XVI
Gerasa (Jerash), 382
Gerizim, mtn...B3 II; D3 VI,
    VII, VIII, IX, X, XIV, XV,
    XVI
Gerizim, mtn., 158, 159
German, ocean.......A6 XIX
Germania.......A7, A8 XIX
Gerrha . . . D6 XI; E8 XII;
    D7 XIX
Geshur...C4 VI, VII, VIII,
    IX, X
Geshur, 202
Gethsemane, 404, 408
Gezer...E2 VI, VII, VIII, IX,
    X, XIV, XV, XVI
Gezer, 221
Gharandel, riv..........C4 V
Ghazra................D12 XII
Ghazzeh...............E2 XXI
Ghazzeh, riv............C1 I
Ghor, El...............B3 II
Ghor, 25, 27 65, 85
Giah, 193
Gibbethon...E2 VI, VII, VIII,
    IX, X
Gibbethon, 272, 273
Gibeah...E3 VI, VIII, IX, X
Gibeah (Gibeathelohim), 143,
    177–78, 180–82, 192
Gibeath-ammah, 193
Gibeon...E3 VI, VII, VIII,
    IX, X
Gibeon, 136–37, 192–94, 198,
    207–08, 213, 317
Gihon (spring).......XVIII
Gihon spring, 295, 300, 301
Gilboa, mtn...D3 XIV, XV,
    XVI
Gilboa, mtn., 188–90
Gilead...B2 I; D4 VI, VII,
    VIII, IX, X, XI
Gilead, 28, 83–84, 161, 191–92,
    204–05, 214
Gilgal...E4 VI, VII, VIII, IX,
    X
Gilgal, 133–34, 149–51, 178,
    180, 337

Gilgal-Goiim . . . D2 VI, VII,
    VIII, IX, X
Giloh, 204
Gimirrai................B3 XI
Ginnesar................B2 I
Ginnesar, 26
Ginnaia...D3 XIV, XV, XVI
Ginnaia (Jenin), 390
Girsu.................C6 III
Gischala (Gush Khalab).......
    B3 XIV, XV, XVI
Gitta...D3 XIV, XV, XVI
Gitta (Jett), 417
Gittaim, 195
Gizeh.................C3 V
Gob, 208
Golan...C5 VII, VIII, IX, X
Golgotha, 367, 406–09
Gomer...............A5 IV
Gomorrah, 70, 71, 72
Gophnah (Gophna)...E3 VI,
    VII, VIII, IX, X, XIV, XV,
    XVI
Gordion.........B3 XI, XXI
Gordium....C5 XII; B3 XIII
Gordyene...C7 XII; D14 XIX
Gortyna, 463
Goshen...C3 III; F2 VI, VII,
    VIII, IX, X
Goshen, 93, 99, 138
Goshen, Land of........B3 V
Gozan, 298, 304
Granicus, riv..........A4 XX
Great Bitter Lake......B4 V
Great Sea...A2 VI, VII, VIII,
    IX, X; B2 XIV, XV, XVI
Greater Zab, riv......B5 XIII
Greece................A1 XXI
Greece, 429
Gurgum...............B4 XI
Gutium................B6 III
Gutium, 328
Guzana (Gozan, Tell Halaf)..
    B5 XI

H

Habor, 298
Hachilah, 185–87
Hadrach, 279
Hadrumetum.......D8 XIX
Haifa.........B1 I; B2 II
Haifa, 453
Ha'il...........D5 XI, XIII
Hala el Bedr...........E7 V
Halaf, Tell......B5 III, XXI
Halah.................B5 XI
Halah, 297, 298
Halak, mtn...D2 II; B6 V;
    G2 VI, VII, VIII, IX, X
Halak, mtn., 140
Halal, mtn...........D1 II; B5 V
Haleb.................C6 XII
Halfa, riv............C5 IV
Halhul......E3 VI, VII, VIII,
    IX, X
Halicarnassus..B2 XI, XIII;
    C4 XII; D11 XIX
Halys, riv...B3 III, XI, XIII,
    XXI; B5 IV, XII; D12 XIX;
    A5 XX
Ham, 67
Hama................B4 XXI
Hamadan, 298
Hamath.........B4 III, XI
Hamath, 200, 215, 292, 294, 298
Hamath Gader, 377
Hamathites...........B5 IV
Hannathan......C3 VI, VII,
    VIII, IX, X
Haradah...............C7 V
Haradah, 110, 115
Haran.......B4 III; C6 XII
Haran, 62, 79, 81–83, 304, 311,
    324, 326
Harbaj, Tell........D2 XXI
Hariri, Tell.........C5 XXI
Harmal, Tell........C6 XXI
Harod (spring)...C3 VI, VII,
    VIII, IX, X
Harod, 155
Haroshethha-Goiim....C2 VI,
    VII, VIII, IX, X
Haroshethha-Goiim, 151
Harra el 'Awarez........E7 V
Harra er Raha..........E7 V
Harran................B4 XI
Hasmonaean Palace....XVIII
Hassuna, Tell.......B5 XXI
Hatra..D14 XIX; B5 XXI
Hattin, Horns of, 373
Hauran, mtn...C6 VI, VII,
    VIII, IX, X, XIV, XV,
    XVI; C4 XI

Hauran, 343
Hauzran...............B3 I
Havilah...............C6 IV
Havilah, 42
Havvoth-Jair...C4 VI, VII,
    VIII, IX, X
Hazarmaveth..........D7 IV
Hazazon-tamar, 68
Hazeroth..............D6 V
Hazeroth, 116
Hazor...E2, C4 III; B4 VI,
    VII, VIII, IX, X, XIV, XV,
    XVI
Hazor, 138, 139, 140, 202, 220
Hebran, riv..........D5 V
Hebron (Kiriath-Arba).......
    C2 I; E2 III; A7 V; E3 VI,
    VII, VIII, IX, X, XIV, XV,
    XVI; D6 XII
Hebron: visited by Abraham, 76–
    77; location of, 78; taken by
    Judah, 146; Samson carries
    gates of Gaza to, 165; scene of
    Abner's death, 193–94; Ab-
    salom anointed king at, 203;
    Rehoboam anointed king at,
    268; fortified by Rehoboam,
    270
Hebron Migdol (Tell el Her)...
    C4 III
Hebrus, riv...........A2 XIII;
    C11 XIX
Hecatompylus......C10 XII;
    B8 XIII
Helal, mtn............D1 II
Helal, mtn., 108
Helam, 201
Heliopolis (Baalbek)...C6 XX
Heliopolis (On)...C3 III, XIII;
    D2 IV; B3 V; D5 XII;
    E12 XIX; C5 XX
Helkath...C3 VI, VII, VIII,
    IX, X
Helkath-hazzurim, 192
Hellas................B1 XIII
Hellespont, strait......A4 XX
Hellespontians (Khuza).....
    B4 XII
Hepher.....D2 VI, VII, VIII,
    IX, X
Hepher, 214
Heptapegon, 380
Heraclea (in Macedonia).....
    A3 XX
Heraclea (in Pontus)...A5 XX
Heracleopolis....A4 V; D3 XI;
    E5 XII; F11 XIX
Heracleopolis, 105, 106
Heracleopolis Magna (Hanesh)
    C2 V
Heres, Ascent of, 157
Hereth, 185
Hermon, mtn...A2 I; A3 II;
    A4 VI; B4 VII, VIII, IX, X,
    XIV, XV, XVI; C4 XI
Hermon, mtn., 25, 38, 474
Hermopolis...E2 V; D3 XI,
    XIII; F12 XIX
Hermus, riv...........B2 XIII;
    A5 XX
Herod I., Kingdom of...C6 XX
Herodium..E3 XIV, XV, XVI
Herodium (Frank mtn.), 363–64
Heroonpolis...........C3 XIII
Heroonpolis, 93, 99, 104
Heroonpolis, Gulf of....D5 V
Heshbon (Esebon)....A7 V;
    E4 VI, VII, VIII, IX, X,
    XIV, XV, XVI; C4 XII
Heshbon, 122, 126
Hesi, Tell el........E2 XXI
Heth.................B5 IV
Hiddekel, 42
Hierapolis...........B4 XX
Hif..................C5 III
Hinatuna, 296
Hinnom, Valley of...........
    XVII, XVIII
Hinnom, valley of, 308–09
Hinnom, valley of, 336
Hippicus.............XVIII
Hippo Regius........D7 XIX
Hippos....C4 XIV, XV, XVI
Hippos, 383
Hispalis.............D4 XIX
Hispalis, 461–62
Hispania.............C5 XIX
Hissarlik............B2 XXI
Hivites.............B5 IV
Hobah, 68
Hodeida.............D6 IV
Holwan..............C6 XI
Holy Sepulcher, Church of the
    XVIII

Homs................C4 XI
Horeb, 100, 108–10, 277–78
Horesh, 185
Hormah...A6 V; F2 VI, VII,
    VIII, IX, X
Hormah, 118, 119, 147
Hor (Jebel Harun), mtn..B7 V
Horonaim, 202
Horus, Way of.......C3 III
Hudherah.............D6 V
Hudrach.............C4 XI
Huldah Gates........XVIII
Hul Girgashtes.......B5 IV
Husn, Tell el........D2 XXI
Hypanis, riv..........B7 XII;
    B12 XIX
Hyrcania (Warkana)..C7 XII;
    B7 XIII
Hyrcanium..E3 XIV, XV, XVI

I

Iberus, riv...........C5 XIX
Ibleam...D3 VI, VII, VIII,
    IX, X
Ibleam, 293
Ibrahim, Tell........C5 XXI
Iconium...C5 XII; B3 XIII;
    D6, D12 XIX; B5 XX
Iconium (Konia), 433–34
Ida, mtn.............B4 XX
Idumaea...C1 I; F2 XIV, XV,
    XVI; C6 XX
Idumaea, 31
Ijon...B4 VI, VII, VIII, IX, X
Ijon, 271
Ilion................B4 XX
Illyria...C1 IV; B2 XII
Illyricum.............A3 XX
Illyricum, 464
Imbros, isl...........A4 XX
Immer, 321
Ina.........B4 XIV, XV, XVI
India...........D3 IV; E12 XII
India, 222–23
Indus, riv...D3 IV; E12 XII
Inner Sea............C3 XX
Ionia, 466
Ionian Sea..D9 XIX; B2 XX
Ipir Omar Gudrun....B6 III
Ipsus................B3 XIII
Iran................C7 XXI
Iraq................C5 XXI
Iris, riv...A4 XI, XIII; A6 XX
Is (Hit)....C5 XI; D7 XIII
Isana (Jeshana).......D3 XV
Isaur Pisidia..........B5 XX
Isfahan.......C7 XI; D9 XII
Ishhuza-scythians.......B5 XI
Isin.................C6 III
Isin, 144
Isla, riv............D5 V
Isles of the Sea.......C4 XII
Ismailieh............B4 V
Israel...D3 VIII; C3, D2 XXI
Israel, 81
Issachar.............C3 VI
Issatis..............C7 XIII
Istros................C1 IV
Issus........C6 XII; B4 XIII;
    B6 XX
Ister................B3 XII
Itabyrion............C3 XIV
Italy (Italia).......C8 XIX;
    A1 XX
Ituraea...A2 I; A4, B4 XIV,
    XV, XVI
Ivernia..............A4 XIX
Ivvah, 305
Iye-abarim (Aiy)......A7 V
Iye-abarim, 122

J

Jabbok, riv......B2 I; B3 II;
    D4 VI, VII, VIII, IX, X,
    XIV, XV, XVI
Jabbok, riv., 27–28, 83–85, 206
Jabesh...E2 III; D4 VI, VII,
    VIII, IX, X
Jabesh, 178–79, 208
Jabneh...E2 VI, VII, VIII,
    IX, X
Jabneh, 294
Jabreel...E2 VI, VII, VIII,
    IX, X
Jaezer.....E4 XIV, XV, XVI
Jaffa: see Japho
Jahaz, 122
Jamnia...E2 XIV, XV, XVI
Janoah...D3 VI, VII, VIII,
    IX, X
Janoah, 296

Japhia...C3 VI, VII, VIII, IX, X, XIV, XV, XVI
Japhia, 359
Japho......B1 I; D2 VI, VII, VIII, IX, X; D5 XII
Japho, 32, 292, 419
Jarmo...............B6 XXI
Jarmo, 53
Jarmuk, riv..........B2 I
Jarmuth...E2 VI, VII, VIII, IX, X
Jarmuth, 137
Jathrib............E4 XIII
Jattir...F3 VI, VII, VIII, IX, X
Jaulan................B2 I
Jaulan, 28
Javar...............B4 IV
Jazer...E4 VI, VII, VIII, IX, X
Jebeil.............C4 XXI
Jebusites...........B5 V
Jedur................A2 I
Jehoshaphat, Valley of, 342
Jehud...D2 VI, VII, VIII, IX, X
Jehud, 273
Jemdet..............C5 III
Jemdet Nasr........C6 XXI
Jemmeh, Tell.......E2 XXI
Jerabis............B4 XXI
Jerash...B2 I; D5 VI, VII, VIII, IX, X; C4 XXI
Jerasus, riv........B11 XIX
Jericho...C2 I; A7 V; E3 VI, VII, VIII, IX, X, XIV, XV, XVI
Jericho, 27, 134–35, 150, 337, 395
Jerishen, Tell ej......D2 XXI
Jermak, mtn...........B2 I
Jeruel, 76
Jerusalem....C2 I; C3 II; C4, E2 III; A7 V; E3 VI, VII, VIII, IX, X, XIV, XV, XVI; D6 XII; C4 XIII, XVII; XVIII; E13 XIX; C6 XX; E2, C4 XXI
Jerusalem: topography of, 195–97; taken by David, 197; acropolis of, 217–18; beseiged and captured by Nebuchadnezzar, 315-17; reconstruction of, 329–30, 335–36; publication of Law of Ezra at, 340; much building by Herod in, 353; visit of the boy Jesus, 365–67; Jesus visits the Temple, 393; Jesus in city for Passover and Last Supper, 401; visits of Paul, 426, 446, 453; importance of, in Judaeo-Christian tradition, 474
Jeshimon, 186
Jezreel......C3 VI, VII, VIII, IX, X
Jezreel, 30, 188, 192, 279, 286–87
Jezreel, Plain of...C3 VI, VII, VIII, IX, X
Jidda...............C5 IV
Jizr, Tell...........D2 XXI
Jobab...............D7 IV
Jocha...............C6 XXI
Jogbehah...E4 VI, VII, VIII, IX, X
Jogbehah, 157
Jokneam, 276
Joktan...............C6 IV
Joppa...E2 III; C3 XI, XIII; D2 XIV, XV, XVI; C5 XX
Joppa................B2 II
Joppa: see Japho
Joppe..............E12 XIX
Jordan (country)...C4,D2 XXI
Jordan, riv........B2 I, III; B3 II; D4 VI, VII, VIII, IX, X, XIV, XV, XVI
Jordan, riv, 25–27, 36–37, 65, 133–34, 156, 370
Judaea...C2 I; E3 XIV, XV, XVI; C5 XX
Judaea, 30, 31, 354–55, 390–91, 394, 409, 453
Judah...F2 VI, VII, VIII, IX, X; C4 XXI
Judah, 309, 338
Judah, Wilderness of.....C2 I
Judah, Wilderness of, 31, 368
Judeideh, Tell (in Israel)...... E2 XXI
Judeideh, Tell (in Turkey)..... B4 XXI
Julias......C4 XIV, XV, XVI

Julias (et Tell), 388
Juliay...............D4 XIX
Juttah...A7 V; F3 XIV, XV, XVI
Juttah, 187

K

Kabul..............D12 XII
Kadesh (Kinza)........C4 III
Kadesh, 98, 109, 113, 117–19, 209, 312
Kadesh-barnea......D2 II; C3 III; B6 V
Kadesh-barnea, 102, 108
Kanah....B3 VI, VII, VIII, IX, X, XIV, XV, XVI
Kanan, mtn...B3 II; C4 XIV, XV, XVI
Kanata....C5 XIV, XV, XVI
Kanatha...C6 XIV, XV, XVI
Kandahar..........D12 XII
Kanesh (Kultepe)......B4 III
Kaptaru (Crete)......B1 III
Karabel...........B2 III
Karatepe...B4 III, XI, XXI
Karduniash..........C6 III
Karim-Shahir.......B6 XXI
Karim-Shahir, 53
Kariukulti-Ninurta.....B5 XI
Karkiya.............B2 III
Karkor, 157
Karnaim (Sheikh Saad)....... C4 III, XI; C5 VI, VII, VIII, IX, X
Karnaim, 297
Karnak.............D3 XI
Karnak, 131, 270
Karnion............C5 XIV
Kar-Shalmaneser.....B4 XI
Karun (Eulaeus), riv...C7 XI
Kashka.............A4 III
Katerin, mtn.........D5 V
Kedar..............C4 XI
Kedemoth, 122
Kedesh...B4 VI, VII, VIII, IX, X; B3 XIV, XV, XVI
Kedesh, 152
Kefr-Bir'im..B3 XIV, XV, XVI
Keilah...E2 III; E3 VI, VII, VIII, IX, X
Keilah, 185
Kelishin Pass.........B6 XI
Kenites....B6 V; F3 VI, VII, VIII, IX, X
Kephar Uzziel, 358
Kerak, Khirbet....D2 XXI
Kerkha, riv..........C6 XI
Kermanshah..........C6 III
Keykavus Kaleh.......B4 III
Kezib, 90
Khabur, riv........B5 III, XI
Khaduttu...........B4 XI
Khafajeh.........C5 III, XXI
Khaibar............D4 XI
Khalman (Aleppo)......B4 XI
Khalab or Khalpa......B4 III
Khalpa, 98
Khanigalibat........B5 XI
Kharput...........B4 XI
Kharuf, mtn.........D2 II
Khatti-land, 313, 314
Khattusha (Boghazkoi)..B3 III
Khayasha...........B4 III
Kheleifeh, Tell el....D3 XXI
Khilaku............B3 XI
Khindan............C5 XI
Khirbet: for names beginning thus see under following part of name
Khorsabad........B5 XI, XXI
Khurri.............B5 III
Khuzistan..........D8 XII
Kidron, valley...XVII, XVIII
Kidron, valley, 196, 203, 342
King's Garden, 316
Kir, 297
Kir-Haresch............C4 XI
Kir-hareseth (el-Kerak)....... F4 VI, VII, VIII, IX, X
Kir-hareseth, 284
Kiriathaim....E4 VI, VII, VIII, IX, X
Kiriath-jearim.....E3 VI, VII, VIII, IX, X
Kiriath-jearim, 137, 175
Kir Moab (el Kerak)...... F4 XIV, XV, XVI
Kish..............C5 III, XXI
Kishon, riv...B2 I; B3 II; C3 VI, VII, VIII, IX, X, XIV, XV, XVI
Kishon riv, 30, 33, 152, 153, 276

Kition.......B5 IV; C3 XI; D5 XII; C5 XX
Kition, 216
Kitron...C3 VI, VII, VIII, IX, X
Kitron, 148
Kizzuwatna...........B3 III
Klysma (Suez)..........C4 V
Kokab.....B5 XIV, XV, XVI
Kokab, 424
Komana (in Galatia)......... A4 XI; A6 XX
Komana............B4 XI
Komara............B6 XX
Koptos.............D3 XI
Koraea...D3 XIV, XV, XVI
Korakesion...........B5 XX
Korasion............B5 XX
Korykos............B5 XX
Koyunjik...........B5 XXI
Ktima, 431
Kue, 223
Kültepe..........B4 XXI
Kummukh............B4 XI
Kuntilla.............C6 V
Kurnub...A6 V; F3 XIV, XV, XVI
Kurse, 383
Kuwait.............D6 XXI
Kyros, riv...........A6 XI
Kystus............XVIII

L

Laban, 116
Lachish......E2 III, VI, VII, VIII, IX, X
Lachish (Tell ed Duweir), 270, 292, 302–03, 315–16
Lahm, Tell el........C6 XXI
Laish..B4 VI, VII, VIII, IX, X
Laish (Leshem), 166–67
Lantulae, 459
Laodicea........B4 XIII, XX; D12 XIX; B6, B5 XX
Laodicea, 449, 472
Laoe...............B4 XI
Laranda............B5 XX
Larissa...B1 XIII; D10 XIX; B3 XX
Larsa............C6 III, XI
Larsa, 323
Lase Matala.........B3 XX
Lauriacum..........B9 XIX
Laxaries..........B12 XII
Lebanon..........C3 XXI
Lebanon, mtn...A2 I; C4 XI; A4 XIV, XV, XVI; C6 XX
Lebanon, mtn., 330
Lebonah...D3 VI, VII, VIII, IX, X, XIV, XV, XVI
Lebonah (el Lebban), 365
Lechaeum...........B3 XX
Legio...C3 XIV, XV, XVI
Lehabim............B4 IV
Lehi (Ramath-lehi), 164
Leja...B3 I; B6 VI, VII, VIII, IX, X; C5 XIV, XV, XVI
Lemnos, isl...........A1 XX
Leontes, riv...A2 I; A3 II; B3 VI, VII, VIII, IX, X, XIV, XV, XVI
Leontes riv., 33
Leontopolis..........C5 XX
Leptis Magna........E9 XIX
Lesbos, isl...B2 XIII; B4 XX
Lesbos, 451
Lesser Armenia........B6 XX
Lesser Zab, riv......B5 XIII
Libba.............E4 XIV
Libnah...E2 VI, VII, VIII, IX, X
Libnah, 286, 303
Libya.......D1 IV; C2 XIII; E11 XIX
Liger, riv...........B5 XIX
Lilybaeum..........B1 XX
Limassol...........C5 XX
Lisht...............C3 V
Little Bitter Lake......B4 V
Lod (Lydda)..E2 III, VI, VII, VIII, IX, X
Londinium..........A5 XIX
Lower City.........XVIII
Lower Zab, riv....B5 III, XI
Lucus Augusti......C4 XIX
Lud...............B5 IV
Ludim, 459
Lugdunensis........B6 XIX
Lugdunum..........B6 XIX
Lugdunum Batavi....B6 XIX
Lukka.............B2 III
Luristan......C6 III; D8 XII

Lusitania............D4 XIX
Lussan, riv..........B6 V
Luxor..............D3 XI
Luz, 64
Lycadnia..........D12 XIX
Lycaonia (Ant.)......B5 XX
Lycaonia (Gal.)......B5 XX
Lycia...B2 XI, XIII; C4 XII; D11 XIX; B4 XX
Lycia, 432–33
Lycian, sea..........B4 XX
Lycus.............C13 XIX
Lycus, riv...A4 VI, VII, VIII, IX, X, XIV, XV, XVI; A6 XI, XX
Lydda (Diospolis)....E2 XIV, XV, XVI; C5 XX
Lydda (Lod, Ludd), 32, 418–19
Lydia........C4 XII; B4 XX
Lydia, 325
Lydian, kingdom.......B3 XI
Lystra.............B5 XX
Lystra, 433–34, 437

M

Maacah, 201
Ma'an...D3 II; B7 V; C4 XI
Mabartha (Nablus)...D3 XIV, XV, XVI
Macedonia..B3 XII; A1 XIII; C10 XIX; A3 XX
Macedonia, 438–41
Macestus, riv........A4 XX
Machaerus..E4 XIV, XV, XVI
Machaerus, 385
Machpelah, 77
Maciya..............D3 XII
Madai..............B6 IV
Madeba...C2 I; E4 VI, VII, VIII, IX, X, XIV, XV, XVI
Madeba map, 370
Madiama...E6 XII; D4 XIII; F13 XIX
Madian............D4 XI
Madian (el Bed)......D6 V
Madon...C3 VI, VII, VIII, IX, X
Madon, 139
Maeander, riv...B2 XI, XIII; B4 XX
Magan.............D3 III
Magdala (Tarichaea)..C3 XIV, XV, XVI
Magdala, 374, 380
Magharah, mtn........D5 V
Magnesia...B2 XI, XIII; B4 XX
Magnesia, 467
Magog..............B6 IV
Mahanaim.D4 VI, VII, IX, X
Mahanaim, 84, 85, 204–06
Mahaneh-dan, 163, 167
Mahra.............D7 IV
Major, isl.........D6 XIX
Makaz, 214
Makkedah...E2 VI, VII, VIII, IX, X
Makkedah, 138
Malaca.............D5 XIX
Malea, cape.........B3 XX
Malta, isl...........B1 XX
Malta, isl., 457, 458
Mamre, 66, 68, 70, 76–77, 85
Mamshath..F2 VI, VII, VIII, IX, X
Mamshath, 307
Manasseh.........C5, D3 VI
Mannai............B6 XI
Maon...F3 VI, VII, VIII, IX, X; D6 XII
Maon, 186–87, 281
Maorah, mtn.........B6 V
Maqam el Arba 'in ("the place of the Forty"), 384
Maqlub, Tell el, 179
Maracanda (Samarkand)..... C12 XII
Marah.............C4 V
Marah, 107, 110
Mardin............B5 XI
Marea...C2 XI; D4 XII
Mareotis, lake.........A2 V
Mareshah (Marissa)...E2 XIV, XV, XVI
Mareshah, 270
Margiana (Margush)...B10 XII
Mari.............C5 III, XI
Mariamne..........XVIII
Marisus, riv.........B10 XIX
Marmarica.........E10 XIX
Marum, 296
Masada....F3 XIV, XV, XVI
Masada, 186, 355†

Mash............B5 IV
Mashkhutah, Tell el..C3 XXI
Massawa.............D5 IV
Massah, 117
Massilia............C7 XIX
Matiane.............C7 XII
Mauretania..........D5 XIX
Mazaca...B4 XIII; D13 XIX;
............B6 XX
Mazaka.............C6 XII
Mecca..............C6 IV
Medain Salih........D4 XI
Medeba, 123
Medhbeh, Khirbet,......A6 V
Media (Mada)...D2 IV; B6
..........XI, XIII; C8 XII
Media, 325–28, 332
Medina.......C6 IV; E4 XI
Mediolanium........B7 XIX
Mediterranean Sea.....A1 I;
...B1 II; C2 III, XI, XIII;
...B3 IV; A3 V; D4 XII; D8
..........XIX; C2 XXI
Megara......B1 XIII; B3 XX
Megiddo...E2 III; C3 VI, VII,
......VIII, IX, X; C4 XI
Megiddo, 21, 152–153, 216, 220,
297, 311
Meiron....C3 VI, VII, VIII,
...IX, X, XIV, XV, XVI
Me-jarkon, riv...B2 II; D2 VI,
......VII, VIII, IX, X
Melid...............B4 XI
Melita, isl..........D8 XIX
Melite..............C6 XII
Melitene...B4 XIII; D13 XIX
Melos, isl...........B3 XX
Meluhha (Nubia)......E3 III
Memphis (Moph, Noph)...
...D3 III, XI, XIII; C3 V;
.........E5 XII; F12 XIX
Memphis, 104, 306
Mendes.............A3 V
Mendes, 341
Mendesic Mouth.......A4 V
Menshiyeh, Tell el, 174
Menzaleh, lake.......A3 V
Meribah, 117
Meroe..............D2, D5 IV
Merom, Lake, 26, 139
Meroz, 153
Mersin.............B3 XXI
Merv...............C11 XIX
Mesene.......B6 IV; D8 XII
Mesha, 52, 53
Meshech............B5 IV
Mesopotamia.......E14 XIX
Mesopotamia, 325
Messana............D8 XIX
Messara, gulf........B3 XX
Messina............B2 XX
Mesta..............B6 XI
Metheg-ammah, 200
Metropolis..........B4 XX
Micah, house of, 166–67
Michmash...E3 VI, VII, VIII,
...IX, X, XIV, XV, XVI
Michmash, 180–82
Michmethath, 293
Midas, Tomb of.......B3 XI
Midian.............D7 V
Midian, 100, 101, 108, 109
Migdal Eder, 88, 362
Migdol (Tell el Her)...B4 V;
..............C3 III, XI
Migdol, 105, 106, 107, 318
Migron, 181
Milet..............B2 XIII
Miletus....C4 XII; D11 XIX;
.........B4 XX; B2 XXI
Miletus, 451
Millo, 197, 220, 290
Minius, riv..........C4 XIX
Minni..............B6 XI
Minnith...E4 VI, VII, VIII,
..............IX, X
Minnith, 161
Minor, isl...........D6 XIX
Misrephoth-maim......B3 VI,
......VII, VIII, IX, X
Misrephoth-maim, 139
Misru..............D3 III
Mitanni (Khanigalbat).....
..............B4 III
Mitanni, 96
Mizpah?...E3 VI, VII, VIII,
..............IX, X
Mizpah, 84, 271, 317, 337; see
also Mizpeh
Mizpeh?...B4 VI, VIII, IX, X;
..............D4 XII
Mizpeh, 140, 161, 175–76, 185;
see also Mizpah

Mizraim............C5 IV
Moab....C2 I; A7 V; F4 VI,
...VII, VIII, IX, X; C4 XI
Moab, 27, 29, 124, 167–68, 283
Moabitis...F4 XIV, XV, XVI
Modein.....E3 XIV, XV, XVI
Moeris, lake.........C2 V
Moesia...........C10 XIX
Moesia, Upper.......A3 XX
Mogentiacum.......B7 XIX
Mohammediyeh.......A4 V
Mokatteb, riv........D5 V
Mokha.............D6 IV
Moladah...F2 VI, VII, VIII,
..............IX, X
Mons Cassius........B5 IV
Mons Casius, 105, 106
Mopsuestia......B4 XI, XIII;
..............B6 XX
Mopsuestia, 436
Moreh, Hill of, 155
Moresheth-gath, 301
Moriah, 76
Mortar, 308
Moschians.........B6 XII
Mosella, riv........B7 XIX
Mosera, 119
Mosul......C7 XII; B5 XIII
Muhhazzie..........E2 III
Mukish.............B4 III
Mukish, 96
Muluchath, riv.......E5 XIX
Muqenna', Khirbet el, 273;
Murabba'at, riv......E3 XIV
Murabba'at, riv., 18
Mursa.............B9 XIX
Musa, mtn., 112–13
Musasir...........B6 XI
Mushki............B3 XI
Mushki (Meshech), 223
Musri.............B4 XI
Mutesellim, Tell el...D2 XXI
Mutesellim, Tell el, 152
Mycenae...........B1 III
Mygdonia..........B5 XIII
Myra.............B5 XX
Myra, 454
Myriandros..D6 XII; B4 XIII
Mysia.......C4 XII; B4 XX
Mytilene...........B4 XX
Mytilene, 451

N

Naacratis...........C2 XXI
Nabataeans.....C4 XIII; F4
...XIV, XV, XVI; E13 XIX
Nabataeans, Kingdom of.....
..............C6 XX
Nablus...D3 XIV, XV, XVI
Naboth, 280, 286
Nacer.............B7 XIX
Nahalol...C3 VI, VII, VIII,
..............IX, X
Nahalol, 148
Nah Araim..........B4 III
Nahor, 79
Nahr Baniyas, riv......A3 II
Nahr ez Zeraa, riv......B1 I
Nahr Rubin, riv...C1 I; C2 II
Nain....C3 XIV, XV, XVI
Nain, 380
Naioth, 184
Napata............D5 IV
Naphtali...........B3 VI
Naphtuhim.........C5 IV
Naqb el Emreikheh.....D6 V
Naqb el Mirad.......C6 V
Naqb Shtar, 119
Narbata (Arbatta)...D3 XIV
Narbo.............C6 XIX
Narbonensis........C6 XIX
Nasbeh, Tell en.....D2 XXI
Nasr..............C6 III
Nations, the, 66
Natrun, riv.........C3 XI
Naucratis...B2 V; C3 XIII;
..............E12 XIX
Nazareth...B2 I; C3 XIV, XV,
..............XVI
Nazareth, 358, 359, 383, 384
Nazianzos.........B5 XX
Neapolis (in Italy)....C8 XIX;
..............A1 XX
Neapolis (in Macedonia).....
..............A3 XX
Neapolis (Kavalla), 438–39
Nebi Mind, Tell.....C4 XXI
Nebi Samwil........C2 I
Nebi Yunis.........B5 XXI

Nebo, mtn...C3 II; A7 V; E4
...VI, VII, VIII, IX, X, XIV,
..............XV, XVI
Nebo, mtn., 126, 127, 132
Nefud.........B5 IV; D5 XI
Negeb...C1 I; D2 II; F2 VI,
......VII, VIII, IX, X
Negeb (Negev), 32, 64, 67
Nejd...............D5 XI
Nejran.............D6 IV
Nemrud Dagh...B4 XI, XIII,
..............XXI
Nemrud Dagh, 364
Neqb Shtar.........C7 V
Nerab.............B4 XXI
Nessana (Auja el Hafir).....
......G1 XIV, XV, XVI
Netophah, 337
Nians.............C4 XII
Nicaea............A4 XX
Nicomedia.........A3 XIII;
............C11 XIX; A5 XX
Nicopolis...E2 XIV, XV, XVI;
............C11 XIX; B3 XX
Nicopolis, 409, 464
Nihawend..........C6 III
Nile, riv.....C5, D1 IV; C3 V;
...D3 XI, XIII, XXI; F5 XII
Nimrud............B5 XXI
Nimrud, 267
Nilus, riv..........F12 XIX
Nineveh...B5 III, XI; B6 IV
Nineveh, 56, 310
Nippur............C5 III, XI
Nippur, 56
Nisibis......B5 III, XI, XIII;
...C7 XII; D14 XIX
Nisir (Pir Omar Gudrun), mtn.,
............B6 III, XI
Nisir, mtn., 44
Niya (Qal at el Mudig)..B4 III
Nob, 184
Nobah (Kenath)...C6 VI, VII,
..............VIII, IX, X
Nobah, 157
Nod, Land of, 43
Noph (Memphis)......D3 III
Noricum...........B8 XIX
Nubia.............E3 III
Nuffar.............C5 XXI
Nukhasse...........B4 III
Numidia...........D7 XIX
Nuzi..............B5 III

O

Oak of Moreh, 63, 159
Oana, riv...........B2 I
Obal..............D6 IV
Oboth (Ain el-Weibeh)...B7 V
Oboth, 121, 122
Oea (Tripoli).......E8 XIX;
..............C1 XX
Oerahi, riv..........A7 V
Olbia.............B12 XIX
Olisipo............D4 XIX
Olives, mount of, 224, 394–98,
404, 414
Olympus, mtn.......A3 XX
Olympus, mtn., 441
Oman.............C7 IV
Oman, gulf of.......C7 IV
On (Heliopolis).......C2 III
On, 92, 93
Ono...D2 VI, VII, VIII, IX, X
Ono, plain of, 338
Ophel.............XVIII
Ophel, 295, 307
Ophir.............D6 IV
Ophrah?......C3, D3 VI, VII,
..............VIII, IX, X
Ophrah, 154, 157–58, 180–81
Ophrah of Abieser, 154
Opis...C5 XI, XIII; D7 XII;
..............E14 XIX
Opis, 328
Orchoe (Uruk, Erech).....
............D8 XII; C6 XIII
Orda......F2 XIV, XV, XVI
Oreimeh, Tell el......D2 XXI
Orontes, riv.......B4 XI, XIII
Orontes, riv., 98, 427–28
Osha, mtn...B2 I; D4 VI, VII,
..............VIII, IX, X
Ossa, mtn..........B3 XX
Ostia.............A1 XX
Ostian Way, 460
Ostrakine..........A5 V
Oxyrhynchus..D2 V; D3 XIII

P

Padus.............B7 XIX

Pahel (Pella)...E2 III; D4 VI,
...VII, VIII, IX, X, XIV,
..............XV, XVI
Palace of Helena......XVIII
Palace of Herod.......XVIII
Palatine Hill, 460
Palegawra.........B6 XXI
Palegawra, 53
Palestine...........C6 XX
Palestine, 24ff., 33–36, 429
Palm Tree of Deborah, 151
Palmyra...E13 XIX; C4 XXI
Palmyra, 215–16
Palus Maeotis.......B13 XIX
Pamir............C13 XII
Pamphylia.....B3 XI, XIII;
...C5 XII; D12 XIX; B5 XX
Pamphylia, 433
Pamphylian Sea......B5 XX
Paneas............C4 XIII
Pannonia..........B9 XIX
Panormus..D8 XIX; B1 XX
Panticapaeum......B6 XIX
Paphlagonia........B5 XII;
...A3 XIII; C12 XIX; A5 XX
Paphos.....C3 XIII; C5 XX
Paphos, 431
Paradise, 42
Paraetacene........C7 XIII
Paraetonium........C2 XIII
Paran.............C6 V
Paran, 75, 187
Paropanisus (Hindukush)....
..............C13 XII
Parsa.............E9 XII
Parthia (Parthava)...C10 XII;
..............C7 XIII
Parthia, 353
Parthenon, 442
Parva..............A4 V
Pasargadae...C7 III; D9 XII;
..............C7 XXI
Pasargadae, 326, 332, 334
Patara.............B4 XX
Patara, 452
Patavium....   ...B8 XIX
Pathros............D3 XI
Pathrusim..........C5 IV
Patmos, isl.........B4 XX
Patmos, isl., 466
Patrae....D10 XIX; B3 XX
Pattala............E12 XII
Pax..............D4 XIX
Pazarli............A4 XXI
Peleg.............B6 IV
Pelion, mtn.........B3 XX
Pella...A1 XIII; D4 XIV, XV,
...XVI; C10 XIX; A3 XX
Pella, 422, 441
Pelusiac Mouth......A4 V
Pelusium...D5 XII; C3 XIII;
...E12 XIX; C5 XX
Pelusium, 102–03, 105–06, 132,
318
Penuel.....D4 VI, VII, VIII,
..............IX, X
Penuel, 85, 268
Peraea.......E4 XV, XVI
Perga.............B5 XX
Perga, 433, 435
Pergamum......B2 XI, XIII,
...XXI; C4 XII; D11 XIX;
..............B4 XX
Pergamum, 432, 447, 467–69
Pergamum, Kingdom of.....
..............B2 XIII
Perinthus...........A4 XX
Persepolis..........D7 XIII;
...E9 XII; C7 XXI
Persepolis, 334–35
Persepolis Gate......D9 XII
Persia............D2 IV
Persian Gulf....D7 III, XI,
...XIII, XXI; C7 IV; E9 XII
Persis (Parsa).......E9 XII;
..............D7 XIII
Pessinus..........B5 XX
Pethor, 125
Petra........C4 XIII, XXI;
...E13 XIX; C6 XX
Petra, 110, 118, 119, 343
Pharan, 111, 116, 118
Pharpar, riv....B5 VI, VII,
...VIII, IX, X, XIV, XV, XVI
Pharsalus..........B3 XX
Phasael............XVIII
Phasaelis...D3 XIV, XV, XVI
Phasis............B7 XII
Phatnitic Mouth (Damietta
...Mouth)...........A3 V
Pherath, 42
Phiala (Birket Ran), lake....
..............A3 II

Philadelphia (in Asia Minor)...
B4 XX
Philadelphia (in Asia Minor),
471–72
Philadelphia (Rabbath Am-
mon).....C4 XIII; E4 XIV,
XV, XVI
Philippi...A1 XIII; C10 XIX;
A3 XX
Philippi, 439, 450, 469
Philippopolis...........B4 XII;
A2 XIII; C10 XIX
Philistaea, 32
Philistines.........C1 I; B5 IV;
E2 VI, VII, VIII, IX, X
Philoteria (Beth Yerah)......
C4 XIV, XV, XVI
Phoeis................C3 XII
Phoenice (Phoenicia)........
E13 XIX
Phoenicia......A2 I; B3 XIV,
XV, XVI; C6 XX
Phoenicia, sea..........C5 XX
Phoenician, sea...........C5 XX
Phoenicians.....B3 VI, VII,
VIII, IX, X
Phoenix...............B3 XX
Phoenix, 455
Phrygia....C4 XII; D11 XIX
Phrygian Kingdom.....A3 XI
Pi-hahiroth, 104
Pillars of Hercules, 461, 462
Pirathon...D3 VI, VII, VIII,
IX, X
Pir Omar Gudrun (Grandfather
Omar Mountain), 44, 45
Pisae.................C8 XIX
Pishon, 42
Pisgah, The, 127, 128
Pisidia...C5 XII; B3 XIII;
D12 XIX
Pisidian-Antioch......B5 XX
Pithom...........C3 III, XI
Pithom, 98, 99
Pithom Heroonpolis (Tell Er-
tabeh)................B3 V
Podandus.............B6 XX
Polemon..............B6 XX
Pompeii...............A1 XX
Pompey's Camp.......XVIII
Pontine Marshes, 459
Pontius...............A5 XX
Pontus...A3 XI; A4 XIII;
C13 XIX
Praetorium, 405, 406
Priene........B4 XX; B2 XXI
Propontis...........A2 XI, XIII;
A4 XX
Prymnessus...........B4 XX
Pteria................B4 XX
Ptolemais (Acco)...C3 XIII,
XIV, XV, XVI; C6 XX
Ptolemais, 452; see also Acco
Ptolemais (in Egypt).........
D3 XIII; E10 XIX
Ptolemaic Empire....C3 XIII
Punon (Felnah).......B7 V
Puqudu-Pekod........C6 XI
Put..................B5 IV
Puteoli..............A1 XX
Puteoli, 458, 459
Putiya...............D4 XII
Pydna...............A3 XX
Pyramo, riv........D13 XIX;
B6 XX
Pyretus, riv........B11 XIX

Q

Qal 'a Sherqat.......B5 XXI
Qal 'at en Nakhl......C5 V
Qana, riv...B3 II; D3 VI, VII,
VIII, IX, X
Qantir...............C3 III
Qarantal (Mons Quarantana),
mtn., 371
Qarqar...............B4 XI
Qarqar, 280, 299
Qatar...............D7 XXI
Qatieh...............B4 V
Qatna................C4 III
Qedal, Tell el......D2 XXI
Qoseimeh.............B6 V
Que..................B4 XI
Qum..................C7 XXI
Qumran, Khirbet, 17–19, 21, 31,
136, 357, 368–69, 474
Qumran, Khirbet....E4 XIV,
XV; E2 XXI

R

Raamah...............D6 IV
Raamses?.............B3 V

Raamses, 98–99, 104–05, 131
Rabbah: see Rabbath Ammon
Rabbath Ammon (Philadel-
phia; Amman)......C3 II;
E5 VI, VII, VIII, IX, X;
D6 XII; E4 XIV, XV, XVI
Rabbath Ammon, 29, 201
Rabbath Moab...F4 VI, VII,
VIII, IX, X
Raetia...............B7 XIX
Raga.................C9 XII
Ragaba....D4 XIV, XV, XVI
Rakkath...C3 VI, VII, VIII,
IX, X
Ram, mtn.E3 II; C7 V; D4 XI
Ramallah.............C2 I
Ramah (Ramathaim)...E3 VI,
VII, VIII, IX, X, XIV,
XV, XVI
Ramah (Ramathaim), 172, 177,
178†, 184, 271
Ramah (NW of Galilee).......
C3 VI, VII, VIII, IX, X
Ramat Rahel, 68, 337, 340
Ramoth (Gilead)...C5 VI, VII,
VIII, IX, X
Ramses, 277, 280, 286
Ramses, Land of, 93
Raphana...C5 XIV, XV, XVI
Raphia...E2 III; A6 V; C3 XI,
XIII; F1 XIV, XV, XVI;
C5 XX
Raphia, 103, 299
Rasappa..............B5 XI
Ras el Abyab...E4 XI; F6 XII
Ras el Ain...B5 XI; D2 XXI
Ras esh Shamra.......B4 XI;
B3 XXI
Ras esh Shamra, 165
Ras Mohammed........E6 V
Ras Safsafeh..........D5 V
Ras Safsafeh, 112, 113
Ras Siyagha, 128
Ravenna.............C8 XIX
Ray.................B7 XXI
Red Sea...D4 III, XI, XIII,
XXI; C5, D2 IV; E6 V
Red Sea, 103–04
Reeds, sea of, 105, 106, 108
Regina Castra........B8 XIX
Rehob...E2 III; D4 VI, VII,
VIII, IX, X
Rehob, 149
Rehoboth...A6 V; F2 VI, VII,
VIII, IX, X
Rekem (Petra)...B7 V; C4 XI
Remeth...C4 VI, VII, VIII,
IX, X
Remphthis, 407
Rephaim, plain........C2 I
Rephaim, plain, 31, 198
Rephidim.............D5 V
Rephidim, 107–09, 112, 117
Retenu...............C3 III
Reuben...............E4 VI
Rezeph (Rasappa)......B4 XI
Rezeph, 304
Rhagae...........B7 III, XI
Rhegium...D9 XIX; B2 XX
Rhegium, 458
Rhenus, riv..........A7 XIX
Rhinocorura..........C3 XIII
Rhodanus, riv........C7 XIX
Rhodes (Rhodus).....C4 XII;
B2 XIII; D11 XIX; B4 XX
Rhodes, 452
Rhyndacus, riv.......B4 XX
Riblah...............C4 XI
Riblah, 311, 316
Rici................D5 XXI
Rihab...D5 VI, VII, VIII, IX,
X
Rimmon (near Ephraim)......
E3 VI, VII, VIII, IX, X
Rimmon, 194
Rimmon (W. of Galilee)......
C3 VI, VII, VIII, IX, X
Rithmah..............C7 V
Robinson's Bridge....XVIII
Rogel, Fountain of, 204
Rogelim, 206
Rome (Roma).......C8 XIX;
A1 XX
Rome, 429, 454, 460
Rosetta...............A2 V
Rosetta Mouth........A2 V
Rub 'a el Khali.......C6 IV
Ruheibeh, 81
Rumeileh, Tell er.....E2 XXI

S

Sabrata..............E8 XIX
Sabta.................D6 IV

Sabteca...............D6 IV
Safed...B4 XIV; C4 XV, XVI
Safed, 360†, 361
Safi, Tell es.........E2 XXI
Sagartians............D9 XII
Saggara...............C3 V
Saint Paul's Bay, 457
Sais..........C3 XI; D5 XII;
C5 XX
Sait, valley of, 291
Sajur, riv............B4 III
Saka Haumavarga (Amyrgian
Scythians)......C13 XII
Sakastan (Sistan)....D11 XII
Saka Tigrakhauda (Pointed
Helmet Scythians)..C13 XII
Saktshegözu..........B4 XXI
Sa'l, riv.............D6 V
Salamis...C5 XII; B3 XIII;
D12 XIX; B5 XX
Salamis, 430
Saldae...............D6 XIX
Salecah (Salkhad)....D6 XIV,
XV, XVI
Salem, 68
Salhieh...............B3 V
Salim....D4 XIV, XV, XVI
Salim, 391
Salmon, mtn., 160
Salmone (Sammonium), cape..
B4 XX
Salmone, cape, 455
Salonae..............C9 XIX
Sam'al...............B4 XI
Samaria, reg...B2 I; D3 VI,
VII, VIII, IX, X, XIV, XV,
XVI; C4 XI; C3 XIII; C5
XX
Samaria, reg., 30, 354–55, 416
Samaria (Sebaste)....D3 XIV,
XV, XVI; C6 XX
Samaria (Sebaste), 273, 285,
297, 416–17
Samarih..............D5 XII
Samega...............E4 XIV
Samosata....B4 XI, XIII;
C6 XII
Samothrace, isl........A4 XX
San..................B3 V
Sana.................D6 IV
Sangarius, riv...A3 XI; D12
XIX; A5 XX
San Tunis............C3 XXI
Sanur, 365
Sardes...............B2 XIII
Sardina, isl.........D7 XIX
Sardis...B2 III, XI, XXI;
D1 IV; C4 XII;
D11 XIX; B4 XX
Sardis, 326, 470
Sarepta...B3 XIV, XV, XVI
Sarid...C3 VI, VII, VIII, IX,
X
Saripul (Behistun).....C6 III
Sarmatia..............A10 XIX
Saros, riv.............B6 XX
Saspeires.............B7 XII
E13 XII
Saudi Arabia.........D5 XXI
Savus.................B9 XIX
Saxones..............A7 XIX
Scallabis.............D4 XIX
Schedia..............C5 XX
Scopus, mtn., 202
Scrolls Caves . . .   E3 XIV,
XV, XVI
Scylla and Charibdis, 458
Scythians (Saka)......C2 IV;
C13 XII; B4 XII
Scythopolis..C3 XIV, XV, XVI
Sealand..............C6 XI
Seba.................D5 IV
Sebaste: see Samaria
Sebastiyeh...........D2 XXI
Sebastopolis.........A6 XX
Sebennytic Mouth......A2 V
Sebennytos...........A2 V
Second Quarter (of Jerusalem),
308
Second Wall........XVIII
Seffuriyeh...........D2 XXI
Segovia..............C5 XIX
Seilun...............D2 XXI
Seir, mount....C3 II; B7 V
Seir, mount, 67, 115–16
Seirah, 150
Sela, 291
Seleucia...B3 XIII; C4 XIV,
XV, XVI; E14 XIX; B5 XX
Seleucia (in Babylonia)......
C5 XIII

Seleucia Pieria.......B4 XIII;
B6 XX
Seleucia Pieria, 427
Seleucis.............B4 XIII
Selinus.....D12 XIX; B5 XX
Selmun, isl., 457
Semechonitis, lake.....A2 I;
A3 II; B4 VI, VII, VIII, IX,
X, XV, XVI; B3 XIV
Senkereh.............C6 XXI
Sepharad (Sardis in Lydia), 343
Sephar, 52
Sepharad.............C5 XII
Sepharvaim, 304
Sepphoris...C3 XIV, XV, XVI
Sepphoris, 354
Sequana, riv..........B6 XIX
Serabit (el Khadem)....D3 XI
Serabit el Khadem......D5 V
Serbal, mtn............D5 V
Serpent's Pool........XVIII
Sewen (Syene, Assuan)..E3 V
Shalim (Shaalim), 176–77
Shalisha (Baal-shalisha), 176–
77
Shamiramalti (Tilke Tepe)....
B5 III
Shammar, mtn.........D5 XI
Shankhar.............B5 III
Shapur...............D7 XXI
Sharon, plain...B1 I; B2 II;
D2 VI, VII, VIII, IX, X,
XIV, XV, XVI
Sharon, plain, 32, 33
Sharuhen...E2 III; F1 VI, VII,
VIII, IX, X
Shasu................C4 III
Shatt el Hai, riv......C6 XI
Shaveh, valley of, 68
Shaveh Kiriathaim, 67
Shebarim, 135
Sheba................D6 IV
Shechem (Sychar)...B2 I; C4,
E2 III; D3 VI, VII, VIII, IX,
X, XIV, XV, XVI
Shechem: no strong defensive lo-
cation, 30; Abraham at, 62–
63; visit of Jacob, 85–87;
Joseph seeks his brothers at,
91; alleged site of Joshua's
farewell address, 143; in time
of Abimelech, 158, 160; seat
of prefecture under Solomon,
213; rebuilt by Jeroboam, 268;
site of Jacob's Well, 391–92
Sheep Gate..........XVIII
Sheikh Sa'ad.........C4 XXI
Sheikh Zuweid........C3 XXI
Sheleph..............D6 IV
Shephelah.............C1 I
Shibah, 81
Shihan, mtn...C3 II; F4 VI,
VII, VIII, IX, X
Shiloah, 295, 300, 301
Shiloh...D3 VI, VII, VIII, IX,
X
Shiloh, 172–73, 269
Shimron...C3 VI, VII, VIII,
IX, X
Shimron, 139
Shimronmeron...B3 VI, VII,
VIII, IX, X
Shinar, 53, 66
Shiraz........C7 IV; E9 XII
Shittim, valley, 342
Shobek...............B7 V
Shuah................C5 XI
Shunem...E2 III; C3 VI, VII,
VIII, IX, X, XIV, XV, XVI
Shunem, 188–89
Shupria..............B5 XI
Shur, 64, 69
Shuruppak, 44
Shush, Shushan: see Susa
Shushan-Susa (Shush)......
C6 XI, XXI
Sibe, 299
Sicilia (Sicily), isl...D8 XIX;
B1 XX
Sicily, 458
Sicyon...............B3 XX
Sicyon, 445
Siddim, valley of, 68, 71
Side....B3 XIII; B5 XX
Sidon...A2 I; A3 II, VI, VII,
VIII, IX, X, XIV; C4 XI,
XI, XIII, XV, XVI; D5 XII;
E13 XIX; C6 XX
Sidon, 139, 149†, 342, 387, 454
Sidonians............B5 IV
Sidreh, riv...........D5 V
Sile.................B4 V
Silis, riv...........B12 XII
Siloam..............XVIII

Siloam, pool of, 393
Simeon................F2 VI
Simonias....C3 XIV, XV, XVI
Sinai (Jebel Musa), mtn......
        D6 V; D3 XI
Sinai, mtn., 100, 113
Sinai, peninsula.........C5 V
Sinai, peninsula, 108–10, 116,
        145
Sinites................B5 IV
Sinjar, mtn............B5 XI
Sinjirh.............B4 XXI
Sinope...D2 IV; A4 XI, XIII;
        B6 XII; C13 XIX; A6 XX
Sin-Pelusium......A4 V; C3 XI
Sippar...........C5 III, XI
Sippar, 328
Sipylus, mtn......B2 III, XI;
        B4 XX
Sirbonis, lake..........A5 V
Sirbonis, lake, 105, 106, 107
Sirhan, riv.....B5 IV; C4 XI,
        XIII
Sirmium............B10 XIX
Siwa (oasis)...........D2 XI
Siyalk...............C7 XXI
Sminthium, cape.....B4 XX
Smyrna....B2 III, XI, XIII;
        D11 XIX; B4 XX
Smyrna, 466, 467
Socoh..E2 VI, VII, VIII, IX, X
Socoh (Shocoh), 183, 270, 307
Socotra................D7 IV
Sodom, 70, 71, 72
Sogdiana (Suguda)...C12 XIX
Solaf, riv...............D5 V
Soli........B3 XIII; B5 XX
Somaliland, 223
Sorek, vale of, 165
Soviet Union.........A5 XXI
Spain, 461, 463
Sparda................C4 XII
Sparta.....C3 XII; B1 XIII;
        D10 XIX; B3 XX
Spring of the Steps, 196–97
Stobi...............C10 XIX
Straton's Tower.....C3 XIII;
        C2 XIV
Strymon.............A3 XX
Subartu.............B5 III
Subur, riv.............E4 XIX
Succoth (Scenae)....D4 VI,
        VII, VIII, IX, X, XIV, XV,
        XVI
Succoth, 85, 104, 105, 106, 219
Sucre, riv...........D5 XIX
Sudr, riv..............C4 V
Suez....................C3 XI
Suez, 102, 104, 109
Sukhu (Shuah).........C5 XI
Sulaimania............B6 XI
Sultan, Tell es....D2 XXI
Sultan, Tell es, 27
Sultan Tepe......B4 III, XXI
Sumer................C6 III
Suph, 116
Sur, riv., 183
Susa (Shushan).......C6 III,
        XIII; D8 XII
Susa (Shushan), 332–34
Susiana.............D8 XII
Sustana.............C6 XIII
Sutu.................C4 III
Syene.....F5 XII; E3 XIII;
        G12 XIX
Sykaminos..C2 XIV, XV, XVI
Synnada.............B5 XX
Syracuse.....D9 XIX; B2 XX
Syracuse, 458
Syria.....C4 XIII; E13 XIX;
        B6 XX; B4 XXI
Syrian Gates.........B6 XX
Syrian Gates, 436
Syrtes, 456
Syrtica..............E8 XIX
Syrtis Major........E9 XIX;
        C2 XX
Syrtis Minor.........E8 XIX

T

Taanaoh...C3 VI, VII, VIII,
        IX, X
Taanathshiloh...D3 VI, VII,
        VIII, IX, X
Ta'anek, Tell.......D2 XXI
Ta'anek, Tell, 152
Tabali................B4 XI
"Table of the Lord," 410
Tabor, mtn...B2 I; B3 II; C3
        VI, VII, VIII, IX, X, XIV,
        XV, XVI
Tabor, mtn., 29, 152, 389
Tabor, plain (oak) of, 177–78

Tabriz...............B6 XI
Tacapae............E7 XIX
Tadmor (Palmyra)....C4 III,
        XI, XIII; D6 XII
Tadmor, 215–16
Tagus...............C4 XIX
Tahae.............D10 XII
Tahpanhes (Daphnae)...B3 V;
        C3 XI
Tahpanhes, 106, 318
Tainat, Tell.........B4 XXI
Takritain...........C5 XI
Tamar, 221
Tamassos............B5 XX
Tamesis, riv..........A4 XIX
Tanis...........C2 III; B3 V
Tanitic Mouth.........A4 V
Tannach, 152
Tannur, mtn..........C4 XXI
Tappuah...D3 VI, VII, VIII,
        IX, X
Tappuah, 293
Tarentum...B2 XII; C9 XIX;
        A2 XX
Tarichaea..C3 XIV, XV, XVI
Tarraco.............C6 XIX
Tarraconeusis.......D5 XIX
Tarshish (Tartessus).......A2,
        B1 IV
Tarshish (Tharshish), 222
Tarsus.....C5 XII; B4 XIII,
        XXI; D13 XIX; B5 XX
Tarsus, 423–24, 426–27, 432
Tatta, lake..........B5 XX
Taurus, mts......B3 III; B4,
        B6 XX
Taurus, mts., 431–32
Tavium.............B5 XX
Taxila...............D13 XII
Tebuk...C5 IV; D7 V; D4 XI,
        XIII
Tehran (Teheran)..B7 III, XI;
        C9 XII
Tekoa...E3 VI, VII, VIII, IX,
        X, XIV, XV, XVI
Tekoa, 270, 336
Teku.................C3 III
Telaim (Telem), 182
Tel Aviv...............B2 II
Tel-assar, 304
Teleilat Ghassui....D2 XXI
Tel-harsha, 321
Tell: for names beginning thus
        see under following part of
        name
Tell-abib, 315
Telloh.........C6 XI, XXI
Tel-melah, 321
Telmissus..........B2 XIII
Tema (Amurru), 325
Tema (Teima)...D4 XI, XIII
Teman (eth-Thuwaneh)..B7 V
Teman, 343
Tembris, riv.........B5 XX
Temple..............XVIII
Temple, 289, 399, 400–01
Temple of Apollo, 444†
Tepe Gawra........B5 XXI
Tepe Giyan..........C6 III
Tepe Hissar........B7 XXI
Thamar...B7 V; G3 VI, VII,
        VIII, IX, X
Thamna...D3 XIV, XV, XVI
Thapsacus...C6 XII; B4 XIII
Thapsus.............D8 XIX
Thasos..............A3 XX
Thebes (Thebae, No Amon)...
        B3 III, XI; D1 IV; E3 V;
        E5 XII; D3 XIII; F12 XIX
Thebes, 306
Thebes (in Greece)....B3 XX
Thebez....D3 VI, VII, VIII,
        IX, X
Thebez, 160
Theku...........B3 V; C3 XI
Theku, 104
Themed...............C6 V
Themiskyra..........A4 XIII
Thessalia (Thessaly)...C3 XX;
        B3 XX
Thessalonica (Thessalonice)...
        A1 XIII; C10 XIX; A3 XX
Thessalonica, 440
Third Wall..........XVIII
This.................D3 XI
Thmuis...............A3 V
Thrace (Thracia), reg....C2 IV;
        A2 XIII; C11 XIX; A4 XX
Thracians (Skudra)....B3 XII
Three Taverns........A1 XX
Three Taverns, 459
Thyatira............B4 XX
Thyatira, 469–70
Tiber, riv.............A1 XX

Tiberias....C3 XIV, XV, XVI
Tiberias, 384†, 385, 393, 410
Tiberis, riv...........C8 XIX
Tibneh, Khirbet, 143
Tiflis...............A5 XI
Tigris, riv....C5 III, XI, XIII,
        XXI; B6 IV; C7 XII;
        D14 XIX
Tigris, riv., 56
Tihamah..........C5, D6 IV
Til Barsip..........B4 III
Til Barsip, 62, 63†
Timnah...E2 VI, VII, VIII,
        IX, X
Timnah, 90, 163, 273
Timnath-serah....D3 VI, VII,
        VIII, IX, X
Timnath-serah, 143
Timsah, lake.........B4 V
Tingis..............D4 XIX
Tingitana...........E4 XIX
Tiphsah (Thapsacus)..B4 XI
Tiphsah (Thapsacus), 214–15
Tiran, isl...........E6 V
Tiras...............B4 IV
Tirga...............B5 XI
Tirhakah...........C5 III
Tiryns..............B1 III
Tirzah (Jemma'in)...D3 VI,
        VII, VIII, IX, X
Tirzah, 127, 154, 269, 272, 293
Tishbe, 274
Tmolus, mtn.........B2 XI
Tob, 161
Tobiah, House of.....D4 XIV
Togarmah...........B5 IV
Toletum.............D5 XIX
Tolosa..............C6 XIX
Tomb of Jesus, 407, 408
Tophel (et Tafileh).....B7 V
Tophel, 116
Toprak Kaleh.........B5 III
Tor..................D5 V
Tower of Babel, 54
Tower of David, 367
Tower of Hananel, 343
Tr (el Kantara).......C3 III
Tr, 103
Trachonitis..........B5 XIV,
        XV, XVI
Tralles.............B4 XX
Trapezus (Trebizond)..A4 XI,
        XIII; B6 XII; C14 XIX
Tripolis.....C4 XIII; C6 XX
Troas..............B4 XX
Troas, 438
Trogyllium, cape.....B4 XX
Troy................B2 III
Trucial Oman........E7 XXI
Tubal..............B5 IV
Tubeigan, Khirbet et..E2 XXI
Tulul...............B5 XXI
Tumilat, riv.........C3 III
Tunip...............B4 III
Turkey.........B3, B4 XXI
Turquoise Mines......D5 V
Tuspa (van Kaleh)....B5 XI
Tuspa Turushpa, 45
Tyaly Drayahya......C4 XII
Tyana...B3 XIII; D12 XIX;
        B5 XX
Tylos, isl...........E9 XII
Tyre...A2 I; A3 II; C4, D2 III,
        D2 IV; B3 VI, VII, VIII, IX,
        X, XIV; D6 XII; C3 XI,
        XIII; C5 XV, XVI, XX
Tyre, 33, 216, 274, 318, 342, 387
Tyrian Ladder...A2 I; B3 VI,
        VII, VIII, IX, X, XIV, XV,
        XVI
Tyropoeon Valley......XVIII
Tyropoeon Valley, 296, 316
Tyrrhenian Sea.......C8 XIX
Tyrus.....C4 XIII; E4 XIV,
        XV, XVI; E13 XIX

U

Ufratu, riv............D7 XII
Ugair, Tell............C5 XI
Ugarit (Ras esh Shamra).....
        B4 III
Ugarit, 96, 131
Ulai, riv.............C6 XI
Ulai (Eulaeus), riv, 333–34
Ulatha...B4 XIV, XV, XVI
Ulatha, 26
'Umair, Tell.........C6 XXI
Umma................C6 III
Umm er Ramamim, Khirbet, 343
Umm Shomer, mtn.....D6 V
Upi.................C4 III
Upper City..........XVIII
Upper Pool, 295, 296

Upper Zab, riv.....B5 III, XI
Uqair, Tell..........C5 XXI
Ur..............C6 III, XI
Ur, 55
Urartu..............B5 XI
Urartu, 299
Urhai (Edessa).......C6 XII
Urmiah, lake...B6 III, IV, XI,
        XIII, XXI; C8 XII
Usdum, mtn., 71
Utica................D8 XIX
Uwaga (Khuzistan)...D8 XII
Uz..................B5 IV
Uzal.................D6 IV

V

Valentia.............D5 XIX
Valetta Melite, 457
Van, lake....B5 III, XI, XIII,
        XXI; B6 IV; C7 XII
Van Kaleh (Toprak Kaleh)...
        B5 III, XXI
Velleq, mtn..........D1 II
Verona..............B8 XIX
Vesuvius, mtn.......A1 XX
Via Dolorosa, 406
Viadua, riv.........A8 XIX
Vindelicorum........B8 XIX
Virunum............B8 XIX
Vistula, riv.........A9 XIX
Visurgis, riv.........A7 XIX
Volubilis...........E4 XIX

W

Wailing Wall, 399
Warka...............C6 XXI
Wassukanni.........B5 III
Water Gate.........XVIII
Well of Jacob, 391, 392†
Well of Job (En Rogel).......
        XVIII
White Nile, riv.......D5 IV
Wilderness of Shur.....B5 V
Wilderness of Shur, 107, 108
Wilderness of Sin.......B5 V
Wilderness of Sin, 111
Wilderness of the Wandering
        (Badiyet et Tih)......C5 V
Wilderness of Zin......B7 V;
        G3 VI, VII, VIII, IX, X
Wilderness of Zin, 108, 117, 118
Wilson's Bridge.......XVIII

X

Xanthus.....C4 XII; B2 XIII

Y

Yadnana (Cyprus), isl..C3 XI
Yalo, 138
Yamkhad...........B4 III
Yamutbal............C6 III
Yarkon, riv., 330
Yarmuk, riv....B3 II; C4 VI,
        VII, VIII, IX, X, XIV, XV,
        XVI
Yarmuk, riv., 27–28
Yazilikaya..........A3 III
Yeb (Elephantine Isl.)..E3 XI
Yehem (Jemrop)......E2 III
Yehud...............D6 XII
Yehudiyeh, Tell el....C2 XXI
Yelleq, mtn..........B5 V
Yenoam...D2 III; C4 VI, VII,
        VIII, IX, X
Ye'or................D3 XI
Yitm, riv.............C7 V
Yorghan Tepe........B5 XXI
Yotapata (Jodephath).......
        C3 XIV, XV, XVI
Yotapata (Jodephath), 373
Yozgad..............B3 III
Ytr, riv.............D3 XI
Yursa...............E2 III

Z

Zaanannim, 152
Zab, riv............B6 XI
Zadrakarta.........B7 XIII
Zagazig.............B3 V
Zagros, mtn.........C6 XI
Zagros, pass........C8 XII
Zalmonah, 121
Zanoah...F2 VI, VII, VIII,
        IX, X
Zanoah, 337
Zaphon (Asaphon)...D4 VI,
        VII, VIII, IX, X, XIV, XV,
        XVI
Zaphon, 162

Zaphon (Casius), mtn...B4 III
Zarephath...B3 VI, VII, VIII, IX, X; C3 XI
Zarephath, 275, 343
Zarethan...D4 VI, VII, VIII, IX, X
Zarethan, 133, 156, 219
Zebillun..............C3 VI
Zeboim, 71, 180–81

Zela, 208
Zelzah, 177–78
Zemaraim, 271
Zemarites............B5 IV
Zered, riv............A7 V; G4 VI, VII, VIII, IX, X
Zered, riv., 29, 122
Zeredah, 224
Zeugma............B4 XIII

Ziklag F2 VI, VII, VIII, IX, X
Ziklag, 188
Zion, fortress of, 195–96
Ziph...F3 VI, VII, VIII, IX, X
Ziph, 182, 185, 270
Zoan.................C3 XI
Zoan, 77, 99
Zoar (Zoara).....F4 VI, VII, VIII, IX, X, XIV, XV, XVI

Zoar, 70, 71
Zobah (Aram-zobah), 200
Zobah-subatu..........C4 XI
Zophim, 126
Zorah (Zora).....E2 III, VI, VII, VIII, IX, X
Zorah, 163, 270
Zosta, 434

A

Abdi-Khepa, 97
Abel, 43
Abiathar, 185, 199, 206, 210–12
Abieser, 154
Abijam, 271
Abner, 191–94
Abram, 54
Abraham, 52, 62 ff., 100
Absalom, 202–07, 342
Achaemenids, 353
Achish, 188
Achsah, 147
Adad-nirari III., 291, 293, 304
Adams, Phythian, 165
Adonibezek, 146
Adonijah, 210, 212
Adonis, 361
Adoram, 268
Adrammelech, 304
Agabus, 429
Agrippa I, 420–21
Agrippa II, 389, 422
Agrippa III, 454
Agur, 343
Ahab, 274–76, 280–81, 286–87
Ahaz, 295, 296, 297
Ahaziah, 281, 283, 286, 287, 289
Ahijah, 224
Ahimaaz, 206
Ahuramazda, 364†
Akhnaton (Amenophis IV), 92–93, 96
Akkad, King of, 310
Albright, William F., 16, 65, 156
Alexander the Great, 41, 54, 366, 447, 452
Alexander Jannaeus, 386
Amalekites, 118, 182–83, 189
Amasa, 204, 206–07
Amasis, 318
Amaziah, of Israel, 293
Amaziah, son of Jehoash, 291
Amaziah of Judah, 291
Amenophis III, 96
Amenophis IV: see Akhnaton
Ammonites, 72, 160, 178, 201, 281, 295, 318, 337
Amnon, 202
Amon, 307
Amorites, 118
Amos, 293
Amyrtaeus, 341
Anani, 340
Ananias, 404
Andrew, 378
Andronicus, 450
Antigonus, 374
Antiochus II, 472
Antiochus of Commagene, 353, 364
Antiochus Epiphanes, 393
Antipas, 386
Antoninus, 384
Antonius Martyr, 20
Aphrodite, 408, 445
Apollos, 448
Apries, 315
Aquila, 445, 446, 448, 449, 450
Arabs, 294, 298
Aramaeans, 145, 200, 224, 267, 279, 285, 291, 309, 341
Archelaus, 353, 354
Arculf, 20
Aretas IV, 425–26
Arioch, 66
Aristrarchus, 454
Arpachshad, 52
Arphaxad, 332
Arsacids, 353
Arsham, 341
Artaxerxes I, 315, 334–36, 338
Artaxerxes II, 336, 339, 341
Artaxerxes III, 342
Artemis, 447, 449
Asa, 271, 272, 278
Asahel, 192
Asenath, 92
Ashdodites, 337
Asher, 155, 192
Asherah, 271, 288
Ashima, 298
Ashurbanipal, 46†, 306, 310, 333
Ashur-nasirpal II, 267, 305
Ashurnirari V, 297
Ashur-uballit II, 311
Athaliah, 218, 286, 289, 290
Attalus I, 468

Attalus II, 471
Augustus, 424, 427
Augustus Caesar, 352–55, 388, 442, 461, 463
Ayab, 343
Azariah, 292, 294
Azriyau of Yaudi, 294

B

Baal, 274, 390
Baalis, 317
Baasha, 271, 272
Bab Kisan gate, 426
Bacchides, 395
Badé, F. W., 271
Bagoas, 338–41
Balaam, 125–26
Balak, 125–26
Baramki, 134
Barnabas, 426–28, 431, 434–36
Bartimaeus, 395
Bathsheba, 201, 210–11
Belshazzar, 325, 327–28
Benaiah, 203, 210
Benhadad, 271, 278–81, 286, 291
Bernice, 389
Berossus, 41
Boaz, 168
Brownlee, William H., 17
Brutus, 352
Burckhardt, 114
Burrows, Millar, 17

C

Caesar, Julius, 352, 442, 444, 461
Caiaphas, 404
Cain, 43
Caleb, 141, 146
Calebites, 191
Caligula, 353, 355, 428
Caliph Hisham, 375
Cambyses, 328, 330
Canaanites, 52, 118
Carites, 289
Carmelite Monks, 276
Carter, Howard, 97
Cassites, 96, 144
Cassius, 352
Chaldeans, 316, 343
Charitan, 371
Chedorlaomer, 66–67
Chemosh, 284
Cherethites, 203
Cicero, 430, 459
Cimmerians, 299
Claudius, 353, 355, 445
Clédat, 69
Clement of Rome, 462, 463
Cleopas, 409
Cleopatra, 352
Commagene, 364
Constantine, 361, 407, 408
Coponius, 354
Copper scrolls, 18, 64, 136
Corinthians, 449
Cornelius, 419–20
Crispus, 446
Croesus, 325–26, 447, 470
Crowfoot, J. W., 417
Crusaders, 363, 374
Cushan-Rishathaim, 150
Cushites, 301
Cutheans, 298
Cyril, 392
Cyrus, 326, 328–30, 332
Cyrus (the Younger), 341

D

Damascus Document, 19
Dan, 163
Daniel, 322–23
Danites, 166
Darius I, 102, 328, 330, 333–34
Darius II, 217, 338
David, 183–212, 224, 295
Dead Sea Scrolls, 15–23, 35, 66, 68, 325
Delilah, 165, 338, 341
Demetrius, 449
Deutero-Isaiah (Second Isaiah), 325–26, 331
Diadochi, 447
Dionysius the Areopagite, 443
Domitian, 465
Dorians, 131
Dositheus of Capernaum, 377
Dusares, 277

E

Eber, 52, 54
Edomites, 78, 89, 343
Ela, 272
Elamite Jews, 399
Eleasar, 143
Eli, 173
Eliakim, 312, 315
Eliashib, 336
Elijah, 38, 275–78, 281
Elisha, 277, 278, 283–86, 291
Elizabeth, 358
Ephraimites, 150, 162, 172
Erastus, 449
Esar-haddon, 304, 318, 335
Esau, 81
Eshmunazzar, 342
Essenes, 17, 368, 369
Esther, 332–33
Etheria, 394
Eusebius, 20, 361, 380, 392, 407, 409, 421, 466
Evil-merodach, 324
Ezekiel, 309, 315, 318, 321–22, 473
Ezra, 335–36, 338–40

F

Felix, 453
Felix Fabri, 405
Fisher, C. S., 416
Free, Joseph P., 92

G

Gaal, 159
Gad, 209
Galilaean Man, 373
Gallio, 445, 446
Gamaliel, 354, 415
Garstang, John, 134, 138, 164
Gaumata, 330
Gedaliah, 317
Genesis Apocryphon, 17, 202
Germanicus, 472
Geshem, 337
Gezrites (Girzites), 188
Ghirshman, 66
Gideon, 154
Gileadites, 162
Gilgamesh, 46
Girgashites, 382
Glaphyra, 354
Glueck, Nelson, 67–68, 70, 89, 117, 119–21, 221
Gog, 321
Goliath, 183–84
Gordon, Charles G., 407
Gregory, Caspar René, 19
Gubaru (Gobryas), 329
Guy, 216
Gyges, 321, 325

H

Hadad, 224
Hadadezer, 200–01
Hadrian, 361, 362, 406, 408
Hagar, 69, 75
Haggai, 331
Ham, 45, 47
Hamath stones, 200
Hamites, 52
Hammurabi, 53, 66–67, 144
Hamutal, 314
Hanun, 201
Hanun of Gaza, 299
Happizzez, 358
Haran, 54
Harmhab, 98
Hattushil III, 98
Hazael, 286, 288, 290, 291
Heber, 152–53
Herod, 416, 430–31
Herod Agrippa, 355
Herod Antipas, 353, 371, 384, 385, 387, 406
Herod of Chalcis, 385
Herod the Great, 273, 295, 353–54, 359, 363–65, 374, 386, 389, 399, 406
Herodias, 386
Herodotus, 20, 303
Herzfeld, Ernst, 334
Hezekiah, 300, 302, 303, 306, 316
Hiddai, 143
Hippocrates, 452

Hiram (Huram), 219
Hiram (of Tyre), 197, 220
Hisham, 134
Hittites, 76–77, 96, 98, 144, 285, 312
Hobab, 115
Holy Innocents, 364
Homer, 467
Hophra, 315, 318, 341
Horace, 459
Horites, 89
Hosea, 293
house of Mary, 421
Hui, 98
Hurrians, 96
Hushai, 203, 205

I

Isaac, 75, 79–81, 88
Isaiah Scroll, 17†, 383†
Isaiah, 273, 295, 301, 302, 303
Ishbosheth (Eshbaal), 191, 193–94
Ishmael, 72, 75, 317
Ishmaelites, 30, 92
Israel Stela, 131
Issachar, 359
Ittai, 203

J

Jaazaniah, 223
Jabin, 151
Jacob, 81–89, 93–94
James (brother of Jesus), 421, 426
James (son of Zebedee), 421
Japheth, 45, 47
Japhethites, 47, 48
Jarvis, C. S., 106, 108
Jason, 441
Jehoahaz, 311, 312
Jehoash, 289–92
Jehoiachin, 314, 315, 324
Jehoiakim, 312, 314
Jehoiada, 289, 290
Jehoram, 283, 284, 286
Jehoshaphat, 280, 281, 283, 286, 342
Jehu, 277, 286, 287, 288, 297
Jephthah, 161
Jeremiah, 308, 309, 317–18
Jeroboam, 87, 224, 268, 270, 271
Jeroboam II, 292, 294
Jerome, 168, 409
Jesus Christ, 351, 354, 375–78, 383–84, 390–93, 398, 406
Jezebel, 274, 276, 287, 470
Jezreel, 287
Joab, 192–94, 206–07, 210–12
Job, 343
Job, Well of, 211
Johanan, 317, 338–39
John, 390, 401, 417, 465–68, 472, 474
John the Baptist, 357, 367–68, 370–71, 385–87, 391, 421
Joktan, 52, 53
Jonadab ben Rechab, 287
Jonah, 292
Jonathan, 181, 184, 212
Joram, 286
Joseph, 90–94, 143, 147, 172, 404
Josephus, 20, 65, 104, 318, 373–74, 376, 382–85, 397, 404, 406
Joseph of Arimathea, 407, 408
Joshua, 132–35, 141–43
Josiah, 308, 311, 314
Jotham, 295, 307
Judah, 90, 92
Judas the Galilaean, 354
Julius, 459, 460
Junias, 450
Justinian, 111, 361
Justin Martyr, 361

K

Kalir, 358
Kandalanu, 310
Kaushgabri, 306
Kelso, James L., 64, 134, 395
Kenites, 188
Kenyon, Kathleen, 134
Khaldians, 45
Khepa, 199
Khnum, 340–41

Khurri, 89
Kjaer, H., 172
Koldewey, Robert, 323
Kyaxares, 310

L

Labaya, 86
Layard, Sir Austen Henry, 267
Lazarus, 393, 394
Lemuel, 343
Lepidus, 352
Levi, 86–87
Lloyd Seton, 57
Loftus, 333
Lot, 64–65
Lucian, 454
Lucius Mumius, 444
Luke, 384, 390
Lydia, 439, 469
Lydians, 52
Lysanius, 354
Lysimachus, 447, 467–68

M

Maacah, 202
Macalister, R. A. S., 221
Maccabees, 365, 409
Machir, 124
Magdalene, 374, 409
Mallon, Alexis, 70
Manahthites, 163
Manasseh, 124, 172, 192, 306–07
Manoah, 163
Mar Athanasius, 16–17
Marduk, 304, 313, 324
Mariamne, 354, 406
Mark, 357, 368
Mark Antony, 352, 364, 367, 399, 464
Marsh-Arabs, 44
Martha, 394
Marullus, 355
Mary, 358, 400
Mati-ilu, 297, 304
Matthew, 357, 380, 398, 404
Medes, 309, 310
Melchizedek, 68
Melito, 471
Melqarth, 274, 279
Menahem, 293, 294, 295
Mephibosheth, 203
Merneptah, 131
Merodach-baladan, 301
Merrill, Selah, 85
Mesha, 122, 123, 126, 273–74, 283–84, 289
Meunites, 281, 294
Michal, 184, 193
Midas of Phrygia, 299, 300
Midianites, 126, 153–55
Mita of Mushki, 299
Mitanni, 144
Mithras, 364†
Mithredat, 329
Moabites, 72, 126, 281, 283, 291, 318
Moloch, 308
Mosaic of Madeba, 20
Moses, 96, 99–101, 119, 127–28
Muilenburg, 134
Murashu Sons, 315
Mushki, 299
Musil, Alois, 101, 109, 115, 140
Musiri, 306

N

Naaman, 284
Nabataeans, 221, 277, 343, 425–26
Nabonidus, 57, 324–26
Nabopolassar, 310–12, 324
Naboth, 279
Nahor, 54
Nahum, 310
Naomi, 168
Naveh, J., 174
Nazarenos, 358
Nebi Yunis, 292
Nebo, 313

Nebuchadnezzar, 312–15, 366
Nebuchadnezzar I, 145
Nebuchadnezzar II, 316–24
Nebuchadnezzar IV, 331
Nebuzaradan, 316–17
Necho, 311, 312, 313, 314
Nehemiah, 301, 309, 330, 335–40
Nektanebos II, 342
Neolithic Man, 36
Nepherites I, 341
Nergal, 298
Nergal-sharezer, 316
Neriglissar, 324
Nero, 443, 461
Nerva, 466
Nicanor Gate, 415
Nicolas, 469
Nimrod, 46
Nisroch, 303, 304
Noah, 44

O

oak of weeping, 87–88
Obadiah, 275, 343
Obed-edom, 199
Octavian, 352, 440, 464
Og, 123
Omar, 218
Omri, 272, 273
Onesiphorus, 433
Orfali P., 378
Origen, 370, 396
Osnappar (Ashurbanipal), 335

P

Padi, 302
Palmer, E. H., 112–15
Paltiel, 193
Parker, 196
Paul, 351, 352, 423–72
Paula, 20
Paul's Prison, 448–49
Pekah, 295, 296
Pekahiah, 294
Peleg, 52, 54
Pelethites, 203
Persians, 309
Peter, 378, 380, 387, 404–10, 417–22, 430, 464
Petrie, Flinders, 21, 111, 318
Peutinger's Table, 21
Pharisaic Teachers, 370
Pharisees, 399
Philip, 389, 417–18, 423
Philip the Evangelist, 453
Philistines, 103, 163, 173, 269, 272
Phillips, Wendell, 111
Philostratus, 441
Phineas (of Tiberias), 428
Phoebe, 450
Phoenicians, 274
Pilate, Pontius, 168, 355, 405, 406, 408
Pilgrim of Bordeaux, 407
Pliny, 382, 386, 468
Polycarp, 467
Pompey, 382, 395, 451, 461
Priscilla, 445, 446, 448, 449, 450
Procurator, 354
Psammetichus, 309
Psusennes II, 213
Ptolemy, 20, 456
Ptolemy II (Philadelphus), 102
Publius, 458
Pul, 293, 294

Q

Qainu, 337
Quirinius, 354

R

Rabbi Meir, 385
Rabshakeh of Sennacherib, 366
Rachel, 88, 364
Rachel, tomb of, 177–78
Ramses I, 98
Ramses II, 164, 312
Ramses III, 46, 131–32, 145

Rawlinson, Sir Henry, 55
Rehum, 335
Rehoboam, 268
Reisner, G. A., 273, 416
Reuben, 88
Rezin, 295, 296
Rezon, 224, 278
Rice, D. S., 57
Rim-Sin, 67, 323
Rizpah, 208
Robinson, Edward, 21, 71, 111, 112–14, 192, 360, 378
Ruth, 167–68

S

Sabaeans, 343
Sadducees, 399
Saladin, 374
Salome, 385
Samaritans, 392
Samson, 162–66
Samuel, 173, 177–78
Sanballat, 336–37, 339
Sardanapalus, tomb of, 424
Sargon II, 297–300, 335
Saul, 176–85, 188–90
Schick, G., 392
Schmidt, A., 172
Schmidt, E. F., 334
Scythians, 331
Seba, 206
Seetzen, Ulrich, 100, 112, 115
Seleucids, 143, 353, 382, 452
Seleucus I, 427, 469
Sellin, E., 134, 152, 160
Semiramis, Queen, 288
Sennacherib, 273, 301, 303, 307
Seneca, 445
Septuagint, 93
Sergius Paulus, 431
Serpent's Stone (stone of Zoheleth), 211
Seth-nakht, 131
Seti I, 98
Shallum, 293
Shalmaneser III, 267, 280, 288, 297
Shalmaneser V, 297, 305
Shamash-shum-ukin, 310
Shamgar ben Anath, 151
Shamshi-Adad I, 145
Shamshi-Adad V, 288
Sharezer, 304
Shebnah, 305, 306
Sheikh Khudr, 389
Shem, 45, 47, 52
Shemaiah, 268
Shemer, 273
Sheshbazzar, 329–30
Shimei, 204, 212
Shimshai, 335
Shishak, 224
Shobak, 201
Shoshenk I, 270
Shunamite Woman, 285
Shutruknah-hunte, 144
Sibe of Musri, 299
Sihon, 122
Silas, 442, 445
Silvia, 20
Simeon, 86–87
Simon the Leper, 401
Simon the Maccabee, 371, 391, 463
Simon Maccabaeus, 196, 419
Simon (the Tanner), 419
Sin, 324
Sin-shar-ishkun, 310
Sion Church (Church of the Apostles), 414
Sisera, 151, 153
Smerdis, 330
Smith, George, 44
So, King of Egypt, 297
Solomon, 210–24
Sosthenes, 446
Stephanas of Corinth, 443
Stephen, 415
Strabo, 20, 462, 466, 472
Straight, street called, 424–25
Sukenik, E. L., 135
Sulla, 352
Sumerians, 53

T

Tabali, 309
Tabel, the Son of, 295
Tabitha, 419
Talmai, 202
Tamar, 202
Tamerlane, 470
Tartan, the, 300
Tattenai, 331–32
Taylor, J. E., 55
Teachers of the Law, 367
Terah, 54, 55, 56
Tetrarch Philip, 384, 385, 388
Teumman, 333
Themistocles, 441
The Twelve, 380
Thoi, 200
Thomas, 409, 410
Tiberius, 353, 355, 463, 470
Tiglathpileser I, 46, 145, 216
Tiglathpileser III, 222, 293, 296–98, 304
Timothy, 442, 445, 449
Tirhakah, 303
Titus, 105, 389, 463
Tobiah, 336–37
Trajan, 408
Trever, John C., 16–17
Tudkhalia, 66
Tukulti-Ninurta II, 267
Tutankhaton (Tuntankh-Amon), 97
Tyrannus, 448
Tyrian ladder, 33
Tyrimnos, 470

U

Umman-manda, 311
Unger, E., 322
Upper Room, 414
Uriah, 201, 314
Ur-Nammu, 56
Ut-napishtim, 44, 46
Uzzah, 199
Uzziah, 292, 294, 295

V

Varus, C. Quintilius, 354
Verethragna, 364†
Vincent, L. H., 392
Virgil, 352
Vliet N. van der, 392

W

Warren, 196, 211
Watzinger, C., 134
Weill, Raymond, 415
Wen Amon, 139, 145
Wilbour, C. E., 341
Wilken, K. E., 381
Wiseman, J. D., 312
Wise Men, 363
Wood, J. T., 447
Woolley, Sir Leonard, 44, 55
Wright, Ernest, 158

X

Xenophon, 341
Xerxes, 328, 332, 334

Y

Yaddua, 366
Yadin, Yigael, 19, 139
Yamani of Ashdod, 300
Yaosh, 316
Yaubidi of Hamath, 298
Yeivin, S., 174

Z

Zaccheus, 395
Zacharias, 358
Zadok, 206, 210–11
Zebul, 159
Zechariah, 293, 331, 401
Zedekiah, 31, 314–16
Zelophehad, 127
Zeno, 442
Zephaniah, 308
Zerah, 272
Zerubbabel, 331–32
Ziba, 203
Zimri, 272